ePublishing with InDesign® CS6

ePublishing with InDesign® CS6

Design and produce digital publications for tablets, ereaders, smartphones, and more

Pariah Burke

WILEY

John Wiley & Sons, Inc.

Acquisitions Editor: Mariann Barsolo

Development Editor: Candace English

Technical Editor: Bob Levine

Production Editor: Rebecca Anderson

Copy Editor: Kim Wimpsett

Editorial Manager: Pete Gaughan

Production Manager: Tim Tate

Vice President and Executive Group Publisher: Richard Swadley

Vice President and Publisher: Neil Edde

Book Designer and Compositor: Maureen Forys, Happenstance Type-O-Rama

Proofreader: Louise Watson, Word One New York

Indexer: Ted Laux

Project Coordinator, Cover: Katherine Crocker

Cover Designer: Ryan Sneed

Cover Image: © Pariah S. Burke

ISBN: 978-1-118-30559-1

ISBN: 978-1-118-33418-8 (ebk.)

ISBN: 978-1-118-46384-0 (ebk.)

ISBN: 978-1-118-33531-4 (ebk.)

Dear Reader,

Thank you for choosing *ePublishing with InDesign CS6: Design and produce digital publications for tablets, ereaders, smartphones, and more*. This book is part of a family of premium-quality Sybex books, all of which are written by outstanding authors who combine practical experience with a gift for teaching.

Sybex was founded in 1976. More than 30 years later, we're still committed to producing consistently exceptional books. With each of our titles, we're working hard to set a new standard for the industry. From the paper we print on, to the authors we work with, our goal is to bring you the best books available.

I hope you see all that reflected in these pages. I'd be very interested to hear your comments and get your feedback on how we're doing. Feel free to let me know what you think about this or any other Sybex book by sending me an email at nedde@wiley.com. If you think you've found a technical error in this book, please visit http://sybex.custhelp.com. Customer feedback is critical to our efforts at Sybex.

Best regards,

Neil Edde
Vice President and Publisher
Sybex, an Imprint of Wiley

To Schentel, Mikayla, Mom, Ma, and Dad. This book exists because of your unflappable faith, love, and support.

Acknowledgments

First and foremost, I want to acknowledge my fans. You honor and humble me.

When you choose to write a book about not one or two but about a dozen different cutting-edge technologies that change faster than the wind…well, if you choose to do that, you must be insane. I can now say that with confidence because I've written this book about the biggest moving target since 1984. Every technology covered in this book changed radically between the beginning of the book and the end. I rewrote everything at least once. The patience and understanding exhibited by the rest of the book team, my family, and my friends were truly amazing.

My wife, Schentel, thank you, thank you, thank you for your bountiful patience, understanding, and faith. Thank you for putting up with my long hours at work, darling, and for being everything I ever wanted in a wife, a best friend, and a partner.

Mikayla, I know you didn't understand why a book takes so much concentration and time, but now your name is in *another* published book that your friends can buy at the bookstore.

Sarah Taylor, Mom. Thank you for teaching me to crawl, run, and pick myself up when I stumble. This—and every book—is because of you.

My friends, Anna Gauthier, Kirsten Rourke, Tom Green, Bob Levine, Samuel John Klein, A.J. Wood, Justin Seeley, Rufus Deuchler, Kevin Stohlmeyer, Scott Valentine, Branislav Millic, Nancy Smith Burleson, Rob Huddleston, Wendy Katz, Jim Babbage, and Joseph Labrecque, thank you for the commiseration, support, and well-timed jokes.

Mike Rankin, thanks for consenting to let me include pages from your book, *The Guide to the InDesign ACE Exam*, as examples in Chapter 7.

Mariann Barsolo, thank you for being excited about this project and helping me redraw the lines on the map…and redraw them again. Oh, and again.

Bob Levine, technical editor and friend, thank you for somehow making it through, too.

Candace English, Kim Wimpsett, and Louise Watson: a tweak here, a pluck there. Thank you for finding and fixing all the little things.

David Fugate, for the Pariah-to-English translations, advice, and advocacy.

I would also like to thank all the fine people—too many to name—at Adobe and Aquafadas for the rapid responses to my "what does this do, exactly?" questions.

Thanks to Lenovo for the loan of the ThinkPad Android tablet.

Thank you to Johannes Gutenberg, Aldus Manutius, Claude Garamond, John Warnock, Chuck Geschke, Paul Brainard, Tim Gill, Steve Jobs, Bill Gates, and everyone else who got us to the ePublishing Revolution.

About the Author

Pariah Burke: Empowering and Informing Creative Professionals

Pariah Burke is a creative professional trainer and a design, publishing, and digital publishing workflow expert and consultant whose passion is empowering, informing, and connecting creative professionals around the world (http://iampariah.com/teaches). As a freelance graphic designer with more than 20 years' experience, Pariah is an Adobe Community Professional and a former trainer and technical lead for Adobe's technical support team for InDesign, InCopy, Illustrator, and Photoshop. A prolific author, Pariah wrote the first Adobe InDesign book for experienced InDesign users, *Mastering InDesign for Print Design and Production*; has written books on epublishing, Creative Suite, Adobe Illustrator, and QuarkXPress (http://iamPariah.com/books); and has published more than 450 tutorials and articles (http://iamPariah.com/articles). He is the coauthor of several InDesign and Illustrator Adobe Certified Expert exams, the tests Adobe administers to gauge the skill levels of InDesign and Illustrator instructors and experts. Pariah is the host of a series of digital publishing, epublishing, and the business of design webinars (http://iamPariah.com/webinars) and is the publisher of a network of websites, communities, and tools for creative professionals, the Workflow: Network (http://workflownetwork.com). When not traveling, Pariah lives in Boston, where he writes (a lot) and creates (many) projects and publications Empowering and Informing Creative Professionals.

Contents at a Glance

Contents

Chapter 7 • Creating PDF Publications for Digital Delivery 225

Introduction

Print is dead! they cry.

They. Are. *Wrong.*

No, print is emphatically *not dead*. Print-*only* publishing, however, *is* dead.

If you (or your clients) publish anything with a larger distribution than a church bulletin only in print, then your publication will be dead before the end of the decade. (In that vein, you can find the electronic edition of this very book at `www.sybex.com/go/epublishingwithindesign`.)

We are hip-deep in the beginning of the largest shakeup in the publishing world since the Desktop Publishing Revolution of the 1980s. This book you're now reading is part of a comprehensive educational system that covers the entire epublishing spectrum, from ebooks to fixed-layout picture books, from print-to-tablet digital replica publications to fully interactive tablet magazines, from periodicals to ecatalogs, and from ebooks to digital yearbooks. I say "comprehensive educational system" because this book is only the tip of the iceberg. *ePublishing with InDesign CS6* is not just a book but a full, ready-to-deploy epublishing curriculum. And it goes beyond that, as well. Digital publishing is a wide and rapidly evolving set of industries. Some segments change so frequently that, had I written extensively about them in this tome, the text would be out of date before you had a chance to get the book. Consequently, I've covered those mercurial topics like fixed-layout ebooks on my website so that I can keep up to the minute with industry, format, and workflow changes so that *you* can stay up to the minute and produce the most powerful, most marketable epublications possible, using the most efficient and cost-effective methodologies available. You can find all the components at `http://abbrv.it/ePubInD`.

How This Book Is Organized

This book covers three overarching topic areas: the world and economics of epublishing, ebooks, and rich-media interactive publications. Each section focuses on a different area of epublishing—from the business, market, devices, and formats of epublications; then going into ebooks; and wrapping up with the area I'm most excited about, fully interactive periodicals, catalogs, and enhanced ebooks.

Chapter 1: Exploring Ereading Devices   The first thing to understand about digital publishing is what devices people use to consume digital content, including what types of publications each device class can support, how people use the devices, and where ereading hardware is headed. You will find a startling array of devices on the market, but ultimately there are only four classes of devices on which digital publications are consumed: ereaders, tablets, computers, and mobile phones. The pros and cons of each, and which epublication file formats each can support, can be maddening without this guide.

Chapter 2: Learning about Digital Publishing Formats   Like devices, epublication formats are numerous and varied, with subtle differences between them but large divergences in purpose, capability, and device support. Consequently, it's most logical and productive to think of epublications in terms of format classes, with each class offering a particular combination of purpose, capability, and device support. This chapter discusses the unique characteristics and publishing experiences of EPUB; Amazon Kindle formats such as MOBI, AZW, and KF8; and PDF, digital replica, interactive-magazine, and HTML5-based epublications.

Chapter 3: Surveying the Digital Publication Types   Now that I've covered the characteristics and capabilities of the available digital publication formats, it's time to think about the kind of content you want to disseminate digitally. In this chapter, I identify the purpose, character, and uses of the ebook, digital magazine, enewspaper, etextbook, and digital comic book publication types as well as explain which format classes are best suited to each type.

Chapter 4: Creating Basic Ebooks   Whether creating ebooks from TXT files or word processor documents or converting existing print publications to EPUB, the basics are all the same. You must learn to think in terms of EPUB, to reevaluate how your content is organized, and to know how to structure it using InDesign's built-in tools in order to produce well organized, readable ebooks. The yellow brick road to becoming a wizard of ebook production starts with this chapter and proceeds through the next several chapters, creating progressively more interesting, more marketable ebooks and other EPUB-based publications.

Chapter 5: Working with Images and Multimedia in Ebooks   Although the majority of ebooks are text-only novels and short stories, a large minority across all genres include photographs, illustrations, charts, graphs, maps, and all sorts of other imagery, and even audio and video. Moreover, even novels and short stories typically have at least cover images. Whether your publication merely needs a cover or requires lots of figures, creating and using them in ebooks differs in several distinct ways from creating and using graphics for print or other digital formats.

Chapter 6: Fine-Tuning EPUBs   Successful, efficient EPUB production begins in, and centers on, InDesign and the tool set InDesign brings to the business of ebook publishing. However, InDesign isn't the *only* tool you'll need to produce ebooks of the highest quality, maximum compatibility, and utmost reader engagement. At a certain point, you'll need to go *inside* the EPUB to edit and massage the components InDesign can't reach, often working in conjunction with the original files in InDesign to build an ebook that takes fullest advantage of ereader hardware and software to provide an ideal reading experience.

Chapter 7: Creating PDF Publications for Digital Delivery   Not to be overshadowed, PDF-format publications are still a viable—indeed, a popular—distribution format. PDFs support rich multimedia, hyperlinks, some pretty cool interactivity, scripting, reflowable text like an EPUB, and electronic forms. PDF viewers are available for all computer and mobile platforms, though feature support varies by platform. In this chapter, I'll use PDF to its fullest epublishing potential while defining the restrictions placed on it by certain devices. I'll also show some successful PDF-based publications that have been going strong for years.

Chapter 8: Covering the Basics of Interactive Magazines   In this chapter, I'll focus on the nuts and bolts of interactive-magazine design—how to plan and build the layouts in both Adobe Digital Publishing Suite and its leading competitor, Aquafadas Digital Publishing System. I cover adapting one layout for multiple devices and orientations (including working with liquid layout behaviors to make that process as easy and quick as possible), building articles and pages the correct way, and filling in the important finishing touches.

Chapter 9: Creating Interactive Magazines with Adobe DPS   Now that you know how to begin and lay out interactive magazines, I can get into the really good stuff—all the different ways in which those publications can be made interactive and engaging with Adobe Digital Publishing Suite. From adding animation and video to immersing your readers in 3D panoramic spaces, from including live web content and widgets to employing advanced content-replacement techniques to put volumes of information on a single page, at your readers' fingertips, I'll go hands-on and step-by-step, including all the interactivity in Adobe DPS and then showing how to build a viewer app for your publication and publish it to the Apple App Store, Google Play App Market, and Amazon Android App Store.

Chapter 10: Creating Interactive Magazines with Aquafadas DPS   Competing head to head with Adobe Digital Publishing Suite is a comprehensive but lesser-known challenger from France, Aquafadas Digital Publishing Solution. Although not as popular as Adobe DPS, Aquafadas offers a much richer set of interactive elements for incorporation into digital magazines. Also working as an InDesign add-in, the Aquafadas system is more polished and professional-looking than Adobe's DPS tools, and, in nearly all other aspects, Aquafadas is arguably a better, more intuitive, more feature-rich system for producing digital magazines. In this chapter, I'll go hands-on through step-by-step instruction for including numerous richly interactive features, including slideshows and galleries, audio and video, read-along text, advanced content replacement, web and HTML content, and prebuilt games and activities.

How to Use This Book

You could, of course, use the print version of this book as a doorstop or to squish a bug—the aqueous coating on the cover will enable the guts to be easily wiped off if you don't leave them sitting too long. It's just thick enough that, should one of the casters fall off your office chair, this book could keep your chair perfectly balanced until it's fixed. If you find yourself trapped in the woods during the winter, there are plenty of pages herein to burn or to crinkle up and use as insulation inside your clothes.

Candidly, I prefer you read the book and use it to help you begin or expand your epublishing efforts. With that in mind, what follows is an explanation of the special way I've handled URLs in the book, a note about the lesson files, and a reminder that there's much more content available than what is directly between the bug-squishing covers of this individual printed book volume.

Aspirin-Free Workflow Sidebars

In addition to the standard tip boxes and sidebars you'll see throughout the book, I've included special Aspirin-Free Workflow sidebars to call extra attention to pointers that will make your production work a little less stressful and more efficient.

SPECIAL URLs

Throughout this book I've included a number of hyperlink addresses. To make it as easy as possible for you to use those hyperlinks while working with this book, they have been specially created and organized.

Each URL is written out so that you can type it into a web browser or make note of it for future use. In most cases, the URLs begin with `http://abbrv.it/`, which is the author's own custom URL-shortening service. These shorter URLs make it easier for you to retype what otherwise might be very long and complicated addresses. Also, because the URLs employ my own URL shortener, should the address on a third-party website change, I can update the shortened URL without invalidating the address provided in this book. Should you discover a broken link, please alert me immediately by emailing `ePublishingIND@iampariah.com` (subject: "Broken Link in *ePublishing with InDesign CS6*") so that I can fix the shortened link.

LESSON FILES

Obviously, the best way to learn some of the techniques presented in this book is by going hands-on, and you will, through numerous step-by-step tutorials. To make your hands-on learning easier, you are, of course, encouraged to work with your own production documents, but I've also provided copious examples you can dig through, manipulate, and test-publish.

Note that I used only the fonts automatically installed with InDesign. That way, when you open the INDD lesson files, you won't have to hassle with font substitution or text reflow; unless you chose not to install the Adobe Fonts or removed or deactivated them later, you already have the fonts I used installed and ready for your use.

How to Contact the Author

Questions?

Criticisms?

Epiphanies?

Consulting inquiries?

Knock-knock jokes?

Examples of your digital publications I can use in a future edition of this book?

Contact me:

Email me:	`ePublishingIND@iampariah.com`
Visit my website:	`http://iamPariah.com`
Follow me on Facebook:	`http://iamPariah.com/Facebook`
Connect with me on Twitter @iamPariah:	`http://iamPariah.com/Twitter`
Follow my InDesign, epublishing, and other pins on Pinterest:	`http://iamPariah.com/Pinterest`

Take Your ePublishing Education Further

As I noted in the "How to Use This Book" section, this book is not the entirety of the epublishing with InDesign material I've produced; it's only one portion. My website offers text and videos on segments of epublishing that update too fast for a printed book, templates, instructor materials, and, most important, updates to the content in this book and all companion materials to make sure you're always ready with the latest epublishing technologies and techniques. The following links will get you to *everything* in the *entire* ePublishing with InDesign system.

The complete *ePublishing with InDesign CS6* system:	`http://abbrv.it/ePubInD`
Updates to this book:	`http://abbrv.it/DigiPubID`
Video tutorials:	`http://iamPariah.com/YouTube`
Customized training and workflow development:	`http://iamPariah.com`

Sybex strives to keep you supplied with the latest tools and information you need for your work. Please check the book's website at `www.sybex.com/go/epublishingwithindesign`, where I'll post additional content and updates that supplement this book if the need arises.

Chapter 1

Exploring Ereading Devices

The first thing to understand about digital publishing is what devices people use to consume digital content, including what types of publications each device class can support, how people use the devices, and where ereading hardware is headed. You will find a startling array of devices on the market, but ultimately there are only four classes of devices on which digital publications are consumed.

In this chapter, you will learn about the following:

- ◆ Device Classes
- ◆ Ereaders
- ◆ Tablets
- ◆ Computers
- ◆ Mobile Phones
- ◆ Hybrid Devices
- ◆ Future Devices

Device Classes

There is an ever-increasing variety of devices on which to read electronic publications. And the more devices that are out there, the more frequently those devices are upgraded, competing with one another, forcing each other to innovate and improve, and driving the price of ereader ownership lower and lower while making electronic content more and more accessible to consumers. That's good for consumers and for content producers like you and me; competition in ereader hardware, ereader software, tablets, and other devices does most of the work of opening up markets for us. More of these devices are being devised and released every month. In fact, by the time you've finished reading this sentence, there will be another—BestBuy.com just listed the newest, greatest ereading device to kill all prior devices! And now—the newest, greatest to kill *that* one!

Of course, there's also a downside to the feverish pace of device creation and improvement: Creating content that takes full advantage of, or even just fits perfectly on the screen of, the current or next generation of devices is like trying to shoot a bull's-eye hanging from the flank of a bucking bronco while blindfolded.

As with all media and business revolutions, the bronco will eventually be tamed and set upon a predictable path around the corral, making bull's-eyes easier to land for everyone. That happened with the Desktop Publishing Revolution in the 1980s as well as the Web Publishing Revolution in the late 1990s and early 2000s. For now, the best strategy for landing bull's-eyes in this Electronic Publishing Revolution lies in understanding *classes* of digital content-consumption devices and the individual characteristics of devices in those classes.

But first, Table 1.1 presents a quick reference of device class capabilities. The specifics of the various publication formats are discussed in Chapter 2.

TABLE 1.1:   Device Class Characteristics

	EREADERS	**TABLETS**	**COMPUTERS**	**MOBILE PHONES**
Can display EPUB/MOBI ebooks	☑	☑	☑	☑
Can display interactive PDFs	◪	◪	☑	◪
Can display digital replicas	◪	☑	◪	
Can display digital magazines		☑		◪
Can display HTML5 epublications	◪	☑	☑	☑
Has full-color display	◪	☑	☑	☑
Can display dynamic, server-fed content	◪	◪	◪	◪

Legend: ☑ Yes, the device class supports this option. ◪ The device class supports some but not all features of the option, and/or some devices in the class supports the option while others do not.

STAY UP TO DATE AS THE LANDSCAPE CHANGES

To keep pace with the changes in the digital publishing landscape, I will provide periodic updates on the latest devices (and many other sections from this book) on my website, `http://abbrv.it/DigiPubID`, and at `www.sybex.com/go/epublishingindesign`.

Ereaders

The first class of digital-content-consumption device is handheld ereaders. These devices support the inclusion of imagery and media to one degree or another, but they're built for reading novels, novellas, short stories, newspaper articles, and other text-heavy content. You wouldn't, for example, target ereaders for your coffee-table picture book or image-laden fashion magazine.

There are more brands and models of handheld ereaders available than most people would imagine—and more are being developed every year. Figure 1.1 shows many ereaders, but the selection goes on well beyond what I've pictured here.

FIGURE 1.1A
A selection of hand-held ereaders

Barnes & Noble
NOOK Simple Touch

Kindle Keyboard

Kobo Touch

Sony Reader

BeBook Club S

Range 3

iriver Story

txtr eBook Reader

Pocketbook Pro

Photos courtesy of the device manufacturers

FIGURE 1.1B
A selection of
handheld ereaders
(continued)

Aluratek LIBRE | PRO

Bookeen Cybook Opus

ECTACO jetBook mini

Jinke Hanlin eReader V5

Onyx Boox M90

Plastic Logic 100

Photos courtesy of the device manufacturers

The popularity of ereaders lies in their simplicity. They don't play movies or have lots of apps. The most used ereaders don't even have color screens; many of the biggest manufacturers do offer color versions of their ereaders, but those are far outsold by their grayscale or black-and-white counterparts. Instead, using proprietary technology and a lack of backlighting, ereaders provide on a handheld screen a remarkably close replica of a printed book page—one that is no more difficult for, or taxing on, the human eye while reading for extended periods than ink on a novel's pulp page. Of course, ereaders weigh only a few ounces—typically 6 to 8 ounces—and can contain thousands of books, making them far more convenient to tote around than a stack of printed books. Bookmarking, full-text searching, user-defined type size, week- and month-long battery lives, and the ability to browse and purchase a vast array of modern books and an ever-increasing library of older titles round out a list of the top advantages over printed books cited by ereader owners.

Tablets

Tablet computers are the youngest but fastest-growing class of digital-content-consumption device. Contrary to popular belief, the device class was not devised by, and did not originate with, Apple; tablets and slates have existed in several forms, most running the Windows Mobile operating system, since the turn of the 21st century. They were, however, very low-profile and marketed primarily to industrial, medical, and high-tech enterprise customers, all but completely ignoring the rest of the potential market. It wasn't until the iPad's sleek form factor and consumer-targeted advertising campaign that the general public saw tablets as potential everyday devices. From there, businesses began adopting them, too—an inverse of the way prior tablet devices (also called *slates*) were marketed.

Kicked off (officially) by the release of Apple's iPad in the spring of 2010, the tablet market has exploded with additional operating systems (see the "Tablet Operating Systems" section) and dozens of different devices being released—and purchased—at breakneck speeds. (See Figure 1.2 for a small sampling of such devices.) In general, tablet devices offer consumers a smaller, lighter device to tote around than a laptop while sacrificing little of the convenience and power of having a laptop on hand. From a tablet device a person can read and compose email, write and collaborate on documents, play games and watch videos, surf the Web and interact with social networks, participate in video conferencing, work with database content such as medical records or pharmacy dispensary systems, manage point-of-sale and retail inventory, edit and organize photographs, and even create and edit new graphic, art, or technical designs. In other words, tablets are becoming a replacement for laptops for many professionals and students and a replacement for *any* standard computer for the average consumer whose computing requirements are limited to these abilities (which is most consumers).

FIGURE 1.2
Three of the many available tablets and mini-tablets. These three are available in 7-inch and 10.1-inch models.

Acer Iconia Tab   Samsung Galaxy Tab   Creative ZiiO

Photos courtesy of the device manufacturers

Of course, tablets are not—at the moment—ready to completely replace computers for everyone. They have their limitations. First, tablets run *apps*, not *applications*. You cannot, for example, run the full version of Photoshop on an iPad or Motorola XOOM. You can, however, run Photoshop Touch, an app built specifically for tablets but lacking much of Photoshop's power, automation, and ability. Creatives and many other professionals still need a desktop or laptop computer to run full applications.

Another big limitation of tablets is their storage capacity—though it's a limitation that is quickly being remedied. The Apple iPad is available with 16, 32, or 64 GB of storage, and that storage capacity is not expandable. Most Android tablets offer the same size internal storage drives but also include SD or MicroSD storage card slots that enable the user to double or even triple the devices' file and app storage capacities. Still, even a maxed-out Android tablet can only offer a top onboard storage capacity of 128 GB for all apps, data files, media, and work files. The average laptop sold today offers internal hard drive storage of 500 GB and is often augmented by one or more external portable hard drives of similar capacity. Tablets just can't hold a great deal of data, and virtually none of them can interface with an external hard drive.

One notable exception to these specs is the Kindle Fire, which is not expandable and offers a measly 8 GB with roughly 1.5 GB required for the operating system and embedded apps. But the Fire and the similarly limited iPad are the vanguards in a movement that will ultimately nullify the consequence of low onboard storage capacities. The *cloud*, you see, is ready and waiting to hold all those files we nowadays put on our hard drives, thumb drives, and removable media. With the purchase of an iPad or Fire, Apple and Amazon give you 5 GB of free online storage in their iCloud and Amazon Cloud Drive online storage services, respectively. For the average consumer, 5 GB is a lot of space, holding approximately 1,000 MP3 songs; 2,000 photos; 20 minutes of HD video; or about 5,000 Microsoft Word documents. If that isn't enough space, both services offer paid upgrades beginning at $20 annually. All those files stored in the cloud are accessible at any time to one or all mobile and standard computer devices—as long as the particular device has an Internet connection. And Apple and Amazon aren't the only ones offering large, instant access and free or low-cost cloud storage. ASUS includes unlimited online storage with the purchase of its Android tablets and tablet-laptop hybrids. Microsoft has offered SkyDrive for years and has made it an integral part of not only Windows Mobile–powered devices but every computer running Windows 8 and newer. Even nontablet makers such as Mozy, Livedrive, SugarSync, and the venerable Dropbox offer cloud storage for making your files accessible from any device.

In short, for the average consumer, tablets are today a perfectly reasonable replacement for standard desktop and laptop computers. As time goes on, tablets will be even more common than standard computers because of their portability. The average person will be connected more often and for longer periods because of the power and portability of tablets.

Additionally, tablets offer support for the largest selection of digital publication formats, including those (such as interactive magazines and digital replicas) that were created specifically, and solely, for tablets. (We'll get into the topic of formats in Chapter 2.) Digital publishers who want to compete in today's and tomorrow's worlds need to target their publications to tablets *now*. The early-adopter mind-set ran tablets in 2010 and early 2011; as of fall 2011, though, all of your readers have or are considering tablets. Tablets are one of the biggest sales items of any holiday shopping season, followed closely by handheld ereader devices.

Ereading on Tablets

When compared to handheld ereaders, there are pros and cons to tablets for ereading.

First, tablets support a much wider variety of epublication formats. With installable or pre-integrated versions of iBooks, Kindle, NOOK, Kobo, Google Books, and more, the entire world of ebooks is available to tablet owners (Figure 1.3). And tablets can have several of those ereader applications and libraries installed at the same time, putting every ebook for sale at Amazon, Barnes & Noble, Kobo, and so on (and on iPads, iBooks) readily available on one device. Typically users stick with one, though, especially if one is preinstalled when they purchase the tablet, like iBooks is on the iPad, Kindle is on Amazon's Fire tablet, Kobo is on the Vox, and Barnes & Noble is on the NOOK tablets. Thus, if you publish ebooks, make them available for sale in all of those stores and consider carefully whether it's ultimately worth it to participate in an exclusivity program offered by one ebookstore or another.

FIGURE 1.3
Various ebook stores available on tablet devices. (All except iBooks are shown on an Android 10.1-inch tablet. iBooks is shown on an iPad.)

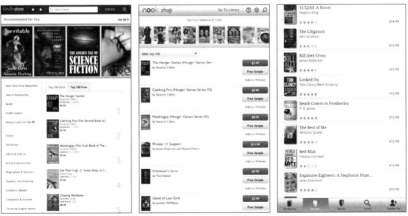

Kindle Store   Barnes & Noble NOOK Shop   Kobo Bookstore

Photos courtesy of the device manufacturers

Google Books   Apple iBooks

    The act of reading for extended periods on tablets is much the same as reading on a computer and nowhere near as friendly as reading on handheld ereaders. Handheld ereaders typically don't include *backlighting,* or illuminated screens; their screens are usually anti-glare, and they use proprietary display technology to simulate the look of real ink on real paper, which enables them to be comfortably read in all the same lighting conditions in which printed books are read comfortably. Computers and tablets *are* backlit, which is why they strain the eyes after a while, and in order to display multimedia, games, and the widest array of content, they use a completely different *anti-aliasing* technology that cannot simulate ink on paper. Tablets, being portable and almost always bearing polished glass faces, often also carry a glare or reflect too much light (or other objects; see Ben Long's "Why the iPad Isn't for Me" in *Macworld*—particularly the "Day Five" section—`http://abbrv.it/150474`) for comfortable reading. Tablets just are not ideally suited to the act of reading long, continuous flows of text like novels and other common ebooks. Despite the science disproving the comfort of reading on tablets, 60 percent of iPad owners report that they read ebooks on the iPad (Simba Information, April 2011 and Imano,

May 2011). Apple, Amazon, B&N, and Kobo are trying to get in on that percentage with their various tablets even though, in the case of all but Apple, the companies also produce handheld dedicated ebook readers.

Magazine, catalog, yearbook, newspaper, and comic book reading is another matter entirely. While the same limitations of backlighting, lack of e-ink–optimized text display, and screen glare still exist no matter what type of publication one is reading on a tablet, these types of publications are not long, continuous, text-only reading experiences. They're usually visually rich layouts augmenting copy with color, imagery, multimedia, and, in the better ones, touch interaction. Tablets are ideally suited for displaying these media-rich publications because the media richness was built specifically for tablets, and consumers adore reading, watching, and interacting with digital magazines, catalogs, yearbooks, newspapers, comics, and even "enhanced" ebooks that go beyond the norm. Figure 1.4 shows a digital replica–format publication (*Redbook*) as viewed landscape; an app-based enhanced ebook (*Rudolph the Red-Nosed Reindeer*) that includes hotspots, read-to-me, and auto-page capabilities; a highly interactive digital magazine-format periodical (*National Geographic*) containing animations, video, hotspots, panoramic pictures, 3D-rotatable imagery, and more; a digital catalog (Brookstone) using TheFind newsstand app, which allows customers to order directly from within the catalog; and an HTML5-based newspaper (*USA Today*) including scrollable and slideshow regions and a preference system that uses the user's desired locations for the weather, sports leagues for scores, and other customizable content. (Go, Bruins!)

If you intend to publish visually rich or media-rich periodicals or other publications, tablets are, and will increasingly be, the primary device class you should target.

Tablet Operating Systems

Just as there are more tablet-class devices for sale than there are web browsers you could possibly install on all your devices combined, there is also a variety in tablet operating systems, which are what drive the tablets and give them their capabilities. I'd like to take a moment to run through what these operating systems are, what devices they drive, and some of the important characteristics of each that a digital publisher should know.

iOS from Apple

iOS runs all of Apple's mobile products, not just the iPad but also the iPhone and the iPod Touch (which is, for all intents and purposes, an iPhone without dialing and texting capabilities).

Apple tightly controls both the hardware and operating systems on its mobile devices, as with its computers. All versions of iOS and all iOS devices may install apps from the Apple App Store and, beginning with iOS 4, iBooks. All content available through the App Store and iBooks is strictly regulated by Apple. Apps and epublications must pass through a review process prior to being made available to iOS users, and Apple reserves (and has often exercised) the right to remove apps or publications for any reason at any time following their initial release into the App Store and/or iBooks. Rumors abound as to reasons every time Apple denies or removes a particular app or ebook, but in general Apple wants content available through iOS to be "family-friendly," legal, and of "the highest quality." The subjectivity of these descriptions has led to many dissatisfied publishers. Ultimately, iOS is what is called a *walled garden*: Only Apple-approved content gets in, which creates a predictable and consistent user experience.

FIGURE 1.4
Tablets display-
ing media-rich
publications

Redbook, August 2011
Creative Director: Amy Dorf

Rudolph the Red-Nosed Reindeer
Developer: Oceanhouse Media

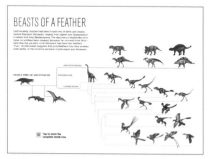

National Geographic, February 2011
Design director: David C. Whitmore

USA Today, January 4, 2012
Developer: Mercury Media

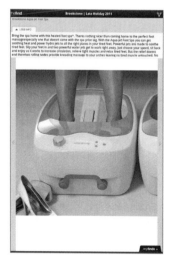

Brookstone Catalog, January 2012

EPUB and PDF digital documents *can* be loaded onto iOS devices without going through iBooks, though the process is too complex for the average iOS device consumer and thus isn't viable for a widespread publication distribution method. Individual users can add EPUB and PDF files to iTunes on their computers, which then pushes those files to the iPad or iPhone iBooks app during device-computer synchronization, that is, of course, if iTunes is used to synchronize the device. iOS 5, recognizing the value of tablets as computer replacements, brought the ability to use iOS devices completely independently of iTunes and computers, using server-based management software in iCloud to update, upgrade, and synchronize iOS devices.

The iPad (all versions) is the gold standard in tablets and tablet publishing (Figure 1.5). It has the highest market share among all tablets—twice that of all Android tablets combined—and is consistently ranked as being the fastest, most responsive user interface, though several Android tablets are ranked as having more user-friendly and intuitive user interfaces.

FIGURE 1.5
An iPad 2

Photo courtesy of Apple

MERGING OF MAC AND IPAD

Following the initial and stellar success of the iPad, Apple began porting many of the tablet's features to its Macintosh line of computers. A Mac App Store was integrated into Mac OS X version 10.6, bringing the ability to purchase apps *and* full major-label applications directly to the screen rather than forcing users to purchase and load CD or DVD installation discs. When OS X updated to version 10.7, codename "Lion," in 2011, the principal way to purchase the upgrade was through the Mac App Store. "Lion" brought with it other iPad features, including the ability to control the computer and applications through *gestures* such as multifinger swiping, turning, and tapping. These gestures required new Apple hardware, specifically laptop touchpads, peripheral touchpads that could be added to desktop computers in place of or alongside a mouse, and a new touch-sensitive mouse whose surface had more in common with the iPad's touchscreen than with other mice. OS X 10.8, codename "Mountain Lion," brought several popular iPad features and integrated apps to Mac in 2012. And, also in 2012, Apple updated its entire line of Mac laptops and desktop displays to the ultra high resolution Retina display that appeared first in the iPhone 4s and then in the iPad 3. Apple is obviously moving toward combining OS X with iOS in all its computing devices or replacing OS X entirely—there are even possible indications of Apple replacing its line of Mac laptops with more powerful iPad-like devices.

ANDROID OS

Android is the big competitor and would-be "iOS killer" in both the smartphone ("iPhone killer") and tablet ("iPad killer") markets. I could give you numbers of Android devices sold versus iPads sold and market share percentages, but they wouldn't be accurate for long. Things change too rapidly; for instance, numerous independent studies noted a sharp 1Q2012 decline in iPad sales. This dip corresponded with rises in Android tablet sales, but one doesn't necessarily have anything to do with the other. In fact, in my learned opinion, iPad 2 sales slumped in 1Q2012 because the market knew full well that the iPad 3 was on its way. When it appeared in March 2012 iPad sales once again skyrocketed while Android sales remained the same, proving that Android sales growth was not directly related to iPad sales fall-off.

The big takeaway from any statistical comparison of tablets is that both iOS and Android are popular platforms, with user bases measured in the hundreds of millions.

Created and sponsored largely by Google (as a member of the Open Handset Alliance), Android is an open source operating system that, like iOS, is obviously moving toward becoming a primary computer operating system as well. The difference is that Google has always *said* Android will become a full-blown computer operating system—with computers adapting to be touch-sensitive and mobile—while Apple hasn't actually said it intends to combine or replace OS X with iOS; it's just *doing* it bit by byte. Because Android is an open source operating system free from licensing fees, many tablet manufacturers use it in their devices. In fact, with the exception of iPad, the BlackBerry PlayBook, the defunct HP TouchPad, and some upcoming Windows Mobile devices, *all* current tablets run on Android (see Figure 1.6). Thus, competition in the tablet market is, as of the moment, primarily limited to iPad vs. Android-powered devices, with the various Android tablet manufacturers competing with one another on hardware capabilities and user-interface tweaks.

The Google Play app store (formerly Android Market) is open, enabling any publisher or developer to distribute her creation to all Android tablets and smartphones. This is a double-edged sword. Unlike with iOS-based content, there are no reviewers or censors to clear content through and no issue with releasing apps and publications that may impact the financial interests of the platform maker. However, the openness of the app store can create the impression that the selection of apps and publications is of an inferior quality to those available in Apple's strictly controlled App Store and iBooks. Regrettably, there's some truth in that perception. The Google Play app store has seen a flood of adult-content apps and publications, many included under ambiguous or intentionally misleading names, as well as an avalanche of unwanted, often duplicate ebooks. Public domain classic books such as *A Tale of Two Cities*, *Moby Dick*, *A Christmas Carol*, and hundreds of others are frequently converted to ebook format of varying qualities by unassociated individuals and placed in the Google Play app store in hopes of making a quick, often unearned buck. On the other hand, the openness of Google Play creates more variety in apps, more choice, and access to apps that Apple wouldn't allow on iOS because the apps' functionality might compete with Apple's or its partners' interests. The average Android app also costs significantly less than its iOS equivalent in head-to-head comparisons.

Because Google Play is open to any content a developer wants to publish, and because the Android operating system is being actively improved by so many different device manufacturers and programmers, it has real potential to improve faster and more often than iOS. Thus, it's entirely possible that Android-powered tablets could at any time take top market share from iPad. From the perspective of an epublisher, that means you must take Android seriously, and even if you don't target Android readers right now (a mistake in my opinion because Android tablets typically account for 30–40 percent of the tablet market), you must at least be ready to do so at a moment's notice.

FIGURE 1.6
A sampling of
Android-powered
tablets

ASUS Eee Pad Transformer

Lenovo ThinkPad Tablet

LG Optimus Pad

Samsung Galaxy Tab 10.1

Sony Tablet P

Photos courtesy of the device manufacturers

AMAZON TABLETS

Amazon debuted a potent entry into the tablet market with its Kindle Fire tablet (and other tablets are reportedly under development). Fire runs on Android, but it's a modified implementation with a uniquely Amazon user interface hiding all but a few small parts of Android (see Figure 1.7). In fact, Amazon doesn't even promote the fact that Fire uses Android; customers don't even think about the Fire's operating system, but those who do just think of it as Amazon's original creation unencumbered by the negatives associated with Android. Next, instead of pricing its 7-inch tablet in the then-standard $350–$600 range for similarly sized tablets, Fire debuted at $199 and was positioned as an entertainment device, not the all-around tablet iPad is marketed as, though the Fire lacks none of the functionality of other tablets (with the arguable exception of a camera). It merely focuses on content, offering books, movies, music, and periodicals exclusively from Amazon's library. Amazon also built a custom user interface on top of Android and limited user access to Amazon's *own* app store rather than to Google Play, thus eliminating the flooding of bad content. Thus, the Fire is an Android-powered walled garden like the iPad but backed by a much larger, long-established, curated collection of Amazon-approved apps, ebooks, movies, music, and more.

FIGURE 1.7
The Kindle Fire: built on Android but with a twist

Photo courtesy of Amazon

Apparently Amazon did everything right with the Fire, because by February 2012, only four months after its debut, the Kindle Fire had captured over 50 percent of the market among all Android tablets (comScore April 2012). Perhaps even more significantly, the cellular provider favorite Samsung Galaxy Tab tablets—all sizes in the line—was the next most popular Android tablet with only 15.4 percent market share.

So significant is Amazon's position in the tablet market that I strongly recommend digital publishers think of it as a completely different operating system. When publicizing that their epublications are available for or "run great on" iPad and Android tablets, I recommend they add Amazon's tablet to the list as if it weren't related to Android at all.

ANDROID 2.2 AND OLDER

The initial batch of Android-powered tablets was based on Android version 2.2 or older, which was an operating system built exclusively for phones. The result was a very slow, very poor, often-crashing user experience on a tablet. Moreover, the fact that Android 2 wasn't built for tablets meant that there weren't many apps available for it that could run on tablet hardware, and most of those that did were designed for a small screen and looked horrible when blown up to a 7- or 10-inch display.

Most such tablets initially were iPad knockoffs, cheap plastic clones of iPads with names like "ePad" and "aPad," though a few big-name manufacturers had early success with Android 2–powered tablets, most notably Motorola with its XOOM and Samsung with the Galaxy Tab. These devices were typically priced far below iPad prices, which is why they sold well.

It wasn't until the release of Android 2.3—better known by its codename "Gingerbread"—in December 2010 that the Android operating system was capable of delivering graphics of decent quality to larger-screen devices such as tablets. With Gingerbread also came apps capable of running on such devices. A surprising number of powerful tablets continue to run on Android 2.3, including the initial release of the Kindle Fire and numerous other devices released well after the Fire's debut.

Unfortunately, there are still Android 2.1 and 2.2–powered tablets in circulation, and new ones sell each week. As of this writing, Bed Bath & Beyond sells one in-store and online for $219.99. BestBuy.com offers 21 different models. Similar units are sold by warehouse clubs and in overstock stores. Average purchasers don't know that they're getting old technology with limited functionality. The boxes for these devices promote their strengths, not their weaknesses; in most cases, the version of Android running on the device is listed only in the fine print on the back—if at all. Pandigital, one of the largest purveyors of this outdated tech in an astonishing variety of big-name online and brick-and-mortar store chains, takes great pains to hide the fact that its line of 7- and 9-inch Novel Multimedia Tablet & Color eReader tablets run on Android 2.1. The product specifications on Pandigital's own site list the operating system as merely "Android," whereas the more expensive Android 2.3–powered devices identify the Android version number in the same place. In fact, the version number of the operating system isn't listed *anywhere* directly. Upon close examination of the product boxes—if you happen to have access to one before you purchase it—you'll see way down on the back of the box it says it "supports…Android 2.0 audio format." And, of course, these devices are not upgradable to any later version of Android.

Digital publishers like you need to know that these devices are out there—that they are being marketed to consumers who (justifiably) don't know any better, even when the operating system version isn't deliberately hidden from them. You must also realize that, well, you can't publish to them. These devices will read ebooks just fine—for now, until the ebook stores upgrade their software and systems beyond the capabilities of these version-stagnant tablets—but they can't read media-rich tablet publications because no one has built a Folio or Issue viewer for them (and never will). The same goes for interactive replica publications—no one is going to build apps for a dead operating system. Even Android *phones* moved up to Android 3.*x* and 4. The browser and HTML rendering engine in Android 2.2 or older won't fully support HTML5, a feature added as of 2.3, so there goes that otherwise universal format. PDFs *can* be viewed on Android 2 with the installation of Adobe Reader or a similar PDF-reading app, but the features of PDFs supported by these Android 2–compatible PDF readers are not complete; audio and video typically work but buttons, rollovers, and other interactivity features tend to break. Of course, that's assuming Android 2 tablet owners can still find Android 2–compatible PDF reader apps on Google Play or the proprietary app stores included with many of these sub-par tablets.

BlackBerry Tablet OS

The first, and thus far only, tablet running the Research In Motion (RIM) BlackBerry Tablet Operating System is the BlackBerry PlayBook (Figure 1.8). BlackBerry phones held a huge, roughly 11 percent share of smartphone sales worldwide and, as of October 2011, included 70 million subscribers to the BlackBerry Internet Service, through which BlackBerry phones and PDAs access the Internet. BlackBerry is a mainstay brand in mobile computing and communication. Thus, when the BlackBerry PlayBook debuted in April 2011 with 50,000 units sold on the first day, it was obvious the PlayBook would be a righteous competitor to the iPad—some called it the "iPad killer" (note how often that name is bandied about).

FIGURE 1.8
The BlackBerry
PlayBook

Photo courtesy of Research in Motion

Although the PlayBook was made available for sale to the general public in April 2011, RIM had been demonstrating it since fall 2010 with the help and cooperation of Adobe, whose AIR and Flash application technologies were central to the functionality of the PlayBook. Weighing less than a pound and featuring advanced multimedia hardware and, of course, being from BlackBerry, the PlayBook should have done well. It didn't.

Six months after public launch and that massive initial sales date, RIM announced that it had shipped half a million units in that first quarter but only 200,000 units in the second. Most people have never heard of the PlayBook. By 4Q2011 it had become a bit player in the big drama of tablets with approximately 3 percent market share; by 2Q2012 that share had dropped to less than 1 percent with no sign of swinging back. Moreover, major app developers stopped developing for the PlayBook or never started. Even Adobe killed development of its Adobe Content Viewer for PlayBook, the technology that allows the display of interactive magazines on the tablet.

For now, digital publishers should recognize that there are close to a million PlayBooks out there and that their owners absolutely love them. The tablet can read ebooks, with available Kindle and Kobo (no NOOK) apps, access the Web for HTML5-based content, and natively read PDF publications, but it can no longer display rich-media app-based publications.

WINDOWS

Microsoft Windows has been powering mobile devices for more than a decade. First there was Windows Mobile, which ran on PDAs (remember those?) and mobile phones, but with the release of Windows 7, the "Mobile" moniker was dropped, leaving a mobile-optimized version of Windows 7, and then Windows 8, just part of the Windows family.

The biggest distinction between Windows-powered tablets and its competitors is Windows's ability to run full applications, not just apps. In fact, at least on the array of tablets sporting Intel chips and possibly those using chips by other manufacturers, Microsoft boasts that if you can run it on a Windows 7 or 8 desktop computer, you can run it on a Windows 7 or 8 tablet. That includes full versions of Microsoft Office applications like Word, Excel, and PowerPoint rather than the limited-functionality Office knockoff apps you'll find available for use on the iPad and Android tablets. Theoretically, you can also run full graphics software like Photoshop or InDesign, though I haven't had a chance to put that to the test because, as of this writing, there are no Windows 7 or 8 tablets available with the necessary hardware capabilities.

Assuming mobile-app developers embrace Windows 8, through the Windows App Store users can install mobile apps, including digital newsstands that would enable them to read interactive magazine- and digital replica–format publications. Therefore, it may come to pass that Windows desktop and laptop computers, which, as of Windows 8, also have access to the Windows App Store, could finally display richly interactive publications formerly available only on tablets.

Combine Windows tablets' full application support with their heretofore unheard-of multitasking and split-screen application-usage features, and you have a tablet operating system ready to grab a significant—even, perhaps, the top—market share.

webOS

I'm including the Hewlett-Packard TouchPad and its webOS here merely for completeness. Yes, webOS is still out there, though you may be more familiar with its previous name, Palm OS, as in Palm Pilot. Hewlett-Packard bought Palm some time ago and, in 2011, renamed the Palm OS to webOS, which makes sense now that just about every device runs from one's palm.

The first webOS-powered tablet was the HP TouchPad (Figure 1.9), released in June 2011 to riotous critical praise. The TouchPad was declared by some as the "iPad killer" *and* the "Android killer!" Sales were abysmal. Best Buy, which marketed the hell out of the TouchPad including top in-store placement ahead of all other tablets except the iPad, still had 80 percent of its inventory by mid-August. Other retailers had the same result. That same month the TouchPad was discontinued, with HP stating that it was dropping webOS entirely. HP then instructed retailers to sell off their remaining units of the TouchPad for $99 for the 16 GB unit and $149 for the 32 GB unit. They sold like hotcakes with every retailer selling out within hours. HP received so many orders for the cut-rate TouchPad that it had to do another manufacturing run just to satisfy demand. In October 2011 HP officially stopped taking orders, offering its few remaining units of the TouchPad bundled with new HP laptops.

FIGURE 1.9
The HP TouchPad

Photo courtesy of Hewlett-Packard

The inventory sell-off didn't resurrect or, in the long run, really even help the TouchPad or webOS, but it did prove that lower-priced tablets would sell. If Android tablet-makers or RIM pay attention, they might carve out big tablet market shares for themselves.

In December 2011, HP made webOS *open source*, giving it to the world to do something with. To date, the world hasn't done too much with it—remember that Android is also open source and has already been open for quite some time to tinkering by any interested programmer or company.

As far as digital publishing is concerned, the TouchPad is a blip on the radar—here and then gone. There's no reason to think about targeting epublication design for the TouchPad screen or features. Many TouchPad owners have already hacked the devices to run Android OS, giving them access to Google Play and all the other abilities of an Android tablet. Those who haven't hacked them don't expect new development on the TouchPad; besides, they can at least read EPUBS and PDFs and use HTML5-based publications through a web browser.

Tablet Sizes

Another important factor to consider when designing for tablets is their screen sizes. Because there are not yet any standards, screen sizes vary wildly, though two brackets have become common. First you have full-sized tablets, those with screens around 10 inches diagonally, with resolutions ranging between 2048×1536, 1024×768, and 1280×800. The second common bracket is about 7 inches diagonally, with screen resolutions in the range of 1024×600 to 800×480; I call these mini-tablets, as they strike me in form and observed consumer usage as being halfway between a smartphone and a full-sized tablet (see Figure 1.10). There are some 5-, 6-, 8-, and 11-inch tablets out there, but most manufacturers seem to be concentrating on the 7- and 10-inch sizes.

FIGURE 1.10
Comparing differ-
ent device screens
at scale. Left to
right: an iPhone 4S,
an HTC Evo 3D,
a Kindle Fire, an
iPad 3, and an
ASUS Eee Pad
Transformer.

Full-sized tablets include the iPad line (9.7 inches), Samsung Galaxy Tab 10.1 (10.1 inches), ASUS Eee Transformer line (10.1 inches), and Motorola XOOM (10.1 inches); they offer a pretty comfortable reading experience for media-rich digital publications. Even with interactive rep-licas, which are basically print magazines displayed on a tablet screen and don't reflow to fit the screen, reading one page displayed full-screen is comfortable for most people. Reading is almost impossible without pinch-zooming when a full spread is shown on the tablet screen, though. In my experience, full-sized tablets are viable replacements for most tasks formerly handled by laptops, which is what makes them marginally more popular than mini-tablets.

On the other hand, mini-tablets like the original Samsung Galaxy Tab, the Kindle Fire, the NOOK Tablet, the Dell Streak, and the HTC Flyer—all 7 inches—are even more portable than full-sized tablets. Many people love the small form factor, easily deposited in a purse, backpack, or large coat pocket. Typically mini-tablets are used for media viewing (Netflix, YouTube, Hulu, and so on) and general Internet usage (browsing, social media, email), but owners of these devices just as often will read digital publications on them. Naturally, ebooks work great as mini-tablets and are about the size of handheld ereaders, which are themselves about the size of paperback books. Although many digital replicas are available on mini-tablets, media-rich digital publications don't often do great on these devices because such publications tend to be designed specifically for larger screens and resolutions. This leaves mini-tablet owners feeling left out by many publications. As an epublisher, that presents an opportunity for you. Given the popularity of smaller tablets, I strongly suggest designing a version of your publication specifi-cally to fit 7-inch screens—especially in light of the dominance of the very successful 7-inch Kindle Fire.

In seeming opposition to the Kindle Fire's hold of more than half the Android tablet market are figures from comScore measuring web page impressions. In findings released by the digital business analytics in April 2012: "10″ tablets have a 39-percent higher consumption rate than 7″ tablets and a 58-percent higher rate than 5″ tablets."

Computers

You might be tempted to skip this section, thinking it's a no-brainer that standard computers would support all the digital publication classes and be ideally suited to display any type of digital publication you might want to publish. If that's what you're thinking, you'd be in error.

True, there are software-based and in some cases even web-based ereaders available. You can download the Kindle, NOOK, or Kobo ereader software free for Windows, Mac OS X, and even for many flavors of UNIX. You can also read many ebooks directly in your web browser, without installing any software, such as with Amazon's Kindle Cloud Reader. Dozens of other ebook readers—some commercial, most free or open source—abound as well. Adobe even makes one, called Adobe Digital Editions; this ebook reader was bundled with other Adobe software and made available as a standalone download, though it hasn't seen widespread use. Despite the selection of ereader software, the big stores like Amazon's Kindle, Barnes & Noble's NOOK, and Kobo dominate ebook reading on desktop, laptop, and netbook computers just as they rule the handheld ereader class (see Figure 1.11).

FIGURE 1.11
Kobo Desktop ereader software displaying an ebook (Jane Austen's *Pride & Prejudice*) on a Windows computer

As reading ebooks becomes more popular in general, so does the portion of consumers reading ebooks on computers. This is deceptive, however, because that's the smallest and slowest-growing segment. More and more people are reading ebooks, true, and naturally many of them start out using their office, school, or home computers for that purpose. However, computer monitors are not built to comfortably accommodate extended periods of reading (trust me, I have to write and edit this book on standard monitors). Eventually, the majority of consumers who read more than the occasional ebook tend to purchase either a handheld ereader or a tablet, doing the bulk of their reading on those devices. Thus, as you begin to create ebook content, you may be tempted to design for the flexible, high-resolution, full-color world of computer-based ereaders, but the reality is that only a small portion of your audience is likely to view your publication within that environment. The rest will be using, in order of frequency, the following: handheld ereaders, tablets, and mobile phones.

The shift away from standard computers for reading digital content is being sped along by the fact that app-based interactive magazines are completely unusable on computers. *Sports Illustrated, Oprah Magazine, Maxim, Popular Science, Wired*, and a host of other big-brand magazines publish digitally only or primarily in formats that work on tablets, as *folios* or *apps*. To date there are no applications or technologies (beyond previewers as you build your own richly interactive publications) to view media-rich digital magazines (and catalogs, enhanced books, and so on) or even most digital replica–format publications on standard computers. The fact that hundreds of popular periodicals are available electronically only on tablets increases demand for, and usage of, tablets while simultaneously reducing demand and usage, at least with respect to consuming epublications of all types, on desktop, laptop, and netbook computers.

As a publisher of electronic content, if you want to include computer-based reading in your publications' reach, you have two choices. First, you can create multiple-format editions of your publication, such as app-based for tablets and PDF- or HTML5-based for computers. Alternatively, you could publish exclusively in PDF or HTML5, relying on those formats' almost universal support across devices to present a single edition to a variety of devices. Of course, there are pros and cons to each option, which we'll get into in Chapter 2, "Learning about Digital Publishing Formats."

Mobile Phones

Because one of the main characteristics of EPUB-format ebooks is their ability to reflow and adapt to the size of any screen, many people choose to do some or all of their ebook reading on mobile smartphones. (Personally I can't; I read rather fast, and with so little text fitting on a phone screen, the result is that I'm nearly constantly swiping to advance pages.)

Again, as with computers, Kindle and NOOK dominate these platforms—with one exception. On iOS-based devices such as the Apple iPad, iPhone, and iPod Touch, Apple's own iBooks is the top ebook reader and store. Its library isn't quite as large as Amazon's or Barnes & Noble's, but iBooks offers support for nonstandard epublication formats such as fixed-layout and picture books as well as other unique features.

Of course, anything but fully reflowable ebooks is harder to read on the small screen of a mobile phone than on any other device. Consequently, very few people will use a mobile phone, even if they don't have ready access to a larger-screened device, to read more advanced, more interactive, or fixed-layout publications. Even Apple's own fixed-layout ebooks are almost impossible to read on an iPhone. Thus, the only two viable formats to use in targeting mobile phone readers are EPUB and liquid layout HTML5 (for a discussion of the latter, see my website, `http://iampariah.com`).

Hybrid Devices

A number of hybrid devices out there merge handheld ereader with tablet or tablet with laptop. Ever since their debut, iPads have been the target (victim?) of attempts to create hybrids. The Crux360 pictured in Figure 1.12 is only one of numerous such insert-iPad-to-make-instant-netbook devices. Tablet-laptop hybrids like the ASUS Eee Pad Transformer line are proving quite popular. They are built with rugged, rounded metal backs and, once attached to the optional keyboard dock, complete the transformation into clamshell-style netbook or laptop. The ASUS Eee Pad Slider harkens back to pre-iPad slates by incorporating the keyboard, USB ports, and other standard laptop and netbook features into a device that can be used as a tablet or slid open to function as a netbook. Similarly, Lenovo's IdeaPad was built to easily slip in and out of a clamshell cover to become a netbook. The ThinkPad line of Android tablets, also by Lenovo, some of which include a built-in precision stylus for drawing and writing on-screen with the familiar feel of using a pencil or pen, come with a docking station into which you can connect a full-sized keyboard and mouse, external speakers, microphone, and other devices; the ThinkPad devices are therefore suggesting themselves as replacements to desktop computers, but replacements you pick up and interact with on the go, like slates. Figure 1.12 shows various hybrid devices.

FIGURE 1.12
Numerous tablets are tasked as hybrid devices, either by design or with after-market add-ons.

The Crux360 iPad case with iPad inserted

The Acer Iconia Tab W500 with its keyboard dock

The ASUS Eee Pad Slider

The ASUS Eee Pad Transformer

The Lenovo IdeaPad

The Lenovo ThinkPad with keyboard

Photos courtesy of the device manufacturers

Other hybrid devices fall squarely in one class but borrow features or characteristics from another. One example of the latter is the appearance of crossword puzzles, sodoku, and other games, as well as EPUB-based periodicals, on ereaders. Another example, going the other way, is tablets from ereader manufacturers. The Amazon Kindle Fire, an Android-based 7-inch touch-screen device, is definitely a tablet but one with ebook reading enhancements drawn from the venerable ereader models in the Kindle product line. Amazon built a custom user interface on top of Android, integrating its Kindle store and ereader into nearly every facet of the device's use and encouraging Fire owners to think of the device as an ereader as well as a tablet. Barnes & Noble did much the same with its NOOK Tablet, as did Kobo with its 7-inch Vox tablet, also based on Android (see Figure 1.13).

FIGURE 1.13
Tablets marketed as more powerful, not-just-reading ereaders, all about the same size as a typical handheld ereader

Kindle Fire   Barnes & Noble NOOK Tablet   Kobo Vox

Photos courtesy of the device manufacturers

Future Devices

In the future of digital-publication–delivery devices, we'll see slimmer, lighter devices; devices without practical internal storage; and devices with not just touch interaction but possibly distortion interaction, too. About a dozen different companies, from LG to MIT splinter foundations, have epaper concepts gradually coming to market. These are one-, two-, or full-color displays ranging from about 4×6-inches (the average size of a handheld ereader) up to 11×17, and they are flexible, rollable, and even foldable. The idea is that content will live in the cloud (yeah, I'm a little sick of that phrase, too, but what can we do?). Instead of storing publications on the device, epaper readers will function more like handheld ereaders do now, with an always-on, dedicated wireless connection similar to today's Kindles, NOOKs, and other ereader devices.

With current ereaders you have to download books, stories, articles, and so on to the device, which are kept in internal storage. Epaper will keep your books and more in the cloud—out on the Internet—and download to the epaper device one page at a time via an always-on background connection. The process will be quick; you won't notice a delay between pages. Some of the epaper solutions under development actually hold the next page in cache so it's already there when you swipe to it. And most epaper is being developed to be as thin as just a few sheets or even a single sheet of regular copier paper. Some can be rolled up and stuck in your back pocket, while others can be folded and slipped into a wallet. Either way, when you want the latest book, magazine, catalog, or even newspaper, with up-to-the-minute article updates, you just have to open the page again.

These ereaders are coming, and they'll become not only the handheld ereaders of the future but also the tablets. LG Philips debuted its first full-color epaper device in 2007 (the black-and-white version demoed a year earlier). At the Consumer Electronics Expo in 2011, Nokia demonstrated the Kinetic, a full-color smartphone device that includes the obligatory touchscreen but also—pardon the pun—a kinetic interface. Users actually bend the phone to zoom in or out on pictures, web pages, and other content and twist the flexible phone to scroll or move through a list such as a photo album, an email inbox, or the pages of a digital magazine. Blow the Kinetic up to 7 or 10 inches, and you have a flexible tablet—Nokia is already working on that.

These devices are coming—some are here already—but fortunately the operating systems seem to have stabilized for now, with iOS, Android, custom-covered Android a la Amazon's offerings, and Windows 8 being the big four. Given the experience of HP's webOS-based TouchPad and RIM's BlackBerry PlayBook, it's not likely that we'll see other whole mobile operating systems debuting for quite some time. What we will see are improvements and refinements of the ones we already have, more makers following Amazon's lead in creating custom user experiences built atop existing operating systems, and expansions of those mobile operating systems to more and more areas of our lives, with less reliance on standard computers.

Chapter 2

Learning about Digital Publishing Formats

Like devices, epublication formats are numerous and varied, with subtle differences between them, but large divergences in purpose, capability, and device support. Consequently, it's most logical and productive to think of epublications in terms of format classes, with each class offering a particular combination of purpose, capability, and device support.

In this chapter, you will learn about the following:

◆ Quick Reference: Format Capabilities

◆ EPUB

◆ Amazon Kindle Formats: MOBI, AZW, and KF8

◆ PDF

◆ Digital Replica

◆ Interactive Magazine

◆ HTML5

Quick Reference: Format Capabilities

Table 2.1 offers a quick reference to the capabilities of each epublication class to help you determine the best format for your epublications. In the future, referring to this chart may save you a lot of rereading just to refresh your memory about what features a specific format class does and does not support.

TABLE 2.1:   Content and Interactivity Support per Format

	EPUB	AMAZON KINDLE FORMATS	PDF	DIGITAL REPLICA	INTERACTIVE MAGAZINE	HTML5
Reflowable text	☑		☑	◪		☑
Audio	☑		☑	☑	☑	☑

TABLE 2.1:   Content and Interactivity Support per Format   *(continued)*

	EPUB	AMAZON KINDLE FORMATS	PDF	DIGITAL REPLICA	INTERACTIVE MAGAZINE	HTML5
Video	◩		☑	☑	☑	☑
Video—Link to specific frames or time points			☑			☑
Hyperlinks (URL, email, telephone, SMS, Apple App Store/Google Play/ BlackBerry App World)	☑		☑	☑	☑	☑
Hyperlinks to internal content			☑		◩	☑
Publication-page thumbnails	◩		☑	☑	☑	◩
JavaScript	◩		☑		◩	☑
Forms			☑		◩	☑
Button actions			☑		☑	☑
Multiple actions per button			☑		☑	☑
Zoomable	☑		☑	☑	☑	☑
Image panning			◩		☑	☑
Image slideshows			☑		☑	☑
Video slideshows			☑		☑	☑
Content replacement			☑		☑	☑
In-page embedded web content			◩		☑	☑
Panoramas					☑	☑
3D rotatable images					☑	☑
In-page scrollable content					☑	☑
Vector graphics	☑		☑			☑
In-page animated objects	◩					☑

TABLE 2.1:   Content and Interactivity Support per Format   *(continued)*

	EPUB	AMAZON KINDLE FORMATS	PDF	DIGITAL REPLICA	INTERACTIVE MAGAZINE	HTML5
Drag-and-drop objects						☑
Dynamic server-fed content	☑		☑		☑	☑
Attachments			☑			

Legend: ☑ Yes, the format supports this type of content or interactivity. ◪ The format supports some but not all features of the content or interactivity, and/or some systems or software that produce the format support the option while others do not.

EPUB

EPUB is the international standard for ebooks as read by ereaders and ereader software. EPUB is a shortened form of "electronic publication," though that's a misnomer because everything you read on a screen is technically an electronic publication. EPUB is the standard for ebooks, which, with a couple of exceptions I'll discuss in Chapter 3, "Surveying the Digital Publication Types," is all it's currently suited for, though that may change in the future.

NOTE   You'll see EPUB capitalized in a variety of ways, including ePUB and ePub, but according to the standards body that maintains it, it is properly written as EPUB.

The current version of EPUB is 3, which was officially ratified in November 2011 by the International Digital Publishing Forum, the standards body that defines the EPUB file specification. Because of the length of time between file spec ratification and updates to ereader software, firmware, and, in some cases, hardware, it's entirely possible that some of your audience will be able to read only in EPUB 2 for some time yet to come. That's OK, because EPUBs degrade gracefully for the most part, meaning that you should design for EPUB 3, and any features not understood by the ereader should be ignored while everything else does display.

EPUB is effectively a web page, albeit with much less ability than the average site you might visit in a browser. The format is structured through *XML* and *XHTML*, the latter being a subset of the former's language, while content is styled within the ebook via *CSS* just like any web page. When viewing an EPUB, you are effectively reading a web page whose entire text, images, and other assets are localized and wrapped up into a single EPUB-format archive file, much like a *ZIP* or *RAR* archive. Inside the EPUB is at least the XHTML comprising the text of the book, a CSS stylesheet file controlling the presentation of the book text, and a manifest file that informs the ereader hardware or software about the existence of the other files. We'll get into those components and others in depth in Chapter 6, "Fine-Tuning EPUBs."

Because EPUBs are XHTML and CSS, they are designed and styled like web pages but without many of the bells and whistles possible with pages on the Web. They can be created from InDesign (of course), Apple Pages, QuarkXPress, and other software without the need to ever touch their XHTML and CSS markup or code (see Chapter 4, "Creating Basic Ebooks," for guidance on doing it with InDesign). To go beyond a basic, bland ebook and add color, font variance, imagery, audio, and more, you'll need to get into the XHTML and CSS markup of the ebook—which isn't as scary or as difficult as many think. In Chapters 5 and 6, we'll do just that, with hands-on, easy-to-follow step-by-steps and measurable results.

Despite the ability to control the layout to a degree with XHTML and CSS, ebook presentation is primarily dependent on the reading device and the person wielding it. EPUB text always adapts to fit the screen on which it's viewed, which is perhaps the greatest strength of the format class, and that text can be dynamically resized by the person reading it, growing or shrinking the font size for that individual's optimal reading experience. The dynamic reflow naturally causes changes in the way elements are displayed; images may get moved around; drop caps may show differently on different devices, at different sizes; columns may or may not show as designed; and so on. The bottom line is that, by design, ebooks are fluid and adaptive to their reading environments. Consequently, the control designers have over their layout and appearance is minimal when compared to print publications and even most other digital publication format classes.

Here is a quick look at the advancements in EPUB 3 compared to its previous version, EPUB 2.0.1.

◆ Support for the CSS3 version specification, including better line break and hyphenation control as well as right-to-left text display for languages such as Hebrew, Arabic, and Japanese

◆ Support for multiple CSS stylesheets, which can be used to alter the display of an ebook for different display devices, sizes, and horizontal and vertical orientations as well as give users a choice of background and foreground colors and fonts

◆ Support for HTML5

◆ Support for *JavaScript*

◆ Expanded metadata

◆ Embedding of fonts in *OTF* and *WOFF* formats

◆ Inline vector graphics in *SVG* format

◆ Direct embedding of *MathML* rather than images of mathematic equations

◆ Inline HTML5 rich-media audio and video elements

◆ Text-to-speech and synchronized text and audio functionality

What EPUB Offers

Here are the big characteristics of the EPUB format:

- Typical use: ebooks, ejournals, enewspapers (see definitions in Chapter 3)
- Ideal for mostly text content
- Text automatically reflows to fit any screen
- User-adjustable font sizes for maximum reading comfort
- CSS-based styling
- Supports images and video
- Supports audio captioning and read-aloud ability (in EPUB3 and depending on reading device)
- Supports server-fed dynamic content (with live connection)
- Supports limited JavaScript functions (in EPUB3 and depending on reading device)
- Very small file sizes
- No publication fees

What EPUB Does Not Offer

Conversely, if you want any of the following characteristics in your digital publication, then EPUB is decidedly not the right format to choose.

- Precise layout control (except in fixed-layout EPUBs, which only a few latest-generation devices support)
- Touch interactivity (beyond tapping to change pages and activate hyperlinks and embedded audio or video)
- Nonlinear reading experience
- Mostly photographic or illustrative book (except fixed-layout EPUBs)
- Embedded games
- A large amount of video content

The Business of EPUB

Is there money in producing EPUB-formatted ebooks? You betcha! Here are some facts to establish that point right up front:

- There were $313 million in ebook sales in 2009 (Association of American Publishers [AAP] and Book Study Industry Group [BISG], April 2010).
- In 2010 ebook sales increased to $1.62 billion (AAP/BISG, May 2011).
- Tablet and ereader ownership in the U.S. doubled during the three-week 2011–2012 holiday season, December 2011 to January 2012 (Pew Internet & American Life Project, January 2012).

◆ 60 percent of iPad owners read ebooks on the iPad (Simba Information report, April 2011).

◆ 19 percent of all U.S. adults own an ebook reader (inclusive of tablets) according to the January 2012 Pew report.

◆ One fifth of U.S. adults report having read an ebook in the past year (Pew Internet & American Life Project, April 2012).

◆ Of those, 20 percent have an annual household income of under $30 thousand, 25 percent have an income of $30–49 thousand, 35 percent are in the $50–74 thousand range, and 38 percent have annual household incomes in excess of $75 thousand.

◆ 89 percent of 16 and older U.S. ereader (and tablet) owners read ebooks for pleasure (Pew Internet & American Life Project, April 2012).

◆ 71 percent of 16 and older U.S. ereader (and tablet) owners read ebooks for work or school; 49 percent report doing so daily (Pew Internet & American Life Project, April 2012).

◆ Forrester Research predicts that one third of U.S. adults will own a tablet and 29.4 million people will own an ereader by 2015 (note that this includes tablets and other mobile devices using installed ereader software).

◆ 49 percent increase in adult (all, fiction and non-fiction) ebook sales between January 2011 and January 2012 (AAP, March 2012).

◆ 150 percent increase in religious segment ebooks between January 2011 and January 2012 (AAP, March 2012).

◆ 475 percent increase in children's and young adult market ebooks between January 2011 and January 2012 (AAP, March 2012).

◆ 30 percent of adult ereader owners have college educations, while approximately 15 percent of ereader owners only report a high school education (Pew report, January 2012).

◆ Nearly half of U.S. publishers expect ebooks to dominate all book sales by 2014 (*PublishingPerspectives.com*, 26 January 2011).

◆ 67 percent of U.S. public libraries offer ebooks for lending to privately owned ereaders, up from 38 percent in 2008 (American Library Association [ALA], *State of America's Libraries Report*, April 2012).

◆ 28 percent of U.S. public libraries lend ereader and mobile devices for ebook consumption (ALA, April 2012).

◆ 82 percent of U.S. public libraries are expected to offer ebooks by 2014.

◆ 94 percent of U.S. academic libraries offer ebooks.

◆ The U.S. Department of Education estimates that 80 percent of academic libraries' budgets will be allocated to purchasing and producing electronic content by 2020.

- 94 percent of academic libraries offer ebooks (*Library Journal* and *School Library Journal* survey, November 2010).

- By 2020 80 percent of academic library budgets are expected to be allocated for electronic content (U.S. Dept. of Education, NCES, Academic Libraries Survey, 2011).

- 61 percent of ebook readers prefer purchasing ebooks to borrowing them (Pew Internet & American Life Project, April 2012).

TIP Need more statistics, demographics, and other hard data about ebook and ereader sales, adoption rates, and annual revenue? Visit my websites, `http://WorkflowEPUB.com` and `http://iamPariah.com`, for constantly updated figures and data as well as epublishing news, tutorials, and more.

EPUB Examples

The best way to understand the characteristics of the EPUB type is to look at examples. If you're familiar with ebooks at all, you've probably already looked at many. If not, refer to Figure 2.1, which shows a few examples across fiction, nonfiction, and children's genres. Naturally you'll need the most modern ereader software you can get your hands on, and you should ideally try the different examples in as many classes of devices as possible.

FIGURE 2.1

Examples of EPUBS: (a) *Mastering InDesign CS5 for Print Design & Production* by Pariah Burke as viewed on a Kindle handheld ereader; (b) *Side Jobs: A Novel of the Dresden Files* by Jim Butcher viewed in iBooks on an iPad; (c) *Richard Scarry's Bedtime Stories* by Richard Scarry viewed in NOOK for Android on a 7-inch Android tablet

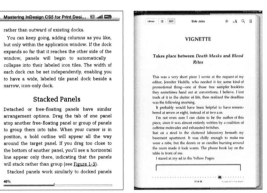

a

b

c

EPUB Production Roles

Because EPUB ebooks may be produced in a wide variety of software and are less difficult to create than the average simple website, like websites, they can be created by individuals or teams. Depending on the content of the ebook, some or all of the following roles will need to be filled by team members or the individual self-publisher:

◆ Author/copywriter

◆ Developmental editor

◆ Copyeditor

◆ Technical editor

◆ Indexer

◆ Compositor

◆ Production artist

◆ Illustrator

◆ Graphic designer

◆ Photographer

◆ Photo retoucher

◆ Videographer

◆ Video editor

◆ HTML/XHTML designer

◆ CSS styler

Amazon Kindle Formats: MOBI, AZW, and KF8

Amazon.com, which parlayed online printed book sales into an emporium offering everything from computer components to clothing, is inarguably one the largest providers of both digital publications and products on which to consume those digital publications.

One of the reasons Amazon became so successful in the digital-publication–distribution space is its creation of proprietary formats that didn't wait for international standards bodies in order to innovate. For instance, while the rest of the world was still trying to define digital rights management, Amazon had already built and implemented its own DRM system within ebooks sold through its Kindle devices and software.

Using Amazon devices and software to read econtent is a seamless, virtually bug-free experience, with digital-content features leading the industry or trailing behind other innovators by only a short time. For publishers, supporting proprietary file formats typically means redundant workflows or at least content-conversion headaches—which is true of fixed-layout ebooks for Amazon devices but not of standard ebooks. Amazon carefully crafted its proprietary formats and its publication system to reduce the amount of work for publishers. While Amazon's Kindle devices don't use the industry-standard EPUB ebook format, Amazon provides several tools free of charge to convert valid EPUB files into Kindle formats without significant work. One such tool is an export plug-in for InDesign; simply export to the Kindle-approved MOBI format, and you're done. The plug-in will even submit the ebook to the Amazon store during export if you want it to do so. Another tool is a command-line utility called KindleGen that will convert EPUBs, even fixed-layout EPUBs, into Kindle-ready MOBI and KF8 formats.

Each of the Kindle formats detailed in the following sections are roughly equivalent to more standardized formats. For example, EPUB has never been a natively supported file format, but MOBI and AZW can do just about everything EPUB can. As long as you read the earlier section on EPUB, you'll understand MOBI as well. For this reason, I'll keep the discussion of the Amazon formats brief, noting similar formats and the differences Amazon's formats bring to the equation.

The chronology and categorization of Amazon proprietary formats follows generations of Kindle devices, which is the best way to explain those formats.

Kindle 1 Generation

The first generation of Kindle devices uses Amazon's DRM-enabled AZW file format, which is based on the Mobipocket type, which can be MOBI or PRC file formats; the Mobipocket type of ebook is most commonly referenced as simply MOBI in recognition of the more commonly seen of the two file extensions. Amazon owns both the Mobipocket books and AZW file formats. MOBI is an unprotected format, free from digital rights management, which is why free online libraries often distribute MOBI files alongside EPUB editions of their ebooks. AZW, conversely, is DRM-restricted, enabling Amazon to control access to paid content, including preventing Kindle ebooks from being opened in other applications or transferred to other Kindle users (outside Amazon's lending system). Consumers never see the AZW file extension and typically have no idea it exists; for them, the experience is that they purchase an ebook through the Kindle store, and that ebook is delivered, ready to read. For publishers, AZW enables content protection without impeding user experience (unlike DRM efforts in other media, such as music and films), creating trust with publishers, and is therefore creditable with building much of the foundation of the ebook industry.

Other than the superior DRM in AZW, both AZW and MOBI in the first-generation Kindle devices contain roughly the same features and functions as EPUB version 1.

Kindle 2 and 3

The second and third generations of Kindle, including the Kindle Keyboard, support a more feature-rich version of AZW (and MOBI), with features on par with EPUB 2.01 and some early EPUB 3 features, long before EPUB 3 was ratified as an official standard.

PDF files can also be viewed on second- and third-generation Kindle devices natively, whereas the first-generation Kindles required PDFs to be converted to AZW.

Kindle 4 and Fire

The latest ebook format for Amazon is *KF8* (Kindle Format 8), built for Kindle tablets and the fourth generation of Kindle handheld ereaders and software, which include the keyboard-less Kindle and the Kindle Touch series. Although these devices still support AZW natively and transparently, Amazon is transitioning away from AZW into KF8. When designing natively for this generation and future Kindle devices, use KF8.

The KF8 format is roughly equivalent to EPUB 3, with support for CSS3, HTML5, fixed layouts, embedded fonts, SVG graphics, and more advanced audio and video inclusion. Thus, KF8 is the format to use when creating fixed-layout ebooks (discussed on my website, `http://iampariah.com`).

Kindle Publishing and Conversion Utilities

Again, for most ebooks it's not necessary to build specifically for Kindle, in Amazon's proprietary formats. Amazon makes several easy conversion tools available, and, in fact, some of the most popular third-party utilities also support relatively easy conversion of standardized formats (EPUB, PDF, HTML, and so on) into these proprietary formats. Calibre, a third-party EPUB editor and converter we'll make extensive use of in later chapters, can convert EPUB and many other formats into AZW and KF8, as can Amazon's own Kindle Publisher Tools, including KindleGen, Kindle Previewer, and the Kindle Export plug-in for InDesign. You can access all of these tools at `http://abbrv.it/DigiToolsIDTools`.

As you get into advanced ebooks or seek to take advantage of the unique capabilities inherent in Amazon's proprietary formats, you will need to work directly with the code of the MOBI, AZW, and KF8 formats.

PDF

PDF has long been the format of choice for a wide array of digital publications, from books and manuals to magazines and catalogs and everything in between. It supports all modern media and a good deal of interactivity, is relatively easy to create, and is readable by just about every screened device.

Ironically, many people dismiss PDF as a viable digital-publication format because of how common and pervasive PDF is in the modern world. We so frequently deal with PDF contracts, user manuals, reports, design proofs, email archives, web page captures, and all sorts of other simple, "flat" PDFs that many forget or never learn that PDFs can be so much more. They can contain audio and video—and with more precise control than that offered in most other formats, including digital magazines; they support in-the-page slideshows, rollover effects, and content replacement; text can be built to reflow to fit the screen on which the PDF is displayed; users can bookmark, highlight, and annotate the content; hyperlinks in PDF can execute multiple actions simultaneously (such as play a video and launch a URL or zoom into a specific area of an image and activate an audio track), something no other format except HTML5 can do; and if the built-in interactivity isn't sufficient, PDFs are scriptable via JavaScript for advanced interaction and function. PDFs also have built-in security features that can be augmented with DRM via the Adobe LiveCycle Server product.

Most importantly, PDF is a near-universal format. Who doesn't have a PDF reader on her computer? Mac OS X even comes with one built in. Everyone else—and Mac users who want the full PDF experience—can easily install the free Adobe Reader, which is available for Windows, Mac, UNIX, iOS (5 and newer), Android, Fire, and so on, for a total of 23 different operating systems and platforms. Just about any Internet-connected screen in the world can display a PDF.

From the design and production point of view, PDF is already a familiar format with which we work every day; making it interactive is a little more work, but far less work than creating tablet-only interactive digital magazines. Designing the interactivity into a PDF happens in InDesign, just like everything else; you add a video here, create a slideshow on this page, and make multistate objects over there (see Chapter 7, "Creating PDF Publications for Digital Delivery").

I am not trying to persuade you to use PDF over any of the other formats discussed in this section. What I *am* pointing out is that PDF is still viable as a digital-publication format, so the newer formats and devices don't automatically make PDF obsolete.

TIP   Subsequent mentions of the Apple App Store, Google Play app store, and BlackBerry App World will use the terms App Store, Google Play, and App World, respectively.

Publishing a PDF also doesn't require any additional licensing fees. It can be distributed through ebook stores, but typically not in the Apple App Store, Google Play app store (formerly Android Market), or BlackBerry App World, which can be a downside depending on your distribution goals. It's also not an either/or situation; you can certainly publish both a tablet-only app version *and* a PDF for everywhere else.

What PDFs Offer

In Chapter 7, we'll go step by step through creating PDF-based magazines, catalogs, and other digital publications while discussing the strengths and weaknesses of the format in depth. For now, here are the big characteristics of PDF-based publications. Note that some of them are not available for all platforms.

- Near-universal device support

- May be distributed via iBookstore, Kindle Store, NOOK Store, and just about any other means

- Precise layout control

- Optional reflow of text to fit any screen

- Highly interactive

- Supports images, audio, video

- Supports vector graphics

- Supports rollovers and content replacement

- Supports integrated forms

- Supports JavaScript

- Supports zooming

- Optional in-publication subscription and ordering system (via integration with web-based ecommerce system)

- Enables user annotation, bookmarking, and highlighting

- Built-in table of contents

- Built-in navigational system

- Linear and nonlinear reading capabilities

◆   Ability to include attachments

◆   Quick conversion from print edition layouts

◆   No publication fees

What PDFs Do Not Offer

The following are features you *won't* get in PDF-based publications:

◆   Multiple layouts for horizontal and vertical device orientations

◆   Scrolling areas

◆   Embedded web content

◆   3D rotatable objects

◆   Delivery via App Store, Google Play, or App World

The Business of PDFs

Several factors minimize the ability of anyone to accurately predict the success or failure of PDF-based digital publications. On one hand, nearly all PDF-based magazines and newsletters failed within their first years—but that was before tablets, media-rich digital magazines, and digital replicas exploded onto the scene, changing the business of digital periodical publishing as a whole. Now, there's some evidence to show that PDF-based periodicals are enjoying a renaissance in popularity.

Next, even as the popularity of PDF periodicals increased following the release of the iPad, the fact that Adobe didn't make an official PDF reader for iOS until late in 2011—and that third-party PDF readers up until that point were mediocre at best—meant that PDF-based publications still couldn't effectively reach 60 percent of tablet users. It's still too early to tell whether iPad and iPhone owners will make use of Adobe Reader for iOS to read PDF periodicals in the long term and whether Adobe will increase the capabilities of Adobe Reader for iOS to allow for more interactivity.

Finally, digital replica publication has grown as a huge segment of periodicals on all tablets. Digital replicas (covered later in this chapter) are, effectively, PDFs wrapped in their own viewers. Thus, people *are* reading periodicals that have the appearance and functionality of PDFs containing minimal interactivity; that may translate into greater popularity for PDFs once tablet owners realize that *actual* PDF publications can offer many features over and above digital replicas—features such as rich interactivity, integrated forms, highlighting and copying of text, annotating, and sharing—and do it all for the same or less cost than producing digital replicas.

PDF Examples

There are several publications going strong in PDF, though, again, it's too soon to tell whether they'll do as well with PDF on mobile devices as they do on standard computers. Figure 2.2 shows a trio of such publications, including an interactive one-off ebook in PDF that I produced.

FIGURE 2.2

Examples of PDF publications: (a) *InDesign Magazine*, issue 45; (b) *Model Railroad Hobbyist* magazine, January 2012 issue; (c) *The InDesign Secrets Guide to the InDesign ACE Exam*, a PDF ebook. Clicking the Reveal Answers button in this practice test shows the correct test answers.

Article by Pariah Burke, design by W+W Design — a

Article by Mike Rose, design by Patty Fugate — b

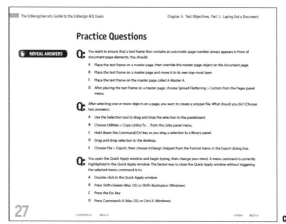

Author: Mike Rankin, design by Pariah Burke — c

ASPIRIN-FREE WORKFLOW: FLASH-POWERED DIGITAL PUBLICATIONS

Flash is dead. Long live Flash. And, no, I don't mean Sam Jones's title character in the 1980 film *Flash Gordon* (ah, ahhh, savior of the universe). I mean Adobe Flash, formerly Macromedia Flash, formerly FutureSplash.

Once upon a time Flash was the future (again, not Flash Gordon, though he's supposed to be from the future, too). Once, Flash was the *de rigueur* technology for website design. An untold number of online games were built in Flash and continue to run in Flash...but not on iOS. That's the crux of it. Apple—specifically late cofounder and CEO Steve Jobs—said no to Flash when the iPad was released, and he and Apple never relented. The ability to play Flash-powered animations, video games, videos, websites, and even web banner ads was never an option on iPads, iPhones, or iPod Touches. Eventually, the popularity of those devices led Adobe to discontinue the mobile viewer for Flash content—for any platform. Thus, iOS killed Flash for every mobile device but only as a delivery format; Flash is still alive and very well as a *development platform*, and some of the most popular games and apps running on mobile devices—even iOS-powered devices—were built using Flash.

Flash also used to be a format option for digital publication delivery. It was extraordinarily well suited to that purpose, in fact, given that Flash SWF files could contain multiple pages (as frames on the timeline), included typographic support that was better than HTML offered, and, of course, supported multimedia and virtually any type of interactivity one could want. Several companies banked on Flash-powered magazines, in fact, offering issue-distribution services and software to create them from scratch or through conversion from PDF. One such company was eDocker, which has since switched to an HTML5-based format and delivery model.

A few Flash-based delivery systems still exist, and for now, Flash is still almost universally supported as a content-delivery format (for web stuff and epublications) on computers, which is why the Flash-based service providers continue to make sales, but without mobile-device support, it just doesn't make sense for a serious publisher to choose Flash for any epublication delivery.

PDF Production Roles

Creating a basic digital-distribution PDF requires no additional skills or personnel beyond what is required to create a print publication. After all, from InDesign, PDF creation is a simple export operation. However, taking full advantage of the format with multimedia and interactivity will require some or all of the following additional skills for an individual or team:

◆ Author/copywriter

◆ Developmental editor

◆ Copyeditor

◆ Technical editor

◆ Indexer

◆ Illustrator

- Photographer

- Photo retoucher

- Videographer

- Video editor

- Voiceover talent

- Audio mixer

- Form designer

- JavaScript programmer

- Web analytics expert

Digital Replica

An increasingly common format in the age of tablets is *digital replica*, which you might also see referred to as *interactive replica*, *print replica*, or other similar names. A digital replica magazine (or other publication) is what I call "an app via PDF"—it is the print version of the publication displayed on a digital device, typically through export from the layout program to PDF, which is then wrapped in a viewer app that is released to the public. Another method of creating a digital replica includes converting all the pages in the publication into JPEG or PNG images and then displaying them sequentially within the viewer app, with or without reflowable text backing up the page image. This latter method is common for digital replicas of books where the appearance of the book page is as important to the book's value as the text in the book—for example, digital editions of historically significant texts.

Digital-replica publications are easy and quick to move to digital formats because they require little extra work as long as the design is already done for the print edition. Depending on the software and service used for the PDF or image conversion, additional features may be added—features such as the inclusion of hyperlinks within the content, the addition of videos and audio as overlays or separate pages, and EPUB-like views of article copy (without images). Digital replicas are not very engaging to readers because they simply mimic the passive reading experience of printed magazines, but if a publication doesn't *need* the extra interactivity and embedded media, a digital replica might be the ideal format. Moreover, priced appropriately and marketed well, a digital replica can be a successful companion or even replacement for a print publication without production workflow retooling. When compared to interactive digital-publication systems, digital-replica publications are also usually quite a bit less expensive to produce and distribute.

What Digital Replica Offers

At a glance, here are the big characteristics comprising the digital-replica publication type:

- Viewable almost anywhere (as PDF) or only on tablets (as app-via-PDF)

- Obtained as single-issue/one-off standalone apps; as single-title, multi-issue, branded newsstand apps; or as part of a newsstand of multiple titles

◆   Available in-publication or in-app subscription ability

◆   Option for issues delivered automatically to subscribers

◆   Precise layout control

◆   Supports limited audio, video

◆   Supports hyperlinks

◆   Optional built-in table of contents

◆   Built-in navigational system

◆   Linear and nonlinear reading capabilities

◆   User-selectable, optional EPUB-like text-only display of articles

What Digital Replica Does Not Offer

Conversely, if you want any of the following characteristics in your digital publication, then digital replica is decidedly not the right publication class to choose:

◆   User-adjustable font sizes (except in optional text-only display of articles)

◆   Text automatically reflows to fit any screen (except with optional text-only article display)

◆   Touch interactivity (beyond simple tap/swipe for page turning and activating hyperlinks, audio, and video)

◆   Embedded games, forms, or web content

◆   A large amount of video content

The Business of Digital Replica

Digital-replica magazines and other publications are only slightly older than rich-media inter-active tablet magazines (discussed later in this chapter) and are still trying to find profitable business models. Some of the techniques being tried include one-week to one-month free trials to entice readers, completely free digital issues given away as a value-add to print-edition sub-scribers, paid digital subscriptions but at a lower rate than print editions, and exclusive content (for example, a separate special issue or audio or video augmentations to standard text and pho-tos) for digital subscribers. Given the low overhead of producing digital-replica editions, many publishers feel justified in offering free or dramatically reduced subscription rates. On the flip side, a digital-replica edition can also be used to sweeten the deal for advertisers—for example: "insert in our print edition and we'll carry your ad in our digital editions free of charge."

The list of periodicals publishing digital replicas to a wide array of devices is staggering, but here is a quick dozen off the top of my head:

◆   *Advanced Photoshop*

◆   *Cosmopolitan*

◆   *Entrepreneur*

- *Esquire*

- *Harper's Bazaar*

- *Maxim*

- *Men's Fitness*

- *Motor Trend*

- *The Nation*

- *National Geographic*

- *Oprah*

- *Rolling Stone*

Digital-Replica Examples

Figure 2.3 shows a few digital-replica publications you should be able to find in the App Store, Google Play, or App World by searching for either the publication name or the system it uses.

Digital-Replica Production Roles

Digital replicas are, as the name implies, merely replicas of print publications. Thus, there is very little work involved in their creation and publication after the print edition has been finalized. Someone merely exports the print edition to PDF, uploads it to a conversion and distribution service, adds a minimum of interactivity, and clicks Publish. Assuming you want to add as much interactivity as possible to your digital replicas, you may need to hire or train for the following additional roles beyond developing the print publication:

- Author/copywriter

- Developmental editor

- Copyeditor

- Technical editor

- Indexer

- HTML/XHTML designer

- CSS styler

- Videographer

- Video editor

- Voiceover talent

- Audio mixer

- Web analytics expert

FIGURE 2.3
Digital-replica–
publication exam-
ples: (a) *SoulM8*
magazine, June
2011 issue, using
the 3D Issue system
and viewed on a
10.1-inch Android
tablet; (b) *Entre-
preneur* magazine,
January 2012,
using Texterity's
system and viewed
on an iPad (note
the pop-up video
box); (c) *WebMD the
Magazine*, Novem-
ber/December
2011 issue, using
the Zinio system
(navigation system
shown) and viewed
on a 10.1-inch
Android tablet

Design by Jane Jackson   a

Design director: Richard R. Olson   b

Art directors: Glenn Pierce, Melissa H. Miller   c

Interactive Magazine

When the iPad was first released, major magazines like *Wired* and *Sports Illustrated* were the first out of the gate, with interactivity and media-rich publications utilizing the full array of touch interactivity inherent in the iPad's design. Because of this, as well as the rapid succession of other magazines to adopt the technology even in its *alpha* and *beta* stages, the format, which actually lacks a formal name, has come to be commonly called the *interactive magazine* format, and for the duration of this book I will use that nomenclature. (However, it is also often described as the *fully interactive, media-rich,* or *app-based* publication format.) The format's use, however, is not limited to magazines. The format class is ideal for ecatalogs, eyearbooks, richly interactive ebooks, and many other types of publications. Unfortunately, its moniker tends to make creators of other types of publications shy away from interactive magazine. I hope that won't be you, now that I've defined the full use of the term.

The biggest publishing-related beneficiary in the age of tablets is the digital magazine. Built specifically for tablets' touch interfaces, fully interactive, media-rich, app-based digital magazines fully exploit the multimedia and user-interactivity features of tablets by offering not only pixel-precise layouts equivalent to print magazines but also audio, video, slideshows, 3D rotating objects, zooming, panning, replaceable content, scrolling regions, live web content, and on-the-page video games. All of these features (and more) function with the reader's direct physical interaction—interaction more involved than simply clicking a mouse button or swiping to turn the page. They draw readers into the content through their interactivity, making the process of reading a magazine more of a collaborative, personal, and active experience than the passive reading experience inherent in print magazines.

Given that this format is exclusively for tablets, with no support whatsoever on computers or handheld ereaders, and the fact that competing technologies use proprietary systems, there is no common file extension to refer to as there would be with PDF or EPUB publications. Some digital-magazine–creation systems create `.Folio` files, others `.Issue` files, but none of those formats are actually used on a tablet; rather, those `.Folio`, `.Issue`, or other intermediary formats are converted into apps for distribution to the App Store, Google Play, and App World. Calling them "app-based publications" would be misleading because several publications are available that don't use this particular class of format but instead have been custom-coded from scratch to do something unique.

CUSTOM-CODED APPS

If none of the other format classes fit your publication's needs, consider hiring a programmer to produce it as a custom app. Custom-coded apps offer the ultimate freedom in functionality, doing whatever you need your publication to do and presenting your publication in any manner you desire. You can locate quite a few custom-app developers with just a moment or two spent with Google, or you can place ads for them on Monster.com, CareerBuilder.com, DesignJobsLive .com, and other common creative and programming job listing sites. The expense of having an app custom-coded is high and usually beyond the means of small and medium-sized publishers.

Because a custom-coded app will be built to your unique requirements and specifications, I won't cover that particular subject in detail in this book.

What Interactive Magazine Offers

Tablet-based interactive magazine-formatted publications can contain a great deal of interactivity, including hyperlinks that open web pages, hyperlinks that send email and SMS text messages, hyperlinks that dial the phone, audio and video, image and video slideshows, panoramic images, 3D rotatable objects, scrollable areas, content replacement to create areas of pages that change based on user interaction, and embedded web content such as live Twitter streams, RSS feeds, video games, web pages, shopping carts, and *anything* else you can do on the Web. All of this is wrapped into an app with swipe-to-page and pinch-to-zoom capabilities and visual tables of contents, with or without page thumbnails.

We'll go step by step through creating all of those types of content and interactivity in Chapters 8 through 10. At a glance, here are the big characteristics of the interactive magazine publication type:

- Viewable only on tablets
- Typically delivered as app
- Obtained as single-issue/one-off standalone app; as single-title, multi-issue, branded newsstand app; or as part of a newsstand of multiple titles
- Available in-publication or in-app subscription ability
- Issues delivered automatically to subscribers
- Precise layout control
- Optional separate or adaptive horizontal and vertical article layouts
- Optional multiple layouts for different tablets and screen sizes published and managed as one unit
- Fully interactive
- Supports images, audio, video
- Supports server-fed dynamic content (with live device connection)
- Built-in table of contents
- Built-in navigational system
- Linear and nonlinear reading capabilities

What Interactive Magazine Does Not Offer

Conversely, if you want any of the following characteristics in your digital publication, then the interactive magazine format is decidedly not the right one to choose:

- User-adjustable font sizes
- Text automatically reflows to fit any screen
- Very small file sizes

- Viewable on computers

- Viewable on handheld ereaders

- Quick conversion from print edition layouts

- No publication fees

The Business of Interactive Magazine

The interactive magazine format, whose use, again, is not limited to magazine-style periodicals, is new and still in a state of flux, businesswise. There is no shortage of digital magazines using the format—as I write this, by my count there are around 700 monthly magazines using the format and another 100 non-magazines—including some of the world's largest publishing brands (see the "Interactive Magazine Examples" section below). The issue (pardon the pun) is that these publications are still trying to find their points of profitability in the format.

Both *Wired* and *Sports Illustrated*, the first proof-of-concept periodicals to begin publishing in the interactive magazine format on tablets, had tremendous initial response, but their numbers quickly fell off. Why? Probably because they were charging print-edition prices in the tablet space and their interactive magazines didn't bring additional content to the format, making them little more than digital replicas that cost a heck of a lot more to produce than digital replicas should. They also failed to interest advertisers in the potential of the medium. Instead of flat, two-dimensional ads straight out of the print editions, both publications could have sold their A-list advertisers on embedded media—at least a car commercial, if not an embedded video game branding experience.

Others did see the potential of the format. Disney used the format to produce 2010's *The Guide to TRON Legacy*, a one-off companion to the *TRON Legacy* film and video game released that same year. Distributed free of charge through the App Store, the publication seemed to do well in that its revenue-generating function was to encourage people to see the film and buy the video game; the publication even included call-to-action buttons on every page that let readers purchase movie tickets and the video game in-app.

Given that it (currently) takes approximately three times as long to produce a fully interactive digital magazine from scratch (or starting from the print edition) as it does to create the print edition, publishers have significant overhead in creating digital magazines. Many of them make the mistake of charging the cost of those extra work hours to the consumer of the magazine. Consumers won't pay the extra cost because print periodicals have been telling consumers for decades that the largest portion of the cover price of a magazine is its paper cost. The average consumer doesn't understand the amount of work involved in creating digital magazines and never will; instead, consumers perceive that cover price as being the cost of nonexistent paper—an excess of profit back in the publisher's pocket.

Publishers who want to succeed need to drop their subscription rates and cover prices to no more than two-thirds of the print equivalents and make their money on advertising, which is where publishers should make money anyway. Sell advertisers on the medium's benefits; get them buying video placements instead of flat ads, get them inserting live product order forms instead of simple links with keyed URLs, and convince them to place branding campaigns, video games, and interactive experiences on the page in your digital magazines. Do that, and the money will flow; do that as well as drop the price of each digital issue, and your magazine will succeed in the tablet space.

Interactive Magazine Examples

As I noted, there are about 800 magazines and non-magazines using this format class as of this writing, with more launching monthly. I couldn't possibly include them all, but Figure 2.4 shows a few you should look at to see what they're doing right and what they're doing wrong.

FIGURE 2.4

Examples of the interactive magazine format: (a) *The Essential Guide to TRON: Legacy*, a one-off ebook produced in InDesign with Adobe Digital Publishing Suite tools, shown on an iPad; (b) *New Guinea Adventure* (Adobe demonstration publication), displayed on a 10.1-inch Android tablet; *Condé Nast Traveller*, on an iPad displaying the "How to Use This App" instruction page common to interactive magazines

a   Designer: Disney Interactive

b   Designed by Adobe

c   Illustration by Oliver Jeffers

Interactive Magazine Production Roles

Interactive magazines are creatively and logistically the most demanding of all types of digital publications to create. They must be designed almost entirely separately from their print editions, with page sizes and orientations specifically geared toward one or more tablets' resolutions and capabilities, often with multiple versions of every article, and interactivity and media features built by hand for each issue, each article. Depending on the content of your particular interactive magazine, some or all of the following roles will need to be filled by team members or the individual self-publisher. The payoff, of course, is a reader experience wholly different from the print edition, one most readers consider worth paying for.

- Writer
- Story editor
- Managing editor
- Layout artist
- Production artist
- Paginator
- Illustrator
- Photographer
- Photo retoucher
- Videographer
- Video editor
- Voiceover talent
- Audio mixer
- HTML programmer
- HTML5 programmer
- Developers for Java, JavaScript, PHP, Ruby, ColdFusion, Oracle, MySQL, IIS, and others
- Web server administrator
- Web analytics expert

HTML5

HTML5—Hypertext Markup Language, version 5—is a radical departure from previous versions of HTML. When the World Wide Web was first devised and used by government agencies and universities, it was text-only, with minimal formatting support—HTML, version 1. Quickly its users realized that, even for academic documentation, they needed to incorporate imagery, tabular data, color, and more customizable content markup; thus, HTML 2.0 was born. The Web continued to improve every few years up through HTML 4.01, which was the version feature-rich enough to spawn Internet application and social media websites like Facebook, Twitter, adaptive content pages, and so on. Think about everything you saw on the Web, all the things that were possible, back between 2007 and 2010. That was all HTML 4.01.

Now enter HTML5, which is as far beyond HTML 4 as HTML 4 was beyond HTML 2. Of course, HTML5 still runs websites and web applications, but it is much more feature-rich than the code needed to produce a simple shopping website, blog, or even microblogging service like Twitter. HTML5 includes a plethora of multimedia and rich interactivity features, features that used to require add-on technologies like Flash, Java, and Virtual Reality Modeling Language (VRML). Complex animation, dynamic content replacement and modification, slideshows, and much more are built directly into HTML5. HTML5 can do just about everything Flash can, but in a file format that is semantic, internationally approved, and fully compatible with modern computers, tablets, smartphones, and even many handheld ereaders.

With such universal support and flexible capabilities, it's no wonder that HTML5 is rapidly becoming one the best formats for digital publications. Many publications are being created in HTML5, and readers are being given access through the Web, which, of course, usually entails no publication licensing fees, App Store, Google Play, or App World royalties, or other expenses common with the creation of apps. Distributing via the Web means publishers have to get creative about enticing mobile users to find and visit the publications, though.

Other publishers are producing HTML5-based publications as apps available for sale in the App Store, Google Play, or App World. Some of these are self-contained, meaning that once the user installs the app and downloads a publication or issue, the entire content of the publication is stored in the device's memory. Some apps are merely wrappers that store none of a publication's content beyond perhaps a thumbnail of its cover; rather, these wrappers are chrome-less, custom-branded web browsers that link directly to HTML5 publications located on publishers' or service providers' websites. In these cases, the removal of the browser chrome, title bar, bookmarks bar, and so forth convince readers that they're reading directly inside a custom app; they'll never realize they're actually reading content sitting on a web server and not on a device's internal storage.

HTML5 content can be designed with almost as much precise control over the layout as you'd have with a PDF or media-rich tablet app or as a layout that adapts to the screen on which it's viewed. With its full support of modern media and built-in code for animations and interactivity, it can be every bit as engaging to readers as any other format.

What HTML5 Offers

At a glance, here are the big characteristics of HTML5 relative to digital publishing:

◆ Viewable on tablets, computers, smartphones, and some handheld ereaders

◆ Can store publication content on the Web or contained within app

◆ Web-based versions can be instantly updated without App Store, Google Play, or App World update notifications

◆ Obtained as single-issue/one-off standalone app; as single-title, multi-issue, branded newsstand app; or as part of a newsstand of multiple titles

◆ Available in-publication or in-app subscription ability

◆ Available issues delivered automatically to subscribers

- Precise layout control

- Liquid (screen-adaptive) layouts

- Supports audio, video, animation, rich interactivity

- Supports forms, games, web content

- Supports dynamic, server-fed content

- Can be database-driven

- Content may be fully customized by reader

- Linear and nonlinear reading capabilities

What HTML5 Does Not Offer

Conversely, if you want either of the following characteristics in your digital publication, then HTML5 is decidedly not the right format to choose.

- Readable by older web browsers

- Readable by older devices (including those running Android 2.*x*)

The Business of HTML5

HTML5-based publications compete head-on with media-rich tablet publications and, for all intents and purposes, are just as young and just as in flux in terms of effective business models. That said, tablets are here to stay, and both publishing formats will be worked out to profitability.

HTML5 Publication Examples

Figure 2.5 shows a few titles published in HTML5, as either web-based or app-based content.

HTML5 Production Roles

Because HTML is a markup language and HTML5 is even more programming-centric than previous versions of the language, you'll need to either learn or hire the requisite skills. Even though InDesign CS6 can create liquid-layout, HTML5-based digital publications, publications that adapt to the screen on which they're viewed, other programs, such as Dreamweaver and Muse, offer HTML5 creation in similarly graphical user interfaces; some even include direct PDF-to-HTML5 conversion ability. Despite the availability of WYSIWYG layout applications that will export to HTML5, it's important to know the HTML5 language itself in order to tweak code and accomplish effects not yet possible via layout application export. Specifically, you'll need your team to cover the following roles, depending on which forms of interactivity and media you want to include:

- HTML5 developer
- Writer

- Story editor

- Managing editor

- Layout artist

- Production artist

- Illustrator

- Photographer

- Photo retoucher

- Videographer

- Video editor

- Voiceover talent

- Audio mixer

- Developers for JavaScript, PHP, Ruby, ColdFusion, Oracle, MySQL, IIS, and others

- Web server administrator

- Web analytics expert

FIGURE 2.5
HTML5-based publication examples: (a) *Blackline* (May/June 2012), running chrome-less on an iPad; (b) *LIFE Wonders of the World* one-off ebook as viewed on an HP Touchpad; (c) *The Sunday Times* (Culture section), December 25, 2011, issue as displayed on a 10.1-inch Android tablet. The snow falling in the background is a full-page, multilayer animation behind the masthead, coverlines, and foreground photo.

a

Designers: Nico Engelhardt and Johannes Ippen

b

c

Chapter 3

Surveying the Digital Publication Types

Now that we've examined the characteristics and capabilities of the available digital publication formats, it's time to think about the kind of content you want to disseminate digitally. It's all rather subjective, but I'll identify the purpose, character, and use of different publication types as well as explain which format classes are best suited to each type.

In this chapter, you will learn about the following:

- ◆ Quick Reference: Publication Types in Format Classes
- ◆ Ebook
- ◆ Emagazine
- ◆ Enewspaper
- ◆ Etextbook
- ◆ Digital Comic Book
- ◆ Designing for Devices

Quick Reference: Publication Types in Format Classes

Table 3.1 provides you with an at-a-glance reference to the format classes and the publication types that will work with them.

TABLE 3.1:   Format classes and suitable publication types

	EPUB	AMAZON KINDLE FORMATS	PDF	DIGITAL REPLICA	INTERACTIVE MAGAZINE	HTML5
Ebook	☑					
Enhanced ebook (text and image)	☑		☑			
Enhanced ebook (multimedia)			☑		☑	☑

TABLE 3.1: Format classes and suitable publication types *(continued)*

	EPUB	AMAZON KINDLE FORMATS	PDF	DIGITAL REPLICA	INTERACTIVE MAGAZINE	HTML5
Fixed-layout ebook	◪		☑	☑	☑	☑
Ejournal (text-heavy, moderate layout control, minimal interactivity)	☑		☑			
Emagazine (absolute layout control, little or no multimedia and interactivity)				☑		
Emagazine (absolute layout control, fully interactive)			☑		☑	☑
Ecatalog (absolute layout control, image-heavy)			☑	☑	☑	☑
Eyearbook (absolute layout control, image-heavy)			☑	☑	☑	☑
Enewspaper (text-heavy, moderate layout control, minimal interactivity)	☑					
Etextbook (nonproprietary system)	☑		☑		☑	☑

Legend: ☑ *The indicated format class is suitable (but not necessarily ideal) for the publication type.* ◪ *Only some devices capable of displaying that format class support the publication type.*

Ebook

An ebook is a publication that is primarily text, such as a novel or other book designed to be read in its entirety, cover to cover. Ebooks may include images or videos here and there but are not by any means considered image-heavy. The content of ebooks follows a simple layout structure. For instance, in the case of a novel, you may have chapter numbers, chapter titles, the first paragraph of a chapter (for example, one that doesn't indent its first line), and then the average paragraph. A nonfiction ebook, say a history book or a book about digital publishing with InDesign, might have a slightly more complicated structure that includes multiple levels of headings and quite a few images and captions. Ebooks can be created using any digital format, but typically use, and are best suited for, the EPUB format, making them readable by a wide range of devices, including handheld ereaders and ereading software available for nearly every computer, tablet, and smartphone (see Figure 3.1).

FIGURE 3.1

Examples of ebooks: (a) *The New Oxford American Dictionary* on a Kindle 7-inch tablet; (b) *The Murder of the Century* by Paul Collins, as displayed in the B&N Nook app on a 10.1-inch Android tablet; (c) *Evangelists of Art* by Rev. James Patrick, B.D., B.Sc., as displayed in iBooks on an iPad; (d) *Gulliver's Travels* by Jonathan Swift, viewed on an iPhone using the Kobo Reader app

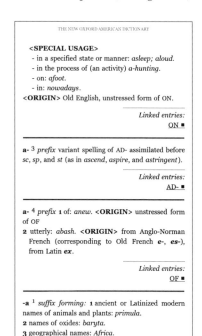

THE NEW OXFORD AMERICAN DICTIONARY

<SPECIAL USAGE>
- in a specified state or manner: *asleep; aloud.*
- in the process of (an activity) *a-hunting.*
- on: *afoot.*
- in: *nowadays.*

<ORIGIN> Old English, unstressed form of ON.

Linked entries:
ON ▪

a- ³ *prefix* variant spelling of AD- assimilated before *sc*, *sp*, and *st* (as in *ascend*, *aspire*, and *astringent*).

Linked entries:
AD- ▪

a- ⁴ *prefix* **1** of: *anew.* **<ORIGIN>** unstressed form of OF
2 utterly: *abash.* **<ORIGIN>** from Anglo-Norman French (corresponding to Old French **e-**, **es-**), from Latin **ex**.

Linked entries:
OF ▪

-a ¹ *suffix forming:* **1** ancient or Latinized modern names of animals and plants: *primula.*
2 names of oxides: *baryta.*
3 geographical names: *Africa.*

a

1.

THE MYSTERY OF THE RIVER

IT WAS A SLOW AFTERNOON for news. The newsboys along the East River piers still readied themselves on a scorching summer Saturday for the incoming ferry passengers from Brooklyn, armed with innumerable battling editions of Manhattan's dailies for June 26, 1897. There were sensational "yellow papers" like Pulitzer's *World* and Hearst's *Journal*, the stately flagships of the *Herald* and the *Sun*, and stray runts like the *Post* and the *Times*. By two thirty, the afternoon editions were coming while the morning papers were getting left in stacks to bake in the sun. But there were no orders by President McKinley, no pitched battles in the Sudan, and no new Sousa marches to report. The only real story that day was the weather:

b

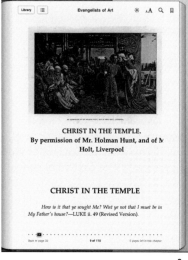

CHRIST IN THE TEMPLE.
By permission of Mr. Holman Hunt, and of M
Holt, Liverpool

CHRIST IN THE TEMPLE

How is it that ye sought Me? Wist ye not that I must be in My Father's house?—LUKE ii. 49 (Revised Version).

c

Thus much I thought proper to tell you in relation to yourself, and to the trust I reposed in you.

I do, in the next place, com-

d

Producing ebooks is relatively easy compared with other types of digital publications and doesn't require much of an investment beyond a computer and an Internet connection. Ebooks may be produced with InDesign or with a variety of other programs, including free and simple text-editing programs. Moreover, there are usually no fees required to publish an ebook in the major ebookstores, unlike more media-rich publications, whose requisite formats often entail a publishing license, costs per copy distributed, and other fees.

SELF-PUBLISHING IS NO LONGER A DIRTY WORD

Self-publishing—aka vanity press—has been as dirty a phrase in literary circles as *military intelligence* is within the military and law-enforcement arenas. For decades, only the most desperate would-be authors, or extremists with manifestos to disseminate, self-published—particularly in ebook format. The conventional thinking was that if you self-published, it was because you weren't a good enough writer to be signed by a publishing house.

Today, that's changed. Now, neither ebook publishing nor self-publishing is the last act of a desperate writer with a drawer full of rejection letters. If you don't believe me, just ask best-selling business and marketing author Seth Godin.

Godin is the author of more than a dozen worldwide bestsellers, including *Poke the Box*, *We Are All Weird*, and *All Marketers Are Liars*. In 2010 Godin announced that he had moved completely away from traditional publishing; all of his future books will be published exclusively in electronic formats.

Granted, Seth Godin will be publishing ebooks through a major publishing house, with the support of a full editorial team, so maybe he doesn't make my point fully. In that case, take Amanda Hocking.

A then-unknown writer in the young-adult paranormal genre, 26-year-old Amanda Hocking began self-publishing ebooks in April 2010 on Amazon.com's Kindle Store for $0.99–3.99 per copy. She averaged 100,000 copies of those books sold per month, earning more than $2 million in 12 months. By early 2011 she was selling an average of 9,000 copies of her nine ebooks per day, and one of her ebook trilogies had already been optioned for a film.

In March 2011 Hocking's desire to publish her works in print started a bidding war between major publishers Random House, Simon & Schuster, HarperCollins, and Macmillan. St. Martin's Press, an imprint of Macmillan, gave her a $2 million contract for a new series of four books.

Did I mention that she was completely unknown and unpublished until she began self-publishing on Amazon?

Hocking's level of success is rare, but many others (previously published and first-time authors) are getting themselves and their work noticed and getting paid by self-publishing—no literary agent, no publishing house, no capital investment...just Kindle, NOOK, and the rest.

Don't be afraid of the self-publishing stigma, whether you intend to write the next great American novel or want to publish a short technical piece that will help increase awareness of your company's brand. *¡Viva la revolución!*

Enhanced Ebook

Enhanced ebook is a nebulous term. When EPUB 2.01 was the current version, *enhanced ebook* was a term often applied to ebooks that used the upcoming but not yet finalized EPUB 3 specification to include things like audio captioning or the equation language MathML. You'll also find apps in the Apple App Store, Google Play app store, or BlackBerry App World that use digital magazine–class interactivity features within a media-rich book; those apps, too, are considered enhanced ebooks. Thus, any book-style content presented in a technology beyond the capabilities common to the ebook publication type or the EPUB standard can be considered an enhanced ebook.

Consequently, there are no hard-and-fast rules about what the enhanced ebook publication type is or is not, nor is there an easy way to define production roles or the business of the enhanced ebook publication type. Rather, you have to look at the definitions and information of the publication type each individual enhanced ebook most closely matches—if it's an EPUB with a little JavaScript thrown in to provide extra functions, then, for all intents and purposes, it's an ebook; if the book includes lots of interactivity, touchscreen features, and multimedia, then it is more accurately categorized as the digital magazine type, and so on.

One exception I would like to specifically discuss, however, is fixed-layout ebooks, which are just as often referred to as picture books and are, thanks to tablets, rapidly approaching a level of popularity that will set them apart as their own unique publication type.

Fixed-Layout Ebook

Fixed-layout or *picture-book ebooks* are those that, unlike a standard ebook, are heavily dependent on imagery. They're so dependent, in fact, that this class of publication often displays on every page background images or full-page photographs or illustrations that serve to tell the story at least as much as included text does. Examples of such publications include many children's books or so-called coffee-table books, wherein imagery is paramount and text is of equal or lesser importance. Although based on EPUB-like text-centric ebooks, fixed-layout ebooks do not automatically adapt to fit the screen on which they're viewed. Most of them are *designed* to fully fit the most popular device screen sizes, but they won't automatically adapt to other screen sizes; instead, readers may have to zoom or scroll horizontally and/or vertically to view the entirety of each page. For more information on fixed-layout ebooks, please visit my website at `http://iampariah.com`.

Ejournal

The ejournal publication type is for multistory periodicals that are very heavy on text with only a few images and illustrations here and there, as one might find in industry, trade, scholarly, or academic publications such as the *Journal of the American Medical Association*, *The Magazine of Fantasy & Science Fiction*, and similar publications (see Figure 3.2). Ejournals are, in essence, ebooks that, instead of being broken into chapters, use the same function to separate articles, with each article having a table of contents entry and, within the EPUB archive itself, created as a separate XHTML file. Images, audio, and/or video are included inline within the content. Issues may be purchased one at a time or delivered to subscribers automatically via subscription.

FIGURE 3.2

Examples of ejournals: (a) *Linux Journal*, September 2011, as viewed in Sony Reader for PC; (b) *National Geographic*, December 30, 2011, as published to Kindle through the Kindle Newsstand; (c) *The Magazine of Fantasy & Science Fiction*, Jan/Feb 2012

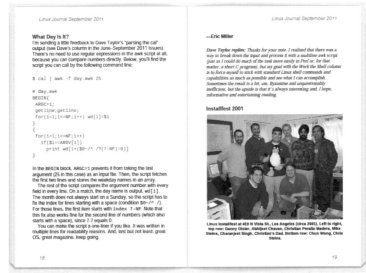

Art director: Garrick Antikajian

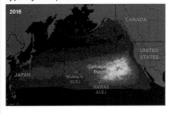

Of course, electronic journals can be published in format classes other than EPUB, as well—as interactive magazines, as digital replicas, as HTML5, as PDF, and so on. Their content, however, makes them ideally suited for publication as EPUB, which maximizes their reach across devices. Many publishers produce them in multiple formats—as visually rich interactive magazines and HTML5 for devices that support those formats, as EPUB for ereader access, and as PDF for general computer use.

On the flip side of the equation, many normally image-heavy periodicals even decoct their stories and photos down to ejournal format to take advantage of the additional distribution channels offered by the EPUB-powered class. *National Geographic* (Figure 3.2b) is the perfect example of this tactic. One would be hard-pressed to name a periodical more renowned for photography than *National Geographic*, yet there it sits on Kindle, NOOK, and other handheld ereaders, in EPUB format, with a scant one image per article. And it does well, commercially, in this format in addition to, and separate from, the other publication format types employed to disseminate the same issues to readers—those classes being print, of course, as well as digital magazine and digital replica editions.

USING EJOURNAL STYLING FOR NONJOURNAL CONTENT

If you want to publish journal-style content, look to the preceding chapter's lists of things the various publication types do and do not offer to help you decide on the best format (or formats) for your journal. Your original content need not be in journal format to be publishable as an ejournal; look to the example of *National Geographic*, discussed in this section.

Emagazine

Emagazines have been around for decades in different formats, but they exploded with the debut of the iPad, expanding as fast as the tablet industry itself—with no signs of slowing (for either industry).

Magazines are multistory publications that mix many photographs and illustrations with text, often with visually rich page design and advanced typography. When moved into the digital realm, all those attributes remain but are augmented by multimedia (audio and video), hyperlinks, and, depending on the format class, often a good deal more multimedia and interactivity.

The best format class for a digital magazine depends on the nature of the content, the level of interactivity desired, the magazine's audience and distribution, and the budget for the publication. Depending on those criteria, digital magazines can use nearly all format classes, including EPUB, PDF, HTML5, digital replica, interactive magazine, and custom-coded app (see Figure 3.3).

FIGURE 3.3

Examples of digital magazines: (a) PDF format: *Proxy*, May 2006, viewed in Adobe Reader on a Mac; (b) digital replica format: *Maxim*, August 2011, viewed in landscape mode on a 10.1-inch Android tablet; (c) interactive magazine format: *Oprah*, March 2011, viewed in portrait mode on an iPad; (d) HTML5 format: *The Sunday Times* (Culture Section), December 25, 2011, displayed on a 10.1-inch Android tablet

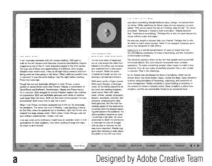

a

Designed by Adobe Creative Team

b

c

d

The most successful emagazines are those that target multiple platforms and devices through several different format classes. For instance, *PC Magazine* (Ziff Davis Media), a monthly for computer, tablet, and gadget enthusiasts and professionals, publishes an EPUB-based version (almost certainly a relatively simple export of an issue's stories, with their lead images inserted at the beginning) through Amazon, Barnes & Noble, and Sony for reading on Kindle, NOOK, and Sony Reader ereaders and ereader software, *and* a digital replica of its print edition (the print edition is exported to PDF and from there converted to flat digital replica), also published through Amazon and Barnes & Noble for viewing on their respective tablets, client software, and web clients, as well as via the Zinio newsstand and viewer app, which reaches iOS, Android, webOS, Windows, and Mac OS X.

The digital replica version doesn't even fully take advantage of the format—the emagazine doesn't include media not in the print edition, and it doesn't make URLs within its content into clickable or tappable hyperlinks. Despite this failure to take full advantage of the medium, *PC Magazine* is reaching a broad audience with its two electronic versions (in addition to publishing articles on its website).

National Geographic has virtually the same multiformat/multidevice distribution method, sending EPUB versions to devices that support them and digital replicas to more advanced devices. Other publications are following suit, but not all of them are stopping at digital replicas. Many are also incorporating the rich interactivity in the interactive magazine format class to exploit the full potential and user interaction possible on tablets.

> As you consider publishing your digital magazine, heed the example set by others: If possible, don't limit your publication to just one format. Publish it in as many formats as possible to reach the widest possible readership.

Ecatalog

A typical catalog is a publication that lists products for sale and provides a means for readers to purchase those products. Tablets represent a tremendous opportunity for publishers to take their catalogs digital, though few have as yet taken advantage of the possibility. Ecatalogs (and electronic *magalogs*) can be produced as ebook-like EPUBs and, of course, the old standby PDFs, though the interactivity and advanced content possible with interactive magazines is often the best way to go.

Just think about it: In a clothing catalog readers could touch color swatches beside a photograph of a jacket to make the photograph change, displaying the garment in the selected color. Perhaps the reader can even watch a commercial for the product right on the product page. Or maybe the reader is a returning customer, whom you ask to log into her account directly *within* the ecatalog. Once a customer is logged in, the ecatalog communicates with a web-based database to populate a sidebar or other section of the page with items based on the customer's previous purchase history. How about a sale? On the Friday after Thanksgiving all the prices in the ecatalog app you began distributing six months ago automatically update to reflect Black Friday or holiday-season sales—without requiring the reader to download an update to the ecatalog app. Conversely, maybe you want to *force* the reader to update the ecatalog app after that edition of the catalog expires, thus making sure that every potential customer is looking at the latest selection of products, the most up-to-date pricing. All of this and a great deal more is possible in the digital magazine publication type, so why limit that type to only *magazines*? It works just as well—if not better—for catalogs.

To date there aren't many interactive ecatalogs out there, though early adopters have taken the relatively easy step of creating digital replicas (apps via PDF) and including them in dedicated ecatalog newsstands such as TheFind and Google Catalogs (see Figure 3.4b and Figure 3.4c). One notable exception is Pottery Barn, which created its own branded newsstand to publish monthly and special-edition catalogs in digital replica format.

FIGURE 3.4
Examples of ecatalogs: (a) Pottery Barn, August 2011, two-page spread in branded library app on an iPad; (b) Crutchfield, January 2012, in Google Catalogs on an Android 10.1-inch tablet; (c) Best Buy weekly newspaper insert (Jan 1–7, 2012 edition), published in TheFind and viewed on an Android 10.1-inch tablet

a

b

c

THE PROMISE OF EYEARBOOKS

The digital magazine publication type could be used to create richly interactive eyearbooks. Instead of giving students, alumni, and faculty flat and costly printed yearbooks that they sign with pens, give them interactive, tablet-based eyearbooks that, upon launch, play the school anthem and that they can sign with a stylus or via form field. Rather than flat grids of headshots and captions, create dynamic fly-bys of student photos, complete with hypertext that, when tapped, locates mentions of the student throughout the entire eyearbook, plays a video greeting by the student, peeks inside the student's virtual locker of mementos, opens the student's resume, or initiates a secure email to the student.

Although the fees associated with publishing a digital magazine type of publication can be high, they can be passed on to students with a minimal cost per student—one that is significantly less than the average student now pays for a single copy of a printed yearbook.

Although the promise of eyearbooks is great, there aren't yet any examples. As I write this book, I've searched high (school) and low(er education) for examples of eyearbooks built in modern formats, for modern devices. I couldn't find a one, though I did find numerous examples of yearbooks as websites and even proprietary software for producing CD-based yearbooks. Don't let the lack of examples fool you; it isn't indicative of the invalidity of producing eyearbooks in the digital magazine format. Rather, it's an opportunity for you to take advantage of that format and blaze the new trail.

Enewspaper

Any publication type or format class can be used to format content like a newspaper or newsletter. When I talk about the enewspaper publication type, I specifically mean publications with lots of articles, running on short lead times between content creation and publication. Not every enewspaper is a daily, but every enewspaper has to move fast to create, edit, publish, and distribute its content.

Most successful enewspapers follow the lead of digital magazines (or vice versa), targeting multiple formats, devices, and distribution channels. For example, *The New York Times* is available on Kindle and NOOK ereaders, ereader software, and tablets by those manufacturers as an EPUB-based collection of articles. Naturally the EPUB version is very stripped down, owing to the limitations of the format and the devices; it offers text articles with minimal imagery and no inline hyperlinks. The *Times* also reaches out to more capable devices with an HTML5-based edition that runs through a branded app on iOS, Android, BlackBerry, and Windows OS phones and tablets, as well as in the Google Chrome Web Store and via the Adobe AIR–based Times Reader 2.0, a desktop app for Windows, Mac OS X, and Linux. Figure 3.5 shows off the January 3, 2012, issue of the *Times* in several formats.

FIGURE 3.5

The New York Times daily newspaper in various distribution channels and formats: EPUB-based running on (a) Kindle and (b) Kindle Fire; HTML5-based presented within (c) the *New York Times* app on a 10.1-inch Android tablet, (d) a web app from the Google Chrome Web Store, and finally (e) in the Times Reader 2.0 desktop app

a

b

c

d

e

Etextbook

An etextbook is mostly prose text but also relies heavily on other types of content, including tables, photographs, illustrations, charts, graphs, mathematic or scientific equations, captions, audio clips, video segments, self-test quizzes, and other features beyond the ken of the average ebook. Often the layout requires absolute control over element positioning in order to effectively present the content. The structuring of etextbook content is more complex than ebooks because the content itself is more complete, requiring not just chapter numbers and names, basic headings, figures, and captions, but numerous other repetitive element styles. Etextbooks can be created from any of the available digital format classes, with varying features and drawbacks.

Even though I consider the etextbook to be one of the four major digital publication types (accompanying books, magazines/catalogs/yearbooks, and newspapers), it's also the most volatile of all the classes. Numerous polls and studies of educators and students from just about every level of education reveal and continuously reinforce two interesting and all but conflicting facts. First, educators and students want more textbooks and educational material made available electronically, on tablets, ereaders, and/or computers. Second, neither educators nor students want to use the electronic textbooks and educational materials widely available today. They don't like the limited layout control of ebook formats, nor do they like the narrow selection of compatible devices for interactive magazine tablet publications. Similarly, PDF, HTML5, digital replica, and other formats fail to satisfy the needs of academia because of those formats' limitations in terms of interactivity, device availability, reader annotation, or content customization by educators themselves, whether in the K–12 or higher education brackets.

Given that the textbook market for higher education alone is worth more than $7 billion (*The San Diego Union-Tribune*, February 27, 2012), several companies are working very hard to build a format and publishing process to address all the needs of educators and students. Though some are predicting that etextbooks will account for 18.8 percent of all textbook sales by 2014 (*ReadWriteWeb*, April 19, 2010, `http://www.readwriteweb.com/archives/digital_textbooks_set_to_capture_almost_20_of_the_market_by_2014.php`), and others predict as much as 50 percent by 2018, as of 2011 etextbooks only claimed 3 percent of the market, which was up from 2009's 0.5 percent (*NextIsNow.net*, February 12, 2012, `http://www.nextisnow.net/blog/e-textbook-market-remains-on-course-to-pass-25-by-2015.html`). Why doesn't digital have a bigger chunk of the $7–8 billion textbook market? Because no one seems to have built the right format yet, though everyone is trying.

Barnes & Noble has been trying for several years, with its NOOK Study etextbook application for Mac and Windows. Unfortunately, NOOK Study requires a computer in a time when more and more students, and even many educators, want to work from tablets. With the advent of NOOK-brand tablets, NOOK Study may break out into a tablet-compatible format.

Amazon is trying to sell textbooks as ebooks for Kindle devices and software, but ebooks lack features critical to academia, features such as full annotation and content highlighting, copying of content with citation, and, of course, advanced layout control.

Two etextbook systems took early leads in the market, though they have no shortage of competition. The first early leader was Kno, which offered etextbooks in a format almost identical to rich-media tablet digital magazines but ran not only on an iPad, but also, because they're HTML5-based, in any modern web browser on any device, including desktop and laptop computers, Android or other tablets, and even smartphones. Kno also offered the same textbooks as PDFs for those who prefer that format and the annotation and markup features inherent in

Adobe Reader and Acrobat. Kno briefly offered its own hardware in the form of a dual-screen, folding tablet aimed squarely at students who want to be able to access two textbooks or two places in a text simultaneously—a common need identified by many students. The device fizzled because it lacked the ability to do much more than work with digital textbooks, and tablet owners, particularly college students, want a do-it-all tablet—astrophysics *and* Angry Birds in Space, if you will.

The other early leader, Inkling, approached the problem of etextbook adoption from the perspective of professors and faculty rather than from that of publishers or even students. Inkling claimed that educators want to be able to fully customize textbooks, dropping chapters or sections the educators don't feel are relevant to their courses and adding material from other sources, often material the educators themselves author. Thus, Inkling offered a library of customizable educational material. Educators could purchase, build, and push to students' tablets digital textbook content à la carte, adding in their own essays, articles, chapters, notes, highlights, text, video, audio, quizzes, and other types of content. Those customized texts could then be saved and reused by professors, shared with their colleagues, or given back to Inkling to offer to its other customers, often with royalties paid back to the original educator for their contributed content. Needless to say, educators loved this approach, though some traditional textbook publishers had difficulty seeing how Inkling's method could ensure protection of their content from intentional or unintentional piracy, as well as secure adequate royalties for them, when educators could customize just about everything within publishers' materials.

Ingram, CafeScribe, CourseSmart, and several others devised their own digital textbook systems, competing to meet the needs of educators, students, and publishers and find that magic combination of features that would make their etextbooks the official system.

In January 2012 Apple introduced its solution to the etextbook market, and, in standard Apple style, declared its solution would "reinvent the textbook." The solution came in the form of iBooks 2.0 and iBooks Author, a free, Mac-only tool that enables anyone to create etextbooks. Targeted first at etextbooks for high-school students, Apple's strategy mentions "potential" for higher-education applications of iBooks etextbooks. The initial response to the announcement was stunning, with 350,000 etextbooks sold through iBooks in the first three days following the announcement (`http://allthingsd.com/20120123/350000-textbooks-downloaded-from-apples-ibooks-in-three-days/`). As was the case with all preceding etextbook technologies, however, educators were quick to point out the flaws in Apple's etextbook strategy. First and foremost, iBooks etextbooks run only on iPads, meaning that until every public-school child in the interested nation owns a personal iPad, the school can't standardize on iBooks. The school can't even incorporate those titles as secondary or even tertiary educational materials, because laws require that every student be given access to the same resources as every other student. Whether you want to call America's tough economic times a recession or not, unemployment and poverty are simply not compatible with 100 percent K-12 iPad ownership.

The CEO of educational publisher McGraw Hill said in an interview that a typical school pays $75 per textbook and uses that same book for five years, working out to a $15 cost per student, per year. Even with an educational discount, Hillsborough County, Florida, paid $479 each for 900 iPad 2s it bought from Apple in May 2011. The iPads were distributed to only two middle schools in the district, and funding for the purchase came from the federal Title I and Magnet Schools Assistance Program grants rather than from the district's own shrinking operating budget (source: *Tampa Bay Times*, May 19, 2011). Assuming students never break their iPads, the same units can be utilized for five years (it's a real stretch for technology of that grade to be usable that long, but let's assume). That makes the cost of one iPad $60 per year, which is just a little less than the five-year cost of a printed textbook. *Now* we can add the per-annum cost of $9.99, $14.99, and $19.99 iBooks etextbooks on top of that, one each for English, math, science, social studies, and so on. Then there are secondary language textbooks, elective class textbooks, and on and on. The cost for one student's iPad adds up pretty quickly.

If Apple provided iPads *and* etextbooks to schools at costs competitive with print textbook purchases—meaning iPads and all the textbooks for less than $200 per year—or if Apple opened iBooks etextbooks up to being read on other platforms like Android tablets, Windows computers, or even Apple's own Mac OS X, then maybe iBooks textbooks could see widespread adoption in K-12 education. As the system stands now, only private schools and more affluent public school districts can take advantage of iBooks. Until every child has a tablet or computer, iBooks etextbooks are all but useless to K-12 on a large scale.

Higher education, which sees a greater number of students able to attend class with tablets or laptops, offers a greater potential for the format in the near future. Of course, requiring a college freshman to buy a new iPad for $399–$829 on top of the cost of books, room and board, and everything else the student needs would be a tough sell to some colleges, but it's a far easier pitch than in the K-12 arena, especially if Apple follows Amazon's lead and offers etextbooks for rent at lower prices than outright purchases.

Costs alone aren't the only problem cited by iBooks critics in the educational industry. Apple maintains absolute control over any content distributed through the iBookstore (or the App Store or iTunes). That means Apple directly controls which etextbooks are available to schools and which aren't; Apple is in a position to subtly or not-so-subtly influence education by tailoring its etextbook offering. Personally, I think a tech company like Apple might do a better job than the U.S. government has done at influencing public education in the U.S., but that's still way too much power to put in the hands of a private-sector company whose primary responsibility is a financial one to its shareholders, not a moral one to its customers.

Are iBooks etextbooks the future? Well, they certainly aren't the present. With changes to Apple's content control policies, government-appointed textbook reviewers, major pricing incentives, and the expansion of iBooks onto other platforms the way Apple did with iTunes, then I can easily see iBooks becoming the standard in etextbooks. But remember that while Apple is rushing to incorporate educational publishing into its empire, Barnes & Noble, Amazon, Kno, Inkling, and more are driving toward the same goal.

Given how fragmented and varied the ecosystem of etextbooks currently is, there is no one system or digital-content publisher I can advise you to use. None of the solutions currently available satisfies all the needs of its would-be markets, and each uses closely guarded proprietary publishing methodologies. If you'd like to distribute your etextbooks in a more open, less proprietary format class, however, such as PDF, digital magazine, or HTML5, then you'll find exactly what you need in this book.

Digital Comic Book

Though people have read digital comic books for years on their computer screens, the advent of the iPad and other tablets rocketed digital comics into their golden age (pun intended). Rather than making a weekly trip to the comic-book shop, which, like the brick-and-mortar bookstore, is a dying breed, comic fans can have digital editions of comic books delivered directly to their tablets. Tablets can store hundreds, even thousands, of comic books in a slim, light, and eminently portable package.

This golden age of digital comic books has lifted the barrier of the previously high cost of entry to would-be comic creators and publishers. Without the cost of printing and mailing their comics, any comic creator can now self-publish or work with one of several emerging small comic publishers and newsstand app makers to distribute their titles. In fact, beyond the cost of the Photoshop, Illustrator, or similar graphics programs that comic creators have to own to design their panels and pages anyway, there are often no additional costs to epublish their comics. This allows them to keep cover prices down, which, of course, drives sales and generates profit.

Unfortunately, the two big comic-book companies, Marvel and DC, haven't yet learned that lesson. You would think that titles like *Spider-Man, the X-Men, Batman,* and *Justice League* would be among the first to find great success as digital comics, but alas, that's not the case—but not for lack of customer interest. Rather, the problem is that Marvel and DC, which now charge a $2.99–$3.99 cover price per printed 32-page comic book, are often charging the same rates for each digital comic. For 60 years the comic-book industry has justified every increase in issue cost by citing the rising cost of paper—and, more recently, fuel for trucks to ship cases of comic books from printers to retail outlets. The paper and fuel costs are irrelevant to the world of digital comics, so how can the big companies justify the same per-issue price? This question perplexes would-be readers, who only started to come around to purchasing digital comics when the prices dropped from the same as print editions to an average of $1.99—at least for Marvel; as of this writing, DC had only dropped its price for new comics issues to $2.99.

Creating digital comics is easy and thus not covered in detail in this book. Digital comic books are almost always simple JPG or PNG images of each page, with all the pages of a given issue compiled into a CBR or CBZ archive file. These two formats are simply renamed RAR and ZIP archives, respectively. Each page of an issue is a separate image, numbered sequentially, and then archived to RAR or ZIP. After archival, the RAR or ZIP file is renamed CBR or CBZ, which is then read by any of several free or commercial digital comic-book readers available for computers and tablets. The series of images is then presented sequentially by the comic-book reader software—a glorified image previewer (see Figure 3.6).

Designing for Devices

As you write and produce digital publications, you'll begin testing on your computer just as a matter of convenience. Computer-based ebook readers, for example, can provide instant results when creating and modifying an EPUB-based publication. Just don't rely on what you see on-screen; computer-based ebook readers, even those such as Kindle, NOOK, Kobo, and Sony Reader, which have corresponding handheld ereaders, contain display and formatting variances that won't match the ebook's presentation precisely between devices. Always test your ebook on as many devices as you possibly can before calling it ready for publication. At the very least, test your ebooks—and explore the differences in other publishers' ebooks—on each class of ereading device.

FIGURE 3.6

Digital comic book examples: (a) *Carnival of Souls: Welcome to the Show,* viewed on a 7-inch Android tablet in self-contained app; (b) *X-Men,* June 1999, viewed in the Perfect Viewer comic book viewer app on a 10.1-inch Android tablet

Creator: Jazan Wild; Artist: Kevin Conrad

Creator: Jazan Wild; Artist: Kevin Conrad

HTML5 Proofing with Adobe Shadow

A convenient way to proof HTML5 content on various devices is to use Adobe Shadow. Once installed on a Mac or Windows computer, Adobe Shadow can connect to all of the iOS and Android devices on your office or home network. And, once connected, Shadow will instantly push the same web page to all those devices—including any changes you make in real time— enabling you to see how your content will look on numerous devices without the usual hassle of uploading the content to a web server and then visiting the content from within each device individually.

You can get Adobe Shadow from Adobe Labs at `http://labs.adobe.com`.

The same holds true, though often with a smaller selection of compatible devices, when creating rich-media publications. Test digital magazines on iPad, Android-powered tablets (several, if you can), the BlackBerry Playbook, and so on. PDF- and HTML5-based digital publications should be tested on, well, *everything*. All computers, the big-name tablets, and most smartphones will display PDFs and HTML5. If a device displays the format, consumers will view your publications on that device. Even if a device doesn't support a given format, consumers will *try* to view your publications on it.

Your Audience Already Told You What Devices They Use

If you have a website—and, really, who doesn't?—then the audience for your digital publications is already telling you what devices they use. Working on the (usually) solid assumption that most of the people who would consume your epublications will also visit your website, then all you have to do is check your site's server logs or analytics. One of the first things a web server logs is the *user agent* through which people access your site. A user agent is the combination of a site visitor's web browser and operating system. For example, you might see an entry like the following, which indicates that the user visited your site on an iPad running iOS version 3.2, a first-generation iPad that hasn't been upgraded (iPad 2s shipped with iOS version 4, iPad 3s shipped with iOS 5, and iOS 5 was released as a free upgrade for all iPads prior to the third generation).

```
Mozilla/5.0 (iPad; U; CPU OS 3_2 like Mac OS X; en-us) AppleWebKit/531.21.10
(KHTML, like Gecko) Version/4.0.4 Mobile/7B334b Safari/531.21.10
```

Use the user agent data to inform your decisions about the devices, operating systems, and file formats to support in your publications.

Most important, know your audience. If you want to distribute a digital edition of the *Journal of the American Medical Association* or a similarly specific trade or academic publication, then you know that nearly all of your affluent audience will be consuming that content on the best-of-breed tablet devices. You can then design specifically for those environments without worrying too much about also designing versions for the features and screen sizes of the second and third most popular tablets. However, if your job is to digitize a general-interest periodical, then you need to take into account, and design for, a much broader selection of devices. That may entail limiting your publication to a single semi-universal file format such as PDF or HTML5, or you may want to create several editions that take advantage of the strengths of each format— separate digital magazine format editions or interactive replicas for iPad, PlayBook, XOOM, Transformer, and Galaxy Tab; PDF or HTML5 for desktop and laptop computers; and EPUB-based for handheld devices.

What and how you design is determined as much by your audience's device preferences as by your desires for the content, presentation, and level of interactivity of your publications. Naturally, you can elect to force your market to adopt one format or another, but that can backfire; people have a tendency to use what they want to use and to expect your content to adapt to their devices rather than the other way around. The demise of Flash as a file format (discussed in Chapter 1, "Exploring Ereading Devices") is proof enough of that.

Chapter 4

Creating Basic Ebooks

Whether creating ebooks from TXT files or word processor documents or converting existing print publications to EPUB, the basics are all the same. You must learn to think in terms of EPUB, to reevaluate how your content is organized, and to know how to structure it using InDesign's built-in tools in order to produce well organized, readable ebooks. The yellow brick road to becoming a wizard of ebook production starts with this chapter and proceeds through the next several chapters, creating progressively more interesting, more marketable ebooks and other EPUB-based publications.

In this chapter, you will learn about the following:

◆ Creating an Ebook from Scratch

◆ Testing Your EPUB

◆ Styling Your Ebook

◆ Converting a Print Publication to an Ebook

Creating an Ebook from Scratch

Starting your first ebook from scratch—from a text document, from a word processor document, or by writing directly in InDesign or InCopy—is the best way to begin learning to create ebooks. (That's not to say you can't start from an existing for-print InDesign publication; we'll convert those to ebook form later in the chapter.) If this is your first ebook, even if you have the content already in another form, start with this section—there's a lot of important information here.

Beginning the Layout

Before bringing any existing content into InDesign, you must start a new InDesign document. Let's do that using options with an eye toward the final EPUB output.

1. Choose File ➢ New ➢ Document. (File ➢ New ➢ Book is tempting, but that's not what you want; I'll talk about that in Chapter 6, "Fine-Tuning EPUBs.")

2. In the New Document dialog, set Intent to Web, which will put the document into the RGB transparency blending space, and set the measurement system to pixels. Again, you might be tempted by the Digital Publishing intent, but that's for digital magazines, not EPUBs.

3. Set the Page Size drop-down to 800 × 600 (pixels), and change the orientation from the default landscape (800 pixels wide) to portrait (600 pixels wide), which will enable you to work within a good approximation of how the average ereader might display your ebook. Ultimately, the page size doesn't matter, however; the ebook content will reflow to fit whatever screen it's viewed on, be that 600 pixels wide, 320, 1,024, or whatever.

Similarly, the margin values in the New Document dialog are irrelevant because margins are given to ebook content by the ebook readers themselves. You *can* add margins via CSS and during the export to the EPUB process in InDesign, but neither of those options has anything to do with the margin values in the New Document dialog (except when exporting as EPUB 3.0 with Layout, which I'll cover in more depth in Chapter 6).

4. Ensure that Primary Text Frame (Master Text Frame in CS5/CS5.5) is checked, and leave the rest of the options at their defaults (Figure 4.1). This option, once enabled, will cause InDesign to automatically create a text frame on the first page and each subsequently created page. Moreover, the primary text frame on the pages will automatically thread together, enabling text to flow freely between them. Click OK to create the document.

FIGURE 4.1
Setting up a new document for creating an ebook

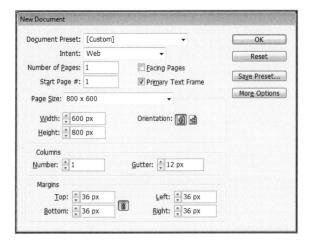

5. If you haven't already enabled Smart Text Reflow, which automatically adds pages when text is too long to fit within the text frames on the existing pages, open InDesign's Preferences by selecting Edit ➤ Preferences ➤ Type. In the bottom section, turn on Smart Text Reflow, set Add Pages To to End Of Story, and enable Limit To Primary Text Frames and Delete Empty Pages (Figure 4.2). Click OK, and then wait; you need to work through preparing the incoming text before proceeding.

FIGURE 4.2
The Smart Text Reflow section of the Preferences Type pane

If you're writing directly in InDesign, you're all set to begin writing. Just select the Type tool, click inside the first page's text frame, and get to work; you can skip to the section "Styling Your Ebook." However, if you'll be writing in InCopy or, as is more often the case, placing existing content from a text, word processor, or InCopy document, read on for specific instructions.

Writing in InCopy

Although you could begin writing directly in InCopy and then create the layout in InDesign later, it's a little more efficient to begin the layout in InDesign and then move into InCopy. You have two options for how to do that.

First, if you are the sole creator in the workflow, you can open the INDD document directly in InCopy and begin writing. There's no need to export anything or link InDesign to InCopy in any way. Both applications can edit INDD layout documents, though InCopy can't create frames; it can only edit content within existing frames, which is why you need to create the InDesign document and then open it in InCopy.

Alternatively, and this is especially useful if someone else will be doing the writing, you can export a story from InDesign to an InCopy document while simultaneously replacing that embedded story with a link to the InCopy document. That's easy with the following steps:

1. In InDesign, use the black arrow Selection tool to select the empty primary text frame on the first page of your new document. As of CS6, this can be done without the Ctrl+double-click/Cmd+double-click that previous versions of InDesign required in order to activate the automatic text frame.

2. Choose Edit ➤ InCopy ➤ Export ➤ Selection. InDesign will prompt you to save an ICML InCopy document. Save it wherever you like, though I recommend putting it in the same folder as the one containing the INDD document or a subfolder of that one.

3. If you haven't yet set up your user identity in InDesign via the File ➤ User command, InDesign will now require you to do so (Figure 4.3). When the User dialog comes up, pick a unique name and color. Both will be used to identify you to the InCopy user and are particularly useful in communicating when you or the InCopy user have checked out the story for editing and during commenting and revision tracking.

TIP   If you're a single user, the same person who will be working in both InDesign and InCopy, you must still specify a username in InDesign that is different from the one you use in InCopy. For example, I typically set my usernames to Pariah Burke (ID) and Pariah Burke (IC), respectively.

FIGURE 4.3
Exporting from InDesign to InCopy for the first time requires that you choose a username and color.

4. InDesign will prompt you to save the INDD document; click OK.

Now you can switch to InCopy and begin writing in the ICML file you exported. Because the ICML is a linked document, both it and the rest of the INDD can be opened and worked on simultaneously, by the same or different people, and edits to the ICML can be incorporated into the InDesign layout the way any modified linked asset can be, by updating the link. Conversely, forgoing ICML export and opening the INDD directly in InCopy allows many people to *view* the file simultaneously, whether in InCopy or InDesign, but only one person can check out and edit the content at a time.

Importing from InCopy

If the book content has already been written in InCopy, all you have to do is import the ICML, INX, or INCD document via File ➤ Place. You won't need to use Show Import Options as you will for the other formats discussed later. InDesign and InCopy share a code base, which means that everything you can do in InCopy translates perfectly to InDesign without the need to set any of the conversion options required for TXT, Word, or RTF files.

Importing from a Text Document

If you (or an editor) haven't already prepared ebook content in Microsoft Word or another word processor, start with a text document. If you don't already have one ready for use, please use the one I provided, L. Frank Baum's classic *The Wonderful Wizard of Oz*, the best known of Baum's 17 Oz books. You'll find it in this chapter's lesson files with the filename WonderfulWizardofOz.txt.

FINDING FREE EBOOK CONTENT

The Wonderful Wizard of Oz, as well as all of Baum's 38 other Oz and non-Oz works, is in the *public domain*, meaning it's free from copyright ownership in the United States because of its age and the length of time since the author's death. Thus, I'm able to distribute it to you, and we're both able to use it, without infringing upon anyone's copyrights. Welcome to Munchkin Land! Note that the laws in countries other than the United States vary; you should check the intellectual property laws of your country before making use of any Project Gutenberg content.

The Wonderful Wizard of Oz, as well as 38,000 other ebooks, are available from Project Gutenberg, whose mission since 1971 has been to "encourage the creation and distribution of ebooks." All of the books you'll find within the Project Gutenberg library (http://gutenberg.org) are free to read, and nearly all are free to build your own ebooks—or anything—from because they're in the public domain. On most books' individual pages you'll find a link to download the plaintext UTF-8 version; that's the one you want for these exercises. Just be sure to check your chosen book's individual license statement inside the book file and to review and understand Project Gutenberg licensing in general.

www.gutenberg.org/wiki/Gutenberg:The_Project_Gutenberg_License

---

Although you're free to work with your own documents—after all, that is the point—within this and the next few chapters, I'll be working with *The Wonderful Wizard of Oz* lesson files. It's ideally suited as a learning example and resource for several reasons:

- The book is in the public domain.

- The book's fantastic illustrations are also in the public domain.

- There is even a public domain recording of the book being read aloud, which will come in very handy in Chapter 5, "Working with Images and Multimedia in Ebooks," when we add read-along functionality to the ebook.

TIP In addition to plaintext versions of ebooks, Project Gutenberg often offers EPUB versions. Although they tend to be simple EPUBs, they can be useful as examples of the format. Crack them open in Calibre or another EPUB editor. (See Chapter 6 for more on that subject.)

PREPARING THE TEXT DOCUMENT

ASCII text files are 1960s technology (yes, they had computers back then). They are the most basic form of textual content available on computers, which is why they're so useful and universally supported. However, they still carry the limitations of their origins, namely, that they are structured to be viewed on incredibly low-resolution terminal screens with no support for punctuation and symbols that *are* part of the English language but *are not* painted on your keyboard's keys. Consequently, to be used effectively in a modern publishing workflow, we have to do some cleanup on the files.

Removing the Project Gutenberg Trademark

If you're using `WonderfulWizardofOz.txt` or another text file from Project Gutenberg, you must remove the Project Gutenberg trademark and license information. Failure to do that will require you to pay a royalty to Project Gutenberg, which isn't a bad thing because the project runs on such royalties and donations. If you'd rather not pay the royalty, follow the instructions here—and don't worry; it's all perfectly legal and acceptable to Project Gutenberg. (You did read the licensing statement I noted earlier, didn't you?)

1. Open the Project Gutenberg text file in a text editor such as Windows Notepad or Mac OS X's TextEdit.

2. Near the top of the file, locate the line that begins with the text *** *START OF THIS PROJECT GUTENBERG EBOOK*.... Delete that line and all lines of text above it.

3. About 400 lines from the end of the document, locate the line beginning with *** *END OF THIS PROJECT GUTENBERG EBOOK*.... Delete it and all lines of text below it. Also look to see whether a second *END OF PROJECT GUTENBERG'S*... line appears above the one that started with asterisks; if so, delete it as well. Your file should now have no reference to Project Gutenberg.

Mending Line Length

Next you have to deal with the problem of text files' line length. The standard for ASCII text files is to include no more than 75–80 characters *and* spaces per line and to use a hard carriage return at the end of each line (see Figure 4.4). The purpose of these rules is to make the documents human-readable on very low-resolution (and old) devices, and Project Gutenberg adheres to these rules for maximum compatibility of its ebooks. For us, it complicates our EPUB production workflow. If you left each line as is, the text wouldn't properly reflow to fit different screens; instead, each line of text would be treated as a separate paragraph. Yuck!

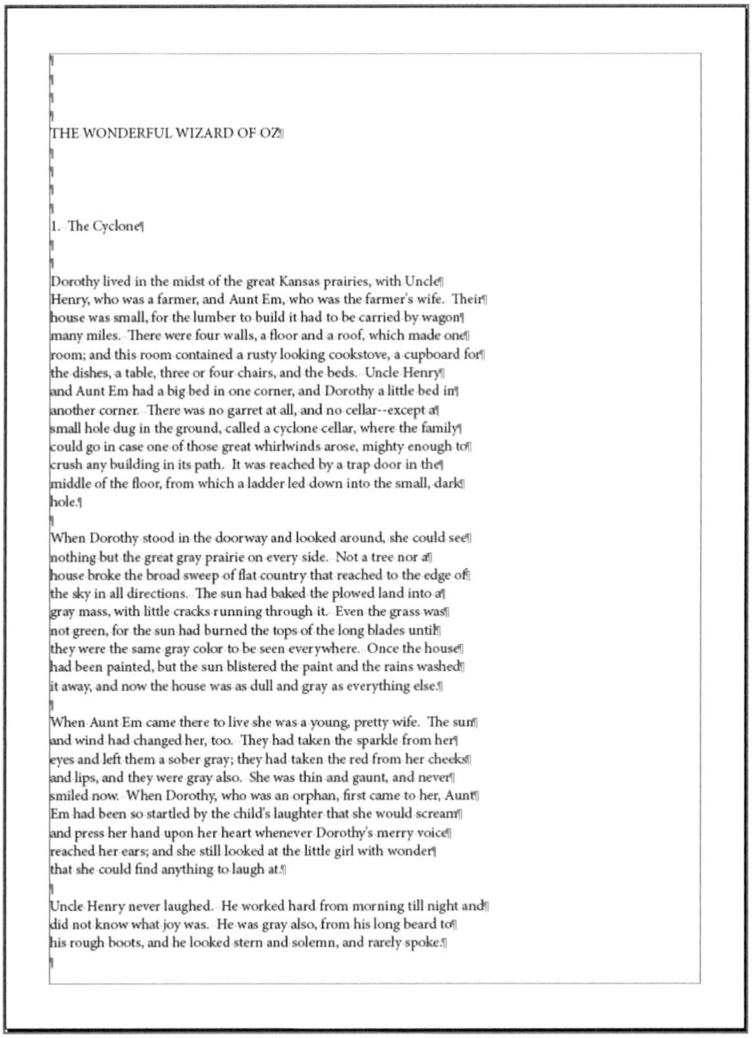

¶
¶
¶
¶
THE WONDERFUL WIZARD OF OZ¶
¶
¶
¶
¶
1. The Cyclone¶
¶
¶
Dorothy lived in the midst of the great Kansas prairies, with Uncle¶
Henry, who was a farmer, and Aunt Em, who was the farmer's wife. Their¶
house was small, for the lumber to build it had to be carried by wagon¶
many miles. There were four walls, a floor and a roof, which made one¶
room; and this room contained a rusty looking cookstove, a cupboard for¶
the dishes, a table, three or four chairs, and the beds. Uncle Henry¶
and Aunt Em had a big bed in one corner, and Dorothy a little bed in¶
another corner. There was no garret at all, and no cellar--except a¶
small hole dug in the ground, called a cyclone cellar, where the family¶
could go in case one of those great whirlwinds arose, mighty enough to¶
crush any building in its path. It was reached by a trap door in the¶
middle of the floor, from which a ladder led down into the small, dark¶
hole.¶
¶
When Dorothy stood in the doorway and looked around, she could see¶
nothing but the great gray prairie on every side. Not a tree nor a¶
house broke the broad sweep of flat country that reached to the edge of¶
the sky in all directions. The sun had baked the plowed land into a¶
gray mass, with little cracks running through it. Even the grass was¶
not green, for the sun had burned the tops of the long blades until¶
they were the same gray color to be seen everywhere. Once the house¶
had been painted, but the sun blistered the paint and the rains washed¶
it away, and now the house was as dull and gray as everything else.¶
¶
When Aunt Em came there to live she was a young, pretty wife. The sun¶
and wind had changed her, too. They had taken the sparkle from her¶
eyes and left them a sober gray; they had taken the red from her cheeks¶
and lips, and they were gray also. She was thin and gaunt, and never¶
smiled now. When Dorothy, who was an orphan, first came to her, Aunt¶
Em had been so startled by the child's laughter that she would scream¶
and press her hand upon her heart whenever Dorothy's merry voice¶
reached her ears; and she still looked at the little girl with wonder¶
that she could find anything to laugh at.¶
¶
Uncle Henry never laughed. He worked hard from morning till night and¶
did not know what joy was. He was gray also, from his long beard to¶
his rough boots, and he looked stern and solemn, and rarely spoke.¶
¶

FIGURE 4.4
The proper formatting of text files, with 75-character lines and hard returns (the ¶ mark is visible in some editors) after each line.

Although you could go through the thousands of lines of a TXT document, manually replacing hard returns within paragraphs with a space (and I have), there are much easier ways. Several industrious individuals have created free or commercial software and website apps specifically for the purpose, and a few minutes with Microsoft Word's or another word processor's Find and Replace utility can make quick work of the replacement. InDesign (and InCopy) also has a utility built in, and it's the easiest and fastest way to fix this problem. Let's use that.

1. Choose File ➤ Place to open a Place dialog and then navigate to the ebook content text file you want to import. *Do not click Open yet!*

2. Check the box beside Show Import Options and *then* you can click Open. Up will pop the Text Import Options dialog (see Figure 4.5).

FIGURE 4.5

Text Import Options configured to fix your text file

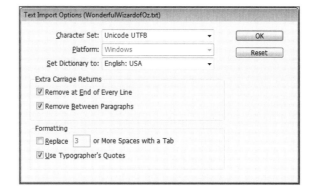

3. Character Set, Platform, and Set Dictionary To should automatically populate with the correct options—Unicode UTF8, Windows or Mac, and English: USA. You may have to enable the options Remove At End Of Every Line, which will rejoin lines broken by hard carriage returns; Remove Between Paragraphs, which fixes the problem of paragraph separation via double carriage returns; and Use Typographer's Quotes, which will replace so-called dumb quotes, which are actually inch and foot marks, with actual quotation marks (often called *typographer's quotes, smart quotes,* or *curly quotes*). Although you could choose to replace a number of spaces with a tab, which would be useful when placing text documents for use in print layouts, it won't benefit you in this case; just disable that option and click OK.

4. You'll be deposited into InDesign with a loaded cursor. Click once inside the empty text frame on the first page. Note that the frame was created by enabling the Primary Text Frame option in the New Document dialog.

   If you turned on Smart Text Reflow—or left it on, because it's on by default—the entire text file will pay out, automatically adding as many pages as necessary. In my case, using `WonderfulWizardofOz.txt`, that's 50 pages, though yours may vary if we have different fonts and sizes selected. Note that the lines wrap nicely to the text frame, thanks to InDesign's import options. If you haven't already enabled Smart Text Reflow per the instructions in the "Beginning the Layout" section, do it now, while the cursor is still loaded and before clicking into that primary text frame, or Shift-click to cause the text to autoflow.

Replacing Substituted Characters

The next big issue you need to resolve in the text document content is the substitution of punctuation and other characters necessitated by ASCII's limited 95-printable-character repertoire. Enabling the Use Typographer's Quotes option in the Text Import Options dialog already replaced inch or minute marks (") with actual quotation marks (""); similarly, it replaced foot or hour marks (') with correct apostrophes and single quotes (''). But now you need to replace things like double hyphens (--) with em dashes (—), three periods (...) with an ellipsis (…), improvised copyright symbols like "(C)" and "(R)" with the correct symbols (© and ®), and so on. To do that, you'll employ InDesign's handy-dandy Find/Change utility.

1. Open Find/Change by selecting it just south of the middle of the Edit menu.

2. On the Text tab, enter two consecutive hyphens (--) in the Find What field (see Figure 4.6).

FIGURE 4.6
Replacing double
hyphens with an
em dash in Find/
Change

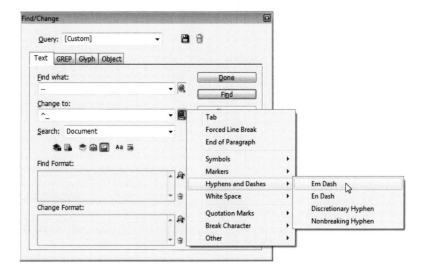

3. To the right of the Change To field, click the asterisk-labeled Special Characters For Replace button to expose a menu containing categories of special characters. From within the Hyphens And Dashes category, choose Em Dash; that should populate the Change To field with InDesign's code for an em dash, which is ^_.

4. Set the Search drop-down menu to Document, and click Change All. InDesign will then replace all double hyphens in the document with their typographically correct better, the em dash. When the replacement is complete, InDesign will tell you exactly how many instances were replaced.

5. Click OK on the results alert to return to the Find/Change dialog, and replace the contents of the Find What field with three periods (...).

6. Delete the contents of the Change To field, and again from the Special Characters to Replace menu, choose Symbols ➤ Ellipsis. Click Change All.

7. Repeat the replacement process for "(C)" and "(R)," which should be replaced with, respectively, the copyright symbol and the registered trademark symbol, both in the Special Characters To Replace ➤ Symbols menu.

8. Now let's get rid of any tabs in the document. That's important because tabs—regardless of the number of consecutive tabs—will be replaced with a single space upon export to EPUB. That's not InDesign's doing, though; it's part of the EPUB file specification, just like HTML. Instead, if you want tabbed lines in your document, you'll need to use a first-line indent or perhaps even tables.

   Delete the contents of both the Find What and Change To fields. Then, from the Special Characters For Search menu (the @ symbol beside the Find What field), choose Tab at the top of the menu. That will insert InDesign's tab code, ^t. Leave the Change To field blank to obliterate tabs, or put a space in it to replace tabs with spaces *if your document needs that to separate columnar data*. Click Change All.

9. If there are any other special characters, punctuation, or symbols fudged in your ASCII ebook content, use Find/Change to fix them as well.

At this point, the text of your ebook might be ready to go. If you're using *The Wonderful Wizard of Oz* text document I provided, then you're done with substituted-text replacement.

With some documents, though, there is another bit of cleanup that is no fun at all, with no way to automate it. Because ASCII text files cannot contain even simple formatting like italics, emphasis has to be shown by the Project Gutenberg transcribers by setting emphasized words in all caps. In a professionally typeset publication, there's no place for all caps. You'll have to go through the document, line by line, replacing all-caps words with their correct case and italicizing them.

Finally, end the cleanup process by fixing any other substitutions or peculiarities in the document, such as the following:

◆ Fix paragraphs that begin with spaces (use Find/Change to look for a carriage return followed by a space, as in "^p ")

◆ Fix paragraphs that end with spaces (" ^p")

◆ Fix paragraphs that include section-breaking symbols such as a bunch of hyphens (or now em dashes) or asterisks (*)

◆ Replace a slash (/) in a fraction with a solidus (/)

◆ Replace *x*'s in mathematic expressions with the multiplication sign (×)

◆ Replace hyphens between ranges of numbers and dates with en dashes (–)

The next step is to test the ebook thus far, but that'll have to wait until after you've worked through starting from a word-processing document.

Importing from a Word Processor

Most ebook content comes from a word processor such as Microsoft Word, Apple Pages, Google Docs, or Adobe InCopy. Thankfully, these programs create documents free of most of the limitations of, and issues encountered with, ASCII text. For one, word-processor writers don't hit Return/Enter at the end of every line (if they do, they should have a house dropped on them). They also don't use a bunch of spaces to indent paragraphs (drop the house on 'em again if they do). And, even if they *try* to use double hyphens where em dashes belong, three periods instead of an ellipsis, or "dumb quotes," the word processor usually fixes the mistakes as the writer types. You still might need to fix a few things in InDesign, though.

Let's get the document into InDesign. InDesign supports Word documents with .doc or .docx file extensions, as well as Rich Text Format (RTF) files—and native InCopy documents, of course. If your word processor saves any other file format, such as Apple Pages' PAGES files or ODT-extension OpenDocument files, you'll first need to export from your word-processor document to Word DOC, DOCX, or RTF.

1. Starting again from a new, blank document with a primary text frame already extant and Smart Text Reflow enabled, choose File ➢ Place to navigate to the ebook content you need to place. Again, before clicking the Open button, ensure that Show Import Options is selected.

2. After clicking Open, the Microsoft Word or RTF Import Options dialog will appear (Figure 4.7), both with very similar options. Set the options as follows:

   ◆ In the Include section, enable Footnotes and Endnotes, but disable Table Of Contents Text and Index Text. The latter two, though probably dynamic in the word-processor document, will import to InDesign only as flat text, meaning the page numbers will not automatically update to reflect the location of the referenced text in the InDesign document. Better to remove them entirely and rebuild them, if needed, in InDesign.

   ◆ Unless the writer didn't use correct quotation marks in the word processor, disable Use Typographer's Quotes to prevent converting *deliberately* used inch/second and foot/minute marks into quotes and apostrophes.

   ◆ Select Preserve Styles And Formatting From Text And Tables.

   ◆ From the Manual Page Breaks drop-down, choose either No Breaks or Preserve Page Breaks; the latter will preserve breaks in the EPUB.

   ◆ Enable Import Inline Graphics, but disable Import Unused Styles and Convert Bullets & Numbers To Text. Whether Track Changes is enabled is up to you; even if tracked changes are in the document, they won't output to EPUB.

   ◆ Finally, choose Import Styles Automatically, leaving both Paragraph Style Conflicts and Character Style Conflicts set to Use InDesign Style Definition unless you want to redefine InDesign's styles with those coming in through the placed document or make new styles from the incoming ones.

FIGURE 4.7
Microsoft Word
Import Options
(left) and RTF
Import Options
(right)

ASPIRIN-FREE WORKFLOW: SAVE A PRESET

If you intend to use Word or RTF source files for additional ebooks in the future, set the options now and then click the Save Preset button to record this exact set of options for rapid reuse later. After you click the Save Preset button, InDesign will prompt you to name your preset; give it a meaningful name like "Word to EPUB" or "RTF to EPUB" and click OK. The next time you need to change options for importing Word or RTF files, you'll find your new preset in the Preset list at the top of the Import Options dialog. Select the preset to reset the options to the way they were when you saved the preset, and then simply click OK to continue the import. You won't need to change any options manually.

3. After clicking OK, you'll be facing the InDesign page with a loaded cursor. Click once inside the empty text frame on the first page. (Note that the frame was created by enabling the Primary Text Frame option in the New Document dialog.)

   If you turned on Smart Text Reflow, the entire document will pay out, automatically adding as many pages as necessary.

4. Now go through the document fixing any substituted characters, all-caps words, and other common errors. Pay special attention to double carriage returns, a common workaround writers use in word-processor applications if that application's paragraph styles haven't been configured to show vertical space between paragraphs or an indented first line.

TIP Refer to the "Replacing Substituted Characters" section for common characters that require replacement and step-by-step instructions. You might also want to choose Type ➢ Show Hidden Characters to see returns, spaces, tabs, and more represented as symbols visible on your screen.

Testing Your EPUB

At this point, you have the most basic, probably unstyled, possibly ugliest ebook content one could imagine. Still, it's important that you see your first ebook *as an EPUB* as early as possible in the process. For that reason, let's zip through exporting to EPUB now.

1. In CS5 choose File ➤ Export To ➤ EPUB. In InDesign CS6, the entire Export To submenu was removed, unifying its output formats with the standard Export dialog. Thus, you should choose File ➤ Export.

2. From the Save As Type (Windows) or Format (Mac OS X) menu in the Export dialog, choose EPUB, name your EPUB file, and click Save. Up will pop the EPUB Export Options dialog (see Figure 4.8).

FIGURE 4.8
The EPUB Export
Options dialog

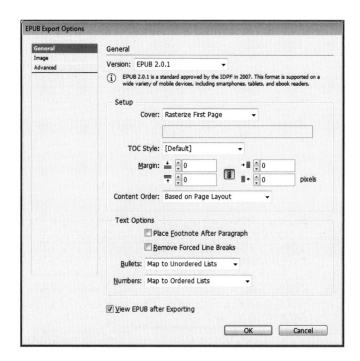

3. There are many settings in the EPUB Export Options, all of which you'll get to in time. At this juncture, however, you have such a rudimentary ebook that all you need are the default options. Make sure that the option View EPUB After Exporting is enabled, but leave all others at their defaults. Click OK.

Assuming you have ereader software installed on your computer, your new ebook should appear momentarily. As you can see from Figure 4.9, the book looks rather hideous, but that's not the point. The point is, you now have an EPUB! Navigate around and check it out. Compare the output in the ereader with what appears on the InDesign page, noting differences. You might want to also resize the ereader software window a few times, noting how the text responds.

FIGURE 4.9
My ebook (dis-
played in Sony
Reader for PC)

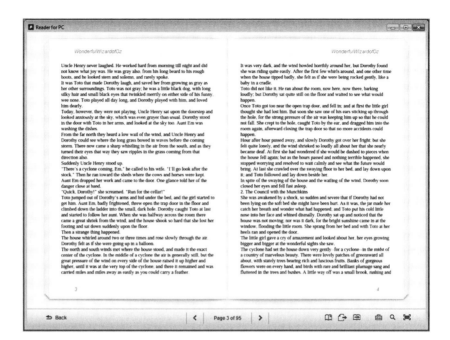

FIGURE 4.9
My ebook (dis-
played in Sony
Reader for PC)

For the most accurate look at your ebook, check it on a handheld ereader or tablet. They all have ways of getting ebooks from your computer onto them; check your particular device's help file, user manual, or support forum for the method.

EREADER SOFTWARE FOR YOUR COMPUTER

All of the big ebookstores—with the current exception of Apple's iBookstore—offer ereading software for Windows, Mac, and often even UNIX computers. You'll find links to some of the biggest ebookstores' ereading software, as well as a couple of popular ebook readers that aren't connected to any particular store, on the *ePublishing with InDesign* ereaders page at `http://abbrv.it/DigiPubIDReaders`.

Although what you'll see on screen in the computer-based ereaders section is often very different from what you'll see in the same manufacturers' mobile ereader software for tablets and smartphones and in their purpose-built handheld ereaders, viewing EPUBs in computer-based ereaders is the first and fastest way of proofing ebooks at early stages. As you near the end of production of a book, however, you'll definitely want to proof directly on the devices on which most consumers will read your content. In fact, you'll want to check your ebook on as many such devices as you possibly can, even if that means buying or borrowing several devices you'll use only for proofing. (At any given time I own about a dozen of the latest and most popular ereaders, tablets, and smartphones that I use strictly for proofing and teaching how to proof digital publications.)

Styling Your Ebook

Using paragraph styles in ebook creation is crucial. Ideally the styles will be used by the author at writing time, even if the content is written in a word processor.

Paragraph Styles

The Wonderful Wizard of Oz is typical of most novels in terms of styling requirements. Each chapter begins with a chapter number and title and then contains prose text. Assuming you want the first paragraph at the beginning of each chapter to vary a little from the style of the rest of the paragraphs—maybe the first paragraph has a drop cap or doesn't indent its first line, whereas the rest of the prose paragraphs do—you'll need to create and apply a total of only four paragraph styles to format the majority of the book. Let's start styling there, leaving the cover, introduction, table of contents, and other front matter and back matter until later in the process.

BODY COPY

Let's begin by styling the majority of the text—the body copy—in one shot.

1. With the Type tool somewhere in the manuscript, press Ctrl+A/Cmd+A to select all the text in the story, chapter, or book.

2. Open the Paragraph Styles panel from the Window ➢ Styles menu and click the Create New Style button at the bottom; the button looks rather like a sticky note. This will create a new style with the unhelpful name of Paragraph Style 1 or another number. Double-click Paragraph Style 1 to simultaneously apply it to the highlighted text (all the text in the manuscript) and to open the Paragraph Style Options dialog.

3. At the top of the Paragraph Style Options dialog, rename the style Body Copy (Figure 4.10), and then click OK. Don't worry about any other options right now.

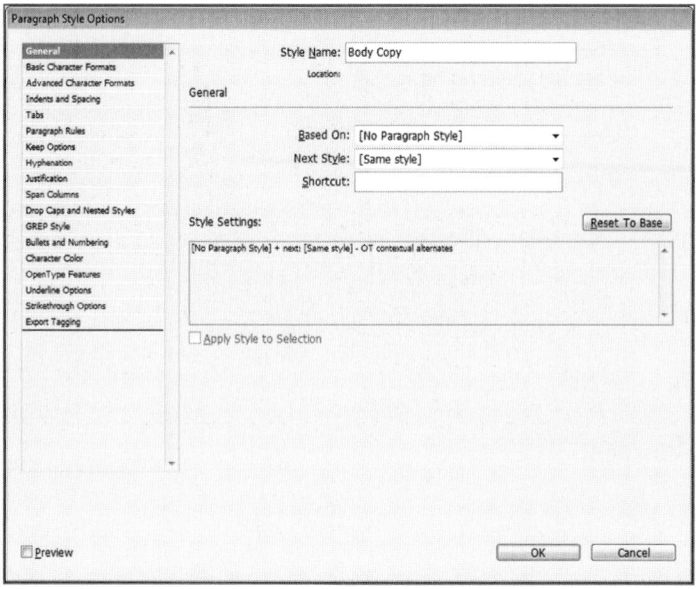

FIGURE 4.10
Renaming the style in the Paragraph Style Options dialog

CHAPTER NUMBER AND CHAPTER TITLE

Now that the majority of the manuscript has been given its required style of Body Copy, you need to format the first chapter's chapter number and name; if you're using *The Wonderful Wizard of Oz*, that would be "1. The Cyclone."

1. Although you can leave the number and name on one line together, for this exercise set them on separate lines, replacing the period and double space between the number and name with a return (Figure 4.11).

FIGURE 4.11
The first chapter number and name (left), reset as separate lines (right)

2. Now style both the chapter number and the chapter title as you'd like them to appear in the ebook. Note that there will be variances, probably in font and relative size, when viewed on different devices. Also, don't worry about vertical spacing at this point. I'll cover that very shortly.

STYLE THE RETURN

When styling a paragraph, remember that the invisible hard-return character at the end of the paragraph (¶, called a *pilcrow*) is treated as a character, too. Therefore, you must also select the pilcrow when styling or risk creating *overrides* (or, worse, paragraph styles based on the formatting of the return character and not the text before it). There are two ways to ensure that you always select the pilcrow along with the rest of the text in the paragraph. First, you can expose invisible characters via Type ➤ Show Hidden Characters in InDesign and then, when clicking and dragging to select text, remember to drag *past* the end of the paragraph text to also highlight that pilcrow. The other method is even easier—with the Type tool, quadruple-click inside the desired paragraph. That will select all the text in the paragraph *and* its return character, whether it's visible or hidden.

As you can see in Figure 4.12, I've chosen to make my chapter number 60pt and center-aligned; my chapter title is italic, 40pt, and also center-aligned. I've left both as InDesign's default serif font, Minion Pro.

3. Highlight the chapter number line, and, on the Paragraph Styles panel, click the Create New Style button to create a style from it. Again, the default style name will be less than informative, so you'll need to double-click the style and rename it Chapter Number.

4. Repeat the previous step to create a paragraph style for the chapter title, named Chapter Title. When you've finished, you should have a total of three paragraph styles—Body Copy, Chapter Number, and Chapter Title—all applied to their respective paragraphs at the start of Chapter 1.

5. Go through the rest of the book setting chapter numbers and titles on separate lines and applying their respective paragraph styles.

FIRST PARAGRAPHS

Finally, before exporting to EPUB again, turn your attention toward the first paragraph of each chapter. Although you could leave it as is, matching the indentation level of every other paragraph in the chapter, it's customary to set the first paragraph a little differently than the rest. You can do quite a bit here—you could use a different color or font for the first paragraph or just the first few letters or line of it, you could change the font size for the whole paragraph or the first few words or line, you could do drop caps, and you could do all sorts of other stuff. I'll get into things like that in later chapters. For now, let's just remove the first-line indent, making the first paragraph start *flush* left.

1. With the Type tool, click inside or highlight the text of the first paragraph at the beginning of Chapter 1.

2. Create a new paragraph style for that paragraph and, in the Paragraph Style Options, name it Body Copy First Paragraph. Don't click OK in the Paragraph Style Options dialog just yet, though.

   Note the Based On field on the Paragraph Style Options' General pane (see Figure 4.13). It should already say Body Copy.

FIGURE 4.13
The Based On field states that this style is based on another style.

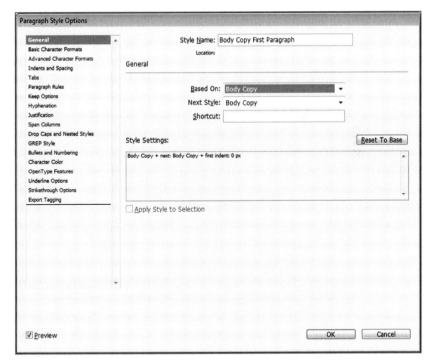

Basing one style on another—in this case basing Body Copy First Paragraph on Body Copy—means that one style, the child, automatically inherits the attributes of the other, the parent style. In fact, all the attributes and formatting of the parent will also apply to the child, except where you've deliberately set differences within the child paragraph style's options. In this case, you're going to merely remove the first-line indent from the Body Copy First Paragraph style, the child; that will be the only difference between it and its parent, the Body Copy style. Thus, if you change the font size, typeface, or any option other than the First Line Indent value in Body Copy, that change will automatically cascade through Body Copy First Paragraph as well.

Typically when you create a new paragraph style, the Based On field reads *[No Paragraph Style]*. You can change it manually. In this case, that field was already populated with Body Copy because you made the Body Copy First Paragraph style from a paragraph that had already been tagged as Body Copy. InDesign therefore interprets your action as a desire to base the new style on the preexisting one.

3. Go to the Indents And Spacing pane and reset the First Line Indent field value to 0 px. Before clicking OK, go back to the General pane. Notice in the Style Settings area that the definition of Body Copy First Paragraph is Body Copy + next: *[Same Style]* + first indent: 0 px. Setting aside the "next: *[Same Style]*" for the moment, the rest of the definition says that this style is whatever attributes comprise Body Copy *except* that the first line indent is 0 px.

4. The value in the Next Style field, just beneath the Based On field, determines what happens when you press Return/Enter while typing. Any time you press Return/Enter, you create a new paragraph, one that must have its own paragraph style assignment. When that field reads *[Same Style]*, hitting Return/Enter will apply the same style—in this case, Body Copy First Paragraph. Although our content is already written, it's just good practice to set the Next Style field to the style you actually want to appear next—Body Copy. Make sure to select Apply Style to Selection and click OK.

5. Now the tedious part: Go through the rest of the document—all 24 chapters plus the introduction—applying the Body Copy First Paragraph style. Alternatively, you could use the GREP tab of Find/Change to style the first paragraphs of each chapter by searching for patterns. Explaining GREP and using GREP in Find/Change is a little outside the focus of this book, though. If you want to learn about those features, you'll find some great information in the book *Mastering InDesign for Print Design & Production*, also by yours truly.

Once all that's done, export another EPUB proof. You should see something akin to Figure 4.14.

If your ebook requires more styles than the four you've created and utilized thus far—paragraph styles for headings, lines of poetry, quoted paragraphs, footnotes, bulleted or numbered lists, and so on, and maybe even character styles for figure references, inline code, URLs, glossary terms, subscript or superscript, or anything else—create and apply those styles.

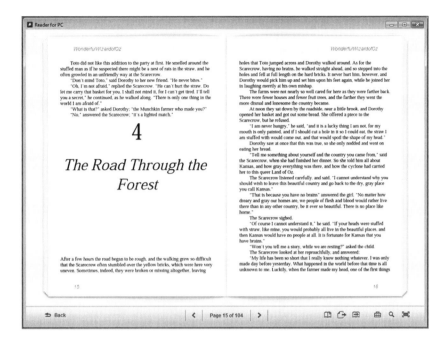

Vertical Spacing

In a printed book, you may choose to create vertical space between paragraphs such as the chapter number and title copy by using (shudder) separate text frames. When it comes to ebook layout, however, that will produce very different results. Take a look at Figure 4.15 to see what I mean. The fact that I linked the three frames is irrelevant; threaded or unthreaded, the result in EPUB will be consecutive paragraphs with no additional vertical spacing between them.

FIGURE 4.15
Space between separate frames in an InDesign story (left) are ignored by EPUB (right).

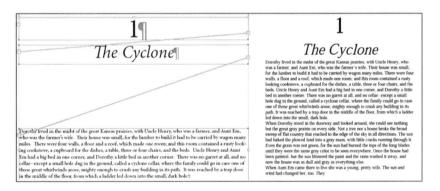

There are two ways to create vertical spacing between paragraphs that *will* translate from InDesign to EPUB.

First, the one I advise *against* using, because it robs you of a tremendous amount of layout control, is multiple returns between paragraphs. Yes, you can hit Return/Enter multiple times, which, just like when converting to a web page, will translate within the EPUB to multiple blank paragraphs created with the <p></p> tags.

The other—and infinitely better—method is to use paragraph vertical spacing. You can, of course, control vertical spacing before and after a paragraph on the Control panel (when working with the Type tool) as well as from the Paragraph panel (Window ➤ Text & Tables ➤ Paragraph). In a potentially lengthy publication like an ebook, though, you won't want to do that manually via those panels for each paragraph requiring vertical separation; rather, you'll want to add space before and/or after within paragraph styles. Let's do that with the existing chapter number and title styles.

1. Open the Paragraph Style Options dialog for the Chapter Number paragraph style. There are several ways you can do that:

   ◆ With the Type tool active, highlight the chapter number or place the cursor within that paragraph somewhere. That will highlight the correct style in the Paragraph Styles panel, whereupon you may simply double-click the style or choose Style Options from the Paragraph Styles panel flyout menu.

   ◆ With or without text selected, you can right-click the style name in the Paragraph Styles panel and choose the command Edit [whatever style name].

   ◆ Again, with or without text selected, holding Shift while double-clicking the style name in the Paragraph Styles panel will enable you to edit the style without applying it to any text or setting it as the default, which is what happens if you double-click a style name without text or a frame selected.

2. In the Paragraph Style Options for Chapter Number, go to the Indents And Spacing pane selectable on the left (Figure 4.16).

3. If you didn't already set the chapter number's paragraph alignment to what you want, you can do that here as the first option. Then move down to the Space Before and Space After fields, setting the amount of space you want, in pixels, before and/or after chapter numbers. If you're unfamiliar with setting vertical spacing between paragraphs, here are a few points to keep in mind:

   ◆ Space before a paragraph is vertical spacing that appears above the paragraph, separating it from previous paragraphs, while space after appears below the paragraph.

   ◆ Typically you want to choose space either before or after, not both, for all of your paragraphs. That prevents odd stacking of vertical spacing. Which you choose—before or after—is a matter of personal preference. I prefer using space after; some designers prefer space before. The key is to settle on one and use it consistently, though there will be exceptions, such as with headers that typically need both space after and more space before.

FIGURE 4.16
The Indents And
Spacing pane of the
Paragraph Style
Options dialog

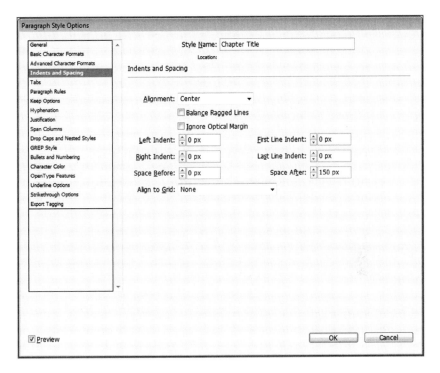

- ◆ InDesign will suppress space before and after at the ends of pages, frames, or columns. For instance, if a paragraph that has a Space Before setting appears at the top of a page, frame, or column, InDesign will ignore the Space Before value, setting that paragraph at the very top of the page, frame, or column. Similarly, paragraphs with a Space After attribute will not show that space after when they appear at the bottom of a page, frame, or column.

- ◆ As a general rule, EPUB does *not* have the intelligence to suppress space before and after paragraphs based on their positions. Some ereaders will follow InDesign's lead, some won't. Thus, it's doubly important that you don't stack space before *and* after.

- ◆ Even though values entered into the Space Before and Space After fields are in pixels and show their absolute values on screen in InDesign, when it comes to ebooks, they're interpreted relative to the size of type chosen by the reader. Thus, if the type size is increased for reading comfort on an ereader device, the actual vertical space between paragraphs will increase commensurately.

With all that in mind, I'm setting the Space After option for my Chapter Number style to 20 px. It's not a lot, actually; I just want a little bump of white space between my chapter numbers and their titles. Speaking of…

4. Once you've set your vertical spacing options for the Chapter Number style, do the same for the Chapter Title style. For my edition of this book, I want lots of space between the chapter title and the first paragraph, so I'm going with a Space After value of 150 px. Note

that, because we're changing the style definitions, *every* chapter number and every chapter title will update to match these changes (see Figure 4.17). This is why using styles in InDesign is crucial—well, this and being able to change them all in the CSS later.

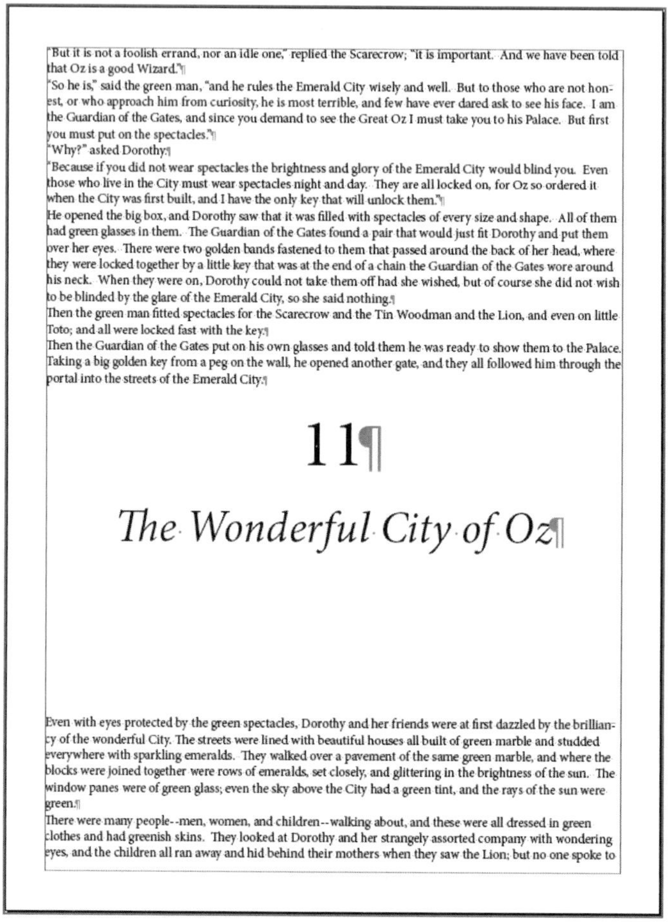

"But it is not a foolish errand, nor an idle one," replied the Scarecrow; "it is important. And we have been told that Oz is a good Wizard."¶

"So he is," said the green man, "and he rules the Emerald City wisely and well. But to those who are not honest, or who approach him from curiosity, he is most terrible, and few have ever dared ask to see his face. I am the Guardian of the Gates, and since you demand to see the Great Oz I must take you to his Palace. But first you must put on the spectacles."¶

"Why?" asked Dorothy.¶

"Because if you did not wear spectacles the brightness and glory of the Emerald City would blind you. Even those who live in the City must wear spectacles night and day. They are all locked on, for Oz so ordered it when the City was first built, and I have the only key that will unlock them."¶

He opened the big box, and Dorothy saw that it was filled with spectacles of every size and shape. All of them had green glasses in them. The Guardian of the Gates found a pair that would just fit Dorothy and put them over her eyes. There were two golden bands fastened to them that passed around the back of her head, where they were locked together by a little key that was at the end of a chain the Guardian of the Gates wore around his neck. When they were on, Dorothy could not take them off had she wished, but of course she did not wish to be blinded by the glare of the Emerald City, so she said nothing.¶

Then the green man fitted spectacles for the Scarecrow and the Tin Woodman and the Lion, and even on little Toto; and all were locked fast with the key.¶

Then the Guardian of the Gates put on his own glasses and told them he was ready to show them to the Palace. Taking a big golden key from a peg on the wall, he opened another gate, and they all followed him through the portal into the streets of the Emerald City.¶

11¶

The Wonderful City of Oz¶

Even with eyes protected by the green spectacles, Dorothy and her friends were at first dazzled by the brilliancy of the wonderful City. The streets were lined with beautiful houses all built of green marble and studded everywhere with sparkling emeralds. They walked over a pavement of the same green marble, and where the blocks were joined together were rows of emeralds, set closely, and glittering in the brightness of the sun. The window panes were of green glass; even the sky above the City had a green tint, and the rays of the sun were green.¶

There were many people--men, women, and children--walking about, and these were all dressed in green clothes and had greenish skins. They looked at Dorothy and her strangely assorted company with wondering eyes, and the children all ran away and hid behind their mothers when they saw the Lion; but no one spoke to

FIGURE 4.17
After adding vertical spacing to my Chapter Number and Chapter Title paragraph styles

For now, don't worry that there isn't much space between the end of one chapter and the number of the next chapter.

5. At this point, you need to decide how you're going to differentiate paragraphs of the main text. The two most common ways are to use vertical spacing between paragraphs or to indent the first line of each paragraph. (Sometimes both approaches are used in concert.) There are other methods, of course, but these are the most common. In ebook publishing, the preferred method is to indent the first line of each paragraph, so let's do that.

   Open the options of the Body Copy paragraph style, and again, go to the Indents And Spacing pane. Instead of altering the 0 px values of the Space Before and Space After fields, enter a positive value in the First Line Indent field. (Refer to Figure 4.16.) Turn on Preview in the lower-left corner of the dialog to see the effect on your text as you change that value.

I'm going to use a value of 25 px, which is larger than I'd normally use for print work but should be perfect for this ebook.

Click OK when you have the value you want, and every paragraph of prose in the book will indent accordingly (see Figure 4.18), thanks to the fact that you assigned the Body Copy style to all of it before working on the chapter number and title.

FIGURE 4.18
Indenting the first line of every paragraph creates distinct separation between paragraphs.

on either side of his funny, wee nose. Toto played all day long, and Dorothy played with him, and loved him dearly.¶

Today, however, they were not playing. Uncle Henry sat upon the doorstep and looked anxiously at the sky, which was even grayer than usual. Dorothy stood in the door with Toto in her arms, and looked at the sky too. Aunt Em was washing the dishes.¶

From the far north they heard a low wail of the wind, and Uncle Henry and Dorothy could see where the long grass bowed in waves before the coming storm. There now came a sharp whistling in the air from the south, and as they turned their eyes that way they saw ripples in the grass coming from that direction also.¶

Suddenly Uncle Henry stood up.¶

"There's a cyclone coming, Em," he called to his wife. "I'll go look after the stock." Then he ran toward the sheds where the cows and horses were kept.¶

Aunt Em dropped her work and came to the door. One glance told her of the danger close at hand.¶

"Quick, Dorothy!" she screamed. "Run for the cellar!"¶

Toto jumped out of Dorothy's arms and hid under the bed, and the girl started to get him. Aunt Em, badly frightened, threw open the trap door in the floor and climbed down the ladder into the small, dark hole. Dorothy caught Toto at last and started to follow her aunt. When she was halfway across the room there came a great shriek from the wind, and the house shook so hard that she lost her footing and sat down suddenly upon the floor.¶

Then a strange thing happened.¶

The house whirled around two or three times and rose slowly through the air. Dorothy felt as if she were going up in a balloon.¶

The north and south winds met where the house stood, and made it the exact center of the cyclone. In the middle of a cyclone the air is generally still, but the great pressure of the wind on every side of the house raised it up higher and higher, until it was at the very top of the cyclone; and there it remained and was carried miles and miles away as easily as you could carry a feather.¶

There is, of course, a great deal more that can be done with your ebook. The next thing I'd do, for instance, is force a page break before every chapter number to avoid a situation like you see in Figure 4.14, wherein a chapter begins in the middle of a page. Alas, you'll have to wait until Chapter 6 for that and a whole lot more. Now I'll talk about converting existing InDesign print layouts to ebooks, and then, in the next chapter, I'll get into working with imagery, audio, and video in ebooks.

Converting a Print Publication to an Ebook

Even more common than creating ebooks from scratch is the need to convert existing print publications to EPUB. That's a fairly easy task, though it isn't as easy as just choosing File ➤ Export. Let's start by looking at what *doesn't* work.

What Doesn't Work

If you open wizardofoz_print_ch4.indd in this chapter's lesson files, you'll see seven pages from a book, including threaded text frames, unthreaded text frames, illustrations, an illustration caption, master page *folios*, and sidebars, which themselves include threaded and unthreaded story frames, background imagery, hyperlinks, and footnotes (see Figure 4.19). This document is Chapter 4 of a theoretical annotated edition of *The Wonderful Wizard of Oz* such as might be produced for print or PDF publication.

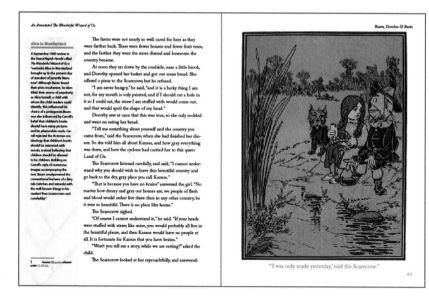

Our task is to convert this to EPUB. Toward that end, let's do a quick export to EPUB test. Just go to File ➤ Export, choose EPUB in the Save As Type or Format drop-down, and click Save. Leave all the EPUB Export Options at their defaults, and click OK. Now open that EPUB in an ebook reader.

Wow! Isn't that a bucket of water thrown on a witch?

Depending on which ebook reader you use, you may see things slightly differently, though it's still pretty bad. In Figure 4.20, you can see a page-by-page comparison between the print layout and the resulting EPUB.

The comparison highlights a number of issues. Some of these can be resolved by altering settings in the EPUB Export Options dialog; the rest you'll have to address manually. Let's list the conversion problems, creating a "to-fix" list for yourself in the process.

Master-page items do not export to EPUB. This is actually a good thing. Ebook readers will add headers from the book metadata (title and author) and enumerate pages according to how they flow on the particular device. The fact that master-page items such as these don't export means you needn't delete or hide them before going to EPUB.

The arrangement of elements is unpredictable. Compare page 1 of the print edition with pages 1, 2, and 3 in the EPUB version. Notice how the main illustration wound up dominating the first ebook page, the chapter number and title became the second page, and the main story didn't start until the third. Even if you used my INDD, exported with identical settings, and also used the same ereader for proofing, you might see a completely different result. In fact, I saw four different arrangements of those elements during six exports—all without changing anything about the document, the export settings, my proof ereader, or my computer. I ran all the exports within minutes of each other, and nearly all of them produced different results. It's a big problem when you don't know in what order elements will export. We'll fix that later in this chapter.

FIGURE 4.20
A page-by-page comparison of the print layout (1–7 at the top) and the resulting EPUB with default values (1–19 below)

Print Edition

page 1 page 2 page 3 page 4 page 5 page 6 page 7

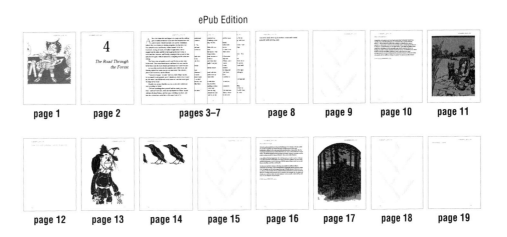

ePub Edition

page 1 page 2 pages 3–7 page 8 page 9 page 10 page 11

page 12 page 13 page 14 page 15 page 16 page 17 page 18 page 19

ASPIRIN-FREE WORKFLOW: THREAD CHAPTER NUMBER AND TITLE

Incidentally, in the print publication I set the chapter number and title in separate, disconnected text frames to help illustrate a point in ebook conversion. Typically, for a book of any media, I'd lay it out with the chapter name and number in threaded frames, using a Start Paragraph In Next Frame attribute on both of them and in the Body Copy First Paragraph paragraph style. I recommend that method to others; it just makes for fewer separate stories to manage.

Images get divorced from text.   Regardless of how they were arranged in the document, the images have all been completely separated from the text. With the exception of the first, very short image in some export tests (not shown here), all the images in the document became their own pages, even so far as leaving the previous pages empty except for one or two lines like you see in pages 8 and 12 of the ebook in Figure 4.20. Even though the images were throughout the print layout—indeed, there's a TIFF or JPEG on every page of the print layout—the EPUB export separated image from text.

Images are exported at full resolution and cropped to the display. Examining W. W. Denslow's illustrations on pages 1, 11, 13, 14, and 17 of the ebook, it may appear as if those images were somehow cropped during export. Not so. They were exported at their full, original dimensions—not the size to which they were scaled in the print layout but the full size. The reader window size, which I've set to simulate the largest of the handheld ereaders, can't fit the images at their full sizes. Moreover, the EPUB export filter, left to its default options, center-aligns every image. Thus, to fit in the ereader window, the images are cropped inward from both sides, and in some cases, the bottoms are cut off, too. The complete images are still in the ebook; they just can't be displayed on most devices (these particular images are small enough that they do show on iPads and other 10-inch-class tablets, however).

If not given one, EPUB will interpret a content hierarchy for itself. Just as the EPUB export operation separated the images from the text, it also gave the images a lower priority than the text. Look at the EPUB pages. With the exception of the first page, which kept the initial image at or near the front, all the other images and the sidebar content don't appear until after the main story on pages 3–7 (I consolidated the thumbnails because those pages are straight text, except for the drop cap *A* that begins the story).

By default, the export process renders content to EPUB in the order of appearance, left to right and then top to bottom. It renders each piece of content *in its entirety* before moving on to the next piece of content. In this case, the main story began before the first sidebar and before the full-page illustration and caption on page 3 of the print layout. Thus, in the EPUB, the order of elements rendered was main story, sidebar, full-page illustration, illustration's caption. Then, of course, it began including the remaining elements in order—the Scarecrow drawing, the illustration of crows, the next sidebar's components, the cottage illustration, and, finally, the components of the final sidebar on page 7 of the print layout. That sidebar's text, having been a continuation of the sidebar in the print layout on page 6, had already been composed in its entirety into the EPUB's page 16, orphaning its background (page 18) and the "Cont'd" line on page 19.

Everything in the print layout—except master-page items and natively drawn InDesign vector elements—will be included in the EPUB, even if, as in the case of the sidebar header on the EPUB's page 19, it has no place in the ebook.

NO SUCH THING AS OVERSET TEXT IN AN EBOOK

When prepping for print output, layout designers and compositors always do a check for overset text—text that doesn't fit within the frames and is thus invisible and unprintable—even if that check is merely to look to the lower-left of the InDesign document window for a warning from the Live Preflight function. Although I certainly don't want you getting into the habit of not checking for overset text, it really isn't necessary with EPUB export. You see, because stories are exported in their entirety, even overset text is exported. Theoretically, you could have a one-page, one-frame InDesign document that outputs to a thousand-page ebook by virtue of the automatic inclusion of any overset text. And that's *all* overset text, whether in the main story or in secondary text frames.

Now that I've identified the problems inherent in simply exporting a print layout to EPUB unmodified and using the default export settings, let's address those problems. I'll leave some of the image-related issues until the next chapter, which is devoted entirely to such things, but address others in this chapter in order to fix overall export issues.

Master-Page Items in Ebooks

Master-page items do not export to EPUB. That's a fact. There's no setting for changing that. If you need items from the master page to export to EPUB, be sure to override them prior to export. Holding Ctrl+Shift/Cmd+Shift while clicking master-page items on document pages will override the items one at a time. Conversely, you could use Override All Master Page Items from the flyout menu on the Pages panel to override all master-page items on the current spread in one fell swoop. Note that the latter option overrides *all* master-page items on the current spread, including folios, headers, footers, page numbers, and so on, and it will export them all to EPUB, probably as stories at the end of the ebook.

Removing Fixed-Layout References

You must remove elements referring to locations within an imposed, fixed layout; these are items such as page-number references in the text, for example "See the illustration on page 26." Page numbers have no bearing in EPUB because the number of "pages" in the book is fluid, changing on the fly to adapt to the size of the screen on which it's viewed and the user-specified size of the text in which it's being read. Many of our documents—particularly periodicals, journals, educational material, and other such publications—have page numbers littered around *outside of folios*. Often a publication includes a *jumpline* ("continues on page *x*") in one or more stories, usually paired with a *carry-over* ("continued from page *y*"). Publications that are heavy on figures, charts, graphs, tables, and so on often have internal references such as "See Figure 13 on the next page" or "Referencing again the 1Q P&L chart on page 16…." Obviously, keep references to the *content*, but not to the *position* of that content. Change them to read "See Figure 13" and "Referencing again the 1Q P&L chart in Section 4…." Also look for any text variables you might have used that rely on page, section, or chapter number.

Content Ordering by Placement

As you learned in the preceding text, EPUB will interpret an order to objects if left to do so on its own. The rule it follows is simple: left to right and then top to bottom…usually. The fact that I got a different arrangement of objects on the first (and sometimes second) pages every time I exported to EPUB from the *An Annotated The Wonderful Wizard of Oz* Chapter 4 layout was because of the placement of my objects on the first page (see Figure 4.21). On that page are four objects—the main story text frame at the bottom, two other text frames holding the chapter title and chapter number, and a graphic frame containing the illustration.

As you can see by the objects' bounding boxes, they're distributed around the page (within my two-column, six-row layout grid). During export, the EPUB filter looked for the leftmost object on the page—the illustration—and determined that this is the first object to render. And the EPUB filter looks at the *bounding boxes* of frames, not their *contents*, to determine left-to-right, top-to-bottom order. Then it looked for the second leftmost object, which, in this case, is two completely separate objects: the chapter title and the beginning of the story. Note that the drop cap *A* is part of the main text frame, just hung out to the left; the export filter looks for the position of frame objects, not the contents within them. Because both of those frames' left edges are at exactly the same horizontal or x-axis coordinate, the filter couldn't determine which was more important by its horizontal position and had to switch to top-down page interpretation. Thus, the chapter title came before the body copy. But, it put the chapter *number*, which is obviously far to the right of the title, *ahead* of the title. Why? Simple: Once the filter switched to a top-to-bottom interpretation of item hierarchy, it noticed that the frame containing the "4" was higher than the frame containing the chapter title. That's how the EPUB turned out, with objects in the order of illustration, chapter number, chapter title, and body copy.

FIGURE 4.21
Note the left-to-right, top-to-bottom order of objects on the first page of the print layout.

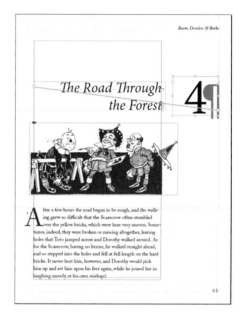

Similarly, when the export filter came to the first sidebar, it was back in left-equals-earlier object-inclusion mode. Because I had built the sidebar as two separate objects—the text frame in front of and smaller than a graphic frame containing the yellow brick imagery—it took the first object it encountered moving in from the left of the page, which was the background image, and *then* the smaller text frame (see Figure 4.22). Because an EPUB won't overlap objects, it rendered the sidebar background images earlier in the ebook than the content of the sidebars.

If you don't want certain elements to appear in the ebook—such as the sidebar background images—delete them or put them on a separate layer and hide that layer.

To control the order of objects as they appear in the ebook, give them a clear left-to-right hierarchy. Moving inward from the right of the page, the first object the export filter encounters becomes the first object in the ebook. If multiple objects have the same left coordinate, then their vertical order determines their importance. Simple. Of course, rearranging and resizing frames all over the place, and deleting or hiding a bunch of objects, is not always the most efficient means of controlling what exports and in what order. This is particularly true if you want to maintain the page geometry for outputting to print or a fixed-layout design format like PDF or interactive magazine. Fortunately, there are other methods of controlling content ordering and inclusion or exclusion—articles and tagging and styles—oh my!

FIGURE 4.22
The two objects comprising the sidebar (left) were rendered in the EPUB in the order in which they appeared from the left of the page (right).

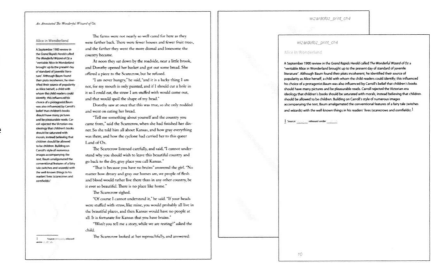

Content Ordering with the Articles Panel

If you lay out a document and export to EPUB without doing anything extra to that document, InDesign follows the left-to-right, top-to-bottom content-ordering rules. Put more simply, page geometry equals item order. In the case of a standard, all-text novel or short story, that's just fine—desired page and object order are the same as actual order in the InDesign document. More complicated layouts, however, like *An Annotated The Wonderful Wizard of Oz*, require a little extra work to produce the correct order of content in ebooks.

That's where the Articles panel comes in (Figure 4.23). It's the first panel on the Window menu in InDesign CS5.5 and newer, and it enables the easy inclusion, exclusion, and ordering of content for EPUB and HTML export and tagged PDFs. Let's open `wizardofoz_print_ch4.indd` again and see whether we can improve its output.

FIGURE 4.23
The Articles panel

1. With `wizardofoz_print_ch4.indd` open, open the Articles panel from the Window menu.

2. Using the black arrow Selection tool, drag the chapter number text frame onto the Articles panel. You'll be immediately prompted to name the article (Figure 4.24).

FIGURE 4.24
The first time you add content to the Articles panel, it will prompt you to name the article.

Articles are merely a way of grouping and ordering content in the ebook (or HTML or tagged PDF). Each separate section of content needs its own article. For instance, with this book, the chapter number, title, main story, illustrations, and any captions assigned to those illustrations need to be in one article, while each of the sidebars would be a separate article. Article names are used only within the Articles panel for your reference; they are never shown in the exported documents. So, go ahead and name this article Main Story, and, of course, leave the Include When Exporting option checked.

After clicking OK, you'll see your new article and its first piece of content in the Articles panel (Figure 4.25). It looks very much like InDesign's Layers panel. In fact, if you had grouped objects, just like the Layers panel, the Articles panel would show the entry "<group>" with an expansion arrow allowing you to see the individual components of the group. In my figure, there are no groups yet, however.

FIGURE 4.25
The Articles panel after creating the article and simultaneously adding the first object to it

3. Forgetting about the chapter title and the main illustration for the moment, drag the first frame of the main story onto the Articles panel. You want to drop it *immediately* below the entry for the chapter number, "<4>" in Figure 4.25. If you're prompted to create a new article, cancel it; it means you tried to drop the text frame into the empty area beneath the Main Story article but not close enough to the bottom of "<4>." When added successfully, you'll have two items inside the Main Story article.

4. Even though there are plenty of items left to be included, let's try a test export. Using File ➤ Export, get to the EPUB Export Options dialog. We need to make a change here.

Because you're now using the Articles panel to control what content appears in the ebook and where, you need to communicate that fact to the export filter. On the General pane of the EPUB Export Options, dead smack in the middle is a drop-down field for Content Order (Figure 4.26). By default, Based On Page Layout is selected; this tells InDesign to export all visible objects that are not master-page items and not vector objects drawn directly in InDesign. It also tells InDesign to order those objects in the ebook based on their left-to-right, top-to-bottom relation to one another. Previously you used this setting; now you want to change the Content Order drop-down menu to the Same As Articles panel.

FIGURE 4.26
The Content Order field specifies whether the layout, Articles panel, or XML structure of the document determines inclusion and ordering of content.

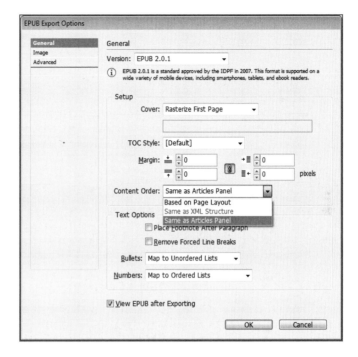

5. Make sure that View EPUB After Exporting is checked and click OK. Up will pop your ebook, composed solely of the chapter number and the chapter's main story in its entirety (Figure 4.27). Notice that nothing you didn't deliberately include in the Articles panel became part of the EPUB. Thus, you don't have to delete or hide elements from your print layout just to keep them out of the ebook.

6. Back in InDesign, let's add the other first-page elements to the article. Drag the chapter title frame onto the Articles panel, too, dropping it *between* the two existing elements. That will place the chapter number first, then the title, and finally the main story. While we're at it, let's also add the first-page illustration to the Articles panel, just below the chapter title. Your Articles panel should now look like Figure 4.28.

7. Running another quick export will show you the results—all four elements included, arranged in the order you specified on the Articles panel. Depending on the size of the ereader software or device on which you preview it, you might see the main illustration on the same page as the title and the story beginning, or the book may be forced to flow the illustration and/or the story start to the second page. Either way, the order is accurate and will be consistent throughout every subsequent export.

FIGURE 4.27
Only items included in the Articles panel were sent to EPUB.

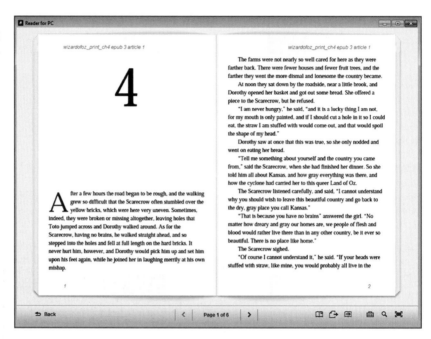

FIGURE 4.28
After adding the remaining first-page components

8. Now let's add the rest of the content you want in the ebook to the Articles panel.

   On the third page of the print layout (numbered 63 in the Pages panel), drag the full-page illustration of Dorothy, Toto, and the Scarecrow into the Articles panel and then the illustration's caption text frame. These should be the fifth and sixth items in the Main Story article, respectively. If they land anywhere else in the list, you can just drag each up or down in the list as you do with layers and objects on the Layers panel.

9. Proceed to pages 4, 5, and 7, adding their illustrations to the article. Leave the sidebars alone for now.

A quick test export will produce an ebook, but unfortunately, all images will be at the end of the ebook. The Articles panel doesn't give you a way to insert images *inside* the main story; rather, it simply runs each object in the article, start to finish, in the order displayed in the document, before adding the next object.

Note page 8 (or thereabouts) of the ebook (Figure 4.29). If your ereader has the space to do so, you'll see the caption directly below the full-page illustration. If you wanted the caption above it, all you'd have to do is drag the caption's entry in the Articles panel ("<I was only made…>") above the illustration's entry ("<oz_ch4_02.tif>").

FIGURE 4.29
Image and caption arranged in the right order

wizardofoz_print_ch4 epub 3 article 1

"'I was only made yesterday,' said the Scarecrow."

5

10. Now turn your attention to the sidebars. On the Articles panel, click the sticky-note-esque Create New Article button at the bottom. Again, you'll be prompted to name the article; name it Sidebar: Alice in Wonderland. Then add the sidebar story—just the text frame, not the yellow brick background image graphic frame—to the new article.

AUTOMATIC AND DUPLICATE ARTICLE INCLUSION

As you create new articles with the Create New Article button, you may notice objects automatically added to what should have been an initially empty article. This is a feature (some say bug) of the Articles panel: If you have one or more objects selected at the time you click the Create New Article button, those objects will be automatically added to the new article. Some people hate that behavior, because forgetting to deselect all objects before creating an article adds those objects to the article and necessitates their removal from that article (drag and drop to the trash can on the Articles panel). Note that content will not be duplicated in the ebook even if it belongs to multiple articles. That content can, however, be included even if some articles to which it belongs are hidden and not exported.

I see this behavior of the Articles panel as a benefit. True, it can get annoying having to delete those accidental inclusions, but so can dragging and dropping a bunch of objects. Sometimes it can be a real time-saver to select a bunch of objects on the page and have them all added to the article at the moment of article creation.

Is it a feature or a bug? You decide.

---

11. Repeat the last step for the final sidebar story, "Illustration & Design," creating a new article for it and adding its first text frame. Remember that the export will grab the entire story automatically; you don't need to include the second text frame of the sidebar. Also be sure to leave out the page 7 sidebar's continuation title.

12. Export a proof again and notice that the sidebar articles appear after the contents of the Main Story article, just as they're displayed in the Articles panel. You could rearrange their order—perhaps even move the illustrations to an article of their own—if you wanted the sidebars to appear before the images.

There are a few finer points to using the Articles panel that you should be aware of.

◆ The check box beside each article name is the Include When Exporting control. If you want to remove an article from a particular export version or media (again, EPUB, HTML, or tagged PDF), uncheck the Include When Exporting box and export.

◆ Deleting an object from an article does not delete the actual object as long as you use the trash-can icon. If you press Delete or Backspace on your keyboard, though, you'll delete whatever object is actually selected in the layout.

◆ You can rename an article either by double-clicking its name in the Articles panel or by choosing Article Options from the panel flyout menu.

◆ If you have an empty Articles panel, holding Ctrl/Cmd while clicking the Add Selection To Articles (plus sign) button at the bottom of the Articles panel will ask you to create a new article and add all content in your entire document—everything—to that new article.

◆ The behavior is similar if you already have an article; Ctrl-clicking/Cmd-clicking the Add Selection To Articles button will add all document objects to the selected article.

◆ To use the Articles panel object order for the reading order in tagged PDFs, you must (annoyingly) take the extra step of enabling the Use For Reading Order In Tagged PDF option on the Articles panel flyout menu.

◆ Double-clicking an object listed on the Articles panel will jump your document window to view that object.

Now that you know how to use the Articles panel to include content, exclude content (note that the sidebar backgrounds never made it to the ebook), and order content, you have a great deal more control over your ebooks, and you have predictability in their export. When you need even greater control—or want images and sidebars to appear not after but at specific points within the main flow of text—then you need to couple the Articles panel (or page-layout ordering) with another technique: anchoring objects.

Content Ordering by Anchoring Objects

One very important thing you've been unable to do thus far is place the images and sidebars within the chapter's main story, near the text they reference and enhance. Fortunately, InDesign can do it.

1. Turn to page 2 of the print layout and select the "Alice in Wonderland" text frame.

2. Notice the blue box in the top-right corner of the frame. Introduced in CS5.5, the official (and unwieldy) name for this box is the Anchored Object control, though most people, including Adobe's own documentation, refer to it simply as "the blue box." It enables you to create anchored and inline objects much more easily than in previous versions of InDesign, which required you to cut and paste objects into the text flow and/or use the Object ➤ Anchored Objects menu. Now you can simply drag that blue box from the top of the container you want anchored—the sidebar text frame in this case—into another text frame and drop it where you want the object anchored.

   Go ahead and do that now. Drag the blue box from the top of the "Alice in Wonderland" text frame and drop it after the first paragraph in the main story on that page, immediately to the right of "country became." Once done, and with Show Hidden Characters enabled, you'll see a yen symbol (¥) at the point of insertion, a blue dashed line leading from there to the bottom-right of the sidebar text frame, and the blue box on the sidebar frame will have been replaced with the anchored object anchor icon (see Figure 4.30).

3. Run a quick EPUB export test. If the sidebar was correctly anchored, you will see it appear in the main flow at the anchor point (Figure 4.31).

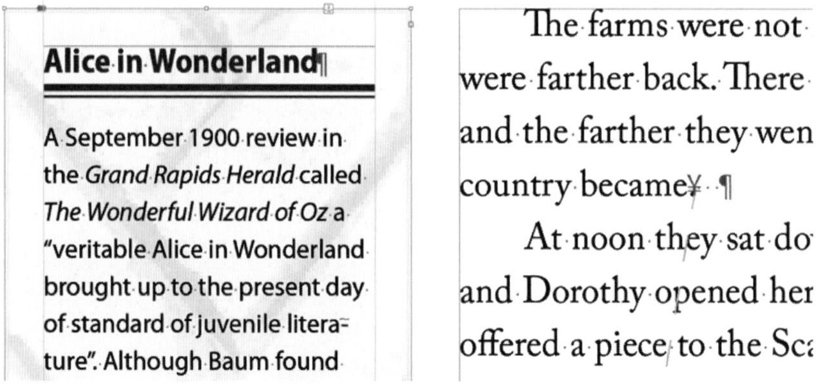

FIGURE 4.30
After anchoring
the sidebar text
frame into the main
body text. Note: I
added extra spaces
between the anchor
and the return
only to make the
anchor insertion
point clearer in this
figure.

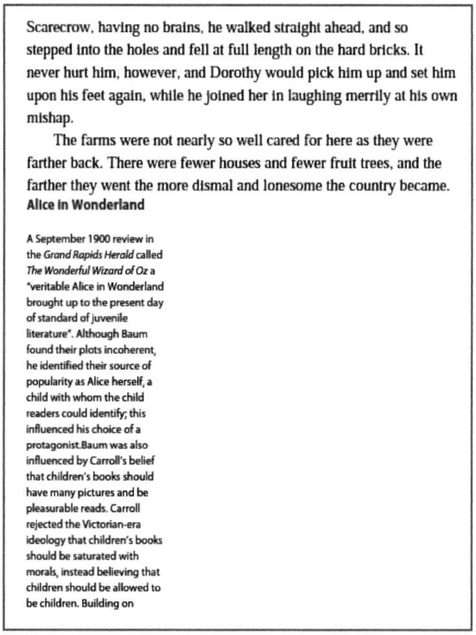

Alice·in·Wonderland¶

A·September·1900·review·in·
the·*Grand·Rapids·Herald*·called·
The·Wonderful·Wizard·of·Oz·a·
"veritable·Alice·in·Wonderland·
brought·up·to·the·present·day·
of·standard·of·juvenile·litera=
ture"·Although·Baum·found·

The·farms·were·not·
were·farther·back.·There·
and·the·farther·they·wen
country·became¥·¶
At·noon·they·sat·do
and·Dorothy·opened·her
offered·a·piece·to·the·Sca

FIGURE 4.31
The sidebar now
appears inline in
the EPUB.

Scarecrow, having no brains, he walked straight ahead, and so
stepped into the holes and fell at full length on the hard bricks. It
never hurt him, however, and Dorothy would pick him up and set him
upon his feet again, while he joined her in laughing merrily at his own
mishap.

The farms were not nearly so well cared for here as they were
farther back. There were fewer houses and fewer fruit trees, and the
farther they went the more dismal and lonesome the country became.
Alice in Wonderland

A September 1900 review in
the *Grand Rapids Herald* called
The Wonderful Wizard of Oz a
"veritable Alice in Wonderland
brought up to the present day
of standard of juvenile
literature". Although Baum
found their plots incoherent,
he identified their source of
popularity as Alice herself, a
child with whom the child
readers could identify; this
influenced his choice of a
protagonist. Baum was also
influenced by Carroll's belief
that children's books should
have many pictures and be
pleasurable reads. Carroll
rejected the Victorian-era
ideology that children's books
should be saturated with
morals, instead believing that
children should be allowed to
be children. Building on

4. Let's try getting an image inline with the text, too. Let's use the illustration on the opposing page. It would be the same technique as anchoring the sidebar but for the presence of
a caption. You *could* anchor both the image frame and the caption text frame separately,
but then there's no guarantee they'd really appear together. A better way is to group the
image and the caption and then anchor the group into the text. Upon export you'll have
something like Figure 4.32.

FIGURE 4.32
Grouping two
objects and then
anchoring the group
helps keep them
together.

As a general rule, grouping objects does not change how they appear in the EPUB or guarantee that they'll be in any specific position relative to one another—despite a popular myth. However, grouping them and *then* anchoring *does* make a difference, clearly. (See the "Captioning Images" section in Chapter 5.)

5. Go through the rest of the document, anchoring the second sidebar and the rest of the images, and you'll have all your content in the order it needs to be presented.

There's more to anchoring, too.

◆ If you drag the blue box into text, you'll anchor the object; even if you put the object somewhere else on the page (or pasteboard) in the layout, it will appear at the tether point in the EPUB.

◆ Holding Shift while dragging the blue box to an anchor point creates an inline object, which moves to the tether point in both the layout and the ebook; this is the same as the old method of cutting the object and pasting it into the text.

◆ Dragging the blue box while holding Alt/Opt will open the Anchored Object Options dialog when you drop anchor. You can also still manually access those options from Object ➢ Anchored Object ➢ Options.

◆ Similarly, Alt-clicking/Opt-clicking the anchor icon on an anchored object will open Anchored Object Options.

◆ To untether an anchored object from text, choose Object ➢ Anchored Object ➢ Release, or choose the same command from the context-sensitive menu when right-clicking the anchored object.

ASPIRIN-FREE WORKFLOW: OBJECTS ON THE PASTEBOARD

Objects on the pasteboard are not included in EPUB (or any kind of) export unless they're anchored. Even if the pasteboard object is included in an exporting article on the Articles panel, it will not actually be exported to EPUB. Note that objects on the pasteboard that touch or overlap the page *at all* will be included in the EPUB; it's only those objects wholly on the pasteboard that are exempt. That offers a workflow enhancement.

The fact that anchored objects don't have to appear on the printed page in order to be included in the ebook means that you can conveniently create ebook-only and print-only content without creating two different InDesign files. Use the Articles panel to include only on-the-page content that you want in both print and ebook, leaving out of the articles the print-only content, and add in as anchored objects living on the pasteboard those items that are EPUB-only. Thus, both the print and ebook versions can be designed simultaneously, using the same layout but different objects.

The ebook doesn't even have to look anything like the print version if you include an EPUB-only CSS style sheet that styles the text and objects differently.

Content Ordering by Tagging

The most powerful and precise way of controlling the order of content is through tagging that content and then ordering the tags in the XML structure of the document. This is not full-on XML coding; in fact, tagging and ordering is 0 percent more complicated than working with the Articles panel. Where you do it is different—the Tags panel and Structure View pane instead of the Articles panel—but the process is almost identical. Moreover, tagging can be completely automated with a minimum of prep work.

If you produce periodicals, catalogs, or other content with a predictable structure, tagging is the way to organize it—and, depending on how you produce that content, it may already be tagged. Many publishers tag and structure their content in XML, particularly those that produce multistory publications comprised of content with regular, repeatable formats and hierarchies. For example, both newspapers and catalogs produce multistory publications with templatelike content. In a newspaper, every article will include headline, byline, deck, kicker, body copy, and possibly photo, photo credit, photo caption, and some other elements. Catalog entries include even more rigidly structured content, with product title, SKU, price, description, and photograph. In those types of publications, the content often lives in a database, which exports the content to tagged and structured XML, which is then imported into and laid out in InDesign. During that layout process, the XML tagging and structure remains unchanged and therefore becomes instantly exportable to EPUB and any number of other formats with the correct content ordering.

By way of example, check out the *New York Times* daily newspaper and the journal *Fantasy & Science Fiction*, both EPUB-based, as viewed on a 7-inch tablet (Figure 4.33). Notice the consistent structure between stories—section/department title, article title, single photo (an actual photo for *The Times*, a graphic element for *Fantasy*), photo credit (for *The Times*), byline, main story, and, unseen, the *end sign*. The order between the two publications' elements is different, but the underlying structure is the same. It's probably even a little more than what you can see here, with additional structural elements such as excerpts, thumbnail photos, and so on.

FIGURE 4.33

The *New York Times* articles (left) and a story in *Fantasy & Science Fiction* (right) both use EPUB-format and XML tagging for consistent content ordering and styling.

INTERNATIONAL · BREIVIK CLAIMS SELF-DEFENSE IN NORWAY KILLINGS

Breivik Claims Self-Defense in Norway Killings

Heiko Junge/Agence France-Presse — Getty Images
Anders Behring Breivik saluted as he entered the courtroom in Oslo on Monday morning.
By MARK LEWIS and ALAN COWELL

OSLO — By turns defiant, impassive and, just once, tearful, the self-described anti-Islamic militant who admitted killing 77 people last year, including scores of young people at a summer camp on a tranquil wooded island, went on trial here on Monday.

In the courtroom, the defendant — Anders Behring Breivik, 33 — proclaimed that he had acted in self-defense, bore no criminal guilt and rejected the authority of the court.

DEPARTMENTS · CURIOSITIES

CURIOSITIES
By Jack Womack | 269 words

THE OUTCAST MANUFAC-TURERS,

BY CHARLES FORT (1909)

IN THE BOOKS for which he is remembered, Charles Fort wrote sublimely about the ridiculous. Earlier he wrote short stories for magazines edited by longtime friend Theodore Dreiser. Although ten years later Dreiser demanded his publisher print *The Book of the Damned*, when *The Outcast Manufacturers* came out in 1909, Dreiser opined that in the author's first book and only novel "the art of luring your readers on" was not in evidence.

Set on the West Side of Manhattan—partly Hell's Kitchen, partly the neighborhood destroyed to build Penn Station— *The Outcast Manufacturers* tells of the Birtwhistle family, their neighbors, and

If you don't know if your publication is tagged or contains XML structure, checking is simple: Choose View ➤ Structure ➤ Show Structure to expose the document Structure pane (Figure 4.34). If there's anything other than Root there, you have at least some structure and tags in your document. Another way to view the same information is on the Tags panel (Window ➤ Utilities ➤ Tags).

FIGURE 4.34

The Structure pane reveals a document's XML tags and structure.

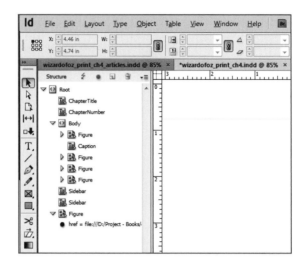

CREATING AND USING TAGS

Let's assume you don't have any tags yet; you'll now build some. You can use your own document or the same *An Annotated The Wonderful Wizard of Oz* Chapter 4 layout you've been using.

1. Open the Tags panel by choosing it from the Utilities submenu on the Window menu. Ignore the Root entry; it's required for semantic XML markup, but you won't be using it directly.

2. Now determine the structure of your document. If you're working on a book like *An Annotated The Wonderful Wizard of Oz* Chapter 4 or that document itself, your structure or content classification, with a little thought about elements and their relative importance, will wind up looking like the following:

```
Chapter Number
Chapter Title
Body
   Image
      Caption
   Sidebar
```

Even though you have more than one image and sidebar in the Oz example, structurally or categorically speaking, all the illustrations are of the Image type of content, and both sidebars are classified as Sidebar content. Ergo, you need to create only one tag for each type no matter how many individual objects will belong to that tag/category.

Now create those tags. Click the New Tag sticky-note icon at the bottom of the Tags panel. It will insert a new tag in the list, automatically choosing a unique color for the tag just like the Layers panel does when creating a new layer. By default the tag will be named Tag1, which isn't very helpful at all. Instead, name it ChapterNumber. Note that you can't include spaces, tabs, or punctuation in tag names.

3. Repeat the creation and naming of tags until you have all of the previously listed items created as tags. You won't need to indent anything on the Tags panel, and, regardless of their creation order, the Tags panel will alphabetize your tags. When finished, your Tags panel should look like Figure 4.35.

FIGURE 4.35
After creating tags representative of the chapter's content classifications

4. Now that you have your tags, you need to assign them to content. That's simple. On the first page of the publication, select the chapter number frame with the black arrow Selection tool.

5. Click the ChapterNumber tag in the Tags panel. The chapter number is now tagged.

6. Select the chapter title frame and click the ChapterTitle tag. Now it's tagged, too.

7. Tag the illustration with the Image tag.

8. At this point, you won't see any difference between tagged and untagged objects on the page. Fix that by selecting View ➤ Structure ➤ Show Tagged Frames. Now that's a horse of a different color! Now you see why each of the tags was given a unique color identifier. Figure 4.36 shows what you should be seeing at this point. These colorings are nonprinting, by the way.

9. Tag the body copy text frame with the Body tag. This is the only body copy frame you'll need to tag. The story, in its entirety, is now tagged; the other frames in the thread don't have to be tagged separately and, in fact, *shouldn't be* tagged separately because tagging the first frame tags the entire story, regardless of how many frames it occupies.

10. Continue through the rest of the document tagging elements—images, captions, and sidebars (just the text frames).

SPECIFYING ORDER WITH TAGS

Now that all the elements of the document are tagged, let's use those tags to specify content order in the ebook.

1. Show the Structure pane by choosing Show Structure from View ➤ Structure (Figure 4.37). What you're seeing are the names of tags identifying pieces of content; you should have multiple entries for Image, for instance.

FIGURE 4.36
With Show Tagged Frames activated, each tagged frame is tinted and outlined in a (nonprinting) color corresponding to its tag.

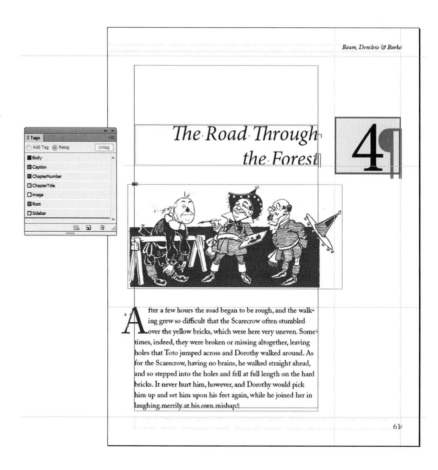

FIGURE 4.37
The Structure pane reveals tagged content.

2. Click the expansion arrows beside each of the Image entries to hide the image file paths, unless you want to see them for some reason.

3. What you now see in the Structure pane is the order the content will export to EPUB. It's not a bad order because you tagged things in order. However, if you want to change the order—maybe to move the first illustration so that it appears between the chapter number and the chapter title—just drag the first Image entry in the Structure pane up above the entry for ChapterTitle.

4. Continue reordering elements as necessary until you get them in the order you want, which is how they'll export.

5. You have to *tell* InDesign to use the XML structure as the ordering for elements in the EPUB. Start a new EPUB export, and, in the EPUB Export Options, change the Content Order field on the General pane to Same As XML Structure. Now when you export, your ebook content will match the ordering in the Structure pane.

TAGGING BY STYLE

Manually tagging a document is fine for short, simple publications like the *An Annotated The Wonderful Wizard of Oz* Chapter 4 layout. A whole book or something more complex, like a catalog, magazine, or technical book like this one, would be a nightmare to tag manually because of all the different elements. For instance, this book contains body copy like this paragraph, numbered and bulleted lists, four levels of headings, several tables, copious figures, captions for all those figures and tables, code snippets, and lots of other formats, all of which need to be tagged for content ordering and CSS styling in the ebook version. Instead of doing it all manually, there are more efficient ways, assuming you use paragraph and/or character styles the way you should.

Take a look at Figure 4.38, which is this very page being laid out in InDesign.

On the displayed page is a third-level heading, "Tagging by Style," which uses the H3 paragraph style you can see on the panel. I'll start with that.

1. Still using the `wizardofoz_print_ch4.indd` file, open the Tags panel by choosing Window ➤ Utilities ➤ Tags.

2. On the Tags panel, create the tags you'll need to structure your document, including H1 (which you'll use in place of Chapter Number), H2 (for Chapter Title), Body, Figure, Caption, and so on.

3. From the Tags panel flyout menu, choose Map Styles To Tags, which opens the identically named dialog (Figure 4.39).

   Here the job is to match tags to paragraph styles. Once done, and after clicking OK, the document will be automatically structured by virtue of the paragraph styles applied to text.

FIGURE 4.38
A technical book is often a complex publication, with numerous paragraph styles, all requiring unique tags.

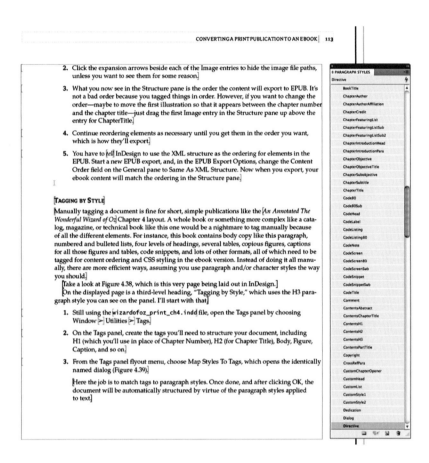

FIGURE 4.39
The Map Styles To Tags dialog

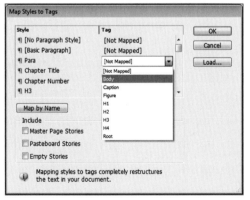

4. The first job is to match the Para paragraph style to a tag, so click the [Not Mapped] entry in the Tag column beside the Para tag entry. Up pops a list of the tags defined on the Tags panel. Choose Body because Para is the style utilized for body copy. Now every paragraph assigned to the Para style will also be tagged with the Body tag.

5. Then there's the Map By Name button. What it does is try to find matching names between tags and styles; finding matching names, it then associates one to the other, saving you the trouble of having to define each pair manually. Clicking the Map By Name button can automatically map headings (H1, H2, and so on) and several other styles to like-named tags. For any styles that aren't automatically mapped to tags, finish up by manually selecting them in the Tag column.

6. Click OK to commit the mapping changes and then check the Structure pane, which can be viewed or hidden with the keyboard shortcut Ctrl+Alt+1/Cmd+Opt+1. The Structure pane is now populated by entries for every text element in this chapter (see Figure 4.40).

FIGURE 4.40
The Map By Name button automatically matches like-named tags and styles, as you can see better in the structure of this chapter than in a fiction piece like *The Wonderful Wizard of Oz* lesson file.

7. Map Styles To Tags does only text (paragraph, character, table, and cell styles), as you might realize after noticing the absence of any images in the Structure pane. It will do all the text, including figure captions, but it won't actually tag the image frames containing the figures. So, whip through the document manually tagging figures with the *Figure* tag.

8. Now in your Structure panel you should have *everything* in the document. Drag an entry for a figure up to after the paragraph in which the figure is referenced. Doing so, of course, means that when exporting to EPUB, that figure will be right where it needs to be in the content order.

   Then proceed to insert all *Figure*-tagged figures where they need to be in the chapter, save the document, and then run a quick EPUB export to verify changes.

You now have absolute control over the order of your EPUB content with zero visible changes to the print layout. You don't even have to use anchored objects, thanks to tagging and structuring!

Also keep in mind these little tidbits about working with the Tags panel and the XML Structure pane.

◆ Tag only the objects you want to include in the ebook.

◆ You can apply tags to one or more frames in several ways:

  ◆ By selecting the frame(s) and clicking the tag in the Tags panel

  ◆ By right-clicking a frame and choosing the correct tag from the Tag Frame submenu

  ◆ By dragging a tag off the Tags panel and dropping it on a selected or unselected frame

  ◆ By dragging one or more objects into the Structure pane. Before you'll be allowed to drop them, InDesign will have you choose a tag to apply to them.

◆ Frames can be untagged in a few ways, too, including using the Untag button on the Tags panel and right-clicking the frame itself or its entry in the Structure pane and choosing Untag Element.

◆ Just like deleting an in-use style or color swatch, deleting an in-use tag on the Tags panel prompts you to pick a replacement tag.

◆ Selecting one or more untagged frames and clicking the Autotag button at the bottom of the Tags panel will have InDesign attempt to identify the type of content selected and create and apply tags for that content. Typically, text frames get the tag Story, while graphic frames get the Image tag, for example. You can alter that behavior by selecting Tagging Preset Options from the panel flyout menu and editing the drop-down lists therein (see Figure 4.41).

FIGURE 4.41
Editing the autotag
presets

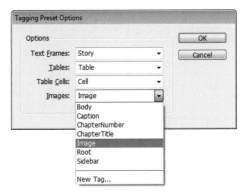

◆ Rename tags and/or change their indicator colors by double-clicking the tag in the Tags panel or selecting the tag and choosing Tag Options from the panel flyout menu.

◆ Choose Show Text Snippets from the flyout menu of the Structure pane to show snippets of text beside the tags for a more informative view of the document structure.

◆ Tagging and ordering by tags is only scratching the surface of what you can accomplish using the Structure pane and XML in InDesign, but that's outside the topic of this book.

Chapter 5

Working with Images and Multimedia in Ebooks

Although the majority of ebooks are text-only novels and short stories, many ebooks—across all genres—include photographs, illustrations, charts, graphs, maps, other imagery, and even audio and video. Moreover, even novels and short stories typically have at least cover images. Whether your publication merely needs a cover or requires lots of figures, the process of creating and using graphics and multimedia in ebooks differs in several distinct ways from creating and using them in print or in other digital formats.

In this chapter, you will learn about the following:

◆ Exporting Images to Ebooks

◆ Preparing Images for Ebooks

◆ Adding Audio and Video to Ebooks

◆ Adding Vector Graphics to Ebooks

Exporting Images to Ebooks

Exporting images to ebooks requires an understanding of the supported formats and how to control the quality of those images during conversion to EPUB-ready formats. I'll start by defining the formats I'm talking about.

Ebook Image Formats

Because EPUB (and Amazon-format) ebooks are effectively self-contained websites, they support the inclusion and display of only web-standard image formats. Specifically, those formats are JPEG (aka JPG), GIF, PNG, and SVG. If you're unfamiliar with some of these formats, allow me to explain.

These four graphics formats are what ebooks use and understand. Of these four, InDesign understands three—it has no concept of SVG, but there are two ways around that, which I'll get to later. Of course, InDesign can import many types of images other than JPEG, GIF, and PNG via File ➢ Place. So, are you locked into making all your images one of those formats, converting the hundreds of TIFFs and PSDs you normally use? Not at all. InDesign will take care of converting them on the way out through the EPUB export filter, though there are reasons you might want to create versions of your images specifically for EPUB output.

JPEG

JPEG (or JPG) is the most popular file format for images that contain many colors and shades, such as photographs of people, scenery, objects, and so on. JPEG supports full 24-bit RGB color, or up to a maximum of 16.7 million colors, which represents the entire range of human vision; if our eyes can perceive the color, JPEG can use it. That makes the format ideal for photographs. JPEG does have one major limiting characteristic, though: JPEG images cannot contain transparency.

All *raster*, or pixel-based, images are rectangular regardless of how the image looks. You may have an image of a circle, but square pixels comprise that circle, and those pixels live inside a rectangular grid. Ergo, the image itself *must* be a rectangle. An image of a circle may *appear* to be a circle in the final product by making its background (the parts of the pixel grid not covered by the circle image) transparent, thus allowing whatever might be behind the image to show through. JPEGs, however, cannot have transparent backgrounds. If you try to save or export a graphic with a transparent background to JPEG, the creating app—Adobe Photoshop or what have you—will automatically add an opaque background to the resulting JPEG image.

Part of the value of JPEG-format images is their ability to compress. Simply put, 24 bits of data in every pixel of a potentially very large image results in a great deal of data for a computer to crunch and a great deal of data to be stored in a single file. Both conditions result in large file sizes on disk and long download and rendering times. To compensate for these factors, compression was built into JPEG, enabling the format to reduce the quality of the image—often imperceptibly—by combining the data for adjacent pixels, thus reducing the total amount of data and thereby reducing the file size. Compression in a JPEG is typically set via a 12-step scale, with a value of 12 equaling no compression, and thus no loss of quality, and a value of 1 equating to the maximum compression level possible, quality be damned. In some software applications and even in different places in the same application, you won't be exposed to a 12-step scale; rather, you'll be given five natural-language choices for quality: Low, Medium, High, Very High, and Maximum. Each of these equates to a percentage of quality, generally as follows: Low = 10% quality/90% compressed; Medium = 30%/70%; High = 60%/40%; Very High = 80%/20%; and Maximum = 100% quality, no compression, or a value of 12 on the 12-step scale. The more you compress a JPEG image, the smaller its file size, the faster it will download and display, but also the lower the quality. When quality degrades in a JPEG, it does so by attempting to combine pixels in 8-pixel blocks. Many times the quality difference isn't noticeable. When it is, the result is often described as "fuzzy," "softened," or, in more extreme cases, "pixelated" or "chunky colored."

GIF

GIF (pronounced like "gift" without the *t*, not "Jif" as in the peanut butter) images are limited to containing a maximum of 256 colors (aka 8-bit). Furthermore, whether or not white and black are used in the image, two of the colors in any GIF image's palette *must* be black and white. The remaining 254 can be *any* colors from within the full 16.7 million color RGB spectrum; if you have an entirely grayscale GIF, you may give it a full complement of 256 shades of gray (including black and white). If you have pie chart graphic with red, green, blue, yellow, orange, and purple slices, several hues of each of those colors will fit comfortably within the 254 palette.

When saving or exporting a GIF from most graphics programs, you will be presented with a list of the colors actually used in the image. If the number of colors is fewer than 256, the program will allow you to reduce the number of color slots to match the number of actual colors used, which reduces the file size of the resulting GIF and thus increases its download and screen-rendering speed.

Another feature of GIF images is that they may contain what's called *1-bit transparency*. This type of transparency is effectively replacing one color in the image with nothing, knocking out that color to show whatever might be behind the GIF when it's incorporated into a page. You don't have to choose the color to hide. Continuing with the circle analogy, simply create your circle on a transparent or empty background in Photoshop (or another raster image editor) and export to GIF; the background will remain transparent in the resultant GIF. The circle will, however, have jagged edges. One-bit transparency means that only a single color will be replaced by transparency, and, since any given pixel may be only one solid color—you can't have a half-and-half or faded pixel, for instance—then only those pixels that are wholly the color chosen to be replaced by transparency will actually become transparent. When you have an object like a red circle drawn in square pixels, the graphics program anti-aliases or fades the edges and colors some pixels 75 percent red and others 50 percent, 25 percent, 10 percent, or 5 percent red to create the illusion of roundness in a shape comprised of squares. Each of these less-than-red pixels is mixed with the hidden background color, resulting in its pink appearance. During export to GIF, the part-red/part-transparent pixels are made solid, mixed with white to create the same color pink in a solid pixel, maintaining the illusion of roundness…well, maintaining the illusion of roundness if the GIF is placed atop a white background on the EPUB or web page. Placed atop any other color, those pink pixels stick out like Waldo in a funeral procession. For this reason, it's best to use GIF transparency only when the background it will be laid atop is the same color as the background used in the image editor or only with rectangular-edged objects that don't use partially transparent pixels.

Another feature of GIFs is that they may contain frame-replacement animation. Viewers see animation—as smooth as you want to make it—but behind the scenes each frame of the animation is another image; when the animation plays, the GIF hides the previous frame, revealing the next one in rapid succession to create the illusion of movement. In other words, GIF animation works just like television and movies. For GIFs, though, the fact that each of those frames is a full-sized separate image increases the file size (and download time) exponentially in relation to the length and smoothness of the animation. The smoother the animation, the more frames needed to create that smoothness, thus the larger the file size.

Two limitations apply to GIF animation. First, all frames must share the same color palette. You can't, for instance, have one frame that uses 256 shades of gray, a second that uses 100 shades of orange, and a third designed in 168 shades of blue. The GIF-creation process will chop those colors down to a unified 256-color palette, probably creating *posterization* in the artwork of each frame. Second, for all intents and purposes, animated GIFs cannot contain transparency. There *are* ways to incorporate transparency into them, but with widespread support for SVG nowadays, the techniques are more trouble than the payout warrants. If you need animation with transparency, use SVG.

PNG

PNG is often pronounced as "ping" because it is simply "P-N-G." It is an oft-used replacement for both GIF and JPEG. PNG comes in two flavors: 8-bit, which is roughly equivalent to GIF, and 24-bit, which bears only a passing similarity to JPEG.

Eight-bit PNGs are limited to 256-color palettes, may use 1-bit transparency, and can be animated using the same frame-replacement process employed by GIF. PNG also contains file compression technology that is newer and more efficient than that in GIF, resulting in usually—but not always—smaller file sizes when the same image is exported to PNG and GIF. They also tend to produce better results when hues and shades must be sacrificed to fit within the 256-color limit.

Like JPEG, PNG-24s support the full visual spectrum of computer-renderable, and human-discernible, colors, which makes the format suitable for photographs and detailed illustrations. Unlike JPEG, PNG-24s may also contain transparency, and that would be 8-bit, or what we call *alpha channel*, transparency. This is the same level and quality of transparency as used to create images in Photoshop or other professional-grade image editors. Thus, in practice, the transparency you see in Photoshop when you create that red circle translates to the same transparency—wholly opaque, fully transparent, and 254 more levels of partial transparency in between them—in the exported PNG. For this reason, PNG is ideal when transparency is desired in situations where the background color onto which the image will be placed is unknown or is composed of more than a single color (such as overlaying the foreground image onto a background or page image).

PNG-24s (aka 24-bit PNGs) tend to be larger in file size than JPEGs—sometimes dramatically so. Both flavors of PNG contain compression algorithms to make their file sizes smaller, but that compression is what we call *lossless*, meaning quality is never sacrificed to reduce file size. JPEG uses a lossy compression method, letting you choose the ratio between quality and compression. Consequently, JPEG images may be highly compressed, whereas PNG-24s have no user-accessible compression controls; you simply export, whereupon compression is automatically applied while preserving maximum quality. What you get is what you get. When exporting the same image to PNG-24 and to JPEG with a quality setting of Maximum or 12, the PNG will be smaller every time because of the built-in compression. However, reducing the quality of the JPEG during export usually results in that file being smaller than its PNG-24 counterpart.

SVG

In a nutshell, SVG enables you to include true vector artwork in ebooks and web pages—think Adobe Illustrator artwork online. In fact, Adobe Illustrator can export to SVG, as can a host of other applications, and SVG can support just about anything you can create in a vector drawing program like Illustrator. The format can display 2D vector graphics, text, and even incorporated raster imagery; like Illustrator, it can also produce the *appearance* of 3D, though not actual 3D. If you need real 3D in an ebook, you're currently out of luck unless you want to swap the EPUB format for interactive magazine or app-based.

EPUB 3, the current version as of this writing, supports SVG graphics, while EPUB 2.01 does not. Therefore, it's important to keep in mind that people consuming your ebook on older ereader devices or software probably will not see your SVG content. I say probably because some manufacturers adopted some or all the features of EPUB 3 early, before it was an official standard.

If your publication could benefit from SVG—meaning, you want something other than static imagery in your book—and your audience can view it, I highly suggest you use it. It has numerous advantages over JPEG, GIF, and PNG in an ebook.

The biggest benefit to SVG is right there in the name: *scalable vector graphics*. Vector, unlike raster, is resolution-independent; you could draw an SVG image at 1 inch by 1 inch, and a reader could blow it up to 10 feet square without ever losing quality. No jaggies. No fuzzy edges. Nada. And, even blown up, that graphic will print at the highest resolution the printer or other output device can render, assuming you allow it to be printed. SVG graphics are infinitely scalable—up or down—without loss of quality (except in any raster-based art that may be embedded within the SVG).

SVG images, being vector and thus not constrained to a pixel grid, have automatic transparency around the edges of nonrectangular objects. Moreover, they support true transparency within the artwork; the center of an *O* would be transparent, or you could make some objects or colors semitransparent via 256 shades of alpha channel transparency or a simple 0 to 100 percent opacity scale.

Another big benefit of SVG is that it can be scripted to do far more than raster-based images using JavaScript and *SMIL*, a markup language developed specifically to control the presentation of multimedia elements. SVG artwork can be animated using SMIL or JavaScript for simple animations, such as a cartoon, or complex content replacements, such as running a playlist of videos and displaying time-coded closed captioning for those videos. It's also useful for incorporating server-fed content into the SVG artwork and then replacing that with other server-fed content or reacting to user interaction with the server-fed content.

I'll talk first about using images already in print publications or ones created using a normal print publication workflow, and then I'll loop back around to the topic of purpose-built images for EPUB.

Automatic Conversion to EPUB Image Formats

Returning to the `wizardofoz_print_ch4.indd` layout from the lesson files that accompany Chapter 4, "Creating Basic Ebooks," you'll notice standard print-ready raster images—high resolution, laid out rather large on the pages, and in TIFF, JPEG, PDF, or PSD format. In this publication, all the images are TIFFs (you can see them in Chapter 4's lesson files, namely, the `Wizard of Oz PRINT - Ch 4\Links` folder). Ebook readers typically can't display TIFFs, but that's OK; InDesign will convert them on export. In fact, if you exported `wizardofoz_print_ch4.indd` to EPUB previously, you've already witnessed the automatic conversion. If you haven't, try a quick export to EPUB now.

Although you can't tell (yet), the images you'll see in the EPUB are a mixture of JPEG and PNG. When left to its own devices, InDesign uses an alchemical formula bordering on sorcery to choose which images become JPEG, which PNG, and which GIF. You may not always agree with InDesign's choice; in fact, more often than not, ebook designers disagree with InDesign's choice of automatic image conversion format. Consequently, I recommend you take control of the conversion yourself.

Asserting Control over Bulk Image Conversion

During the EPUB export process, once you've arrived at the EPUB Export Options dialog, you can choose several options that affect the format and quality of all exported images in the Image pane (see Figure 5.1). I'll go through these options one at a time, top to bottom, and explain what they could mean to your ebooks.

FIGURE 5.1
The Image pane
of EPUB Export
Options

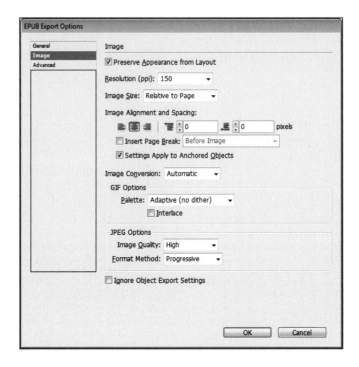

PRESERVE APPEARANCE FROM LAYOUT

If enabled, the Preserve Appearance From Layout option will make the exported images look like they do on the InDesign page. Turn it off, and the appearances of the *original* linked images are used instead. Any effects—drop shadow, outer glow, transparency—are lost with Preserve Appearance From Layout disabled, as are tints on grayscale images, transformations such as rotation or skew, and even crops. The full and complete image will appear in the ebook regardless of how the image was cropped in InDesign.

Typically you'll want to leave Preserve Appearance From Layout checked, but deselecting it could be beneficial to your workflow. Let's say you've done what I've done with this *Wizard of Oz* chapter: placed grayscale TIFFs and then tinted them with a color for the print layout. Perhaps for the ebook you don't want them tinted; that's simple—just uncheck Preserve Appearance From Layout, and then the original grayscale TIFFs will be used regardless of what I've done to them in InDesign. Another scenario where that option could prove even more useful is for ebook-only imagery. While producing the print edition, you could place ebook-only images where they need to go but change their opacities to 0 percent. Because exporting to EPUB with Preserve Appearance From Layout disabled also ignores opacity settings, those invisible images become quite visible in the EPUB export. (At the same time, you could set print-only images to not export to EPUB, but I'll talk about that a bit later in this chapter.)

IMAGE RESOLUTION

When using images in a print book layout, it's important to make them high resolution, which is accomplished either by making the original image high resolution or by scaling the image down in InDesign so that pixels pack more tightly into the smaller space and the image becomes higher resolution. This is the difference between Actual PPI and Effective PPI, as displayed in the Links panel (see Figure 5.2). The value beside Actual PPI is the native resolution, in pixels per inch (PPI), which is effectively the same as dots per inch (DPI), of the linked image; this value can't be changed in InDesign. Scaling down the image increases the output resolution or Effective PPI because reduction of pixel-based images always equates to increased resolution; conversely, scaling up the image reduces its resolution because the pixels comprising the image are stretched over a greater area. For example, taking a 300 PPI image and scaling it down in InDesign to 50 percent of its original size makes the image's Effective PPI 600 PPI. Taking that same 300 PPI image and doubling its size on the InDesign page decreases its resolution to half of the original, or 150 PPI.

FIGURE 5.2
On the Links panel, the Actual PPI and Effective PPI fields display an image's native and in-use resolution.

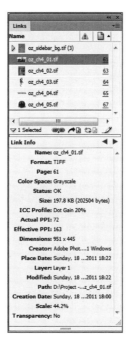

TIP Images created by InDesign's EPUB export often look poor (low resolution, fuzzy, blurry) when viewed in computer-based ereader software but great on ereader devices themselves. Therefore, I recommend you proof on-device before making quality assessments of images.

The Image Resolution field in EPUB Export Options determines the resolution of exported image files. It doesn't accept typed-in values, instead offering a drop-down menu of four presets: 72, 96, 150, and 300 PPI. Which you choose is largely dependent on how poor the images look at other resolutions and whether you want readers to be able to zoom in to view your images or whether you want the images to automatically scale to the ereader's screen. Using 300 PPI gives you the highest-resolution image, able to be zoomed quite a bit before quality degrades, but also pretty big image file sizes. Moreover, if your original image Actual PPI (or Effective PPI with Preserve Appearance From Layout selected) has a resolution lower than 300 PPI, choosing 300 here won't improve it; it's quite the opposite.

A couple of rules of thumb will help here. First, set the export resolution to, at most, match the effective resolution, up to 300 PPI. Once that's done, if your image's effective resolution is 96 PPI or greater, choose whether you want to include the images only at screen resolution (72 PPI) or whether you'd like to go with a higher resolution (and larger file size) to enable zooming and/ or scaling.

IMAGE SIZE

Let's take a moment to revisit the one image-related problem that occurred during EPUB export in Chapter 4 that I haven't addressed. That would be the issue of images exporting at full resolution and then getting cropped to the display size of the ebook. If you don't recall this, Figure 5.3 might jog your memory. Of course, you can always flip back to the "What Doesn't Work" section of Chapter 4.

FIGURE 5.3
This image was cut off during the export tests in Chapter 4.

wizardofoz_print_ch4

What's really going on here is that the full-sized image is being exported within the EPUB, but the ereader screen isn't large enough to display that full-sized image. In this particular case, these images do show in their entirety on large screens, such as a 10-inch tablet or desktop monitor.

Within the Image Size field in EPUB Export Options, you have two options: Fixed and Relative To Page. By default, Fixed is selected, which exports the images at their on-the-InDesign-page sizes. If they don't fit on the ereader-size pages, they're cropped by the display. That was the problem with the images during the test in Chapter 4. Changing the Image Size field to Relative To Page scales the images dynamically in the EPUB relative to the viewable area in the ereader. The images will shrink or grow with the screen on which the book is read—assuming the ereader supports that particular function of CSS, and *most* of them do. Those that don't will default to cropping them. Figure 5.4 shows the same, previously problematic image, displayed after enabling the Relative To Page option upon export.

FIGURE 5.4
With the Relative To Page option checked, the image in the resulting EPUB scales to fit the page without cropping.

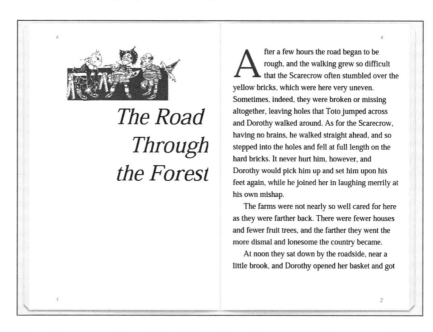

Now, I don't want to get you all excited and then drop a house on you, but as appealing as the Relative To Page option sounds—and often *is*—you may decide not to use it, opting instead to create fixed-sized images specifically for ebook export. I'll talk about how to do that later in the chapter, but the reason you may elect to follow that particular yellow brick road is to ensure maximum image quality. Leaving it to ereaders to scale images is like leaving it to web browsers to scale images—they can do it, but not always well, and some downright gruesomely. As a general rule, e-ink devices, such as handheld ereaders, do a pretty good job scaling images as a result of their advanced rendering technologies, but other devices, such as tablets, smartphones, hybrid tablet ereaders, and ereader software on computers, might do a great job, a decent job, or a terrible job. As always, testing your ebook on a variety of devices will reveal which way you should go with image sizes.

IMAGE ALIGNMENT AND SPACING

By default, images are center aligned when exported to an ebook, and that's a very common way they'll stay. Sometimes, though, you might want your images to be flush left or flush right in the ebook. The three alignment buttons under Image Alignment And Spacing in EPUB Export Options let you choose, just as you'd choose paragraph alignment from the Paragraph or Control panel. Also in this section you can use the adjacent Space Before and Space After fields to give images a little vertical breathing room from the paragraphs or other images that precede and succeed them. The values, measured in pixels, translate to the `margin-above` and `margin-below` attribute values in the EPUB's resulting CSS markup.

For extra space—particularly if you have full-page images like the one on page 63 of `wizardofoz_print_ch4.indd`—you can also insert page breaks before images and/or after images. Without breaks, ereaders that use a paged or side-to-side swipe methodology will jump large images to the next page if they can't fit wholly on the previous page anyway. Those ereaders that use a vertical scrolling system, however, will show whatever part of an image fits and let the user slide down to see the rest. With one or more automatic page breaks enabled, these vertical scrollers will "jump" from one page to the next even if the image would have fit in the whitespace on a preceding page. That can be jarring for some people—it's up to you to decide whether potentially splitting an image across a page or jumping to a new page prematurely is your preference.

Not only can automatic page breaks be useful for full-page images, they can also be employed to easily break up sections or chapters. Say you have an ebook that begins each chapter with an image, even ahead of text components such as chapter titles, numbers, or whatever. Instead of making sure that the line into which the image is anchored—if it's anchored—is assigned to a paragraph style containing an automatic break, you can simply choose the break option in EPUB Export Options to automatically break up the ebook by its chapters or sections. At other times, it's just nice to have images always start at the top of a page.

TIP   Page breaks will separate images from their captions, which is why it's recommended to make captions part of the images (see "Captioning Images" later in this chapter).

Also of note is the Settings Apply To Anchored Objects check box. Anchored or inline objects may have their positions, alignment, spacing, and breaks set via the Anchored Object Options dialog (from InDesign's Object ➢ Anchored Object menu). The options chosen there will survive export unless Settings Apply To Anchored Objects is enabled, which then applies the settings selected in EPUB Export Options to anchored and inline objects as well.

IMAGE CONVERSION

In this section, I'll return to those image formats supported by EPUB and how to choose which format(s) you want. Within the Image Conversion drop-down menu, you're offered the choice of exporting all your images—or all images not given specific object export settings—as JPEG, PNG, or GIF. The fourth option, Automatic, employs that alchemical formula that leaves it to InDesign to choose whether your images become lead or gold.

If you select Automatic, both the GIF Options and JPEG Options sections below remain available, whereas choosing GIF or JPEG from the Image Conversion drop-down menu grays out the other's corresponding section. PNG has no options to set—you automatically get a PNG-24.

Between them, the GIF Options and JPEG Options areas give you four options to set (see Figure 5.5).

FIGURE 5.5

The GIF Options and JPEG Options sections of the Image pane

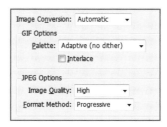

GIF Options Palette   Choose the color palette to use for generated GIFs. Adaptive (No Dither) offers the fullest range of color but does not dither, which is to say that it will not smooth the edges of color transitions by mixing pixels of one color with pixels of the other. The Mac and Windows system palettes each include 256 colors, like Adaptive, but are specific to the unique 256-color palette of the respective operating system. There are 40 colors that are close, but not identical, between the platforms. The web palette is solely the 216 colors that match identically between Mac and Windows computers.

GIF Options Interlace   Interlace causes generated GIF images to progressively load, creating the perception of a faster image load, although it actually takes longer for the full image to render.

JPEG Options Image Quality   As a lossy compression method, the relative size of a JPEG image is in direct relation to its quality. The higher the quality, the larger the file. Low (10%), Medium (30%), High (60%), and Maximum (100%) quality are your choices (Very High [80%], the most common one I use in other circumstances, is frustratingly left out of the selection choices).

JPEG Options Format Method   Multiple flavors of JPEG are available. Baseline is the oldest and most commonly supported, though Progressive is widely supported in ereaders, browsers, and other rendering software of the last 10+ years. Progressive has the added benefit of rendering the JPEG in stages, creating the perception of a faster image load.

Asserting Control over Individual Image Conversion

Even if the settings on the Image pane of EPUB Export Options produce exactly the image output you want for most of your graphics, you may find yourself wanting different settings for specific images here and there. If you've been at this a while, epublishing from several versions of InDesign, then you might be thinking that individual image control is a pipe dream, or at least requires after-export modification of the images. Not so.

Added in InDesign CS5.5 is the ability to control the export options for individual images. All of the options in the EPUB Export Options Image pane can be set per image. All you have to do is select an image, choose Object Export Options from the Object menu, and switch to the EPUB And HTML tab (Figure 5.6). There you'll find all the same options—image size, resolution, format, and GIF- and JPEG-specific options, as well as alignment, space before and after, and page break controls. Just enable the section you'd like to manipulate for the current image, either Custom Rasterization or Custom Layout or both, and begin setting options.

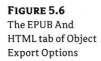

FIGURE 5.6
The EPUB And
HTML tab of Object
Export Options

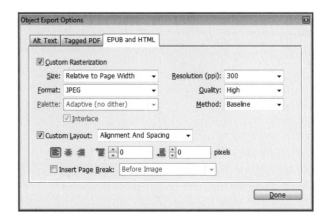

There's even a bonus here. With the check box beside Custom Layout checked, a drop-down box becomes available. By default this drop-down displays Alignment And Spacing, which lets you set the aforementioned left, right, and center alignment; spacing before and after the image; and whether there are page breaks before and/or after the image. Below Alignment And Spacing in the list are two other options: Float Left and Float Right. Choosing one of those will float an image one way or the other, causing text to wrap around it (rectangularly) on the other side. This is the only place outside of directly editing the CSS that you can create text wrap and floating objects; Adobe didn't even include the floating options in the standard EPUB Export Options dialog.

Once you've set the desired options, click OK to apply them, and then you can move on to the next image to set its individual export options. Unfortunately, Adobe also forgot to include the Object Export Options fields in object styles, so you'll have to set all the options manually or write a script to do it. Thankfully, you can set the options for multiple images in one shot, as long as they're on the same page or spread so that you can select them together.

Preparing Images for Ebooks

In addition to choosing formats and setting export quality and alignment options, you might want to take other steps in preparing graphics and images for optimal results when used in ebooks. Furthermore, these extra steps are often the solution to the most common image-related ebook problems, including those I talked about in Chapter 4 when converting a print publication to an ebook.

Let's start by making images accessible and valid.

Adding ALT Tag Alternate Text

You may have heard the term *ALT tag*—or you may not have. It's common in web design. ALT is an abbreviation of "alternate text" and is used within IMG (image) tags in HTML, which, of course, means the Web and ebooks. ALT tags describe images when those images aren't seen—deliberately, because of technical difficulty, or as a consequence of a disability.

For example, let's say your ebook includes the image in Figure 5.7 and that the content of that image is crucial to understanding the message of nearby text. If images were not available as a communication medium, how would you describe the content of the image in writing? That's the ALT tag, a textual description of the content of an image for those who, for one reason or another, will not see the image itself. Even nonessential images such as those that are merely decorative elements, like colored boxes, rules, or flourishes, need ALT tags. Why? It's so that the viewer who can't see them knows they're nonessential. Otherwise, he's left wondering what he might be missing, because his software will tell him there's a picture that isn't displaying even if your text doesn't reference the image.

FIGURE 5.7
An image like this may contain information crucial to the reader's understanding of the material.

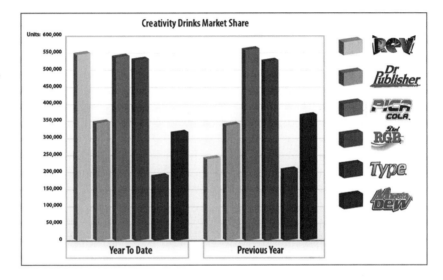

I'm just going to go ahead and say it: *Every image you put in an ebook must have an ALT tag.* Who says? I say. I have some very important reasons why you should agree with me.

First, there's a little thing called Section 508. Its full title is Section 508 Amendment to the Rehabilitation Act of 1973, which was enacted in the United States in 1998. Among provisions about operating system access, telephone TTY services, and others, the technical standards of Section 508 require, in a nutshell, that electronic content be made accessible to visual- and hearing-impaired people using accessibility devices. For example, this means images must have ALT tags describing the content of the image so that the visually impaired, who use keyboards with Braille tickers or text-to-speech systems, can access the information inside the image or, at the very least, be informed that the image doesn't contain any substantive information, as would be the case with a decorative element. Another example is video. Video needs to have closed captions available to make the content accessible to both the audibly impaired and the visually impaired, the latter by use of a Braille ticker or a text-to-speech engine.

Does Section 508 say we all have to use ALT tags, closed captioning, and other such services? No. Specifically, it limits enforcement of compliance to government agencies and companies that have government contracts. Other countries have taken the ideals of Section 508 further, making it a requirement of nongovernment affiliated commerce, education, and, in some cases, content produced by individuals. And some of those countries are fining for noncompliance and threatening imprisonment for repeated noncompliance. Advocacy groups for people with disabilities are pushing for the United States to follow the lead of its peers in that respect.

If that doesn't sway you, this might: Relative to population size, the visually impaired are the largest consumers of ebooks. The format is ideally suited for them—light, portable content in valid XHTML that can be easily read by any text-to-speech engine available on even mass-market devices such as smartphones and tablets, but especially on ebook readers built specifically for the visually challenged. Sighted people typically have the option of buying print and ebooks at the same time. Braille books, however, are rarer, and when they are released, it isn't typically until weeks or months after the other editions. Moreover, books printed in Braille are huge and heavy, owing to the thicker, usually one-sided pages required to convey the raised Braille dots. Who wants to wait for, or lug around, a Braille book when the weightless ebook is already there? If you don't add ALT tags to the images in your ebooks, you'll lose your book's visually impaired audience.

If you're curious as to how an image without ALT text is presented to a visually impaired person, you can easily replicate the experience, the confusion, and the frustration. Just pick up your iPad and go to any website using Adobe Flash as the front end of its site—there are plenty of them out there. Because iOS does not display Flash and because many of the people who develop Flash-powered websites don't bother to create non-Flash alternate versions, you'll see a big blank area and the now infamous (but totally useless) Get Adobe Flash Player button that communicates that there's something, some kind of content, there, but you can't see it. You'll have no idea what's supposed to be in that blank area; you don't know if it's just a decorative animation or if it's a data-driven Flash chart or graph conveying exactly the information you need to get from the site. I guarantee you'll be confused, I'm almost certain you'll be frustrated by your inability to see that content to dispel your confusion, and I bet you'll never return to that same site if given a choice. That's the experience of the visually impaired when they run across an image without ALT text.

Adding ALT text is easy—just return to the Object Export Options dialog and, on the Alt Text tab, choose where the ALT text is coming from. You have several options (see Figure 5.8).

Custom Custom lets you type in the ALT text that could be something as simple as repeating the caption—because the caption might not be connected to the image by an assistive device that someone with impaired vision might use; because the caption may be a pixel-based part of the image (see "Captioning Images" a little later in this chapter), a quick description such as "an illustration by W.W. Denslow depicting Dorothy, Toto, and the Scarecrow sitting on the embankment of a stream"; or because, for images that are merely decorative, it might be something like "[decorative rule]" or "[colored box]." In the case of something as informative as the column chart in Figure 5.7, the ALT text should reiterate the data for those who cannot see the image (see Figure 5.9).

From Structure If the document is structured using XML, then in order to have valid, complete XML, the image element should already have an ALT tag value in the XML structure. Selecting From Structure for Alt Text Source pulls in that preexisting alternate description.

FIGURE 5.8
Alt Text Source
options

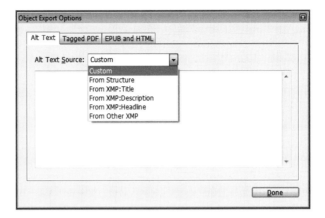

FIGURE 5.9
A custom ALT-text
caption explaining
the contents of the
image

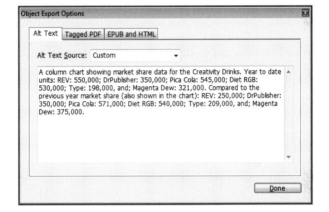

From XMP There are four options in this category, including From Other XMP. All four refer to an image's metadata, specifically the technology Adobe created to encompass and expand on standard metadata fields: Extensible Metadata Platform (XMP). An image's XMP metadata can be accessed and edited in a variety of programs, from asset managers such as Adobe Bridge and Lightroom, where many images' metadata can be changed in batches, to image editors such as Photoshop (via File ➢ File Info). Figure 5.10 shows the metadata for an image as viewed in both Bridge and Photoshop. InDesign documents themselves have XMP, also accessible from File ➢ File Info. Images (and other documents) may have written into their metadata such information as a title, author, copyright status and notice, and a description, the last of which often serves as the caption or ALT text of an image. By selecting one of the From XMP options on the Alt Text Source drop-down menu, you can have the ALT text automatically populated from the image's Title, Description, or Headline metadata fields. If the desired ALT text is contained within a different metadata field, choose From Other XMP, and then, on the right, enter the name of the field whose value should be returned.

FIGURE 5.10

Metadata for an image shown in Photoshop's XMP dialog (left) and in Bridge's Metadata panel (right)

Just as you can set export format options on multiple images at once, you can also set ALT text options. As long as you can select more than one image at a time—which means images limited to sharing a page, spread, or pasteboard—you can set them all to autopopulate ALT from XMP or structure or, in the case of multiple decorative elements, give them the appropriate custom text ALT tag.

Sizing for Ebooks

As I discussed, you can set images to scale with the page during export. If you don't want to do that because of quality concerns, because of compatibility with ereaders that can't scale, or just because as a designer you absolutely must know how your design will look, then you might elect to specifically size your images for ebook publication. Naturally you'll do this if you're starting an ebook from scratch instead of repurposing a print edition.

To resize the images, I'm going into Photoshop. If Photoshop isn't your forte, never fear: I'll walk you through resizing an image and then show you step-by-step how to automate image resizing for ebooks so you never have to open Photoshop for that task again.

CHOOSING YOUR IMAGE SIZE

The first thing you need to do when creating images for ebook publication is set your standard for dimensions, at least the width, in pixels. Remember all those different devices I showed you in Chapter 1, "Exploring Ereading Devices"? From those—and all the ones out there that I didn't show—there are nearly as many different combinations of screen width and height (reference the e-updates to this book at `http://abbrv.it/DigiPubIDUpdates` for a regularly updated list of common devices' screen resolutions). Unfortunately, it's not possible to make EPUBs that look fantastic on all of those screens. Ergo, your job becomes to make EPUBs that look *decent* on every screen and fantastic on as many as possible in terms of imagery. That starts with picking a size for your images and sticking with that size, at least throughout a single publication; you can change sizes for every ebook if you want.

This book, the e-updates, and keeping your ear to the ground will tell you which devices are the most popular at any given time, but ideally your book will be wildly popular on a variety of readers and for much longer than any one ereader dominates the fickle market. Thus, you need to pick a standard image size that works best on most devices available now and those likely to come out in the near future.

Some people like to use very small images, like 480–300 pixels wide, to produce ebooks with very small file sizes. Others swear by making them 600 pixels wide because the average ereading device's screen resolution in portrait (taller-than-wide) mode is 600 pixels. I disagree with both ideas.

I recommend the following as a guideline: Make your images 800 pixels wide for the following reasons:

◆ As noted, many ereaders and 7-inch mini-tablets have 800×600-pixel displays, and though people tend to read in portrait mode as they read a novel, if the device is rotated to landscape mode, 600-pixel-wide images will be scaled up, losing quality, or left with empty spaces to either side that look odd in relation to the text.

◆ A resolution of 800×600 pixels is a display aspect ratio of 4:3, which is the most common display aspect ratio for handheld devices of many classes (including iPad).

◆ For those devices that use larger resolutions still within the 4:3 ratio, 800×600-pixel images scale up or down without distortion; though, of course, scaling them up might result in a loss of resolution.

◆ As of this writing (but ideally finally fixed by the time you read this), iPad has a problem scaling images up in iBooks. By "problem," I mean it won't do it. Just about every other ebook consumption device will respect a CSS `width` or `max-width` and `height` or `max-height` attribute larger than the image's actual pixel dimensions, but the iPad won't; it will display the image no larger than its actual size. It will scale *down*, though. Thus, making an image 800 pixels wide means it will fit the iPad's 8×768×1024-pixel (iPad 1 and 2) or 1536×2048-pixel (iPad 3 and later) portrait mode well with minor scaling and will scale down even more nicely in the device's two-page landscape mode display.

◆ That width, 800 pixels, scales nicely to the other most common screen widths and/or heights—800, 768, 600, 540, 480, 320, and 240 pixels.

◆ Reducing an image to fit a smaller screen increases its resolution, making it look better.

◆ Enlarging reduces resolution, so using, say, a 320-pixel width and blowing it up to 1280 pixels cuts the quality down by 75 percent.

The most important thing is to set a size and stick with it throughout the book. Otherwise, images will appear in different sizes and the perceived quality (if not the actual quality) will vary.

RESIZING AN IMAGE IN PHOTOSHOP

In the unlikely event you're drawing every image from scratch in Photoshop, Illustrator, Corel Painter, or some other program, start each new image file with the standard dimensions you've chosen. Otherwise, you'll most likely need to resize some existing images. Open one in Photoshop, and you'll do that faster than you can say, "We represent the lollipop guild."

1. With the image opened in Photoshop, go to the Image menu and choose Image Size (not Canvas Size). In the Image Size dialog box, there are lots of fields and options, but you

need concern yourself with only four for the task of resizing images for ebook production (see Figure 5.11).

FIGURE 5.11
The Image Size dialog in Photoshop

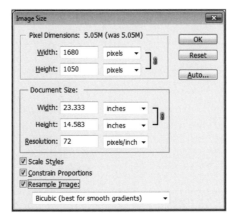

2. The first set is the width and height of the image in pixels. As long as the Constrain Proportions check box is enabled at the bottom of the dialog, changing either the Width or Height value will alter the other proportionately. Replace whatever value is in the Width field by highlighting that value and typing in your chosen image standard—800 or whatever you've selected; Height will update to match. If at all possible, do not enter a width that is larger than the original value by more than 10 percent; doing so will degrade the quality of your image. If your average image is smaller than your chosen size standard by more than 10 percent, you might have to reduce your size standard to the next closest step (for example, 768, 600, and so on) or use a nonstandard step such as 575 pixels and adjust all images to that new standard.

3. In the Document Size section you can ignore the set of Width and Height fields. Beneath that, however, is the Resolution field showing the image PPI. What resolution have you chosen for your images? Decrease—never increase—this value to the resolution on which you've chosen to standardize unless it's already there. Note that changing the resolution will also alter the pixel dimensions, so you may have to reset them to the correct width. (Once you're familiar with the steps, you can change the Resolution field before Width and Height, but I wanted to walk you down the dialog in order.)

4. Finally, you'll want to enable the Resample Image check box and select an interpolation method from the drop-down box below it (Figure 5.12). Any time you reduce the size of an image (*downsample*) or increase it (*upsample*), you, respectively, reduce or increase the number of pixels in the image. Photoshop must therefore take the existing pixel data—the colors and transparency values—and figure out how to squeeze them into fewer, or expand them into more, pixels to accomplish the resize. This is the process of *resampling*, which attempts to produce a resized image whose quality and content match those of the presized version as closely as possible. Photoshop can employ several different algorithms or interpolation methods while resampling. The one it uses, the ideal one for your image, is determined by your choice in the drop-down list. Any good Photoshop book

will go into great detail about the processes at work in resampling, so if you want to know all the science behind them, look for a good Photoshop book; I'll just give you the *Reader's Digest* version of what each interpolation method means to your image and when to choose one method over another.

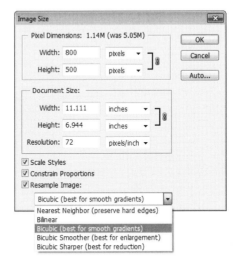

Nearest Neighbor   As the parenthetical explanation in the Image Size dialog states, the Nearest Neighbor method is best used for hard edges. That means this method looks for areas of contrast—for example, a blue square within a yellow background—and preserves those sharp demarcations. Nearest Neighbor does not do so well, however, with subtle color shifts or the anti-aliased edges of colors that blend together. If large areas of solid color separated by sharp edges comprise your picture, then Nearest Neighbor is often the best choice of resampling interpolation method.

Bilinear   The Bilinear method is rarely the best choice. It is once in a great while, though, so I'll describe its *modus operandi*. Bilinear averages the colors between two adjacent pixels. For example, if you had that blue square within a yellow background, using the Bilinear method would result in green pixels along the edges. Sometimes that's great—it helps the blue square blend into the yellow background—but in most cases the quality is not as good as a Bicubic method.

Bicubic   Bicubic interpolation is like Bilinear after taking that weird, transparent supersmarts pill in the movie *Limitless*. Instead of examining and building (or removing) pixels based on just the pixels immediately adjacent to one pixel, it looks at pixels further out too, attempting to gain a—pardon the pun—big-picture view of how one pixel fits into the overall image and therefore how best to create or destroy pixels to accomplish the resizing.

Bicubic Smoother and Bicubic Sharper   Bicubic Smoother and Bicubic Sharper are Bilinear on the *improved* super-smarts pill that Bradley Cooper's character creates after his brain is already improved on the first-generation NZT-48 super-smarts pill. They're specifically optimized for the processes of image enlargement and reduction, respectively. Sharper works by maintaining sharp edges separating areas of color, while Smoother softens those edges. Typically these are your best choices for downsampling and upsampling.

Choose the interpolation method that best fits your image and the action you're taking on it, and click OK.

If the result is less than desirable, undo the resize with Ctrl+Z/Cmd+Z and resize again using a different interpolation method. When you're satisfied, it's then time to save the image as a new file optimized for EPUB.

From the File menu, choose Save For Web & Devices; up will pop the Save For Web & Devices dialog, which offers more visual and intuitive options for your EPUB-optimized image creation than would the options within the Save As dialog (see Figure 5.13). This dialog lets you choose whether to save your image as JPEG, GIF, or PNG, and then it gives you precise control over the colors, quality, and other features of those formats. Ignore the Preset menu for the time being, and choose the correct format for your image—JPEG, GIF, PNG-8, or PNG-24—from the menu just below it. Refer to the "EPUB Image Formats" section for descriptions of the features and limitations of each file format to help you make the choice of formats—or just experiment here in Save For Web & Devices. The main window will preview the image in the format you select and with the options you change.

FIGURE 5.13
The Save For Web & Devices dialog in Photoshop

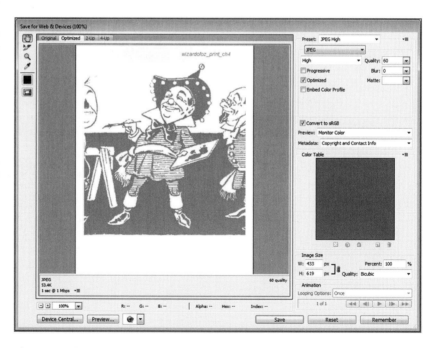

Speaking of options, the JPEG options are mostly the same as those offered within the Image pane of the EPUB Export Options dialog. Here, for example, you're offered the same quality level as a natural-language expression preset (with Very High this time!) or numeric percentage, as well as the choice to make the image optimized and progressively rendered. New here is the Blur field, which softens edges and can repair many negative pixelation effects resulting from lower-quality levels, as well as the Matte field, which enables you to select the background color to fill in any areas of transparency in the original image. Embed Color Profile is also an option, which I typically recommend you do. I won't get into color profiles and color management in this book, though you can find out everything you need to know about it—in InDesign, Photoshop, and other Creative Suite applications—in my *Mastering InDesign CS5* book.

Selecting GIF from the Optimized File Format menu, you have the previously discussed choice for interlacing, but the rest of it varies quite a bit from InDesign's EPUB Export Options (see Figure 5.14).

FIGURE 5.14
Photoshop's GIF options are much more detailed than InDesign's.

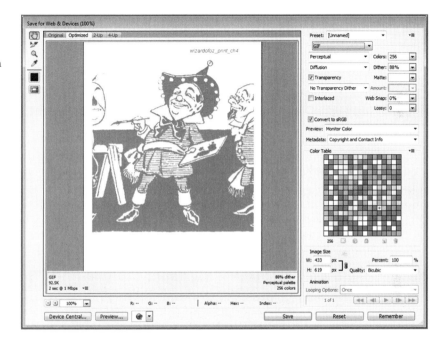

Color Reduction Algorithm The first drop-down field, set to Perceptual by default, is Color Reduction Algorithm. Because GIF images may contain no more than 256 colors, you must choose a method for reducing the colors in the document to fit. Again, there's a good deal of discussion to be had on these choices, but I'll distill it to my recommendations.

Ignore the choices for Mac OS and Windows. These correspond to the 256-color palettes specific to those operating systems. No one uses only 256-color displays on Mac or Windows these days, and they have no correlation to other ereading devices, so these options are completely irrelevant. So is Custom, unless you want to define all the colors included in the GIF by hand. Use Black – White and Grayscale if your images are black and white (without grays) or grayscale. Otherwise, stick with the top four methods. Typically, Perceptual, which tries to preserve the appearance of colors from the original to the reduced color set GIF, is the best choice. Sometimes, however, Selective, Adaptive, or Restrictive, which pick colors based on their locations within the numerically based RGB gamut, produce the best results. Try each of them, and then examine the preview to the left.

Colors To the right of the Color Reduction Algorithm field is a field for setting the number of colors to output in the GIF. You can choose any of the presets, up to a maximum of 256. Reducing the color count reduces the file size, so if your image doesn't need all 256 colors, try reducing the number here.

Dither Algorithm Dithering is the process of simulating one color by mixing pixels of two adjacent colors. For example, dithering can simulate purple by alternating blue and red pixels. You have four choices for dithering: None, which does not dither to simulate colors that could not be included in the allotted 256; Diffusion, which dithers colors according to their directions in the original art, usually producing the best results; Pattern, which dithers in a regular pattern even if that isn't the best way to blend colors; and Noise, which uses random digital noise effects to blend colors.

To the right is a Dither percentage field that lets you control the amount of dither. Experiment with this value. Raise it if you see blotchy areas of color that don't dither together; reduce the value if you see too much dithering.

Transparency If the Transparency check box is enabled—and the original image is on a transparent background—the background of the image will disappear. Note that one of the available 256-color slots is occupied by transparent. Also, once Transparency is enabled, you can choose below the check box the dither algorithm used to blend transparent into semi-transparent and that into opaque. Again, a field to the right—this time labeled Amount—lets you set the dither percentage.

Matte The matte color is the background color for the GIF, if it doesn't already have one. Even when the background is transparent, semitransparent pixels need to be rendered as opaque, blending with what would be the background color. Set here the color you expect the GIF will sit atop—for ebooks that's probably white.

Web Snap Ignore this. It's about as relevant today as a 28.8 BPM modem. Why? Because a positive value in this field will cause colors that are similar to the 216 web-safe colors to change to one of those 216 colors. That web-safe color palette was relevant when people used 256-color monitors and display settings. No one does any more. Even cheap cell phones use 65,000 colors, if not the full 16.7 million.

Lossy By default, GIF doesn't sacrifice quality for compression like JPEG does. However, you can make it act like a JPEG in that regard by entering a positive value in the Lossy field. Any value other than 0 will reduce the file size even further but will degrade the image, though not necessarily noticeably. Often a 5 percent, 10 percent, and up to 25 percent value can be used without any noticeable loss of quality.

TIP The options between Lossy and Animation Controls—Convert to sRGB, Preview, Metadata, Color Table, Image Size, and so on—aren't relevant to preparing images for ebooks, so they are not discussed here.

Animation Controls If your GIF is animated, the controls at the bottom will activate. The rewind, skip backward, play, skip forward, and fast-forward buttons let you preview the animation, while the Looping Options field lets you choose whether the animation loops or restarts itself when it reaches the end and how many times it does so before stopping.

Choosing PNG-8 from the Optimized File Format menu will create an 8-bit, 256-color PNG image with all the same features as a GIF, except a Lossy option.

Opting for PNG-24 offers GIF-like options for Interlaced, Matte, and Transparency (see Figure 5.15). Bear in mind, though, that PNG-24 uses genuine alpha channel transparency. Unlike GIF's 1-bit, invisible or wholly opaque transparency, PNG-24 can use any level of transparency from 100 percent transparent (invisible) to 0 percent (opaque) and every level in between.

FIGURE 5.15

Sparse but appropriately so—the PNG-24 options don't leave much to configure.

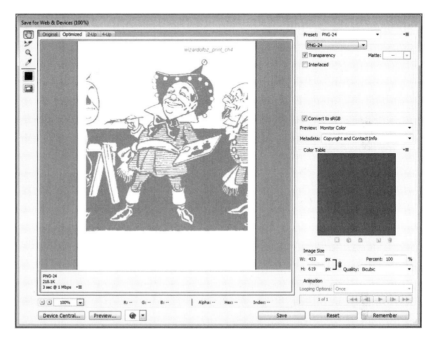

Don't use the WBMP file format, incidentally. It's a defunct file format used for old Windows Mobile–powered phones and PDAs. Windows—including the mobile versions—have long since abandoned WBMP in favor of PNG-8 and PNG-24. Its continued presence in Save For Web & Devices is probably just the result of someone at Adobe forgetting to delete it.

As you choose different file formats and adjust their various options, the preview window on the left shows you the results of your alterations in real time. That is, it shows them to you if you're viewing the Optimized tab. Notice that at the top of the preview window there are four tabs: Original, the original image exactly as you see it in the normal Photoshop document window; Optimized, showing the result of format and option changes; and 2-Up and 4-Up, each of which arranges multiple views of the document on-screen. While 2-Up lets you compare the optimized to the original to check for quality degradation, 4-Up lets you compare three separate sets of optimized image options to the original (see Figure 5.16). Click within each pane of the 4-Up tab to change settings for that preview.

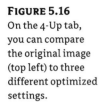

FIGURE 5.16
On the 4-Up tab, you can compare the original image (top left) to three different optimized settings.

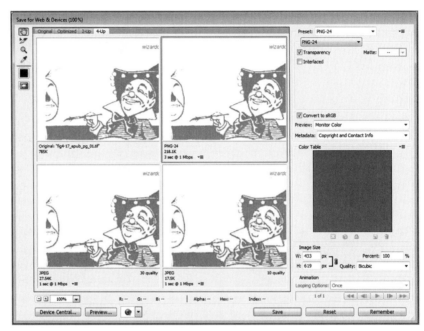

Also of note is the bottom left of Save For Web & Devices. As you change options, the bottom left of the preview window shows the file size of the image that would result with your current settings. In the 4-Up pane, each preview pane contains its own file size.

TIP Ignore the Device Central (if you have it) and Preview buttons as well as the drop-down to the right of the Preview button, because they aren't relevant to this discussion.

Once you have your image exactly the way you want it in your ebook, click Save to save the image. You can then place it into InDesign.

SEMI-AUTOMATING IMAGE RESIZING FOR EBOOKS

As promised, in the next section ("Fully Automating Image Resizing for Ebooks"), I'm going to show you how to resize only one image and never have to do it again by hand—as long as you're using the same width (or height). But that section is predicated on this one. Before you can fully automate, you have to semi-automate.

1. Once again in Photoshop, open an image in need of resizing, but don't actually resize it.

2. Open the Actions panel from Photoshop's Window menu. Photoshop actions are *macros*, or recordings of steps and actions, that can be replayed to automatically execute those steps and actions in the future with little or no manual effort.

3. On the Actions panel's flyout menu (top right), ensure that there is not a check mark beside the Button Mode command at the very top of the menu. If there is a check mark,

click the command to clear that check mark and switch the Action panel out of button mode into normal mode. You can't create or edit actions in button mode (see Figure 5.17).

FIGURE 5.17
The Actions panel in button mode (left) and normal mode (right)

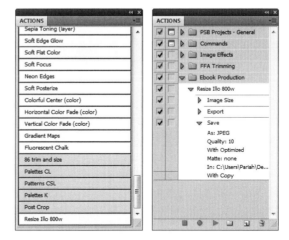

4. At the bottom of the Actions panel, click the Create New Set button (the folder icon) to initiate a new action set. When the New Set dialog appears, call your set Ebook Production, and click OK. You'll now have a new, empty set in the Actions panel.

5. Click the Ebook Production set to highlight it, and then click the New Action button at the bottom of the panel. The New Action button is beside the Create New Set button and looks like a sticky note.

6. In the New Action dialog, ignore the Function Key and Color fields. The Set field should say Ebook Production. Name the action according to the width you've chosen as your ebook image standard. For example, because my chosen standard is 800 pixels wide, I'm naming my action Resize Illo 800w.

Click OK when finished and *halt.*

You might notice at this point that there's a depressed red circle button at the bottom of the Actions panel (Figure 5.18). That's the Record Action button. The fact that it's depressed and red (lit up) indicates that you are now recording an action. Anything you do in Photoshop from this point forward will become part of the macro. Fortunately, actions don't record the time between actions, so don't freak out if it's sitting there recording while you read this. (Mine is recording while I *write* this, which is probably longer than it takes you to read it.)

FIGURE 5.18
When this button is depressed and red, Photoshop is recording an action.

7. With the action recording, select Image ➢ Image Size.

8. Set the options for resizing your image, including the resolution, pixel dimensions, resampling interpolation method, and so on. Once they're correct (double-check them), click OK to both resize the image and record the action of resizing the image.

9. Select File ➢ Save For Web & Devices (or use the Ctrl+Alt+Shift+S/Cmd+Opt+Shift+S keyboard shortcut), and choose the file format and options for the image. Ideally you should be choosing the format and options for the average image in your workflow, not necessarily this particular image. When done, click Save, and in the Save dialog, navigate to—or create—an outbox-type folder where new, ebook-ready images can be regularly dropped. Save the image there.

10. At the bottom of the Actions panel click the gray square, the Stop Playing/Recording button, to stop recording the action. This will save your action containing two steps—the one to resize the image and the other to save it, complete with all the options set in both tasks.

11. Open another image you need to resize for your ebook.

12. In the Actions panel, click the Resize Illo 800w action and then the Play Selection button (the right-facing arrow) at the bottom of the panel. Faster than a three-card monte dealer can shuffle, your image will seemingly resize and save a copy of itself to your outbox folder.

You have now semi-automatically resized the second image. It's semi-automatic because you still had to manually open the image and deliberately run the action. Each subsequent image will need the same semi-automatic treatment of opening, running the action, and then closing the original. Assuming you're happy with the result of the action, let's make it run fully automatically.

FULLY AUTOMATING IMAGE RESIZING FOR EBOOKS

The action you just created is the foundation of several more-automatic-yet-still-semi-automatic and actually-automatic techniques for resizing images singularly or in batches. I'll start with the former and work my way toward less and less human interaction.

Resizing a Batch of Opened Images

To resize a batch of opened images, follow these steps:

1. In Photoshop, open several images that need to be sized for ebooks. You can do that in several ways, but the easiest is to just drag and drop those images atop Photoshop's title bar (Windows) or its icon in the Dock (Mac OS X). All of the images will appear as document window tabs (see Figure 5.19).

FIGURE 5.19
Multiple images opened in Photoshop appear as tabs across the top.

2. On the File menu, select Automate ➢ Batch to open the Batch dialog (see Figure 5.20).

FIGURE 5.20
The Batch dialog, with the options in steps 3 through 5 set

3. In the Set field, choose the new action set you created, Ebook Production, and then select the Resize Illo 800w action from the drop-down menu below it.

4. In the Source field, change it from Folder to Opened Files. Do *not* click OK!

5. Change the Destination drop-down from its default, Save And Close, to None. The action is going to take care of saving copies of the images after resizing, so you don't need to have the Batch function do it. In fact, if you had clicked OK with Save And Close as the destination, the action would have resized the image and made its copy, but then the original, resized as it was, would have been saved in that state, too; each of your opened original images would be permanently resized, with no hope of ever getting them back to their previous sizes and/or resolutions.

6. Now click OK and sit back. Photoshop will run the Resize Illo 800w action on all opened images, creating EPUB-ready copies in your specified outbox folder, and then stop. Then you have to close all those opened images *without saving them* because, if you did save them, you'd overwrite the original images (that's a very bad idea).

Resizing Images in Batch without Opening Them

An even more automated way of doing this would be to not open the files.

1. In Photoshop, with or without any documents open, choose File ➢ Automate ➢ Batch.

2. Select the correct set and action.

3. In the Source drop-down, choose Folder, and navigate to the folder containing the images that need to be processed. If you also want to process images in that folder's subfolders, check Include All Subfolders beneath the Choose button.

4. Change Destination to Folder also, and then navigate to the folder where you'd like all the resized and converted images placed. This can be same outbox folder you created earlier, or it can be somewhere else.

5. Check the option Override Action "Save As" Commands, and click OK to the warning. Now click OK and wait for the destination folder to fill up with the processed copies of your images.

Resizing Images in Batch via Bridge

As you may have guessed from the Bridge option in the Batch dialog's Source menu, you can also execute the script as a batch operation from the asset manager Adobe Bridge. Doing it in Bridge enables you to visually select images instead of brute-forcing an entire folder for conversion and to process images from multiple locations in one shot.

1. Open Adobe Bridge, and navigate to a folder containing images. If this is your first time running Bridge, you may have to wait a few moments while it creates thumbnails of your images. Now, you *could* simply select images in the main Content area of the application and then run the batch action on those selected images, but let's take this a step further.

2. In the top right of Bridge's window is a search field (see Figure 5.21). Enter there some part of the filenames of images you want to convert (for example, **fig5_**). If the images haven't been given consistent filenames corresponding with their usage in the book (tsk, tsk), you can enter a filename mask such as ***.jpg** or ***.tiff** to find all JPEG or TIFF files in the selected folder and its subfolders. Hit Return/Enter and wait while Bridge compiles a list of files.

FIGURE 5.21
The search field in the top-right corner of the Bridge window helps you search for images.

3. When the search is finished, the results will show in the Content pane as thumbnails of images that may not necessarily be in the same folder. Select the ones you want to convert by holding Ctrl/Cmd while clicking each desired image. You can select all images by using Ctrl+A/Cmd+A or a range of images by clicking the first one, holding the Shift key, and then clicking the last; all the intervening images will also be selected.

4. From Bridge's Tools menu, select Photoshop ➢ Batch. Up will pop Photoshop, if it wasn't already running, and Photoshop's Batch dialog. The source will already list Bridge. Now you just have to set the other options and run the batch operation.

Executing the batch is obviously still done by Photoshop, but initiating it in Bridge gives you the opportunity to run the batch on more files or, at the least, select images based on their contents rather than filename or location.

Batch Image Resizing with No Button Pushing

And, finally, there's a way to process images automatically via simple drag and drop with no button pushing or menu navigating (well, after a couple of menu commands and buttons pushed to *make* it drag and drop).

1. In Photoshop, select File ➢ Automate ➢ Create Droplet. Up will pop a dialog almost identical to the Batch dialog (see Figure 5.22).

FIGURE 5.22
Creating a droplet

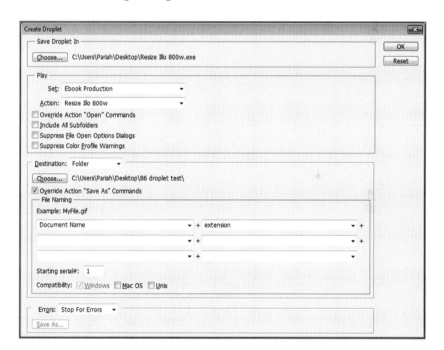

2. Set all the options in the Play section accordingly for your Resize Illo 800w action.

3. In the Destination section, you must choose Folder and then set the location to an outbox folder. Again, check the box beside Override Action "Save As" Command.

4. At the top of the Create Droplet dialog, click the Choose button. Photoshop will then ask you to name and choose the location for the droplet. To make those choices, it might help if I explained exactly what a droplet is.

A *droplet* is effectively a self-contained action—in this case, the action to resize and export images for EPUB compatibility. It's an applet or mini program that sits on your desktop or somewhere else on your system just like a program shortcut or alias (Figure 5.23). To use it, you merely drag one or more images and drop them on the droplet, whereupon Photoshop will run in the background, processing the images and depositing their copies into your specified outbox. From there you simply move the processed images to wherever they should really go. You can even make the outbox a network folder so that processed images are delivered to a teammate automatically instead of to your computer.

FIGURE 5.23
The completed droplet for this action is a standalone applet icon that can be placed on the desktop, put in a folder, or added to the Dock or Quick Launch toolbar.

Resize Illo 800w.exe

The droplet can be placed anywhere you like. Many people like to put them on their desktops, but I use so many that I personally prefer to keep them in my project- and type-of-work-related folder structure. For example, my droplets for resizing and exporting images for EPUB compatibility I keep in my `Projects - Ebooks` folder, while droplets for processing figures for this book sit in the main project folder for this book right beside the `Figures Processed` outbox into which the droplets deposit them.

Select the location to save your droplet, name it, and click Save to finish creating your droplet.

You may now quit Photoshop or continue making additional droplets. For example, you might want to make several actions—and from them, droplets—for creating JPEGs, GIFs, and PNGs—maybe a few for each, all using different options. You might also want to create a droplet for sizing cover images or whatever you need. You can have droplets process a single image or many, an entire folder or several folders, or, heck, even an entire hard drive full of images.

Using Cover Images

Cover images are required elements of ebooks for many ebookstores. That may sound odd if you're an experienced consumer of ebooks because, typically, ebooks open onto their first pages, not their covers. Covers are shown in a number of other locations throughout ebookstores and ereading devices, however. Consequently, ebooks distributed through the major ebookstores must have cover images.

Some ebookstores are lenient with their cover image dimensions, and others are strict. As a matter of course, it's best to design one cover that meets all the stores' requirements rather than produce multiple editions of the cover and thus the entire ebook. The size to use is 600 pixels wide by 800 pixels deep or tall. That's the standard 800 × 600-pixel measurement again, but deliberately rotated for the way book covers are presented on ereaders, that being portrait mode.

When you consider what normally goes on a printed book cover, particularly for a technical book like this one, dimensions of 600 × 800 are pretty paltry. For example, a technical book will have a title, possibly a subtitle, the name of the author(s), the name of the publisher, possibly the publisher's tagline (for example, "Serious Skills" for Sybex), an illustration, deck and/or cover lines, maybe even a blurb about "Foreword by So-and-So," and, if the book is not in its first edition, perhaps quotes about, or awards won by, previous editions. Now cram all that *legibly* into 600 × 800. You can't. Figure 5.24 shows you this book's print edition cover, then the same cover scaled to relative ebook dimensions.

FIGURE 5.24
This book's print edition cover (a) and the same cover squished into ebook dimensions (b)

Ebook covers are different animals than print covers. You cannot put all the same content on them and expect the digital version to be legible. Therefore, you have to approach ebook cover design not as a conversion process but as a completely new design task. Design the ebook cover separately from the print book cover. Of course, use the same imagery if you can, but if you can't, look for smaller-form alternatives. For example, if the cover image of the printed book is a painting of a forest with a dozen people visible in between the trees, try a cropped version depicting one or two people between the trees or even a close-up on one face beside a tree trunk. Or consider a separate illustration commissioned specifically for the smaller display area.

You'll also likely have to cut down the cover text. Work with your marketing department on this task. The purpose of an ebook's cover image is to sell the book in ebookstores. While it would be nice to have the publisher's name and tagline on the cover, is that absolutely necessary to make the sale? Could it work with just the iconic version of the publisher's logo? Are cover lines more important than the cover illustration; is it worth it to cut into that illustration for the cover lines? Can you use one cover line instead of the print edition's three? Approach the design process with those types of questions, evaluating the relative importance of every cover element anew specifically for the ebook medium.

Once you've designed a cover image, here's how to use it:

1. In your ebook's INDD document, place the cover image as the first page of the publication.

2. Select File ➤ Export, and begin exporting your EPUB.

3. On the General pane of EPUB Export Options, select Rasterize First Page from the Cover drop-down field, and then finish the export (Figure 5.25).

FIGURE 5.25
Choosing a cover option in EPUB Export Options

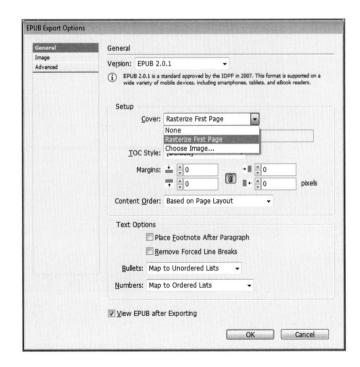

The Cover field offers two additional choices: None and Choose Image. None, obviously, omits a cover image entirely. Choose Image allows you to browse for a cover image and use it, which means you don't need to place it as the first page of the publication.

Including Native InDesign Artwork

Exporting to EPUB does not include graphical elements drawn directly in InDesign, elements such as rules, paths drawn with the Pen tool, shapes like rectangles and ellipses, decorative frames without text or imagery inside them, type on a path object (the type exports but as standard inline text), or even many vector objects copied and pasted from Illustrator. Look to Figure 5.26; by default, most of those elements will not export—at least, not as you see them there. The text from the map callouts (top) will export, but they won't be associated with the image. Similarly, the text from the Type On A Path object (on the lower left) will export, but will do so as normal text, not in the shape of the house. The rule (on the lower right) won't export at all.

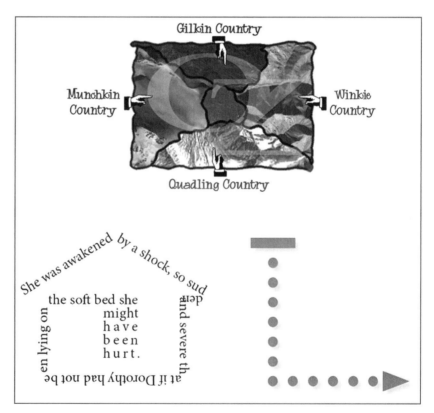

In some cases, this behavior is ideal—you don't want native objects like print-edition-only decorative page elements exporting to ebook. In other cases, however, you do want those objects to come through. The solution is once again Object Export Options. Just select the native object and activate Custom Rasterization in Object Export Options (Figure 5.27). Upon export to EPUB (and HTML), the native objects will be converted to raster-based JPEGs, GIFs, or PNGs, according to the options you choose. At all times, they'll remain editable native vector objects in InDesign, however, so you can always work on them further.

FIGURE 5.27
Using the Object
Export Options'
Custom Raster-
ization options
allows even native
InDesign objects to
export as images.

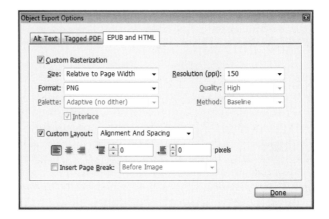

TIP When you add all unassigned content to the Articles panel, InDesign automatically sets native vector objects to rasterize and export to EPUB. Of course, InDesign chooses the format and options for the objects. You can change them individually via Object Export Options and remove them from the Articles panel.

While you're setting the export options, remember to also use the Alt Text tab to fill in the image ALT text. This is especially important in this case because rasterizing a caption means it is no longer searchable text; the ALT text, however, is searchable along with the main book text.

Captioning Images

As you probably noticed with your quick EPUB exports in Chapter 4, captions don't always stay with their images. Sometimes captions appear above or below their images when the caption and the image are separate from the main story, and sometimes they wind up pages apart.

Grouping a caption text frame with the image it accompanies doesn't do much to help. However, grouping them and then anchoring the group into the text does keep them together on about half of the ereaders out there. The other half? Well…

FORGET PHOTOSHOP FOR COMBINING IMAGES AND CAPTIONS

If you've created ebooks containing images and captions with versions of InDesign prior to CS5.5, you're probably familiar with the Photoshop method of combining images and captions (you might have even gotten the method from me, because I've written about it for a couple of magazines). That method entails making the captions *part of* the images they accompany so that the whole thing—image and caption and/or photo credit—is rasterized and thus a simple placed image in InDesign and a solid image in the EPUB. That method is no longer needed, thankfully.

Click your left and right mouse buttons together three times while repeating, "There's no place like InDesign." Say it with me now: *"There's no place like InDesign. There's no place like InDesign. There's no place like InDesign...."*

Making Captions and Images Stick Together

Captions and their images can now be made to stay together directly in InDesign. Let's give it a try.

1. Open the `wizardofoz_print_ch4.indd` layout from Chapter 4's lesson files.

2. On the third page (page 63 in the Pages panel), note the full-page illustration and its caption. You need those to stick together, so select both with the black arrow Selection tool.

3. Group them, either by choosing Object ➢ Group or by using the keyboard shortcut Ctrl+G/Cmd+G.

4. Anchor the group into the text where it should appear. Otherwise, during export, the illustration (and caption) will appear after the entire text of the chapter.

5. With the group still selected, choose Object ➢ Object Export Options, and go to the EPUB And HTML tab.

6. Enable the Custom Rasterization check box, which is the secret to the whole process. That one little check box tells InDesign to rasterize the group, making the caption part of the image, when it exports to EPUB (and HTML). The objects will remain separate, an editable pair of graphic and text frames, within InDesign, but they will combine on export.

7. Now set your desired options for the output graphic format and quality and the layout.

8. Click Done, and run a quick EPUB export. Ta-da! The caption is now part of the image in the EPUB and thus always where it should be!

That's much easier than combining caption and image in Photoshop or Illustrator.

If the output quality of the text looks less than ideal, remember that computer-based ereader software often shows poorer-quality images (and rasterized text) than the average device on which the ebook will be consumed. If you're worried about the quality of the output, send the test EPUB to your ereader, tablet, or other device to proof it as readers will see it.

Using Live Captions

Introduced in InDesign CS5, Live Captions are semi-automatically generated text frames that can expose the metadata contained within images. For example, a common image metadata field is Description, which is often the same text you would use as a caption. InDesign can be told to use the Description field text as a visible, exportable caption, and it can keep that caption in sync with any changes to the Description field metadata. Similarly, Live Caption objects can be created for photo credits, copyrights, location data, and just about any kind of information you might want to store and display about an image. Thus, Live Caption objects can dramatically increase the efficiency of captioning and labeling images, particularly if you're dealing with a large number of images.

Viewing and Editing Image Metadata

First I'll cover how to view and edit image metadata. Open Adobe Bridge or another digital asset manager. Because Bridge is installed automatically with InDesign, as well as Photoshop and a number of other standalone CS applications, and as part of the Creative Suite, I'll use Bridge to explain this process. In my work, I use Bridge only about 25 percent of the time, relying on more robust digital asset management applications most of the time.

1. In Bridge, navigate to and select one image. If you don't have one readily available or simply want to see one with metadata already filled in, navigate to the Chapter 5 Lesson Files folder where you'll find oz_ch4_02.tif, the full-page illustration on page 3 of wizardofoz_print_ch4.indd.

2. On the right side of the Bridge window, you should see the Metadata panel. If not, show it by choosing Metadata from the Window menu. Select the image to see the metadata in the IPTC Core section populate (see Figure 5.28).

FIGURE 5.28
The metadata for the full-page illustration as shown in Bridge

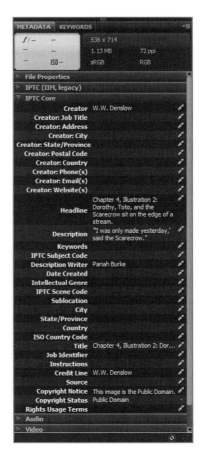

You can see that I've already filled the Creator, Headline, Description, Description Writer, Title, Credit Line, Copyright Notice, and Copyright Status fields.

3. To change any of that information or to add data to an empty field, click inside the field on the Metadata panel, or click the pencil icon beside the field. Give it a try with the Keywords metadata field. You'll know you're editing when the field turns white (see Figure 5.29).

FIGURE 5.29
When editing a document's metadata, all the fields turn white.

4. Now enter comma-separated keywords for the illustration. In this case, enter **Dorothy, Toto, Scarecrow**. Keywords make the images easier to find and sort in Bridge or other digital asset managers.

5. When you've finished entering keywords and editing any other fields, click the image or in an empty area of the Content pane on the left. You'll be prompted to choose Apply or Don't Apply for the changes to the metadata. Of course, you want Apply, which will write your metadata alterations into the image file. You've now edited the image metadata.

You can also edit the metadata of more than one image at a time to, for instance, add a copyright notice or creator credit to a folder or entire drive full of images. Just select them all and edit the appropriate fields in the Metadata panel. When you apply those changes, Bridge will update all the images' metadata—which may take a while.

Another way to edit the metadata of an image is to right-click the image and choose File Info from the context-sensitive pop-up menu. That will open the XMP dialog, which shows you the same metadata fields but arranged differently (Figure 5.30). Note that it's easier to use the Metadata panel when working with multiple images.

FIGURE 5.30
Editing an image's metadata in the XMP dialog

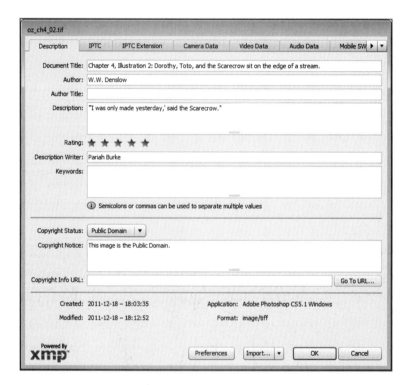

If any of those images were already placed in InDesign, you'll need to update them via the Links panel in order to have InDesign use the new data.

Creating a Caption from Metadata

Now that you know how to add and edit image metadata, you'll learn what you can do with it in InDesign.

1. In InDesign, place oz_ch4_02.tif into a document. It can be a new document or your own edition of *The Wonderful Wizard of Oz*.

2. Right-click the image and choose Captions ➢ Caption Setup from that context-sensitive menu. If you prefer, you can also access the Captions submenu and Caption Setup command from the Object menu. Up will pop the Caption Setup dialog (see Figure 5.31).

FIGURE 5.31
The Caption Setup dialog

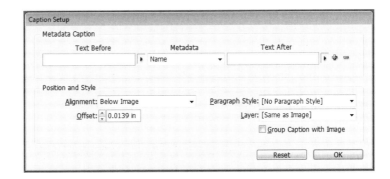

3. Leave the Text Before and Text After fields blank, but change the Metadata drop-down field to Description, which is roughly halfway down the nonalphabetically ordered list of metadata fields. Leave all other options at their defaults, and click OK. Nothing will happen.

4. Right-click the image again (or use the Object menu again), and open the Captions submenu. Notice that now you have three available choices: Caption Setup, to make changes to the setup we just finished configuring; Generate Live Caption; and Generate Static Caption. I'll talk about the last shortly. For now, choose Generate Live Caption. Instantly a new text frame will appear beneath the illustration, containing its caption (see Figure 5.32).

FIGURE 5.32
The Live Caption object exposes the metadata Description field as the image's caption.

5. Return to Bridge, and edit the image's Description field. Change it so that it reads as follows, including all quotes:

```
"'I was only made yesterday,' said the Scarecrow."
```

Apply the change in Bridge, and return to InDesign.

6. InDesign will alert you via a yellow caution sign on the Links panel and on the image frame itself that the image has been updated outside of InDesign. Click once directly on the yellow caution sign in the top-left corner of the graphic frame to update the link (Links panel not necessary). *Voila*! The caption instantly and automatically changes to reflect the new metadata. That's a Live Caption! (You'll make it look pretty shortly.)

Creating an Illustration or Photo Credit Caption Object

Let's try that again. This time you'll create a second Live Caption object to hold the illustration credit (or photo credit for photographs).

1. Once again, get to Caption Setup by one of the two means. You don't really need to have an image selected at this point or even have images in the document, because any changes to Caption Setup are document-wide. Still, it can be beneficial to get in the habit of working with Live Captions only when an image is selected.

2. In Caption Setup, type into the Text Before field **Illustration By:** (see Figure 5.33). This is static text that will precede the metadata pulled in from the file.

FIGURE 5.33
My illustration credit Live Caption setup, fully filled out

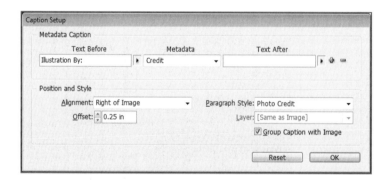

3. Set the Metadata field to Credit, which is just above where you found Description last time. Note that the Credit field listed here corresponds to the Creator field visible in Bridge's Metadata panel. (See the sidebar "Live Captions In Depth" for the location of a complete explanation of that discrepancy and everything else to do with Live Captions.)

LIVE CAPTIONS IN DEPTH

For more detail on the ways Live Caption can help your workflow, including techniques for reusing Live Caption objects for easy, pain-free application and ways to get around its built-in frustrations, pick up a copy of *Mastering InDesign CS5*, in which I devote 11 pages in Chapter 5 to all the ins and outs. And, don't let the "CS5" worry you; Live Captions haven't changed at all since CS5. Find out more about the book here: http://abbrv.it/Mastering.

---

4. Leave the Text After field blank, but focus on the Position And Style section. The Alignment field lets you choose where the Live Caption text frame is generated in relation to the image. Choose Right Of Image, which will rotate the caption object to run up the right edge of the image.

5. If you have a particular paragraph style you'd like to use for the illustration credit, choose it from the drop-down menu to the right. Live Caption objects can use any text formatting, including spacing before and after, indents, paragraph rules, and anything else that can be defined in a paragraph style.

   Leave the Layer field set to Same As Image. That field allows you to place Live Caption text frames on separate layers, which can be quite convenient for print work, but for EPUB export you need the caption and its image to stay together. In fact, to facilitate that, check the option Group Caption With Image. That will automatically group the two objects together, doing half the work needed to set the image and caption(s) to rasterize together upon export to EPUB. Click OK.

6. Again, nothing will happen. So, select the image and choose Caption ➤ Generate Live Caption to actually create the illustration credit. Ta-da! Instant illustration credit (see Figure 5.34)!

FIGURE 5.34
The illustration credit becomes the second Live Caption object attached to the same image.

You can put up to four Live Caption objects on any one image—well, technically you can have more than four, but there are only four sides from which to choose, thus more than four means some overlap others.

WRAPPING CAPTIONS

If the metadata you want to display is longer than a single line at the font size chosen, you have to do something slightly different. In the Live Caption object, the entire metadata field value is treated like a single character, which means it won't wrap across lines. If you need wrapping, choose Generate Static Caption from the Caption menu. That will create a caption that does wrap, that is real text, but that won't update to match changes in the image's actual metadata.

The trick to Live Captions is that a Live Caption object must *touch* the image it describes. That's why, when Live Captions are generated, their text frames abut the graphic frames of their images. If the text itself is too close to the frame, don't move the frame. Instead, increase the value of the Offset field in the Caption Setup dialog.

If you moved the Live Caption frame away from the image so that it didn't touch it, the metadata would be replaced with "<No intersecting link>." That means the Live Caption isn't touching anything with metadata it can use. Of course, that does suggest the Live Caption object isn't limited to the image for which it was created. It's not. If you move that same Live Caption frame so that it touches a different image or if you relink oz_ch4_02.tif to a different graphic, the Live Caption will update to reflect the metadata contained in *that* image's Description or Creator field. In other words, you can create just a single Live Caption object, copy it, and then paste it onto all the other images in your document; there's no need to individually select all the images and then use menu commands to generate a Live Caption anew. For an even more convenient bulk–Live Caption method, see the sidebar "Aspirin-Free Workflow: Live-Caption All Images at Once."

Static Captions

Speaking of generating, I didn't talk about the Create Static Caption option. It will create a "dumb," or nondynamic, caption text frame that will *not* update with changes to an image's metadata or, if moved, touch a different image. Static captions are generated once, as normal text, and then divorced from the Live Caption process. This is useful if you know the metadata will never change or if you want to move the caption frames away from the images they describe.

ASPIRIN-FREE WORKFLOW: LIVE-CAPTION ALL IMAGES AT ONCE

If you have many images requiring captions, save yourself a headache by creating Live Caption objects on them *all* in one step. Instead of right-clicking an individual image, go to the Links panel and highlight its entries for all the images requiring captions, photo credits, or other live or static caption objects. Now right-click one of those Links panel items. On the context-sensitive menu, you'll find a Captions submenu, complete with the commands Generate Live Captions, Generate Static Captions, and Caption Setup. Executing one of the former pair of commands will generate a caption on all the highlighted objects in one fell swoop.

TIP   A problem since InDesign CS5 is that Live Captions, once created, cannot be altered via Caption Setup. Instead, the existing caption object(s) must be deleted and a new one(s) generated. Check *Mastering InDesign CS5* for the details of that and other Live Caption strengths and weaknesses, as well as workarounds.

Adding Audio and Video to Ebooks

You might think that it's difficult to include audio and video in ebooks, but it's surprisingly easy, especially with InDesign. In fact, there's a lot more to preparing and using static image graphics than there is to preparing and using audio and video files.

Ebook Audio and Video Formats

Ereading devices that support audio and video all support the same two standard formats (and may support others). Ergo, you should always use these two standards. For audio, the standard is MP3; that's right—common, everyday, all-over-your-iPod MP3s. For video, the standard format is the easy-to-produce-but-complicated-sounding H.264 video with AAC audio compression, otherwise known as MPEG4 M4V video, the same format you'll find on YouTube.

CONVERTING AUDIO FORMATS

If you've been producing audio or video content for a while or are buying the content from a stock media agency, it's possible you may receive audio that isn't in MP3 format and, even more likely, video in something other than H.264/AAC MPEG4. There are numerous methods for converting audio and video from one format to another. Any modern video-editing application can save to H.264, and any decent-quality audio editor can create MP3. If you're having content created, have it delivered to you in those formats. However, if you already have audio or video content in a different format, then you need to use another free utility that was installed with InDesign, Photoshop, and/or the Creative Suite: Adobe Media Encoder.

Adobe Media Encoder's entire *raison d'être* is to convert multimedia files—from one format to another or from one size or quality to another. The user interface is very simple, as you can see in Figure 5.35. (The interface of Adobe Media Encoder in CS5.5 or earlier is arranged differently, but has all the same controls.) I'll run through using the CS6 version on one of this chapter's lesson files.

TIP   Audio and video file size is crucial because EPUBs cannot be larger than 2GB.

1. In Adobe Media Encoder, click the plus sign in the top-left corner of the Queue pane. You'll then be prompted to open a file. Navigate to where you saved the Chapter 5 lesson files, and open wizardofoz_04_baum_64kb.wav. The file will be added to the queue list.

FIGURE 5.35
Adobe Media
Encoder

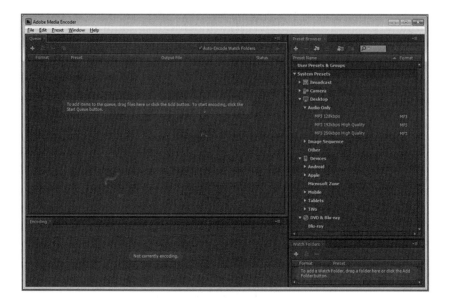

2. Underneath the filename in the queue you should see a second line, one with orange text. If not, click the expansion arrow beside the filename. Regardless of whatever is displayed on that second line in the Format column, click the arrow in that column. From the pop-up menu, choose MP3 à la Figure 5.36.

FIGURE 5.36
Choosing the con-
vert-to format for
the WAV audio file

3. Changing the format changes the preset as well. In the Preset column, ensure that the format is MP3 128kbps.

4. In the Output File column, you should see the same path from which you opened the file, but with an .mp3 file extension instead of .wav. If not, click the path, and navigate to where you would like to save the converted audio file. Your settings should look like those in Figure 5.37.

5. In the top right of the Queue window, click the green playlike button, the Start Queue button. Adobe Media Encoder will begin converting the sound file. When it's finished, it will play a sound, and the Encoding pane will return to listing "Not currently encoding."

You have now converted the old-tech, incompatible WAV audio file to a modern-format, EPUB-ready MP3. Unfortunately, you also made an MP3 with double the quality of the original recording—note that you couldn't tell that from the WAV file other than by the _64kb in its file-name. You see, audio-file quality is called *bit rate*. Table 5.1 lists the available bit rates and defines each one's approximate quality.

TABLE 5.1: Common MP3 bit rates and quality

BIT RATE	QUALITY
32 kbps	1980s landline telephone quality
64 kbps	AM radio/spoken word quality
96 kbps	High-range spoken word quality
128 kbps	FM radio quality
160 kbps	Medium quality
192 kbps	Near CD quality
256 kbps	CD quality
320 kbps	High-def CD quality
kbps = kilobits per second	

Because `wizardofoz_04_baum_64kb.wav` is spoken word—a public-domain reading of the text in *The Wonderful Wizard of Oz*'s Chapter 4, "The Road Through the Forest"—it doesn't need to be 128 kbps. The 128 kbps MP3 came out to be roughly 7.5 MB, which is twice the quality and file size it really needs to be for the content of the recording (the WAV of the same audio at half the quality was a whopping 42 MB!). Ideally, the recording should be 64 kbps; it might even sound decent at 32 kbps. Still, we'll stick with 64 kbps.

Unfortunately, Adobe Media Encoder doesn't include a preset for anything less than 128 kbps. No worries; it's easy to create one.

1. In Adobe Media Encoder, in the Preset Browser pane, click the New Preset plus-sign button. Up will pop the Preset Settings New Preset dialog (see Figure 5.38).

FIGURE 5.38
Creating a new audio preset for lower-quality MP3 sound files

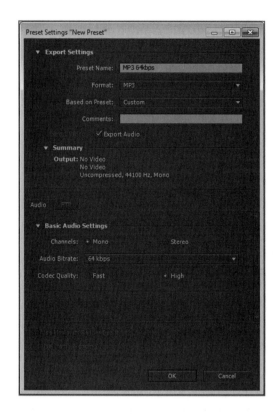

2. Name your preset. A name like MP3 64kbps would work well.

3. Set Format to MP3 and change Based On Preset to New Preset. Feel free to enter comments if you want. The comments are text that shows when the preset is examined. So, for instance, you could enter **creating because a book told me to**, and then you'd know in the future why you created the preset.

4. On the Audio tab at the bottom, change Audio Bitrate to 64 kbps—note that you have lots of choices, should you ever want to make even smaller MP3 files or need ones of higher quality than the top out-of-the-box preset of 256 kbps.

   You have two other choices to make in this section: Channels and Codec Quality.

5. Channels is rather self-explanatory; one option puts your audio in stereo, and the other makes it mono so that the same audio comes out of both speakers. For music, always use Stereo—unless the source music was already in mono. For spoken word, however, Mono just might do the trick, and it will further reduce the resultant file size significantly. Set this as appropriate for your file.

6. Codec Quality offers you a simple choice: Convert the file fast and risk slight deviations in quality, or ensure the quality is high and consistent regardless of the fact that conversion will take longer. I usually go with High, but choose whichever suits you.

7. Click OK to create your new preset.

Your new preset will now be available from the Preset column on the Queue tab when converting files. Go ahead and re-convert the `wizardofoz_04_baum_64kb.wav` file using your new 64 kbps preset. The file size should top out around 3.7 MB. The proof, of course, is in the pudding, so give a listen to both the 128 and 64 kbps versions and see which you like better. They should sound about the same, since the original file from which I created the WAV was actually a 64 kbps MP3 (that original is also in the `Lesson Files` folder).

CONVERTING VIDEO FORMATS

Video can be converted the same way as audio formats.

1. Still in Adobe Media Encoder, add `folgers_13_512kb.mov` to the queue.

2. Set its format to H.264, click the down arrow in the Preset column, and then pick your jaw up off the floor.

   Yes, there are many, many options there, including options for a number of phones and tablets, YouTube and Vimeo, Apple TV and TiVO, HD TV, and the older television standards of NTSC and PAL (see Figure 5.39). Don't worry about that dizzying array of options. I'll explain your choices in a minute. For now, select Android Phone – 360p 29.97.

3. Set the output location and run the conversion. You'll end up with a 4.7 MB MP4 file ready for ebooks.

FIGURE 5.39
Converting a Quick-Time MOV movie to EPUB-ready H.264

When converting video for ebooks, file size is very important because, even at 360p, one minute of video is about 4.5 MB, give or take a few hundred thousand kilobytes. You do *not* want to embed 720p or 1080p (television-size) HD-quality video in ebooks, even for tablets, because the resulting ebooks will be huge and potentially unusable (again, there's that 2 GB limit). Thus, the preset you typically need for video embedded in ebooks is either Android Phone – 360p 29.97, which will create a movie that is 360 pixels wide with 29.97 frames running per second (the standard for television and film), or Android Phone & Tablet – 480p 29.97, which will create a 480-pixel-wide video with the same frames per second. There are similar options beginning with Apple TV, iPad, iPhone, and so on, so feel free to use those options if the notion of Android bothers you; they're pretty much the same.

If you right-click the name of the preset in the Preset column before converting and then choose Export Settings, you can see exactly which video and audio settings will be applied to your converted video, and you can make some rather useful changes to the output video. The main area of the Export Settings screen is a pair of preview tabs that let you watch and examine the video in its original form on the Source pane and with export settings and filters applied on the Output pane (see Figure 5.40).

FIGURE 5.40
Examining the export settings of the Android Phone – 360p 29.97 preset

AUTOMATING AUDIO AND VIDEO CONVERSION

If you have many audio and/or video files to convert, you can do them all at once by dragging and dropping them into the Adobe Media Encoder Queue pane. A more efficient way, however, is to create a watch folder. Any file dropped in a watch folder will be automatically queued for conversion by Adobe Media Encoder, no manual action required. Follow these steps to create a watch folder:

1. In the Watch Folders pane (bottom right) of Adobe Media Encoder, click the plus sign, whereupon you'll be asked to select (or make) a folder to watch. This folder will serve as the inbox; any media dropped into it will be converted with the preset you choose next and saved to an output folder you choose. The watch folder can be on your computer or a network drive, as can the output folder, making it easy for an entire workgroup to convert files automatically through a single copy of Adobe Media Encoder running on one machine, assuming Adobe's end user licensing agreement (EULA) allows for this as interpreted by your company's compliance or legal department.

   Pick (or create) your watch folder for audio that you want to make 64 kbps MP3 (or whichever preset you intend to use). When you click OK, that folder will be added to the Watch Folders pane (Figure 5.41).

FIGURE 5.41
My Watch Folders pane after adding an inbox for audio I wanted automatically converted

2. Set the format, preset, and then output folder for converted files. Note that every file in a watch folder, except those already in the output format, will be converted to the same format. Therefore, you need to have a separate watch folder for each desired output format and/or preset.

3. Drop one or more files into your new watch folder and wait a moment. Adobe Media Encoder will automatically begin converting whatever files are in the folder, saving converted files to the output folder, and removing the originals—which is why you need to *copy*, not move, original-format media into the watch folder.

4. Repeat the first three steps as many times as needed to set up watch folders for each of your desired output format and preset combinations. As long as Adobe Media Encoder is running, it will automatically convert any media dropped into those watch folders.

   To remove a watch folder, select it in the list and then click the minus sign above the list.

ASPIRIN-FREE WORKFLOW: CONSTANT CONVERSIONS

If you or your department is constantly working with audio and video for producing ebooks, digital magazines, other epublications, or any type of project, it might behoove you to run Adobe Media Encoder with watch folders constantly. In that case, consider installing Adobe Media Encoder on a server or an otherwise unused network-connected computer and making Adobe Media Encoder automatically run when that system starts up. That way, you'll have always-ready watch folders to which you and your colleagues can copy to-be-converted media without having to use your own system resources for running Adobe Media Encoder.

RATIOS AND DIMENSIONS FOR DIGITAL PUBLICATIONS

I'd like to say a few words about the "wide-screen" video options. Remember when I noted that the average ereading device, including tablets and smartphones, uses a 4:3 aspect ratio? That's the aspect ratio of standard, non-HD, non-wide-screen television—y'know, the TV you had as a kid. What you probably watch the Super Bowl or the season finale of *American Idol* on is wide-screen, which is actually an aspect ratio of 16:9. Even the iPhone, which *records* wide-screen video, does not actually *have* a wide-screen, er, screen; its display ratio is 3:2. Of course, you can play wide-screen video on just about any of these devices, but when you do, they often show black bars at the top and bottom of the screen—*letterboxing*—because the 16:9 aspect ratio of the film doesn't fit without letterboxing on the 4:3 ratio screen. In other words, unless you start with wide-screen video, don't use a wide-screen preset for conversion. And, even if you do have wide-screen video, you might consider having its sides chopped off to convert it to 4:3—that is, if there isn't any important action or information on those sides. Doing so will not only remove the letterboxing if the video is played full-screen but will also cut the video file size.

Another option, which might strike you as totally off the wall but is in fact quite practical and gaining in popularity, is what we call *tall-screen video* or *vertical video* (Figure 5.42), which is taller than it is wide, or portrait orientation. Typical video is landscape-oriented, wider than it is tall, formatted for movie theater screens, television screens, and other common video playback devices. Books, however, are not landscape oriented; the format of books is nearly always portrait—whether in print or digital form. This presents a unique challenge when combining the two mediums. You can easily create full-page illustrations and graphics, which fill the portrait-mode page in ebooks, but when it comes time to include video, you're stuck with one that may reach across the page but will never fill it vertically. Moreover, if the video is played in the optional full-screen mode, the device must be rotated by the reader in order to watch the film. Enter tall-screen video.

Many ebook creators are now shooting video in portrait mode—often by simply rotating the camera 90 degrees—and inserting that into ebooks as full-page video without black boxes on the top and bottom and without forcing readers to rotate their devices in order to watch the video full-screen. In other words, instead of a 16:9 or 4:3 ratio, the video is displayed in a 9:16 or 3:4 ratio. It's a radical idea and one that suits ebook publishing perfectly.

FIGURE 5.42
Tall-screen video
(3:4 aspect ratio)

Note that most video-editing programs are still accustomed to landscape-mode video, though in all the better ones you can rotate the entire video through the video project settings or somewhere else in the program. Check your video-editing application's documentation for how to change rotation, width and height, or aspect ratio. Unfortunately, you'll have to shoot and/ or edit the video to be vertical; you can't simply rotate a landscape mode video in InDesign and expect it to play for users tall-screen.

Inserting Audio

Once your audio is in MP3 format, adding it to an ebook is, surprisingly, no more difficult than adding an image, and in some ways, it's easier. Let's do it.

1. In InDesign, choose File ➤ Place, select an MP3 file, and then place it into the document—on the page or out on the pasteboard. You're more than welcome to use `wizardofoz_04_baum_64kb.mp3`.

2. Just as with an image, click and drag the blue box in the media frame's top-right corner (Figure 5.43) to a location in the text to anchor the audio to that point. If you're inserting audio that doesn't connect to a specific portion of text—for instance, if you want background music or read-along audio—anchor it to the top of the first page, ahead of any text.

FIGURE 5.43
Placing an audio file

3. Export to EPUB and try it. In an ereader that supports embedded audio, you should see a small sound controller (see Figure 5.44). Tap the Play button to start the audio playing.

FIGURE 5.44
An audio control-
ler appears in the
ebook when viewed
in a compatible
ereader—in this
case, iBooks on an
iPad.

You can use a few options to set the behavior of your audio. In addition to letting you pre-view your audio file directly in InDesign, the Media panel (Window ➢ Interactive ➢ Media) offers several options (see Figure 5.45).

FIGURE 5.45
The Media panel
when a placed
sound file is
selected

Play On Page Load, if enabled, will begin playing the audio file as soon as it comes on-screen in the ereader. Automatically playing a sound file can be quite useful for several types of audio, such as atmospheric music or sound effects, narration of the text, speech that introduces the text or imagery, and, in the case of children's books, just about any kind of experience-enrichment audio.

Stop On Page Turn will terminate playback as soon as the reader moves to the next page or screen. Enabling this option is useful if the audio has no relevance beyond the text immediately surrounding it. Some would argue that most audio should be set to cease playing when the reader leaves the page, but I disagree. The reader will see a player control and can stop the audio playback at any time—on the initial page—with the controller. Many readers, in my experience, appreciate the ability to listen to a lecture, interview, cultural recording, or other types of audio while continuing to read past the point where the recording begins.

Loop will rewind the audio, playing it in a continuous loop, without cessation. There is no way in InDesign to specify a certain number of repetitions before the audio stops playing. Finally, you have the Poster drop-down field. It has no relevance at present to ebooks. When adding audio files to PDF, Flash SWF, interactive magazines, and other formats, however, it's possible to choose a *poster*, which is an image to visually represent the audio file. Posters are particularly important for user-activated playback when controllers are not automatically shown, such as in the digital magazine format. A poster—whether a custom image or the "standard" speaker icon—communicates to the reader that tapping that location will initiate audio playback. In ebooks, however, posters are simply not supported at this time. In fact, the use of a poster sometimes *replaces the actual audio* on some devices and software versions, resulting in a picture that does not activate the embedded audio when tapped. The best practice for ebooks is to leave the Poster field set to None; devices will automatically show tiny controllers to help readers initiate and control playback.

Including Video

The method of inserting, and the options for controlling, video are very similar to those of audio, except that video *does* work with posters.

1. In InDesign, use File ➢ Place to locate and place a video. Feel free to use folgers_13_512kb.mp4, a public-domain commercial from the 1950s, as shown in Figure 5.46 (the classic *The Wizard of Oz* film is not public domain, unfortunately).

FIGURE 5.46
The video placed into InDesign

2. Once the video is placed and its frame shown, click and drag the blue box into the main story to anchor the video to a place in the text.

3. In the Media panel (Window ➤ Interactive ➤ Media), preview the video at the top, using the Play/Pause button to ensure it's the video you want. Then, below the previewer, set your options (discussed in a moment).

4. Export to EPUB and try it. Within ereaders that support video, you'll see the video appear as a still image; tap it to start playing the video.

The following options are available to you in the Media panel, as shown in Figure 5.47.

FIGURE 5.47
When a video object is selected, the options in the Media panel are different from those available with audio objects.

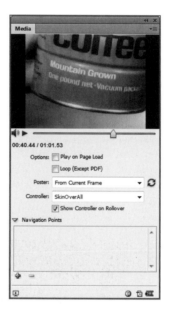

Play On Page Load   Activating this control automatically plays the video when it moves into view in the ereader. The user will not have to initiate playback manually.

Loop   In all media except PDF, activating this option will cause the video to replay continuously until the page is turned.

Poster   A static image poster will be shown before the video plays or if the video is stopped. By default, InDesign assigns the first frame of the video as the poster, though you aren't stuck with that. Using the preview slider at the top of the panel, you may advance to any spot in the film, pause, choose From Current Frame from the Poster drop-down menu, and then click the Refresh button to the right of the field to make the current frame the movie's poster. Alternatively, you may use the Standard option, which displays a simple filmstrip icon, or Choose Image, through which you can load any external image. See the section "Making Good Video Posters" for more information.

Controller   From this menu, you can choose which types of video controllers appear and when. There are quite a few options, though I typically pick SkinOverAll, which adds all controls (play/pause, fast-forward, rewind, full-screen toggle, caption toggle, and so on) on top of the video.

Show Controller On Rollover   When a controller is set to display in the Controller menu above this check box, this option lights up. If checked, it will cause the video controller to hide until and unless the user moves her mouse over the video or taps it once on a touch-screen device. This enables the reader to experience the video without user interface elements, or what is commonly referred to as the *chrome*.

Navigation Points   Navigation points are references to specific frames in a video, enabling you to link to those places rather than always forcing a reader to begin the video at the beginning. Sadly, these don't work in ebooks, so I'll talk more about them later in the book when discussing the formats in which they do work.

Making Good Video Posters

If your video isn't going to play on page load—and, honestly, most of them *shouldn't* unless they're full-page vertical video—then the reader may misinterpret the standard or even a frame poster for a static image. Help the reader identify that the media is video by creating a custom poster with a familiar video device. Think about videos from YouTube, Vimeo, or any video-hosting site, either on those sites or embedded into Facebook or other sites. How is it that you always know that the nonplaying video is, in fact, a video and will play when clicked? Right— the videos have that familiar Play arrow within them (see Figure 5.48). In the absence of player controls or a "tap to play video" caption, which many will ignore anyway (sadly, many people don't read image captions), including that unmistakable arrow on the video poster will make it instantly clear to people that the content is playable.

FIGURE 5.48
A video embedded in a website from YouTube presents the familiar Play button over the video poster. In this case, it's one of my videos from my *Copyright for Creative Professionals* series.

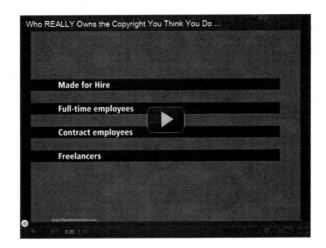

Unfortunately, though creating a Play icon in InDesign is child's play (pun intended), you can't simply stick a vector object atop the video. In many cases, ereaders and other devices and formats (including PDF) place multimedia objects on a higher layer than static page elements. Thus, even if you put a graphic atop a video in InDesign, the video may appear on the top layer, completely hiding that graphic when the electronic publication is viewed.

There are two techniques I commonly employ to show that video is playable and not merely a graphic.

Though this first technique doesn't work with EPUB, it is useful to know about for other media, such as PDFs, digital magazines, and even some fixed-layout ebooks. Simply include the Play symbol (and an optional poster graphic) *behind* the video and give the video no poster whatsoever. The video will be transparent until played, showing the symbol behind it. I use this technique about 20 percent of the time; for the majority, I employ the next method.

For EPUB, and as an alternative for including video in other formats, create a new image to use as the poster for the video. That gives you complete control over the appearance of the poster, including adding symbols to differentiate the video from static imagery.

1. Open the desired video in a media player and pause it on the frame you'd like to use as the poster. You can also just use InDesign's Media panel directly, without loading the video into an external player.

2. Take a screenshot of the current frame of the paused video. On Mac OS X, use the keyboard shortcut Opt+3 to copy the screenshot to the clipboard. On Windows, use the Print Screen button on your keyboard, which is typically located near the Pause/Break key and may be labeled PrtScn, PrSc, or something similar. Pressing the Print Screen button will take a screenshot of your entire screen area, including all monitors. If you like, use Alt+Print Screen (on Windows) or Opt+4 (Mac) to capture only the currently selected window, either the media player or InDesign.

3. Open Photoshop.

4. In Photoshop, go to File ➤ New. The New dialog should automatically choose the Clipboard preset and set the Width and Height fields equal to the size of the monitor or application you captured (see Figure 5.49). It usually does, but if not, manually set the Width and Height fields to at least the size of the monitor you captured, and click OK.

FIGURE 5.49
Photoshop should automatically detect the dimensions of the image on the clipboard, which will be the full screen or the area of the screen you captured.

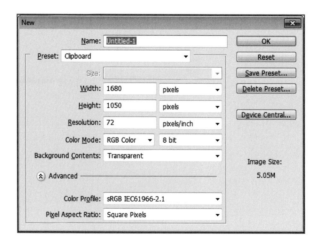

5. Paste the screenshot into the new document with Ctrl+V/Cmd+V. If it doesn't paste, go back to the application playing the video and repeat step 2. Then return to Photoshop and paste.

6. Using whatever means is most appropriate—Crop tool, Canvas Size or Trim commands, Marquee tool and then Crop command, whatever—reduce the Photoshop document to just the video frame.

7. Switch to the Type tool, and click inside the image, right about at the center of the video frame. This creates a new Type layer in Photoshop's Layers panel.

8. Locate a symbol font with an arrow or triangle in it. Perhaps the easiest way to find the right symbol within such a font is back in InDesign using the Glyphs panel (Window Type & Tables ➤ Glyphs), which is shown in Figure 5.50. Use InDesign's Glyphs panel to insert the triangle glyph into a text frame, and then copy the glyph from the text frame and paste it into Photoshop as live text on your newly created Type layer.

FIGURE 5.50

Photoshop's Glyphs panel with the Marlett font selected

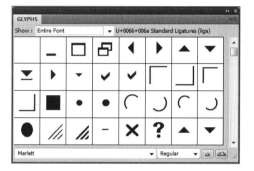

9. Close the Glyphs panel and format the arrow—your Play button—however you see fit. For instance, you'll probably want to adjust its type size, color, opacity, and so on. You may even want to employ Photoshop's layer blending options to make the arrow beveled or embossed, glow or fade, and so on.

10. Save the image from Photoshop as a PSD, TIFF, JPEG, or other raster image, and close Photoshop.

11. In InDesign, use the Media panel's Poster field to choose the image you just created as the poster for your video. Ta-da! You now have a frame from the actual video with a Play button built in (see Figure 5.51). Of course, you can go back to Photoshop and tweak it, especially if you saved it as a PSD.

Before you worry about using a PSD and whether EPUB supports it, remember that, upon export to EPUB, InDesign will automatically convert the poster image to JPEG, PNG, or GIF just like all the other images in the publication.

VIDEO FROM URL

If you've done any video work before or are simply the type to explore panel menus, you may know that InDesign can include online videos by reference using the Video From URL command in the Media panel flyout menu. Alas, that doesn't work with ebooks. That command requires video to be compliant with, and will ultimately use when embedding, Flash Player. You might recall that iOS doesn't allow Flash; neither does the official EPUB file spec.

If you want to include video hosted online, you'll need to add the reference directly in the EPUB code after export from InDesign. You can see how to do that in Chapter 6, "Fine-Tuning EPUBs."

Adding Vector Graphics to Ebooks

Scalable Vector Graphics (SVG) let you do things that raster images can't. For one, a vector is *resolution-independent*, meaning it can be scaled—or zoomed—up or down to infinity without loss of quality. That makes it ideal for detailed illustrations such as maps, floor plans, graphs, and charts that readers may want to interact with in the overview as well as zoomed in for detail. Another big advantage to vector over raster in ebooks is that text contained within SVG images is searchable; thus, if a reader searches the ebook for a term that appears in an SVG image, that SVG is returned as one of the locations for the term. SVG is also accessible, meaning its content can be interpreted by alternative-access devices for people with disabilities, and its file size is generally smaller than a raster image of equivalent creation dimensions and content.

Creating SVG Graphics

In many arenas, SVG is a competitor to Adobe's Flash technology and Microsoft's Silverlight technology; thus, its creation and use are only begrudgingly supported, if at all, by these big software publishers and by other software publishers that market to the same customers. You can create SVG in Adobe Illustrator, but it is, honestly, functionality left over from when Adobe wanted to use SVG to compete with Macromedia's Flash format (in other words, don't look for Illustrator's SVG capabilities to be greatly improved in future versions).

1. In Adobe Illustrator CS2 or newer, create (or open) your vector artwork as normal.

2. From Illustrator's Save, Save As, or Save a Copy As dialog (all on the File menu), choose SVG as the Save As Type or Format and save the artwork.

3. In the SVG Options dialog that appears, choose SVG 1.1 from the SVG Profiles drop-down, SVG from the Type drop-down, and, unless your artwork uses custom fonts, None (Use System Fonts) from the Subsetting drop-down (see Figure 5.52).

FIGURE 5.52

The SVG options when saving to SVG from Illustrator

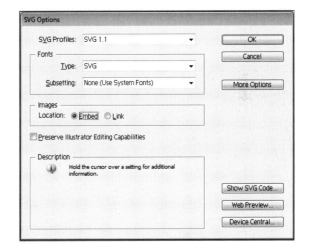

4. If your SVG artwork uses placed or embedded raster images, choose Embed from the Images Location field. Disable Preserve Illustrator Editing Capabilities because it could cause issues with the SVG display in ereaders.

5. Click OK to save the SVG image.

You can also apply various filters and effects to SVG graphics, for instance to give them drop shadows or have them animate in one way or another. Illustrator includes a set of standard (but by no means complete) filters on the Effect ➢ SVG Filters menu. From the same menu, you can also import other and more recent filters.

If you'd rather not use Illustrator, there are alternatives, including Inkscape (`http://inkscape.org`), an open source (read: free) vector editor that builds only in SVG. Note that while Inkscape and programs like it are often easier to learn for vector drawing novices, they can't hold a candle to a professional-grade drawing program like Illustrator in terms of artwork quality and workflow.

Using SVG in InDesign

Now that I've sold you on using SVG, I must regrettably inform you that InDesign can't import or export SVG graphics. I told you that Adobe doesn't much care for SVG. Fortunately, there are two ways around that.

First, you can insert SVG graphics manually within the code of the EPUB after creation. The second method makes it so SVG *does* work within InDesign. You'll need to purchase Scand Ltd.'s SVG Kit for Adobe Creative Suite from `http://svg.scand.com`. Once it is installed, you can then place SVG images into InDesign via the standard File ➤ Place operation, *and* those same images will export as SVG to EPUB during the normal export process. Even InDesign's native effects, such as drop shadow, outer glow, and so on, will apply to the contents of the SVG just as they apply to the contents of text and graphics frames. Moreover, installing the SVG Kit automatically enables SVG support in InCopy and Photoshop, too.

Chapter 6

Fine-Tuning EPUBs

Successful, efficient EPUB production begins in, and centers on, InDesign and the toolset InDesign brings to the business of ebook publishing. However, InDesign isn't the *only* tool you'll need to produce ebooks of the highest quality, maximum compatibility, and utmost reader engagement. At a certain point, you'll need to go *inside* the EPUB to edit and massage the components InDesign can't reach, often working in conjunction with the original files in InDesign to build an ebook that takes fullest advantage of ereader hardware and software to provide an ideal reading experience.

In this chapter, you will learn about the following:

- ◆ Getting Inside the EPUB
- ◆ Editing Files inside an EPUB
- ◆ Editing Ebook Metadata
- ◆ Creating Multiple-Chapter Ebooks
- ◆ Creating Tables of Contents

Getting Inside the EPUB

An EPUB is not a file per se; rather, it's an archive of several files, like a ZIP or RAR archive. In point of fact, EPUB *is* ZIP. We'll unzip an EPUB in a moment.

Inside the EPUB are all the files comprising the ebook, including the actual book text, a CSS file to define the presentation of the book text, any images and multimedia used in the ebook, the fonts used if you've chosen to embed some, and a couple of files containing a manifest and the book metadata such as title, author, publisher name, ISBN, and so on. Each of those files has a specific purpose, and each can be edited manually in a variety of applications, which is one of the many things you'll do in this chapter. First, let's get *to* those files.

DOWNLOAD EPUB-EXTRACTION AND EDITING TOOLS

You can download all of the EPUB-extraction and editing tools mentioned in this chapter from a single page on my website. Just visit `http://abbrv.it/DigiPubIDTools` to access the latest versions of WinZip, Sigil, Calibre, the OSX Terminal scripts, the NCX playOrder renumbering scripts, and lots more.

Unzipping and Zipping an EPUB on Mac

If you're working on a Mac, don't skip this section. True, EPUB is ZIP, but in some cases *treating it like* a ZIP can cause the EPUB to fail to validate or even fail to open.

UNZIPPING

Double-clicking a ZIP archive in Mac OS X typically results in the identical behavior to Windows—extracting or viewing the archive contents. You might even have StuffIt, MacZip, or another ZIP extractor installed to handle those tasks for you. *Don't use them.* Don't rename an `.epub` file `.zip` and then double-click it. While you will get an extraction, there exists a significant chance that, upon rearchiving back to ZIP and then EPUB, the ebook will be altered to the point that it won't validate as EPUB, preventing it from being distributed and sold through the ebookstores; there's even a chance that the EPUB won't open in one or more ereaders. Unfortunately, to extract and work with the contents of an EPUB on the Mac, you must take a more circuitous route than you would on a Windows-based computer.

1. Create a new folder wherever you like and copy the EPUB in question to that folder. I usually put it within the main ebook project folder and title it something like Extracted_ EPUB. Make note of where you place the EPUB.

2. Open the Mac Terminal app, which you'll find in Applications ➢ Utilities.

3. On the Terminal command line, enter the Change Directory command, **CD**, followed by a space and then the path to the folder containing the EPUB. Press Return/Enter. (To get the path of a folder, navigate to that folder in Finder, right-click, and choose Get Info from the context pop-up menu. When the Get Info dialog appears, note the Where field under the General info, as shown in Figure 6.1; that's the path to the folder, exactly what you need to retype at the Terminal command prompt.)

FIGURE 6.1
Choosing Get Info on the folder shows the path I'll need in Terminal.

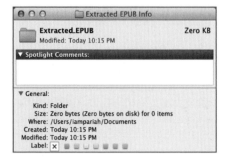

Figure 6.2 shows exactly what I mean; the third line from the bottom is the command I just described, and the bottom line is the new command prompt showing that Terminal is now in the Extracted_EPUB folder.

TIP The Nacre you see in the figure is the name of my Mac (bonus points if you can figure out why), and iampariah is my username on that Mac. Obviously your computer name and username will replace mine in your Terminal window.

FIGURE 6.2
After changing the directory to the correct folder path

4. Now that you know almost everything you need in order to hack my Mac, on the new command-prompt line, type the **unzip** command followed by the name of your EPUB, including its file extension. Terminal will list all the files extracted from the EPUB. Figure 6.3 shows unzipping an EPUB.

FIGURE 6.3
The unzip command extracts all files in the EPUB.

```
Nacre:Documents iampariah$
Last login: Mon May  7 16:21:21 on ttys000
Nacre:Documents iampariah$ cd /Users/iampariah/Documents/Extracted_EPUB/
Nacre:Extracted_EPUB iampariah$ unzip wwoz_ch4.epub
Archive:  wwoz_ch4.epub
 extracting: mimetype
  inflating: OEBPS/wizardofoz_print_cover.xhtml
  inflating: OEBPS/toc.ncx
  inflating: META-INF/container.xml
  inflating: OEBPS/css/wiz_cover_ibooks_test.css
 extracting: OEBPS/font/ACaslonPro-Regular.otf
 extracting: OEBPS/font/BookAntiqua.otf
 extracting: OEBPS/font/Dollhouse.TTF
 extracting: OEBPS/font/MinionPro-It.otf
 extracting: OEBPS/font/MinionPro-Regular.otf
 extracting: OEBPS/font/MyriadPro-BoldSemiCn.otf
 extracting: OEBPS/font/MyriadPro-Regular.otf
 extracting: OEBPS/font/PortlandLDO-Bold.TTF
  inflating: OEBPS/image/8170.png
  inflating: OEBPS/image/oz_ch4_01_fmt.jpeg
  inflating: OEBPS/image/oz_ch4_02_fmt.png
  inflating: OEBPS/image/oz_ch4_03_fmt.png
  inflating: OEBPS/image/oz_ch4_04_fmt.png
  inflating: OEBPS/image/oz_ch4_05_fmt.png
  inflating: OEBPS/image/oz_sidebar_bg_fmt.png
  inflating: OEBPS/image/oz_sidebar_bg_fmt1.png
  inflating: OEBPS/image/tumblr_lxd265nwRm1qahnd_fmt.png
  inflating: META-INF/encryption.xml
  inflating: OEBPS/content.opf
Nacre:Extracted_EPUB iampariah$
```

5. You're done with Terminal; quit it.

ZIPPING

At some point, you're going to want to rezip that EPUB. This is as good a place as any to tell you how to do that.

1. Make sure you've deleted or moved the original EPUB from your `Extracted_EPUB` folder (or whatever you've named it). You don't want to compress an EPUB inside an EPUB, after all.

2. Open Terminal, and on the command line enter the Change Directory command, **CD**, followed by a space and then the path to the folder containing the extracted EPUB. Press Return/Enter.

3. For consistently best results, you must include the MIME type, uncompressed, and the rest of the EPUB, compressed, separately. First comes the MIME type.

   At the command prompt, type the following and then press Return/Enter:
   ```
   zip -0Xq book.epub mimetype
   ```

4. Add the rest of the files to the EPUB with compression by executing the following command (when it finishes, you'll have an EPUB ready for testing or publication):
   ```
   zip -Xr9Dq book.epub *
   ```

ASPIRIN-FREE WORKFLOW: GRAPHICAL ZIP AND UNZIP ON MAC OS X

Designer and InDesign scripter Dan Rodney created a pair of scripts to make it even easier to unzip (and later zip again) EPUBs. Download EPUB Zip and UnZip from `http://abbrv.it/DigiPubIDTools` and extract the two `.app` files inside. Running the EPUB UnZip script presents you with a graphical user interface for selecting the EPUB to unzip, while running EPUB Zip lets you choose which files to archive into an EPUB.

Unzipping and Zipping an EPUB on Windows

On Windows, unzip and rezip away! Find an EPUB, copy it, and change the copy's file extension to `.zip`. Now double-click the ZIP archive. Windows should automatically extract all the files within the archive, prompt you to do so, or at least show you the contents of the archive in an Explorer window. (On Windows 7 and newer, you can just right-click a ZIP and choose Extract All.) If you get an error, then your computer needs a ZIP-extraction program like the popular WinZip or one of dozens of similar ZIP extractors.

Editing EPUBs without Unzipping Them

A handful of programs allow you to work with the individual files inside EPUBs without the need to actually unzip (and later rezip) the EPUB. Sigil, a free editor for Windows, Mac, and Linux, is among the best EPUB editors available.

Throughout the chapters on EPUB, you'll see me sometimes using Sigil, editing the contents of an EPUB without extracting any files from it; at other times, you'll see me editing files I've extracted in other applications. Sigil is an excellent tool, but I typically use it for relatively simple editing tasks; anything requiring heavy coding or major changes to the EPUB I'll do within the unzipped files and then rearchive them back to EPUB when I'm done editing. You may disagree with my preferences or where I draw the line between when to use Sigil and when to unzip. Give both methods a try and decide for yourself.

Editing Files Inside an EPUB

Regardless of whether you're on a Mac or Windows, you'll find the same files inside every EPUB. In this chapter's Lesson Files folder, you'll find one of the EPUBs generated in an earlier chapter already unzipped—wwoz_ch4.epub. If you don't have an EPUB of your own on hand, check out that one by opening the various files in an XML or HTML editor or a text editor like Windows' Notepad or Mac's TextEdit. The following sections discuss what each of the files are, what they do, and why you need them.

MIME Type

Located in the root of the EPUB archive—and the root folder of the expanded EPUB—is the MIME type file. You might already be familiar with the term *MIME type* from web-design work, and you may have even seen it in email messages with attachments. A MIME type simply defines a specific file extension as belonging to a common file type so that software can decide how to act on that file. Within every EPUB's MIME type file you'll find only the following line: application/epub+zip. That tells the device on which the EPUB is viewed that the ebook should be treated as an EPUB in ZIP archive format.

The MIME type file must be present in the root of every EPUB.

Container.xml

Within the META-INF folder is the container.xml file, whose job it is to direct the XML processor (ebook-reading software) to the metadata information and the content of the book within the OEBPS folder. Typically the container.xml folder looks like the following code:

```
<?xml version="1.0" encoding="UTF-8" standalone="yes"?>
<container version="1.0" xmlns="urn:oasis:names:tc:opendocument:xmlns:container">
    <rootfiles>
        <rootfile full-path="OEBPS/content.opf" media-type="application/oebps-
package+xml"/>
    </rootfiles>
</container>
```

The first line is the declaration statement required for all XML and XML-based documents (including HTML files). It tells the processor the markup language being used (XML), the version of that markup language, the encoding method, and, with the standalone attribute, that the document is self-contained and does not require external elements because all pieces of the ebook are contained in the rootfile path (line 4).

The second line is the opening of the root element, which closes itself as the last line of the file, and the namespace. The root element and namespace won't change; they'll be the same for all EPUBs, as will the presence of the <rootfiles></rootfiles> parent container within the root element. The rootfile child element path declaration is where things might differ between ebooks and where you may want to make manual changes.

The rootfile declaration is the full path from the root of the EPUB to the content.opf file as well as a MIME type definition of that OPF file. Conventionally, the full path is OEBPS/content.opf, which is how it appears in the code here. You can change that location, however.

OEBPS is an abbreviation for Open eBook Publication Structure. Within the OEBPS folder is all the content comprising the ebook, including the OPF file that manifests all the other files. As the presence of the word *structure* implies within Open eBook Publication Structure, placing all those files into the OEBPS folder is standard practice; it's not a requirement, however. If you wanted to change the name of the OEBPS folder to CONTENTS, for example, you could do that—just remember to also change the rootfile declaration in the container.xml file from OEBPS/content.opf to CONTENTS/content.opf.

TIP You must not change the name of the META-INF folder. It's required by EPUB file specifications to be in every EPUB and named as such.

Encryption.xml

Also in the META-INF folder you might find an encryption.xml file. There are two reasons this file may exist: The ebook has digital rights management (see the sidebar "Adding DRM Protection to Ebooks"), or it includes embedded fonts.

If this file is present, you—or your readers—may not be able to open the EPUB on certain devices or desktop ereader software. Unless the EPUB is backed by a DRM-management server, many ereaders see the EPUB as something that has protection but that has had the link to its protecting server severed; whether the ereader has permission to view the EPUB cannot be ascertained. In other words, the ereader thinks you pirated the ebook, and it won't enable your thievery. Ironic, I know. If the encryption.xml file is there because you added DRM, make sure your DRM server is fully functional and accessible. If font embedding created the encryption.xml file, delete the file.

You should also delete the encryption.xml file if your book doesn't have direct DRM.

All the other files from here on out are contained in the OEBPS folder.

XHTML Files

Within the XHTML or HTML files you'll find the actual text of your ebook, including standard HTML references to images, multimedia, and hyperlinks, as well as the HTML markup code needed to structure the document into paragraphs (<p></p>), headings (<h1></h1>, <h2></h2>, <h3></h3>, and so on), and containers of various purposes (<div></div>). Put simply, the XHTML files are your ebook converted to HTML.

ADDING DRM PROTECTION TO EBOOKS

Without getting into whether DRM is effective, let's say you want to add DRM to your ebooks, which will prevent at least what I call *ignorance piracy*, or people who copy and share your book with a friend or two out of ignorance of the law, not out of some deliberately avaricious bent or damn-the-man-information-should-be-free idealism. That latter group engages in what I call *deliberate piracy*, which you simply can't stop with DRM. The ways to defeat DRM in EPUB are widely known. Yup. Not only can you learn how to build a nuclear bomb on the Internet, but with slightly more effort, you can learn how to crack open any current method of DRM for ebooks.

Assuming you do want to add DRM to your ebooks, first ask yourself how your ebooks will be distributed. If you'll sell them only through the big ebook stores like iBooks, Kindle, NOOK, Sony, Kobo, and so on, don't worry about DRM. All those stores automatically add DRM protection to ebooks they distribute. If, however, you'll be distributing your ebooks directly to consumers or through other distribution channels, then you might want to invest in a DRM solution. There are several out there, not the least of which is Adobe Content Server (`www.adobe.com/products/content-server.html`), which enables copy-protection and content-expiration options on PDFs as well as EPUB. Its ability to expire content after a certain number of days or on a specific date is one of the greatest appeals of the system, making it ideal to manage lending libraries as well as time-sensitive content.

Every ebook must have at least one XHTML file, though many have multiple such files. Multichapter books, for example, are most often published with each chapter occupying its own XHTML file. Later in this chapter we'll go through the whys and hows of making multichapter ebooks.

CSS Files

One or more CSS—Cascading Style Sheet—files define the appearance of the text in the ebook by specifying attributes for each tag within the XHTML files. Such attributes can be as simple as setting a font or text color or can include a number of attributes to, for example, separate a note or tip box from the main part of the text, placing a colored box and outline around the note or tip box and indenting and styling the text within that box.

Your ebook may have one or multiple CSS files, and they may be in the same OEBPS folder as the XHTML files or in a subfolder of OEBPS. If you elect for the subfolder option, what you name that folder—and, indeed, what you name the CSS file—is entirely at your discretion. You just have to make sure that each CSS file is listed in the content.opf file (discussed in depth very soon) and that each CSS file is referenced from within each XHTML file that uses it.

If you open one of the XHTML files, you'll see within the <head></head> container a link tag referencing the full path to each CSS file. If you add or alter the folder or filename of any CSS file, you must include a link line in the XHTML file(s) that needs that CSS. The following is an example link tag:

```
<link href="css/style.css" rel="stylesheet" type="text/css"/>
```

NCX File

The NCX file, which stands for Navigation Control for XML, creates the pop-up or on-demand table of contents (TOC) presented by most ereader devices and programs. It's not *the* table of contents, but *a* table of contents. For example, in Figure 6.4, you can see the on-demand TOC for an ebook in iBooks. This is not a dedicated TOC page as you might create in InDesign, but a structured list of navigational elements that the ereader device and software then formats and presents to the human reader. InDesign will make a `toc.ncx` file during export if you tell it to, with or without a standard on-the-page TOC generated from InDesign's Layout ➤ Table Of Contents menu. That's how the `toc.ncx` file in the `Lesson Files` folder came about.

FIGURE 6.4

iBooks displays an on-demand table of contents.

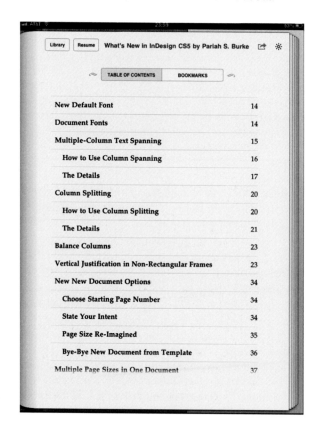

TIP   The NCX file can be named whatever you like—`toc.ncx`, `nav.ncx`, `billy-bobs-giant-world-of-epub-internal-linking-goodness.ncx`—as long as the file has the `.ncx` extension, doesn't include spaces and other characters illegal on the Web, and is properly identified in the `content.opf` manifest and spine (discussed later in this chapter).

Take a look at the (abbreviated) content of a typical NCX file—the one that iBooks displayed in Figure 6.4—and then let's examine each section.

```
<?xml version="1.0" encoding="UTF-8" standalone="no" ?><!DOCTYPE ncx PUBLIC "-//
NISO//DTD ncx 2005-1//EN" "http://www.daisy.org/z3986/2005/ncx-2005-1.dtd"><ncx
xmlns="http://www.daisy.org/z3986/2005/ncx/" version="2005-1">
    <head>
        <meta content="urn:isbn:978-0-9825083-3-6" name="dtb:uid"/>
        <meta content="2" name="dtb:depth"/>
        <meta content="0" name="dtb:totalPageCount"/>
        <meta content="0" name="dtb:maxPageNumber"/>
    </head>
    <docTitle>
        <text>What's New in InDesign CS5</text>
    </docTitle>
    <docAuthor>
        <text>Pariah S. Burke</text>
    </docAuthor>
    <navMap>
        <navPoint id="navpoint1" playOrder="1">
            <navLabel>
                <text>New Default Font</text>
            </navLabel>
            <content src="Text/Chapter1.xhtml#toc_marker-1"/>
        </navPoint>
        <navPoint id="navpoint2" playOrder="2">
            <navLabel>
                <text>Document Fonts</text>
            </navLabel>
            <content src="Text/Chapter1.xhtml#toc_marker-2"/>
        </navPoint>
        <navPoint id="navpoint3" playOrder="3">
            <navLabel>
                <text>Multiple-Column Text Spanning</text>
            </navLabel>
            <content src="Text/Chapter1.xhtml#toc_marker-3"/>
            <navPoint id="navpoint4" playOrder="4">
                <navLabel>
                    <text>How to Use Column Spanning</text>
                </navLabel>
                <content src="Text/Chapter1.xhtml#toc_marker-3-1"/>
            </navPoint>
            <navPoint id="navpoint5" playOrder="5">
                <navLabel>
                    <text>The Details</text>
                </navLabel>
                <content src="Text/Chapter1.xhtml#toc_marker-3-2"/>
            </navPoint>
        </navPoint>
    </navMap>
</ncx>
```

METADATA

The first part is the required root element and declaration statement; then the <head> and </head> tags containing the document metadata come next.

InDesign generates the toc.ncx file with four default meta fields.

The unique identifier (name="dtb:uid") is discussed in depth in the "Identifier" section later in this chapter. This value must precisely match the value between the <dc:identifier id="bookid"> and </dc:identifier> tags in the OPF file's metadata section.

Tables of contents are hierarchical listings sections within a document. For example, Figure 6.5 compares the display of a single-level table of contents on the left with a three-level table of contents on the right. The value for the depth metadata (name="dtb:depth") is the number of levels in the TOC, minus 1 (in other words, 0 in the first example and 2 in the other). Failing to match this value to the levels of TOC entries in the <navMap></navMap> section will result in all entries being presented as the same level.

FIGURE 6.5:
On-demand tables of contents as displayed in Sony Reader—(a) a single-level TOC and (b) a three-level TOC

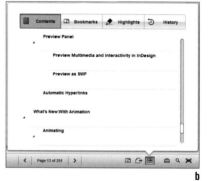

The page count and maximum allowable number of pages fields (name="dtb:totalPage Count" and name="dtb:maxPageNumber") are pretty much irrelevant. They talk about the page count and maximum page number, respectively, for the table of contents itself, not the book as a whole. They have no real bearing at this stage, so leave them at their default 0 values.

TITLE AND AUTHOR

The docTitle and docAuthor fields are fairly self-explanatory—the title of the book and its author, respectively.

NAVIGATION MAP

The navigation map is the meat of the NCX, containing the actual TOC entries and linking them to the content they describe. The outer container is the <navMap></navMap> tag pair, and each TOC item is a <navPoint></navPoint> that contains the title for display in the on-demand TOC (<navLabel><text>*Entry Title Here*</text></navLabel>) and the location of the content it describes (for instance, <content src="Text/Chapter1.xhtml#toc_marker-1"/>).

Each `navPoint` must have a unique ID, and if a `playOrder=` attribute is used, that value must be unique and numerical as well.

The `playOrder` attribute is really useful only if you have multiple tables of contents in the ebook—for example, the main on-demand TOC, a TOC that lists all the tables in the book, another that lists all the illustrations, and so on. The point of the attribute is to enable more advanced navigation than most ereaders currently do. Let's say, for instance, that you're publishing a cookbook. You'll naturally have the main TOC listing the full contents of the book, but you may also elect to have separate TOCs that index vegan dishes, fat-free dishes, and low-sodium dishes wherever those recipes happen to fall in the normal structure of the book (for example, some in this chapter, some in that). Those three extra TOCs could be very helpful to readers, and if the ereading device supports it, readers could jump from one fat-free dish instantly to the next via a "next fat-free dish" link or button. That link or button would actually be calling back (probably via JavaScript) to the specific TOC for those types of dishes and asking for the next `navPoint` according to the `playOrder` number. *And*, the `playOrder` doesn't necessarily have to match the logical appearance of the recipes in the book; simply by altering the `playOrder` values you could connect dishes in a manner independent of their page numbers, jumping from a recipe in Chapter 5 to one in Chapter 2, then to Chapter 8, and on to Chapter 4. Situations like that, multiple TOCs, are the reason the `playOrder` attribute exists.

`playOrder` is optional if you aren't using multiple TOCs, but removing it isn't advised for two reasons. First, removing it requires you to alter the root element declaration statement so that it no longer points to the ANSI/NISO Document Type Definition (DTD), which can cause other issues. Second, InDesign will reinsert all those `playOrder` attributes if you reexport to EPUB.

What gets most people thinking about removing `playOrder` attributes in the first place is that any time you manually add TOC entries, some or all of the `navPoint`'s `playOrder` values have to be changed, which is about as fun as counting things on your co-worker's toes. Many people will add boilerplate or template content XHTML files to the beginnings or ends of their ebooks—sections such as "About the Publisher," "About the Author," "How to Use This Book," and other content that may not change with every ebook. Each of those inserted sections must have a `navPoint` and thereby a `playOrder` value.

ASPIRIN-FREE WORKFLOW: AUTOMATIC PLAYORDER RENUMBERING

On the highly useful `http://abbrv.it/DigiPubIDTools` page you'll find links to a few scripts that help you quickly (and without reaching under the cubicle wall for a foot) renumber the `playOrder` values in the navMap.

So, now that you know far more than you ever wanted to about `playOrder`, let's look at the rest of the structure of a `navPoint`.

The markup for `navPoint` items is patterned after HTML list items (`<li></li>`). Each item begins with an opening `<navPoint>` tag and ends with the closing `</navPoint>` tag. Anything in between those tags is considered a single item and indented or otherwise styled as such. Should you nest one pair of `<navPoint></navPoint>` tags inside another, you'll create a second-level TOC entry, indented twice, and stylable via CSS just like you would use the nested pairings of two list element tags—`<li><ul><li></li></ul></li>`—to create a nested bulleted list. You can see that sort of nesting in the item whose ID is navpoint3 (see the following code snippet). Because the opening tag for navpoint4 comes before the closing tag for navpoint3, navpoint4 and subsequently navpoint5 are displayed as second-level TOC entries. I've indented them here to help make their hierarchy easier to interpret.

```
<navPoint id="navpoint3" playOrder="3">
   <navLabel>
      <text>Multiple-Column Text Spanning</text>
   </navLabel>
   <content src="Text/Chapter1.xhtml#toc_marker-3"/>
   <navPoint id="navpoint4" playOrder="4">
      <navLabel>
         <text>How to Use Column Spanning</text>
      </navLabel>
      <content src="Text/Chapter1.xhtml#toc_marker-3-1"/>
   </navPoint>
   <navPoint id="navpoint5" playOrder="5">
      <navLabel>
         <text>The Details</text>
      </navLabel>
      <content src="Text/Chapter1.xhtml#toc_marker-3-2"/>
   </navPoint>
</navPoint>
```

To create a third level of navigation—say, a subsection of navpoint5 ("The Details")—you'd nest another <navPoint></navPoint> item before the closing </navPoint> tag on navpoint5. You could keep going, adding fourth and fifth levels, but I don't recommend that for two reasons. First, it makes the on-demand TOC overly complex for readers and their ereader devices, the latter of which sometimes render such deep nested items so slowly that the device may appear to have locked up; it's better to ensure that your first- and second-level headings are descriptive enough that they succinctly communicate what content and subsections readers will find within them. Second, some ereaders don't support more than three levels of TOC headings, which means, in some cases, any level deeper than the third will be ignored, while in other ereaders subsequent entry levels will be shown but forced to look like level-two or level-three headings, which is about as confusing for a reader as the end of *Inception*.

OPF File

I saved perhaps the most important required file for last. Within the OEBPS folder you'll find an OPF file, probably content.opf. Like most of the other files within the EPUB, the name of this file isn't important as long as the .opf file extension is used. OPF stands for Open Packaging Format, and within this file are four sections, three of them crucial to the EPUB; should any one of those three sections be missing or incomplete, your ebook will almost certainly be rejected by ebookstores and may not even display on ereader devices (though most desktop ereader software tends to be more forgiving of omissions).

When you open an OPF, you'll find four sections—three, if the OPF was created via export from InDesign. All the sections are contained within a <package></package> container element, which is preceded by the standard XML declaration line. Each section has a distinct function.

Metadata

The metadata section contains all the metadata about the ebook, including the book title, publisher name, date of publication, language of the ebook, and lots of other information highly useful to you, the reader, or the ebookstore (see the following code example). I'll cover each piece of metadata, as well as how and why you might want to edit it, in the "Required Metadata" section a few pages hence.

```
<metadata>
    <meta name="generator" content="Adobe InDesign"/>
    <meta name="cover" content="x203.png"/>
    <dc:title></dc:title>
    <dc:creator></dc:creator>
    <dc:subject></dc:subject>
    <dc:description></dc:description>
    <dc:publisher></dc:publisher>
    <dc:date>2012-01-11</dc:date>
    <dc:source></dc:source>
    <dc:relation></dc:relation>
    <dc:coverage></dc:coverage>
    <dc:rights></dc:rights>
    <dc:language>en-US</dc:language>
    <dc:identifier id="bookid">urn:uuid:7256fj62-db2e-4694-ba77-f95836b8c357</
dc:identifier>
</metadata>
```

Manifest

Within the manifest section is a series of item lines, each containing three pieces of information about one of the files used in the EPUB. As you can see in the following sample code, each item identifies the filename of the NCX, the CSS, the XHTML, and any images, video, and audio files used in the ebook via the id attribute. Next the href attribute lists the relative path from the OPF file to the identified asset; in this case, everything is within the OEBPS folder or a subfolder of that. Finally, the media-type attribute identifies the MIME type of the file in question.

```
<manifest>
    <item id="wizardofoz_print_ch4" href="wizardofoz_print_ch4.xhtml" media-
type="application/xhtml+xml" />
    <item id="ncx" href="toc.ncx" media-type="application/x-dtbncx+xml" />
    <item id="wizardofoz_04_baum_64kb.mp3" href="audio/wizardofoz_04_baum_64kb.
mp3" media-type="audio/mpeg" />
    <item id="with-audio-video.css" href="css/with-audio-video.css" media-
type="text/css" />
    <item id="ACaslonPro-Regular.otf" href="font/ACaslonPro-Regular.otf" media-
type="application/vnd.ms-opentype" />
    <item id="oz_ch4_01_fmt.jpeg" href="image/oz_ch4_01_fmt.jpeg" media-
type="image/jpeg" />
```

```
    <item id="oz_ch4_02_opt.png" href="image/oz_ch4_02_opt.png" media-type="image/
png" />
    <item id="folgers_13_512kb.mp4" href="video/folgers_13_512kb.mp4" media-
type="video/mp4" />
</manifest>
```

Every file in the OEBPS folder must be included in the manifest as a separate item listing. If you attempt to publish an EPUB containing unmanifested files through any of the major ebook stores, your publication will be rejected. Moreover, some of those ebook stores, reportedly, will flag your account for closer scrutiny of all your existing publications and future submissions. Why? For the security of readers. See the sidebar "Manifest Density."

MANIFEST DESTINY

Unmanifested files contained within an EPUB could be content illegally distributed, such as pirated media. More important, EPUBs can execute JavaScript on devices that support it. JavaScript can be and has been used to deliver viruses and worms, to steal sensitive data, and to wreak all sorts of other havoc with people's devices, which is why web browsers and operating systems have such strict controls over what JavaScript can and cannot be allowed to do when you visit a web page containing a script. When a JavaScript is listed in the manifest, the major ebook publishers' systems scan that script for any malicious code prior to publication. Some people have tried to circumvent the code scanners by including and referencing from within ebook JavaScripts without listing them in the manifest of the OPF. Moreover, malicious code can be executed from scripts that don't bear the .js file extension. Consequently, a policy was adopted by most ebook stores to automatically reject any submission containing unmanifested files of any type.

If you add additional CSS files, if you break up one long XHTML into chapter- or section-based XHTML documents, if you manually add fonts for embedding, if you hand-code in any audio, video, or SVG files, then remember to list each of those new files as an item in the manifest.

SPINE

The spine section lists the order in which text content files should appear in the book. Each entry is merely an internal reference citing an item ID from the manifest. If your ebook contains only one XHTML, you'll find only one itemref entry in the spine section. Multiple-chapter books will have XHTMLs listed in the order in which they should be read.

GUIDE

The guide section, which is completely absent from any EPUB generated by InDesign, lets you define the role of each XHTML. For example, take the following code, which tells an ereader device or software that cover.xhtml is the cover page of the book (an additional cover beyond the cover image itself), `fm1.xhtml` is the copyright page of the book, and `chap1.xhtml` begins the book's main content:

```
<guide>
    <reference type="cover" href="cover.xhtml"/>
    <reference type="copyright-page" href="fm1.xhtml"/>
    <reference type="text" href="chap1.xhtml"/>
</guide
```

Several reference types are available (note case and punctuation for proper usage):

- cover
- title-page
- copyright-page
- acknowledgments
- dedication
- epigraph
- preface
- toc
- loi
- lot
- foreword
- text
- bibliography
- notes
- index
- glossary

Most are self-explanatory, but I should note that `loi` stands for list of illustrations, `lot` is for list of tables, and `text` is used for main content files. With the exception of `text`, which should be used for all chapter files as well as all other types of files that don't otherwise have a separate type, all reference types should be used only once, each referring to a separate XHTML file. You don't have to use all of them, though.

In fact, the entire guide section is optional, which is why InDesign omits it. Apple recommends its use for iBooks, and I recommend including it for all your EPUBs, bound for iBooks or not. Including the guide won't break any ebook reader, but it helps many devices properly identify and direct readers to your content. This is particularly important when publishing nonfiction, such as textbooks or scholarly works, because the sections become all the more important to human readers and their devices.

Image, Audio, Video, and Font Folders

Depending on the content of your book, you may have subfolders containing graphics, audio or video files, and font files embedded via InDesign's EPUB export and/or the `encryption.xml` file in the `META-INF` folder.

While the EPUB is exploded is an excellent opportunity to check on the quality of the images InDesign automatically generated for you, as well as the file size and quality of any multimedia files. If you need to make any replacements or adjustments, keep the same filenames; if you change file formats—for example, convert a JPEG image into a PNG—make sure to change the file extension on all references to the image in the XHTML and CSS files as well as within the OPF manifest. And, of course, delete the old JPG version so you don't wind up with an unmanifested file in the EPUB.

Filenaming

As you explore and edit files within an EPUB, it's important to remember that there are restrictions on the names of component files and assets. Improperly named files can cause the EPUB to fail validation, be rejected by ebook stores, behave strangely in ereaders, and/or fail to open at all in ereaders.

The International Digital Publishing Forum (IDPF), the standards body that defines the EPUB specification, sets forth the following rules for filenames within EPUBs:

♦ Filenames must be unique within a given directory and should not have the same name as another file with different case. In other words, don't use `MyPicture.png` and `mypicture.png`.

♦ Filenames must not exceed 255 bytes, which, with "double-byte" Unicode, equates to a maximum of about 127 characters, including the file extension and preceding period.

♦ The full path name (`path/filename.ext`) must not exceed 65,535 bytes.

♦ Filenames must be Unicode UTF-8 encoded (which includes standard ASCII characters) except for the following characters (this list Copyright © 2010, 2011 International Digital Publishing Forum):

  ♦ Solidus: / (U+002F)

  ♦ Quotation Mark: " (U+0022)

  ♦ Asterisk: * (U+002A)

  ♦ Full stop as the last character: . (U+002E)

  ♦ Colon: : (U+003A)

  ♦ Less-than sign: < (U+003C)

  ♦ Greater-than sign: > (U+003E)

  ♦ Question mark: ? (U+003F)

  ♦ Reverse solidus: \ (U+005C)

  ♦ DEL (U+007F)

- C0 range (U+0000...U+001F)

- C1 range (U+0080...U+009F)

- Private Use Area (U+E000...U+F8FF)

- Non-characters in Arabic Presentation Forms-A (U+FDD0 ... U+FDEF)

- Specials (U+FFF0...U+FFFF)

- Tags and Variation Selectors Supplement (U+E0000...U+E0FFF)

- Supplementary Private Use Area-A (U+F0000...U+FFFFF)

- Supplementary Private Use Area-B (U+100000...U+10FFFF)

Here's my rule of thumb when naming files: Use only alphanumeric ASCII characters and, if needed, hyphens and underscores. I recommend that publishers avoid all other characters in filenames, including spaces and other punctuation, just as you would with files on the Web. Readers won't see the component filenames anyway, so they don't have to be pretty—just something that validates and makes sense to publishers when editing the contents of EPUBs.

Editing Ebook Metadata

Metadata is a crucial component of any ebook. It's from the metadata that ereaders and ebook stores pull the title, author, publisher, ISBN, and a host of other details needed to identify and classify the ebook within, well, within *everywhere* ebooks are displayed—ebook store listings, the ereader's bookshelf, the ereader while reading the book, Books in Print (`http://booksinprint.com`), the Library of Congress, and so on and so forth. Even while you're editing the EPUB contents, the metadata is essential to the function of programs such as Sigil and Calibre.

Editing Metadata in the OPF

All the metadata for an EPUB is written as individual lines within the `<metadata></metadata>` block in the EPUB archive's OPF file. For example, the following code shows metadata exported from InDesign to EPUB. (It is included for illustrative purposes, but it is not complete in terms of either the fields that could be there or the data within each field.)

```
<metadata>
  <meta name="generator" content="Adobe InDesign" />
  <meta name="cover" content="x203.png" />
  <dc:title></dc:title>
  <dc:creator></dc:creator>
  <dc:subject></dc:subject>
  <dc:description></dc:description>
  <dc:publisher></dc:publisher>
  <dc:date>2012-02-22</dc:date>
  <dc:source></dc:source>
  <dc:relation></dc:relation>
  <dc:coverage></dc:coverage>
  <dc:rights></dc:rights>
```

```
<dc:language>en-US</dc:language>
<dc:identifier id="bookid">urn:uuid:7256fj62-db2e-4694-ba77-f95836b8c357</
dc:identifier>
</metadata>
```

Each opening (for example, `<dc:title>`) and closing (for example, `</dc:title>`) tag defines a specific metadata field. The text between the tags is the value of that field, the metadata itself. Notice that InDesign completes the `date` metadata field (at least, it does starting with InDesign CS5.5), as well as the `identifier` and `creator` fields, but leaves all the other requisite fields empty. Thus, you cannot simply export from InDesign and expect a fully functional, press-ready ebook. You must edit the EPUB metadata subsequent to export from InDesign.

Completing the existing metadata fields, as well as adding those not included by InDesign, is very easy. You can edit the metadata code directly in a text, HTML, or XML editor, such as Windows Notepad or Notepad++ or Mac TextEdit or BBEdit, or in a cross-platform, EPUB code editor such as Sigil. To edit a line, either complete the data between the opening and closing tags or edit the `content=` attribute of the tag. To add an absent field, just type it on a new line within the `<metadata></metadata>` section.

Required Metadata

Some metadata is required in order for the EPUB to validate as a correctly formed EPUB, for ebookstores to accept the EPUB for publication, and/or for ereaders to display the EPUB. This section covers the hows and wherefores of these required pieces of information. Note that there is no required order to these elements; they may appear together at the beginning of the meta-data section, at the end, or scattered about, mixed with optional elements.

PACKAGE NAMESPACE DECLARATIONS

The package line (shown next) identifies the namespaces to use, the book's unique identifier, and the version of EPUB in which the book is built. All of these elements are required, so a quick definition of each is in order.

```
<package xmlns="http://www.idpf.org/2007/opf" unique-identifier="bookid"
version="2.0" xmlns:dc="http://purl.org/dc/elements/1.1/">
```

XMLNS   XMLNS is an abbreviation for Extensible Markup Language namespace. The `xmlns` line tells the interpreting ereader or software that the markup within the `<package>` `</package>` container should be evaluated against the specified Open Packaging Format (OPF). The statement informs the software about the conventions to use for the OPF file, including the fields that begin with `opf:`, `meta`, `item`, `itemref`, and so on.

MISSING OPEN PACKAGING FORMAT SPECIFICATIONS

It's important to note that the specifications are no longer located at www.idpf.org/2007/opf, though no one, it seems, has alerted Adobe to that fact. If you try visiting the URL, you'll get a 404: Not Found error—or, at least, you will as of the time of this writing. Ideally someone will have discovered the problem and activated a redirect to the correct OPF specification. Make sure you change the incorrect address to the correct one in your EPUBs.

XMLNS:DC The metadata section can contain a great many other pieces of information that are not accounted for directly in OPF but use a more universal system called the *Dublin Core Metadata*. The `xmlns:dc` attribute tells the interpreting software to use a particular version of the Dublin Core specification located at `http://purl.org/dc/elements/1.1/`. Any metadata elements that begin with `dc:` are those interpreted by the Dublin Core specification.

Unique Identifier This field lists a word, phrase, or number that uniquely identifies the book within its own code. Typically that's the book's ISBN, but if you aren't publishing through an ebookstore or for general sale, this identifier can remain the generic `bookid` InDesign slaps in there. The identifier won't be used outside the code of the book but must match its uses in the package definition, the `dc:identifier` line, and any other lines that reference one or the other.

Version Given its placement, the `version=` attribute may seem like it refers to the version of your book. It does not. Rather, it notes the version of the EPUB specification in use—the one you selected in the InDesign CS6 and later EPUB Export Options dialog. Thus, if you chose EPUB 2.0.1 from the Version drop-down on the General tab, the `package` line will list `version="2.0"` (only two-digit versions are listed), whereas that would become `version="3.0"` if you opted for EPUB 3.0 or EPUB 3.0 with Layout.

Meta Cover

According to the EPUB specification, the cover image is technically optional, not required. That said, several major ebookstores require its presence. Ergo, I consider it a requirement element.

The basic format of a cover-image reference is `<meta name="cover" content="x203.png" />`, with the `content=` attribute referencing the ID of the cover image. The actual path to that image will be listed in the manifest lower in the OPF—for example:

```
<item id="x203.png" href="image/203.png" media-type="image/png" />
```

It's the `id=` attribute of the cover-image item line to which the `meta name="cover" content=` refers.

Not all stores and ereaders use that field to show the cover image, however. For example, Amazon and Barnes & Noble use that field to create the cover image of the book that is shown in several locations—in the ebook itself as the cover page and in the ereader library and store as the book's thumbnail cover image—but iBooks does things completely differently.

If you created your cover in InDesign as the first page of the ebook's INDD and then, during EPUB export, told InDesign to rasterize that first page, then iBooks will *not* display that first page as rasterized. Instead, it will display the constituent components of that cover as individual elements, possibly spread across several pages (Figure 6.6). Image a, rasterized during export, will become a solid image to be used as the cover in the other major ebookstores and ereaders; within iBooks, however, the result will be the pages in image b, which are the components of the cover displayed separately and unrasterized.

FIGURE 6.6
(a) The full cover
image and (b) what
iBooks does to it

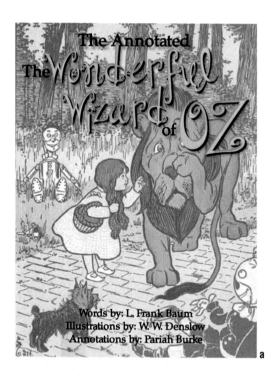

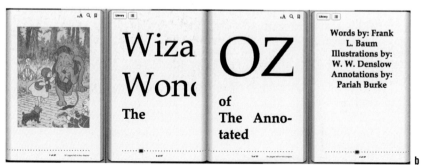

To make iBooks match the presentation of other ereaders, you have to go through a few extra steps before exporting to EPUB.

1. In InDesign, select all the pieces of your cover page—background image, publisher logo, title, author, cover-line text frames, and everything else.

2. Group the objects with Object ➢ Group or Ctrl+G/Cmd+G.

3. Choose Object ➢ Object Export Options and go to the EPUB and HTML tab (Figure 6.7).

FIGURE 6.7
Setting the raster-
ization and layout
options on the cover
design group to
account for iBooks's
peculiar treatment
of the cover

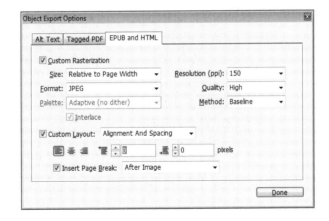

4. Enable Custom Rasterization and set the options as you see fit, selecting the best format, resolution, and other options for your document's unique cover.

5. Enable Custom Layout and, within that section, the Insert Page Break check box. Choose After Image from the drop-down menu beside Insert Page Break. Leave the Space Before and Space After fields (indicated by the left-most line-spacing icon) at their default 0 values, and then click Done.

These steps will force a page break after the cover image, effectively making the first page of the document a duplicate of the cover image—which is also a slick trick for ensuring that your cover is seen even though most ereaders, not just iBooks, actually begin displaying pages *after* the cover image.

IDENTIFIER

Every EPUB must have a unique identifier, which is typically, but not always, an ISBN or ASIN (Amazon's proprietary) number.

Just as citizens of the United States are identified by their unique Social Security numbers (and other countries have similar systems), books are identified globally by a unique International Standard Book Number (ISBN). No two books, and no two significantly different editions or revisions of the same book, may have the same ISBN. In fact, even the print and ebook editions of the same book must have different ISBNs. By way of example, compare the ISBNs (ISBN-13) for different editions and formats of my *Mastering InDesign for Print Design and Production* books:

♦ *Mastering InDesign CS3 for Print Design and Production* (paperback printed edition): ISBN: 978-0-470-11456-8

♦ *Mastering InDesign CS5 for Print Design and Production* (paperback printed edition): ISBN: 978-0-470-65098-1

♦ *Mastering InDesign CS5 for Print Design and Production* (ebook edition): ISBN: 978-1-118-01658-9

If you intend to publish an ebook for widespread distribution, the identifier must be the ISBN and should be merely the numbers, without spaces or hyphens, and preferably the ISBN-13 instead of the ISBN-10.

To add the ISBN in InDesign, simply enter it in the Unique ID field in the EPUB Export Options dialog. (See `http://abbrv.it/DigiPubIDTools` for how to obtain an ISBN, rules about doing so, and what to do after purchasing one or more ISBNs.)

If you haven't obtained an ISBN or you intend to produce ebooks for limited distribution— say, as internal training manuals—then you can use either a universal unique identifier (*UUID*) or a uniform resource identifier (*URI*).

A UUID is a very large number designed to provide a unique identifier without registration of any kind (which means UUIDs aren't *really* universally unique because there's no agency or system to ensure singularity of any generated number). You can create a UUID in a number of ways, including with scripts, via `http://random.org`, by repeatedly and blindly mashing your fist or forehead down on the keyboard, or with InDesign. To have InDesign do it, all you have to do is leave the Unique ID field in the EPUB Export Options blank upon the first EPUB export; InDesign will automatically generate a UUID for you, and it will retain the same UUID through subsequent exports of the same document to EPUB.

> **TIP** As with UUIDs as a whole, there's no guarantee that a UUID InDesign gives you is unique in the world. The number will be random, however, and (supposedly) unique among the numbers InDesign generates on your particular computer.

You can also use a URI, which is simply a more up-to-date way of saying universal resource locator (URL). URI identifiers are rare because they rely on website addresses and page structures remaining fixed pretty much forever, something few websites, no matter how big or small, actually do. One successful implementation of URIs is Project Gutenberg, whose EPUB-format ebooks are all identified by the unique URI for the ebook's page; for example, `www.gutenberg.org/ebooks/55`.

An ISBN identifier looks like this:

```
<dc:identifier id="bookid" opf:scheme="ISBN">urn:isbn:9780470650981
</dc:identifier>
```

An InDesign-generated UUID looks like this:

```
<dc:identifier id="bookid">urn:uuid:7256fj62-db2e-4694-ba77-f95836b8c357
</dc:identifier>
```

And a URI identifier looks like this:

```
<dc:identifier id="bookid" opf:scheme="URI">http://www.gutenberg.org/ebooks/55
</dc:identifier>
```

The use of the `type=` or `opf:scheme=` attribute in the identifier is optional. However, if you elect to employ multiple identifiers, you must include within each a `type=` or `opf:scheme=` attribute or add one as a meta refine line, such as in the following code:

```
<dc:identifier id="pub-id">urn:uuid:7256fj62-db2e-4694-ba77-f95836b8c357
</dc:identifier>
        <meta refines="#pub-id" property="identifier-type" scheme="xsd:string">uuid
</meta>
```

```
<dc:identifier id="isbn-id">urn:isbn:9780470650981</dc:identifier>
        <meta refines="#isbn-id" property="identifier-type"
scheme="onix:codelist5">15</meta>
```

The id= attribute of the identifier—or the primary identifier if you're using more than one, as I did in the preceding code—must be present and must match the unique-identifier= attribute in the package tag at the top of the OPF. So, feel free to change the id=, but make sure you update the unique-identifier= too.

TITLE

Your book must have a title, which you enter between the <dc:title> and </dc:title> tags. Remember not to use special characters like colons, ampersands, and so on in the Title field. If you need to include additional elements to the title, such as a subtitle or qualifier, see the "Title Refinements" section later in this chapter.

Notice that InDesign does not, by default, furnish a value in the <dc:title></dc:title> area. It will if you presupply InDesign with the document title via the XMP metadata inside the INDD document. To do that, choose File ➤ File Info and then complete the Document Title field in the dialog that results (Figure 6.8). Click OK and then export the EPUB to see that InDesign has translated the INDD's metadata into the EPUB's metadata.

FIGURE 6.8
Editing the INDD's metadata in the XMP File Information dialog

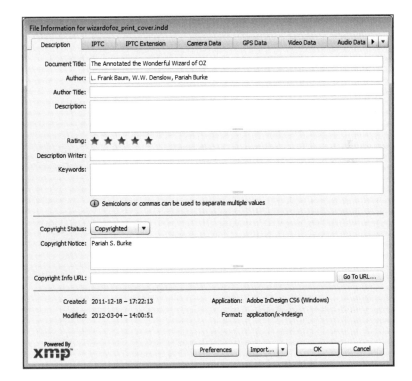

FOLLOW HTML CHARACTER RULES

It's important to remember that metadata fields in an OPF are the same as metadata fields in any HTML file for display on the Web. That means they're limited to standard ASCII text characters—upper- and lowercase letters, numbers, and a limited set of punctuation marks. Follow the same rules as in the "Filenaming" section a few pages back or, better yet, my rule of thumb therein. Note that you *can* use colons, semicolons, quotation marks, question marks, and periods (full stops) in most metadata fields, though dc:title is not one of those.

Failure to follow those rules in metadata fields can result in unexpected behavior. For instance, merely using an ampersand (&) in the dc:title metadata field will make some ereaders display your ebook without a title!

LANGUAGE

Each EPUB is required to list the language in which the majority of the book is written, according to ISO 639 and/or ISO 3166-1 language codes. The former, ISO 639, identifies all printed languages as two-digit codes, for example "EN" for English, while ISO 3166-1, which identifies countries as two-digit codes, enables the identification of country-specific language, such as "EN-US" for English as used in the United States as opposed to "EN-GB" for *u*-heavy British English.

Consult http://abbrv.it/DigiPubIDISO639 and http://abbrv.it/DigiPubIDISO3166 for more information on language and country codes you can use in the dc:language field.

DATE

InDesign CS5 and older failed to enter any data in the dc:date field, leading to significant frustration. Subsequent versions now fill in the date of export in the logical YYYY-MM-DD format. Note that this is not the date the INDD was created or the date it was modified but rather the date of export to EPUB. According to the EPUB specifications, the date of the ebook must be its date of publication, which is not always the same as its date of export. Books from major publishers, for example, are published a few weeks before their official dates of publication to give retailers time to place the books on sale.

A value is required between the <dc:date> and </dc:date> tags and must conform to the ISO 8601 standard of dates and times (see http://abbrv.it/DigiPubIDISO8601). At a minimum, the value must be a four-digit year—for example, 2013—but may also include any or all of the following: month, week, day, hour, minute, second, and time zone values, such as in the following examples:

```
<dc:date>2013</dc:date>
<dc:date>2013-01-01</dc:date>
<dc:date>2013-W01-1</dc:date>
<dc:date>2013-01-011200-0700</dc:date>
```

The average one-off, standalone ebook requires no more than the four-digit year but often includes the full date written as YYYY-MM-DD. Serialized EPUBs or those frequently updated nearly always include the YYYY-MM-DD format date as a minimum, but also often include the time of publication or update.

When an ebook is based on a print edition or a previous work, it's important to include the publication dates for both versions. You can do that by including multiple `dc:date` tags and adding `opf` qualifiers as attributes to them. For instance, in the following code for *The Wonderful Wizard of Oz*, I list the date the original book was published, followed by the (theoretical) date my edition would be published in print and then as an ebook edition.

```
<dc:date opf:event="original-publication">1900</dc:date>
<dc:date opf:event="publication">2013-01-01</dc:date>
<dc:date opf:event="epub-publication">2013-02-01</dc:date>
```

Optional or Special-Case Metadata

Beyond the required metadata elements are a number of other items that are optional but quite helpful in different circumstances.

VERSION IDENTIFIER

Revising the content of an ebook beyond minor content changes requires that the new version have an identifier different from the previous edition. But for minor revisions—which include fixing typos and other minor typographic changes, styling alterations such as modifying the HTML or CSS without changing the text they style, and switching image format or quality settings without altering the content of an image or its placement relative to the text—you can keep the same ISBN or UUID, but you should add a version identifier line to properly classify the revision.

To identify a specific version of a publication, you'll need to add a `refines` line beneath the `dc:identifier` line, such as the following code. Note that the `refines=` attribute must match the `id=` from the `dc:identifier` field (plus a hash sign to reference the ID) and that the actual version number (or name) must appear between the `<meta>` and `</meta>` tags, as shown. You may use numbers, letters, dates, or whatever scheme you like to identify the versions. There is no specification limitation here, though logically you should use a consistent version system that makes sense to readers of your publications. For a more consistent system, employ an ONIX code list (`www.editeur.org/14/Code-Lists/`), as used in the following example.

```
<meta refines="#bookid" property="identifier-type" scheme="onix:codelist5">03
</meta>
```

TIP   ONIX for Books, incidentally, is the international standard for presenting book industry product information in electronic form. You can read more about it at `http://abbrv.it/DigiPubIDONIX`.

PUBLISHER

The publisher field is fairly self-explanatory: In this field enter the full name of the publisher as you want it to appear in the ebook and ebook listings. This name should be the full legal name of the publisher entity—for example, Pariah Press, Inc., if the publisher is a business—or the name of the individual as he want to be identified if the publisher is a person rather than a business, say John Q. Public. The publisher name in the ebook metadata should always match the name of the book's ISBN owner.

AUTHOR, CO-AUTHORS, AND CONTRIBUTORS

Most books have an author—or editor, for anthologies. She would be identified in the `dc:creator` field; however, oddly enough, you aren't required to include a value. It's a good idea to include one, though; otherwise, would-be readers can't search ebook stores by author/editor. For single-author titles, enter the author's name in human-readable format—First Last, as in Jane Doe—between the `<dc:creator>` and `</dc:creator>` tags.

In the case of multiple authors or books with contributors, you have to add additional fields and attributes. Someone must be listed as the primary author within the first `dc:creator` field. This is usually the anthology editor or the book's primary author. For example, I wrote several chapters in the last edition of *Real World QuarkXPress* (Peachpit Press, 2007), as did eight other publishing-expert authors. The editor of the project was listed as a creator, but so were those of us who actually wrote the book chapters. That listing would have looked something like the following, which is abridged for brevity:

```
<dc:creator opf:role="edt">David Blatner</dc:creator>
<dc:creator opf:role="aut">Pariah S. Burke</dc:creator>
<dc:creator opf:role="aut">Claudia McCue</dc:creator>
<dc:creator opf:role="aut">Chuck Weger</dc:creator>
```

Each co-author was listed within a separate set of `<dc:creator></dc:creator>` tags. Moreover, the contribution of each to the project is identified via the `opf:role=` attribute. The first entry is identified as the editor (`edt`) of the project, while the next three are noted as authors (`aut`). There is no special designation for co-authors; merely the presence of multiple author roles establishes the fact that they are co-authors.

When an individual or entity has added to the ebook in some way other than as a co-author or anthology editor, that person or company should be identified within a set of `<dc:contributor></dc:contributor>` tags, and, as with `dc:creator`, the role that contributor's work plays in the publication should be identified.

Let's look at another example, this one a fictitious textbook containing material written by two primary authors; small sections written by another writer; a preface written by a fourth writer; and illustrations, photographs, and other materials provided by various people. Its EPUB metadata could include the entries in Table 6.1.

TABLE 6.1:   Textbook Creator and Contributor Metadata Entries

ROLE	METADATA ENTRY
Co-author	`<dc:creator role="aut">Jane Doe</dc:creator>`
Co-author	`<dc:creator role="aut">John Smith</dc:creator>`
Contributing writer	`<dc:contributor opf:role="clb">Bob Roberts</dc:contributor>`

TABLE 6.1:   Textbook Creator and Contributor Metadata Entries

ROLE	METADATA ENTRY
Illustrator	`<dc:contributor opf:role="ilu">Illustrations R Us, Inc.</dc:contributor`
Cartography	`<dc:contributor opf:role="ctg">Dusty Rhodes</dc:contributor>`
Photographer	`<dc:contributor opf:role="pht">Flip Filmcan</dc:contributor>`
Preface author	`<dc:contributor opf:role="aui">Dr. Samuel Mudd</dc:contributor>`

The `opf:role=` attribute uses the almost exhaustive MARC Code List for Relators main-tained by the Library of Congress here: `http://abbrv.it/DigiPubIDMARC`. If you're curious, MARC is an acronym for Machine Readable Cataloging, a 40-year old system that helps comput-ers make use of bibliographic data.

Each contributor or author should be listed within her tags exactly as the name would appear within the book or within its catalog listing, such as First Last names. Obviously, that is not how they'll be sorted in a book catalog or ebookstore, though. To enable sorting by last name, you'll need to add the `opf:file-as=` attribute, which should be added for each creator tag. For example, within the metadata of *The Wonderful Wizard of Oz*, you'd want to write the author credit creator tag as follows. Note that I've omitted the `opf:role="aut"` attribute because it isn't necessary for a single-author work.

```
<dc:creator opf:file-as="Baum, L. Frank">L. Frank Baum</dc:creator>
```

TITLE REFINEMENTS

Not always does a work have a single title. For example, this very book has a title, *ePublishing with InDesign*, but it also has a subtitle, *Design and Produce Digital Publications for Tablets, Digital Magazines, and More*, which is also important. In the ebook edition, the publisher and I will need to identify the title and the subtitle, but not in the same `dc:title` field. Instead, by using the `title-type` property along with a `meta refines` line, we can communicate to ereader devices and ebookstores which is the title and which is the subtitle, as in the following code. The `display-seq` property defines the hierarchy of the title contents, placing the main title first and the subtitle second.

```
<dc:title id="title">ePublishing with InDesign</dc:title>
        <meta refines="#title" property="title-type">main</meta>
        <meta refines="#title" property="display-seq">1</meta>

<dc:title id="subtitle">Design and Produce Digital Publications for Tablets,
Digital Magazines, and More</dc:title>
        <meta refines="#subtitle" property="title-type">subtitle</meta>
        <meta refines="#subtitle" property="display-seq">2</meta>
```

Let's go a step further.

Although rare in fiction, in nonfiction it's common to have a multipart title for a book, particularly one that is part of a larger volume of works. For example, the IDPF provides this example: *The Great Cookbooks of the World: Mon premier guide de cuisson, un Mémoire. The New French Cuisine Masters, Volume Two. Special Anniversary Edition.* When creating the metadata for a title such as that it's important to break it apart hierarchically and then reproduce it piece by piece in metadata tags of a matching hierarchy. The primary title of the book is *Mon premier guide de cuisson, un Mémoire,* so that must be listed as the primary title of the book, and, if a device supports only a single-part title, that one, identified in the following code as the first dc:title, will be shown. From there each piece of the collection title, such as the volume, and so on, is added on like building blocks. Finally, the complete name is reiterated in an extended title field for those devices that support the display of an extended title, such as in the following code (an example provided by the IDPF).

```
<dc:title id="t1" xml:lang="fr">Mon premier guide de cuisson, un Mémoire</
dc:title>
    <meta refines="#t1" property="title-type">main</meta>
    <meta refines="#t1" property="display-seq">2</meta>

<dc:title id="t2">The Great Cookbooks of the World</dc:title>
    <meta refines="#t2" property="title-type">collection</meta>
    <meta refines="#t2" property="display-seq">1</meta>

<dc:title id="t3">The New French Cuisine Masters</dc:title>
    <meta refines="#t3" property="title-type">collection</meta>
    <meta refines="#t3" property="group-position">2</meta>
    <meta refines="#t3" property="display-seq">3</meta>

<dc:title id="t4">Special Anniversary Edition</dc:title>
    <meta refines="#t4" property="title-type">edition</meta>
    <meta refines="#t4" property="display-seq">4</meta>

<dc:title id="t5">The Great Cookbooks of the World:
Mon premier guide de cuisson, un Mémoire.
The New French Cuisine Masters, Volume Two.
Special Anniversary Edition</dc:title>
    <meta refines="#t5" property="title-type">extended</meta>
```

Also note that, because the primary title, *Mon premier guide de cuisson, un Mémoire,* is in French, an xml:lang="fr" was added to denote that fact and use the device's French dictionary for spell checking, hyphenation, and proper display of accented characters. Each line could be specified as being in a different language if so desired, using the same language and/or country codes as dc:language.

Codewise, there is no limit on the number of dc:title entries or their refinement entries. And there's no limit on the types of titles that can be used, as long as you specify within the line containing the property="title-type" value a scheme that contains the used title-type. Without a specified scheme, most ereaders will recognize the following default title-type values: main, subtitle, edition, collection, extended, and short. Short, which is not shown in the preceding example, would be the shortest version of the title acceptable. For example, the short title *Gray's* might be used in the EPUB version of the famous medical text *Gray's Anatomy.*

SOURCE

Another commonly used element is the source element. It specifies the print edition of a publication from which the ebook was created. Unlike elements like dc:creator, dc:title, and so on, only a single instance of dc:source is allowed. If the ebook is a compilation of multiple printed sources, you can either omit all references to the sources in the metadata or list the source documents' authors within dc:creator or dc:contributor entries. The dc:source may be listed standalone (just the first line in the following example) or with the meta refines tag to identify the scheme; with the tag is better.

```
<dc:source id="src-id">urn:isbn:9780470650981</dc:source>
    <meta refines="#src-id" property="identifier-type"
scheme="onix:codelist5">15</meta>
```

TYPE

Currently there isn't much guidance for the type element. Its job is to differentiate specialized publications, such as a dictionary or reference book or a compilation of annotations. Use it as shown here, if you choose, but recognize that there isn't yet, as of the time of this writing, a list of accepted types. Rather, it's still wide open as to what publishers might use as the type of a publication.

```
<dc:type>Annotations</dc:type>
```

SUBJECT

Just as with dc:type, dc:subject is wide open. It's another way to categorize an EPUB, but there's no universally accepted list of subjects. If you use this tag, I recommend employing common genre titles—for example, Mathematics for an algebra textbook, Self-Help for a book about using orange hair and aggressive real estate development tactics to market yourself into a national TV show where you get to fire people who don't really work for you, Young Adult Fiction for a novel about an awkward teen girl with a sparkly boyfriend and his rejected rival for the girl's affections, who also has an allergy to shirts, and so on.

```
<dc:subject>Publishing and EPUBlishing</dc:subject>
```

RIGHTS

This tag indicates the copyright status of the work. Acceptable values include Public Domain, *Creative Commons* notices, and the always acceptable Copyright So-and-So.

```
<dc:rights>Copyright 2013, Alias Smith and Jones</dc:rights>
```

DESCRIPTION

Here's where you want to provide a synopsis of, or the marketing blurb about, your ebook. The contents of dc:description are often displayed within ereader bookshelves and ebookstores, and sometimes within samples certain ebookstores make available for free download ahead of purchasing the entire book.

```
<dc:description>It was the best of times, it was the worst of times. This book
delves deep into the subject of…</dc:description>
```

COVERAGE

This tag indicates the specific subject matter covered in your publication. Although useful for period fiction, the `dc:coverage` metadata element is used primarily for historical or scientific texts and other nonfiction that discusses a particular time period or geographic region. If, for example, you've produced an ebook about the 19th-century art and lifestyles of the Inupiat people in Barrow, Alaska (personally, one of my favorite places on the planet), then you'd want to enable your ebook to be found during a search for that region and time period—even if you've not used the location name or time period in any `dc:title` elements. The following lines, added to your metadata, would affect optimal findability of your ebook in libraries and catalogs.

```
<meta name="dc.coverage.placeName" content="Barrow, AK">
<meta name="dc.coverage.placeName" content="North Slope Borough">
<meta name="dc.coverage.placeName" content="Utqiagvik">
<meta name="dc.coverage.placeName" content="Ukpiaġvik">
<meta name="dc.coverage.placeName" content="Ukpeaġvik">
<meta name="dc.coverage.placeName" content="The place where we hunt snowy owls">
<meta name="dc.coverage.y" content="71d17N">
<meta name="dc.coverage.x" content="156 45 59">

<meta name="dc.coverage.periodName" content="19th century">
<meta name="dc.coverage.periodName" content="between 1801 and 1900">
```

The first six lines all communicate the name of the location discussed in the book, using different terms that may be employed as search terms by researchers and would-be readers. Specifically, these are as follows:

- *Barrow, AK*, the common name of the city and state

- *North Slope Borough*, the larger geographic and political body encompassing the city

- *Utqiaġvik*, *Ukpiaġvik*, and *Ukpeagvik*, all variations on the native Inupiak language name for the city as expressed in Latin language characters

- The translation of the native Inupiat name for Barrow, "the place where we hunt snowy owls"

Then, the next two lines, those bearing `dc.coverage.x` and `dc.coverage.y`, are the geographic coordinates for Barrow, AK, which, given Barrow's significance to numerous fields of scientific study, are important to include in the metadata for findability and cross-reference purposes. The *Y* coordinate is the longitude of the city, while the *X* coordinate is its latitude. In this case, I've used two different content formats as examples, whereas you would typically want to use the same format for both longitude and latitude. In the first, the *Y* value, I've entered the value 71d17N, which is 71 degrees, 17 minutes North. Note the use of the *d* to denote degrees but the lack of *m* for minutes. The last value doesn't need an identifier because system is obvious—minutes always come after degrees, just as, in page layout, points always come after pica, such as in the measurement "12p6." However, if you included seconds in the coordinate, you *would* use the *m* after the minutes and before the seconds, but you would leave off the *s*, or seconds, notation.

In the latitude value in the next line, I've employed a different format, separating degrees, minutes, and seconds with spaces and without notations. Notice, too, the absence of an East or West identifier. In this format such isn't necessary. Rather, you would employ positive values for locations east of the Prime Meridian and negative values for locations west of the Prime Meridian.

The final two lines, those containing `dc.coverage.periodName`, identify the time period the book discusses. Either or both of those lines could be used, or several options employed. The first temporal identifier notes the century, while the second specifies an exact range of years, offering a more specific value than a full century (though I've used it as a full century, too).

The `dc:coverage` metadata element is quite advanced, offering far more granular geographic and temporal specification than I've employed here. If you'd like to learn everything you can do with these tags, take a look at the official definition at `http://abbrv.it/DigiPubIDdcCoverage`.

META GENERATOR

This one is entirely optional and all but superfluous. Meant for future (human) editors of the metadata more than any application or the reader, the `<meta name="generator" content="Adobe InDesign" />` line is merely to indicate which program created the metadata. PDFs have similar creating application values in their metadata, but that can actually prove useful in troubleshooting problem PDFs. Within EPUB, InDesign doesn't even list its version number, just "Adobe InDesign," not that the presence of such would make this line any more useful. You can leave the line or delete it, leave the `content=` value as `Adobe InDesign` or change it to `Red Bull and Cheetos` if you like.

Editing Metadata in InDesign

During EPUB export in InDesign, on the Advanced pane of EPUB Export Options, there is a tiny little section called EPUB Metadata, which contains only two fields: Publisher, which corresponds to `dc:publisher`, and Unique Identifier, which, of course, is `dc:identifier`. InDesign CS5.5 and newer will automatically fill in the `dc:date` value as the date of EPUB export and doesn't expose that field to you within the user interface.

Additional pieces of metadata, such as book title, description, copyright status, subject, and a few others, may be added to the INDD document by editing the corresponding XMP metadata fields accessible via File ➤ File Info (refer to Figure 6.8). It isn't possible, however, to include multipart titles, co-authors and contributors, coverage data, or refinements of any metadata field directly within InDesign.

Editing Metadata in Calibre

Calibre, a free application, enables editing of EPUB metadata in a graphic user interface without extracting the contents of the EPUB. To access and edit the metadata fields, you'll need to first open the EPUB in Calibre and then click the big blue Edit Metadata button in Calibre's main window.

Note that Calibre enables access to all the basic metadata as well as some advanced features, including the ability to specify multiple authors, set sort order per author, change the cover image, and set dates via a pop-up calendar (see Figure 6.9).

FIGURE 6.9
Editing EPUB metadata in Calibre

Editing Metadata in Sigil

Sigil also lets you edit EPUBs with or without first extracting their constituent parts. Part code editor, part previewer, Sigil is like Dreamweaver for EPUB editing. Editing or adding to the metadata in Sigil is simply a matter of opening an EPUB and double-clicking its OPF file in the left Book Browser pane. After a warning that only advanced users should manually edit an OPF, you'll see the OPF code, helpfully color-coded, in the main area of Sigil, enabling you to edit the code by hand and add metadata Calibre can't, with total freedom (see Figure 6.10).

FIGURE 6.10
Editing the OPF metadata in Sigil

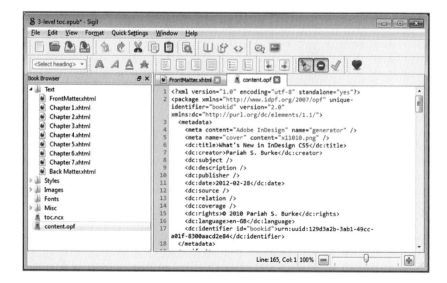

Creating Multiple-Chapter Ebooks

Although many ebooks are short enough to not need chapters or sections, the vast majority of ebooks include content broken into chapters. Given that many older ereaders cannot display XHTML files larger than 300 KB, breaking longer books into separate, chapter-based XHTML files is often a necessity. You can start creating chapters in the original content before it gets to InDesign, create chapters by making an INDD break at specific points, or, after InDesign, break your ebook into chapters by hand in the EPUB's files.

Using Multiple InDesign Documents

A typical multichapter book is *written* as multiple chapters. Take this book, for instance. It isn't practical for a 400–500 page book to be written entirely in one continuous InCopy or Word document. Rather, my editors and I work in chapters. Here I am writing Chapter 6 while one of my editors takes a pass through the first draft of Chapter 5, another editor is doing the second review of Chapter 4, and a third editor is reviewing my changes to Chapter 3. Chapter 2 will be coming back to me soon for a final review before layout, while Chapter 1 has already gone to the compositor for layout in InDesign. That first chapter will be laid out in its own INDD document. When Chapter 2 reaches the compositor, he'll lay it out in a separate INDD. Each subsequent chapter and appendix, the glossary, the index, the table of contents, the front matter, and the back matter will all be given their own individual INDD documents. All those INDDs will be tied together with an INDB book file.

That's how most longer books are produced, and that's the easiest way to translate chapter-specific INDDs to chapter-specific XHTMLs.

Take Figure 6.11, for example. It's the Book panel of a seven-chapter ebook with separate files for the front matter and back matter. (Book panels are covered in more detail in the next section.)

FIGURE 6.11

The Book panel for a multichapter ebook

Because each file is linked through an INDB Book panel, the page numbering is consecutive between chapters and remains that way in response to changes in page count in any of the individual chapters, which, of course, isn't all that important to ebooks. The following *are* important advantages to ebook creation via a Book panel:

♦   Export of the entire book to EPUB.

♦   Upon export, each INDD automatically becomes a separate XHTML inside the EPUB.

- Output of the entire book, or portions, to PDF and print for proofing or, when using a single set of files for print, PDF, and/or EPUB production.

- Preflight of the entire book or components thereof.

- Packaging of the entire book or components thereof.

- Synchronization of standardized elements—master pages, swatches, and paragraph, character, table, cell, TOC, and object styles—across all INDDs in the book.

- Separate chapters may be worked on by different workgroup members simultaneously.

- The Book panel itself provides the publication lead or production manager with a live overview of the readiness of each portion of the book.

- Fast opening of individual INDDs.

BOOK PANEL POWER IN-DEPTH

There's more to working with a Book panel than what I've discussed in this section. The information herein is meant more as a review for experienced InDesign users and to help less-experienced users get up to speed quickly with using a Book panel in an ebook workflow. To learn everything the Book panel can do for your documents, for you, and for your workflow, whether for ebooks, other digital output methods, or print, check out *Mastering InDesign for Print Design and Production* (http://abbrv.it/MasterInD), which will give you a soup-to-nuts understanding of the Book panel, plus examples of how the Book panel saves real working companies hundreds of hours and thousands of dollars.

CREATING A BOOK PANEL

Creating a Book panel is a breeze. In fact, you might have previously created one by accident by choosing File ➤ New ➤ Book in InDesign, thinking the command was suited for creating a book-length single InDesign document. Follow these steps:

1. Choose New ➤ Book from InDesign's File menu.

2. You'll be immediately prompted to name and save an INDB file. I recommend you name it with the title of your book and save it in the same folder that contains, or will contain, the constituent INDD chapter or section documents.

   Clicking Save produces a blank Book panel but no document. The panel itself is the INDB you just saved and is more accurately thought of as an index of INDDs than a document unto itself.

3. At the bottom of your Book panel, click the Add Documents button (the plus sign) and browse for the book's component INDD files. Although they don't have to be all in the same folder to be managed by a Book panel, it's helpful when adding them. In the Add Documents dialog, you can select multiple files by holding Ctrl/Cmd while clicking them, or, to select a sequential list of files faster, click to select the first in the list, and then

hold Shift while clicking the last in the list; all the files in between will be selected as well. Click Open to incorporate those files into the book.

Inserting documents into a book requires the Book panel to examine and then paginate (number) each document and its pages, so you may have to wait a few moments for InDesign to do this after adding documents.

4. Repeat the last step if you need to add additional INDDs to the book from other folders.

5. If the files are out of order in the Book panel, simply drag and drop them up or down into their new positions. Again, InDesign is going to repaginate after each change. You can disable the automatic numbering, which can get tiresome quickly, by selecting Book Page Numbering Options from the Book panel's flyout menu and then disabling the option Automatically Update Page & Section Numbers (Figure 6.12). With automatic numbering disabled, you'll need to initiate the renumbering before final output (or any time ahead of it) by selecting Update Numbering ➢ Update All Numbers from the Book panel's flyout menu.

FIGURE 6.12
Disable the frequent renumbering of all Book documents by unchecking the last option in this dialog.

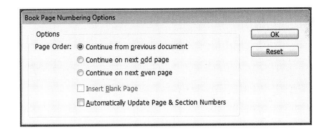

6. From the Book panel flyout menu, choose Save Book to commit the file additions and changes to the INDB.

TIP If you accidentally included a file you don't want in the book, highlight that file in the list and click the Remove Documents button (minus sign) at the bottom of the Book panel.

Now, any time you need to work on a chapter, just double-click its entry in the Book panel. The INDD will pop open in InDesign without you having to use File ➢ Open or scrounge around in Finder or Explorer.

SYNCHRONIZING STYLES, SWATCHES, MASTER PAGES, AND MORE

Just as good typography is essential for good page design, consistent use of styles, swatches, and master-page items is essential for good book design. Maintaining that consistency across multiple INDD documents in a book under production, one wherein anyone from the publisher through several editors and even the author may require a bookwide stylistic change, can be murderous. If, for example, you're laying out the final chapter in a 20-chapter book and you get an email from the production editor that all first-level headings throughout the 20 chapters need to have three more points of space before them, you could be in for a head-rapidly-and-violently-meets-desk moment. If you're managing those chapters in a Book panel, however, the change is fairly easy.

1. Open one of the chapter documents, preferably one that has all the styles, swatches, and master pages used by any of the other chapters.

2. Edit the paragraph style as needed in that chapter's INDD and do a quick Ctrl+S/Cmd+S to save the chapter with changes.

3. On the Book panel, click in the box to the left of the opened chapter's name to set that document as the book's style source (see Figure 6.13).

FIGURE 6.13
The style source icon in the far-left column designates one document as the style source for the entire book.

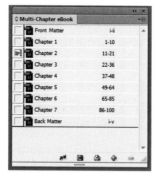

4. Ensure that no chapters are selected in the Book panel file list; click inside the empty space at the bottom of the list if necessary to deselect any highlighted files.

5. From the Book panel flyout menu select Synchronize Options. Up will pop the Synchronize Options dialog wherein anything that's checked will be synchronized across all documents in the book to maintain consistent appearance and, in some cases, behavior. Check the options you want to synchronize (see Figure 6.14). Unless you have a reason not to, I recommend checking them all.

FIGURE 6.14
All checked items will be synchro-nized across all documents in the book.

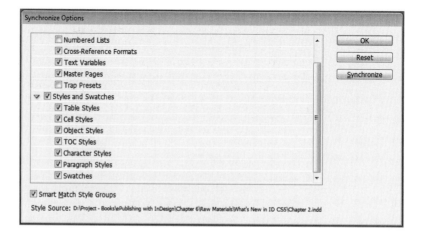

6. Click the Synchronize button to force all the other documents in the book to update their styles, swatches, master pages, text variables, and so on to match those in the document you defined as the style source.

Ta-da! Every chapter now updates its first-level-heading style (or whatever you changed) to match the one document's (Chapter 2 in our example).

To resynchronize in the future, after you've set the options once as to what to synchronize, just choose the Synchronize Book command from the Book panel flyout menu.

EXPORTING THE BOOK TO EPUB

Exporting a book to EPUB or PDF as well as printing, packaging, and preflighting couldn't be easier. Just select the appropriate command from the Book panel's flyout menu (Figure 6.15). Choosing Export Book to EPUB, for example, begins a process identical to exporting a single document to EPUB, with all the same options. The rub, as they say, is in *what* you select in the Book panel prior to choosing the Export command.

FIGURE 6.15
The Book panel's flyout menu in two different circumstances: (a) when no documents are selected and (b) with one or more documents selected

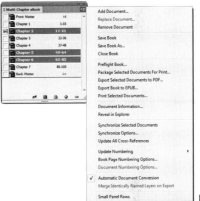

Compare the images in Figure 6.15. Image b is my Book panel and its flyout menu showing what happens when I open the flyout menu while I have several chapters selected in the list; image a is the same panel and menu revealing that the commands change—slightly in verbiage, significantly in effect—when I haven't highlighted any of the files in the list. If one or more files is selected in the Book panel's file list, then all output commands become specific to those selected files. For example, if I chose Print Selected Documents, it would print only those selected documents, which is perfect for proofing, among other things. However, to print the entire book, I need to make sure I don't have any files highlighted in the list. Clicking within the empty area of the file list below the last file will deselect any files, returning the panel flyout commands to versions that control output of the entire book instead of portions of it.

ASPIRIN-FREE WORKFLOW: EXPORTING PARTS OF A BOOK PANEL TO EPUB

Can you export only portions of a book to EPUB from the Book panel? Frustratingly, no. Adobe goofed on that one. Even with fewer than all the files selected, the Export Book To EPUB command remains the Export Book To EPUB command. If you want to proof or test only certain chapters in EPUB, you'll have to remove all the chapters you don't want exported from the Book panel. That may sound extreme, but here's a slick tip: A single INDD may belong to any number of INDB Book panels. Therefore, you could create another Book panel just for selective chapter testing. Choose Save Book As on the panel's flyout menu, save a new copy of the INDB, and then remove the files you don't want to output. Meanwhile, the original Book panel, though now closed, remains completely unaltered. You could even open it up alongside your new testing Book panel.

The only caveat to including an INDD in multiple book panels is that InDesign will attempt to renumber the pages in the INDD to match its position in the most recently used Book panel. If the content is strictly for EPUB export, that's inconsequential because ebook pages don't have fixed numbers.

Exporting a Book panel publication to EPUB automatically turns every INDD into its own XHTML inside the EPUB. You can see in Figure 6.16 how that looks in Sigil, with the file structure on the left, the OPF file in the center showing the chapter XHTML files' entries in the manifest, and, on the right, the table of contents InDesign automatically generated to point the reader to each chapter.

FIGURE 6.16
A multichapter, multi-XHTML ebook as viewed in Sigil

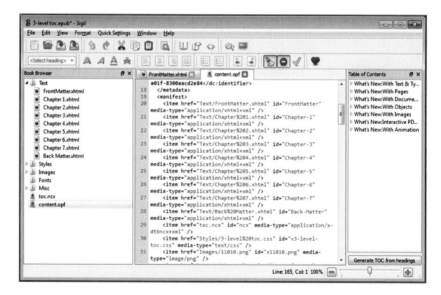

Whatever you name the individual INDD documents will become their names as XHTML files and in the automatically generated TOC. Consequently, you want to name the INDD files themselves according to the filenaming conventions I talked about at the end of the "Editing Files inside an EPUB" section of this chapter. You may also want to edit the chapter titles because they'll be displayed to readers. You can do that inside the EPUB's NCX file by changing whatever appears between the `<text>` and `</text>` tags for each instance of the following code:

```
<navPoint id="navpoint3" playOrder="3">
    <navLabel>
        <text>Chapter 1</text>
    </navLabel>
    <content src="Text/Chapter1.xhtml"/>
</navPoint>
```

Breaking by Paragraph Style

I highly recommend using a Book panel whenever you possibly can. The advantages are numerous. For those times when you can't, such as when an entire manuscript comes to you in one Word or InCopy document, or if you just prefer to work on an entire book in a single INDD, there is a very simple way to create chapter breaks—and thus separate XHTML files—during export. The key rests in the proper use of paragraph styles.

You must insert into your InDesign document some element that appears at the start of each chapter—often the chapter number or chapter title. Naturally, you're going to create a paragraph style to consistently style and update all the chapter numbers (or titles), maybe one called Chap Num. Now, on the InDesign page and in PDF and print output, forcing text assigned to a particular paragraph style to start on a new page is a trivial matter of changing the Start Paragraph field value in the paragraph style's Keep Options pane (Figure 6.17). Unfortunately, that value will not translate to EPUB; the next instance of the Chap Num style will simply start beneath the last line of the previous chapter. If it does happen to break to the next page, well, that's a coincidence of the length of the preceding text and the amount of space left for the Chap Num.

FIGURE 6.17
Setting the Start Paragraph value to On Next Page or another option can force the chapter to begin on a new page during print and PDF output.

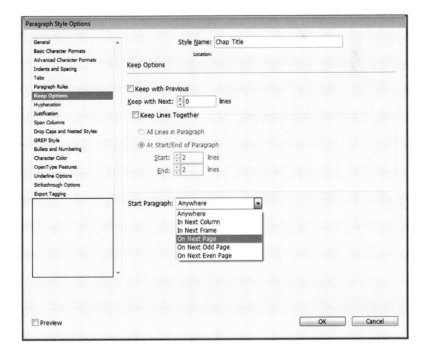

The way to break to the next page (and a separate XHTML) at each instance of the Chap Num or another style in EPUB is easy. On the Advanced pane of the EPUB Export Options dialog, at the very top, is a drop-down menu for Split Document (see Figure 6.18). By default the field reads Do Not Split, which will create a solid, single XHTML EPUB. Clicking the down arrow on that field reveals all of the document's paragraph styles. Choose Chap Num or whatever other style signals the start of a new chapter in your document, and, well, that's it. You're done. When you export, InDesign will now begin a new chapter and XHTML file beginning with each instance of the selected style, and it will take whatever text is tagged with that paragraph style as the TOC entry title.

FIGURE 6.18
The Split Document drop-down menu enables you to create multiple chapters simply based on instances of a particular paragraph style.

Breaking by Tags

In the Split Document drop-down, just beneath Do Not Split, is the option to break Based On Paragraph Style Export Tags. In the next chapter, I'll talk about paragraph style export tags, but I'd like to briefly define that document-splitting option. Each paragraph style can be mapped to a standard HTML tag such as <p> for standard paragraphs or <h1>, <h2>, <h3>, and so on for headings. When you've accomplished this mapping via the Paragraph Style Options Export Tagging pane, as of InDesign CS6, you can also specify right there that each instance of this style—or, more specifically, the HTML tag to which it's assigned in the event multiple styles are assigned to the same HTML tag and/or class—instigates the beginning of a new chapter (Figure 6.19).

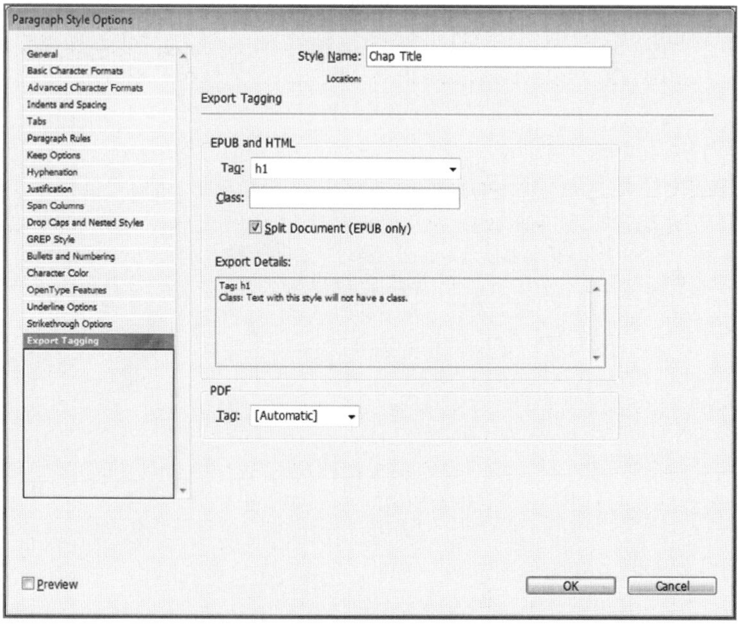

FIGURE 6.19
The Export Tagging pane lets you define in the style itself whether a new XHTML is created upon use of the style.

Creating Tables of Contents

Whether you're using one or multiple XHTMLs, longer documents need a table of contents to help readers reach the section and information they desire. There are two kinds of, or locations for, tables of contents—one for ebooks and PDFs and one for everything other than ebooks, including PDFs. Beginning the average print publication with a table of contents is usually quite important. The kind a reader might encounter as a page before the beginning of a book's main content is what I refer to as an on-the-page TOC because a designer deliberately places the TOC on one or more pages in InDesign. This type of table of contents typically directs readers to a specific page and, if the format supports it, hyperlinks TOC items to the locations in the document they reference. You'll see these in virtually every type of publication except an ebook—and knowing how to make an on-the-page TOC is necessary for making the "on-demand" TOCs that appear in ebooks.

Ebooks don't have page numbers per se, because the number of pages in a publication varies depending on how many pages are needed to display the full content on a given screen at the user-specified font size. Consequently, ereader makers and the EPUB specification allow for what I call an "on-demand" TOC, which doesn't actually appear on a page within InDesign. The on-demand TOC is the NCX file inside an EPUB.

Although we're talking strictly about EPUBs in this chapter, generating an on-demand TOC uses the same dialog and almost every step of the process as creating an on-the-page TOC. So, let's go through that process first. Along the way I'll explain the differences with EPUB (on-demand) TOCs and how to make them.

YOU'LL BE BACK

Even if you're producing other digital format epublications or print publications, this section about generating a TOC will come in handy because it, and the walk-through of InDesign's Table of Contents dialog box, applies equally to creating print, PDF, digital replica, digital magazine, and HTML5-based publications. You might want to dog-ear this page because I'll refer to it from within sections relevant to producing those other types of digital publications as well.

Building an On-the-Page TOC

Creating a table of contents for a document (or book) is easy as long as you practiced efficient composition by assigning paragraph styles to the elements that should be listed within the TOC. The basis for TOC generation is paragraph styles; in other words, any text assigned to *this* style or *that* style will be included or excluded based solely on its paragraph style.

Begin creating an on-the-page table of contents by creating an empty page to hold the TOC or, in the case of a Book panel–managed collection of documents, by creating a new document just for the TOC and then adding that to the Book panel. Once you have the space for a TOC, choose Layout ➢ Table of Contents, which opens the Table Of Contents dialog (Figure 6.20). Click the More Options button to reveal the full depth of the dialog.

FIGURE 6.20
The Table Of Contents dialog (with More Options shown)

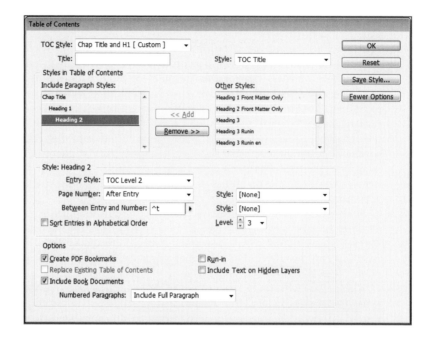

TOC Style All of the options incorporated into the Table Of Contents dialog may be saved as a preset called a TOC style. Creating a TOC style here and now is crucial to on-demand TOCs for EPUB export. After setting the options, click the Save Style button on the right and give the style a name. TOC styles can also be created and edited by choosing Layout ≻ Table Of Contents Styles. If a style has been precreated, it will appear in the TOC Style list; choose it, and all the options below it in the dialog will fill in with their style-defined values.

When exporting to EPUB, you'll need to select a saved TOC style from the TOC Style field in the middle of the General pane of the EPUB Export Options (Figure 6.21). This is why it's so important to set your TOC options in the Table Of Contents dialog and to save those options as a TOC style. Those options are not merely for the look of your TOC but also its contents, as you'll see as we move down through the controls and options in the Table Of Contents dialog.

Title When the TOC is generated and placed, it will have a title as the first line of the InDesign story. By default, the title will be *Contents*, but it can be anything you like. Leaving the Title field blank removes the title from the generated TOC entirely, without leaving a blank line where it would have been.

Style This is the paragraph style for formatting the TOC title. Look at the Style list; you should see *TOC Title* in there. Using that will create the *TOC Title* paragraph style and assign it to the title.

Styles In Table Of Contents This is the crux of creating a TOC. On the right, in the Other Styles list, are all the paragraph styles defined in the document. Click a style on the right to highlight it, and then use the Add button to move it to the left to the Include Paragraph Styles list. You can also double-click an entry in either column to move it to the other.

FIGURE 6.21
Choosing a TOC style to control on-demand TOC structure, content, and appearance in the ebook

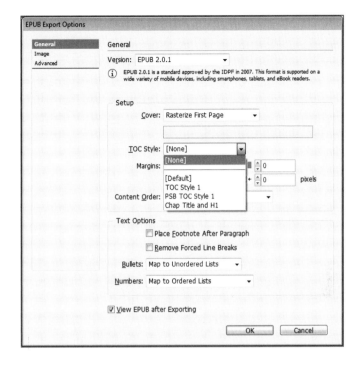

Each style included under Include Paragraph Styles will cause all text assigned to that style to be listed in the resulting TOC; styles not in the list will not have their dependent text referenced by the TOC. The order of styles in the Include Paragraph Styles list establishes the TOC hierarchy. In other words, the first listed style is the most important, highest level of the generated TOC, with the next appearing below it, the next below that, and so on.

If you insert styles in the wrong order, drag them up or down in the list just as you would reorder styles in the Paragraph or Character styles panel. But you must also change their Level value in the Style section below. Figure 6.22 shows an example of the Include Paragraph Styles list and the TOC it would generate.

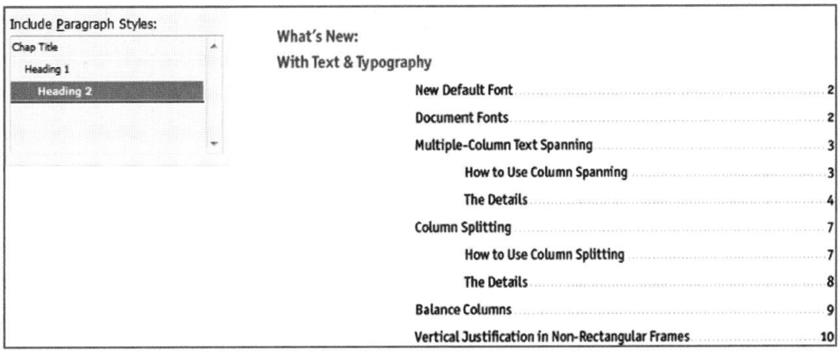

FIGURE 6.22
At left, the Include Paragraph Styles list, and at right, the resulting TOC

Include Paragraph Styles:

Chap Title
Heading 1
Heading 2

What's New:

With Text & Typography

New Default Font 2
Document Fonts 2
Multiple-Column Text Spanning 3
    How to Use Column Spanning 3
    The Details 4
Column Splitting 7
    How to Use Column Splitting 7
    The Details 8
Balance Columns 9
    Vertical Justification in Non-Rectangular Frames 10

Click to highlight a style in Include Paragraph Styles to set its options below in the Style section. Each included style may have its own entry style, page number options, and so on.

Entry Style   When the TOC is generated, the text for each entry can have its own paragraph style. There is already an entry on this list for *TOC Body Text*, which InDesign will assign to entries if you select it. You can also create a new paragraph style from scratch by choosing the last option on the menu, New Paragraph Style, which will launch the New Paragraph Style dialog. Alternatively, leave the default of [Same Style] to include the same style in the TOC as on the document pages—that is, the actual H1, H2, and H3 styles.

Page Number   Choose whether to place the page number before or after the entry text or to omit the page number entirely. When exporting to EPUB, the page numbers will be omitted from the on-demand TOC automatically, even if all page number options (Page Number, Style, Between Entry And Number, Style, Level, and the Sort check box) are enabled here. Note that iBooks will actually add page numbers to its rendition of the on-demand TOC, and those page numbers will match how iBooks arranges the content into pages to reflect the size of screen, the reader's font size preference, and other options.

ASPIRIN-FREE WORKFLOW: ONE DOCUMENT WITH A TOC FOR PRINT AND EBOOK

If you're using the same document to produce both EPUB and another format—PDF, print, whatever—there's a handy way you can handle both types of output: Create a Book panel for the document, using an INDD to hold the TOC document for print (or other) output. Then, just before you export to EPUB, remove the TOC document from the Book panel. Because ebooks don't use page numbers, you don't even have to update the page numbering of the other documents in the Book panel!

Between Entry And Number   Used for non-EPUB output, the Between Entry And Number field is the separator character or characters to appear between the entry text, the Heading 1 title, for example, and its page number. The pop-up menu to the right (the right-facing arrow) offers many symbols, markers, and special characters. To create a dot leader separator, specify a tab (^t) in the field and then modify the paragraph style (outside of the Table Of Contents dialog) to include a leader dot separator at that tab stop. The drop-down Style menu at the right allows assigning a character style to the separator itself, enabling any unique styling to be applied to just the separator.

Sort Entries In Alphabetical Order   By default, and in most cases, TOC entries are sorted in order of appearance in the document. However, especially when creating documents for electronic distribution as PDFs or EPUBs, this option opens numerous other possible uses for the table of contents feature beyond creating a standard TOC.

When InDesign generates a TOC, it creates hyperlinks connecting the TOC entries to the text they reference. Exporting to interactive PDF preserves these hyperlinks, enabling a reader of such a digital document to click the TOC entry and jump to the content. Thus, the option to sort entries alphabetically rather than logically opens the possibilities of creating vastly different lists, such as lists of product names, an advertisement index, personnel referenced in the document, or even a replacement for a standard index—without having to manually create index entries. The only significant limitation to using the table of contents functions in place of index and other features is that InDesign's table of contents is dependent upon paragraph styles; it cannot create an entry from a character style or a specific word in the middle of a paragraph.

Level   In a hierarchal TOC such as the one at the front of this book, entries from each successive style are considered inferior to their predecessors—Heading 1, for instance, is superior to Heading 2, which is superior to Heading 3. The Level field defines that hierarchy. Because each style is moved from the Other Styles list to the Include Paragraph Styles list, InDesign automatically assigns a successive level. If you have reordered the include list by dragging and dropping, you will also need to change the level for each affected style.

The Level field is nonexclusive, meaning that you are not required to have only a single level-one or level-two entry. If you have two or more equally important styles, they can all be set to the same level.

Create PDF Bookmarks   Similar to the way each TOC entry on the page will be hyperlinked to the associated section's content, InDesign can automatically generate PDF bookmarks, which are hidden until PDF export time. Adding these, and choosing to include bookmarks when exporting to PDF, creates something akin to Figure 6.23—a Bookmarks panel sidebar TOC-style list of topics that, when clicked in a PDF reader like Acrobat or Adobe Reader, become hot links and jump the reader to the referenced content.

FIGURE 6.23
The TOC-style bookmarks in this InDesign-created document were built by checking the Create PDF Bookmarks option in the Table Of Contents dialog.

This option has no relevance whatsoever to EPUB export because entries in an on-demand TOC are always hyperlinked to their destinations.

Replace Existing Table Of Contents If you have previously generated and placed a TOC, this option will replace (not update) it. The option is active only if you already have a TOC in your document.

Include Book Documents When generating a TOC for documents managed through an InDesign Book panel, check this option to generate a single TOC that points to all instances of the included paragraph styles in all documents within the book. If you aren't working with a book, this option will be grayed out.

Run-In By default, all TOC entries are given their own line, with a carriage return at the end. An alternate style is to use the run-in method that separates only by top-level styles. All entries lower in the hierarchy will be placed together in a paragraph (see Figure 6.24).

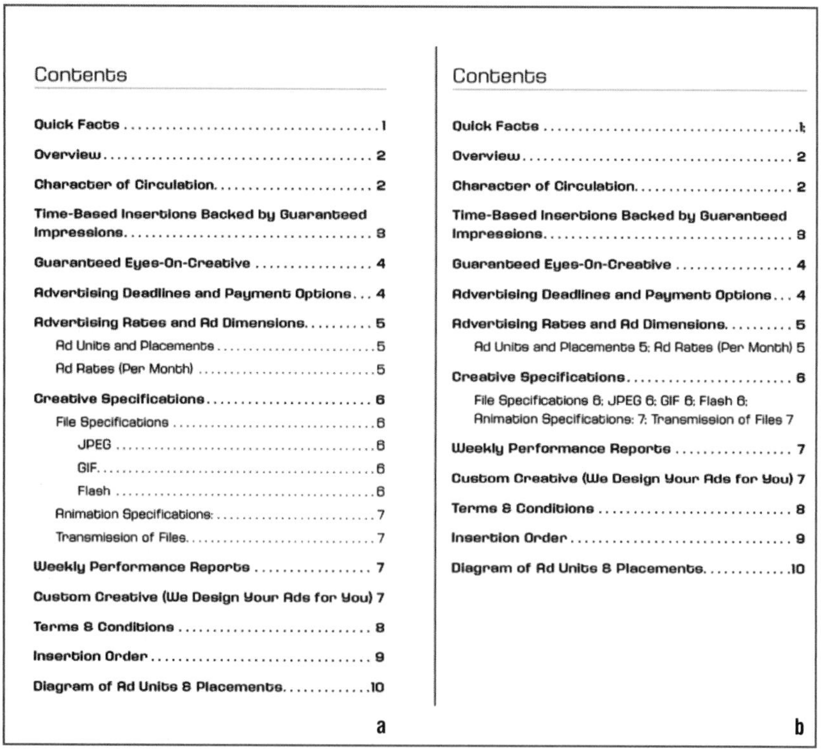

Contents

Quick Facts 1
Overview 2
Character of Circulation 2
Time-Based Insertions Backed by Guaranteed Impressions 3
Guaranteed Eyes-On-Creative 4
Advertising Deadlines and Payment Options ... 4
Advertising Rates and Ad Dimensions 5
Ad Units and Placements 5
Ad Rates (Per Month) 5
Creative Specifications 6
File Specifications 6
JPEG 6
GIF 6
Flash 6
Animation Specifications: 7
Transmission of Files 7
Weekly Performance Reports 7
Custom Creative (We Design Your Ads for You) 7
Terms & Conditions 8
Insertion Order 9
Diagram of Ad Units & Placements 10

a

Contents

Quick Facts 1
Overview 2
Character of Circulation 2
Time-Based Insertions Backed by Guaranteed Impressions 3
Guaranteed Eyes-On-Creative 4
Advertising Deadlines and Payment Options ... 4
Advertising Rates and Ad Dimensions 5
Ad Units and Placements 5; Ad Rates (Per Month) 5
Creative Specifications 6
File Specifications 6; JPEG 6; GIF 6; Flash 6; Animation Specifications: 7; Transmission of Files 7
Weekly Performance Reports 7
Custom Creative (We Design Your Ads for You) 7
Terms & Conditions 8
Insertion Order 9
Diagram of Ad Units & Placements 10

b

FIGURE 6.24 A standard hierarchical TOC (a) places each successive level of entry on its own line. A run-in version (b) places only the top level on its own and bunches lower levels together in a paragraph.

Include Text On Hidden Layers Choose whether to include in the TOC text that appears on hidden layers. This is useful if you're creating an index to advertisements or advertisers in your publication, for instance, and you've put the display names of those items on a hidden layer that readers won't see. In terms of EPUB export, content on hidden layers will not export at all, so this option isn't truly relevant; even if it's enabled, the export will omit any TOC entries that point to the nonexported hidden layer content.

Numbered Paragraphs   This option tells InDesign how to handle paragraphs that have been numbered through the List and Numbering functions. Note that InDesign does not recognize numbers that have been converted to standard text and will include them in the TOC regardless of this setting. The options are as follows:

Include Full Paragraph   Lists the text in the TOC exactly as it appears on the page, with all text automatic numbering intact. For example, the ninth table in a chapter whose number is defined within the paragraph Numbering options to include the prefix *Table 9* and whose table caption is *Four-Star Coruscant Cantinas & Tapcafs* will list in both the main text and the TOC as *Table 9.9 Four-Star Coruscant Cantinas & Tapcafs.*

Include Numbers Only   Ignores the text in the paragraph and includes only the automatic number and any prefixes. For example, to include a TOC entry for *Table 9.9* without the table's caption, choose Include Numbers Only.

Exclude Numbers   Includes in the TOC the text of the paragraph but not the automatic number. The TOC output using our example would therefore be simply *Four-Star Coruscant Cantinas & Tapcafs.*

Click OK in the Table Of Contents dialog to return to the document with a loaded cursor ready to place the TOC story, which may be placed and flowed like any story. If any stories in the document contain overset text assigned to the included styles, you will be prompted after clicking OK in the Table Of Contents dialog whether to include those overset instances in the TOC. If you were defining a TOC just for EPUB export, drop it on the pasteboard, whereupon you can leave it there or delete it. Items on the pasteboard will not export to EPUB (as long as they don't overlap a page at all). Having the TOC story on the pasteboard enables the Update Table Of Contents command.

If the contents of the document or book change, you needn't go through the entire generate process to update a TOC. Instead, select a text frame holding the TOC style, and choose Layout ➢ Update Table Of Contents. Shortly, an alert dialog will inform you that the table of contents has been updated successfully.

Styling the Table of Contents

All the paragraph-level elements comprising a table of contents have or can have styles assigned to them. In EPUB that styling translates to CSS formatting and class names.

If you've already generated a TOC, you'll most likely find on the Paragraph Styles panel one or more styles beginning with *TOC*. These can be edited to your heart's content, altering the display of elements within both the on-the-page and on-demand tables of contents—or at least as much styling as the ereader will support, which varies per device. If you haven't yet generated a TOC, you can set up your styles in advance.

1. Choose Layout ➢ Table of Contents Styles to open the Table Of Contents Styles dialog (Figure 6.25).

2. If an appropriate TOC style already exists, highlight it and click Edit. If not, click the New button.

3. In either case, the familiar Table Of Contents dialog will appear. The difference is that this instance will not generate a TOC itself but merely allow you to set all the options necessary for building a TOC *style* for later use. Set all your options as needed.

FIGURE 6.25

The Table Of Contents Styles dialog

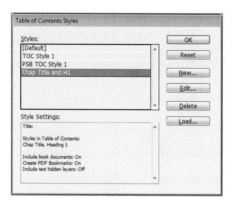

4. In the Entry Style drop-down menu, you'll find all of your document's paragraph styles. If what you want isn't there, the very last option on the list will let you create a new paragraph style without having to leave the Edit Table Of Contents Style dialog box. Thereby, you can create your TOC Level 1, TOC Level 2, and other styles right there, as you pick all the other options for the appropriate inclusion levels.

5. When you've set all the options the way you want them, click OK to save that style and then OK again to return to your document.

Generating the On-Demand TOC

Actually, there's very little you need to do in order to generate an on-demand table of contents. It's an automatic consequence of creating an EPUB with any type of automatic chapter or section breaking—in other words, multiple-document ebooks exported from a Book panel, breaking by paragraph style, and breaking by tags. InDesign also automatically creates an on-demand TOC if you create an on-the-page TOC—even if that on-the-page is actually on-the-pasteboard. Ergo, there's nothing else you need to do in order to generate the on-demand TOC. It's another matter entirely if you want to control or customize that on-demand TOC.

Even if you aren't going to implement an on-the-page TOC, use InDesign's Table Of Contents dialog to build the structure for your on-demand table of contents. Follow the same procedures, using all the same options discussed previously, to add the correct paragraph styles cum TOC entries and their hierarchy. Before finalizing it, however, click the Save Style button and save all those settings as a TOC style. I recommend naming the style Ebook On-Demand TOC or something else that will make perfect sense to you when you're 10 cans of Red Bull into an all-nighter to meet deadline. Then, after you click OK, resulting in a loaded cursor, press Esc to clear the cursor of the TOC you don't want to place on the page.

To use the TOC style you just created in your ebook's on-demand TOC, choose it from the TOC Style list in EPUB Export Options.

Editing the TOC.NCX

The methods discussed in this chapter generate the on-demand TOC as the EPUB's Navigation Control for XML (NCX) file. Like all the other components of the EPUB, the NCX is an XML file containing human-readable—and editable—text and markup. You can, and may at some point, need to edit the NCX file in Sigil or a text or HTML/XML editor. Refer to the "Editing Files Inside an EPUB" section of this chapter for the skinny on editing the NCX.

Chapter 7

Creating PDF Publications for Digital Delivery

Portable Document Format (PDF) publications are still a viable—indeed, a popular—distribution format. PDFs support rich multimedia, hyperlinks, variable-visibility objects, some pretty cool interactivity, scripting, reflowable text like EPUBs, and electronic forms. PDF viewers are available for all computer and mobile platforms, though feature support varies by platform. In this chapter, I'll show how to use PDF to its fullest epublishing potential while defining the restrictions placed on it by certain devices. You'll also look at some successful PDF-based publications that have been going strong for years.

In this chapter, you will learn about the following:

◆ Planning a PDF Publication

◆ Starting a New Document

◆ Exporting to Interactive PDF

◆ Adding Audio and Video

◆ Creating External Hyperlinks of All Types

◆ Devising Intra-Document Navigation

◆ Creating Advanced Interactivity

◆ Finalizing the Publication

Planning a PDF Publication

As you begin to plan your digital publishing workflow, you should be asking yourself the following series of questions:

- ◆ To what device classes do I want to publish?

- ◆ Within each class of device, which are my top target devices?

- ◆ On what devices will people want to read my publication regardless of what *I* want them to do with it?

- ◆ Ideally, what types of media and interaction would my publication employ?

- ◆ What is the least amount of media and interaction my publication can have and still be viable for its purpose?

Of course, you should also be asking yourself a lot of questions regarding content, distribution channels, financing, production logistics, and so on, but those questions are beyond the scope of this chapter. For now, I will focus on whether PDF has a place as one of your publication's distribution formats.

Choosing the Place for PDF in a Digital Publishing Workflow

As I discussed way back in Chapter 2, "Learning about Digital Publishing Formats," there is a massive installed user base of PDF readers, including those for desktop computers, laptops, netbooks, ultrabooks, tablets, smartphones, and even many ereaders. The support for PDF features varies with each device class, however. In general, you can assume that PDF viewers will show the PDF, including imagery and text, and most will work with forms and enable annotations of some kind, but few handle interactivity and multimedia. The only devices you can rely on having support for the full range of PDF features are computers, and then only if you are using Acrobat or the free Adobe Reader.

Mac OS X Preview, a common preinstalled all-around file viewer, is one of the most horrible ways to view a PDF. It lacks just about everything mobile clients do but doesn't bother to tell users they're missing out on the major features that are most relevant to digital publishing. Consequently, I recommend specifically telling readers not to use Preview to read your PDF publications.

Obviously, devices running full computer operating systems support the largest number of PDF features—all of them, in fact—while devices that run mobile OSs drop support for some things you might find crucial for your publication. It would be even more confusing—unwieldily so—if I start talking about PDF feature support in all the various PDF viewer apps that are available for mobile platforms. One might support video but not do forms, another does forms and JavaScript but not embedded video, and so on. And, of course, all of this is subject to change over time. New developments will be covered in my digital updates to the information in this book (at `http://abbrv.it/DigiPubIDUpdates`), but the best thing you can do is to test the features you want on the devices you think might be used to read your PDF publication.

Depending on the content you want to produce, the devices you want to target, your budget for the publication, and your skill set, you generally want to build for as many platforms and device classes as possible, using the format best suited for each of those platforms and device classes. For publication dissemination on computers, for example, you can't get better than PDF. On tablets, though, digital magazine or digital replica is the format to pick, just as HTML-based EPUB (or Kindle Format 8) is the way to go for ereaders.

InDesign has features that can help you repurpose pages for different output formats, adjusting object positioning and relations without the need to design every page for every version from scratch.

For the rest of this chapter, I'm going to make two assumptions about you and your goals: First, you want to produce epublications with the widest possible reach; and second, you intend to make PDF one of the (or *the*) formats for your epublication.

Targeting to Screen

A *successful* PDF publication cannot be the print edition exported to, and distributed as, PDF. It's a very, very (very) common mistake many, many (many) publishers make, and their circulations pay the price for it. If you're going to distribute your content in PDF, even if it's only one of several formats for the same content, design the PDF version of the publication for PDF.

PDF TO IPAD: CREATING DIGITAL REPLICAS

Of course, if what you really want is to get your print edition onto tablets quickly, efficiently, and with little cost, PDF is not the format for you. Instead, you want to use the digital replica format, which I discussed in Chapter 2. Given that there are a number of successful digital replica creation systems but that those systems are in a state of very rapid evolution and enhancement, I couldn't write about them in this book—the information would be out of date by the time you tried to use it. For current information on the technology, please visit my website at http://iampariah.com.

PDFs are meant to be read on-screen. Whether that's a computer desktop screen, a laptop screen, a tablet screen, or even a smartphone screen, none of those screens is 8.375×10.875 inches, which is the average trim size of printed magazines and catalogs. Neither is the average screen a match for a digest size publication (5.5×8.25 inches). Let's visually compare different page displays to scale in Figure 7.1. All are the same magazine page, viewed in Adobe Reader on various platforms (and in Acrobat Pro in the first one). Starting with a print-ready magazine layout and then trying to scale it to fit a common screen doesn't look so great, does it? Even viewing a full spread with landscape orientation doesn't help (Figure 7.2).

If you start with a print-ready layout and simply export that to PDF, not only will you sacrifice a lot of screen real estate to black or gray bars, but you'll also clearly communicate to readers that the publication wasn't designed to be read on-screen. That alienates your readership and won't inspire them to return for the next issue or even to spend much time with the current issue.

Not incidentally, the magazine used in the previous examples is *not* an old one. Its issue 4 of *The Great Wen*, published in September 2011, which really isn't that long ago. Certainly the creators were well aware of the then-18-month-old iPad and the rapidly expanding competition of Android, webOS, and Blackberry OS tablets, and, more important, of modern computer screens. Unfortunately, they created a print-ready publication and distributed it in PDF. Reading should never be that much work.

FIGURE 7.1

A pretty-close-to-standard-sized 8.27 × 11.69-inch print-ready magazine page displayed on four devices

The page as viewed on a 22-inch, 1650 × 1080-resolution monitor—a little larger than average for computer and laptop monitors. The text is mostly illegible despite the fact that the magazine is marketed for on-screen reading.

Even with the Retina display's superior resolution and text presentation, the page is unreadable at 100 percent on an iPad 3.

Viewing the print-ready PDF on a 7-inch-class tablet (the Kindle Fire) is horrible.

On a smartphone? Fuggetaboutit.

FIGURE 7.2
Pages from the
same magazine,
in landscape
orientation

Unreadable without zooming on the iPad 3

The spread on the 7-inch Kindle Fire

Deciding on Resolution

Think about the size of the screens on which you want readers to consume your publication. And don't think in inches. Digital screens are measured most precisely in terms of their resolution, which is expressed in pixels.

Let's talk delivery resolution—image quality vs. screen quality. With printed publications, you're working with 300–2400 dpi, depending on the publication content and paper and ink choices. In the digital realm, it used to be all just 72 ppi, which is pretty much the same as dpi, but that's changing. More importantly, ppi depends on the screen size of the device and the distance for viewing. For instance, the iPhone 4S has a resolution of 326 ppi, while the iPad 3 is 264 ppi. Apple's Retina display, debuted in the iPhone 4s, then in the tablet-sized iPad 3, and then in all Apple displays, is a gauntlet thrown down in the market; now all mobile device manufacturers are seeking a way to increase their devices' resolution. No longer is it a simple matter of 72 ppi for everything (Windows was usually 96 ppi anyway). Even among like devices—the iPhone 4 and iPad 3, for instance—the number of pixels contained in screen inches isn't identical. Thus, instead of targeting for a screen resolution of 72 ppi, go with a print resolution of 300 ppi. That will then scale to look great on any current-generation mobile device. If you're working from an existing print layout with high-resolution images, then don't change a thing; they'll be downsampled during export to PDF, which I'll cover later in the chapter.

If, however, you're making new images for digital distribution or designing only for digital PDF distribution, choose your image size before you take the lens cap off the camera or open Photoshop. Make them 300 ppi regardless of the devices you're targeting, but choose the dimensions based on the pixel display dimensions of the highest-quality screen you want to target. In most cases, that would be the iPad 3 with its 2,048 × 1,536-pixel screen. If you want a full-screen image to look crisp and high quality on an iPad 3, make it at least 2,048 × 1,536 pixels. If you want an image to look crisp and high quality when the reader zooms into it on an iPad 3, make the image larger than 2,048 × 1,536 pixels. How much larger depends on how far you want them to zoom before loss of quality occurs, weighed against how large you'll allow the image's file size to be.

In a nutshell, use a resolution high enough to look good on the highest-resolution tablet out there, that being the iPad 3 and newer, and to account for zooming to at least 200 percent (even though most people likely won't zoom).

Even if you don't include full-screen images, use the resolution as the basis of your page size, sizing all images appropriately, to maintain consistent quality. With resolution in mind, now it's time to choose a display aspect ratio and an orientation for your pages.

Selecting Display Aspect Ratio

To be perfectly honest, screen resolution, while quite important, isn't the most important measurement to arrive at when deciding on page and image size. The primary measurement with which digital publishers should be concerned when using any format, when targeting any device, is the display aspect ratio.

Display aspect ratio is the proportional relationship between the width of the screen's viewable area and its height. For example, iPad 1 and 2, when held in landscape orientation, have a resolution of 1,024 × 768 pixels, which is a ratio of 4:3. The third-generation iPad, with its Retina display, offers a screen resolution far above that, 2,048 × 1,536 pixels, but the exact same 4:3 aspect ratio. Just reduce 1,024 × 768 and 2,048 × 1,536 to their lowest common denominators, and you'll arrive at 4×3, better expressed as 4:3, on all counts. It's the same with the iPhone and the iPod Touch. Many Android tablets also share the 4:3 display aspect ratio.

The kinds of TVs many of us had as kids—and, for those of us who aren't videophiles, also hung onto into the 00s—had the same 4:3 aspect ratio, but today's HD TVs offer the very different, much-wider-than-tall, 16:9 aspect ratio. That's also the aspect ratio of the average wide-screen computer monitor, whether desktop or laptop, though there's still a lot of variation in the monitor space; for instance, some popular monitors give a bit more vertical space at roughly 16:10, often with a native resolution of $1,650 \times 1,080$ pixels. Thanks in no small part to HD television and HD film, 16:9 is the most widely used "high-definition" or "wide-screen" format for screens of all kinds, with 16:10 (which is correctly written as 8:5, though I'll stick with 16:10 here to show the close association to 16:9) running a close second and 4:3 making up an equally popular screen ratio among mobile devices.

As you plan your PDF-based publication, do so armed with the display aspect ratios of the devices on which you expect your audience to view the publication. Actual pixel measurements of any device are available from the manufacturer's website or from the product listing in common estores like Amazon or TigerDirect. With the pixel resolutions, you can then easily compute the aspect ratios using a ratio calculator like the one at `http://abbrv.it/DigiPubIDRatio`.

Designing for the aspect ratio is crucial because digital publications will be uniformly scaled down to fit the screens on which the publication is viewed. Of course, readers can zoom in and out as they see fit—that's one of the great advantages to PDF, along with the live vector type that looks sharp at any zoom percentage—but a large portion of the population won't zoom. Naturally, the depth of interaction with content varies with the content and the market segments to which it's distributed, but the average human being who reads digital content just doesn't zoom.

First find the resolution you need to meet, and then determine the display aspect ratio of the primary device you want to target. With the variance of screen aspect ratios on the market today, you sometimes just have to target the one you think will be most popular and hope for the best on the rest. Orientation is the final factor in deciding a page size, and it can help or hinder the readability of the publication on all screens.

My first-choice recommendation would be a 4:3 aspect ratio. First, 4:3 accounts for non-wide-screen computers, which include many laptops, netbooks, and ultrabooks. Second, even on wide-screen computers, the 4:3 aspect ratio allows users to open the Bookmarks or Pages panel in Reader or Acrobat without squishing the pages down.

Choosing Reading Orientation

Tablets, phones, and other mobile devices can typically display PDFs in either landscape or portrait orientation. While orientation doesn't have much to do with image resolution either way, it does have a huge impact on display aspect ratio. Consider a 16:9 device. In fact, let's convert that ratio directly to page dimensions. At 1,600 pixels wide and 900 pixels deep or tall, you have a very wide page—an HD page, if you will—one that fills the screen of a 16:9 device. Rotate the device, however, and suddenly you have 1,600 pixels squished into only a 900-pixel space with giant black or gray bars at the top and bottom of the page (see Figure 7.3). Unlike the digital magazine format, PDFs can't be made to switch from portrait-optimized layout to landscape-optimized in correspondence with device rotation. It's one or the other.

FIGURE 7.3
A 16:9 display ratio
page in portrait
orientation on a
16:9 display ratio
device

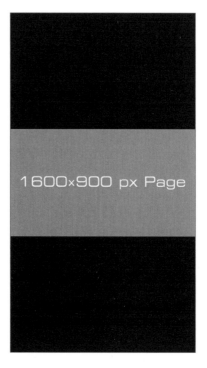

Therefore, you have to pick one orientation to target, and I recommend you make that landscape for the following reasons:

◆ Computer screens, the top device for PDF consumption, are almost always landscape oriented, which is the major reason merely exporting portrait-oriented print magazines to PDF does not create the ideal PDF reading experience.

◆ Adobe Acrobat and the free Adobe Reader on computers, as well as most competing PDF viewer products, default to fitting a page's width in the window when the document is opened. With portrait-oriented pages, that creates a fold, an area at the bottom of the page that isn't initially visible, below which the reader may never venture; a fold is much less likely to occur in a landscape-oriented cover or page.

◆ Landscape orientation instantly communicates that the publication was designed for on-screen use rather than a printed page exported to PDF and marketed as yet another useless, after-thought alternate version.

◆ Because the bottom of the page is much less likely to be cut off by the view, readers can progress from the bottom of one text column to the top of the next without cumbersome vertical scrolling.

TIP I recommend building the layout nonfacing, so that only a single page at a time is viewed and so that you *design* for a single-page display rather than being tempted to create layouts that work well only when viewed as spreads.

Determining Page Size

Taking all these factors into account, I often recommend designing PDF publications with a page size of or near 3,000-pixels wide by 2,250-pixels deep, which is the same as 15 × 11.251 inches. That size works very nicely on computers and tablets, allows zooming (because it displays initially zoomed *out* because of its larger-than-monitor size), and also enables the use of 72 ppi images that result from screen captures on computers, tablets, ereaders, and other digital devices without having to scale them up and lose quality. Of course, the types of materials I usually write are technically oriented for creative professionals and use many screenshots; therefore, my average figure or graphic is captured at 72 ppi, which means my page sizes must be created to support 72 ppi original images. If your publication doesn't include any device screen captures, you probably don't care too much about 72 ppi, but that same 15 × 11.251-inch measurement works just as well for higher-resolution images, too.

Starting a New Document

Obviously I'm not going to tell you how to design your publication—text, images, vector objects, and so on. The average reader of this book is already quite experienced in designing within InDesign for print and maybe even for digital publications of one type or another. If you *do* need help learning to design or design efficiently within InDesign, check out my book *Mastering InDesign CS5 for Print Design and Production* (Sybex, 2010). Later in this chapter, I'll go deep into adding multimedia and interactivity to the PDF layouts, but I'll leave the basic design and layout up to you.

What I *do* want to cover in this pretty short section is the process of starting a new INDD document specifically for PDF publications. Some of the options you'll choose in the New Document dialog and elsewhere will be different from those for your standard print publication. Let's walk through it section by section, and along the way I'll explain why I'm asking you to make certain choices.

Stating Your Intent

Within InDesign, either click New Document from the Welcome screen or go the menu route by choosing File ➤ New ➤ Document. Figure 7.4 shows the resultant New Document dialog.

In the New Document dialog's Intent pull-down, select Web, not Digital Publishing. The Web intent automatically activates two options useful for creating PDF-based publications. First, it makes the working color space RGB, which is absolutely crucial for the best quality imagery, and, second, it sets InDesign's document measurement system to pixels. If you don't like working in pixels, well, you aren't required to; you'll have to leave the system as set until you click OK in the New Document dialog, but after that, you can restore the measurement system to inches, pica, millimeters, or whatever you like by choosing, on Windows, Edit ➤ Preferences ➤ Units And Increments, and on Mac, InDesign ➤ Preferences ➤ Units And Increments (see Figure 7.5). You can also right-click the ruler in the InDesign document window and change the measurement system for that ruler; just remember that you'll need to set the measurement system on both the horizontal and vertical rulers.

FIGURE 7.4
The New Document
dialog

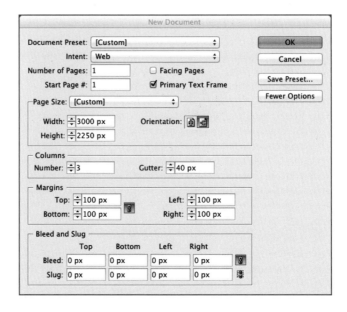

FIGURE 7.5
Changing the
measurement
units in InDesign's
Preferences

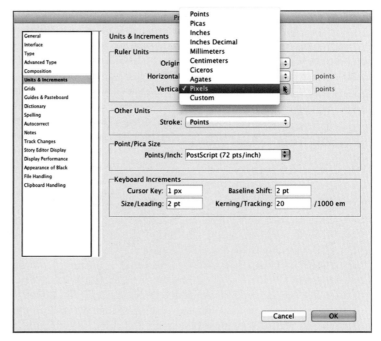

The Digital Publishing intent might seem like the logical choice for a new digital publication, but it's not for PDF-based digital publications (or for digital replica format, for that matter). Its role is specifically to create digital magazine–format publications, which I'll cover in Chapters 8 through 10.

Choosing Page Options

Obviously, the Number Of Pages field in the New Document dialog lets you presupply the number of pages of your publication. You aren't required to put a value in there, and even if you do, you can always add and remove pages later via the Pages panel or the Layout ➤ Pages menu. Rather, the Number Of Pages field is merely there as a convenience; if you know in advance how many pages your publication needs to be, which is often the case with print PDF-based publications, you can save yourself the steps of adding a bunch of blank pages later by filling in this option here, causing InDesign to start the document with that number of blank pages.

The Start Page # field might require a little thought. InDesign defaults to filling the field with a 1, meaning a new document will start at page 1. That's usually just fine. However, PDFs support all the same page and section numbering options you can set in InDesign. For instance, if you're creating a PDF-based ebook, maybe you want the front matter and table of contents of the book to number with lowercase Roman numerals (for example, i, ii, iii, iv, and so on) and then begin the content of the book proper with the Arabic numeral 1. Maybe you're creating an issue or installment of a journal whose numbering continues sequentially month to month until the entire volume is published. For example, the January edition of the journal would begin numbering at page 1 and end on page 32, and the February edition would start with page 33. If for these or any other reason you need the publication to begin at something other than page 1, enter the number in the Start Page # field. Note that the value must always be in Arabic numerals, regardless of the page numbering scheme you want to use, and can be set after the New Document dialog. In other words, if you want to start numbering at i or A, you must still enter 1 in the field because i and A are the Roman and alphabetic-style equivalents of 1.

Once you've clicked OK in the New Document dialog and are now looking at the document, you can change the numbering system in the Numbering & Section Options dialog (Figure 7.6). Just choose Numbering & Section Options from the Layout menu, and then change the page numbering Style field to the system you'd like to employ. To change the document's starting number, letter, or symbol, change from Automatic Page Numbering to Start Page Numbering At and supply the starting value. Whatever you set in this dialog will appear in the Pages panel *and* within a PDF viewer (see Figure 7.7). Note that you must choose Pages, not Spreads, as the export format in the Export To Interactive PDF dialog in order for the page numbering scheme to carry over into PDF. (See the "Exporting to Interactive PDF" section later in this chapter.)

FIGURE 7.6
InDesign's Numbering & Section Options dialog enables you to change the numbering style.

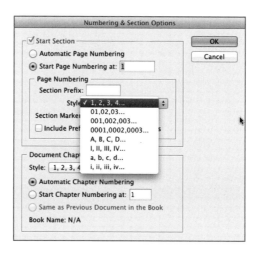

FIGURE 7.7
After you set the
page numbering
style to lowercase
Roman, both InDe-
sign and Acrobat
use that numbering
system.

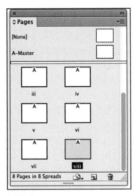

InDesign

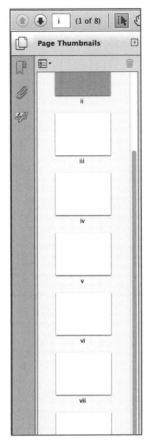

Acrobat

Leave Primary Text Frame checked (as it is by default in the New Document dialog), which replaces the pre-CS6 Master Text Frame option that allows you to easily flow text across pages.

In the Page Size section, you'll want to supply the page size you've decided on for your publication. It's likely not already on the Page Size menu—at least, not the first time you need it. If this is a one-off publication and you don't expect to make any other PDF-based epublications in the near future, just enter the width and height of the pages in the appropriate fields. Even though the fields show pixel measurements, you can enter values using whatever measurement system you're most comfortable with; just append the appropriate symbol after your measurement. For example, to use my recommended page size, just type into the Width field **15 in** and into the Height field **11.251 in**. InDesign will convert the inch measurements to pixels.

If you *do* expect to use the same page size more than just this once, save yourself some trouble in the future. Instead of entering the dimensions in the Width and Height fields, follow these directions to add your desired page size to the Page Size drop-down menu for instant selection later:

1. Choose Custom from the Page Size drop-down menu. Up will pop the Custom Page Size dialog (Figure 7.8).

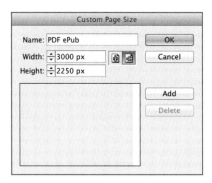

2. Set the Width and Height fields as needed. You can ignore the orientation buttons; all they do is swap the Width and Height values.

3. At the top of the dialog, supply a name for the new page size. If you don't, InDesign won't save the page size, so try entering something like **PDF ePub** or whatever will communicate to you and/or colleagues that this is the page size you want for certain projects.

4. If you want to create only the one page size, click OK; if you need to make several custom page sizes, click Add instead, which will save the custom page size and keep you in the dialog, ready to set up additional sizes.

Setting Columns, Margins, Bleed, and Slug

How you configure columns and margins is entirely up to you, but there are a few things you should remember. First, your type size will need to be larger in PDF epublications than in counterpart print publications. Reading 10.5-point body copy or 8-point caption text in print is just fine, but trying to read that on-screen is a vastly different experience. I recommend you consider 12-point type as the base size for your publication, along with generous leading. If you're creating your page size large enough to zoom—such as with my recommended 3,000×2,250-pixel size—you'll need to dramatically increase font sizes to give them the *appearance* of 12 points when the page is scaled to fit the screen. Increasing type size and leading, of course, may alter many aspects of your page geometry, including the number of, and gutter distance between, columns. Also remember that the number of columns you choose in the New Document dialog will not only create column guides but also set the number of columns inside the primary text frame if you enabled the option for that.

Margins, of course, only help you compose the page; both within InDesign and in the exported PDF, you can place objects outside the margins, including full-bleed images. Still, with bigger type, you might want wider and taller margins.

That brings me to the Bleed and Slug measurement fields. Simple: Don't use them. Because you're creating a digital publication, you have no need of a slug area to communicate to print service providers instructions for bindery and finishing, designer contact means, or tracking information. You could use a slug area for internal tracking and revision control—many production departments include modification and sign-off information in the slug area, for example— but that slug area could become visible in the PDF if the reader changes a few options in Acrobat or Reader. Consequently, I recommend not using a slug area at all, or, if you must, use a slug area but put all the data on a separate layer that you disable prior to exporting to final PDF.

Bleed guides, which help extend bleeding (edge-to-edge) objects and artwork out beyond the trim size to account for paper shifts on a cutter after printing, have absolutely no place in digital distribution, so ignore them entirely.

ASPIRIN-FREE WORKFLOW: CREATE A PRESET FOR THE FUTURE

If you think you might reuse the settings you've just configured in the New Document dialog for a future project—even if that project is expected to be months away—save yourself the trouble of remembering (or looking up) those options and setting them again. Once you have everything set the way you want it, click the Save Preset button. You'll then be prompted to name your preset and confirm its creation. Forevermore, that preset will be available in the New Document dialog's Document Preset menu. Choose it, and your intent, page options, columns, margins, bleed, and slug—*everything*—instantly repopulate with the settings you had to do manually this time.

Exporting to Interactive PDF

I'll cover the process of, and options inherent in, exporting epublications to PDF right up front, so that you can easily test the features I'll cover throughout the rest of the chapter, features such as adding audio and video, variable-visibility objects, hyperlinks, and so on.

As of CS5, Adobe split what was a unified PDF export process for any type of PDF into two distinct procedures: exporting a PDF for print or press and exporting one intended to be used as an epublication. The options for the two intents, which you can see in Figure 7.9, are vastly different. Although the change can be initially jarring, the separation actually makes epublication PDFs easier to create; all the relevant options are presented in a single, smaller dialog box. To reach that dialog, all you have to do is choose File ➤ Export, set the File Format or Save As Type to Adobe PDF (Interactive) option, name the file, and click OK. Up will pop the Export To Interactive PDF dialog. Let's go through its options.

Pages   Choose to export all pages or only some. The Range field can accept any arrangement of pages, in any order. Use hyphen-separated numbers (for example, 2-7) to send a sequential range of pages, or use comma-separated numbers (for example, 8,6,4,2) to send nonsequential, or out-of-order, pages. You can also combine both methods, for example, 2-7,20,18,16,10-14.

Pages or Spreads   You can also choose to export as individual pages or spreads. Again, I recommend exporting as individual pages (not that you had the choice in single-page export-only CS5 and CS5.5).

View After Exporting   Proofing an exported document before sending it out is always a good idea. Checking this option saves you the trouble of launching Acrobat and hunting down the file you just created; as soon as the PDF is finished generating, Acrobat (or Reader, whichever you have associated in your operating system to handle PDF files) will launch with the file loaded and ready for inspection.

PDF for print output...   ...and for Interactive PDF.

Embed Page Thumbnails   Each page of a PDF may be navigated visually via thumbnails in Acrobat's Pages panel. This option creates those page thumbnails—snapshot images of pages—so that they're ready and waiting for the PDF's audience. If you don't create them, the file size of your exported PDF will be smaller, but the reader will have to wait the first time she opens the Pages panel (if she ever does) while Acrobat generates the thumbnails.

Create Acrobat Layers   This option can create layers in the PDF from the top-level layers in InDesign. For instance, if your document is multilingual, with separate layers for English, French, and Russian text, this option will preserve those layers in the PDF document, enabling readers to toggle the various languages on or off, much like layers in InDesign or Photoshop. If you're going to use buttons that control the visibility of layers, make sure you enable this option.

View   When a PDF is opened in Acrobat or Adobe Reader, it can be set to automatically zoom to a particular percentage or to fit one or both dimensions of the page. How your PDF looks the very first time someone sees it is important—it could determine whether the would-be reader dives right in or immediately closes the document and never opens it again. How the view is zoomed has a good deal to do with that first impression. You have several options.

Default   Shows whatever the reader has set as the default view within Acrobat or Adobe Reader. For the vast majority of people out there, that default value is Fit Width.

Actual Size   If the page is 11×8.5 inches, for example, it'll be zoomed regardless of screen size to approximately 11×8.5 inches, cropping out of the view whatever doesn't fit.

Fit Page   Zooms to fit both the width and height of the document in the application window. This is often a good choice for epublications because it opens the document with the full cover fitting in the view like a splash screen.

Fit Width and Fit Height   Chops off the other dimension if necessary and requires the user to scroll in order to see that other dimension.

Fit Visible   Zooms to include the visible portion of the page in the application window.

Fixed Zoom Percentage   Regardless of the screen size, this zooms to the specified percentage of the document dimensions.

Because of the vast difference in screen sizes, I strongly advise against using a fixed zoom percentage; instead, put your best foot forward with Fit Page, Fit Visible, or Fit Width.

Layout   Similar in importance to View, Layout determines the initial view on your document. Both the view and layout can be changed by the reader in the PDF client, but rarely does the average PDF consumer know how to do that. Thus, you should be very careful in changing the layout. You can choose from the following options:

Single Page   Shows one page at a time, jumping from the bottom of one page to the next

Single Page Continuous   Shows one page at a time but scrolls smoothly between pages rather than jumping

Two-Up (Facing)   Puts two pages side by side like a spread

Two-Up (Cover Page)   Shows pages side by side except for the first page, which is assumed to be a cover that displays solo

The Two-Up layouts are available to choose as either standard (jumping pages) or continuous (smooth-scrolling) behavior.

Presentation   For slideshow or kiosk presentations, consider presetting the PDF to Open In Full Screen Mode. This has the effect of immediately placing Acrobat or Adobe Reader into its full-screen Presentation mode, thus hiding the application scrollbars, toolbars, and so on. If your PDF is a kiosk presentation—a self-running set of slides meant to be left unattended—you can set the interval between the advancement of slides by enabling the Flip Pages Every *x* Seconds option.

TIP   Full-screen mode can be toggled in Acrobat or Adobe Reader by pressing Cmd+L/Ctrl+L.

Do *not* set the PDF to open in full-screen mode if it's a standard epublication and is for wide distribution. Doing so is as distressing to the average user as a website that resizes the browser. Readers who aren't tech-savvy get confused and don't know how to leave full-screen mode (Esc or Cmd+L/Ctrl+L), while those who are tech-savvy get annoyed because some document takes over their screens.

Page Transitions   Sticking with the idea of a PDF as slideshow or presentation or, even better, to liven up epublications (if placed in full-screen mode), you can add page transitions that perform wipes, fades, and other effects as the reader, you, or the timer advances from one page or slide to the next. Choose From Document if you've used the Pages panel or Page Transitions panel to add transition effects, or select one from the list. Unfortunately, the Page Curl transition effect is not available for use in PDFs; it's Flash SWF only.

Forms And Media   If your document contains any embedded audio or video or interactivity features, you must choose Include All if you want those elements to be live. If you *don't* want such media live in the PDF—say, if you want to send a nonfunctional, flat proof of the interactive PDF to your client ahead of the client paying your invoice—choose Appearance Only. That option will effectively turn videos and buttons into pictures, using their current appearances in the layout or using the poster image you may have selected for video and audio files.

Tagged PDF   If your InDesign document contains structure tags, you can have them translated to PDF tags.

Create Tagged PDF   Even if you didn't pre-create tags in InDesign, if Create Tagged PDF is enabled, performing the export will tag common elements in text such as paragraphs, tables, lists, basic formatting, and so on. Tagged PDFs are more accessible to people with disabilities and are easier for PDF readers on alternate devices (in other words, cell phones, PDAs, tablets) to reflow for optimal reading. This option must be enabled if you want readers to use Reflow View (see "Preparing the PDF for Reflow View" later in the chapter).

Use Structure For Tab Order   If the document includes XML tagged elements, the Use Structure for Tab Order check box will order the tags to match the order of the XML tags from the document Structure pane.

Image Handling   The Image Handling section sets the options for converting raster images from the layout to PDF. (Note that vector elements will remain vector in the PDF.) Choose the type of image under Compression, either JPEG or the lossless PNG format, and then the output resolution in ppi. Choosing JPEG as the compression format also enables the JPEG Quality field, where you can set the quality of the resulting JPEGs.

Compression   The Compression field offers you three options: JPEG (Lossy), JPEG 2000 (Lossless), and Automatic. In reality you have only one choice, JPEG (Lossy). JPEG 2000 isn't supported by most devices, and even Acrobat and Reader themselves don't always correctly render JPEG 2000 images. The Automatic choice lets InDesign decide whether images should be converted to JPEG or JPEG 2000, which means you can't use Automatic either. By the process of elimination, your only choice is JPEG (Lossy).

JPEG Quality   As a lossy compression method, the relative size of a JPEG image is in direct relation to its quality. The higher the quality, the larger the file. Low (10 percent), Medium (30 percent), High (60 percent), and Maximum (100 percent) quality are your choices.

Resolution   Set the resolution for your images and rasterized effects in this field. Although the field looks like you can type any value into it, doing so will cause an error. Instead, you have only the choices presented in the drop-down: 72, 96, 144, and 300 ppi. I recommend sticking with 300 ppi for the reasons discussed earlier in this chapter.

Security   The Security button gives you access to the various security options available for the PDF. Rather than cover them here, however, I'll wait until the "Finalizing the Publication" section later in this chapter.

Adding Audio and Video

One of the easiest ways to distinguish a PDF epublication from a simple PDF export of a print publication is to add multimedia in the form of audio or video. InDesign and its accompanying Adobe Media Encoder make it easy to prepare, place, and include in your layout any audio or video your publication needs.

Preparing Audio and Video Files

PDF files support the inclusion of only MP3 audio, but will accept video—standard and high definition—in any of the following formats, all of which can be placed within InDesign:

◆ Flash in FLV, F4V, and SWF formats

◆ MPEG-4 (MP4 and M4A)

◆ Other video files encoded in H.264

LEGACY FORMATS

PDFs will accept other audio (AIFF, WAV) and video (MOV, AVI) files, but these are what we call *legacy formats*—older, usually proprietary digital media formats that are being rapidly replaced by more modern, standardized formats like MP3 and MPEG-4. Many devices have stopped support for legacy formats altogether, whether in PDF or outside it. Consequently, I recommend you stick with the modern formats mentioned here.

For quite a while now, PDF has been able to support the inclusion of full Flash content in the Flash Video FLV and F4V formats, as well as the full breadth of what Flash can do—audio, video, animation, games, scripting, and so on—in SWF format. I strongly caution against using any Flash content, however. The reason is simple: Flash is not supported at all on iOS devices and, because of that, is dying as a delivery format on all screens. Refer to the sidebar "Flash-Powered Digital Publications" in Chapter 2 for more on this.

In terms of features, device support, and file compression versus quality, the best formats to use with PDF are MP3 for audio and H.264-encoded MP4 for video. If you have content in other formats, you'll need to convert them. Rather than reiterate everything I covered previously about using Adobe Media Encoder to convert audio and video files from other formats into those ideal for PDF, I will refer you to the relevant portions of the "Adding Audio & Video to eBooks" section in Chapter 5, "Working with Images and Multimedia in Ebooks." Although that section is about adding audio and video to EPUBs, the information about audio and video formats, as well as the instructions for using Adobe Media Encoder to convert them, is right on point for working with multimedia for any digital publication format.

If you don't have any multimedia files of your own to work with, you'll find a public-domain MP4 video clip and several free-to-use instrumental MP3s in this chapter's Lesson Files folder.

TIP In the "Creating Advanced Interactivity" section in this chapter, I'll explain how to have audio and video play based on events other than the reader directly clicking them.

In addition to the details in Chapter 5, a few hidden options are available for controlling video in PDFs. From the Media panel's flyout menu in the top-right corner, select PDF Options to bring up the PDF Options dialog (see Figure 7.10). Here you can give the video a description so that the tagged structure of the PDF identifies the video (or audio, as the Description field is available for audio as well) to people with disabilities who cannot view (or listen to) the content directly. Beneath the Description field you're given options to allow the playing of the video at hand in a floating or full-screen, as videos often play on tablets. To achieve that effect, enable the Play Video In Floating Window option and then select the magnification level from the Size drop-down (Max will utilize the whole screen), and, if needed, set the Position field to align the video pop-up where it should go.

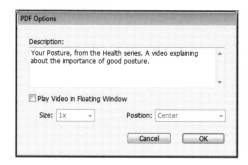

Adding Navigation Points to a Video

As I mentioned earlier, navigation points are markers to specific frames in a video. Once these markers have been created, you can link to them, jumping your audience to specific points in a video, from hyperlinks, buttons, and other interactive elements. I'll get into the specifics of linking to navigation points in the "Creating Advanced Interactivity" section a little later in this chapter, but while you're already hands-on with the Media panel, I'd like to work through creating navigation points.

1. After placing a video, select it with the black-arrow Selection tool, and open the Media panel.

2. Using the preview and the timeline slider at the top of the Media panel, navigate to the first place in the video to which you'd like to directly link viewers. If the movie is playing, pause it at that point.

3. Just below the Navigation Points section of the Media panel, click the plus sign–adorned Add Navigation Point button. This will add a navigation point titled Point 1 just above it in the Navigation Points list.

4. Although you can leave the navigation point with its default name of Point 1 and subsequent markers named Point 2, Point 3, and so on, I recommend giving the navigation points names that communicate the content that they mark. Readers of your epublications will never see your navigation point names, but you will when you link to them; giving them meaningful names will make it easier for you to connect a button action to the correct navigation point.

5. Repeat the previous three steps as needed to fill in all the navigation points you want in your video. If you add one by mistake, use the minus sign button, which is the Remove Navigation Point button, to delete whichever point you highlight in the list.

Once your navigation points have been defined, you can link to them through various methods—again, discussed later in this chapter. It's important to note that navigation points are attributes only for use within InDesign and only on that specific instance of the video object; navigation points will not be written back into the video asset. If you want to create more universal navigation points, ones that *are* part of the video itself and may be used within InDesign as well as a number of other programs, then you'll need to add the navigation points as markers in a video-editing application.

Including Video from a URL

The Media panel's flyout menu offers two items: PDF Options, which I've already talked about, and Video From URL, which I haven't. If you choose Video From URL, you'll open the Place Video From URL dialog (see Figure 7.11).

FIGURE 7.11
Inserting a video
hosted online

This feature allows you to insert into your PDF a video that resides online rather than on your hard drive. Obviously, to insert the video, you must have an active Internet connection, as must the reader of your publication when he attempts to view the video. Assuming those two things, just enter into the URL field the full address of the video (not simply the web page through which you might view the video). Videos linked to in this format can be only Flash Video FLV and F4V formats, which means they may not play on some devices. If that's not a concern for you, enter the full URL from a web server beginning with http:// or the video as served from a Flash Media Player or Flash Streaming Service using the rtmp:// prefix.

Once placed, the video acts like one residing on a local drive—you can preview it, resize it, and so on.

MEDIA PANEL BUTTONS

Although I've mentioned the menu locations of things like Video From URL and PDF Options, there are also buttons for them at the bottom of the Media panel. There you'll also find a Preview Spread button, which will instantly convert the current spread into a Flash SWF and show it within InDesign's SWF Preview panel. The final button, on the far right at the bottom of the panel, lets you place audio and video files. It's just like File ➤ Place, but it limits the file types it will show in the Place dialog to audio and video files. Personally, I never use it. I simply hit Ctrl+D/Cmd+D and use the normal Place dialog; afterwards, I can differentiate between the icons and files extensions of images, text documents, and audio and video files.

Creating External Hyperlinks of All Types

The first and most basic level of interactivity is hyperlinks, but these don't have to be merely hyperlinks to web pages. Oh, no. You can also include hyperlinks that initiate emails, text messages, and phone calls and hyperlinks that jump readers to other pages within the PDF, to specific objects, and even to specific zoom levels onto objects.

Defining Hyperlink Styles

Digital publications are obviously an interactive medium; you embed hyperlinks with the expectation that readers will click or tap them. The question therefore becomes, *how do you, as a designer, communicate that expectation to readers?* You have to indicate that hyperlinks are clickable in some manner, whether the linked text is itself a URL or just prose phrasing. Following the example of the Web, you can offset hyperlinked text with color and an adornment like an underline. Moreover, there are different types of resources to which you might create hyperlinks, and often you'll want to communicate those differences visually in the linked text. For example, a PDF epublication might contain links to pages within the same PDF, links to the company website and documents thereon, and links to outside resources and partner websites. How are your readers to know which link will take them where?

Take a cue from better web publishers and use different colors and/or underline styles to instantly identify your publication's different types of hyperlinks.

1. Place or type your text—including the hyperlink candidate.

2. With the Text tool, highlight the text to be linked, which will be underlined to show the link.

3. Open the Character panel, and from its panel flyout menu, select Underline Options, toward the bottom. This will open the Underline Options dialog box (see Figure 7.12).

FIGURE 7.12
The Underline
Options dialog

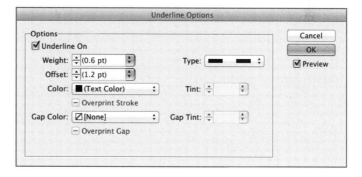

4. First, check the Preview box on the right, and then check Underline On. You should immediately see your selected text underlined.

If you've ever used paragraph rules or even strokes, the controls in this dialog should be familiar. Weight is the thickness of the underline, with a drop-down list of common sizes, or you may type in any value. Offset is how far below the baseline the underline should begin. Again, you may choose a common preset value from the drop-down list or type in your own. Both the Weight and Offset value fields may also be controlled with the up and down arrow keys. Type is InDesign's stroke types—identical to those on the Stroke panel. Any preexisting swatch may be used as the color of the underline, or it may be left at its default, which is the same color as the text. Choosing any swatch but Text Color, None, and Paper will enable the Tint field. Gap Color and Gap Tint activate only if the underline type is one that includes gaps of some sort—anything but Solid, really. Gap colors take the place of having to layer multiple objects to achieve a two-tone dotted stroke.

5. Set up your external hyperlink underline the way you like. Most users are accustomed to a solid, single underline that is the same color as the text (which you should change from black to a contrasting color such as blue, green, or red). When ready, hit OK.

6. Now, on the Character Styles panel, which you can open via Window ➢ Styles ➢ Character Styles, create a new character style called Hyperlink or Standard Hyperlink to store the underline and color settings. This will be the style for hyperlinks to external websites and resources.

Now what other types of destinations might you want to link to in your PDF? Will you link to other pages in the same document? How about linking figure or illustration references so that, when clicked, they jump the user directly to the image, map, or chart that is being described? Of course, once there at the figure, you might want to add a hyperlink within the image's caption to jump the reader back to the text that sent him there in the first place.

Will you be including hyperlinks to start emails? If you expect the PDF to be viewed on phones or other devices with dialing and text-messaging capabilities, will you include hyperlinks that dial the phone or send texts (or "sexts" if you're targeting a publication toward the ex-Disney child-actor crowd)?

Help your readers identify the different functions and destination types of hyperlinks by using different styles for each. Maybe internal hyperlinks, ones that go to different locations or zoom levels within the same PDF, could be colored in blue with dashed underlines, while standard hyperlinks use red and a solid underline. Perhaps links to your own content—the publisher's website, other issues of your publication, and so on—could be colored green with a double underline. For each of these different types of hyperlinks, follow the step-by-step exercise, setting slightly different color and underline options, and make separate character styles. Figure 7.13 shows an example of different hyperlink styles in use.

FIGURE 7.13
Different color and underline styles denoting three types of links

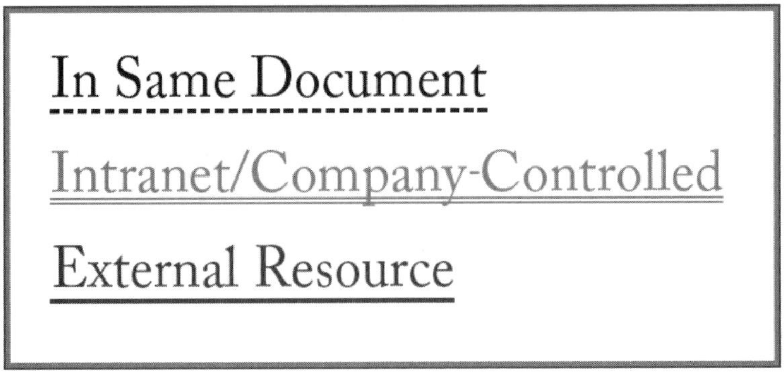

In Same Document
Intranet/Company-Controlled
External Resource

Creating a Basic Hyperlink

Now that you have the style for hyperlinks, let's make a link live, starting with a simple hyperlink to a web page. After this, you'll get into those more exotic types of hyperlinks I mentioned.

1. Create some text in a new or existing INDD, and highlight a word or phrase within that text that you'd like to hyperlink to a web resource.

2. Open the Hyperlinks panel (see Figure 7.14) by selecting Window ➢ Interactive ➢ Hyperlinks.

3. At the bottom of the Hyperlinks panel, click the Create New Hyperlink button, which looks like a few links of chain accompanied by a ship's navigation wheel (the old Netscape web browser logo).

4. Up will pop the New Hyperlink dialog (see Figure 7.15). The Link To field offers several options, all of which I'll get to shortly. For now, set it to URL.

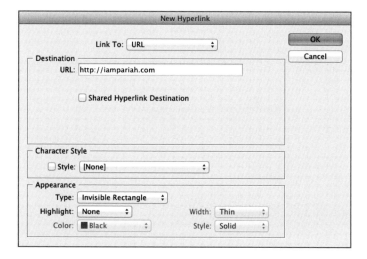

5. In the Destination URL field, enter the URL of your favorite website. Naturally my favorite is `http://iamPariah.com`.

6. Uncheck the box beside Shared Hyperlink Destination. Enabling Shared Hyperlink Destination adds the URL to the Hyperlinks panel for easy reuse in other locations in the document, which sounds very convenient, right? Unfortunately, links created as Shared Hyperlink Destinations often fail in PDFs, so you want to make sure not to use them.

7. From the Character Style section's Style drop-down field, choose the hyperlink character style you created previously.

8. In the Appearance section, choose the options you want to add over and above the character style, if any. You can choose to put outlined rectangles around the hyperlink or highlight them (which can look very nice) when they're clicked; you can even invert when the hyperlink is clicked, causing white to become black, blue to become yellow, and so on. The Width, Style, and Color fields let you refine these on-click/on-tap appearances.

9. Click OK, and do a quick PDF export to test your hyperlink.

IMPORTING HYPERLINKS FROM MICROSOFT WORD

Typing URLs and email addresses in Microsoft Word and then inserting spaces, punctuation, or returns tells Word to hyperlink those URLs and addresses by default. If you're importing Word documents containing live hyperlinks into InDesign and you haven't stripped out Word's styling via the Microsoft Word Import Options dialog, then the incoming Word-format hyperlinks will convert to InDesign-format hyperlinks, populating the Hyperlinks panel. The character formatting will also be preserved. Note, however, that hyperlinks from Word have a tendency to come into InDesign as shared-destination hyperlinks, which, again, often makes the hyperlinks fail in PDF. You'll need to manually edit each of those links by double-clicking them in the Hyperlinks panel and disabling the Shared Hyperlink Destination option.

Creating Email Hyperlinks

Another popular type of hyperlink is one that initiates an email. Creating one is simple.

1. Highlight the text to be hyperlinked, and start a new hyperlink via the Hyperlinks panel.

2. In the New Hyperlink dialog, change the Link To type to Email (Figure 7.16).

3. In the Destination area, disable Shared Hyperlink Destination and fill in the Address field with the email address that should be the recipient of the message. (Do not enter the `mailto:` prefix as you would within HTML; in the background InDesign will automatically prepend `mailto:` to the email address you supply.)

FIGURE 7.16
Creating an email
hyperlink

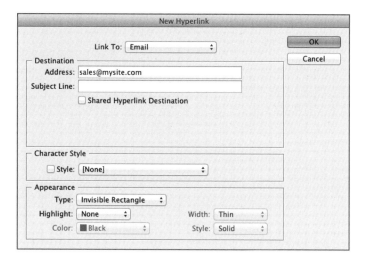

At this point, you can move on to set your style and appearance options, or you can prepopulate the email Subject line. For general "contact me" links, no, you typically don't want to prepopulate the subject. In many other circumstances, however, it's a good idea.

Let's say you're providing the reader with an email address specifically for finding out more information about advertising in your publications. Naturally you'd have a specific email address just for advertising inquiries—maybe sales@yourdomain.com or advertisers@yourdomain.com—but those addresses undoubtedly also get mail that isn't from first-time contacts. Help those who watch the email addresses' inboxes prioritize contact from new advertising prospects by prepopulating the email Subject field with something like "New Advertising Inquiry." If you publish multiple titles, you could also identify the publication to which the advertising prospect is responding by adding the publication title into the email subject; something like "New Advertising Inquiry – *My Pub Title*" would work nicely. You could even add the issue and volume or date information if you wanted.

For advertisers themselves, the subject line can be used to key responses to particular ads from specific publications. Instead of setting up multiple email addresses to track how different ads pull, use the Subject Line field in the Hyperlink dialog to insert a key of some kind, something like "Pre-Sales Inquiry About Gizmo 3.0—Food & Wine, Feb 2013, p100" would tell you which publication, which issue, and which page's ad (if you have multiple ads in the same publication).

The Subject Line field can be anything you want, and its value is designed to help you, the publisher and recipient of the email, not so much the sender or publication reader. In all of my own digital publications (and websites) where I include email addresses for specific purposes (for example, sales, customer service, technical support, press inquiries, advertising sales, and so on), I prepopulate the subject so that, when the emails hit my inbox, I know instantly what they're in reference to—y' know, instead of reading through a six-page email to find a point in the last two lines.

Aspirin-Free Workflow: Automatically Convert URLs to Hyperlinks

If your text contains URLs, including email addresses, you can automate the process of converting those URLs and addresses into live hyperlinks *and* styling them.

1. Create your hyperlink character style.

2. From the Hyperlinks panel flyout menu, choose the Convert URLs To Hyperlinks item.

3. In the resulting dialog, which you can see here, choose the scope of the replacement in the Search field. You can hyperlink URLs just in the current story or in all stories in the document in one fell swoop.

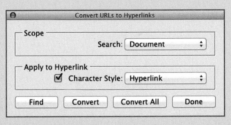

4. Pick your hyperlink character style from the Character Style drop-down menu, which will also automatically activate the check box to the left, telling InDesign to apply that style to all hyperlinks it creates from your text.

5. Now execute the action. If you're a little timid about sweeping automatic changes, click the Find button, and when InDesign shows you the first URL or address to hyperlink, click the Convert button and Find again to go to the next hyperlink candidate. If you're confident in InDesign's acumen, click the Convert All button and watch as InDesign live-links all your URLs and email addresses.

Voila! Instant and automatic conversion of URLs, although you may have to go back into each and deactivate the Shared Hyperlink Destination option that causes so much trouble in PDFs.

InDesign will convert URLs in any of the following formats into hyperlinks:

◆ domain.com

◆ www.domain.com

◆ http://domain.com

◆ https://domain.com

◆ ftp://domain.com

◆ [prefix]domain.com/page

It will also convert any email addresses into proper mailto: hyperlinks. For example, me@domain.com would be converted to mailto:me@domain.com.

Creating Other Types of Hyperlinks

Once the New Hyperlink dialog's Link To field has been set to URL, you can type just about any protocol link into the URL field. Of course, the most common protocol most of us will use is HyperText Transfer Protocol—good ol' HTTP—but that's far from the only protocol that makes up the Internet. There's News Network Transfer Protocol (NNTP) for Usenet Newsgroups, File Transfer Protocol (FTP) for accessing file servers, and TELNET, which is similar to FTP but is a more robust and secure method of accessing and controlling remote servers (of any kind), just to name a few. Hyperlinks can connect to addresses prefixed by any of these protocols. Acrobat or another PDF viewer will send the hyperlink to the operating system, asking the operating system to launch the address in the application configured to handle the particular protocol. Unless the reader has a specific application configured—say, an FTP program or TELNET client—that will be the web browser, which can handle all of those protocols, depending on the security settings of the browser, the OS, and the server to which they're connecting.

You can also type into the URL field non-Internet-standard prefixes and data that have become, or are on their way to becoming, standards in the mobile world. These include URLs for dialing the phone and initiating text messages and links to apps in the various app stores.

To include a link that dials the phone (on phone devices), use the format of `tel:` country code, area code, three-digit exchange, four-digit number. Here's an example: `tel:1-212-555-1212`.

Starting a text message on devices with that capability requires the use of the `sms:` prefix. Using `sms:` all by itself will cause the device's text messaging application to appear with a blank text message waiting to be written and addressed. Specifying a phone number after the `sms:`, such as in the example `sms:1-212-555-1212`, will start a blank text message with the Send To or Recipient field prepopulated.

Link to the Apple App Store by beginning the URL with `itms://` and following it with a full link to the app under the `itunes.apple.com` domain. Here's an example: `itms://itunes .apple.com/us/app/angry-birds/id343200656?mt=8&uo=4`. If you don't know how to link to an app in the App Store, just visit `http://abbrv.it/DigiPubIDTools`, where I've included a link to a handy little App Store link maker.

For the Android Google Play app market, the format is similar, using the prefix `market://` instead. All of the following examples will work. In order, they are a link directly to an app's page in the market, a link that shows all apps by a particular publisher, and a general query that enables searching by any term or name.

```
market://details?id=<package_name>

market://search?q=pub:<publisher_name>

market://search?q=<query>
```

To link to an app in the BlackBerry App World, use this format: `appworld://content/ <app ID number>`.

Devising Intra-Document Navigation

The major PDF readers on all platforms are not designed around the concept of epublications; they're built to read printlike documents in short spurts. Adobe might disagree with me on that point, but I'd merely have to point them to the page navigation user interface of Acrobat and Reader (see Figure 7.17). It almost looks like an afterthought, doesn't it? No wonder the average person has such trouble navigating PDFs for long reading sessions. Basically they're left with scrolling, which they hate doing for more than a few pages in nonlinear publications like magazines and catalogs and when referencing only sections of a book.

FIGURE 7.17
The page-navigation controls on the toolbar in Acrobat X and Reader X

That means it's up to publishers to build a much more intuitive, user-friendly navigation system directly into their publications. It's rather easy, as a matter of fact, and enables you to make your publications even more engaging and appealing.

Adding Global Navigation

Don't leave it to readers to figure out how to navigate your epublication using the tools in their PDF viewers. Even something as simple as controls for advancing to the next page and backing up to the previous page can be done better by you, in a way that makes more sense to readers. And, if you're going to add Next Page and Previous Page navigation buttons, you should also add a means for readers to return to the table of contents instantly from any place in the PDF. If your publication contains clearly delineated sections, say, like a book, then you might even want to put buttons for each of those sections on every page to allow rapid movement between sections. While you're at it, a button or link to the publication's or publisher's website among those other buttons certainly couldn't hurt. That way, if the PDF got around beyond direct customers or subscribers, you have a good chance of converting those unexpected readers into customers or subscribers.

Take a look at Figure 7.18 for some examples of global navigation systems designed into different PDF publications (some I designed and built). Aren't they much better than relying on Acrobat's built-in navigation? Readers sure think so.

All of these navigation systems and more are surprisingly easy to build in InDesign and can greatly ease readers' ability to move throughout your publication. You can even hide the default Acrobat and Reader navigation tools, something I'll talk about in the "Finalizing the Publication" section later in this chapter.

FIGURE 7.18

Examples of global navigation systems designed for PDF

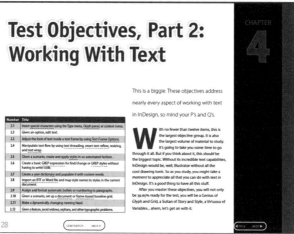

A simple four-button system combining text and iconography in the *Guide to the InDesign ACE Exam* helps the reader move from page to page, access the contents and, via the Info button, access the publisher's website.

A twofold navigation system in *Digital Magazine News* (September 2005). At the bottom, text links offer page navigation and additional features, while at the top each page of the publication is individually linked.

In *The Best of Planet PDF* Volume 2, text links in the colored bar at the top offer jumps to different sections, while buttons beneath the logo provide page navigation.

continues

FIGURE 7.18
Continued

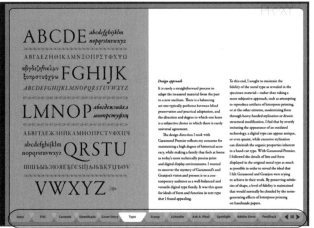

In *Adobe Proxy Magazine* (May 2006), even Adobe itself didn't trust Acrobat's navigation system; it built a tab-based section navigation, used arrows around the page number to enable page turning, and hid Acrobat's and Reader's native page navigation toolbars.

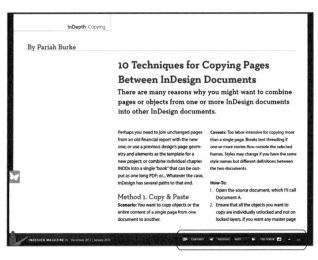

InDesign Magazine (December 2011) uses more graphically oriented buttons to give readers page navigation as well as a quick return to the issue's table of contents.

CREATING NEXT PAGE AND PREVIOUS PAGE BUTTONS

The first thing you might want to do is create buttons to move readers to the next page and back to the previous page.

1. With your publication layout opened in InDesign, double-click the master page used for all your document pages or the master page on which other master pages are based.

2. Using the Type tool, create a small text frame in the margin to serve as the "go to next page" button. Enter the label for the button in that text frame—Next, Next Page, Forward, or whatever.

3. Repeat the process of creating a new text frame and labeling it for the "go to previous page" button. Style the text in both frames as you like.

4. Switching to the black-arrow Selection tool, select the Next Page text frame.

5. Choose Window ➤ Interactivity ➤ Buttons And Forms (just Buttons in CS5.5 and earlier) to open the Buttons And Forms panel (see Figure 7.19).

FIGURE 7.19
The Buttons And
Forms panel

6. At the bottom of the panel, click the Convert To Button button, which will change the text frame into a button object, as indicated by the frame's bounding box turning dashed instead of solid and, if the frame is large enough, the appearance of an icon of a hand with a finger displayed as if pushing a button (see Figure 7.20).

FIGURE 7.20
When an object has
been converted to a
button, its bound-
ing box becomes a
dashed line and a
finger-push icon
appears in the
lower-right corner.

7. Now that the text frame is a button, everything from here on out will be accomplished in the Button And Forms panel. First rename the button to match its label (Next, Next Page, Forward, or whatever) by typing **Button 1** in the Name field.

8. Leave the Event field at its default of On Release Or Tap.

9. Beside the Actions label, click the plus sign to add an action. It will show a pop-up list of available actions for the button (see Figure 7.21). Choose Go To Next Page.

10. That button is done. Now follow the same steps with the Go To Previous Page text frame, converting it to a button, renaming it, and giving it the Go To Previous Page action.

FIGURE 7.21
The available
actions in the Add
Actions menu

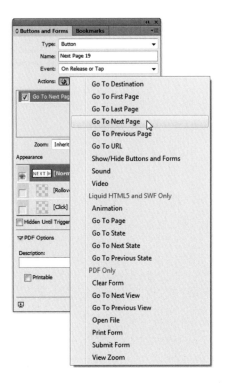

You now have navigation buttons that enable movement forward and back one page in the PDF. Because you created them on the master page, they'll appear on all document pages in InDesign and the PDF. Export to Interactive PDF, and give them a try. You—and your readers— can now move page by page through the publication. If you want, you can also create buttons that use the Go To First Page and Go To Last Page options to move readers to the very beginning and end of the document, respectively.

CREATING BUTTONS TO NAVIGATE TO THE TOC, COVER, AND OTHER LOCATIONS

The process of creating buttons that go to specific locations, like the publication's table of contents, cover, chapters, sections, or other specific locations, is a little different from making simple "next page" and "previous page" buttons. Creating the text frame and converting to a button are the same, but how the action is configured and how you prepare for that action depend on the way you've structured your document.

If you've built your publication using a Book panel and made the table of contents (or cover, chapter, section, or whatever) its own INDD within that Book panel—which is the preferred method for dealing with longer documents—then open that document and switch back to the current one so that you have both documents opened at the same time. After that, you don't have to do anything except to jump down in *this* book to the second step-by-step tutorial in this section.

If all of your content is in one file, then you'll need to define a destination before you can configure a button to send readers there.

1. Navigate to the page in the document to which you want to link your readers via a button.

2. Using the black-arrow Selection tool, highlight one or more objects on that page.

3. From the Hyperlinks panel flyout menu, select New Hyperlink Destination. A dialog with the same name will appear (see Figure 7.22).

FIGURE 7.22
Setting a hyperlink
destination

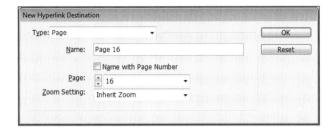

4. Make sure that the Type field is set to Page, and then name the hyperlink destination. Typically you want to use either *Page X*, where *X* is the actual page number, or the title of the page, such as Table of Contents.

5. Ensure that the Page field shows the correct page number, and then set the Zoom Setting field as you see fit. Which option you choose in the Zoom Setting field will cause the page to zoom in the PDF reader to meet that setting. I typically use Inherit Zoom because that brings the reader to the page using the zoom and fitting method *she* chose. I don't want to annoy my readers by overriding their zoom preferences.

When ready, click OK. It will look as if nothing happened, because hyperlink destinations aren't listed in the Hyperlinks panel. Trust me, though; something happened.

Now let's create a button to reach the table of contents from anywhere in the publication.

1. Return to the master page on which you created your previous buttons.

2. Create and style a text frame-to-be-button containing the text you want to display—Contents, TOC, Cover, or whatever.

3. Turn that into a button by clicking the Convert To Button button at the bottom of the Buttons And Forms panel.

4. Name the button appropriately, ensure that Event is On Release Or Tap, and click the plus sign to add an action. This time, choose Go To Destination.

5. You'll now have a Go To Destination action in the Actions List, as you can see in Figure 7.23, but you still have to configure that destination using the fields below the list.

The Document field lists all opened documents, including the current one. If your destination is in another file, like, say, the book's table of contents, choose that file from the Document list. If you went with the method of creating a hyperlink destination, choose from the Document list the file in which you made that destination—probably the one you're working with. Then, in the Destination field, choose the name of the hyperlink destination you created. If you're linking a separate file, it may not have hyperlink destinations, disabling the Destination field. That's just fine; it means when the reader clicks the link, he will be jumped to the first page of the target PDF.

FIGURE 7.23
Configuring the
Go To Destination
button

If you forgot to open the file to which you want to link before creating the button, fret not; just click the folder icon beside the Document field to browse for and open any other INDD.

6. Now set the view you want the reader to have on the destination page from the Zoom field. Again, I prefer to leave this at Inherit Zoom so that the reader reaches the page using the same zooming and fitting options she had before the jump.

You now have a button that will jump the reader to wherever you want her to go. You can add as many of these as you want to help the reader get from here to there, there, and there; to the table of contents; to the cover; to each individual chapter or section; to an order or subscription form; to a dedication page you've written in my honor for showing you how to make navigations buttons; or to wherever.

MAKING NAVIGATION BUTTONS MORE GRAPHIC

So far, you've simply made text frames and converted them to buttons. Maybe you want to make more graphic buttons or add icons beside the text or create buttons that *look* like buttons. You might even want buttons to change their appearance when cursors roll over the buttons or when they're clicked or tapped. All of that's pretty easy.

Any InDesign object may become a button. It doesn't have to be a text frame. If you want to place an image of a button that you created in Illustrator or Photoshop and *make* that a button, then do it. You can also draw vector shapes right in InDesign and make those into buttons. Readable text, icons inserted from symbol fonts via the Glyphs panel, drop-shadowed frames— any object can be turned into a button using the same procedure you walked through moments ago. In fact, you don't have to use just *one* object; the more interesting buttons are created as multiple objects, grouped with Ctrl+G/Cmd+G, and *then* converted to buttons. Just make sure you remember to group them first; if you select a bunch of ungrouped objects and then click Convert To Button, each individual object will become its own button, which is a power-user tip you might want to keep in mind.

Assuming you're happy with the appearance of your button but you want it to change its appearance when clicked/tapped or when the cursor rolls over it, then follow these instructions to add additional appearances to the button:

1. Begin by designing the button's default unclicked, not highlighted, appearance and converting the object or group to a button object.

2. In the Buttons And Forms panel you'll notice the Appearance section in the middle of the panel. Any button object may have three different appearances or looks: the normal appearance, which is how the button looks when it isn't highlighted or actively being clicked or tapped; how the button looks when the mouse cursor rolls over it or it's highlighted; and the button's appearance while it's being clicked or tapped or pressed. In Figure 7.24, you can see the three appearances of a button I created for another ebook. Only Normal is active by default.

FIGURE 7.24
Buttons can have
three appearances.

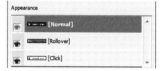

Click the Rollover appearance to activate and highlight it.

3. In the document you should see that the button object is still selected. With the Rollover appearance highlighted in the Buttons And Forms panel, what you are now seeing in the object itself is its rollover appearance. Unless something went wrong, it looks exactly like the Normal appearance. Change something about the object—its fill or stroke or type formatting or effects or whatever.

4. Now, back in the Buttons And Forms panel, click the Normal appearance. Your button object should revert to its prior appearance. Click the Rollover appearance, and the new version reappears, right? You can toggle back and forth between them. What you did in the previous step was to create the new look of the button when the button becomes highlighted or the mouse cursor rolls over it.

5. Now add the Click appearance and change something else about the button. This is how the button object will look as it's being pressed.

6. Export to Interactive PDF, and give the button a try. Mouse over it, and then move the cursor away to watch it toggle between the Normal and Rollover appearances. Click (and hold) the button to observe its Click appearance. It will revert to Normal after you've released it.

The three button appearances can be as similar or different as you like. You can even change the text in each one, making the same button say, for example, "Move the Mouse Over Here," then "Great! Now Click," and finally "You're clicking me! I feel loved!" Similarly, if your button includes a graphic frame, you can insert different linked images for the various states. By altering strokes and/or effects, you can make a button that appears raised in 3D off the page for its Normal appearance, glowing internally for its Rollover appearance, and then depressed into the page in 3D for its Click appearance. Use your imagination.

ASPIRIN-FREE WORKFLOW: OBJECT STYLES AND BUTTON APPEARANCES

You can't save multiple appearances into one object style, but you can create multiple object styles, one for each appearance. Design your first button and all its appearances. Then highlight the button object and create a new object style. Switch to the Rollover appearance and create a second object style; repeat for Click. In the end, you should have three object styles, one each corresponding to the button's Normal, Rollover, and Click appearances. For subsequent buttons, just apply the correct style to the correct appearance. Changes to the object style will automatically reflect across all button objects.

Indicating the Current Section or Page

If you're using a global navigation system that shows all the page numbers or chapter or section names, like *Adobe Proxy Magazine*, *Digital Magazine News*, or *The Best of Planet PDF* (refer to Figure 7.18), then just as those publications do, instead of just linking to those sections or pages, you might want to indicate to readers when they are already within those sections or on those pages. You can do that with a little more master page work. It's so simple, in fact, that you don't even need a step-by-step. Just create separate master pages for each section (or page), and on each master page set the Normal appearance for that section's or page's button to be the same as the Rollover appearance or to differ in some other way from the Normal state of other sections' or pages' buttons. You can even turn the current section or page button back into a standard, non-clickable object with the Convert To Object button at the bottom of the Buttons And Forms panel.

Connecting Content Interactively

One of the most overlooked but powerfully useful types of navigation possible in PDF is intra-content hyperlinks, which are hyperlinks that move readers from one place in the content to another, directly related place. This is very different from a global navigation system that allows movement between pages, sections, and chapters. It's also different from the basic intra-document navigation created automatically by the inclusion of a table of contents; when you add a TOC to InDesign and export to PDF, the TOC entries link to the content they track, unless you deliberately disable the linking. PDF-based epublications can—and often should—also include intra-content hyperlinks throughout the publication. Imagine the following scenarios in relation to your publication:

♦   Within a technical or trade publication, a reader runs across a new word whose definition isn't immediately clear; clicking that word jumps the reader to the publication's glossary for an explanation.

♦ In a PDF-based magazine, a reader encounters a jump line (such as "story continues on page x"), but instead of having to scroll down through a bunch of pages to continue reading, the reader merely clicks the jump line itself and is suddenly at the continuation of the story.

♦ Looking at a map of the trade show floor, a reader clicks a location marker icon and is jumped to a detail page containing text, imagery, and even video about the booth in that space, the company hosting that booth, and the products or services offered by that company.

♦ While reading a paragraph discussing sales data, a hyperlink lets readers jump right to a full-screen view of the chart that visualizes that data.

♦ After springing from one place in the document to another—to a chart, to a map's location detail, to a story continuation, to a glossary definition—the reader can instantly return to the previous location by clicking a button or hyperlink.

These types of intra-content movement can make a good publication great; they can mark the difference between the reader somewhat getting the message of the content and full understanding. And intra-content hyperlinks are easy to create—you already know how if you've gone through this chapter's preceding sections.

CREATING A JUMP TO ANOTHER PLACE IN THE TEXT

The first two scenarios in the bulleted list you just read through are simple text jumps. One moves the reader from an unfamiliar word to that word's definition in the glossary, while the other enables the reader to follow a story from one page to another deeper into the publication. The directions for accomplishing either are the same.

1. Start by locating the destination text, the text you want to jump the user to. For a glossary or index of advertisers or whatever, this would be the entry in that feature. For a jumping story, the destination would be the carryover, the point at which the story continues after the jump.

2. Highlight the destination text—a word or two at the beginning—and open the Hyperlinks panel from Window ➢ Interactive ➢ Hyperlinks.

3. From that panel's flyout menu, choose New Hyperlink Destination.

4. In the New Hyperlink Destination dialog, set Type to Text Anchor, which it should be by default, and then decide whether you need to edit the destination's Name field. It will prepopulate with the text you highlighted, which, in the case of a glossary or some kind of index, might be just perfect. If it's not exactly what you'll need to later identify that destination, enter something here that will help you remember. Click OK when done.

5. Now go to and highlight the source text, the text that will be hyperlinked to take the reader *to* the destination.

6. At the bottom of the Hyperlinks panel, click the Create New Hyperlink button.

7. In the New Hyperlink dialog, change the Link To field to Text Anchor and the Document field to the current document name if you have multiple INDDs open; otherwise, it shows only the current document. Then, from the Text Anchor field, select the text anchor you just made.

8. Choose from the Character Style section a character style you pre-created to make the text appear to the reader as clickable, and then set any desired Appearance section options.

9. Click OK and do a test export of the PDF. Clicking the source text in the PDF should jump you to the page of the destination text.

CREATING A FIGURE REFERENCE THAT JUMPS AND ZOOMS TO THE FIGURE

Let's create the scenario wherein a hyperlink within the text takes the reader to imagery described by or augmenting that text.

1. Open either your own document or `Figure Reference Link.INDD` in this chapter's `Lesson Files` folder. Figure 7.25 shows a page in the latter.

FIGURE 7.25

A page containing figure references that link to, and zoom in on, the figures referenced

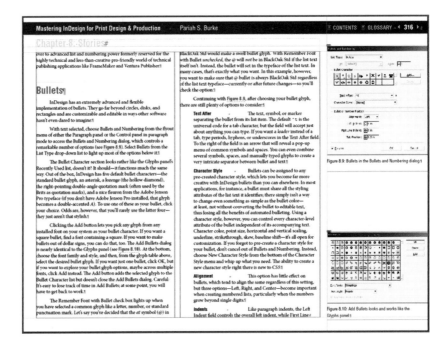

THE LESSON FILE

It's a short excerpt from one of my other books, which I thought was a rather clever way of sneaking in here some additional information you might find useful when building PDF-based epublications—specifically, how to create jump lines and carryovers as well as how to use characters from any symbol font as custom bullet characters.

Please don't judge the design of the lesson file layout too harshly. I created it quickly just for this exercise; it never went to print, er, screen this way. In fact, even the images aren't optimized for on-screen usage.

2. You'll want to have as much of the formatting and layout done as possible before you start creating hyperlinks. You should also create paragraph styles for the image or figure captions, as well as character styles for the figure references within the main text and the return hyperlinks in the captions.

3. If you merely selected the figure (and its caption text frame) and tried to create a hyperlink destination from them, InDesign would allow you only to make the *page* a destination, which isn't very helpful when you're trying to move the reader from elsewhere on the page to the specific area of the figure. Consequently, you need a different method.

    Create a new, empty, small text frame, and position it over the figure. Align the text frame to the top-left corner of the image (see Figure 7.26).

FIGURE 7.26
A new text frame will serve as the hyperlink destination. I've filled the text frame only for clarity in this figure.

4. Switch to the Type tool, and click inside the new text frame so that you see the blinking I-beam cursor. Don't type anything. Instead, from the Hyperlinks panel's flyout menu, choose New Hyperlink Destination.

5. The New Hyperlink Destination dialog will appear with Type already set to Text Anchor. If that isn't the case, then you don't have the Type tool within that text frame; cancel and try again.

    In the Name field, give your text anchor a name more meaningful than the default Anchor 1. If your figures are numbered like mine, enter the name of the figure, for example **Figure 8.8**. Click OK.

6. Now that you've created a text anchor and a hyperlink destination to it, move to the figure reference in the main flow of text. In the sample file I provided, that would be "see

Figure 8.8" at the top of the second column on page 315. Highlight the reference text, the text you want readers to click in order to jump to the figure itself.

7. Back in the Hyperlinks panel, click the Create New Hyperlink button at the bottom.

8. In the New Hyperlink dialog, make sure that the Link To field shows Text Anchor, and then select the current document and the text anchor you just created.

9. At the bottom of the New Hyperlink dialog, pick the appropriate character style for the internal hyperlink (I used one that included a dashed underline rather than a solid), and set any of the other Appearance options. Click OK. Figure 7.27 shows my New Hyperlink settings for your reference.

FIGURE 7.27
After setting the hyperlink options on the figure reference

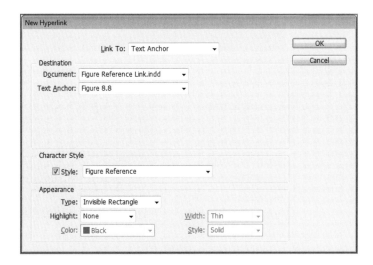

10. Export the document to PDF and try the link. If you see that nothing is happening when you click the figure reference link, zoom into the page far enough that you can't see the destination, the figure, while looking at the figure reference. Click the reference again. *Now* you should see the view change to include the figure.

By default, the hyperlink defined in InDesign has one action or function assigned to it, that being to make sure the figure—or, more specifically, the empty text frame atop the figure—is visible on the page. If you're already viewing the entire page, the hyperlink won't do anything because its function is already accomplished. InDesign can't set the hyperlink to simultaneously ensure that the destination is in view *and* zoom in on it—but Acrobat can.

11. Within Acrobat, activate the Select Object tool. How you do that tends to vary quite a bit between versions. In Acrobat X (not *ex*—10, like Wolverine is Weapon 10), you'll find it in the Tools sidebar in the Content section (see Figure 7.28). With the tool activated, right-click the now-visible box around the figure reference, and select Properties (see Figure 7.29).

FIGURE 7.28

The Acrobat X Tools sidebar and its Content section of tools

FIGURE 7.29

Editing the figure reference hyperlink properties

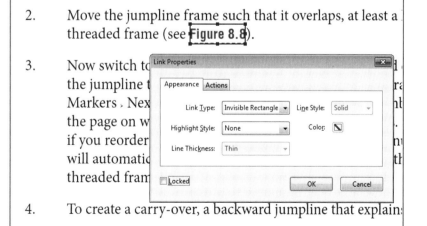

2. Move the jumpline frame such that it overlaps, at least a threaded frame (see **Figure 8.8**).

3. Now switch to [...] the jumpline t[...] Markers › Nex[...] the page on w[...] if you reorder[...] will automatic[...] threaded fram[...]

4. To create a carry-over, a backward jumpline that explain[...]

12. On the Actions tab of the Link Properties dialog, your Actions List should look like mine in Figure 7.30, with the single action of Go To A Page In This Document followed by the destination specifics. In the Add An Action section above, set the Select Action menu to Execute A Menu Item, and click the Add button.

FIGURE 7.30
InDesign inserts a single action on a hyperlink, but Acrobat can add more than one.

13. From the Menu Item list that appears, choose View ➤ Zoom ➤ Actual Size, and click OK. This will add a second action to the Actions List, beneath the Go To A Page In This Document action.

14. If you left this as is, the hyperlink would, in order, ensure that the destination page is showing and then zoom it to actual size, and since you're using very large page sizes (from the "Planning a PDF Publication" section of this chapter), zooming to actual size means it will zoom in pretty far on a section of the page. Unfortunately, it won't necessarily be the *figure's* section of the page because Acrobat zooms to and from the center of the page, and you told Acrobat to make sure the figure was showing *before* it zoomed.

You need to reverse those actions, zooming first and then instantly recentering the view on the figure. To do that, highlight the Execute A Menu Item action in the list, and click the Up button in the dialog. That should move the zoom action above the Go To A Page In This Document action (Figure 7.31). Click OK to exit the Link Properties dialog.

15. Switch back to the Hand tool to interact with the document as a reader would, and click the hyperlinked figure reference. Ta-da! Now it zooms the figure!

If for some reason your document isn't behaving correctly, open my PDF—Figure Reference Link.pdf—and examine my Figure 8.8 hyperlink with the Select Object tool.

FIGURE 7.31
After adding the
Zoom action and
making it the first
action to fire

CREATING MULTIPLE REFERENCES TO JUMP AND ZOOM TO DIFFERENT PARTS OF ONE FIGURE

Taking the idea of text that links to imagery one step further to make complex imagery such as maps, floor plans, charts, graphs, schematics, and other such content vastly more communicative, you can place several links in the text that jump to specific places within the figure. For example, let's say you're producing a PDF-based book that educates children about the basic geopolitical structure of Eastern Europe. You might create a single vector map illustration but want to link to different parts of that map rather than showing the entire map and having to identify specific regions or countries with words alone. The same process you used previously can be employed to create just such interaction.

Oh, and by the way, this can be done *without editing the links afterward in Acrobat!*

1. Begin with the text and imagery laid out and ready to go, as they are in a document like Figure Zone Hyperlinks.INDD in the Lesson Files/Figure Zone Hyperlinks folder. You can have the detail image on the same page or on a page separate from the text; I chose the latter for Figure Zone Hyperlinks.INDD (see Figure 7.32).

2. Create an empty text frame atop the first section of the image to which you'd like to link (see Figure 7.33).

3. With the Type tool still selected and an I-beam cursor in that frame, use the Hyperlinks panel's flyout menu to access the New Hyperlink Destination dialog box.

4. Set the type of the destination to Text Anchor, and name the destination something you'll remember. Click OK to create the hyperlink destination.

FIGURE 7.32
Two pages of the publication; the first page contains the text that describes and will link to the colored regions of the vector map on the second page.

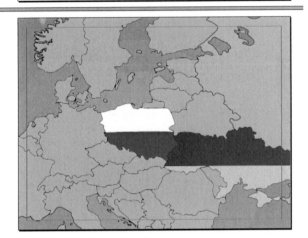

FIGURE 7.33
The text frame encompassing my first hyperlink destination zone

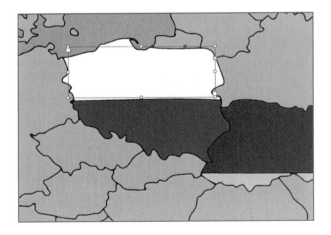

5. Repeat the previous three steps for each of the other destinations you want to create in your image. Using `Figure Zone Hyperlinks.INDD`, that would be four frames and destinations in total, one each for the northern and southern halves of Poland and the Ukraine. The result should look like Figure 7.34.

FIGURE 7.34
After creating all four text frames to serve as hyperlink destinations

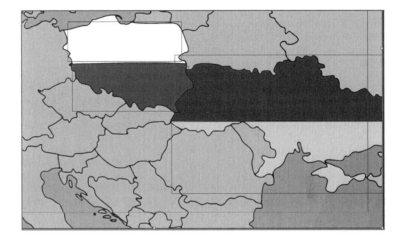

6. Turn your attention back to the text that references those zones of the image. Depending on your layout, you might want to add hyperlinks to the text as you did in the previous exercise, or you might want to create buttons. I'm creating buttons, not just for the visual appeal to young readers but also because using buttons enables me to set multiple actions within InDesign, without having to edit anything in Acrobat directly (see Figure 7.35).

FIGURE 7.35
This button will connect the text to the described region of the map.

North Poland

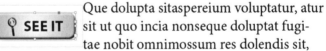

Que dolupta sitaspereium voluptatur, atur sit ut quo incia nonseque doluptat fugitae nobit omnimossum res dolendis sit, nos esed que veritassunt et pa non eum autem quat recearias expe velitem ant distrum fugitat quidemodit volorem estiorem natempos digni vendit illorruptam quam, qui corepel luptam cus, serio doluptat eum reictatus cum quas reperuptas doluptaeped ea volut pediore prestorpores dolenim oloritat.

7. If you'd like to follow my lead with buttons, design your button however you like—mine are single text frames with plain *See It* text, a symbol from the Webdings font, a gradient background, rounded corners, and bevel and emboss and drop shadow courtesy of

Object ➤ Effects. I then gave them a basic text wrap so they'd move the paragraph text out of the way.

8. Once the buttons are created, select the first one with the black-arrow Selection tool and, using the Convert Object to Button button at the bottom of the Buttons And Forms panel (that really is laboriously alliterative, isn't it?), convert the selected object to a button.

9. Name the button, of course, and set its Event option to On Release Or Tap.

TIP You can even skip clicking Convert Object To Button. With an object selected, just click the plus sign beside Actions on the Buttons And Forms panel and choose an action. This will simultaneously convert the object to a button and assign the action you've selected.

10. Click the plus sign beside Actions to open the Actions List. *Don't* choose Go To Destination, not yet. Unlike hyperlinks, buttons created in InDesign may have multiple actions assigned to them. For you that means you *can* set the zoom *and* the jump-to destination right in InDesign without having to later edit the links in Acrobat! Hooray!

First, choose View Zoom near the bottom of the Actions List. When that's added to the Actions List, you'll see a Zoom menu beneath the list; change it to Actual Size.

Now add the Go To Destination as a second action, which will appear after the View Zoom action, the order in which you need it. As a refresher, after you add the Go To Destination action, select the correct document and destination in the relevant fields. Make sure you set the Zoom field to Inherit Zoom, which means it will stick with the zoom level set by the View Zoom action that fires previous to the Go To Destination action. Your Buttons And Forms panel should now look like mine in Figure 7.36.

FIGURE 7.36
After setting the options on my first button

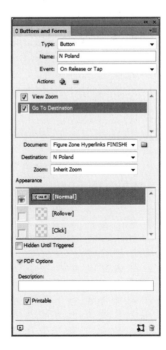

11. Repeat the button creation process for all the other buttons you need, and then export to PDF and give it a try. If something went wrong, examine how I did things in `Figure Zone Hyperlinks FINISHED.INDD` and its exported PDF file, `Figure Zone Hyperlinks.pdf`.

LINKING PARTS OF AN IMAGE TO ADDITIONAL CONTENT

Another example is a map of a trade show floor wherein clicking any booth space or other marker jumps the reader to a page of details about the booth's occupant. Creating that is very similar to the previous technique, though you'll invert things a little bit. I don't have on hand a trade show map that I can legally distribute in the lesson files, so I'll use some house images I picked up from the royalty-free and actually free stock photography site Stock.Xchng (`http://sxc.hu`) in the file `Image Map.INDD` in the `Chapter 7/Lesson Files/Image Map` folder. You're welcome to use that or follow along in your own documents. By the way, I called the file *image map* because, if you're familiar with web design, the process of creating multiple hyperlinks within the area of a single image is called *image mapping*; you're going to do the same thing in InDesign.

1. With an appropriate file open, go first to the destinations, the content to which you want your image to link. In the case of the `Image Map.INDD` file, that would be page 2, "Living Room" (see Figure 7.37).

FIGURE 7.37
The destination of the first hyperlink I want to create

2. For each page, build a hyperlink destination just as you did in the previous exercises. It can be a text anchor or a page destination, as you prefer.

3. Once you have all the destinations defined, go to the image from which you want to link to other locations.

4. Create your buttons however you want them to look. They can be text labels—simple text frames converted to buttons—placed graphics like thumbtacks, map location markers, logos (for the trade show map), or something you draw directly in InDesign. Naturally, what you choose for buttons will vary per project so that the buttons make sense in context. And, using the previous techniques, link those buttons to the hyperlink destinations.

5. Finished. Export to PDF and try it.

In the case of Image Map.INDD, I'm going to create invisible buttons for two reasons. First, they make sense for the artwork. Second, I wanted a reason to show you how to make invisible buttons.

Your buttons don't have to be visible. They'll work just as well if they aren't. Depending on the artwork of your image map, you might be able to create empty rectangular or elliptical graphic frames to serve as buttons. In the case of my 3D house, wherein I want readers to be able to click the rooms themselves, which aren't nicely rectangular, it would be ideal to draw the exact shapes of the rooms and have those be room-shaped buttons à la Figure 7.38. Alas, upon converting the paths to buttons, they'd become rectangular hyperlink areas anyway. So, you can draw the exact shapes with the Pen tool, or you can draw rectangles that approximate the shapes. Either way, I recommend doing it on a separate layer, locking to the original artwork's layer, to make drawing and selection easier.

Once the drawing is done, all I have to do is convert each of those paths into a button object that jumps to my previously defined hyperlink destinations, one each for the corresponding bedroom, living room, and garage detail pages.

If I wanted, even though the buttons are initially invisible, I could add Rollover and Click appearances in the Buttons And Forms panel so the room areas light up further—a fill color with a low opacity and maybe a blending mode to make it react a certain way to the artwork behind it—or even create a text label that appears to guide the reader by saying "click here to read about the living room." Again, you can do anything you want in the different appearances, even if the Normal appearance is only an object with no fill or stroke color.

FIGURE 7.38
Unfilled paths in the shape of each room will serve as my buttons.

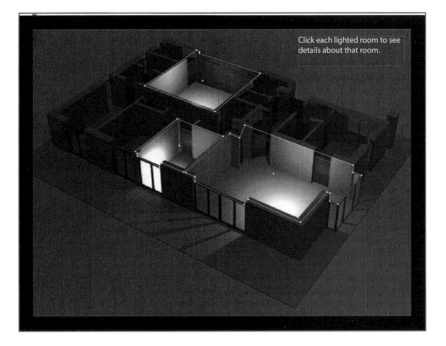

Click each lighted room to see details about that room.

CREATING A LINK TO JUMP BACK

You may want to give readers a way *back* from the destination of a hyperlink to where they were. That way, after they've looked at your chart, defined the word they didn't know, or read about the booth or room on the image map, they can pick up where they left off without having to flip through the document hoping to find it. The prospect of creating hyperlinks that return readers to where they were may sound daunting, but it's actually very easy.

Wherever you send readers, create a hyperlink or a button to send them back. You might, for example, put a hyperlink in every figure caption that says something like *Click here to return to where you were.* In the glossary, on the figure zone image, and in other places, you might just want a single button at the top of the page or somewhere else close by that, when clicked, sends the user back to the location of the original hyperlink. How is it possible to use a single button or link to send readers back to their origins if, as with a glossary page, there are potentially dozens of links that could have gotten them there?

Acrobat (and other PDF viewers) keeps track of the current and previous *views*, with views meaning the page number, zoom percentage, and what part of the page was visible in the program's viewport. Thus, you can create a button that simply returns the reader to the previous view, which, unless the reader moved around or navigated after jumping, will be the source of the original jump. Just define your button's action as Go To Previous View via the Button And Forms panel's Add Action button.

The catch is that the Go To Previous View function is available only within InDesign by using buttons; it's not something you can assign to a hyperlink. You can assign it to a hyperlink in Acrobat, however. Just edit the properties of the hyperlink in the PDF, and on the Actions tab, add the Execute A Menu Item action and select the View ➤ Page Navigation ➤ Previous View menu item.

Another alternative, if you didn't want to edit every hyperlink in Acrobat, would be to create an invisible button above the text that would be hyperlinked with the "return to previous view" ability.

USING ACROBAT TO GAIN ABSOLUTE CONTROL OVER JUMPS AND ZOOMS

Use the absolute control of Acrobat's Go To A Page View action when you need to zoom readers further in (or out) than the Actual Size zoom level allows, or when the artwork or other content to which you're sending them is so complex that you need to restrict their views to a very specific portion, such as with data charts and graphs, schematics, and so on.

I saved this for last, not just because it helps to have learned all the other stuff first but also because this technique can be accomplished only in the PDF and therefore should be used only after the PDF is otherwise finalized. Re-exporting to PDF from InDesign will wipe out the results of this technique.

1. Open in Acrobat any of the PDFs with which you've previously been working. You need one that includes at least one hyperlink or button.

2. Switch to the Select Object tool, select the hyperlink frame or the button object, and then open its properties from the right-click Context menu.

3. Go to the Actions tab, and expand the Select Action drop-down field.

4. Toward the top is the Go To A Page View action. Select it and click Add, whereupon a little dialog box will appear. (See Figure 7.39.)

FIGURE 7.39
Selecting Go To A
Page View from the
Select Action drop-
down list opens the
Create Go To View
dialog.

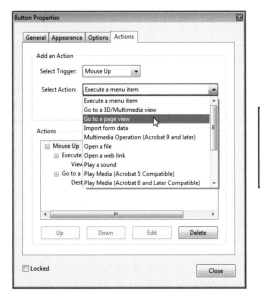

5. At this point, go to the page of the destination for the hyperlink or button, zoom in (or out) to the point where you want readers to be zoomed in (or out), and set the object(s) you want them to reach in the viewport of the application. In other words, navigate, zoom, and align the window so that how *you* see the content is the way you want *them* to see it (see Figure 7.40). The Go To A Page View action basically records the view you set up and plays it back for readers who activate that action.

FIGURE 7.40
If I click Set Link at
this point, with this
precise view in my
window, then this
is exactly how my
readers will see the
document when
they click the but-
ton to which I've
assigned the Go To
View action.

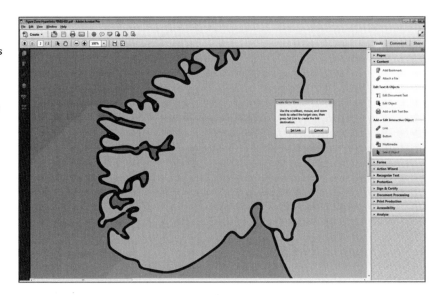

6. When you're happy, click the Set Link button to commit the view to the link.

7. Test the button or hyperlink. Does it bring you to exactly the view you want readers to experience? If not, edit the action.

Creating Advanced Interactivity

Now that you understand the basics of creating and working with hyperlinks, and especially buttons, let's go through tutorials for creating more advanced interactive features and effects.

Creating a Print Button

You might want to let readers print your publication (or you might not; the very last section in this chapter talks about securing PDFs to, in part, restrict printing). Assuming you want to allow printing, why not add a custom-designed Print button into your global navigation system?

1. Create a button that readers will click when and if they want to print the publication.

2. On the Buttons And Forms panel, add the action Print Form (see Figure 7.41).

FIGURE 7.41

Adding the Print Form action to enable printing of the PDF—with or without forms

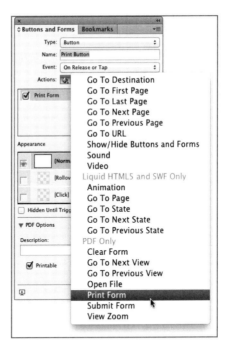

3. Save and export to PDF.

Although InDesign calls the function Print Form, it's really just a shortcut to Acrobat's main Print dialog. The InDesign engineers labeled it the way they did because they expected the average person to create the button as part of a PDF form. Don't let that deter you.

Creating a Full-Screen Mode Button

Full-screen mode in Acrobat offers certain advantages to readers of publications. Specifically, it hides the entire Acrobat or Reader user interface, filling the screen with the document itself—just like pressing Shift+W in InDesign hides the InDesign UI and shows just the document. Another advantage is that full-screen mode will show page transitions when the reader moves from page to page, if you've enabled page transitions in the Export To Interactive PDF dialog or in the Pages or Page Transitions panel. Page transitions are better suited for using PDFs as slide-shows, though.

Still, if you want to point out to the reader that she has the ability to put the document into full-screen mode, *without* trying to force it on the reader (see my admonishment about that in the "Changing Window Options" section later in this chapter), you can create a button that puts the PDF into full-screen mode. The reader can also do this herself, without your help, if she knows about the Ctrl+L/Cmd+L shortcut, but so few of them do.

1. Create a button designed to communicate to readers that it will put the publication into full-screen mode. You might also want to include directions on how they can get out of full-screen mode.

2. In the Buttons And Forms panel, set the button's action to View Zoom.

3. In the Zoom field under the Actions List, choose Full Screen (see Figure 7.42).

FIGURE 7.42
Giving the View
Zoom a Full Screen
action

For inspiration, I'd like to point out the magazine *What Matters Now* from Seth Godin. Rather than trying to force the reader into full-screen mode, *What Matters Now* includes, on a page before the content begins, a large diagram and button encouraging readers to click and place the publication into full-screen mode (see Figure 7.43). Although the magazine should have been a little more informative, explaining not just the Windows shortcut key for exiting full-screen but also the Mac and maybe even the universal Esc shortcut key, this page was still a very good idea. Nothing else appears on the page, which makes the button and instructions command attention; thus, most readers will voluntarily go into full-screen mode, which the publisher prefers, rather than be forced into it and potentially become confused and dismayed by the automatic transition and the "This document is trying to put Acrobat in full screen mode" alert that ensues.

FIGURE 7.43
What Matters Now asks its readers to voluntarily enter full-screen mode.

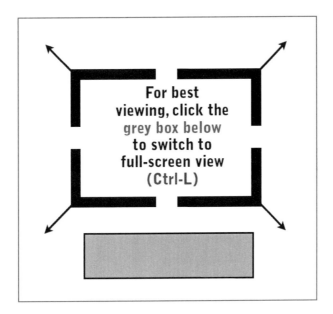

Creating Facebook, Twitter, and Sharing Buttons

How cool would it be to include, as part of your publication's global navigation system, buttons that let readers share the publication—or the publication's subscription page address—with their friends and colleagues through social media? Just think about adding common web page buttons such as Facebook's Like button, Twitter's Tweet This button, and other common social sharing buttons. It's relatively easy.

1. You'll have to write the JavaScript code—or hire someone to do it—though you could use the standard Facebook Like (`https://developers.facebook.com/docs/reference/plugins/like/`) and Twitter Tweet button (`https://dev.twitter.com/docs/tweet-button`) creator codes as bases from which to start.

2. Armed with the right code, create a button either with no action assigned or with an action you'll replace.

3. Export to PDF.

4. In Acrobat, right-click the button with the Select Object tool, and choose Properties.

5. Go the Actions tab, remove any preexisting action, and add from the Select Action menu the option Run A JavaScript.

6. Once you click Add, up will pop Acrobat's JavaScript Editor (see Figure 7.44). Paste into it the script you created for the button, and then click OK.

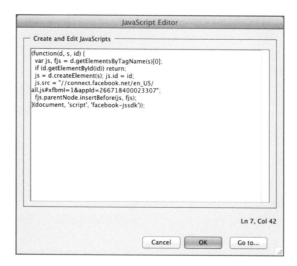

7. Switch to the Hand tool to test the button. If something goes wrong, return to the Button Properties, highlight the Run A JavaScript action, and click the Edit button to return to the JavaScript Editor.

Making Print-Only and Screen-Only Objects

Want to create objects like global navigation buttons that appear on-screen but disappear if the document is printed? Or maybe you'd rather go the other way, impressing your publication's domain name and other information on printouts where there was a blank area or other information on-screen. With buttons, it's easy.

1. Create your print-only and/or screen-only content in InDesign. If you have both types of objects and they occupy the same space, you might want to build them on separate layers so that you can hide and show them individually.

2. Convert each of these conditional display objects to buttons. Unless they're buttons that do something else—like navigation buttons would—don't assign them any actions.

3. Export to PDF.

4. In Acrobat, access the properties of the first conditional display button, and go to the General tab.

5. At the bottom of the General tab, the Form Field field will probably read Visible, but that's not the only option available to you (see Figure 7.45). Take your pick; Visible But Doesn't

Print means the button object displays only on-screen, while Hidden But Printable creates an object that isn't there on-screen but magically appears if the document is printed. And of course, the Hidden option hides the button object completely, which isn't intended for use with buttons; the Hidden option is intended for use with form fields, for calculation fields, or to capture the date of printing or submission or other automatic data in a form without the form respondent knowing it's being captured.

FIGURE 7.45
The Form Field field lets you choose whether an object appears on-screen, in print, both, or not at all.

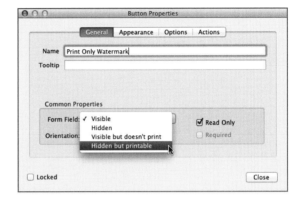

Connecting to Video Navigation Points

Earlier in this chapter you created navigation points in a video so that you could help readers get to specific points within a longer video. Here's where you create the means by which the reader accesses the video navigation points.

1. Place a video into InDesign and create one or more navigation points using the Media panel and the directions from the "Adding Navigation Points to a Video" section in this chapter.

2. Create a button to access the first navigation point. Hyperlinks in text can't be used for this purpose, unless you edit the hyperlinks later in Acrobat, but if you want the *function* of hyperlinking text to a video navigation point—while remaining in InDesign—then style the text like a hyperlink and above it place a button object with no fill or stroke (an invisible button). When the reader clicks or taps, the effect will be the same as if it were the text itself firing the action.

3. In the Buttons And Forms panel, choose simply Video as the button's action. Other fields will appear below the Actions List (see Figure 7.46).

4. From the Video field, select the appropriate video, if there's more than one.

5. Within the Options field, choose not Play but Play from Navigation Point, which will enable the Point field beneath it.

FIGURE 7.46
Assigning a video-navigation action to the button

6. Finally, choose the correct navigation point from the Point field drop-down menu. Once in PDF form, the button will begin playing the video from that navigation point.

7. Repeat as necessary to add and configure buttons for any remaining navigation points in the video.

Creating Pop-Up Lightbox Images

Using Adobe Reader on every platform, readers can zoom in on images—or any part of the document—but a much slicker effect is to give readers the ability to click or tap thumbnails and have a larger version of an image pop up, as images do on Facebook, Pinterest, Flickr, and countless blogs. The big, "zoomed" images can be styled however you like; Figure 7.47 shows a few styles I quickly whipped up, but one of the most popular, thanks to Facebook, Pinterest, Flickr, and countless blogs, is the lightbox effect (Figure 7.48), which shows the image but dims the content behind the image. Why don't you create that?

1. Place your image onto the page or out on the pasteboard *twice*. You can either place the same image twice or duplicate the first instance.

2. Size and position one copy as the thumbnail onto which readers will click to show the pop-up, large version. It should be exactly where you want it on the page. Leave it alone for now.

3. Using the Rectangle tool, draw a box that completely covers the entire page. I recommend doing this on a separate layer just to make it easier to work through step 6 and beyond.

FIGURE 7.47
You can create almost any image-zooming or pop-up effect with a little button work.

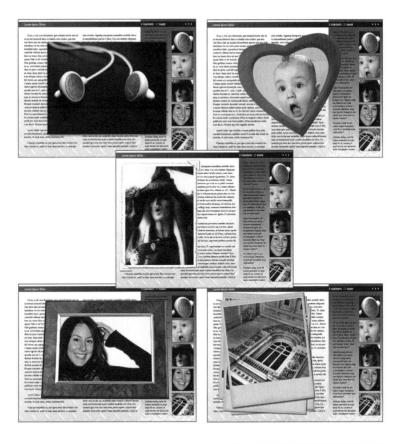

FIGURE 7.48
A lightbox image pop-up effect

4. Fill the rectangle with black, remove any stroke, and, using the Effects panel (Window ➤ Effects), drop the rectangle's overall opacity (or just the Fill opacity) to around 75 percent to 95 percent, whatever you like (see Figure 7.49). This rectangle will create the page-dimming effect. You can also fill it with white to get the Pinterest lightbox effect or any color, pattern, or image you desire. Regardless of its appearance, call this object the *screener*.

FIGURE 7.49
The screener frame overlies and dims the page.

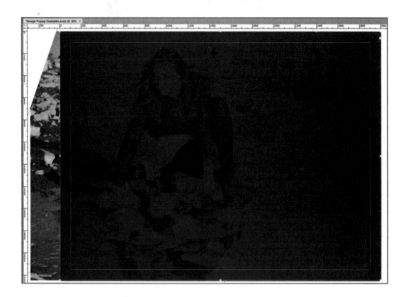

5. Returning to the second copy of the placed image, move it atop the screener and center it to the page and the screener rectangle. Resize the image until it's as large as you want it to appear in the pop-up. Feel free to apply any effects or styling at this point—say, a drop shadow, a large stroke, or padding in the frame to create the look of a printed photo or a Polaroid; you can even rotate the image a little, something I've never seen any of the web-based lightboxes do. This is also the time to add a caption, photo credit, or whatever else you might want to appear with the pop-up image. In mine, I added both a photo credit and a caption (see Figure 7.50); notice that the other objects don't have to be opaque and don't have to be completely—or even partly—within the area of the image.

6. With the black-arrow Selection tool, select the large image, the screener frame, and any other objects you may have added to the pop-up view and group them with Ctrl+G/ Cmd+G.

7. Turn this new group into a button, and name it whatever you like. I named my pop-up group Lightbox Pg 60. Next is where the magic happens.

8. From the plus-sign Add New Action button, choose Show/Hide Buttons And Forms near the top. You will now see the Visibility list beneath the Actions List. All the buttons and form fields contained on the active spread will be listed here—including the button you are actively creating (see Figure 7.51).

FIGURE 7.50
My finished light-box effect—large photo, screener, caption, and photo credit

FIGURE 7.51
Setting the options on the pop-up image and screener group button

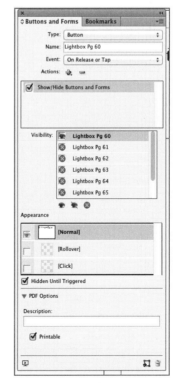

9. Beside each button's entry in the Visibility list is a gray circle with an *X* through it. That symbol means the button is ignored—our action will neither show nor hide it. That's fine for everything else in that list except the button you *want* to show. Find this button in the list, and click its visibility icon twice. Clicking it once will show an eyeball, meaning the button will be shown by the action, while clicking it twice will show the eye with a slash through it to signify that this action will hide the button. That's what you want: to hide the button. In other words, when the reader clicks the lightboxed big image, it will hide itself. (I'll talk about a variation on this after the initial step-by-step.)

10. Tucked away beneath the Appearance list is an innocuous check box labeled Hidden Until Triggered. Check it.

11. Select the thumbnail version of the image and turn it into a button. (This is where working on separate layers becomes convenient.)

12. For its action choose Show/Hide Buttons And Forms, and in the Visibility list, click the visibility icon beside the big image's button *once*. This will show the lightboxed big image (and the screener behind it) when the thumbnail is clicked or tapped.

13. Because of a quirk in PDF, there's one more thing you have to do. As you can see in Figure 7.52, the thumbnail button, being the one just clicked, gets shoved to the top instead of being covered by the lightbox. After clicking a button, Acrobat makes that button the topmost object. I don't know why.

FIGURE 7.52
The original thumbnail button appears above the button that was created before it, the lightbox pop-up.

To prevent that scenario from happening, go back to the thumbnail button and configure it to *also hide itself*, just as you configured the lightbox button to hide *it*self. That will keep it from appearing when the lightbox does. If you want the thumbnail to be visible behind the lightbox, create a second copy of the thumbnail image—but not a button—behind the version that is a button. You'll also want to add to the lightbox button the action to show the thumbnail button again.

14. Now do a test export to PDF. The initial view on the page should be the thumbnail with whatever other content you included. Clicking the thumbnail will make the large image appear in its lightbox, complete with screener dimming the page behind. Clicking the lightbox—anywhere, the image or the screener—will make the lightbox disappear.

Very cool, isn't it? I haven't seen anyone use that effect in PDF publications yet. In fact, *I* haven't even used it (except to create the `Lightbox Popup FINISHED.INDD` in the `Lesson Files/Lightbox Popup` folder), because I came up with it while I was writing this chapter.

I also promised you a variation on this technique. The way it is now, clicking the large image or the screener will close both, returning the reader to the main page with the thumbnail. You can change that behavior, though. What if, when the large image is clicked, it launches a URL? Maybe it's an image of a product you're trying to sell, and clicking the image takes the reader to the online product page or shopping cart. At the same time, only the screener if clicked would be configured to hide itself and the larger image. Here's how to do that:

1. Perform the same tasks all the way through step 5. Skip step 6, and don't group the large image with the screener frame.

2. Turn the screener frame into a button, and turn the large image into a wholly separate button. Name them both appropriately to make the rest of this easier on yourself.

3. Returning to the screener button, give it the Show/Hide Buttons And Forms action, and set it to hide *two* buttons in the Visibility list—itself and the large image. Make sure to check Hidden Until Triggered under the Appearance list.

4. Select the large picture button, and give it a Go To URL action; then fill in the URL beneath the Actions List. If you want it to do something other than access an online resource, use the appropriate action. Again, make sure to check Hidden Until Triggered so the image will be initially hidden.

5. Go back to the thumbnail image, convert it to a button, give it the Show/Hide Buttons And Forms action, and then configure it to show both the screener and the large image buttons.

6. Export to PDF and give it a try. Clicking within the image should launch the URL; clicking anywhere outside the large image, which, of course, means the full-page screener, will close both objects, exiting the lightbox effect.

Building Image Galleries

The Show/Hide Buttons And Forms action can be used to create even more interesting effects, as you'll see in the next couple of sections. For one, it can be used to create image galleries wherein several images occupy the same space. Let's make one.

1. Place into InDesign all the pictures you want to include in your gallery. I'm going to use a series of antique clock images, as you can see in Figure 7.53 and in `Image Gallery FINISHED.INDD` in the Chapter 7 `Lesson Files/Image Gallery` folder. After this point, though, I'm going to incorporate big numbers into the images to help the figures make more sense throughout this tutorial.

FIGURE 7.53
These clocks will
form the content of
my image gallery.

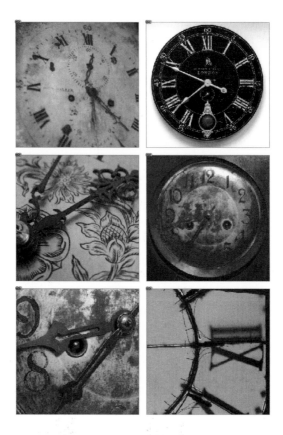

2. Each image frame needs to be the same size, with the images filling the frames, so size and fit them appropriately. Change any of the other attributes of the frames at this point—adding effects, and so on.

   If you want to add a drop shadow, outer glow, or any other effect that will extend beyond the frame edges, *don't*. Instead, create a new frame just for those effects and stash it off to the side for now. The reason I don't want you to use any out-of-frame effects is because you're going to stack all of the pictures on top of one another, which would cause their effects to compound with each other.

3. Convert each image to a button. I recommend naming them in the order you intend readers to view them. For example, the first image you want them to see should be named something like Gallery Pic 1, the second image to appear would then be Gallery Pic 2, and so on.

4. Move all the images so that they overlap *a little bit*. The goal here is to be able to see their stacking order.

5. Using the Object menu's Arrange submenu items or the corresponding keyboard shortcuts, set the stacking order of the objects to match their naming scheme—in reverse. Figure 7.54 should help you do that. You want Gallery Pic 1 at the bottom and the highest-numbered button on the top.

FIGURE 7.54
The correct order of
the gallery picture
buttons

6. Select Gallery Pic 1 again, and assign it the Show/Hide Buttons And Forms action. In the Visibility list, you want to enable or make visible Gallery Pic 2 and make Gallery Pic 1 itself invisible. Also, and this is important, make sure you check the Hidden Until Triggered option (below the Appearance area) for Gallery Pic 1 and all subsequent image buttons. Figure 7.55 shows the settings in the Buttons And Forms panel.

FIGURE 7.55
The settings for the
first image button

7. Moving on to Gallery Pic 2, give it the same action to make itself invisible, and make visible the next image in the sequence, Gallery Pic 3.

8. Repeat the previous step for the rest of the images. Each one should have an action that hides itself and shows the subsequent button, and each should have Hidden Until Triggered enabled. When you get to the last image in the series, go to the next step.

9. The last image requires a decision. What do you want to happen after the reader views the last photo in the gallery? You can leave it on-screen, unchangeable, or you can have it loop back to the first image, beginning the gallery sequence over. I'm opting for the second choice—restarting the gallery with the first image.

   To make the last image show the first image, you merely have to set it to hide itself while showing Gallery Pic 1; the cycle then starts all over.

10. Now you put it all together. Select all the image buttons and, using the Arrange panel (Window ➢ Object & Layout ➢ Arrange) or the arrangement buttons on the Control panel (when the Selection tool is active), align all the images to each other so that they stack perfectly. If the stacking or z-order of the objects is correct, you should see only the last image in the gallery.

11. Position these images on the page where you want the gallery to appear. If you created a separate frame for a drop shadow or other effect, position that behind all the image buttons.

12. Export to PDF and try it. Clicking each image should show the next, with a click on the last image rewinding to the beginning of the gallery. You can test it in my `Image Gallery.PDF` file in the `Lesson Files/Image Gallery` folder.

A variation on this technique is to make the gallery appear in a lightbox pop-up by combining this and the previous technique. To do that, you'd need to make the following modifications to the pop-up gallery technique:

♦ On the initial page thumbnail or another button you create to display the pop-up gallery, set the Show/Hide Buttons And Forms action to show not only Gallery Pic 1 but also a screener frame.

♦ Change the visibility options on the button that will close everything—the screener button in the "Creating Pop-Up Lightbox Images" tutorial—to hide all gallery images as well as itself.

Another variation is to use navigation buttons within the gallery as in Figure 7.56. Instead of clicking the photos themselves to advance or rewind, readers would click the arrow buttons. That would require a little more modification.

1. Move the image buttons around so that you can see them all and there's enough space around each one for the inclusion of the navigation buttons you want to create.

2. Give the image buttons no action at all except to activate their Hidden Until Triggered options—all of them, even Gallery Pic 1.

3. Design your first set of gallery navigation graphics, and turn them into buttons.

4. Duplicate the set—forward and back—so that you have a second set of navigation buttons. Keep duplicating. You'll need a new set for every gallery image.

FIGURE 7.56
Galleries can also
be navigated with
arrows or other
image devices.

5. Name or number them in the Buttons And Forms panel's Name field so that they correspond to the image buttons they'll accompany.

6. Position the first set of navigation arrows around Gallery Pic 1.

7. Selecting the Next Image 1 button (or whatever you called it), go to the Buttons And Forms panel, and—of course—give it the Show/Hide Buttons And Forms action.

8. In the Visibility list, things get a little complicated. This one Next Image 1 button has to do a lot of work. It has to hide all of the following:

   ◆ Gallery Pic 1

   ◆ Prev Image 1

   ◆ Itself, Next Image 1

   At the same time, Next Image 1 must show all of the following:

   ◆ Gallery Pic 2

   ◆ Prev Image 2

   ◆ Next Image 2

9. Configure each subsequent "next image" button the same way so that it shows the next set of buttons—the image and its navigation buttons—and hides its own set of buttons, which includes the image button, the "previous image" button, and itself.

10. For the "previous image" buttons, do the reverse. For instance, the first "previous image" navigation button, Prev Image 1, must hide the following buttons:

    ◆ Gallery Pic 1

    ◆ Next Image 1

    ◆ Itself, Prev Image 1

    Simultaneously, it must show the last set of buttons in the gallery so that clicking Prev Image 1 moves to the end of the gallery, showing, in the case of my six-image gallery, Gallery Pic 6, Next Image 6, and Prev Image 6.

11. Go through the rest of the navigation buttons, configuring each to show the next or previous set, and hide the rest. The result will be a nice image gallery with navigation buttons. Don't forget to add tooltip text to the navigation buttons (see the "Adding Tooltip Text" section).

One more variation, and then I'll quit, I promise. Take a gander at Figure 7.57. It's an ecommerce-style image gallery for use in PDF. Instead of using navigation arrows or clicking one image to linearly move to the next image, this style uses the thumbnails as activation buttons—click a thumbnail, and the main image changes to that. Each thumbnail button shows one image button but hides all the others, which is the only way to make nonlinear gallery navigation work. If you tried using the previous technique of relying on stacking order to block out previous images, the whole thing would fall apart. You have to add the hiding of all image buttons except the one requested into each button's actions.

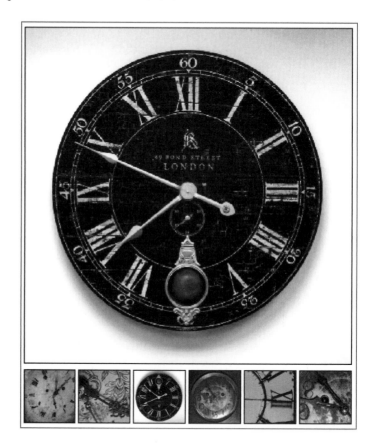

FIGURE 7.57
Thumbnails can also be used to allow more visual navigation between slides in the gallery.

Creating Self-Test Exams

This is one of my favorite ideas. Take a look at Figure 7.58, which is a PDF-based ebook I developed and designed. Written by Mike Rankin, the book is *The Guide to the InDesign ACE Exam* (now in its third edition) and helps people prepare to take the InDesign Adobe Certified Expert exam (which I co-wrote) administered by Adobe and its partners so that Adobe can endorse the skills and knowledge of those who pass the exam as being certified InDesign experts. I wanted readers to be able to take self-assessment exams at the beginning of the book, to gauge their knowledge levels starting out, as well as at the end of each chapter to judge how well they learned that chapter's material. At the end of the book is a longer self-exam patterned after the multiple-choice ACE exam. My challenge was figuring out a way to make several self-assessment exams work within a PDF. I didn't want to use the old print textbook or course method of including an answer key at the end of the book; I wanted readers to be able to compare their answers with the correct ones directly on the exam pages—without forcing them to flip their monitors or heads upside down to read the other old standby of inverted small-type answers at the bottom of the page.

FIGURE 7.58

A self-exam in *The Guide to the InDesign ACE Exam*

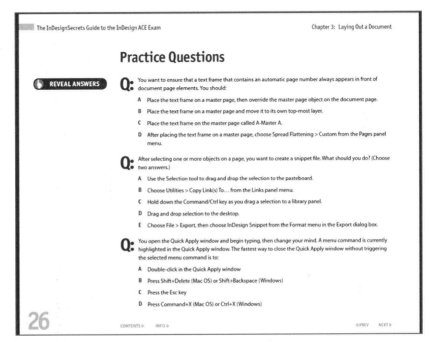

My solution was conditional appearance buttons: Show/Hide Buttons And Form actions.

Figure 7.59 is the InDesign layout of that same chapter-end self-assessment quiz. The checkmark correct-answer indicators—a circle with a text frame atop it—are themselves buttons (grouped first, of course). Each of them is aligned beside its correct answer and configured in the Buttons And Forms panel to have no action, but with the Hidden Until Triggered option selected (see Figure 7.60). The Reveal Answers button, which has multiple appearances, carries the Show/Hide Buttons And Forms action and is configured to make visible all the check-mark buttons for that exam (Figure 7.61). That way, when a reader has finished writing down her answers, or using Acrobat's annotation tools to indicate them in the PDF, she can click the Reveal Answers button to show the check marks. At the same time, the Reveal Answers button hides itself and shows a similarly designed and configured Hide Answers button that will make all the check marks invisible again, hide itself, and reshow the Reveal Answers button, ready to start the self-exam all over again.

FIGURE 7.59
The self-exam lay-out in InDesign

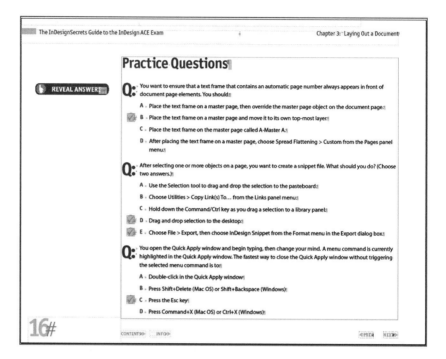

FIGURE 7.60
The correct answer check marks are buttons with no actions.

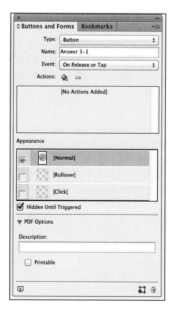

FIGURE 7.61
The Reveal Answers button shows all the correct answer check marks at once; it also includes multiple appearances.

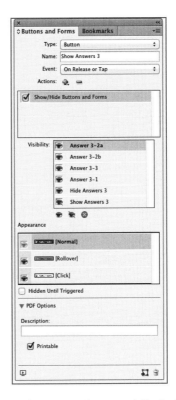

Note that the Show/Hide Buttons And Forms actions aren't limited to buttons on the same page. In this case, the self-assessment exam extends onto a second page.

If you'd like to examine the buttons and how they work, you'll find the two-page self-assessment test I've been showing in the `Chapter 7/Lesson Files/Self Test` folder—in INDD and PDF.

Changing the Color of Video Controllers

When including videos in PDFs, it's often nice to enable the video to pop out of the page and fill the screen. As I mentioned earlier, you can use the PDF Options dialog (refer to Figure 7.10) to activate the ability of a video to play in a floating window. And, from the Controller drop-down menu in the Media panel, you can configure what type of controller appears above the image. What you cannot do in InDesign, however, is change the controller's color. It will always be a 75 percent opaque dark gray controller background...unless you want to change it in Acrobat.

1. In Acrobat, switch to the Select Object tool.

2. Right-click the video, and choose Properties. Up pops the Edit Video dialog.

3. Switch to the Controls tab to change the skin—you'll see options similar to those in InDesign's Controller field—as well as the color and opacity of the overlay player. To change the color, just click the color swatch, which will open a list of swatches you can choose from (see Figure 7.62). If none of those is what you want, click the Other Color option at the bottom to open a standard color picker and mixer.

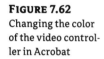

FIGURE 7.62
Changing the color of the video controller in Acrobat

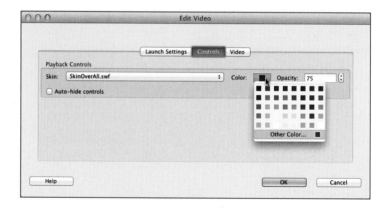

TIP While you're in the Edit Video dialog, check out the tabs and options, which let you toggle via the Playback Style field whether the video plays in place on the page or in a floating window, whether to include a border around the playing video, and more.

Making Buttons Click

To wrap up the advanced interactivity section, here's a short technique to make your buttons really cool. Remember that any button can carry multiple actions. Therefore, in addition to whatever else you may have the button doing, why not make it *click*?

1. Place a sound file—a *click* or whatever you want to use—onto the same page containing a button, and make the media frame as small as possible. I like to use the Transform panel or transform controls on the Control panel to resize the frame down to 0.1×0.1 pixels, which is virtually invisible in a 3,000×2,250-pixel page.

2. Select the button you want to click, and in the Buttons And Forms panel, add the Sound action.

3. Drag the Sound action up in the Actions List so that it's the first action to fire. This is important because the audio file must be loaded into Acrobat's (or Reader's) memory on its first play, which causes a slight delay, and if it's the last action to fire, your reader might experience a noticeable delay between clicking the button and hearing the click sound.

4. In the Sound field below the Actions List, select the audio file and then set the Options field to Play.

5. Export the PDF and give it a try. If everything worked, assign the same sound to all your buttons.

There are catches and caveats with adding sounds to buttons. If you follow the tutorial precisely, it will work every time. However, smart designers will start looking for ways to make things more efficient; unfortunately, quirks within Acrobat/Reader or PDF itself cause the obvious efficiency tips to fail. Here are the first things that pop into my head when I think about adding a sound effect to all the buttons in my multipage publication:

◆ *I should place all my 0.1×0.1-pixel sound media frames on one page, somewhere inconspicuous, so that I can manage them all together.* Unfortunately, buttons won't activate sounds unless the sounds' media frames are on the same page.

◆ *I should put the frames for sounds that I'll be using throughout the document onto the master page, so that they are on every page on which I'll use them but still easily manageable from a single location.* Alas, this doesn't quite work either. The first time a button tries to play a sound included as a master page item, the sound will not play; the second time the same sound is requested on the same page, it will play. It seems that the first time causes Acrobat to activate and ready the media frame, which you can tell because you'll see the media frame's controller appear if the frame is large enough to see the controller. It won't be until the second time, however, that the readied player will actually play. The same behavior occurs even if you override the master page media frame. You actually must place the file on every document page and set the buttons on that page to use that instance of the sound.

Note that buttons on the master page also won't play sounds unless those sounds appear directly on the document pages on which the master page buttons appear.

◆ *Since I'm stuck putting my sound media frames on every page of the document, I should make them a size I can easily work with but hide them behind some other opaque object(s).* It's a good thought, but no. Multimedia content—sound and video—is placed on a layer above everything else in the PDF, and it's not a layer that can be controlled. Basically, PDFs make multimedia the highest object in the stacking order no matter how you lay them out in InDesign. Therefore, in the PDF the audio frames will appear *above* whatever objects you've set them *behind* in InDesign.

So, if you want to use sound effects, you're stuck putting them on every page on which they'll be called and making their media frames small enough that they won't be noticed.

Finalizing the Publication

Before distributing your publication to the world, there are few finishing touches you might want to add.

Adding Metadata

I've talked about adding metadata throughout the book, so I'll be brief here. First a reminder: metadata makes the world go round. Actually, love does that, but metadata makes a smile...no, wait, that's Coca-Cola. Forget it. Look, metadata is important. It helps your publication get properly indexed and attributed, it communicates copyright and ownership, and it spells out exactly who to sue for infringement.

Fill in as much metadata as is relevant before publishing the PDF. You can furnish all the metadata within the PDF itself by going to File ➢ Properties in Acrobat, but it's much better to supply the metadata to InDesign, which will then include it in PDF and other exports. To do it within InDesign, just choose File ➢ File Info to open the XMP metadata dialog in Figure 7.63. Then complete all the fields you feel are relevant for your document. If you find yourself entering the same metadata often, do it just once and then, next to the OK button, click the down arrow and choose Export. You can then save all the fields' metadata to an XMP file that is easily re-imported in future documents.

FIGURE 7.63
Setting metadata
on the INDD file via
InDesign's XMP
metadata (File
Information) dialog

File Information for Lightbox Popup FINISHED.indd

| Description | IPTC | IPTC Extension | Camera Data | GPS Data | Video Data | Audio Data | ▶ ▼ |

Document Title: Lightbox Popup Demo for ePublishing with InDesign

Author: Pariah Burke

Author Title:

Description: A demonstration of creating a popup lightbox image effect in InDesign for display in PDF-based digital publications.

Rating: ★ ★ ★ ★ ★

Description Writer:

Keywords:

ⓘ Semicolons or commas can be used to separate multiple values

Copyright Status: Copyrighted ▼

Copyright Notice: © Copyright 2012 Pariah Burke

Copyright Info URL: http://iamPariah.com   Go To URL...

Created: 2012-04-07 – 13:47:58   Application: Adobe InDesign CS6 (Windows)

Modified: 2012-04-07 – 16:24:31   Format: application/x-indesign

Powered By
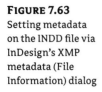

Preferences | Export... ▼ | OK | Cancel

Hiding Acrobat's Toolbars

If you want to hide Acrobat's own navigation buttons in favor of the custom navigation system you built into the publication, or if you'd just rather hide all extraneous parts of Acrobat or Reader not needed by your publication, you can do that pretty easily. On the Initial View tab of the Document Properties dialog in Acrobat (Figure 7.64), you can activate options at the bottom that let you hide the reader's menu bar, the toolbars (all of them, not just the Page Navigation bar), and even the window controls—the Close button and such.

Changing Window Options

Above the User Interface Options on the Document Properties' Initial View tab is the Window Options section (refer to Figure 7.64). It lets you set three options I heartily caution you to never set, as well as one I recommend you do set.

Resize Window To Initial Page, if enabled, will resize the Acrobat or Reader application window to fit the first page of your publication. While that might sound cool and does look a little nicer on Mac than on Windows, resizing people's software tends to annoy them. I know it annoys me like a swarm of mosquitos on a summer night. Similarly, activating the Center Window On Screen and Open In Full Screen Mode options seeks to override the reader's preference with yours; readers don't like that. I mean, they *really* don't like that and have a tendency to immediately quit out of PDFs that have those options enabled. Moreover, because it's such an annoyance to users and creates so much confusion when they lose the Acrobat or Reader interface controls, Adobe configured the software to now warn people if a PDF tries to put itself into full-screen mode. The mere appearance of that warning can be distressing enough to unsophisticated computer users that they'll fear a virus and immediately quit your publication, never to open it again. Obviously, I recommend you leave all three of those options off.

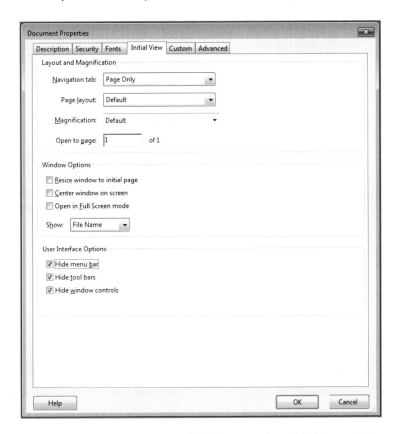

FIGURE 7.64
The Document Properties dialog's Initial View tab in Acrobat lets you hide parts of the Acrobat and Reader user interface.

I do suggest you change the value in the Show field, however, from File Name to Document Title. In the title bar of the document window your readers will see *[filename] – Adobe Reader* or *[filename] – Adobe Acrobat Pro*. If your filename is TBEv2n9.PDF, well, that's not very informative, is it? It certainly doesn't reinforce your brand. What would be both informative and good branding practice is to show the title of the publication—*The Best ePublication, Vol. 2 Issue 9*. Setting the Show field to Document Title will display whatever you entered in the Title metadata field.

Preparing the PDF for Reflow View

Did you know that PDFs can be set to reflow text such that it adapts to the screen on which it's viewed, wrapping to the screen without ever requiring the user to scroll horizontally? Well, they can. In fact, all editions of Adobe Reader and Acrobat can do that, whether on a computer or a mobile device. Give it a try on your computer by opening Image Map FINISHED.pdf from the Chapter 7/Lesson Files/Image Map folder. Move down to page 2 (page 1 has the house image map), and choose View ➤ Zoom ➤ Reflow. You should now see the page content reformatted into a single column that wraps to the window à la Figure 7.65. Pretty cool, huh? Try resizing the window; the text will adapt.

FIGURE 7.65
In Reflow View, text and imagery adapt to fit the width of the PDF viewer and/or screen.

The PDF's Reflow View is especially useful on small-screen devices. Figure 7.66 shows the comparison between the `Image Map FINISHED.pdf` file shown normally and in Reflow View on a smartphone. Shockingly, the original layout is actually legible, but it becomes a much easier read in Reflow View.

On mobile versions of Adobe Reader, Reflow View can be activated or deactivated by tapping the screen once to show the title bar and buttons, tapping the View Modes button at the top, and then selecting Text Reflow, Automatic, Continuous, or Single Page from the View Modes menu that appears (see Figure 7.67).

FIGURE 7.66
The PDF as shown on a smartphone

In normal view

linatuam in tessedet; essiliciam. Sendam serce con rent, inu ius conirta L. Ic re publiam pra perbere nerus, quam.

2/4

In Reflow View

FIGURE 7.67
The View Modes menu on the mobile Adobe Reader

Preparing your content for Reflow View is pretty easy and in many cases automatic. Acrobat takes your text and imagery (no multimedia in Reflow View) and, like an EPUB, presents them in physical order. If the document starts with a headline text frame followed by an image and then the body copy text thread, Reflow View shows them in the order of headline, image, complete body copy. If there's a figure on page 10 of the body copy, Reflow View will show that image around the location of the text from page 10—this makes it smarter than EPUB, which would have put the page 10 image at the end of the document. For the most part, Acrobat will correctly order elements in Reflow View. When it doesn't, you might need to touch them up a bit.

The absolute best way to define content ordering for Reflow View is to tag all the content elements in InDesign using the Structure pane. I covered that and the process of tagging and structuring InDesign content in Chapter 4, "Creating Basic Ebooks," so I won't waste your time by reiterating it now. If you don't want to use that method, or if your document is already in PDF form with changes made directly in Acrobat such that re-exporting from InDesign would invalidate a lot of work, then you can do it all within Acrobat.

1. With the PDF opened, access the Accessibility pane of the Tools sidebar. If your Tools sidebar doesn't have an Accessibility section, click the tiny little Show Or Hide Panels button at the top of the sidebar, and choose Accessibility.

2. Select the TouchUp Reading Order tool, which, if you're using a version of Acrobat before X, you'll find on the Accessibility toolbar. As soon as you select that tool, the TouchUp Reading Order dialog will appear (Figure 7.68).

3. Starting with the first page of your PDF, draw a rectangle around the very first element you want to appear in Reflow View.

4. Now, in the TouchUp Reading Order dialog, click the button that best describes the type of content you just encircled. Is it a heading, a figure, or standard body text?

FIGURE 7.68
The TouchUp Reading Order dialog

5. Move on to the next object, drawing a rectangle around it and defining its type. Don't miss anything you want to appear in Reflow View; if you have a figure with a caption, encircle and define the figure and then the caption, or do them together (and use the Figure/Caption identifier button). In the case of multiple columns of text, select and tag the first column, then the second, then the third, and so on, in order. Continue until the entire document is done.

You'll see gray boxes corresponding with the areas you highlighted. Inside those boxes will be numbers (Figure 7.69). The numbers are the reading order, the order in which the elements will be displayed in Reflow View. They also appear in Acrobat's Order panel (see Figure 7.70), which you can show as you would any panel or by clicking the Show Order Panel button in the TouchUp Reading Order dialog. If you make a mistake in setting the reading order, you can correct it in the Order panel—just drag one tagged object up or down in the list to the place it's supposed to be; all other objects will reorder to compensate.

FIGURE 7.69
The reading order of page 2 is now defined.

FIGURE 7.70
The reading order of elements on the page is reflected in the Order panel.

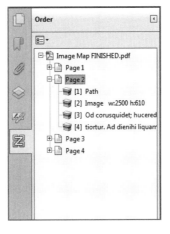

Obviously, leave out of the reading order any objects you don't want to appear in Reflow View. The currently selected reading order box will be highlighted in blue, by the way, in both the layout (Figure 7.69) and the Order panel (Figure 7.70).

Adding Tooltip Text

If you're using any buttons—and after this chapter told you all the cool things buttons can do, how could you *not* use them?—or form fields, you should fill in their tooltips. Tooltips, as you probably already know, are the little informative pop-ups that appear when you hover your cursor over buttons and parts of computer programs or web pages. You can see examples of tooltips by hovering your cursor over any tool on InDesign's tools panel or over the icon beside any field in any of InDesign's panels.

In PDFs you can create tooltips to help guide readers into taking the actions you want them to take. Ask any usability expert or anyone whose mother tells the neighbors that her child is "a computer expert" (that's most of us reading this, I'm sure): people don't always understand what a designer expects them to do no matter how obvious the designer thinks it is. That's not a slam at designers or users; it's just a statement of fact. Therefore, the more help you can give your readers, the more likely they will be to do what you want them to, and the more confident they will be doing it.

To add a tooltip to a button, form field, or hyperlink, follow these easy steps:

1. In Acrobat, switch to the Select Object tool, and right-click the object needing a tooltip.

2. Choose Properties from the context menu and switch to the General tab.

3. In the upper section of the dialog, fill in the Tooltip field with clear, concise instructions explaining exactly what you want the reader to do (see Figure 7.71). For example, for a button that initiates printing of the file, even if the button is actually labeled *Print*, you might want to create a tooltip that says *Click here to print this document.* Another example would be a hyperlink on a jump line; its tooltip could be something like *Click to continue reading on page 43.*

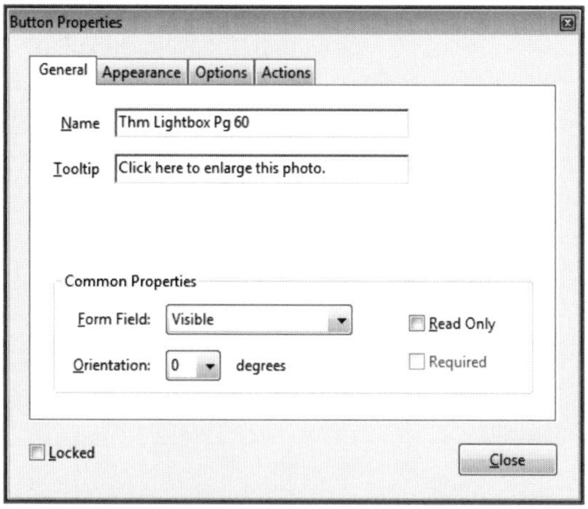

FIGURE 7.71
Adding a tooltip to a button helps readers recognize what you expect them to do.

TIP   You can also supply the tooltip to buttons and form fields directly in InDesign by completing the button or field Description field in PDF Options, which is accessible in CS6 and newer at the bottom of the Buttons And Forms panel and in previous versions of InDesign in the PDF Options dialog, accessible from the Button panel's flyout menu.

Attaching External Files

Not only can you convert just about any type of file to a PDF, you can also attach files to PDFs. This feature is very popular with many modern PDF art journals and culture periodicals because it enables them to distribute MP3s from indie bands (with permission, of course) as well as other materials. Like MP3s, those materials can be saved out of the PDF and loaded into iTunes or the like. True, you can embed audio and video to play within the PDF, but the reader can't get the portable files out that way. By attaching them to the PDF exactly as you might attach them to an email, you can distribute files that readers can save easily. That is popular not only for MP3s but also for wallpaper images, freebie files, demo software, mobile apps, and much more.

Attachment has to happen in Acrobat, so make it part of your after-export segment of the workflow. Here's how to do it:

1. With your PDF publication loaded in Acrobat, open the Attachments panel (see Figure 7.72). Depending on your version of Acrobat, you might find the Attachments panel listed in the View menu or in the context menu that appears when you right-click the panels bar on the far left of the Acrobat window, beneath the icons to show or hide the Page Thumbnails and Bookmarks panels.

FIGURE 7.72
The Attachments panel, with a few files attached

2. Click the Add New Attachments button at the top—it looks like a paper clip with a sunburst over it.

3. When the Add Files dialog appears, select the file or multiple files you want to attach, and click Open. These can be virtually any type of file, including other PDFs.

4. Repeat as necessary to attach all the files you need.

5. Because most people who use PDFs in any context have no idea that you can attach files to PDFs, they won't even think to open the Attachments panel to discover your attachments. You can rectify that situation by *making* the Attachments panel appear when your PDF is opened. There are a couple of ways to do that, depending on your version of Acrobat.

The easiest way, if available to you, is to right-click inside the Attachments panel. On the context menu, ensure that there's a check mark beside Show Attachments By Default, indicating that that option is active (see Figure 7.73).

If you don't have that command, access the PDF's Document Properties dialog by choosing File ➤ Properties or just pressing Ctrl+D/Cmd+D. Then, on the Initial View tab, set the Navigation Tab field to Attachments Panel And Page (see Figure 7.74). Click OK, and you've set the PDF to always open the Attachments panel. Note that in Acrobat X and Reader X and newer, that panel is a sidebar, while in earlier versions it runs along the bottom of the PDF viewer window.

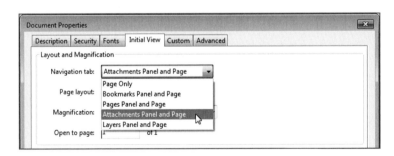

If you don't want to show the Attachments panel, there's another way to attach files, one that allows you to put them in specific places within the content.

1. Open the Annotation tools. In Acrobat X, they're part of the Comment sidebar on the right (see Figure 7.75). Within Acrobat 9 and earlier versions, they were located on the Commenting or Advanced Commenting toolbar accessible by right-clicking any other toolbar.

FIGURE 7.75
The Comment
sidebar offers more
than just text inser-
tion and deletion.

FIGURE 7.75
The Comment
sidebar offers more
than just text inser-
tion and deletion.

2. Among the Annotation tools are the standards people use all the time—tools like Add Sticky Note, Add Or Delete Text, and my favorite, one of Acrobat's most undervalued but most customizable utilities, the Stamp tool. Overlooked among these is the Attach File tool, which, again, looks like a paper clip. Select that tool, and then click somewhere within a page of your publication.

3. When the Add Attachment dialog appears, pick a file—unlike with the Attachments panel, you can't add more than one at a time here—and click Open.

4. An icon of a paper clip will be inserted onto the page at the point you clicked, but the File Attachment Properties dialog will also appear (see Figure 7.76). On the Appearance pane of this dialog you can choose from among four uninspired icons—a graph, a paper clip, a thumbtack, and what looks suspiciously like a coroner's toe tag. You can also change the color and opacity of the icon you choose on the right; click the color swatch to open a color picker.

FIGURE 7.76
After attaching a
file, you can change
the appearance of
the attachment
icon.

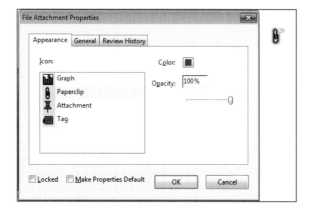

5. Switch to the General tab, and fill in any missing metadata. Ignore the Review History tab; it has no relevance in this situation. If you're done, click OK to commit the changes, or you can first check the box beside Make Properties Default to ensure that future attachments use the icon, color, and opacity you set on the Appearance tab.

You now have a file included inside the PDF and accessible to readers at the location of that icon. Double-clicking the icon (with the Hand tool, as readers will) results in the three options in Figure 7.77.

FIGURE 7.77
Double-clicking the attachment icon offers to open the file, to always allow opening of the file type, and to always disallow opening of the file type.

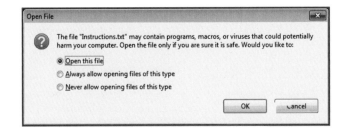

While the icon is tiny and you can't increase its size, you can make it and its function more obvious in two ways. First, if you know you'll be attaching files to various places in the document as you're designing it, design an area on the page in InDesign that spotlights the attachment icon, possibly with a big arrow and instructions that say *Click Here to Download!* Second, you can also insert, somewhere at the front of the document, sort of a "how to use this publication" page that explains conventions like the paper clip (or whatever) icon and how to use them. That sort of instructional page is very common in tablet publications (to train people how to use them), so why not take advantage of the trend in your PDF-based publication?

Ensuring Accessibility

Make sure your PDFs—all of them, not just magazines, catalogs, or whatever—are accessible to people with disabilities. The PDF file format is built to help with accessibility. (In the United States, it's called Section 508 compliancy, meaning that Adobe built PDFs to have as much accessibility as they possibly can in accordance with Section 508 of the Americans with Disabilities Act. Among everything else I do, I've had to become an expert on digital document creation with Section 508 compliancy.) What that boils down to for PDF publishers like you and me is ensuring that we've taken a few extra steps and provided a few extra pieces of information so that our PDFs are useful to people who maybe suffer from vision problems or total blindness or hearing problems. Accessibility is a whole chapter's topic on its own—I know, I've written those chapters in other books and as serial articles—so I'm going to give you just a list of the basics to address that will make 99 percent of the types of digital publications I'm talking about here compliant.

- Make sure all images in the publication have alternate text. That can be added into images by either editing their metadata (document info) in an image-editing program like Photoshop or Illustrator or in a digital asset manager like Bridge, Lightroom, or Extensis Portfolio, or, in InDesign, by selecting an image, choosing Object ➤ Object Export Options, and then filling in the Alt Text tab. (Refer to Chapter 5, "Working with Images and Multimedia in Ebooks.")

- Video and audio objects must also have alternate text descriptions or, better yet, transcripts. Most professional-grade, and many consumer-level, video- and audio-editing applications will allow you to embed transcriptions into, or associate them with, the multimedia files.

- If you use buttons or form fields, ensure that they all have descriptions, titles, and/or tooltips.

- In the Document Properties dialog, on the Advanced tab, make sure the Language field is set to the correct language of the publication.

If you're unsure about whether your PDF is accessible, you'll find in Acrobat the Accessibility Checker. It will analyze your document and look for common problems. If it finds any, it will provide you a report—usually in a sidebar, depending on the Acrobat version—allowing you to zero in on problems and fix them. In Acrobat X you'll find buttons for Quick and Full accessibility checking in the Accessibility section of the Tools sidebar. If you don't see the Accessibility section in your Tools sidebar, well, it's hidden by default. Click the tiny little Show Or Hide Panels button at the top of the sidebar, and choose Accessibility.

Defining PDF Security

Before you get into the settings accessible from the Security button at the bottom of the Export To Interactive PDF dialog, I need to provide a warning. PDFs are *not* entirely secure.

No matter how you may secure your PDF—if you restrict printing or making changes, even if you require a password just to open the document—I can break that security and print your PDF, change it to my heart's content, or peek into that PDF without knowing the password. True, I'm a PDF expert, but I'm not the only one who can crack open a secured PDF. *Anyone* can do it with a little knowledge, a freely available application, and even an application that comes *preinstalled* on one of the world's two largest operating systems. It would be irresponsible of me to explain how to break PDF security, but trust me; it's not difficult to do. That said, it does take a certain level of knowledge to do it—a level of knowledge that the vast majority of the people who might want to read your PDF do not possess. The following security options (Figure 7.78) are for those people and will keep them from doing whatever it is you don't want them doing with your PDF. Just keep in mind that a minority of potential readers will be able to do everything you don't want them to do, if they choose. Bottom line: don't bet the farm on PDF security.

FIGURE 7.78
InDesign's PDF
Security dialog

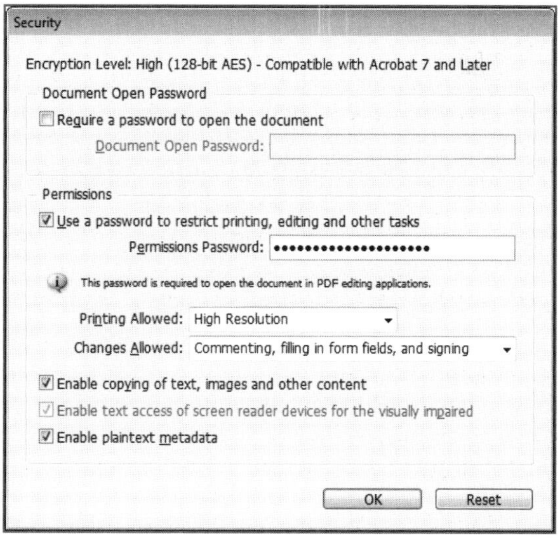

Security

Encryption Level: High (128-bit AES) - Compatible with Acrobat 7 and Later

Document Open Password
☐ Require a password to open the document
    Document Open Password: [   ]

Permissions
☑ Use a password to restrict printing, editing and other tasks
    Permissions Password: ●●●●●●●●●●●●●●●●●●●●

ℹ This password is required to open the document in PDF editing applications.

    Printing Allowed: High Resolution ▾
    Changes Allowed: Commenting, filling in form fields, and signing ▾

☑ Enable copying of text, images and other content
☑ Enable text access of screen reader devices for the visually impaired
☑ Enable plaintext metadata

[OK] [Reset]

PASSWORD PROTECTION

PDFs can have two types of password protection. A password can be required to open the document, and it can be required to change printing, modification, and other permissions. For the former, simply check the Require A Password To Open The Document box and supply a password. With the latter, check the Use A Password To Restrict Printing, Editing, And Other Tasks check box. These two options can be used separately or together. Before security is fully applied, you'll be prompted to reenter and confirm the password by InDesign (or by Acrobat if you're applying security there on an existing PDF). If you forget the password, there is no official, legal way of retrieving it; you'll be locked out of your own PDF. Don't forget your password.

CONTROLLING PRINTING

Once you've elected to restrict printing, editing, and other tasks, you can choose to control whether and how your PDF is printed. By choosing None from the Printing Allowed field, you'll disable the File ➤ Print menu item in Acrobat, Adobe Reader, Illustrator, or any other Adobe product capable of reading and/or editing PDFs.

Choosing Low Resolution (150 dpi) from the Printing Allowed drop-down lets people print only a low-quality version of your PDF, even if the on-screen version is high quality. This is useful for enabling the average reader to print out portions of the PDF for hard-copy reading, sharing, notation, and so forth, all without exposing the PDF to the risk of being scanned back in from paper as a means of circumventing security restrictions.

High Resolution lets the reader print the document normally, without restriction.

CONTROLLING CHANGES

An unsecured PDF can be commented on, can have pages added and removed, and can have form fields inserted and filled in, among many other tasks. If you don't want every Tom, Dick, and Harry to be able to do that to *your* PDF, disallow certain changes. The following are the options in the Changes Allowed drop-down menu:

None Choosing None disallows any type of change to the PDF whatsoever. I advise against using this, though. The reason is simple: people often highlight information they want to reference later and add margin notes. The ability to mark and augment a PDF's information for my own use is very important to me, as it is to a great many PDF consumers. If you are distributing a form for data collection, highlights and notes are not important; however, if your PDF is disseminated information or a publication, you want to encourage, not discourage, people from rereading it, and that requires enabling them to add their own notes, highlight passages, circle and make arrows pointing to segments, and all sorts of other things collectively called *commenting* in the world of PDF.

Inserting, Deleting And Rotating Pages The Inserting, Deleting And Rotating Pages option allows only those functions, disallowing commenting, filling in form fields, digitally signing, and so on.

Filling In Form Fields And Signing Choose Filling In Form Fields And Signing when you're sending out a form or a final contract. In such situations you want people to be able to fill in the form fields and digitally sign the document, but they don't need the ability to add notes or do anything else to the document.

Commenting, Filling In Form Fields, And Signing Commenting, Filling In Form Fields, And Signing is the option you should generally choose when building PDFs for content distribution. Even if the document doesn't have form or signature fields, the important part is the commenting permissions. Readers will be able to make their notes and call out interesting passages and images in a variety of ways. It's also the ideal set of allowed changes when your PDF is a form or contract but still in draft status. It will enable other parties to comment and mark it up without deleting whole pages or inserting others.

Any Except Extracting Pages   The Any Except Extracting Pages option lets PDF readers do anything their software can to the PDF, except save portions of the document to separate PDF files.

OTHER OPTIONS

Below the Changes Allowed field in the PDF Security dialog are three additional options:

Enable Copying Of Text, Images And Other Content   When selected, this option will let PDF consumers highlight and copy out of the PDF just about any element within it. They can then paste that content into Word, InDesign, email, or wherever they like. They can also get your images out of the PDF and reuse them. I always disable this option for PDF publications but enable it for things I want people to copy, such as press releases, schedules, and so forth.

Enable Text Access Of Screen Reader Devices For The Visually Impaired   Hear me now: there is no good reason to turn off this option. All it does is enable those who cannot read your PDF normally to have their Braille keyboards or screen readers do it for them. Unless your PDF is a tasteless collection of Helen Keller jokes, it's foolish to elect to lock the visually impaired, a small but significant minority of potential readers, out of the content.

Enable Plaintext Metadata   Just about every type of document created by Adobe and other creative professional software can contain metadata these days. In InDesign, you can access your document's metadata via the File ➤ Info menu item. Metadata can describe the document, when it was created and by whom, and what it's about, as well as a great deal more data. All of the metadata in your InDesign document becomes part of the PDF you export. But that metadata is in XML format, which some older systems (web servers, search engines, and so on) don't yet fully grasp. By including a second set of the metadata in plain-text format, even the oldest PDF-aware software can get to the important document information. That translates into your PDF being indexable by databases and search engines, out on the Web or within the intranet. It's usually a good idea to leave this option checked.

Chapter 8

Covering the Basics of Interactive Magazines

In this chapter, I'll focus on the basics of interactive-magazine creation with InDesign as a lead-in to the following two chapters, which delve into the nuts and bolts of interactivity using Adobe Digital Publishing Suite and its principal competitor, Aquafadas Digital Publishing System.

In this chapter, you will learn about the following:

- ◆ Planning an Interactive Publication
- ◆ Creating Multiscreen Layouts
- ◆ Working with Pan, Zoom, Slideshows, and Galleries
- ◆ Adapting Designs to Various Layouts and Tablets
- ◆ Using Liquid Layout Behaviors
- ◆ Utilizing Hyperlinks of All Types
- ◆ Inserting Audio and Video
- ◆ Adding Animations and 3D Rotating Objects
- ◆ Employing Scrolling Page Regions and Content Replacement
- ◆ Integrating Live Web Content

Planning an Interactive Publication

Although it's quite common to adapt an existing print layout to an interactive magazine, I advocate planning, and thinking about, the interactive magazine as a completely new publication separate from any companion print edition. The reason why should become clear as soon as you read the section "Understanding the Unique Behavior of Interactive Magazines." A little later in this chapter I will talk about a print-to-digital content-repurposing workflow, but even that must begin by planning the digital edition as a whole new publication.

Getting the Right Tools

If this and one of the next two chapters are your primary reason for buying this book—in other words, if creating interactive magazines is what you want to do—then you really should have InDesign CS6 (or newer). EPUBs can be created just as well in InDesign CS5.5 as in CS6 and newer, building digital replicas requires only a minimum of CS5, and creating PDF-based digital publications can be done quite well in just about any version of InDesign. However, when it comes to creating interactive magazine–format publications, CS6 provides major workflow improvements in the form of liquid layouts and alternate layouts and orientations in the same document. While generally you can get by just fine with CS5 or CS5.5, if you plan to build interactive magazine publications for more than a single device and a single orientation, you'll greatly benefit from CS6 or newer.

In addition to InDesign, you'll need to install the add-ons that enable InDesign to create interactive magazines. Although new systems are in the works, as of this writing two full-featured choices are available: Adobe Digital Publishing Suite (Adobe DPS) and Aquafadas Digital Publishing System (Aquafadas DPS). Their prices and features vary, but they are competitive. (See the following two chapters for a deep discussion of each.)

> **TIP**   There are other capable systems, such as PressRun, Mag+, and Twixl, but they aren't yet on the level of Adobe DPS and Aquafadas DPS in terms of functionality. When and if they get there, I'll write a definitive guide to using them. Keep an eye on `http://iamPariah.com` for announcements of such books and ebooks.

Understanding the Unique Behavior of Interactive Magazines

Interactive magazine publications behave differently than any other format. First, they are always viewed one page at a time; you cannot display spreads. There simply is no such convention as spreads in the interactive-magazine format. Note that the digital-replica format can show spreads, but, as you may recall from Chapter 2, digital replica isn't the same as the interactive-magazine format.

Something else you must recognize before you design a single pixel is that tablets can be held in two orientations, and that greatly affects the design of your publication. Readers could read your publication with a tablet in portrait (taller-than-wide) orientation or in landscape (wider-than-tall) orientation. And, they may not keep the tablet in the same orientation throughout the entire reading session. You have to decide up front whether you want to allow readers to rotate their devices or force them to view your publication in one orientation or the other. If you design only for landscape, for instance, readers will not be able to rotate their devices unless they want to read sideways; the page will always display landscape. For the ideal reading experience, you may want to enable reading in either orientation, which means creating two separate versions of every page—one for landscape, one for portrait. When the reader rotates the tablet from one orientation to the other, in the background the image of the landscape-designed page is swapped out for the image of the portrait-designed page. They're two completely different layouts and can be as similar or dissimilar as you like. Of course, that means twice the work for you and your creative team. So, ask yourself: does your publication *need* dual orientation? Many publications opt to stick with just one orientation unless they can bring something unique to the alternate orientation.

Before going any further, I need to define some more terms. More accurately, I need to *redefine* terms you know from print publishing into their specific uses in digital publishing.

> **Story**   The term *story* in this context refers to the complete content of a particular story, feature, article, or segment and all layouts in which that content is presented. All elements

of a particular narrative are part of the story. For instance, the headline, deck, kicker, byline, complete body copy, illustrations, captions, sidebars, pull quotes, tip and note boxes, and so on are all considered elements of a story. Moreover, the main text flow or body copy of a piece is wholly part of the story; there are no jumps in interactive magazines, such as jumping the last few paragraphs of a story to a page later in the publication. The entire story must be presented linearly and sequentially. The story is then presented in its entirety on a single layout, with or without vertical or horizontal scrolling through multiple screens, but never flowing across actual multiple pages.

Layout   A *layout* in interactive-magazine creation means one size and orientation of a story. For example, if you produce both landscape and portrait designs of a single story for an iPad 3, then each of those designs is a layout, while landscape and portrait orientations for 10-inch Android tablets are another pair of layouts in addition to the pair for the iPad 3.

Article   *Article* in this context refers to all layouts used to present a single story, whether that's a single layout or many. For instance, a single article might contain four layouts—two landscape and two portrait layouts, one of each orientation for iPad 3 and 10-inch Android tablets.

Screen   Substitute *screen* for just about everywhere you would normally say "page." Every time a reader swipes to turn the "page," she is actually moving from one article to the next. If an article is too long to fit on a single *screen*, then the reader scrolls down or to the side, not flips pages, to continue reading. Articles that are too large to fit entirely within the device screen are extended, usually vertically but sometimes horizontally, to multiple screens, which is the more direct corollary to what people typically think of as pages. If an article is three screens deep, readers will scroll down (or to the right) from the initial screen to two subsequent screens. Thus, each article can be considered as having its own page, but there is only one page per article, with one or more screens.

Figure 8.1 shows thumbnails from a live interactive magazine. Note the height differences between the thumbnails; that difference is the length of the articles, with each occupying a single page, but page depths vary by the number of screens required to display the entire page. This is not print publishing; this is digital publishing, which behaves more like web pages than like signatures and leaves.

Folio and Project   Although Aquafadas uses the term *project*, the Adobe DPS-centric *folio* is the one I use, not as a bias toward Adobe DPS but because of its specificity—I can say "folio" to a group of people and receive much greater recognition and less confusion over my intent than if I say "project."

A folio refers to a segment of, or the entire digital publication, prepublication. Upon publication, interactive magazines are turned into apps or issues; before that, they're called folios. Also called folios are self-contained partial publications. For example, full-page ads—interactive or not—are often created by advertising agencies and delivered to publication staff as self-contained folios. Technically these ads are *articles* in the vernacular of interactive magazines, but because they are saved and delivered as self-contained files, they become folios. The layouts within those ad folios are then incorporated into an interactive magazine's own folio in a procedure not unlike adding another INDD file to a Book panel.

FIGURE 8.1
The thumbnails of several pages in the April 2011 *Vogue Exclusive*: Rihanna, made in Adobe DPS and shown on an iPad

Figure 8.2 shows a diagram to help coalesce these terms into an understandable hierarchical system.

FIGURE 8.2
This diagram iden-
tifies the different
parts of a folio,
including the arti-
cle, screen, story,
and layouts.

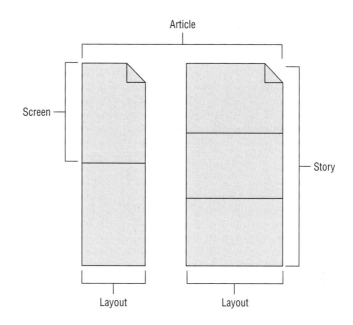

Choosing Resolutions

Once you understand the unique qualities of the format, you must decide on the resolution and dimensions for your publication—for each device you want to target. Table 8.1 lists the physi-cal screen sizes, display dimensions (in pixels), and display aspect ratios of some of the most popular 10- and 7-inch-class tablets on the market. Naturally, the information in this table will change as new tablets are introduced and new display technologies are developed, so keep up with the latest dimension information in the digital updates to this book at `http://abbrv.it/DigiPubIDUpdates`.

TABLE 8.1:   Display dimensions of common tablets

DEVICE	SCREEN SIZE*	DISPLAY WIDTH*	DISPLAY HEIGHT*	DISPLAY RATIO
iPad (third generation)	9.7	2048	1536	4:3
iPad (1 and 2)	9.7	1024	768	4:3
Kindle Fire	7.0	1024	600	128:75
Kindle Fire HD 7	7.0	1280	800	16:10*
Kindle Fire HD 8.9	8.9	1920	1200	16:10*
Google Nexus 7	7.0	1280	800	16:10*
NOOK Color and Tablet	7.0	1024	600	128:75

TABLE 8.1: Display dimensions of common tablets *(continued)*

DEVICE	SCREEN SIZE*	DISPLAY WIDTH*	DISPLAY HEIGHT*	DISPLAY RATIO
Kobo Vox	7.0	1024	600	128:75
Asus Transformer line	10.1	1280	800	16:10*
Acer Iconia Tab line	10.1	1280	800	16:10*
Samsung Galaxy Tab 10.1	10.1	1280	800	16:10*
Samsung Galaxy Tab 8.9	8.9	1280	800	16:10*
Samsung Galaxy Tab 7	7	1024	600	128:75
HTC Flyer 7	7.0	1024	600	128:75
Motorola XOOM	10.1	1280	800	16:10*
Toshiba Thrive	10.1	1280	800	16:10*
HP Slate	8.9	1024	600	128:75

Screen size refers to the physical dimensions of the screen as measured diagonally and is listed in inches. Display width and height values are in pixels.

**16:10 is more correctly written as 8:5, but it is listed here as 16:10 to highlight the comparison with the popular 16:9 HD TV display ratio.*

TIP Please refer to "Planning a PDF Publication" in Chapter 7, "Creating PDF Publications for Digital Delivery," to learn about resolutions, display ratios, and targeting to screen. However, keep in mind that although you *can* design one layout (or two: portrait and landscape orientation) and let that layout scale when viewed on other devices, you really shouldn't.

Lots of different resolutions are available in even the small selection of devices in Table 8.1. There are also three distinct display ratios. That means if you wanted to produce the best possible design for all 15 of those devices—and numerous others that share one of the three display ratios—you have to design only three separate versions of each page. Design one layout in 4:3 display ratio, another in 16:10 (aka 8:5), and a third in 128:75, and your publication will look the best it can on all of them. True, three versions of every page sounds like a lot of work—and six versions, a portrait and landscape version for each, sounds like a lot more—but later in this chapter I'll show you how to design once and efficiently adapt to the other display ratios with very little manual work.

Creating Multiscreen Layouts

Content that won't fit on a single screen-sized page in InDesign may be set in multiple pages in either Adobe DPS or Aquafadas DPS. Adobe DPS also offers an option called *smooth scrolling* to lay out the article on a single tall page instead of multiple pages. I'll explain where to activate the smooth scrolling option within Adobe DPS articles in Chapter 9, "Creating Interactive Magazines in Adobe DPS," in the "Applying Finishing Touches" section. In this section, however, I'll explain how to build for both multiple pages and a single smooth scrolling page.

With smooth scrolling disabled, thus having the reader jump from one page to the next when scrolling vertically, simply lay out your content as you normally would, using multiple pages in InDesign. Each page will become a screen of the layout, seemingly stacked and continuous. This method precludes smooth scrolling.

If you want smooth scrolling, then content that won't fit on a single screen-sized page must be included, not on additional pages but on the same page by extending the height or depth of that page. Figure 8.3 shows an example of a smooth scrolling layout versus a multipage layout.

FIGURE 8.3
Comparing the layout for jumping pages (a) and smooth scrolling (b)

a   b

To extend a page from a single-screen height to a multiple-screen height for smooth scrolling, you must resize the page. If you'll frequently use multiscreen page sizes, the best thing to do is create one or more additional master pages whose heights are set for multiscreen articles. For here-and-there resizing of pages, switch to the Page tool and, while holding Alt/Opt, drag the bottom-center control corner of the page container downward until you've achieved the desired depth. For the best reading experience, you'll want to resize your pages in full-screen increments; in other words, if you're designing for an iPad in portrait mode, each screen is 1024 pixels in height, so you should lengthen the page in increments of 1024 pixels—1024 pixels for one screen, 2048 pixels for two screens, 3072 pixels for three screens, and so on.

Working with Pan, Zoom, Slideshows, and Galleries

Good use of photographs, illustrations, and other image elements is fundamental to publication design for both print and digital delivery. Traditional print publishing imposes certain limitations on the usage of imagery, limitations that the interactive-magazine format lifts. For example, in print, images are limited in size to what fits within the physical dimensions of the page; if an image is too large for the page, it must be scaled or cropped to fit, often sacrificing detail that would be better left in. Interactive-magazine, on the surface, may seem like it includes the same limitation—after all, the page size of the publication and screen size of the device on which it's viewed are fixed sizes. By way of compensating for imagery better presented larger than the area in which it must fit, interactive magazines offer two options print can't: the ability for readers to zoom in on images and for them to pan images, seeing more of the image than will fit in the frame containing the image (something like Figure 8.4). When viewed, the reader simply has to drag the image with one or two fingers to pan and pinch to zoom in and out.

FIGURE 8.4
Using pan and zoom effects enables readers to see the parts of the image that don't fit in the frame.

Another limitation of print publications lifted by interactive-magazine format is that only one object—in this case, a single image—can occupy a given space on the page. It's a common dilemma: you have a big A-roll of images you'd like to use but not enough pages available to the feature to use all those photos. Thus, you spend hours agonizing over them to get only the best few that will fit; maybe you even spend a few more hours trying different arrangements and scales on the page to see how many you can fit. Ultimately, a few great photos are left out of the issue.

Just as common—particularly with catalogs—is the inverse problem: a requirement to include a large number of images, with maybe color, style, or size variations of the same product or detail and isolation imagery. The necessity for a large number of images in the world of print publication, where every page costs money, often results not in increased page count but in shrinking images below their ideal size just to fit them. Text is often reduced in size to help fit images as well, and often layouts are built too tight, cramping content together just to fit all those needed images without raising page count.

Interactive magazines solve both of these problems. Any number of images can be presented in a single space, at their ideal sizes.

A slideshow is a series of images displayed sequentially. They can transition from one image to the next automatically after an interval of time, when a reader taps or swipes on them, or both. By contrast, a gallery in this realm means a series of images that can also be navigated nonsequentially, usually by the reader tapping thumbnails of the images or buttons.

Adapting Designs to Various Layouts and Tablets

Once you have a completed layout, with all the article content on the page or a set of pages, it's *almost* time to create additional layouts for different orientations and devices. (The next chapters cover creating interactive overlays and enrichments, but for the purposes of this discussion, let's assume you've already read through that and added whatever interactivity your article needs.) There's something important you should consider doing before beginning to adapt the design to a new layout—get sign-off on the layout.

Before Adding Layouts

One of the reasons interactive-magazine creation is considered so time-consuming and costly is because participants in the process don't optimize their workflows. Most digital publishing teams—enterprise down to freelancer—work on the portrait and landscape versions for each device simultaneously or, in an only slightly more efficient workflow, create the portrait and landscape versions for just one platform (usually the iPad) first and then base the other platforms' iterations on that pair.

In both of those workflows, because two separate layouts using largely the same content are created and then sent for editing and proofing, when changes come back, the same content must be edited twice, once for the landscape and once for portrait layout, causing an unnecessary duplication of effort. Additionally, because reviewers are being presented with largely the same content in two different layouts, those reviewers often miss errors in one or both layouts, and designers have to scrutinize the feedback on both versions; revision requests can easily slip through the cracks if the majority of changes are written in both layouts, but a few, here and there, appear in only one layout.

In short, producing two layouts for initial editing and proofing unnecessarily doubles the work for everyone and significantly raises the chances of errors. It gets exponentially worse if you design and proof for multiple devices simultaneously.

Don't do the second layout yet.

Instead, follow the workflow shown in Figure 8.5. Create one layout—either portrait or landscape for a single device—and send that out for editing and proofing, however many rounds it takes. The content will be identical or largely the same for all layouts, so why ask clients, editors, and other reviewers to proof the same content in two different arrangements? Get the first layout polished and perfect and *then* adapt the edited and approved content to the next layout, adding any unique elements for that second layout. Then, when you send that out for proofing, it will be to review only the design itself and any content that differs from the first layout. All the carryover elements and content will have already been finalized, speeding the review process by effectively eliminating the editing and proofing of content and elements already approved.

FIGURE 8.5
The most efficient digital publishing workflow available with today's systems, tools, and devices

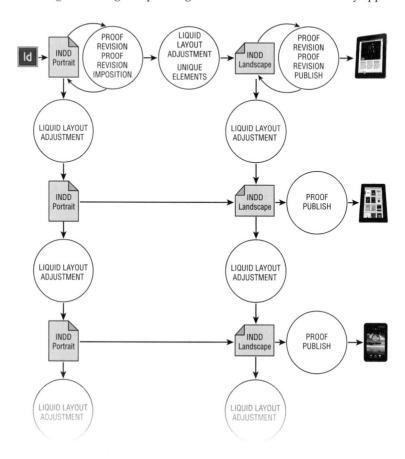

This workflow will save you significant time over the more common one of building, proofing, and correcting multiple layouts at once. On those (ideally rare) occasions when a late change does require you to make changes to two or more layouts, there are tools available to make that easier, too. I'll discuss them when I talk about adding layouts and synchronizing content across them.

Designing for Multiple Devices

Although the iPad dominates the market, it is not the only device your potential readers use to consume interactive magazine–format publications. Market share among tablet operating systems and individual tablets fluctuates radically from month to month, depending on who released a new version, whose commercials are running in heavier rotation, and all the other usual factors that drive competition in the consumer electronics space. Designing for a single device, even if it is the market leader, is ill-advised. Not only will you sacrifice the millions of potential readers on other devices, but should the future find the current market dominator falling to a minority share, all of your back issues will be inaccessible to the then-majority of readers. It's best to hit the ground running by designing for a handful of top mobile operating systems and devices at the start. In the current economy, that means the higher-resolution iPad 3 and newer, iPad 1 and 2, 7-inch Android tablets such as the crowd favorite Kindle Fire and Kindle Fire HD as well as the Google Nexus 7, 10-inch Android tablets, and 10-inch Windows tablets. I'll refer you to Chapters 1, 2, and 3 for figures and more information to help you make decisions about device support.

If budget is a limitation, target iPad (all versions), Kindle Fire and Kindle Fire HD, and the generic 10-inch Android tablet class at the very least. iPads are the most popular, of course, and Kindle Fire alone accounts for more than 50 percent of all Android tablets on the market (according to comScore, April 2012). Also, Fire's screen resolution is the same as the NOOK Color, NOOK Tablet, Kobo Vox, and other popular 7-inch Android tablets, which means a publication designed for Fire will work well on the other leading tablets in the class. Creating a version for 10-inch-class Android tablets targets full-sized Android alternatives to the iPad.

Fortunately, the work of adapting an existing layout to other publication dimensions is easy with Aquafadas DPS's integrated orientation states, synchronized content, and the ability to easily copy articles between projects. Adobe DPS is similarly easy with alternate layouts, synchronized text, and liquid layout *behaviors*, which are not liquid layouts.

Using Liquid Layout Behaviors

Liquid layout behaviors replace the old Layout Adjustment feature in InDesign, which sought to help you adapt frame and other object positions and sizes from one page size or orientation to the next. It was kind of hit-or-miss. Layout Adjustment wouldn't give you great results; you'd still have to do a lot of tweaking and manual cleanup, but it did a lot of the heavy lifting and basics of reworking page geometry, potentially saving you a lot of work. Liquid layout behaviors do everything Layout Adjustment did and more, but they do it better, more reliably, and with less need for manual cleanup afterward. Think of it like this: Layout Adjustment was automatic page geometry 1.0, and liquid layout behaviors is automatic page geometry 2.0. There's still room for improvement in 2.0, but it's head and shoulders above the function of 1.0, and it can save you hours or days you would otherwise spend reworking object positions and relationships.

Liquid layout behaviors can be employed for any type of publication that might need to be reformatted for another output type, not just digital publications. For example, you can use liquid layout behaviors to make the objects on a portrait-oriented digital magazine design adapt automatically to a portrait-oriented variation of the same design, and you can also employ them to take a hardcover book layout and, with almost full automation, adapt the content to fit within the new dimensions of a paperback version layout and within the EPUB layout of a third document. You can also couple liquid layout behaviors with alternate layouts to build multiple versions for digital output, print, or both in a single InDesign document—if you're using Adobe DPS for any interactive-magazine components. If you're using Aquafadas DPS for your interactive-magazine output, you can still use liquid layout behaviors to help adapt content between the landscape and portrait states of the publication and between multiple documents sized for different devices.

Technically, Layout Adjustment is still in InDesign, but liquid layout and Layout Adjustment are incompatible with one another in much the same way Neanderthal and Cro-Magnon man were mismated. One birthed the other, and they had some common strands of DNA, but the later evolutionary branch ultimately supplanted the earlier one. If you enable Layout

Adjustment, it stops liquid layout behaviors from functioning, but Layout Adjustment is destined for extinction, to be replaced by liquid layout.

Using liquid layout you can save hours, days, and even weeks of work adapting publications from one format or size to another. Here are just a few of the things liquid layout behaviors can do when taking a laid-out page and changing that page's size or orientation:

◆ Scale objects up or down

◆ Move objects outward when page size increases or inward when page size decreases

◆ Keep objects positioned the same distance from one or two margins while increasing the space between the objects and the other margins

◆ Keep the content fixed to one or two margins and stretch or resize objects in the direction of other margins

◆ Resize text inside frames while also changing the size of the text frames

◆ Add or remove columns from text frames to maintain a consistent column width while resizing text frames

◆ Resize images within their frames instead of just moving them

Accessing Liquid Page Rules

Liquid layout behaviors are governed by directives called Liquid Page rules. To use liquid layout behaviors, you must tell InDesign which rule to employ. Each page can have its own rule, or the entire document can be reworked according to the definition of a single rule. Master pages can also be assigned Liquid Page rules (except the Controlled by Master rule, unless the master page in question is based on another master page).

You'll work with each of the rules shortly, but first you must know how to get to them. Selecting the Page tool transitions the Control panel into page mode (Figure 8.6a). One of the controls in this mode is the Liquid Page Rule drop-down menu offering you access to all the rules, but none of the object-level options you may want to set. To access the full set of controls, choose Window ➤ Interactive ➤ Liquid Layout to display the Liquid Layout panel (see Figure 8.6b). You can also open the Liquid Layout panel by selecting the Liquid Layout command on the Layout menu. Note that you must also have the Page tool selected in order to access and change the Liquid Page Rule field on this panel; the field is grayed out if you have any other tool selected.

FIGURE 8.6
You can access the Liquid Page Rule drop-down menu and several other options on the Liquid Layout panel.

a

b

You can set the Liquid Page rule on multiple pages at one time by selecting the pages' thumbnails on the Pages panel and then choosing a rule on the Liquid Layout panel or Control panel in page mode.

Using the Controlled by Master Rule

Selecting the Controlled by Master rule makes document pages rework their geometries in response to page size (or orientation) changes on their master pages. Controlled by Master is the simplest rule and works very much like Layout Adjustment worked. Give it a try.

1. Beginning with a simple portrait-orientation page such as the one in Figure 8.7, which includes a simple two-column text frame and an image with text wrap assigned, switch to the Page tool.

2. Open the Liquid Layout panel, and set the Liquid Page Rule field to Controlled By Master.

FIGURE 8.7
A simple portrait-orientation layout

3. Go to the master page that defines that document page, and, with the Page tool still selected, change the master page's orientation to landscape using the appropriate button on the Control panel.

4. Switch back to the document page and examine the changes. You can use Ctrl+Z/Cmd+Z and Ctrl+Shift+Z/Cmd+Shift+Z to toggle between the before and after views.

Figure 8.8 shows my page after changing orientation; compare it with Figure 8.7. Notice that the primary text frame stayed glued to all four margins, resizing to do so, but it also remained two columns, widening to fit the landscape orientation. The photo didn't resize at all; in fact, it fell off the page. The text frame adapted better than it would with Layout Adjustment, but that's the only advantage over Layout Adjustment in this instance.

FIGURE 8.8

After changing the orientation of the master page, while the document page was assigned the Controlled by Master Liquid Page rule

Let's take things a little further.

Using the Scale Rule

An easy way to understand the Scale rule is to think about manually resizing several objects at once. If you select multiple objects, hold Ctrl+Shift/Cmd+Shift, and then click and drag one of the group's control corners, you'll resize the objects' frames and their contents. The Scale rule causes that same scaling behavior in objects, but automatically, in response to page size changes. Let's try it.

1. Start with any layout. For this example, I'll use one a little more complicated than the last (see Figure 8.9). It has two image frames, a multicolumn text frame, and four unthreaded text frames comprising the title and byline.

FIGURE 8.9

A slightly more complex layout

2. Activate the page, and set the Liquid Page Rule field to Scale.

3. Still using the Page tool, drag one of the page's control corners outward, enlarging the page. The content will scale in real time to adapt to the new page size.

4. When you release the mouse button, the page will snap to its original size. That's the page-resizing preview. If you actually want to resize the page, hold Alt/Opt while dragging a control corner.

   Yeah, I uttered a few expletives over that myself. The idea, says Adobe, is that people will want to *preview* the effect of a page resize—particularly in light of liquid layout output—more often than they'll want to *actually* change the page size with the Page tool.

When the Scale rule is applied, all the objects—frames and content—on the page scale up or down proportionately to fit the new page dimensions. They'll enlarge or reduce as needed, maintaining their relative sizes and positioning with one another, but only as long as all objects fit within both the horizontal and vertical dimensions. If you alter one dimension disproportionately to the other, you'll wind up with empty space on one dimension—the same as if you set an image to the Fit Content Proportionately fitting option and the frame wasn't in scale to the image it contained (see Figure 8.10).

FIGURE 8.10
While using the Scale rule, resizing the page dispropor- tionately can leave empty space along the sides or the top and bottom.

The Scale rule is ideal to use when the major difference between two layouts is scale, such as when converting an iPad 1 or 2 layout to a layout for the iPad 3 or to a layout for 10-inch Android tablets with similar display aspect ratios to the iPads. Even when the display aspect ratios aren't exact, it's very useful. Typically you'll do much less work by extending a background frame to fill in empty sides, adjusting the positioning of the main text frame, or performing other fixes to compensate for scaling mismatches than you would scaling every page's content by hand. The rule's suitability to this purpose is further enhanced by the fact that it's the only Liquid Page rule that will resize type. The other rules will change only the dimensions of text frames, not the size of the text within.

Using the Re-center Rule

The Re-center rule does not resize anything. Rather, it merely keeps the content perfectly centered both horizontally and vertically to the page edges. It would be pedantic to walk you through a step-by-step exercise just for that, so I'll merely show you Figure 8.11, the result of selecting the Re-center rule and then enlarging the page. Note that Re-center is really suited only to enlarging. If you reduce the page, the objects will not scale; they'll spill off the page edges.

FIGURE 8.11
With the Re-center rule applied, objects remain centered on the resized page.

Using the Guide-Based Rule

Here's where you start getting to the real potential of liquid layout behaviors. Thus far, using Controlled by Master, Scale, and Re-center rules, I've scaled and moved the content around, always keeping the same relation between the component objects. The objects themselves really haven't adapted to page sizes and orientations—they haven't been liquid, if you will. Guide-based and object-based rules control how liquid layout transforms individual objects to make truly adaptive layout changes.

InDesign now includes two kinds of guides that can be dragged from the rulers—our old friend the ruler guide and its new sister the liquid guide. Placing a liquid guide on the page such that the guide touches one or more objects causes those objects to expand or contract, grow or shrink, in different ways to adapt to changes in the page dimensions. It's simpler—and much more powerful—than it sounds, so let's try it.

1. Begin with a mixed-content layout like the ones you've been using thus far. If you don't have anything suitable on hand, you can find the layouts in the preceding figures in the `Liquid Layout Test Layouts.INDD` file in the Chapter 8 `Lesson Files` folder. In fact, that file contains both of the layouts you've worked with so far.

2. Switch to the Page tool, drag a vertical guide from the vertical ruler, and drop it on the right side of the page, well past the *Spotlight*, *Cheng Wu*, and *by Gayle Mintz* text frames, but touching the headshot graphic, the two-column body copy frame, and, of course, the background image frame. Figure 8.12 shows you where I placed mine. Notice that your guide is a dashed line instead of a solid one; that's the appearance of liquid guides.

FIGURE 8.12
The dashed line is a liquid guide.

3. Still using the Page tool, hold Alt/Opt, and drag the control corner on the right side of the page outward to widen the page. You should see something like Figure 8.13.

Notice what happened? The objects touched by the liquid guide resized while the ones the guide didn't touch stayed exactly where and how big they were. The liquid guide tells InDesign to resize objects beneath it, adapting them to the new dimensions. It's basically a growth indicator, freezing everything else. Try reducing the width of the page now so that it's narrower than the original version (Figure 8.14). Again, you'll see the guide-touched content resize and rework itself while the other objects remain constant.

Think about practical uses for that feature, such as for background images or colored frames that always fill the background, titles that automatically become single lines in landscape mode but multilined in portrait, and images and figures—text wrap applied—that always fit. It has so many uses, and not just for digital publications but all types of layouts you might create in InDesign, for any output method or medium.

And you aren't limited to a single liquid guide or one dimension for scaling.

1. Try resizing the page both horizontally and vertically. With the first liquid guide in place, you'll see that touched objects adapt horizontally just fine, as I've already established, but they won't budge on their vertical measurements. That's a problem. Reset the page with Ctrl+Z/Cmd+Z.

FIGURE 8.14
After narrowing the page, the layout still looks good, thanks to liquid layout behaviors and the guide-based rule.

2. Again, using the Page tool, drag a guide from the horizontal ruler this time. You want to position the horizontal liquid guide so that it's close to the bottom of the page, touching the body copy text frame (and the background image graphic frame, of course).

3. Now resize the page diagonally to see that the background image and main text frame adapt in both width and height (Figure 8.15).

FIGURE 8.15
Liquid guides help objects grow and shrink, not just horizontally but vertically as well.

You can add as many liquid guides as you want, but after a certain number, they'll negate themselves. The idea is to use liquid guides to control the items that most need to be resized. You probably wouldn't, for example, place a liquid guide over the *Spotlight*, *Cheng Wu*, and *by Gayle Mintz* text frames, too. That would cause too much automatic resizing and not enough layout adjustment. A horizontal liquid guide that touches the main photo, though, might not be a bad idea; it would then allow the main photo to scale in proportion to the body copy text frame.

Dragging a guide from the ruler with the Page tool automatically creates a liquid guide, but that's not the only way. If you drag from a ruler with any other tool, you'll get our old buddy the normal ruler guide. If that isn't what you want, you can convert a ruler guide into a liquid guide, and vice versa.

1. Using any tool but the Page tool, drag a guide from one or the other ruler onto the page.

2. Switch to the black arrow Selection tool, and hover your cursor over the ruler guide you just made. When the cursor is over the guide, you'll see the guide change color as usual; right-click and choose from the context menu Guide Type ➤ Liquid Guide (see Figure 8.16). The guide will then become dashed to identify it as a liquid guide.

FIGURE 8.16
Hovering over the
end of a ruler guide
reveals this icon.

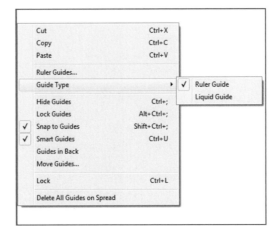

So far, I'm getting excellent results with adaptive content. Still, something is nagging at me. When I widened the page containing the two-column text frame, the frame widened to fit. The type stayed the same, as did the number of columns, but the columns got pretty wide. Having designed just about everything that can be published in my career, I know that there are rules governing the optimal width of columns; widen columns too much, and readers' eyes have to turn uncomfortably far, particularly when those too-wide columns are displayed on back-lit tablet screens. Wouldn't it be great if liquid layout could adjust not just the width of a text frame but also its number of columns?

It can.

Automatically Adding and Removing Text Columns

Now this is a stroke of genius. When a text frame resizes, it can also be set to increase or decrease its number of columns automatically. It enables the number of columns to change based on screen orientation and size—a single column for small screens such as smartphones, two-column text for medium-sized screens such as 7-inch tablets or even larger tablets in portrait orientation, and three or four columns for landscape or other wider views.

The secret is an easily overlooked addition to the Text Frame Options dialog.

1. Select the body copy text frame in the layout you've been working with or any multicolumn text frame you happen to have on hand.

2. From the Object menu, select Text Frame Options (or use the Ctrl+B/Cmd+B shortcut).

3. On the General tab, which you can see in Figure 8.17, click the drop-down arrow beside the Columns field. The two options are now three. The new one is Flexible Width; select it.

FIGURE 8.17
Selecting Flexible
Width on the Text
Frame Options
General tab

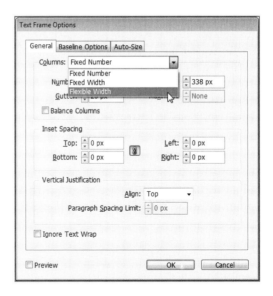

4. With Flexible Width selected, the Maximum field beneath the Width field becomes available. At the same time, the column Number field locks. The Flexible Width setting lets you choose a desired width for columns and a maximum acceptable width, measured in the document's measurement system, so pixels if you're working within the Interactive Magazine intent. InDesign—or whatever is viewing the output from this document—will then keep the width of the columns between the desired width (the Width field) and the maximum, adding or reducing the number of columns accordingly.

Try reducing the value in the Width field and see what happens (remember to activate Preview in the lower-left corner of the dialog). If nothing happens, keep reducing the value until you see the number of columns in the text frame increase.

5. Set your desired values in the Width and Maximum fields, and then click OK. Make sure there's a vertical liquid guide touching the multicolumn text frame you just modified.

6. Now, using the Page tool, resize the page or change its orientation. You should see columns automatically come or go within your text frame.

Set Flexible Width and Width and Maximum settings in the object styles you employ for your body copy, primary, or other text frames, and all your text frames will automatically increase or decrease the number of columns in response to liquid layout resizing or reorientation. Amazing!

Using the Object-Based Rule

The final liquid page rule is the most powerful, albeit the one with the steepest learning curve. The Object-Based rule lets you define individual adaptation behaviors per object. It does that, in part, with the Liquid Layout panel but primarily through the use of symbols and constructs on individual objects.

Let's walk through using the Object-Based rule with the same very simple (read: an easier-to-see-all-the-funky-new-symbols-layout) page in Figure 8.18.

FIGURE 8.18
This overly simple layout will help you understand the Object-Based rule.

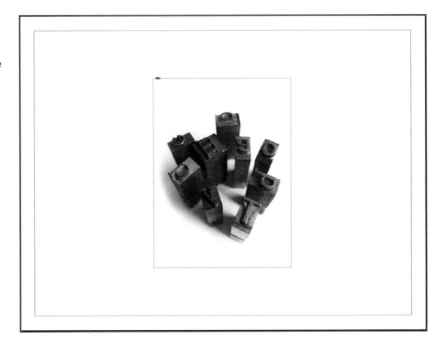

1. Create a document or page like the one in Figure 8.18, with a single image frame aligned to the center of the page horizontally and vertically.

2. Switch to the Page tool, and with it select the graphic frame (yes, I know that sounds like an oxymoron, but that's how it works).

3. In the Liquid Layout panel, set the Liquid Page Rule field to Object-Based.

4. Mimic the options in Figure 8.19 in your Liquid Layout panel—specifically, enable Auto-Fit, Height, Top, and Left.

FIGURE 8.19
Mimic these settings on the Liquid Layout panel to complete this exercise.

5. Now, still using the Page tool, click and drag one of the page's control corners, and enlarge the page diagonally so that its height and width enlarge. Note what happens to the graphic frame. It lengthens but doesn't widen because you chose only the Height option under Resize With Page on the Liquid Layout panel, and it maintains a constant distance from the left and top page margins because those are the two options you enabled in the Pin section of the Liquid Layout panel.

Now that you've seen the Liquid Layout panel options in action, here's what they mean. Refer to Figure 8.19 as you walk through the sections.

Content   The only option in the Content section is Auto-Fit. As you might have already intuited, activating the Auto-Fit option causes images inside graphic frames to resize with their frames. The Auto-Fit option reapplies whatever fitting setting is in effect on the frame—Fill Frame Proportionately, Fit Content to Frame, Center Content in Frame, and so on—with each resizing of the frame.

Resize With Page   You can activate either the Width and Height options or both to have objects scale along one or both axes in response to the page.

Pin   The act of pinning locks the distance of one or more sides from the corresponding page margin. For example, the tutorial you just walked through used the Top and Left options to pin the frame's top and left edges to the top and left margins; thus, when the frame resized, it did so toward the right and downward. You can pin one or two sides but not opposing sides. If you are going to allow an object to dynamically adapt to page size changes, then you must allow it to do so in at least one direction horizontally and one direction vertically. Pinning both the left and right sides but then activating the Width option under Resize With Page creates a paradox—don't resize horizontally, the Pin options say, but do resize horizontally according to the Resize With Page option.

Pinning is most often useful for ensuring that the relationship between two or more objects remains constant. For instance, you might pin the top and left sides of text frames that form a title, deck, and byline, as well as the background image, to ensure that those objects all stay together, aligned properly, while they potentially scale from the right and bottom edges.

Alas, other than Auto-Fit in the Frame Fitting Options pane (see Figure 8.20) and the Text Frame Auto Size Options settings within the options for an object style, Liquid Layout object settings cannot be saved in object styles.

Figure 8.21 shows all the new symbols and adornments that correspond with the Liquid Layout object settings and are visible when an object is selected with the Page tool. To make it easier to understand, on the object shown I've used the same Liquid Layout panel settings as in the step-by-step exercise you went through.

Outside the frame, on the top and left, solid lines connect the top and left object edges with the matching margins. These solid lines with filled-circle terminuses communicate that the object is pinned to those margins. Conversely, on the bottom and right sides, the lack of lines and the open circles indicate that the object is not pinned to the margin on those sides, enabling the distances between the bottom and right edges and the bottom and right margins, respectively, to change based on page size changes.

FIGURE 8.20
Auto-Fit is an option within object styles.

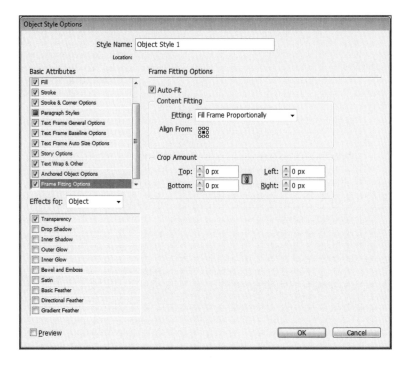

FIGURE 8.21
When objects are selected with the Page tool and the Liquid Page Rule is set to Object-Based, these symbols and lines communicate the Liquid Layout settings and the behavior of the object.

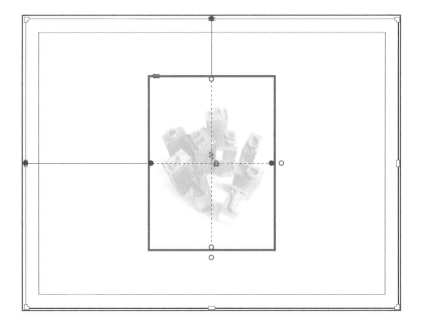

Inside the frame you have dashed lines indicating the horizontal and vertical planes of the frame. On the horizontal line is a padlock icon, while the vertical displays a spring. These two symbols, respectively, communicate that the width of the frame will not change in response to the width of the page changing, while altering the page height will modify the object's height. That's because I disabled the Resize With Pages Width option in the Liquid Layout panel but enabled the Resize With Pages Height option. So, the frame will always be however wide it is, no matter how wide the page gets, but it will grow or shrink in depth along with the page height changes. The filled circles communicate the same thing—notice they're on the line with the padlock—as do the open circles for the liquid or springy dimension.

Now, imagine setting these object-specific movement and sizing options on all the objects within a complex layout destined for multiple outputs—a print-edition magazine or catalog and digital magazine–format editions bound for the iPad, the Kindle Fire, 10-inch Android tablets, and so on, in portrait and landscape versions for each device. Imagine how much time and energy you could save over manually reworking every article and layout for each new device and orientation. If you prep each object carefully, setting autofit options on the images and flexible-width options on text frames, you could almost entirely automate the process of adapting the one layout you actually have to design to all those other devices and orientations. A few minutes of prep time in advance and a few minutes of minor cleanup after wholesale layout resizing or reorienting, and you've just saved yourself hours, days, or maybe even weeks of tedious hand manipulation (ministration has to do with ministering) of the objects.

Can I get a hallelujah?

Utilizing Hyperlinks of All Types

Now that you know how to begin and lay out interactive magazines, I can get into the really good stuff—all the different ways in which those publications can be made deeply interactive and engaging. The obvious place to start with deep interactivity is with the most basic—hyperlinks. Interactive magazines can contain hyperlinks that, when clicked, open web pages, initiate file downloads, start dialing a phone number, send a text message, begin an email, and link to other apps you might have for sale. Any or all of these types of hyperlinks you may use to leverage your own products and services or offer to advertisers as a means of promoting theirs.

Regardless of whether you're using Adobe DPS or Aquafadas DPS add-ins, creating and working with hyperlinks functions the same way—using InDesign's native Hyperlink panel and other features rather than any feature of the respective systems' add-in panels.

The intimate details of defining hyperlink styles and creating hyperlinks from basic to more sophisticated were covered in Chapter 7. The same information applies to interactive magazines, so it is not reprinted in this chapter. Please refer to the step-by-step instructions in the section "Creating External Hyperlinks of All Types" in Chapter 7 to learn the ins and outs.

TIP The only exception to the instructions in Chapter 7 is in step 7 of the "Creating a Basic Hyperlink" procedure. Ignore the Appearance section, because those options are relevant only to PDF-based epublications.

Inserting Audio and Video

Because interactive magazines are displayed on multimedia devices, they can—and whenever appropriate *should*—go beyond the merely visual. Audio can become an important component in digital publications and, along with video, which I'll cover in the next section, can move your interactive publication out of the realm of "print plus" and closer to a broadcast medium.

The following are among the many ways you might choose to incorporate audio:

◆ Including background music to create a reading soundtrack

◆ Building into your publication a digital jukebox that presents readers with a selection of music tracks they may play

◆ Adding a spoken narrative to the publication to augment copy and imagery and to fill in information that can't as easily be presented in prose or imagery

◆ Enhancing elearning titles with sounds, music, and spoken word that relates directly to the material being taught by the publication

◆ Enhancing digital catalogs by including excerpts when they sell products that are, or are related to, audio and video works

◆ Including the full recordings of an interview in interview articles

◆ Including audible critiques captured live at premiere events or even by call-in voicemail in product, entertainment, and other reviews

◆ Adding simple sound effects to enhance the user experience, for instance clicking sounds when buttons are tapped, short "swoosh" or paper rustling sounds when pages are turned, and triumphant horns when readers select correct answers in integrated quizzes

Note that some of the preceding examples, such as adding sound effects to buttons, require a few steps not covered until the "Adding Buttons and Actions" sections in later chapters, but even those begin with the basics of audio inclusion discussed in this section.

ASPIRIN-FREE WORKFLOW: DON'T EDIT MP3S

Both Adobe and Aquafadas prefer that you use MP3-format audio files, but you shouldn't *edit* in MP3 format. MP3 is the JPEG of audio file formats, meaning that MP3 is a lossy compression format—quality is lost to achieve compression. Unlike JPEG, however, you can't choose a maximum MP3 quality setting to disable the loss of audio data. Therefore, every time you edit an MP3 file and save it, that audio loses a little more quality.

Before long, the degradation can become quite noticeable as a flattening of music and spoken-word highs and lows, as well as an increasingly pronounced hissing within the track.

To properly edit audio, avoid MP3 until the audio is fully edited and ready to be included in your publication. Work within native, lossless audio formats such as WAV that can be edited *ad infinitum* without quality degradation and can easily be converted to MP3 for final output.

The ability to include video in interactive magazine–format publications blurs the lines between print and broadcast even further. Consider your static images; indeed, consider your process of *taking* photographs. Can a static image do the subject justice, or would a video be better? This isn't print, and your publications aren't just print anymore. If you're covering a fashion show or a tech expo or even selling a product, wouldn't video of the models, the exhibitors, or the product in use—maybe even a full infomercial—be more engaging to readers than static photos of the same? With this medium, you have all the advantages of static content—long text flows, clickable hyperlinks, images galore—and all the advantages of full-motion video.

TIP   Before you place video, make sure it's in the right format: H.264-encoded video files, usually in the MPEG4 format with MP4 or M4V file extensions. If you need to convert your video from other formats, use Adobe Media Encoder, which is discussed in depth in Chapter 5, "Working with Images and Multimedia in Ebooks."

Adding Animations and 3D Rotating Objects

Whether you're selling products or showing off movie props, letting readers interact with objects in three-dimensional space is a fun and engaging experience for them. It's especially useful when you need to present multiple sides of an object; instead of doing that with static photographs in a gallery or slideshow, present the object as 3D, and let readers explore all the sides themselves.

Before you begin making this type of effect, take a look at the examples, `ex_360rotate` `.indd`, in both `Lesson Files\Adobe DPS\Animation and 360 Rotate` and `Lesson Files\Aquafadas\Animation and 360 Rotate` in this chapter's lesson files. You can open and test one or both of those files. In the testing environment (Adobe Content Viewer or myKiosk), you'll be able to tap/click and drag to rotate the book in three-dimensional space. This is the interactivity you'll be creating with the help of Adobe DPS or Aquafadas DPS. It might look nothing like the animation you have planned, but, trust me, it's very much the same. And it might look like adding this 3D rotating book is a straightforward matter of dropping in a 3D object created in a program like AutoCAD, 3Ds Max, or SketchUp. Alas, it's not quite that simple, which is why you'll tackle the creation of this interactivity in stages in the following two chapters.

Employing Scrolling Page Regions and Content Replacement

If you create a text frame in InDesign, fill that frame with placeholder text, and then reduce the size of that frame, what happens? Assuming Smart Text Reflow is not enabled for that frame, you'll have the same single frame, now containing some visible text and some overset text, correct? The overset text portion of the story hasn't been destroyed; it still exists, in a limbo of sorts, but it won't be made visible to the reader. The interactive-magazine format can make that overset text visible to the reader by enabling the reader to scroll the content within that text frame. Therefore, digital publications may include more content in a given space than will actually fit in that space.

Continuing with the notion of including more content than will fit on the page all at the same time is another type of interactivity called *content replacement*. In Chapters 9 and 10, I'll get into intricate replacement of content, such as the following:

◆ Product pages can replace one color or style of a product image with another.

◆ In a children's epublication, tapping letters such as *A, B, C*, and so on can reveal images of objects or animals whose names begin with the chosen letter.

◆ A reader can tap a location in an interactive map to reveal a pop-up containing information and/or photographs related to that location.

◆ Self-tests in elearning publications can be set to reveal correct answers for all questions with a single button tap.

◆ The entire content of a page—all text, imagery, and background elements—can be replaced by alternate content in response to taps on buttons, images, or text.

Integrating Live Web Content

The ultimate trump to any limitation of interactive-magazine creation systems is the inclusion of web content. Anything Adobe DPS and Aquafadas DPS can't do, HTML5 and related technologies almost certainly can, and anything you can do with web technology can be incorporated into the publication as if it's a native part of the publication…well, except for Flash content, which will never work in iOS.

There are two types of web content integration: including HTML files as assets directly within the interactive magazine and creating in-page portals to live web content. First I'll talk about the more powerful integration of live web content. I should note that what both methods can do is Herculean, and when I say "more powerful," I mean by just a smidge, like Superman versus Captain Marvel (aka Shazam).

Any content on the Web can be incorporated into your publication in real time. Just imagine what can be done by putting the Web on and *in* the page of a digital publication, making web-based content as much a part of the page as that placed image, with readers unable to discern a difference between live web content and native content or interactivity. Off the top of my head, here are only some of the truly limitless possibilities:

◆ Embed your live Twitter feed or even your Facebook page, plus associated Like and Tweet buttons.

◆ Push the latest announcements, news, and other content directly into the interactive magazine without the need for readers to update the app.

◆ Include a form in the publication that collects reader demographic data or even asks them to sign up for your email newsletter.

◆ Embed a web-based game inside your publication to get people to stay in it longer.

◆ If you run an ad-supported publication, you can stop selling a single ad space to only one advertiser at a time and rotate ads in the same space.

- Allow current advertisers to insert into back issues without having to alter and redistribute those back issues.

- Instantly correct errors and misprints.

- Time-sensitive content (coupon codes, daily specials) can be incorporated into the publication, changed as needed, and expired at the right time without the fear of having to uphold out-of-date promises or prices.

- Content can be customized on the fly, instantly, to match database records from subscribers' preferences or customers' prior purchases.

- You can also build a shopping cart into the magazine or catalog, catch interest, and close the sale, complete with purchase confirmation number and shipping tracking, all *inside the catalog or magazine.*

The only drawback to incorporating live web content is that, in order for it to appear, the reader must have a live Internet connection. Smartphones will nearly always have a live connection, as will many tablets, but those using WiFi-only tablets will need a hotspot in order to view your live web content. It may sound like a big drawback, but it isn't really; most readers will open your publication immediately after receiving it, and they have to be online to receive it.

TIP   More and more *widgets*, or prebuilt pages or chunks of web technology, are emerging specifically for inclusion in interactive magazines, reducing the amount of work for creating engaging interactivities.

Chapter 9

Creating Interactive Magazines with Adobe DPS

Adobe Digital Publishing Suite is the tablet publishing system almost everyone has heard about. It's also the most widely used, with more than 850 publishers using it to produce more than 1,700 titles worldwide. This capable system offers strong interactivity integrated tightly into InDesign.

- ◆ Installing Adobe DPS
- ◆ Starting a Publication
- ◆ Adding a New Layout
- ◆ Live-Testing Your Publication
- ◆ Panning and Zooming Images
- ◆ Creating Slideshows and Galleries
- ◆ Incorporating Audio and Video
- ◆ Adding Animations and 3D Rotating Objects
- ◆ Creating 3D Panoramas and Spaces
- ◆ Using Content Replacement
- ◆ Adding Live Web Content
- ◆ Including Offline HTML
- ◆ Applying the Finishing Touches

Installing Adobe DPS

If you're planning on using Adobe DPS, install the following:

- ◆ InDesign CS6 or newer by itself or as part of the Adobe Digital Publishing Suite, which includes InDesign, thus automatically installing the Folio Builder and Folio Overlays panels. The normal software update process will keep these upgraded to the latest version for you.

- ◆ Or, if you have InDesign CS5 or CS5.5, download and install the free Folio Producer tools and Folio Builder panel. You'll find links to download these and other tools at `http://abbrv.it/DigiPubIDTools`.

Starting a Publication

Creating an interactive magazine for publication through Adobe Digital Publishing Suite begins the same way as any InDesign publication, with the New Document dialog available by choosing File ➢ New ➢ Document.

Set the Intent field to Digital Publishing, which, like Web, automatically makes the document color space RGB and the measurement system pixels. It also disables the Facing Pages option because there's no such thing as facing pages in an interactive magazine.

In the Page Size drop-down you'll now see an abbreviated list of page size presets with an emphasis on common tablet device sizes (in Figure 9.1, note that the two sizes at the top are custom page size presets I created; see the sidebar "Create Custom Page Size Presets"). Choose which device you want to target—iPhone, iPad, Kindle Fire and B&N Nook Touch, or 10-inch-class Android tablets. Note that each of these options is merely a set of pixel dimensions; nothing else is changed by choosing iPad over Android 10" or Kindle Fire/Nook over iPhone. If the size you need isn't among the Page Size presets, change the Width and Height fields manually, using pixel-based measurements. For instance, the iPad preset uses the 1024 × 768-pixel resolution of the iPad 1 and 2; if you want to create for the iPad 3, then you'll need to manually enter its resolution of 2048 × 1536 pixels.

FIGURE 9.1
When Digital Publishing is chosen as the document intent, the Page Size drop-down displays common tablet presets.

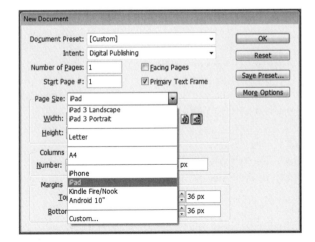

TIP Throughout, I've used *iPhone* to refer to both the iPhone and the iPod Touch; after all, the latter is simply a dialer-less version of the iPhone.

CREATE CUSTOM PAGE SIZE PRESETS

If you'll be creating layouts for the same device in the future, choose Custom from the bottom of the Page Size drop-down menu and create a preset for the device in question—such as for the iPad 3. Then, for future projects, you'll merely have to select your custom preset from the Page Size drop-down to save time.

The rest of the settings in the New Document dialog are standard—choose the number of desired columns and the gutter between them and set margins as desired. Bleed and Slug values (not shown in Figure 9.1) must be all at 0. Slugs are meaningless in this context, but the parts of certain objects that extend into the bleed area will actually appear on subsequent screens, so it's crucial that all Bleed settings be 0. Click OK, and you'll have your first layout for the digital magazine. The Pages panel should even indicate the device and orientation—H for horizontal or landscape and V for vertical or portrait (see Figure 9.2). If the H or V is omitted, which may happen when using custom page sizes without a preset, you can add it manually by double-clicking the layout column heading and typing a new name. Later you'll add additional layouts for other orientations and devices.

FIGURE 9.2
After you create a landscape-orientation iPad layout, the Pages panel indicates the device and orientation.

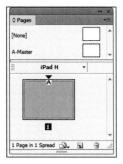

At this point, what you have is merely an InDesign document. Despite the sizes and labels on the Pages panel, this document is not yet considered part of an interactive magazine. To rectify that, you need to create a folio, add an article into that folio, and define the current page(s) as a layout within that article.

Creating the Folio

From the Window menu in CS6 and newer or the Window ➤ Extensions menu in CS5.5 and older, choose Folio Builder. That will pop up the Folio Builder panel, which may (frequently) ask you to update or prompt you to log into Adobe Digital Publishing Suite using your Adobe ID, as in Figure 9.3.

Your Adobe ID is the username (typically your email address) you use to access any online Adobe property. If you've ever registered Adobe software, posted on the Adobe User Forums, bought something from `http://store.adobe.com`, subscribed to Creative Cloud, or created an account for any other Adobe property, including Acrobat.com and Business Catalyst, then you already have an Adobe ID. Log in using it. If you can't remember your password or have other questions or concerns about your Adobe ID, visit the help page linked to from `http://abbrv .it/DigiPubAdobeID`.

TIP   If you already have an Adobe ID, *do not create a new one*; all interactions with Adobe and its products are tied to your Adobe ID, so managing your products, services, purchases, and even your own content hosted through Adobe servers can be nightmarish if you wind up with multiple Adobe ID accounts.

FIGURE 9.3
The Folio Builder panel requires you to log into or create an Adobe Digital Publishing Suite account before it can be used.

If you really don't have an Adobe ID, click the Sign Up link, which will take you to a web page where you can create one. The sign-up process appears to be specific to Adobe DPS, but it isn't; you'll be creating an Adobe ID for use anywhere and everywhere across Adobe properties.

If you aren't connected to the Internet when you go to create your first folio, you can click the New button at the bottom of the Folio Builder panel to create a local folio without logging in. You must log in later, however, to get that folio from your system up to the Adobe DPS server.

Once you're signed in, any other active publication or issue folios will appear in the Folder Builder panel (Figure 9.4). Of course, the list will be empty if this is your first time creating a folio. In that case, click the New button at the bottom of the panel; up will pop the New Folio dialog (Figure 9.5).

FIGURE 9.4
After you've signed in, the Folio Builder panel shows your active folios. The icon of the little people on the last two folios here indicates that those folios are shared with me or by me with others on my team.

FIGURE 9.5
When creating a
new folio, you're
asked to set several
options.

Folio Name   This is the name by which you and your collaborators will refer to the folio. This is not the name of the publication readers will see. Think of it as a filename rather than a document title.

Size   Fill in the Width and Height fields to match the dimensions of your new document. Note that if you're using renditions, which I'll cover in a few pages, your folio dimensions may be different from your document dimensions.

Orientation   A folio may be either landscape or portrait orientation or both. Choose that option here. If you want just one orientation, select the appropriate button; if you want to enable both orientations, select the third button. Keep in mind you can't mix and match single-orientation articles in a single publication; all articles must be either portrait or landscape or both portrait and landscape.

Create a Local Folio   Folios are uploaded to, and managed via a live connection to, Acrobat .com. Ergo, if you want to be able to work with a folio, you must have a live Internet connection. Enabling the Create a Local Folio option lets you save the folio to your local computer, enabling you to work on it without an Internet connection (when traveling, for example). The drawback, of course, is that only you have access to the local folio; you can't let others work with or even see it until you've moved the folio up to the Acrobat.com servers.

Default Format   This is a crucial decision; what you choose from the Default Format drop-down can greatly affect quality, file size, and whether the reader can zoom in on your content.

You see, the static content of your page—the text frames, the noninteractive imagery, vector shapes, page numbers, and so forth—get flattened upon folio export. Depending on your Default Format settings, the content is usually rasterized (type included) into a single flattened image. Interactivity is then added above this image of your page—thus the reason Adobe calls interactivity features *overlays*. There are quality and feature differences to be considered when choosing the format that will be created from the static content of your pages. Each article can be given a separate format, so in the Default Format field you should choose an option for the majority of your pages, overriding only for individual articles. You have three format choices.

JPEG   This option uses the lossy JPEG compression scheme to reduce the size of the rasterized page image at the possible expense of quality, especially if the page is scaled up during display. If you choose JPEG, also select a quality—Minimum, Low, Medium, High, or Maximum—from the Default JPEG Quality drop-down.

PNG   PNG graphics have built-in lossless compression, meaning, unlike JPEG, they don't suffer quality degradation as a consequence of compression. The result is that PNGs usually can't achieve the same level of compression as JPEGs, and they are often much larger in file size than JPEG. Despite the probable larger file size, most publishers opt for PNG format because of the high quality of output.

PDF   Choosing PDF as the default format keeps vector-based objects like text as vector based rather than flattening and rasterizing the entire page. This offers the advantage of allowing readers to zoom in on PDF-based pages, something they can't do with JPEG- or PNG-based pages. PDF pages are typically smaller than PNGs in terms of file size and offer ultra-sharp text rendering on any sized device and any zoom level. And by "any sized device," I mean any iOS device, iPad, iPhone, or iPod Touch. As of this writing, Adobe has not yet made the Content Viewer for Android capable of displaying PDF-based pages. To publish to Android, all your articles or the renditions of those articles for Android must use either JPEG or PNG.

Automatic   The Automatic option leaves it up to InDesign whether to choose JPEG, PNG, or PDF per page. Given that I don't like using JPEG at all, I never leave the setting as Automatic.

After you set the folio options and click OK, InDesign will generate the folio, either on the Adobe DPS server or as a local folio, depending on your choices. The Folio Builder panel will then move you inside the folio, ready to add articles.

Adding an Article

At bottom of the Folio Builder panel, the Add button should be enabled. Note that it's disabled if there are no InDesign documents opened. Clicking the Add button adds the currently active InDesign document as a layout within a new article and provides several options you must set via the New Article dialog (see Figure 9.6).

Article Name   The title you specify in the Article Name field *will* be seen by readers in the table of contents and elsewhere within the publication, so set it appropriately.

FIGURE 9.6
Setting the options
for a new article

Default Format   Here you can choose JPEG, PNG, PDF, or Automatic for the format of this individual article. If you select JPEG, you can use the JPEG Quality drop-down menu.

Horizontal Swipe Only   This option enables horizontally scrolling articles. Instead of the reader swiping up and down to move between screens, the reader swipes laterally, to move between screens in the current article. At the end of that article, continuing to swipe horizontally moves on to the next article. If you enable Horizontal Swipe Only, then vertical screen transitions are disabled; you can't mix them.

After you click OK, the article is created on your local folio, or on the server if you're not working locally. You might experience a slight delay as the content uploads. At this point, you can click the article you just created and use the Preview button at the bottom of the panel to view the article on a connected device or generate a temporary local folio and open it in the Adobe Content Viewer installed with the Folio Producer tools, click Add to create a new article, or add additional layouts to the article for other orientations or devices. The last option I'll hold off on for now and cover shortly. At this point, all the Adobe DPS–specific settings have been taken care of, and you're ready to design this article's layout just as you would any other publication.

Adding More Articles

In addition to following the same procedure you used to create the first article, you—or a collaborator—can create articles outside Folio Builder. Just create InDesign documents of the correct dimensions and save them to a location where you, or whoever is managing the folio, can access those files. Then import these external documents as new articles.

1. Open the Folio Builder panel, and enter the desired folio by clicking the arrow to the right of the folio's name.

2. Inside the folio, choose Import from the panel flyout menu. The Import Article dialog will appear (see Figure 9.7).

FIGURE 9.7
The Import Article dialog

3. If you are importing a single article, fill out the Article Name, Default Format, and other fields. If you are importing multiple articles, you will not have any of these options.

4. In the Location field, either type or paste in the location of the article INDD file(s) or click the folder icon and navigate to that location. When you click OK, the article(s) will be added to the folio. If you have built multiple layouts for the article(s), all those layouts will be added to the article as well. Only the person adding the article will be able to work on it. If you put it in a folder accessible to others, like a Dropbox folder, you can use the Relink feature to work on and update the article.

TIP Articles will be included in the interactive magazine in the same order in which they appear in the Folio Builder. Fortunately, rearranging in both places is a simple matter of dragging and dropping. In the Folio Builder panel you can rearrange articles by dragging up or down in the list.

Designing for Multiple Devices via Renditions

When the iPad 3 first appeared, it came into a world of 1,500 or so existing interactive magazine–format publications—none of which (except *Vogue*) were prepared for the higher resolution of the iPad 3's Retina display. iPad 3 owners immediately complained that interactive magazines looked lower quality, with "fuzzy" text. At issue was the fact that publishers designed for the 1024 × 768-pixel iPad 1 and 2, not the until-then-super-secret 2048 × 1536 pixel iPad 3 display. Because the entire page background, all noninteractive parts of it, is exported as a raster-format PNG or JPEG, magazines looked great on iPad 1 and 2 but degraded quickly in the double resolution of the iPad 3.

So, you might think you should start designing all your publications for the iPad 3's high-resolution display, relying on automatic scaling to fit the double-sized 2048 × 1536-pixel issue into the iPad 1 and 2 1024 × 768-pixel screens. Unfortunately, if you do that, it will bomb faster than Adam Sandler's *Jack and Jill*. Folios built specifically at 2048 × 1536 pixels will display only on iPad 3 and will not function on earlier versions; often they won't even download to earlier-generation iPads.

If you want your publication to be available to all generations of iPads, you have three workflow options—scale from the lowest common denominator or use one of two rendition techniques.

The easiest method is to simply design for the lowest common denominator—the non-Retina 1024 × 768-pixel displays of the iPad 1 and 2. When the publication is displayed on an iPad 3, it will be blown up to 200 percent to fit that device's double-resolution Retina display. Of course, that means you run a serious risk of quality degradation and the aforementioned "fuzzy" text about which consumers complained.

A rendition is a resolution- or aspect ratio–specific version of a folio. For instance, to create separate editions of an article or layout optimized for the iPad 3's 2048 × 1536-pixel display and one for the 1024 × 768-pixel iPad 1 and 2 display resolutions, you would create two separate folios—one at each at those resolutions. The content of the two renditions would be the same, although you have a choice as to whether you merely scale one INDD document to each of the two devices or create separate INDD documents specifically sized for the individual devices. Both folios will carry the exact same title, and when the reader requests to download your publication, the Adobe Content Viewer will detect the resolution of the device and download to it the correct rendition.

There are two methods of employing renditions: two publications/two folios and one publication/two folios.

In the first method, you design each article's layout (or layouts, if using dual orientation) specifically for the resolution of the target device. Thus, you would have one layout built for 2048×1536 pixels and another for 1024×768 pixels. You would then create two folios with the same name but different device target dimensions, add into both an identically named article, and then include in that article the appropriately sized INDD document layout(s). Naturally this means you have to manage at least two sets of identical artwork, copy, and overlays—four, if you're using dual orientations for both renditions. This method provides you with absolute control over each rendition's design, quality, and output, but does entail extra work and a risk of content falling out of sync between the renditions and layouts.

The other method is one in which you design a single layout and include that layout in both renditions. You would create the two folios as in the previous method, but include in them the same INDD article layouts rather than separate versions at different resolutions. The Content Viewer software then downloads the correct rendition and adjusts the display resolution of the layout where it can to meet the requirements of the device. Because a 2048×1536-pixel publication will not be displayed on an iPad 1 or 2—it won't even download, thus eliminating all iPad 1– and 2–based readers from your prospective readership—this means you'll need to design at 1024×768 pixels; that publication will then be scaled up when viewed on an iPad 3.

Don't dismiss this option yet, though. You can do two things to mitigate and possibly eliminate any quality degradation when the layout is scaled up. First, make sure that all your images have an effective PPI measurement of 144 PPI or greater as used in the 1024×768-pixel InDesign layout. That way, when they're scaled up 200 percent on the iPad 3, the pictures will have a minimum effective resolution of 72 PPI, which isn't horrible. Second, use PDF format for the document pages. That will keep the text and native vector objects as resolution-independent vectors, but only in the background page—overlays will always be rasterized (at least at the time of this writing that's the rule).

To publish your interactive magazine to non-iPad devices with different aspect ratios, you'll need to create additional renditions—probably with separate layouts created for the specific display ratio. For instance, to publish to Kindle Fire, Nook Tablet, and similar 7-inch Android tablets, you'll need to produce a folio in 1024×600 pixels containing versions of your layouts designed in 1024×600 pixels. Again, create a folio with the same name as the one(s) for the iPad(s), but with the correct dimensions and orientations in the New Folio dialog box. After publishing your magazine, the Content Viewers on devices that have 1024×600-pixel resolution, or another resolution in the same 128:75 display aspect ratio, will download that rendition.

The more renditions you create, the more individual device resolutions and display ratios you can target for the ideal reading experience on those devices. You *can* include separate renditions for each of the devices listed in Table 8.1, but that's more work than it's worth. Instead, focus on display aspect ratios—separate versions for 4:3, 16:9 or 16:10, and 128:75 (the aspect ratios of the devices in Table 8.1, plus the wide-screen computer/TV aspect ratio). Also, because Adobe's Android-version Content Viewer currently can't display PDF-format pages, you're unable to rely on vector saving the quality of text if scaled up. Therefore, I recommend you design to target the highest-resolution device in any of the aspect ratios you plan to hit. That will ensure a quality experience on those highest-resolution devices and, because raster image resolution increases when scaled down, also on the lower-resolution devices in the same display aspect ratio.

However, don't merely design a single 2048 × 1536-pixel folio hoping it will scale nicely on the iPad 1 and 2. It won't. In fact, it often won't even download. Folios built specifically at 2048 × 1536-pixel will display only iPad 3 and will not function on earlier versions. If you want your publication to be available to all iPads and to other devices, you'll need to use renditions.

Adding a New Layout

There are two methods of creating separate layouts for other orientations for Adobe DPS—three if you count creating a liquid layout, but I'll discuss that separately later in this chapter.

Creating a Separate Document Layout

Before InDesign CS6, there was only the method of using separate INDD files for each layout. Even with the introduction of the Alternate Layout system in CS6 that allows all of an article's layouts to exist side by side (so to speak) in a single document, many creatives prefer to stick to the separate-document method. This preference usually arises because of the need to incorporate layouts created prior to CS6 or because only the multiple document method allows for other designers to work concurrently on the different layouts.

To create a new layout as a separate document, follow these simple instructions:

1. Open the INDD containing your first layout.

2. Choose File ➤ Save As and save a new copy of the INDD in the same folder as the first one, changing the name of this new copy to somehow indicate that it's a different orientation or for a different device. For example, many append _h and _v to filenames (before the period and file extension) to specify horizontal/landscape or vertical/portrait, respectively. Others use a space and then w or wide and t or tall to mean wide and tall, which are holdovers from earlier versions of the Adobe DPS Folio Builder; now _h and _v are the accepted standards.

3. Now that you have a new copy of your layout saved under a different filename, go to the master page in use (or the base master page if you're using several).

4. Switch to the Page tool, which will also put the Control panel into Page mode.

5. Select the appropriate Liquid Page rule from the drop-down field bearing that label (Figure 9.8). (Again, I'll talk in depth about liquid layout and the Liquid Layout rules later in this chapter.)

FIGURE 9.8
The Liquid Page Rule drop-down offers five rules.

6. Using either the orientation buttons, the Width and Height fields, or the Page Size drop-down menu on the Control panel, change the orientation or size of the master page as

desired. This change will affect not only the master page but also any document pages based on it.

7. On the Folio Builder panel, double-click the folio and then the article within it to which you want to add the new layout. You'll see within the article any layouts you added previously (see Figure 9.9).

FIGURE 9.9
Inside the article is the first orientation layout.

8. At the bottom of the Folio Builder panel, click the Add button. You may be prompted to save the file, after which the Folio Builder will upload the new layout to Acrobat.com and add it into the Folio Builder panel as a new layout within the article.

TIP Remember, if you need to add layouts for other devices, resolutions, and display aspect ratios, employ renditions, which I covered in the "Designing for Multiple Devices via Renditions" section earlier in the chapter.

Adding an Alternate Layout in the Same Document

The more modern (CS6 and newer) method enables creation of multiple layouts within a single InDesign document. Adobe calls these *alternate layouts*, which, in addition to placing all of an article's layouts within a single document, also enable the synchronization of the article content across layouts.

When you set the intent of the document to Digital Publishing in the New Document dialog, InDesign automatically starts a labeled layout on the Pages panel. Figure 9.10 shows a document I began as a landscape-oriented, iPad-sized document, which InDesign conveniently labels for me in the Pages panel as iPad H, with the *H* meaning horizontal or landscape.

TIP Alternate layouts are actually sections in the document and are treated the same as if you'd gone to the Numbering & Section Options dialog and checked the box beside Start Section.

FIGURE 9.10
Using the Digital
Publishing intent
sets the Pages panel
to label the layout.

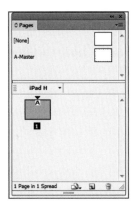

To create a new alternate layout, such as the portrait orientation layout for iPad or a layout sized for the Kindle Fire, NOOK Color, and NOOK Tablet, all of which share the same resolution and pixel dimensions, you add the layout directly into the Pages panel rather than creating a separate document.

1. Beside the label of any layout is a tiny black arrow indicating the presence of that layout's menu. Click the black arrow and choose Create Alternate Layout. You can also access the Create Alternate Layout command by using the Pages panel flyout menu, by using InDesign's Layout menu, or by right-clicking a page thumbnail within the Pages panel.

2. When the Create Alternate Layout dialog appears, choose the correct option from the Page Size menu and/or set the Width, Height, and Orientation options as needed (see Figure 9.11). Select the rest of your desired options—which I'll discuss in detail right after the next step—and click OK.

FIGURE 9.11
Creating an alter-
nate layout

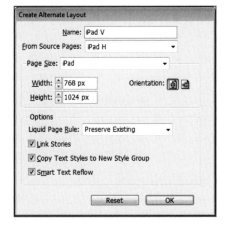

3. The Pages panel will now show your existing layouts and the new one you just created side by side, as you can see in Figure 9.12. Repeat steps 1 and 2 as needed to include additional layouts, and then use those layouts as the bases for your renditions to serve other devices.

FIGURE 9.12
After adding the
alternate layout,
the Pages panel
shows two separate
vertical sections—
alternate layouts.

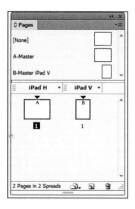

As you work to adapt the content from one layout to another, or as you make changes across layouts, you might want to avail yourself of the very handy Split Window To Compare Layouts command. You'll find the command on the Layout drop-down menu (the black arrow beside the layout name). Similar to the Window ➢ Arrange ➢ Split Window command, Split Window To Compare Layouts divides the InDesign document window in two so that you can see and work on two layouts at a time. Actually, it *is* the Window ➢ Arrange ➢ Split Window command. Because alternate layouts are merely sections within the same document, the two commands do the same thing—split the current document window and allow you to navigate the document in either independently.

Synchronizing Text across Layouts

Alternate layouts all exist within the same INDD, which opens up some very powerful possibilities for content synchronization and reuse. For one thing, all the copies of an image, video, or other external asset across all layouts can be managed simultaneously through the Links panel. With multiple documents, you'd have to open up each INDD to update a modified file or replace a linked asset. Another convenience is the ability to use Find/Change across all layouts concurrently, replacing text, graphics, or object attributes. (However, you could do that with multiple documents, too; as long as they were all open, you couldn't use and update text variables, swatches, object styles, text styles, and hyperlinks across all those layouts if they were separate, at least not without using circuitous routes like a Book file.) Then, of course, there's the pseudo-automatic update of text across all alternate layouts by changing the text in the original layout.

With the creation of the Alternate Layout system, Adobe also enabled layout text synchronization and several other handy features. The way it works is simple: if you edit text in the original or source layout, those edits will propagate across all alternate layouts…after you, um, manually update them…. All right, well, it's still pretty useful, despite the manual updating. Let's try it.

1. Within a digital publishing document with one layout, begin to create an alternate layout, but pause at the Create Alternate Layout dialog (refer to Figure 9.11).

2. In the From Source Pages field, choose the first layout. If you choose All Pages from this list, it will copy all pages from all layouts into a single new alternate layout, which is typically not what you want. You want to copy all the pages from a single layout, usually the one closest in size and orientation to the one you're creating, which you select in this list.

3. Set your desired Page Size options for the new layout, and choose which, if any, Liquid Page rule you'd like to employ to help adapt your content to the new layout.

4. Enable the Link Stories check box to link all text from the source layout to the alternate layout so that edits to the former occur (semi)automatically within the latter.

5. Set the other two options as you like.

Smart Text Reflow, if enabled, will add and remove pages in the alternate layout as necessary to fit all the text, which will almost certainly flow differently between the two layouts.

Choosing the option Copy Text Styles To New Style Group takes all the text styles from the source layout—character, paragraph, table, and cell styles—and copies them as new, but identically named, styles applied to the text (and tables) of the alternate layout, organized into new folders on the Character, Paragraph, Table, and Cell Styles panels (see Figure 9.13 for the Paragraph Styles panel). This offers easy modification of styles for just one layout, which is, frankly, a brilliantly helpful device.

FIGURE 9.13
On the Paragraph Styles panel and other styles panels, styles used in the source layout are collected into a group named for the source layout, while copies of those styles are deposited into a group named for the alternate layout.

Click OK to create the alternate layout.

6. Now that you have an alternate layout, return to the source layout and change some text element. Figure 9.14 shows a large text frame that originally read "This is My Text Frame." I've since changed that to "This is My Synchronized Text Frame." Note that not a darn thing happens to the text on the alternate layout; it still reads "This is My Text Frame."

FIGURE 9.14

A text frame on my source layout originally read "This is My Text Frame."

b

a

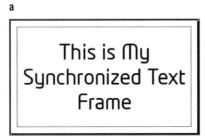

Even though I changed the text on the source layout...

...it didn't update on the alternate layout.

7. Switch to the alternate layout by double-clicking its first-page thumbnail in the Pages panel. Something *has* changed (scrutinize Figure 9.14b carefully). Although the text itself hasn't been updated, the text frame now bears the familiar yellow caution sign indicating that the content has been modified and needs to be updated. A quick glance at the Links panel shows the same thing where the text frame on the alternate layout is listed as a linked asset—linked from the original location in the source layout (see Figure 9.15).

FIGURE 9.15

Changing text on the source layout causes the linked copy on the alternate layout to become out-of-date.

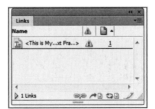

8. To update the alternate layout text, treat the frame like any out-of-date asset. Highlight its entry in the Links panel and click the Update Link button—hold Alt/Opt while clicking to update all out-of-date assets—or click directly on the yellow caution sign on the text frame. Whichever method you choose, the text in the alternate layout will now resynchronize with the original on the source layout.

Obviously, the linked stories behavior is intended for more than a simple, single text frame, which could have been updated throughout the entire document with a simple Find/Change operation. It enables any text change, from replacing a single glyph to overhauling paragraphs and pages worth of copy, things that *can* be done in Find/Change, but only with complex GREP formulas. Synchronized text is like making all of your text a text variable but with paragraph composition and line wrapping and without the instant update.

> **DELETING ALTERNATE LAYOUTS**
>
> If you make a mistake, you can undo the creation of an alternate layout. You can also find the Delete Alternate Layout command in all the same places you can find the command to create one. Be advised, though, that if you delete the first layout, the one to which subsequent layouts are slaved in terms of content and style synchronization, you'll also delete the content and styles attached to the first layout and to all synchronized alternate layouts. In other words, you could totally bork your publication.
>
> Another way to handle removal of the first layout is to not remove it. Instead, delete the pages in that layout just as you'd remove any pages (or spreads) from an InDesign document. The content will then overset but still exist, as will the styles, and they'll live on in the alternate layouts.

Importing Existing Separate Document Layouts

If you already have layouts created as separate InDesign documents, whether from older interactive magazines, by creating layouts before adding them to a folio, or, most commonly, because you've received layouts such as full-page ads from outside agencies, you can import them into your folio without having to re-create anything. As long as the external documents match the aspect ratio of your current publication, follow these steps to import them:

1. If your publication allows device rotation, meaning it has separate layouts for portrait and landscape, ensure that the articles you want to import also have portrait and landscape layouts. Remember that you don't need to have both orientations in a publication, but all articles must contain the same single orientation or both orientations. If there are two orientations in the layouts you're importing, make sure the files are named with a common suffix that the Adobe DPS importer will recognize. For example, use _h, <space>w, or <space>wide for landscape and _v, <space>t, or <space>tall for portrait.

2. In the Folio Builder panel, double-click the name of the folio into which you want to import external articles and layouts. This will place you in the Articles view. Stay there; don't double-click an article title.

3. From the Folio Builder panel's flyout menu, choose Import.

4. When the Import Article dialog appears, choose the appropriate option at the top to specify whether you're importing a single article with one or more layouts or multiple articles, each with one or more layouts (see Figure 9.16).

    If you choose to import a single article, fill out the Article Name field, choose the page format (and JPEG quality if applicable) and Smooth Scrolling option, and then supply the location of the folder containing the INDD layout.

TIP   The PDF format is supported only in smooth scrolling articles up to two screens deep. In other words, in a 1024 × 768-pixel horizontal orientation article, if you make the page more than 1536-pixel high, you can't use PDF. Even if you specify it, Adobe DPS will render the page as PNG.

    If you're importing multiple articles, selecting the Import Multiple Articles radio button offers a much smaller Import Article dialog. Just supply the folder containing the INDD layouts or containing subfolders with the INDD documents in them.

FIGURE 9.16
The Import Article
dialog in single-
article (a) and
multiple-article (b)
modes

a   b

Click OK.

5. A single-article import is finished at this point, but a multiple-article import requires another two steps. In the Folio Builder panel's Article view, highlight the first imported article, and choose Properties from the Folio Builder panel's flyout menu.

6. Fill out the title and options for the article, and then repeat for each of the other imported articles. Initially each article will be named for the folder that contains it. You can also specify properties like the title and much more using a `sidecar.xml` file, which I'll discuss in the "Applying the Finishing Touches" section later in this chapter.

Copying Articles between Folios

Many types of publication reuse articles and layouts. For example, masthead, department, and ad pages are commonly reused—with some degree of change—in periodicals, while book-like interactive magazine–format publications might reuse even more content such as the About the Author, How to Use This Publication, and other common pages. There's no need to re-create everything from scratch. Instead, you can copy articles between one folio and another.

1. In the Folio Builder panel, double-click the folio containing the article you want to copy to another existing folio.

2. Within the Article view, highlight the article you'd like to copy.

3. Choose Copy To from the Folio Builder panel's flyout menu and, in the dialog that appears, select the destination folio, the one to which you want to copy the article. After clicking OK, you'll likely experience a delay while InDesign uploads the article and its layouts to the server as part of the new folio. After that, any changes to the article in one folio automatically apply to the other, keeping them in sync, because the article is in the same layout document.

Live-Testing Your Publication

To test an Adobe DPS publication on your computer screen, make sure you have the latest Folio Producer tools installed; then, with the document you want to test opened in InDesign, click the Preview button at the bottom of the Folio Overlays panel and select Preview On Desktop. InDesign will then generate a local folio from the current document and open it in the Adobe Content Viewer on your computer (see Figure 9.17). The Adobe Content Viewer provides a very accurate preview, though it isn't as touch-friendly as a tablet would be.

FIGURE 9.17

Previewing the interactive magazine with the desktop Adobe Content Viewer software

Previewing the current layout or article, or the entire folio with all its articles and layouts, live on a tablet you have in front of you, is just as easy.

1. Install on your device the free Adobe Content Viewer app you'll find in the iOS App Store, the Amazon Appstore for Android, and the Google Play App Store.

2. Inside the Adobe Content Viewer app, tap the Sign In button and provide your Adobe ID and password, the same one you use to access your Adobe DPS account.

3. Connect the tablet to your computer via USB and ensure that it's recognized by the computer.

4. At the bottom of the Folio Overlays panel, click the Preview button, which should now offer you a choice of Preview On Desktop and preview on your connected mobile device, whatever name you've configured for that device (e.g., "Pariah's iPad 3"). After a moment or two while Adobe DPS generates your publication and transfers it down the USB line, it should appear on the device in the Content Viewer app.

If that doesn't work, which it may not because the desktop-based Adobe DPS doesn't always properly recognize attached devices, you can still preview your folio on mobile devices by syncing them to your Acrobat.com server account (without the need to hardwire-connect them to a computer).

1. Ensure that the folio you want to test is synchronized with the server and not a local folio.

2. Install on your device the free Adobe Content Viewer app you'll find in the iOS App Store, the Amazon Appstore for Android, and the Google Play App Store.

3. Inside the Adobe Content Viewer app, tap the Sign In button, and provide your Adobe ID and password (the same one you use to access your Adobe DPS account).

4. Within a few moments, you'll see all your active folios displayed as thumbnails in the main screen of the Adobe Content Viewer app. Tap a folio to load it and use it just as your readers will once it's published.

If you'd like to enable your team members or clients to preview the folio on their devices, they will need to have Adobe IDs and the Adobe Content Viewer app installed on their devices. Then follow these steps to share the preview:

1. In a web browser, visit DigitalPublishing.Acrobat.com and sign in to your account. Even if you've never been to Acrobat.com before, you have an account via the Folio Builder panel. As of this writing, Adobe DPS publications are managed through Acrobat.com.

2. After logging in, you'll be taken to your personal dashboard. On the left you'll find a set of Publishing tools (see Figure 9.18). Click the Folio Producer link to be taken to the Folio Producer: Organizer screen, which you can see in Figure 9.19.

FIGURE 9.18
My Digital Publishing Suite dashboard

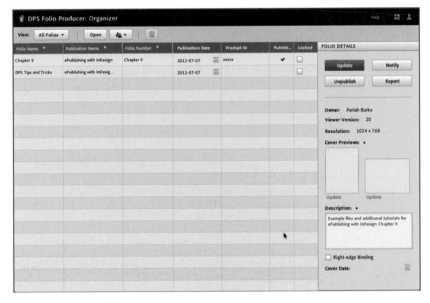

3. Your active folios are all listed, along with important data about each. I'll explain all those columns and controls in the "Applying Finishing Touches" section later in this chapter. For now, find the folio you want to share and click it.

4. In the row of buttons above the folio list, click the people-adorned Share Folio button and then click Share to pop up the Share dialog (Figure 9.20).

FIGURE 9.20
Sharing my folio

5. Enter the email addresses of the people with whom you want to share the folio for review in the Share Folio With field. Note that the email addresses you enter must be the exact ones those people used as their Adobe IDs. Separate multiple addresses with semicolons.

6. Choose whether to customize the subject and message of the email invitations invitees will receive and then click the Share button. Each invitee will receive an email from Acrobat.com inviting them to review the workspace. Upon acceptance of that invitation, the folio will appear inside the person's Adobe Content Viewer on a tablet device (see Figure 9.21) as well as within that person's Folio Builder panel inside InDesign.

FIGURE 9.21
All folios to which you have access will appear within the Adobe Content Viewer app on tablets.

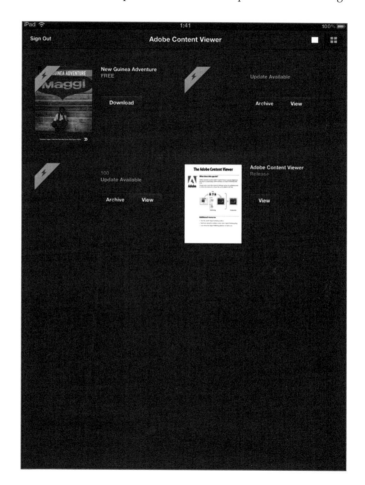

Panning and Zooming Images

Now that you know how to begin and lay out interactive magazines, I can get into the really good stuff—all the different ways in which those publications can be made interactive and engaging. Let's start with one of the simplest and most powerful interactivities: panning and zooming images.

Allowing an image to pan and/or zoom is an extraordinarily simple matter.

1. Perform any essential cropping of your desired image in Photoshop. Because panning enables the entire image to be displayed and all but negates cropping affected by leaving parts of the image outside the image frame, *before* placing it into InDesign you'll need to physically remove any parts you don't want readers to see.

2. Place the screen-ready JPG or PNG image into InDesign using File ➢ Place (Ctrl+D/Cmd+D).

3. Position and scale that image as necessary. If you want to enable image panning—the reader moving the image around within the viewing aperture of its frame—ensure that the image frame is smaller than the image it contains, thus cropping out parts of the image. If you want to enable zooming in on the image, scale the image down in InDesign, making its Effective PPI measurement on the Links panel larger than its Actual PPI value (see Figure 9.22).

FIGURE 9.22
The Links panel's Link Info section shows the Effective PPI and Actual PPI values for the selected image.

4. Select the image object with the black arrow Selection tool.

5. On the Folio Overlays/Overlay Creator panel, choose the Pan & Zoom overlay, and activate the On radio button as in Figure 9.23.

There are a few other things you should know about creating panning and/or zooming images.

◆ Like audio and video overlays (see the appropriate sections just a little further into this chapter), images that pan and zoom employ a temporary placeholder called a *poster*. When your reader first turns to the page containing the pan and zoom image, what she will actually see in the page is a static poster image generated from the part of the main image visible in the graphic frame. That poster always remains in the background on-screen, though it's covered by the actual Pan & Zoom overlay. This is important to note because, should your pan and zoom image contain transparency (in PNG form), the poster will show through the transparent areas of the panning/zooming image. Consequently, using an image with transparency is ill-advised.

FIGURE 9.23
The Pan & Zoom
overlay options in
the Folio Overlays
panel

◆ Adobe recommends you limit the size of images to a relatively paltry maximum of 1024 pixels, either horizontally or vertically or both, to avoid memory issues.

◆ Adobe further sets the maximum image size to 2000 pixels in either direction.

◆ Given the higher resolution of second-generation tablets (starting with the iPad 3, Kindle Fire HD, and so on), maintaining an effective PPI of 72 can cause noticeable quality degradation on these higher-resolution devices. To adjust for those higher qualities, I recommend you maintain an effective PPI value of 144, which may mean scaling the placed image down to half its original dimensions.

Creating Slideshows and Galleries

Like many interactive effects, creating slideshows and galleries using Adobe Digital Publishing Suite is not as streamlined a process as it should be. Both types of image display require you to do the majority of the work outside the Folio Overlays panel, using standard InDesign features that weren't necessarily created with this use in mind.

1. Prepare your slideshow images, and then place them all into InDesign.

2. Size and fit all the images to fit within the space the gallery will need to occupy and so that the dimensions of all the image frames match (see Figure 9.24). Note that they don't *have to* match in size, but images of mismatched sizes replacing one another creates a very unprofessional look when the overlay is executed.

FIGURE 9.24
My slideshow's
selection of
images all placed,
sized, and fitted
appropriately

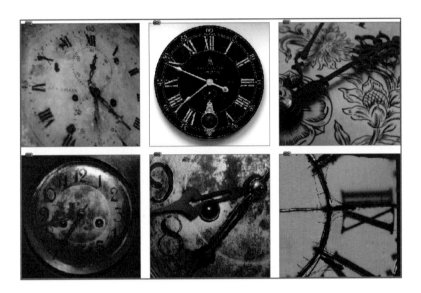

ASPIRIN-FREE WORKFLOW: PLACE, FIT, AND MATCH SIZE ALL IN ONE STEP

You already undoubtedly know that you can place multiple images at one time into InDesign—simply press Ctrl+D/Cmd+D and select multiple images instead of one, or drag multiple images into InDesign from Bridge, Lightroom, Explorer, Finder, or whatever other external program you like. What you may not know is that you can also, in a single step, place all the images on the page (or pasteboard), within frames that all match each in height and width, *and* fit all those images to those frames using the Fit Image To Frame Proportionately option. This method makes *very* quick work of placing a bunch of images for use in multistate objects, slideshows, image galleries, membership grids, catalogs, and a host of other uses.

All you have to do is bring in several images as usual—using Place or drag and drop—and then use just a couple of modifier keys as you click and drag to define the area for the images. Do not click and release to drop the first image from your loaded cursor. Instead, click and drag to define the area, and *while still holding the left mouse button*, press your keyboard's Up arrow to add rows and Right arrow to add columns. When you release the left mouse button, InDesign will have created multiple matching frames arranged in rows and columns, with each graphic frame containing an image fitted to the frame. If you didn't get all the pictures in one shot, undo with Ctrl+Z/Cmd+Z, and use the Up and Right arrow keys to add enough rows and columns to account for all the images. If the frames are too small, enlarge the overall area by dragging the cursor out to the right and downward to increase the size of each frame in the grid.

Reduce the number of rows and columns, respectively, by using the Down and Left arrow keys. Remember that all this has to be done *after you begin dragging* with a loaded cursor and *while continuing to hold down the left mouse button*.

3. Align all the frames such that they stack neatly, with the topmost frame completely blocking out all images and frames beneath it.

4. Select all the image frames. If you had one already selected, with the black arrow Selection tool active, click away from the frames to deselect all of them, and then click and drag a selection rectangle such that it touches the stack, thus selecting all the frames in the stack.

5. From the Window menu choose Interactive ➤ Object States.

6. At the bottom of the Object States panel, click the sticky-note-like Convert Selection To Multi-State Object button (see Figure 9.25). You should now see something like Figure 9.26, wherein the stack of frames has been converted to a multistate object—denoted by the dashed frame and the icon overlay in the bottom right corner—and that the Object States panel now shows each of your images as a separate state (see Figure 9.27).

FIGURE 9.25
The Object States panel

FIGURE 9.26
The six images have now been converted to a single multistate object, as denoted by the dashed line bounding box and the icon in the lower-right corner.

FIGURE 9.27
After converting the images to a multistate object, the Object States panel shows each image as a state of the whole.

Each image is now a state or appearance of the multistate object. All the images coexist within the one object, and each is revealed only as its state is selected. Try it by clicking the various states in the panel; you'll see the corresponding image appear within the object itself. They're all treated as a single object now, occupying the same space, and a slideshow will sequentially change which state is visible.

7. In the Object States panel, change the Object Name field so that your new multistate object has a name more meaningful than *Multi-state 1*. Something like Slideshow or Clocks Slideshow would be good.

8. With the multistate object still selected, you may now go to the Folio Overlays panel. If it hasn't already set itself into Slideshow mode, choose the Slideshow Overlay from the list.

9. Set the appropriate options—discussed in detail next—and then click Preview to test your new slideshow in the Adobe Content Viewer.

TIP   If the slides appear in the wrong order, you can reorder them by dragging and dropping their respective states in the Object States panel.

Understanding the Slideshow Overlay Options

Creating a multistate object and making it a slideshow overlay presents a number of options to help you fine-tune the display, behavior, and interactivity inherent within the slideshow (see Figure 9.28).

FIGURE 9.28
Options for the
Slideshow overlay

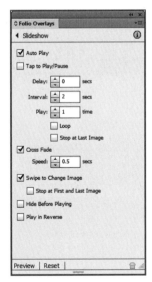

Auto Play   If Auto Play is enabled, the slideshow will automatically begin playing, transitioning between object states or images. With this option enabled, suboptions below Tap to Play/Pause become available.

> **Delay**   Enter in the Delay field a value in seconds to wait before beginning the automatic play of the slideshow.

> **Interval**   Also measured in seconds, the Interval field is how long to wait between slide transitions or the length of time each slide remains on-screen before beginning to transition to the next slide.

> **Play**   The Play field, which accepts whole numbers, is the number of times the slideshow will automatically play before stopping. A value of 1 means the slideshow will play through all the slides once and stop. This field is disabled if Loop is selected.

> **Loop**   If Loop is enabled, the slideshow will cycle indefinitely, automatically starting over again when it reaches the end.

> **Stop At Last Image**   If Loop is disabled, the Stop At Last Image option becomes available, allowing you to specify that, after the final automatic play of the slideshow, it ends by showing—and staying on—the last image in the slideshow rather than reverting to the first image, which is the default behavior.

Tap To Play/Pause   Activating the Tap To Play/Pause option enables the reader to start or stop automatic state/image transitions by tapping the multistate object. Interval is the only suboption enabled when Tap To Play/Pause is enabled but Auto Play is not.

Cross Fade   Cross-fading is a transition effect wherein each slide seems to melt or fade into the next (or previous). Activating the Cross Fade option makes slides transition more smoothly, rather than each subsequent image instantly replacing its predecessor. With the option enabled, you can also change the speed or length of the transition, in whole second or tenth of a second values, using the Speed field.

Swipe To Change Image   The Swipe To Change Image option must be enabled if you want readers to be able to transition between slides manually. If this is disabled, slides will advance only as part of auto playing.

The suboption, Stop At First And Last Image, stops reader-driven slide transitions at the first and last slides. Thus, when a reader swipes from right to left, advancing in the slide deck, she will not be able to advance past the last slide. She can, however, swipe left to right to go backward through the slide deck until she reaches the first slide.

Hide Before Playing   When using the Auto Play option and an initial delay, it's sometimes useful to make the entire slideshow invisible until the delay has expired and the automatic play begins. The same thing can be useful even without the Auto Play option enabled, with a slideshow set not to begin until tapped (using the Tap To Play/Pause option). For example, you may want to display a static image, text, another object, or a "tap here to play" directive of some kind in the same space as the slideshow until the slideshow begins. Setting the Hide Before Playing option accomplishes that by making the slideshow invisible until and unless it begins playing or is activated by a tap.

Play In Reverse   The Play In Reverse option flips the order of the slides, playing through the states from the bottom up rather than the default of from the top down.

Creating a Gallery

A gallery, such as the one pictured in Figure 9.29, offers readers the ability to move through the images nonsequentially, using thumbnails, other images, or buttons to jump directly from any state to any other state rather than having to move through all the intervening states as with a slideshow.

FIGURE 9.29
An image gallery with graphical button triggers

1. To make a gallery, create a multistate object of the desired images and then make that multistate object a slideshow overlay.

2. Set your slideshow overlay options as desired; again, you can make the gallery behave just like a slideshow with autoplaying, cross-fading, and so on, but *also* be navigable non-linearly. When we create the thumbnails or buttons to target individual states, they will cease any auto play and looping so the reader isn't yanked away from the image he specifically chose to see.

3. Place your thumbnail or button images. If you're using thumbnails of the actual slide images, place all the same images again into InDesign and order them such that they match the order of the slide images on the Object States panel. If instead you'll be using some other imagery—such as my software icons for the T-shirts in my example—then place those onto the page in an order that matches the object states. You can also use text frames, vector objects created in InDesign, or groups of objects as the triggers for changing states. Whatever you're using for your trigger objects, size and position them where you want them in the final design.

4. Choose Window ➣ Interactive ➣ Buttons and Forms (just Buttons in versions prior to CS6) to open the Buttons And Forms panel (see Figure 9.30).

5. Select with the black arrow the object you want to trigger your first state or slide, and, at the bottom of the Buttons and Forms panel, click the Convert To Button button. Your selected object (or group) will change its appearance to have a beefy dashed outline and display a button icon in the lower right (see Figure 9.31).

FIGURE 9.30
The Buttons And
Forms panel

FIGURE 9.31
After converting
the InDesign icon to
a button

6. On the Buttons And Forms panel, the button object will be listed as Button in the Type field and given an automatic, generic name (see Figure 9.32). You can leave the name as is or change it. Leave the Event field set to On Release Or Tap (merely on On Release in CS5.5 and older).

7. In the Actions area, click the plus sign to expose the Actions menu (see Figure 9.33). Within that menu are the various actions you can have button objects perform—some of which work only within PDFs, others only within HTML5 and SWF, and still others in those formats and interactive magazines. Down under the Liquid HTML 5 and SWF Only section (SWF Only in CS5.5 and older) is the command to Go To State. It's erroneously labeled; it is *not* just for Liquid HTML 5 and SWF. Go To State, Go To Next State, and Go To Previous State all *do* function when used in interactive-magazine and interactive-PDF output.

Select Go To State.

FIGURE 9.32
The Buttons And
Forms panel after
converting the
InDesign icon to a
button

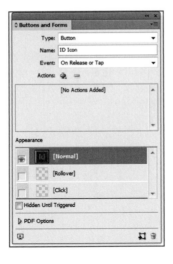

FIGURE 9.33
The Buttons And
Forms panel's
Actions menu

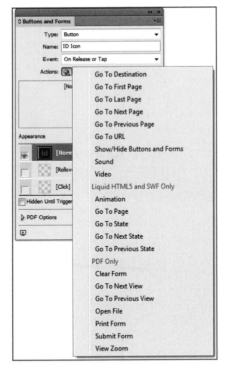

8. The Actions list beneath the plus (Add New Action) and minus (Delete Selection Action) buttons lists the actions currently assigned to the button object. Your Go To State action should already be highlighted, which caused two fields to appear beneath the Actions list (see Figure 9.34). In the first field, Object, select your multistate object from the list.

FIGURE 9.34
With the Go To
State action added,
the Object and State
fields appear.

TIP   You aren't limited to a single action. You can assign main actions as well as secondary ones—
say, showing a different object state while also changing the state of another multistate object
from a single button.

9. The State field is now populated with the states in the object you just chose, so pick the
    state you want to be shown when the reader taps the selected button.

10. Repeat the last five steps (steps 5 through 9) for each of the other trigger objects, convert-
    ing each to a button and setting that button to show one state in the same multistate
    object. When you've finished, you'll now have a fully functional gallery; there's no need
    to do anything in the Folio Overlays panel.

ASPIRIN-FREE WORKFLOW: NAME YOUR STATES

Naming your multistate objects (using only alphanumeric characters and underscores) in the
Object Name field in the Object States panel, as well as the individual states of that object, can
make it much easier to choose exactly which multistate object and which state is desired when
you're creating buttons to trigger display of those states—especially if your publication contains
many multistate objects or multistate objects with many states. Rename individual states on the
Object States panel the same way you'd rename layers in the Layers panel—rapidly double-click
their existing names, which will change the name display into a name edit field, and then type
in the new name; press Enter/Return or click away to commit the name change.

Incorporating Audio and Video

As discussed in the preceding chapter, audio and video can be deployed in your interactive publications to ratchet up the interest level and offer content you couldn't present in static form. Here's how to do that with Adobe DPS.

Inserting Audio

Because Adobe Digital Publishing Suite is so tightly integrated into InDesign—and vice versa—adding an audio file isn't much different from placing an image. At least, that's how it begins; giving your reader a means of controlling the playback of that audio gets into some strange territory, but first, let's worry about adding the audio.

1. Using File ➤ Place or Ctrl+D/Cmd+D, place an MP3 file into the document exactly as you'd place an image.

2. At this point, you have a media frame (as opposed to a text frame or graphic frame) that contains no visuals—MP3s have no visual component, and the frame, by default, has no fill or stroke (see Figure 9.35). Leave it that way if you want autoplay audio without a visible controller (more on that later in this section). If you want to make the audio on-demand, playing only when the reader taps it, then you'll need to include some kind of visual to communicate that fact.

FIGURE 9.35
Placing an MP3 file results in a media frame.

Open the Media panel by going to Window ➤ Interactive ➤ Media. While the MP3's frame is selected, the Media panel will display a standard speaker icon in the preview area (see Figure 9.36). It will also give you a play/pause button and a progress indicator so that you may preview the track without having to leave InDesign.

FIGURE 9.36
Working with the audio file in the Media panel

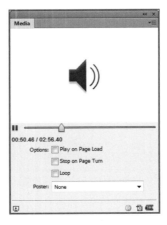

Down at the bottom of the panel you have the Poster drop-down field. A poster visually represents the audio file when it isn't playing, which is particularly important for user-activated playback. A poster—whether a custom image or the "Standard" speaker icon—communicates to the reader that tapping that location will initiate audio playback. From the Poster drop-down you can choose that speaker icon by selecting Standard; Choose Image, which enables you to navigate to a graphic—say, a photograph of the person speaking, a custom play icon, or an album cover—to import, which will fill the media frame and visually represent the MP3. Selecting None, which is the default, leaves the media frame empty. Note that the size of the multimedia frame you draw will be the size of the poster that represents the audio.

3. The Folio Overlays panel should have automatically switched itself into showing the options for Audio & Video overlays with the audio file's frame selected (see Figure 9.37). Obviously you want to focus on the upper section. At this point you have one relevant option and its singular suboption: Auto Play. Activate Auto Play if you want the audio to begin playing automatically when the reader reaches the page. Set the Delay field to however many seconds you want to wait between the time the reader reaches the page and the audio begins to play. Note that there is no way to loop the audio; whether Auto Play is enabled or not, the sound clip will play through once and stop.

FIGURE 9.37
The Audio & Video options in the Folio Overlays panel

4. Click the Preview button at the bottom of the panel to test the overlay. Note that the audio overlay is invisible—there is no player, no visual representation. If you click the space where the multimedia frame would be, however, you can pause and play the audio.

If you've included simple background music or ambient sounds that readers won't need to control, you might want to stop here. However, at some point, you might want to include audio that has some means of readers controlling it. As I noted, there is an inherent control built in—clicking the audio pauses and plays it—but readers won't know that. You could write a caption or draw an image to be placed behind the audio overlay that communicates this ability, which is a great idea, but there's another way to communicate that fact as well as to provide a basic controller with an optional progress bar.

TIP   If you want to use only a simple image that doesn't change with the state of the playback or its progress, use InDesign's Media panel and the Poster field to fill the audio frame with either a standard icon of a speaker or a custom image you choose.

Although device operating system makers like Apple, Google, and so on have already built standard player user interfaces for audio and video, Adobe DPS doesn't make use of those interfaces for audio playback, though it does for video playback. You'll have to create your own user interface if you want an audio controller—which can be seen both as a pain in the neck and as an opportunity to get creative.

Each state of the controller must be its own PNG file, labeled a specific way. If you look in this chapter's Lesson Files folder, in the Adobe DPS\Audio\Links folder, you'll see the PNG files I created for a very basic controller (see Figure 9.38). The AudioAsset portion of the name is arbitrary—it can be anything you want. The numbers, however, as well as _play and _pause, are required components of the filenames. To present an audio player, you must create at least one _play graphic to appear when the audio is stopped and one _pause graphic to appear while the audio is actively playing. If you want to present a progress bar that communicates how far the audio has progressed vs. its total length, then you'll need to make multiple _play and _pause graphics that include imagery that looks like a progress bar (such as the one I included beneath the symbols in Figure 9.38). Each _play and _pause pair should include the progress bar and must be numbered the same, with higher progression images numbered higher. The Adobe DPS viewer will then load those images in order to present the illusion of a moving progress bar. In my case, I created five progress stops for a one-minute music MP3. Therefore, when the music begins to play, AudioAsset001_pause.png is displayed to indicate a very early point in the music. Fifteen seconds into the clip the Adobe DPS viewer replaces that graphic with AudioAsset002_pause.png; 15 seconds after that it displays AudioAsset003_pause.png and then AudioAsset004_pause.png 15 seconds later, and as it nears the end of the audio, it displays the final AudioAsset005_pause.png image. Pausing the playback at any point replaces the _pause image with the _play image of the corresponding number.

FIGURE 9.38
The individual player images

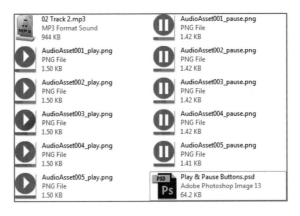

All you have to do is create the correctly named PNG images, place them together in a folder, and then, on the Folio Overlays panel, provide the path to that folder in the Controller Files field. You can either type the path or click the little folder button above the field to browse to the correct folder. Adobe DPS will then use the correctly named PNG images it finds in that folder to create the player. Note that Adobe DPS will ignore any other files in the folder that aren't properly named PNGs, so you might want to include the actual MP3 file and the Photoshop PSD (or other file type) from which you create the PNGs in that same folder.

You can include audio in your interactive magazine in the following other ways:

◆ Create a button that plays an MP3 file (see the "Adding Buttons and Actions" section of this chapter).

◆ Link to an external audio file via a hyperlink (see the "Creating Hyperlinks of All Types" section in Chapter 8, "Covering the Basics of Interactive Magazines").

◆ Include audio that is embedded within or controlled by a page on the Web (see the "Adding Live Web Content" section of this chapter).

USING THE SOUND AND VIDEO ACTIONS

From the Actions menu in the Buttons And Forms panel, the Sound action controls the playback of sounds. A compatible MP3 audio file must have already been placed onto the page somewhere before selecting this action. Then, selecting the action exposes two fields, the Sound field for selecting the sound to control and the Options field that lets you choose whether to play, pause, resume, or stop the playback of the audio.

Choosing Video as the action works the same as choosing Sound but, of course, controls the playback of video objects already placed on the page. Once Video is selected, it offers the same Options field with Play, Pause, Resume, and Stop controls, as well as two others that cannot be used with Adobe DPS: Play From Navigation Point and Stop All. Adobe DPS does not, as of this writing, support playing from navigation points embedded in videos, so ignore the Point field as well.

Including Video

Video is just as easy to incorporate in the publication as audio, but *does* include a player control strip provided by the operating system (see Figure 9.39). Note that Adobe DPS does not have the ability to add animated images like Aquafadas DPS (except 3D rotating objects, which are beyond the scope of this book); if you want animated images, you'll need to first convert them to video and then embed the video object. Let's add a video to the layout.

1. In InDesign, use File ➢ Place to locate and place a video. Feel free to use the one in this chapter's Lesson Files/Adobe DPS/Video/Links folder, which has the added benefit of helping your kids achieve good posture.

2. On the Media panel (Window ➢ Interactive ➢ Media), preview the video at the top, using the Play/Pause button to ensure it's the video you want (see Figure 9.40).

FIGURE 9.39
The controller on this video from *The Essential Guide to TRON Legacy* is automatically displayed by the device—in this case an iPad.

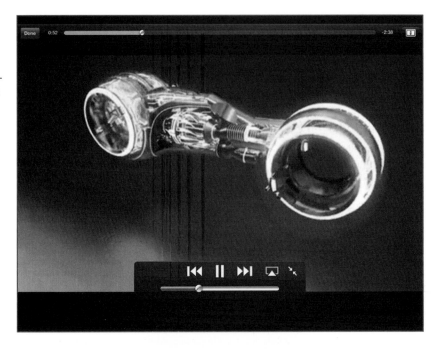

FIGURE 9.40
Working with the video on the Media panel

3. Working with video objects is one of those very rare occasions when the Folio Overlays panel correctly integrates with the rest of the InDesign user interface. If you activate the Play On Page Load option on the Media panel, it will also activate the similar Auto Play check box option of the Folio Overlays field—and vice versa. If you want your video to begin playing immediately upon the reader reaching that page, activate that option on either panel.

4. Also in the Media panel, set the Poster field as discussed in the "Inserting Audio" section previously in this chapter. Again, the poster is the visual representation of the video when it isn't playing. By default InDesign automatically creates a poster from the first slide of the video, which isn't always the best choice. You can choose Standard, which is a basic filmstrip icon, from the Poster drop-down menu. You can choose Image and then load an external, static image—preferably one with a "play" arrow icon or something that communicates to the reader that tapping on the image will initiate playback of the video. Or you can choose From Current Frame, which will take whatever frame of the video is displayed in the previewer at the top of the Media panel and create a poster from it. To change the frame that generates the poster, use the progress slider beneath the preview to reach the desired frame, and then click the refresh button to the right of the Poster field when From Current Frame is selected.

TIP   You can also include videos in Adobe DPS slideshows and galleries! See the "Creating Slideshows and Galleries" topic earlier in this chapter, and instead of importing images—or only images—throw some video files into the mix. They'll play just like images.

In Figure 9.41 you can see the poster I used. It's one I created in Photoshop from a specific frame of the video and some native Photoshop objects. By using an external image, I'm able to immediately communicate to readers that this a video rather than simply a flat graphic.

FIGURE 9.41
To help readers differentiate the video object from a static image, I created a poster image.

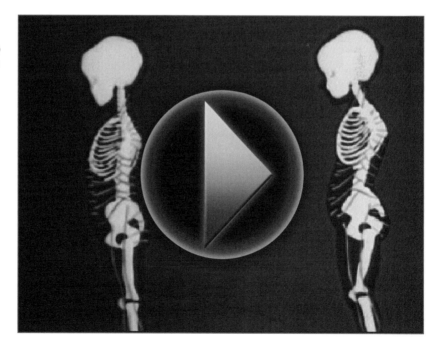

5. Switch to the Folio Overlays panel now, which should already be displaying the options for Audio & Video overlays. Just like with audio files, you have in the Video section the options to set the video to Auto Play and, if that is set, to specify a delay interval in seconds before the video automatically plays after page load (see Figure 9.42).

FIGURE 9.42
Setting the video options in the Folio Overlays panel

6. Set the other two options as desired, on or off. Play Full Screen will automatically launch the video in full-screen mode the instant it begins to play, whether via the Auto Play setting or by a reader tapping to activate playback. If this option is disabled, the video will play on the page within the space you've allotted via the multimedia frame, but it will also include a button enabling the reader to manually place the video into full-screen mode. Tap To View Controller will make the OS-created video player controller initially invisible, but will show it when the reader taps the video; with this option off, the controller is always visible.

TIP   As of this writing, only iOS supports inline video. All other devices play video only as full-screen.

CREATE A VIDEO MAGAZINE COVER

Want to really grab your audience's attention? Consider turning the cover of your publication into an autoplaying video. Doing that is simple: just place a video on the cover page of the publication and set it to Auto Play and to Play Full Screen—or use a video sized to the page dimensions and play it within the page. When the video finishes playing, you can leave the reader looking at the first or last frame or the poster, or have a pop-up, full-screen video close itself and reveal the normal cover content. If you employ this technique, just remember to account for different orientations.

Adding Animations and 3D Rotating Objects

At first blush, topics of this section's title might sound like two totally unrelated types of inter-activity. Bear with me, though; you'll soon see that, while the intent is different, they're actually both built the same way. You'll start with the 3D rotating object; even if you only want to use animation, please go through the 3D rotating objects tutorial, because the steps are the same for other types of animations.

Preparing 3D Rotating Objects

The first thing you need in order to add a 3D rotating object overlay is, of course, your 3D rotating object. Typically these objects are created in 3D drawing programs like the applications available from Autodesk (`http://autodesk.com`), which include industry standards such as the AutoCAD line of products, 3Ds Max, Maya, and pretty much every other go-to name in 3D design and rendering. Although Autodesk is the big name, and has bought up many of its competitors over the years, alternatives like SketchUp (`http://sketchup.google.com/`) from Google and Rhino 3D (`www.rhino3d.com/`) are also available. You can even create basic 3D in Photoshop Extended. And then you can capture 3D objects via photo or video cameras moving around the object in sequence.

However you get your 3D object, you or your 3D designer will need to make a video of that object rotating in all the ways you want the reader to see. For instance, if you want the reader to merely move laterally, rotating the object only horizontally (as with the book example I provided in `Lesson Files\Adobe DPS\Animation and 360 Rotate`), then film it rotating only horizontally; if you want readers to be able to rotate it vertically, film it that way. Filming is the easy part: 3D drawing and rendering programs let you rotate not the object but the *camera*, the view on the object, within a full 360-degree sphere. Those programs also let you record the camera movements to digital video. Naturally, photographs and live-action video captured with moving cameras will already be in digital video format.

That's what you need at this point, a video of the object rotating in three-dimensional space. Moreover, that video must be in a format that Photoshop can open. The list of compatible formats is much too long to include here—especially after Photoshop CS6—so I'll point you to Photoshop's documentation for that list. However, I will say that it'll open pretty much any common format 3D programs, and video-editing applications will render, including standards such as QuickTime MOV, Windows AVI, H.264 MPEG4, MP4, and M4V, 3GP, AAC, and plenty more. Once you have the video of your object rotating, it's time to make the frames.

Preparing Other Animations

If you're aren't working with 3D rotating objects but instead are using any other type of animation—everything from a cartoon character changing expressions and moving in a fixed space to text or another object traveling across the page—the preparation is a little different. First, ask yourself whether you need to use this, the Image Sequence overlay, for your animation or if it would be better as an embedded video, which has its own characteristics. If video is not the way to go, then let's look at the current state of your animation.

If it's in video format, then you must work through the "Making the Frames" section that follows this one. If your animation is already in a series of separate images, then make sure they are either JPEG or PNG image files, with or without transparency in the latter format, and that all the individual images comprising that animation are numbered sequentially and are in the same folder.

MAKING THE FRAMES

When you create the 3D rotating object, you need to do so as a movie clip, which, you may think from testing the overlay in Adobe Content Viewer, is what actually gets embedded in the interactive magazine. In a perfect world, you'd be right; in this world, Adobe DPS doesn't allow that level of interaction with video. For readers to experience the draggable 3D rotation as if it *were* video, you actually have to convert the video to a selection of static images. The Adobe DPS rendering engine then shows those images like a slideshow, *simulating* video. As a reader drags a finger across the overlay, Adobe DPS replaces one static image with another, each image being a frame from the video of the object rotating, thus giving the appearance that the reader is actually moving the object in three-dimensional space. When you interacted with my 3D rotating book, you were actually switching between the 75 different JPEG images in the `Lesson Files\Adobe DPS\Animation and 360 Rotate\Links` folder (see Figure 9.43).

FIGURE 9.43
Some of the 75 individual images comprising the frame of the 3D rotating book animation

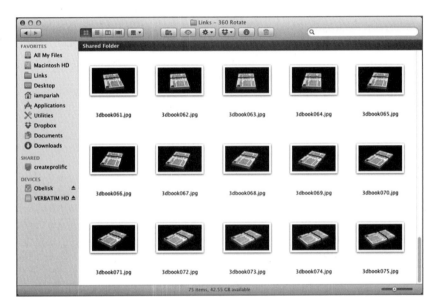

Converting the video file into those individual frame images may look daunting, but it's actually just a few clicks, relying on automation features built into Photoshop to do all the repetitive and complicated steps. Let's open Photoshop (just about any version, at least as far back as CS4) and create those images.

1. In Photoshop choose File ➤ Import ➤ Video Frames To Layers. In the Open dialog, navigate to, and open, your video file.

2. The Import Video To Layers dialog appears next (see Figure 9.44). It shows you a preview of your video, including a Play/Stop button, buttons to move to the beginning and end of the film, and a timeline to show the progress of the film as it plays. Beneath the timeline are two black arrow start and stop markers. If you want to import frames from across the entire video, leave these markers where they are—at the beginning and end. If, however, you want to import only a range of frames, say, to limit the reader's ability to rotate the

object to seeing only three sides instead of four, move the markers such that they include only the portion of the video you want to include in the interactive magazine; any frames before the left marker and after the right marker will be excluded. Moving the markers automatically switches the Range To Import option in the top-left corner of the dialog from the default From Beginning To End option to the Selected Range Only option.

FIGURE 9.44
The Import Video
To Layers dialog

3. Now set the limit of frames.

All video, whether digital or on film, is merely a series of static images played so quickly that our brains fill in the transitions between those images, creating the illusion for us of full-motion—thus the older but more accurate description of film as "motion pictures." When we're talking about movies and television shows shown on any device—movie theater screens, television screens, mobile device screens, and so on—we need to include a high number of frames displayed rapidly, measured in frames per second (FPS). That's not what I'm talking about here.

In this case, you're not working with full-motion video. What you're creating is video that will be driven by the reader's finger, not by a projector or media player. Consequently, the transitions between frames or states of the object during rotation don't need to be as smooth as they would for movies or television. You can use fewer frames and still rely on the reader's brain to fill in the transitions between them. Fewer frames means fewer separate JPEG images, which means less disk space and bandwidth required for the reader to obtain the publication.

Instead of importing every frame and then subsequently making every frame its own JPEG image, tell Photoshop to import fewer frames. You do that by activating the Limit To Every [Blank] Frames option and filling in the blank beside it. If you enter **2** in the blank, Photoshop will import only every second frame of the movie, giving you half the number of images as frames that make up the original movie.

Determining how many frames you must include is largely a matter of trial and error. Start by setting the Limit To Every [Blank] Frames field to a high number like 6 or 8, work through the rest of the tutorial, and test the overlay live on a mobile device. If you see the rotation stutter between frames, then you've chosen too high a number and need to go back through this section with a lower number in the Limit To Every [Blank] Frames field.

4. Disable the Make Frame Animation option, which is really useful only if you're turning a video into an animated GIF or PNG (like how I snuck that cool tip in there?), and then click OK. After a few moments of processing, Photoshop will create a separate layer in the Layers panel from each imported video frame (see Figure 9.45).

FIGURE 9.45
When the video import to layers has finished processing, you'll find each frame as a separate layer on the Layers panel.

5. Now is the time to do anything to the frames if you need to—things such as color correction, special effects, and what-not. Obviously, with so many layers, you'll want to automate such processing with an action file.

6. Now choose File ➤ Scripts ➤ Export Layers To Files to have Photoshop automatically generate a separate image from each of the layers in the document. Up will pop the Export Layers To Files dialog (see Figure 9.46).

FIGURE 9.46
Exporting all the frame layers to individual images via the Export Layers To Files script dialog.

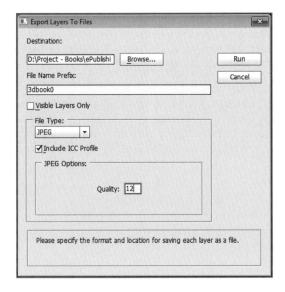

7. Set the options for output and then click Run to begin creating those individual frame images that InDesign's Folio Overlays panel requires.

Here's what those options mean in terms of the project you're currently working on:

Destination   The Destination field tells Photoshop where to save the images. To save a little time, you want to set this to be an otherwise empty folder near or under the folder containing the INDD that will house the overlay.

Filename Prefix   Adobe DPS doesn't much care what you name the images as long as they're sequentially numbered, which they will be automatically by Photoshop (sort of—see the "Filename Reversal" sidebar). Whatever you enter here as the prefix for your images, the name before the numbering, is for your reference only; Adobe DPS has no interest in it, and readers will never see the filenames.

Visible Layers Only   The Visible Layers Only check box gives you another way to limit the range of motion in the 3D rotating object. If you had noticed in the Layers panel frames that you didn't want included in the overlay, well, you probably deleted them. Alternatively, you could have simply hidden the layers, and activating this option would only export the layers that aren't hidden.

File Type   Choose JPEG or PNG-24 from the File Type list, and then set the appropriate options below the field. If you select JPEG as the export file type, then your option will be a numeric field for JPEG quality—0 to 12. If you opt for PNG-24, you'll be given three check boxes: Transparency, Interlaced, and Trim Layers. Disable all three. The first two are incompatible with the overlay, while the third will crop empty space from each layer/ image individually, resulting in the frames of your object not lining up and the whole illusion failing faster than *The Smurfs* movie did.

When Photoshop finishes the process, you'll have a folder full of images ready for use in InDesign (just like the one in Figure 9.43).

FILENAME REVERSAL

As a consequence of this process, first generating layers from the frames in a video and then exporting those layers to individual files, the resulting files are in reverse order; if the object rotated clockwise in the original video, it will now rotate counterclockwise in the overlay. For example, 3dbook_0001_Layer 75.jpg, one of the rotating book's output files, begins numbering at 1 (0001, technically) even though that same image is the last layer, which is the last frame converted to a layer, as identified by the layer name, Layer 75, in the filename. In most cases, this reversal isn't a big problem, but if it is for your publication, you can fix it in InDesign with one option or use a file-renaming utility to rename all the images into their inverse (correct) order.

Adding the Objects

Now that you've filmed your object rotating in 3D space and then converted the frames of that film into individual images, it's just a hop, skip, and a Hulk jump to finish off the effect in InDesign.

1. In InDesign, create a graphic frame sized and positioned as you want the 3D rotating object to appear in the interactive magazine.

2. Decide how you want that frame to look when the reader first reaches the page. If you want it to automatically show the first frame of the 3D rotating object animation, then leave the frame blank. If, however, you want to include a different image, maybe one that includes an icon or text instructing the reader to drag a finger across the image to explore the depicted object in three-dimensional space, then place that static image into the frame using File ➢ Place.

3. Select the frame with the black arrow Selection tool, and choose Image Sequence from the Folio Overlays panel.

4. In the Load Images field, supply the path to the folder containing the frame images, set any additional options (explained shortly), and the overlay is finished.

Here's what the other options in the panel mean. Figure 9.47 shows the panel for your reference.

FIGURE 9.47
The Image Sequence overlay options

Show First Image Initially If you want the first frame of your 3D rotating animation to appear as the poster image, activate the Show First Image Initially option. With this option disabled, you'll need to place an image into the graphic frame using good old File ➢ Place.

Auto Play Activating Auto Play will run through the image sequence, rotating the object, automatically. It will continue to rotate and may be paused or stopped by the reader, based on the options you set further down in the panel.

If you enable the Auto Play option, the suboptions Delay, Speed, Play, Loop, and Stop At Last Image will activate; enabling Tap to Play/Pause activates everything except Delay.

Delay Delay enables you to set an interval, measured in seconds, before the animation begins to automatically play.

Speed   Speed sets the number of frames shown per second (FPS), which is how fast the animation plays. The higher the FPS rate, the faster the frame images go by, which means the shorter the overall animation or the faster the object rotates, but also the less noticeable the missing frames.

Play   The Play field determines how many times through the animation should play before stopping. This field is disabled if you choose Loop beneath it.

Loop   Activating Loop plays the animation in perpetuity, starting over immediately upon ending, which is a great way to just let your object rotate or to use an animation design element with which readers won't directly interact.

Stop At Last Image   Enabling Stop At Last Image, when Loop is not enabled, will stop the animation on the last frame. The default is to return to the first frame image.

Tap To Play/Pause   Toggle the Tap To Play/Pause option to enable the reader to tap the animation to start, pause, and restart it. If you don't want the reader to control the animation—for instance, if you want an animated background or self-running design element animation—keep this option turned off and disable the Swipe To Change Image check box as well.

Swipe To Change Image   If you're producing a 3D rotatable object, you'll typically want to enable the Swipe to Change Image option. This is what enables readers to swipe or drag their fingers back and forth and seemingly rotate the object in 3D space or, in the case of standard animations, control the playback of the animation manually. If you're working with a decorative animation or just want the object to rotate without reader interaction, you can disable this option.

Stop At First And Last Image   Stop At First And Last Image is a suboption of Swipe To Change Image. If enabled, Stop At First And Last Image causes the animation to not loop when the reader swipes or drags forward to the last image or back to the first. With this option disabled, a 3D rotating object will continue to rotate smoothly, restarting the frame sequence at the first view or frame after the last, and vice versa. However, if you've limited the rotation of your object such that the animation does not rotate all the way around, or if you're working with a non-3D animation that has a distinct start and end, you'll want to disable this option.

Play In Reverse   The Play In Reverse option, if enabled, reverses the display order of the frame images. If Photoshop's export reversed the order of your frame images, activating this option will fix that problem without you having to rename all those JPEGs or PNGs.

Creating other types of animation is an identical process, except, perhaps, not allowing readers to control the animation—to have the animation play automatically. For instance, open and test (via the Preview button at the bottom of the Folio Overlays panel) the ex_animation.indd file from the Lesson Files\Adobe DPS\Animation and 360 Rotate folder. Sure, the little guy running across the bottom is rather spastic (see Figure 9.48), but he demonstrates animation in a way you can't miss. Also notice that you can't interact with him. He's an autoplaying animation, one used for decoration.

Adding animations such as that guy is even easier than including 3D rotating objects. Follow the same steps, but with these simple modifications: in the Image Sequence overlay options, enable Auto Play and Loop, and disable Tap To Play/Pause and Swipe To Change Image. If your animation will "travel," as the man runs across the page, then create *all* frames of the animation at the same size, including empty spaces. To better explain that, take a look at Figure 9.49, which is three frames/images from my animation. Notice that, although the man starts out on the right, the image encompasses the full area he'll travel, all the way across to the left edge of the page. Those areas are simply left empty, with the frame-images created as PNG-24 with transparency enabled to enable the background elements to shine through.

FIGURE 9.49
Three frames of the 17-frame animation, all of equal width

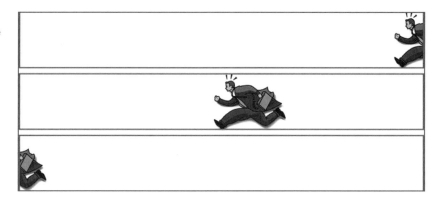

Creating 3D Panoramas and Spaces

Why limit your audience to a single shot of scenery or even a series of images when you can immerse them in the experience as if they were out there seeing it for themselves, turning around and taking in the entire 360-degree view of your subject matter? You can enable readers to explore three-dimensional interior spaces such as rooms in hotels, prison cells, cockpits, or other spaces, like Iron Man's helmet or the interior of a human heart.

Imagine placing a panoramic image inside a box. What you're actually seeing are the six interior surfaces of a cube. The viewer is placed inside this cube, looking around the inside through the portal of the graphic frame.

Creating the 3D panorama overlay means wallpapering some or all of the interior walls of that cube. You can fill them all, letting readers explore all sides, the floor, and the ceiling of the cube, or you can limit which surfaces they get to see. For each surface you will need one image numbered to match the surface on which it's to be displayed. The filenames don't matter beyond the fact that they must all match and be suffixed by an underscore and a number, 1 to 6. Adobe DPS will then stitch them together to create a seamless interior to the box. Even if you don't want to let people see every surface, you must include images for them, sized to match the other images, even if they're simply blank pictures.

TIP Shooting panoramic photos can be accomplished using a variety of techniques. Consult photographer resources—user groups, forums, camera stores, and so forth—for the details and pros and cons of each.

Once you have your panorama photo stitched and separated into the six panel images, creating the overlay is very easy.

1. Create and position a graphic frame to hold the panoramic overlay's poster. Once activated, the panorama overlay will launch full-screen.

2. Select the frame with the black arrow, and choose the Panorama overlay in the Folio Overlays panel, which will present you with all the options in Figure 9.50.

FIGURE 9.50
Options for the Panorama overlay in the Folio Overlays panel

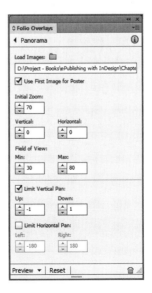

3. In the Load Images field, enter the path to the folder containing only the six panel images.

4. Set the poster image for the overlay, which is the image readers will see before interacting with the panorama, either by checking the option Use First Image For Poster or by placing another image into the graphic frame with File ➤ Place. I recommend the latter method because that allows you to create a special image communicating that the object is a panoramic overlay and what action you expect the reader to take—such as tapping and dragging a finger across the image—in order to interact with the overlay.

5. Set the remaining relevant options—defined next—and finalize the overlay.

The options for the panorama overlay let you define zoom level but, more important, allow you to limit the area of the panorama readers can see. Limiting is important if your image isn't a full 360-degree spherical panorama; for instance, if it doesn't have a ceiling and floor, you want to limit it so readers can't rotate their view up or down. The options, and how to use them, are as follows:

Initial Zoom As the name implies, the Initial Zoom control sets the percentage of zoom on the initial view on the image within the range of 30 to 80 degrees.

Vertical and Horizontal These are offsets. The first image readers see in the panoramic cube is image 1, the shot straight in front of the camera. What if you want them to see the right wall first, image 2? In that case, you'd want to set a horizontal offset to rotate the camera away from the front, from the 0 point, 90 degrees, to display image 2 first.

Each image represents 90 degrees out of the full 360, so offsetting the initial view from one image to the next is a simple matter of using positive or negative multiples of 90 degrees—270, 180, 90, 0, –90, –180, and –270. But that's only if you want to move the view by whole sides; you can partially rotate the view to any whole degree value. If you want the initial view to be half of image 1 and half of image 2, thus centering their join, use a value of only 45 in the Horizontal field.

The Vertical field works the same way, but instead of turning the camera laterally, positive and negative values in the Vertical field rotate the camera vertically. If you want the ceiling or floor—or parts of them—to be in the initial view, set a value other than 0 in the Vertical offset field.

Limit Vertical Pan If your panorama doesn't contain ceiling and floor images—or those images aren't very interesting, like maybe just blue sky and gravel, respectively—you might choose to focus the point of the panorama by limiting the reader's ability to pan vertically. Activating the Limit Vertical Pan option and then setting degree measurements in the Up and Down fields will accomplish that. To remove the ceiling and floor entirely, limiting the reader to rotating laterally, set the Up field to –90 degrees and the Down field to 90. You can also make those values less than 90 (or more than –90) to allow some vertical panning.

Limit Horizontal Pan The Limit Horizontal Pan field functions the same way as its vertical counterpart. It is useful when the lateral view of the space isn't a full 360 degrees around, such as might be the case when photographing only two or three walls or angles in the panorama. Limiting the horizontal pan hides nonexistent or undesirable portions of the photograph (for instance, where the photographer was standing) by trimming degrees off the left (from image 4 in toward image 1) and/or the right (from image 3 in toward image 1).

Using Content Replacement

Using multistate objects and trigger images as you did in the "Creating Slideshows and Galleries" section is the basis of Adobe DPS's content-replacement technique. If you haven't yet worked through creating galleries using Adobe DPS, please do so now and then come back here.

Same-Space Content Replacement

Done with creating your first gallery? Good, because content replacement is entirely the same workflow. When you build your variable content as multistate objects, with each state being the content (one or more objects) you want to show at a given time, each trigger will show a particular state in that multistate object. Those triggers can be all in the same place, like a list of items to tap on the sidebar, or they can be spread out across the artwork or page. They can even be contained within a scrolling frame.

Take the companion images in Figure 9.51, which are from the functional example `ex_animal_alphabet.indd` in the `Lesson Files\Adobe DPS\Content Replacement` folder. Very much like the T-shirt product gallery you created earlier in the chapter, this one uses images converted to buttons to trigger the display of different states of a multistate object that reveals the antelope when A is tapped, the beaver when B is tapped, and so on.

FIGURE 9.51
Using letters for trigger buttons and grouping multiple text and graphic frames as different states of a multistate object

Tapping A shows the "A" state of the object… …and tapping B shows the "B" state.

Relative-Location Content Replacement

Moving on to the next logical step, look at Figure 9.52, which is demonstrative of any kind of map, diagram, or detailed illustration or photograph on which a lot of information needs to be presented. In this case, it's a section of a bicycling route map with various geographic features called out with icons, features such as sights, shopping areas, information kiosks and agencies, boat excursion launches, and so on. Tapping each marker icon reveals a pop-up with additional information about, and a photograph from, that marker's location.

The details about the locations are all created, grouped, and then converted to a multistate object; each location's group of objects is a single state. Note that the different states of the object don't have to be aligned. The information balloons can be positioned near the areas of the map they describe rather than always in the same place on the page. They can even be placed to cover other buttons.

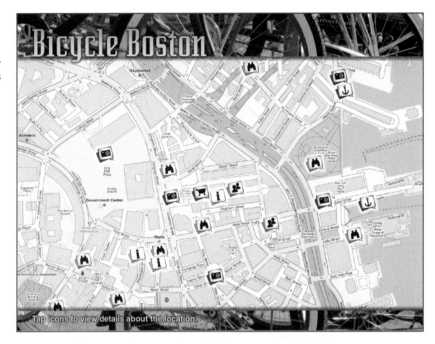

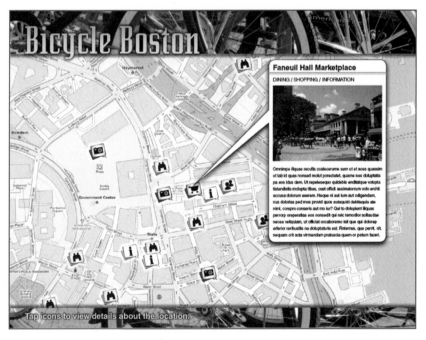

Let's go through how to create relative-location content replacement. You can either build your own document as you go or start with ex_bicycle_map.indd, which already has two completed buttons and pop-ups and the hide-all button I'll talk about in a few moments.

1. Begin your document with the map, diagram, or other image in place on the page. I recommend putting this and any other static elements on a layer by themselves and locking that layer to prevent accidental repositioning. Create all interactivity on subsequent layers.

2. Identify the first area that will trigger the display of variable content. In this area, create or place an image, vector path, or frame (text, graphic, or unassigned) to serve as the button.

3. Repeat step 2 until you've created all the buttons you'll need. (You can add and remove buttons later, but it's more efficient in the long run if you build as many as you can now.)

4. Set your buttons aside—again, it's often easiest to put these to-be-button objects on a layer by themselves and then lock or hide that layer.

5. On a new layer, create or place the content that will be shown by the first button. This content can be a single placed image, a single text frame, a single vector path or shape drawn in InDesign, or any number and combination thereof.

6. Once you've finished creating the first variable-content instance, group all the objects so that they all become one state when converted to a multistate object.

7. Create all the other variable-content elements, remembering to group each. Note that they don't have to align or be anywhere near each other; each set of content can be anywhere on the page, touching or overlapping other content or completely separate from other content.

8. Select all the variable content elements with the black arrow Selection tool, and on the Object States panel, click the sticky note–esque Convert Selection To Multi-State Object button. All but one set of variable content will disappear from the document view because all the content will have become states of one object.

9. Return to the buttons art you created earlier, locking or hiding the multistate content object if necessary. One at a time, convert each button art object (or group of objects) into an actual button with a Go To State action that displays the correct state of the multistate content object.

At this point, if you export a preview using the Preview button at the bottom of the Folio Overlays panel, you should have a series of buttons that trigger the display of different sets of variable content. Whatever the first state of the object, as determined by the order in the Object States panel, it will appear immediately upon the page loading. Each button you click or tap thereafter will show the correct content and hide the previous content because the multistate object can display only a single state at a time.

That's all well and good if you always want one state showing. It's a problem, though, if you want to initially display just the map (and so on), without any variable content visible, and if you want to enable readers to hide the pop-up content so that it doesn't obscure the map. Take the Bicycle Boston map, for instance. Its pop-ups are quite large and obscure large portions of the map. If a reader is reading about the New England Aquarium, he can't access the button to show the pop-up about Faneuil Hall Marketplace, which is a problem...unless you plan for that. How can you make it so that none of the content pop-ups are visible, so that readers can return to a view of the entire map or diagram or whatever? There's a trick.

1. Back in InDesign, select the multistate content object.

2. At the bottom of the Object States panel, click the Create New State button. It's the same button that converts single-state objects to multistate objects. It will create a new state of the object by duplicating whatever state was already selected in the panel.

3. Using the black and white arrow tools, the Selection and Direct Selection tools, remove almost all objects from this selected state. You want to leave a single empty frame with no fill and no stroke. You also want to resize and move that frame so it's not in your way if you want to work on other objects in the document.

4. In the Object States panel, double-click the name of the state and rename it to NONE SHOWING or something else that communicates that it contains no visible content. Then drag the state upward so it's the first listed state. That will make it appear—or disappear, if you will—when the page is first loaded. Figure 9.53 shows the Object States panel for the variable content in the Bicycle Boston layout.

FIGURE 9.53
After adding, editing, and renaming the state that shows no variable content

5. Grab the Rectangle tool, and on the layer containing the buttons, create a rectangle that fills the page from edge to edge both horizontally and vertically.

6. Set both the fill and stroke on this frame to None.

7. Convert the now-empty frame to a button and assign it the Go To State action such that it activates the empty or invisible state of the variable content multistate object.

8. Use the Object ➤ Arrange commands or shortcuts to move this new full-page button behind all the other buttons that trigger state changes.

Now, when a reader taps *anywhere* outside the pop-up content, the content will change or disappear. If the reader taps another button, its corresponding variable content will appear; if the reader taps an empty area, the variable pop-up will simply disappear because that "empty area" is actually covered by a button that activates the empty state. Give it a try by exporting a preview from `ex_bicycle_map.indd`.

ASPIRIN-FREE WORKFLOW: MAKING BUTTONS FROM EXISTING IMAGE FEATURES

Although adding button graphics (the icons) works in the Boston bicycle route map to call out specific features, adding graphics or separate button objects would not be ideal when you want readers to click directly on features of a photo, map, diagram, or what-have-you. For example, in the case of a building or house floor plan, you might want readers to click directly on a feature or area already part of the map, such as the area inside a room. Obviously, if the map (or whatever) is a solid image, you can't make just parts of buttons that trigger state changes of a multistate object. But you can make it *act* like parts of the image are actually buttons.

The trick is to draw empty paths atop the map in the shape of the areas that have variable visibility content. Draw rectangles with both fills and strokes set to None. Then turn each of those empty paths into buttons, each one with an action to show the corresponding state of the multistate object containing the information balloons or whatever information you need to display. While it would be *very* nice to have nonrectangular paths covering nonrectangular areas, Adobe DPS understands only rectangular MSOs. Readers will experience a background image that behaves like multiple buttons; you'll have a background image with individually selectable button objects.

Multiple Object Visibility Toggle

Now in elearning or magazine-style self-tests, you can create a content-replacement effect that is even easier than the other examples I've gone through. In this case, revealing all the correct answers on a page involves a simple two-state multistate object and one trigger, a button that toggles the display of those two states.

1. Begin with a self-test type document, or, if you haven't one on hand, you can start with just a new blank document or with `ex_self_test.indd` in the Lesson Files\Adobe DPS\Content Replacement folder.

2. Create your correct answers if your self-test will provide answers like `ex_self_test .indd`; or, if you'll be creating a multiple-choice exam, create an icon or symbol to indicate the correct answers to the questions (see Figure 9.54). This icon or symbol will be displayed beside or on top of each correct answer. If you make it out of multiple objects, remember to group them together. Duplicate the correct-answer indicator as many times as needed, and position those indicators where they belong.

3. Select all the answers and/or indicators, and group them. Although you could do this without grouping, it's usually easier to work with them as a group.

4. Choose Window ➢ Interactivity ➢ Object States and then convert the selected group of answers or indicators into a multistate object. You should wind up with two states in the object, both containing all answers or indicators (see Figure 9.55).

FIGURE 9.54
A self-test exam
with answers (a) and
a multiple-choice
exam with answer
indicators (b)

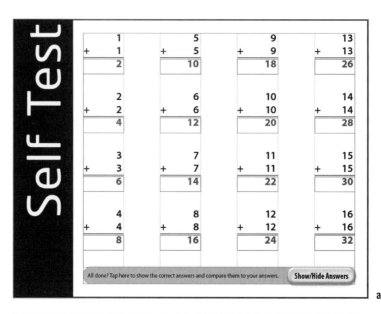

a

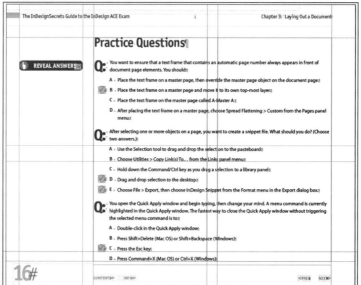

b

5. Double-click the name of the first state and rename it Hidden; similarly, rename the second state Shown.

6. Click the Hidden state to show the objects in that state. You need to make these disappear, but you can't just delete them because a state must have some content.

FIGURE 9.55
After initially converting the group of answers or indicators to a multistate object, the object will have two identical states.

If your indicators are very simple, you can leave them as they are but set their fills and strokes to None. If that's not an option, try using the white arrow Direct Selection tool to selectively delete all but one indicator and as many components of that indicator as possible; you must leave one object of some type, which is ideally something whose fill and stroke you can set to None. If you have text-frame answers, leave one frame there but empty of text.

If even this is not an option, do this instead:

1. Setting aside the multistate object for the time being, create a simple rectangle with no fill and no stroke.

2. Select the rectangle with the black arrow and cut it with Ctrl+X/Cmd+X.

3. In the Object States panel, select the Hidden layer.

4. Also on that panel, choose Paste Into State from the panel flyout menu. Your empty rectangle should now appear within the Hidden state.

5. Delete all other objects from the Hidden state, leaving only your empty rectangle.

7. Create your state-changing trigger. This can be a single object or a group of objects, a placed image, a vector object, a text frame, or a combination thereof. This is what readers will tap in order to show *and* hide the correct answer indicators, so keep in mind it must serve both the purposes of showing the answers and of hiding them again. You might want to label it something like Show/Hide Answers.

8. Choose Window ➤ Interactivity ➤ Buttons And Forms (just Buttons in CS5.5 and earlier) and then convert the trigger into a button. Name the button in the panel just to reduce any confusion with other buttons.

9. Click the plus sign Actions menu, and choose Go To Next State—ignore the erroneous notice that that action works only with PDFs.

10. Beneath the Actions list, ensure that the Object menu correctly lists the name of your correct-answers indicator multistate object and that the option Stop At Last State is disabled.

Figure 9.56 shows my Show/Hide Answers button and the Buttons And Forms panel options for it.

FIGURE 9.56

A Show/Hide Answers button and the settings to toggle visibility of the answers or indicators from it

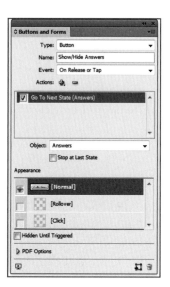

11. Before previewing the folio, make sure you can't currently see the correct answers or indicators. If you can, select the multistate object and click the Hidden state of the object in the Object States panel.

When you do preview the folio, you'll see that tapping the trigger once shows the answers and tapping it a second time hides them again. It works because the multistate object is a simple two-state object, one with all the answers hidden and one with all of them shown. Thus, by telling the button to go to the next state, it simply toggles between Shown and Hidden.

THE SKY IS THE LIMIT

A somewhat more ambitious content replacement would be to change the entire page. This can be very practical, such as asking readers to choose their genders and ages from a set of buttons and then having those buttons change visual elements and the content of the page to a version created specifically for that age group. For example, a catalog selling posters might display *Twilight* star images for female readers who report their ages among preteens while female older readers are treated to shirtless Captain America and Thor.

Whatever your goal, the content replacement can be done the same way as everything else: create the variable content as states of a multistate object accessed via buttons carrying the Go To State, Go To Next State, or Go To Previous State actions.

Adding Live Web Content

Adding live web content to an Adobe DPS layout is no more involved than adding a video overlay. Take Figure 9.57, for example. That's a digital magazine page containing imagery and text and, on the right, the live feed of my Twitter timeline. You can try it for yourself by opening `ex_twitter.indd` from the `Lesson Files\Adobe DPS\Web Content` folder and using the Preview button at the bottom of the Folio Overlays panel to generate a preview for the Adobe Content Viewer. You can then interact with my Twitter feed and your own Twitter account, including signing up for an account if you don't already have one. Just make sure you're online when you try to view the preview.

FIGURE 9.57
Integrating live web content like my Twitter feed, shown on the right, makes updating readers instantaneous and eliminates the need to resubmit to app stores.

1. Create, position, and size a graphic frame. This frame will be the container that holds the live content pulled from the Web. It can be filled and stroked, given a drop shadow and transparency, or left empty and plain. It can look however you want it to, though its interior will be styled by your web content.

2. Select the frame with the black arrow Selection tool, and in the Folio Overlays panel, choose Web Content.

3. In the URL or File field, enter the full address to the web content you want to incorporate, including a prefix like `http://` (see Figure 9.58). Any online resource can be listed here, even content on secure servers; if your website asks visitors to log in to reach that address, the interactive magazine will also.

FIGURE 9.58
The Web Content
overlay options

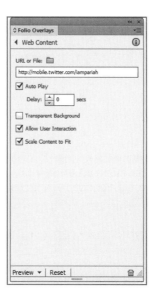

4. Activate Auto Play to enable the device to automatically connect to the Web and begin loading the linked content when the reader reaches the page. Disable this, or add a delay, to have the web content not immediately begin loading.

5. Set the remaining options (discussed next) and preview your publication. When you preview it, you'll see that the web content becomes part of the interactive-magazine page; it's a chrome-less web browser embedded inside the page.

USING THE GO TO URL OPTION

With the Go To URL action, which works just like text hyperlinks (see "Creating Hyperlinks of All Types" in Chapter 8), you can specify any online resource, using any standard Internet protocol, such as `http://domain.com`, `https://domain.com`, `ftp://domain.com/file.ext`, and `mailto:me@iampariah.com`. You can also assign specialized URLs such as those to send text messages, dial the phone, or open App Store or Google Play app store pages for other apps.

There are three options I haven't yet covered.

Transparent Background By default, web content has an opaque background. Enabling the Transparent Background option will allow the background of the folio page to shine through any web content, assuming the web-based content is set to have a transparent background via CSS or another method.

Allow User Interaction In most cases, you'll want to enable the Allow User Interaction option that allows users to touch, scroll, and otherwise interact with the web-based content. If, however, you're using the web-based content merely as decoration—say, serving up the latest imagery or prices—turning off that option makes the web-based behavior like any static element on the page.

Scale Content To Fit   Web pages may or may not match the size of the magazine page or the frame through which the web content is shown. Activating the Scale To Fit option will automatically scale that web content uniformly to fit within the width of the frame. Disabling this option on content that is wider than the frame will make it scrollable if Allow User Interaction is also enabled; if Allow User Interaction is disabled, the content will be cropped by the frame.

TIP   To help readers understand that they can't access your content when they're not connected to the Web, place an informative image into (or text behind) the frame holding the web content overlay or enrichment. Your readers will thank you for it.

Including Offline HTML

The ability to include HTML in, or *as*, pages in your interactive magazine lets you do just about anything Adobe DPS's overlays can't natively do, without the need to require readers to have a live Internet connection. These HTML pages can be HTML version 3 or 4 or HTML5 and may include scripting, such as JavaScript.

Adding In-Page HTML Content

The process of adding local web technology content onto the page is identical to the way you add live web content, but instead of putting a URL into the URL or File field in the Web Content overlay option of the Folio Overlays panel, put in the path to an HTML file on your local computer or network. Adobe DPS will then incorporate that content into the graphic frame as if it were live web content, but without the requirement for the reader to be online. You'll have all the same options, too—Auto Play, Transparent Background, Allow User Interaction, and Scale Content To Fit. Adobe DPS will also include any assets or external files referenced by the HTML, such as image files, one or more CSS style sheets, external JavaScript files, and so on, as long as they're located in the same folder as the HTML file or in a subfolder thereof, and as long as any references to those files is relative (e.g., `images/picture.png`) rather than absolute (e.g., `MacDrive :Documents:Folder:Subfolder:images:picture.png`). The included HTML (and whatever other web technologies are incorporated thereby) can be part of the page or the whole page, depending on the size of the graphic frame you create to house it. However, if you're going to use HTML as full pages, there's a more efficient way.

Using HTML as Pages

As amazing as Adobe DPS's overlays are, you can do far more with HTML. In fact, you can build any given page or range of pages—heck, your entire interactive magazine if you want—directly *as* HTML files without ever touching the Folio Overlays panel.

1. Create your HTML and related content in an HTML editor like Dreamweaver.

2. Save your HTML into a folder structure that looks like Figure 9.59, with each article having its own folder containing an HTML file for each layout that will be in that article

and all the assets required by the HTML file(s) contained within subfolders of the article folder. Specifying the _h and _v locks in an orientation, but to create a single HTML file that reflows and adapts to the device orientation, leave off both suffixes.

FIGURE 9.59
Organize your
HTML pages and
assets into this
folder structure so
that Adobe DPS will
understand them
during import.

3. Zip all the article folders and their contents into an archive named HTMLResources.zip. Note that this is case-sensitive.

4. In InDesign, open the Folio Builder panel, and create or select the folio into which the HTML files will be incorporated.

5. From the flyout menu in the Folio Builder panel, select Import HTML Resource, which will open a pop-up dialog explaining how the file must be named, which I covered in step 3. Click the Browse button.

6. Browse to the location of your HTMLResources.zip archive in the Select HTML Resource dialog. Select that archive, click Open, and wait while Adobe DPS imports the contents, creates the articles and layouts, and synchronizes with the Adobe DPS server.

Your HTML content is now part of the publication. You won't be able to see the content in InDesign as you would a layout created in InDesign, but you can see and reorder the HTML-based articles on the Folio Builder panel. And you can preview those articles using the desktop Adobe Content Viewer by clicking the Preview link at the bottom of the Folio Builder panel.

Applying the Finishing Touches

In this section, you'll give your publications those final touches that can make the difference between mediocrity and greatness. As readers grow more accustomed to using interactive magazine–format publications, they will use the built-in nonlinear navigation systems more and more. Thus, most of the finishing touches you need to focus on include presenting articles well in these navigation systems, identifying the contents of those articles when all that can be seen is a short blurb and a thumbnail image, and ensuring that noneditorial content stays out of the navigation systems.

Supplying Article Details

After carefully designing each article, you need to supply a few additional details to present the article accurately and well in various navigation systems, such as tables of contents and scrubbers.

Each article in a folio has a number of details that can (and, unless the article is an advertisement, *should*) be set. Fortunately, all these details are in a single dialog. Select an article within a folio, and from the Folio Builder panel flyout menu, choose Properties. Up will pop the Article Properties dialog (see Figure 9.60). The details you supply in this dialog control the appearance of the article in the publication's table of contents, content scrubber, and other areas.

FIGURE 9.60
Filling in article details in the Article Properties dialog

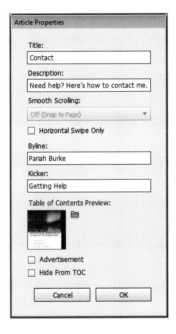

Each of the constituent images in Figure 9.61 presents the same article in different areas of a publication—in the table of contents, in the thumbnail scrubber, and in the scrollbar previews—and correlates each displayed feature with the Article Properties field that controls the feature.

Title The Title field is fairly self-explanatory—it's the title of the article as you want it to appear in all contents and navigational systems.

Description Often overlooked by publishers is the Description field. Leaving it blank means, in some areas, relying entirely on the title of the article to catch readers' attention. That's usually a foolish mistake. Take advantage of this field! You can populate it with the article's dek, a hook paragraph, or just a basic description that tells readers more about the content than the title might.

FIGURE 9.61
Examining the various places article details are displayed in the viewer app

In the table of contents

In the thumbnail scrubber

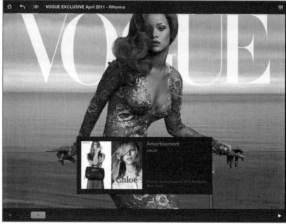

In the scrollbar previews

SCREEN CAPTURES FROM VOGUE EXCLUSIVE, APRIL 2011

Smooth Scrolling   When a reader moves between screens in a longer layout or when he moves around a zoomed-in view of a layout, the behavior of the window (the way the content scrolls) can occur smoothly or a page/view at a time. The difference is the same as changing Acrobat or Adobe Reader from Single Page view to Scrolling View—the former "jumps" between pages, while the latter enables parts of page 1 and page 2 to be viewed simultaneously. Within folios, turning Smooth Scrolling on enables the reader to move smoothly between screens, seeing parts of the first and second screens concurrently, while turning Smooth Scrolling off jumps from one screen to the next, always showing a full-screen (or page). You can also choose to enable Smooth Scrolling only for horizontal or vertical movement, which is useful when zoomed in.

Horizontal Swipe Only   Like the Smooth Scrolling field, I already touched on Horizontal Swipe Only during the construction of the digital publication earlier in this chapter. To review, however, activating the Horizontal Swipe Only option makes subsequent screens of a multiscreen article appear horizontally rather than vertically. Thus, readers don't swipe *down* to continue reading the same article; they swipe to the *right*, just like moving between different articles.

Byline   The Byline field, which identifies the author or authors of the article, is optional because noneditorial content doesn't often have bylines or authors credited within the piece itself.

Kicker   Another common feature of editorial content is the kicker, which is a short phrase that precedes the title of the article. Kickers can be used as hooks or to further explain titles, and they can be used to present a section or classification of the content. For example, in a digital newspaper, an "Op-Ed" or "Opinion" kicker would be used to classify the article as an editorial opinion rather than a news article. (This distinction used to be more important when the average news agency actually reported fair and balanced arguments and counterarguments to news items instead of skewing the average story into the agency's or its corporate sponsor's opinion.) Kickers are optional, but I highly recommend using them when relevant because of the additional information they provide the reader in all the places reflected in Figure 9.61 (the medium gray text such as "Cover Story," "Audio Exclusive," and "Fashion").

Table Of Contents Preview (Thumbnail)   The Table of Contents Preview section is a misnomer: it's a preview of the article thumbnail, not a preview of the complete TOC entry, which would include the title, kicker, and so on. You can stick with the default thumbnail Adobe DPS automatically generates as an image of the full article or supply a custom thumbnail you've created (see the sidebar "Creating Article Thumbnails" for the whys and hows). Assuming you've already created your thumbnail graphic, click the tiny folder icon to the right of the preview. This will let you browse to and select the thumbnail graphic to represent the article.

Advertisement   In an editorial publication, advertisements should never be included in the main navigation systems. It's common, of course, to include an index of advertisers at the back of a periodical, but it's never OK to include them among the article navigation methods. By checking the Advertisement box, you will communicate to Adobe DPS that the selected article is an advertisement and should therefore be excluded from the TOC, the thumbnail scrubber, and so on. Advertisements will also be tracked separately from editorial in the Adobe DPS analytics system.

Hide From TOC   Similar to the Advertisement option, Hide From TOC will keep the selected article out of the table of contents. It will, however, include the article in the thumbnail scrubber and as editorial content in the Adobe DPS analytics system.

CREATING ARTICLE THUMBNAILS

By default, Adobe DPS creates a thumbnail from the entire article or from the first screen of a multiscreen article. Sometimes that's what you want, and you don't need to change anything. But often you can represent an article better with a cropped or custom thumbnail. Save your thumbnail images in PNG format (144×144 pixels for the iPad 3's Retina display and 70×70 pixels for renditions targeted to the iPad 1 and 2, Kindle Fire, and all other tablets) and use the Article Properties dialog or sidecar.xml file to associate them to individual articles.

Adding a Sidecar

There are so many sections in this chapter where discussion of sidecar.xml is relevant, but I kept it for here so that it would make the most sense after reading about adding articles and editing article details in other ways. In brief, sidecar.xml is an optional file you can include within your folio to accomplish any or all of the following:

◆ Import one or many articles into the folio

◆ Change the order of articles in the folio, which is something you can do only via sidecar.xml or newer, in the Adobe DPS dashboard's Folio Producer: Organizer (discussed shortly)

◆ Add or replace article metadata

◆ Add or replace TOC preview images to articles

The sidecar.xml file follows a simple XML tagging structure based on the following example, which you can use as a template.

```
<?xml version="1.0" encoding="UTF-8" standalone="yes"?>
<sidecar>
  <entry>
    <folderName>Article 1</folderName>
    <articleTitle>title</articleTitle>
    <byline>byline</byline>
    <author>author</author>
    <kicker>kicker</kicker>
    <description>description</description>
    <tags>tag1, tag2</tags>
    <isAd>false</isAd>
    <hideFromTOC>true</hideFromTOC>
    <smoothScrolling>never</smoothScrolling>
    <isFlattenedStack>false</isFlattenedStack>
  </entry>
  <entry>
    <folderName>Article 2</folderName>
    <articleTitle>title</articleTitle>
    <byline>byline</byline>
    <author>author</author>
    <kicker>kicker</kicker>
```

```
            <description>description</description>
            <tags>tag1, tag2</tags>
            <isAd>false</isAd>
            <hideFromTOC>true</hideFromTOC>
            <smoothScrolling>never</smoothScrolling>
            <isFlattenedStack>false</isFlattenedStack>
        </entry>
    </sidecar>
```

As you can see, most of the tags are self-explanatory now that you've worked with article metadata. There are a couple of details I should point out, though. Between the `<tags></tags>` tag pair, enter comma-separated keywords. The `<isFlattenedStack></isFlattenedStack>` pair is Boolean, accepting either `true` or `false`. A value of `true` activates Horizontal Swipe Only for the article. Acceptable values for `<smoothScrolling></smoothScrolling>`, which activate and set the type for smooth scrolling instead of paged scrolling, are `always` (smooth scrolling always, both orientations), `portrait` (smooth scrolling only in portrait oriented layouts), `landscape` (smooth scrolling only in landscape orientation), and `never` (smooth scrolling is off, using page-at-a-time scrolling).

Build the entries in your `sidecar.xml` file in the order in which you want articles to appear in the final publication and table of contents. This is one of the big advantages of using `sidecar.xml`, because articles appear in the Folio Builder panel—and thus in the folio itself—according to their order of creation and cannot be reordered except by using a `sidecar.xml` file or in the online Folio Editor: Organizer, which is not an ideal interface for doing a lot of article re-ordering.

The main thing about the `sidecar.xml` file is to know how articles and layouts imported or controlled by it must be organized on disk. As you may have inferred from the example, the value between the `<folderName></folderName>` tag pair is the name of the folder in which the article layouts reside. This imports those layouts into the article by reference. Because the import must follow the rules of Adobe DPS, specifically that each article must have the same size and orientation layout(s) and the same number of layouts, you must organize your files into the folder structure reflected by `sidecar.xml`. This holds true even if you aren't importing new articles but are merely changing the order or metadata of existing articles.

Each article must be in its own folder named identically to the value in `<folderName></folderName>`. Note that the folder name isn't the published title name; you specify the published title name in `<articleTitle></articleTitle>`. Therefore, feel free to use shorthand or abbreviations in folder names, but do not use special characters. Within each article's folder must be one or two INDD documents in the dimensions of the rest of the publication. If you're using single-orientation layouts, you'll have just one INDD; dual-orientation publications will require two layouts—one in landscape and one in portrait—both matching the dimensions of all the other landscape and portrait layouts in the publication. Whether you're using one or two layouts per article, modify their filenames to include the suffixes _h and _v for landscape and portrait, respectively. Also, don't use special characters in INDD filenames—stick with letters, numbers, and underscores for safety. Any assets used by the INDD layouts should be within a Links folder inside the article folder.

Figure 9.62 shows a properly structured set of articles for inclusion via `sidecar.xml`. It also shows several PNG images. These are the TOC preview images for the articles, which will be incorporated merely because of their presence in the folder of articles added or updated by `sidecar.xml`; you won't need to manually add those images to the Article Properties dialog. If you don't include a TOC image, Adobe DPS will fall back on its default behavior of automatically generating one from the layout itself.

FIGURE 9.62

Layouts, assets, and TOC images properly organized for control by the sidecar.xml file

The sidecar.xml file itself needs to go in the root folder of the folio, the same folder that contains all the article subfolders. At any time you can update the sidecar.xml—and any of the articles and TOC images it references—and reimport it via the Import command on the Folio Builder panel's flyout menu to effect changes to article ordering, metadata, and TOC imagery or to add new articles to the folio.

TIP   If you create the sidecar.xml file after creating the folio, which is perfectly acceptable, you would put the sidecar.xml file in its own folder, use the Import Multiple Articles command, and browse to the folder with the sidecar file.

Defining Folio Options

Even more important than the information you supply for individual articles are a few pieces of data needed for the overall publication or issue. These are crucial because they will be the first—and possibly only—parts of your publication would-be readers will see. If you choose Folio Properties from the flyout menu on the Folio Builder panel, you'll see Figure 9.63, which is (almost) all the information that will be presented about your publication in readers' copies of your issue library, the Apple Newsstand, the Kindle Fire Newsstand, the Google Play store, and anywhere else readers will be able to find your publication. I say "almost" in the preceding statement because there are some additional options you can set, and other information you can provide, within the server-side Adobe DPS control panel, which I'll discuss just a bit later.

For now, let's go through the options available in the Folio Properties dialog.

Publication Name   At the risk of being labeled Captain Obvious, the Publication Name field is where you provide the publication title as you want it displayed to readers. What may not be obvious is that you should *not* include a volume or issue number or date in this field. If you're publishing a periodical, you'll supply issue-identifiers such as volume number, issue number, or issue date in the online control panel, not in the Folio Properties. Here, just put the actual title of the publication. If it's a periodical or other serialized publication, enter the title of the series.

Right Edge Binding   English and many other languages are read left to right; that's not true of all languages, however. Japanese, Hebrew, Farsi, and other languages read right to left, and books published in those languages are read right to left, meaning they have a right-edge binding instead of the left-edge binding used by English, French, Spanish, and so on. Activating the Right Edge Binding option on the folio simulates the correct page ordering for right-to-left printed languages, enabling readers to progress through a publication by swiping left to right rather than the default of right to left.

Viewer Version   Choose from the Viewer Version drop-down the version of the Content Viewer with which your publication should be compatible. For the reasons as to why this is important, see the sidebar "Aspirin-Free Workflow: Folio Versioning." Leaving the field at its default value of Unspecified automatically sets the folio to compatibility with the latest version of the viewer.

FIGURE 9.63
Setting Folio
Properties

ASPIRIN-FREE WORKFLOW: FOLIO VERSIONING

Frustratingly, often Adobe creates the situation wherein the version of the Folio Producer Tools (Folio Builder panel, Folio Overlays panel, the desktop Content Viewer, and so on) is incompatible with the version of the Content Viewer available on iOS. That means publications created with the latest version of the Folio Producer Tools can't always be viewed on the iPad, iPhone, and iPod Touch. Folio Producer Tools upgrades are mandatory, as witnessed by the Folio Builder panel disallowing you from accessing your folios until you've upgraded to the latest version. The problem stems from the fact that Adobe releases updates to the Folio Producer Tools and the viewers on all platforms simultaneously, but because Apple tests and reviews every app and update to every app before that app can be added to the App Store, there's always a delay between the iOS Content Viewer becoming available and all the other components being available. Sometimes—and not as rarely as you'd think—it's a long delay because Apple rejects the Content Viewer update, requiring Adobe to recode something about it and resubmit it for evaluation. This delay can sometimes last weeks. All the while, publications created with the latest tools, in the latest format, are unusable on iOS except when fully published as custom apps.

Save yourself a terrible amount of frustration during such times by using the Viewer Version control in the Folio Properties dialog to set the version of your folios back to the previous version, the version of the Content Viewer that already passed Apple scrutiny and is available on iOS. You may lose the latest, greatest features and bug fixes, but at least you'll be able to preview your publications and demo and proof them to your clients and staff.

Cover Preview Every interactive magazine–format publication is required to include cover thumbnail images in both orientations. The sidebar "Creating Cover Thumbnails" explains the proper dimensions and format. Click the folder icons in the Folio Properties dialog to navigate to and select the portrait and landscape cover images.

Once you've logged into your Digital Publishing Suite online dashboard (see Figure 9.64), you can access the Folio Producer: Organizer to set all of the same options from the Folio Properties dialog and more (see Figure 9.65). Click a folio to select it and be able to edit the options for that folio on the right and inline on the left. All fields marked with an asterisk (*) are required. I won't explain the ones I covered already, but I do want to discuss the ones absent from the Folio Properties dialog as well as a few differences in the behavior of the same fields between that dialog and this online interface.

CREATING COVER THUMBNAILS

Every interactive magazine–format publication is required to include both portrait- and landscape-orientation thumbnails of the publication's cover. These will be used in newsstands, in app stores, in viewer libraries, and on the desktop or home screen of mobile devices (icons will be generated from the cover preview thumbnails).

Although cover thumbnails may look like and be presented at the same size as article thumbnails, they are emphatically not. Do not create cover images at 144×144 or 70×70 pixels. Instead, cover images must be the same size as the pages in the publication (or the pages in the particular rendition). In other words, if your article pages are 1024×768 pixels, then your portrait cover image must be 1024×768 pixels, and your landscape cover image must be 768×1024 pixels. These images need to be flattened PNG or JPEG images set in the resolution of the rest of the document.

Because cover images are merely flattened versions of the cover, the easiest way to create them is to export the actual cover page straight from InDesign. Choose File ➢ Export in InDesign; then from the Save as Type drop-down, choose JPEG. You'll then be prompted to choose the page range to export as well as the quality and resolution settings for the JPEG.

FIGURE 9.64
The Adobe DPS
dashboard

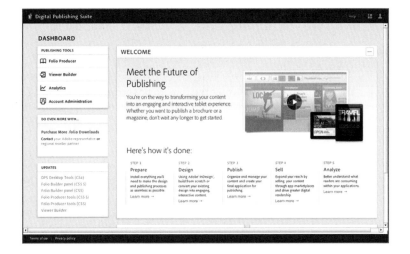

FIGURE 9.65

The Folio Producer: Organizer

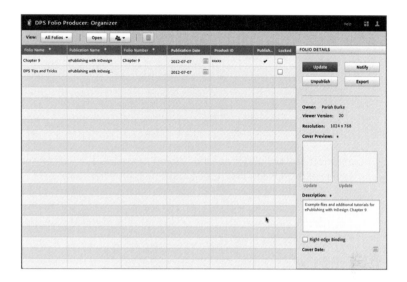

Cover Previews   In the Cover Previews section of the Folio Details column, clicking the empty preview boxes or the Add or Update link will let you choose preview images not just from your local computer but also from anywhere on the Web, from Google, and from your Flickr account.

Cover Date   At the bottom of the Folio Details sidebar is the Cover Date field. Clicking the calendar icon pops up a calendar where you can click a date to set the exact cover date for the issue. This may or may not differ from the Publication Date field on the left.

Publication Name   In the main view on the left, the Publication Name column is the same as the matching field in the Folio Properties dialog. To edit the Publication Name here, simply double-click within the field and type your edits.

Folio Number   The Folio Number field is where you supply the volume number, issue number, issue date, or some other identifier for the individual issue or edition. It can be in any format you like, from "Vol. 1 Issue 6" to "No. 6" to "March 2013." This field is required, so even if you're publishing a one-off publication, you must fill in something—"First Edition" works. As you publish subsequent issues of periodicals, their Publication Name fields will be the same, but the Folio Number fields is what will differentiate them.

Publication Date   By clicking the calendar icon under Publication Date, you can choose the publishing date. Setting the date in advance and publishing will prevent that issue from going live until publication date. Note that folios are sorted by Publication Date values, in descending order, with the latest date first.

Product ID   The Product ID field lists the ID number assigned to the folio automatically when it's published. The ID number may be seen by readers, but it won't matter much to them; it's primarily so that you, the platform's app store, and Adobe's servers can uniquely identify your publication.

Published   A Boolean field—either checked or not—the Published field tells you at a glance whether a folio has been published. Published can mean the issue currently available to your subscribers or a document you've set to be distributed at a future date.

Locked   Using the Locked field, you can lock a folio to prevent changes to the article metadata and uploads of newer versions of articles.

The four buttons you see on the right are as follows:

Update   When a published folio has changed, you must click the Update button to replace the older version of the folio with the newer version on the Adobe Distribution Service. Thereafter, the updated version will be delivered to readers as a new download, and if you send a push notification to subscribers, the revised folio will be made available as an app update.

Notify   Use the Notify button to send a push notification to subscribers of the publication or update of a folio. This action is important after publishing a folio because the act of publishing does not automatically send a push notification to subscribers; you must do that manually.

Unpublish   Clicking the Unpublish button removes the selected, published folio from the Adobe Distribution Service.

Export   To make a folio available to others, for example, to send it to another entity for inclusion in other publications, click the Export button.

Clicking the Open button at the top of the Folio Producer: Organizer will open the Folio Producer: Editor (Figure 9.66), which gives you all the same options (and more) as the Article Properties dialog accessible from the Folio Builder panel inside InDesign. Here in the Article Properties sidebar you have Title, Byline, Kicker, Description, and so on, but also two additional options I didn't cover previously: Tags and Protected. The Tags field allows you to enter keywords or tags by which someone might search for your article, and the Protected check box, once activated, prevents accidental changes to the selected article.

FIGURE 9.66
The Folio Producer: Editor

Use the buttons at the top of the editor to add folios from another publication, import an HTMLResources.zip file (see the "Including Offline HTML" section earlier in this chapter), and switch between viewing the portrait and landscape layouts in the article (if it's a dual-orientation article). Drag the articles around in the main area to reorder them. You can also change the size at which the page thumbnails are displayed inside the editor and switch between Thumbnail and List views with the other two buttons beside Add and HTML. Once you've finished editing, click the X beside the folio name in the title bar to return to the Folio Producer: Organizer.

Using the Viewer Builder

The Viewer Builder, which runs only on Mac OS X, is how you configure, customize, and build the branded Content Viewer app that will present your interactive-magazine publications to readers. The easiest way to install and access the Viewer Builder is by logging into your Adobe DPS dashboard at http://digitalpublishing.acrobat.com and selecting Viewer Builder from the Publishing Tools. That will launch the Viewer Builder desktop application. If you don't already have Viewer Builder installed, you'll be prompted to install it the first time you click the button on the dashboard.

The first time you use Adobe DPS Viewer Builder, it will launch looking like Figure 9.67, with no custom viewer builds. Click the New button at the bottom to begin designing your first viewer build, which will take you to the screen in Figure 9.68. Here you must choose your target device: iPad or iPhone on iOS, or Android. iOS and Android each needs its own viewer build, though both iPad and iPhone can share the same build or have separate builds. In other words, if you intend to build viewers for all three, you'll need to build two or three separate viewers, which is why the main Viewer Builder window offers so many rows. For now, pick the first one you want and click Next in the bottom right to begin the guided build. I'll use the iPad/iPhone viewer builder as the main example here. Most of the options you'll set during this process for Android devices are identical to those required for iOS devices, so I'll describe only the differences.

FIGURE 9.67
The Viewer Builder during its first launch

TIP   Prepare all your viewer build materials and mobile provision files in advance. Once building has begun, Adobe DPS allows you only two options, to continue all the way through submitting the build and canceling the building process. You cannot save midstream.

FIGURE 9.68
Selecting devices
for this version of
the builder

VIEWER DETAILS

After selecting iOS as the operating system and either iPad and iPhone, or both, and clicking
Next, you'll be presented with the Viewer Details screen in Figure 9.69. I'll discuss what all of its
options mean.

FIGURE 9.69
The Viewer Details
screen

Viewer Name   The Viewer Name field is misleading. You're not being asked for the title of the viewer while it's opened but rather for the name to appear underneath the app icon on the device's home screen and, for Android, within the app list. Because of the limited length of icon labels on mobile devices, you'll want a short (13 or fewer characters) name here.

Viewer Version   The Viewer Version drop-down list lets you target the latest version of the Content Viewer (by default) as well as certain previous versions. Custom viewer builds are not dependent on the version of the stand-alone Adobe Content Viewer app and therefore are not limited by the issue of the Content Viewer app being out of sync with the version of the Folio Producer Tools because of Adobe's release cycle and Apple's approval process. You can always use the latest version of the viewer in a custom build. The reason you might want to select a previous build from the Viewer Version field is to update an app in that version already under review by Apple but not yet approved.

Viewer Type   Interactive magazine–format publications come in different types and use different kinds of subscription and entitlement systems. Ergo, viewers can be created in several types to fit the needs of the publication. For example, if you're producing a one-off publication, it's characterized as a single issue, and the viewer must reflect that, effectively removing any perception of separation between the app and the issue. The *Essential Guide to TRON Legacy* is an example of a single viewer. Periodicals and other serialized or multi-issue publications must be contained within an app that enables readers to purchase and view all the issues of that title, which means you'll need a multi-issue viewer that includes a built-in library and, optionally, one of several forms of subscription and issue purchase methodologies.

The options available on the Viewer Type menu vary with the level of Adobe DPS account you have. Single and Professional accountholders, for example, will not be able to use entitlement options, which are available only to Enterprise Adobe DPS accounts.

From the Viewer Type menu, select the viewer type you need, noting that your selection will alter which other fields and options appear below the field.

Adobe Content Viewer   Choosing Adobe Content Viewer alters the screen to look like Figure 9.70. Its purpose is to let you build your folio *into* its own Adobe Content Viewer app—typically for publication but also as a means of previewing the publication on a mobile device before actually building it into an app. From the Viewer Version field, select the latest available Content Viewer version or, if you prefer, one version back to maintain compatibility.

Built-In Single Issue   Built-In Single Issue is the type of viewer you want to create if your publication is a one-off, such as a book, catalog, yearbook, or other nonserialized content. From the reader's perspective, there will be no separation between the app and the content it contains; when the reader launches your single-issue app, the cover of the publication appears. Choosing this type of builder enables the options shown in Figure 9.71.

Multi-Issue   Opting for Multi-Issue, which is the default, creates an app that includes a library from which readers may download additional issues or titles. All the publications available through the library are hosted on the Adobe Distribution Service. Refer to Figure 9.69 for the remaining options enabled by selecting Multi-Issue.

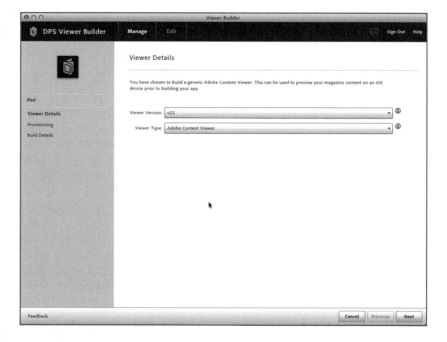

Multi-Issue With Entitlement   Multi-Issue With Entitlement, which is available only to Enterprise accountholders, enables the use of a custom entitlement server for managing customer access to titles and issues rather than using the Apple App Store/Newsstand or Adobe's Distribution Service entitlement servers. Your ability to use this option may be contested because of Apple's policies regarding periodicals and the Newsstand because this type of viewer is not compatible with Newsstand. Before building this type of viewer, you'll want to communicate with Apple to ensure that it won't reject your viewer.

All multi-issue viewer types offer the same options on the Viewer Details page, so I'll forego additional screenshots and refer you to Figure 9.69. That said, different multi-issue viewer types require additional *screens*. All types except the plain Multi-Issue require the completion of the Entitlement Details and Subscription Details screens, and those that use iTunes as an entitlement method also require completing the Newsstand screen, all of which are discussed in depth a little later.

Multi-Issue With iTunes Subscription   Selecting Multi-Issue With iTunes Subscription uses the Apple App Store/Newsstand to manage customer access to your titles and issues based on subscriptions or issue-at-a-time purchases. This type is available to Enterprise and Professional accountholders.

Multi-Issue With Entitlement And iTunes Subscription   The Multi-Issue with Entitlement And iTunes Subscription type combines the ability to use your own or a third-party entitlement service with the ability to use Apple's App Store/Newsstand. Because of the entitlement option this type is available only to Enterprise Adobe DPS accountholders.

Title (Library View)   The Title (Library View) field is where you enter the title that will actually display at the top of the viewer app. Try to keep it to less than 35 characters to avoid the risk of cutting off parts of the title when the app is viewed on smaller screens in portrait mode.

Title ID   Another poorly labeled field is the Title ID. You might think it's asking for the ISSN or an ISBN. It isn't. It's asking for your Adobe ID, typically your email address, the one you use to access the Adobe DPS dashboard and the Viewer Builder. This will secure the viewer app so that it can be modified only by your account.

Password   Enter in the Password field the password you use to log into the Adobe DPS dashboard, corresponding with the Adobe ID entered in the Title ID field.

PDF Zooming Enabled   One of the key advantages to using PDF format pages while building your folios instead of PNG or JPEG is that PDF format allows readers to pinch and zoom. The PDF Zooming Enabled check box, if left empty, will override that behavior, preventing readers from being able to zoom. Really, though, why would you want to disable it? In most cases, you'll want to make sure this option is enabled.

Bookmarks Enabled   Activating the Bookmarks Enabled check box lets readers create bookmarks within your publications so that they can return to specific places in the content at a later time.

Folio Auto-Archiving Enabled   Regularly published periodicals can very quickly fill up the storage space available on a subscriber's device. To prevent that from happening, Adobe DPS offers the ability to automatically delete older issues without maintaining the subscriber's access to those old issues if desired; Adobe calls this *archiving* of older issues.

Checking the box beside Folio Auto-Archiving activates the ability for your app to automatically delete older issues. It also enables two other options, Archiving On By Default and Archive Threshold, which control if and how archiving happens.

Archiving On By Default   Once Folio Auto-Archiving Enabled has been, um, enabled, then subscribers can choose to turn automatic archiving on or off within their copies of your viewer app. You can make the option on by default, meaning auto-archiving will happen until and unless subscribers intentionally turn it off, by activating the Archiving On By Default check box.

Archive Threshold   When auto-archiving is enabled, you should choose a threshold number for local issues to be retained on subscribers' devices before issues begin archiving. For example, if you set the Archive Threshold field to 10, then up to 10 issues will remain on subscribers' devices. Once the 11th issue is downloaded, the oldest (meaning least recently updated, not necessarily the oldest cover date) issue will archive (delete). Adobe DPS imposes a minimum active number of issues of 5 and a maximum of 90. Therefore, valid values for the Archive Threshold field are any number between 6 and 90.

Optional URL Scheme   The Optional URL Scheme field lets you specify a custom URL scheme that you can use on the Web to launch your app. For example, if you enter in the Optional URL Scheme field com.mypub.issue9, you can create a hyperlink like com.mypub .issue9://on your website, Twitter, or anywhere else; when that link is clicked or tapped in a mobile browser, it will open your app.

Optional iPhone Welcome Screen   Enterprise Adobe DPS accountholders can optionally include an HTML-based welcome screen that appears to iPhone users only the first time your app is launched. Typically this screen is used to enable subscribers to restore previous purchases. The Optional iPhone Welcome Screen expects you to locate a ZIP archive containing the HTML and assets for the welcome screen. See http://abbrv.it/DigiPubIDTools for resources for creating an iPhone welcome screen.

Supported Languages   In the Supported Languages area, check the box beside any and all languages in which your *content* appears. The viewer app interface itself will automatically translate into other languages.

As revealed by the absence of controls on the Viewer Details screen, Content Viewer for Android isn't as robust as its iOS counterpart. If you compare Figure 9.72 with the view of the iOS version of the Viewer Details page (Figure 9.69), you'll notice that the entire auto-archive system is not controllable, nor are PDF zooming (because Android Content Viewer doesn't support PDF format pages) and language specifications. Even the built-in help bubbles, which are quite informative in the iOS screens of the Viewer Builder, are Spartan in the Android screens. What is unique to this version of the viewer are the following fields.

Marketplace   From the Marketplace menu you must select which Android app market will be hosting this viewer, either Android Market (now called Google Play App Store), Amazon Appstore for Android (the only way to get your app onto the Kindle Fire), or None. The last option is for limited or internal distributions of your app without making it available to the general public.

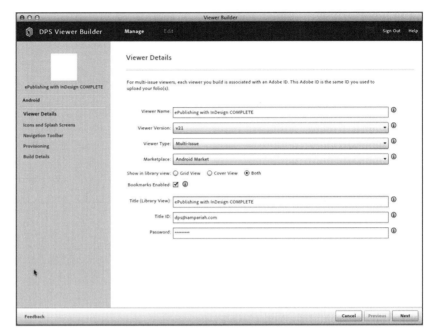

Show In Library View   Library View, which is the screen showing all the issues available in your app, can display issues in either a grid or cover view. Set the radio button beside Show In Library View for one mode or the other; or, to leave the choice to the subscriber, select Both, which will create buttons in your viewer that let subscribers switch between the two views.

ENTITLEMENT DETAILS (ENTERPRISE ONLY)

If you are an Enterprise accountholder and chose one of the entitlement viewer types on the preceding screen, you will next be presented with the Entitlement Details screen (see Figure 9.73). The following is the definition of those fields.

Service URL   Enter in the Service URL field the main URL to the entitlement service you are employing.

Service Auth URL   An authentication service, which is typically part of the entitlement system, tracks customer logins. In the Service Auth URL field, enter the URL to the authentication service.

Integrator ID   When you set up your Enterprise account with Adobe, the company assigned you an Integrator ID to enable access from Adobe's servers to your entitlement service. Supply that Integrator ID value in the field of the same name.

Create Account URL   Enter in the Create Account URL the address to which would-be subscribers will be sent when they tap the Subscribe button in your app.

FIGURE 9.73
The Entitlement
Details screen

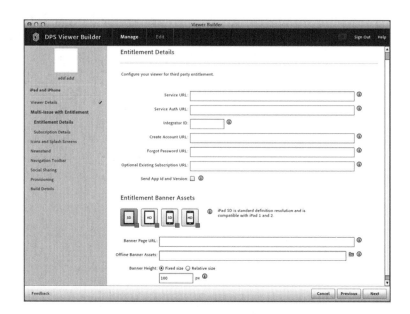

Forgot Password URL   Subscribers need a way to recover their passwords should they lose or forget them, so enter in the Forgot Password URL the address to a system that will let subscribers recover or reset their passwords.

Optional Existing Subscription URL   If your publication is paired with a print edition and print subscriptions, you may want to enable existing print subscribers to access your digital content, a la *The New York Times*. If so, provide the URL for subscribers to verify their existing print subscriptions in the Optional Existing Subscription URL field. Otherwise, leave the field blank.

Send App ID And Version   Some entitlement services will use the ID and version number of the app in which content is being requested to further secure access to issues. If you've configured your entitlement server thusly or would like to have the entitlement server receive that information for analytics tracking purposes, check the option Send App ID And Version, whereupon your app will add that information to any API calls from the app to your server.

Entitlement Banner Assets   Banners display in the app viewer's library view to help brand the app and promote subscriptions. Depending on whether you selected to build the viewer for iPad and iPhone or just one or the other, you may have four or two buttons displayed under Entitlement Banner Assets. Clicking each lets you set the Banner Page URL, Offline Banner Assets, and Banner Height values for each one.

Banner Page URL   In the Banner Page URL field, enter the URL to the HTML comprising the banner. When the subscriber's device is connected to the Web, this live banner will display.

Offline Banner Assets   When subscriber devices are in offline mode, you can still show an HTML-based banner by compressing the HTML and all assets (images, CSS style sheets, JavaScript, and so on) into a ZIP file and giving the location of that ZIP archive in the Offline Banner Assets field.

Banner Height   In the Banner Height area, specify the height of the banner as you've designed it by first choosing Fixed Size, which enables you to dictate the height of the banner in pixels, or Relative Size, which lets you define a percentage of screen height to be used for the banner. When using Relative Size, make sure your HTML is designed as "fluid," meaning without exact width and height values in the CSS or HTML markup.

SUBSCRIPTION DETAILS

Depending on the level of your account (Enterprise, Professional, or Single Edition) and your selection in the Viewer Type field, you may next be presented with the Entitlement Details screen. The following is the definition of those fields:

Subscription Tiles   In the Subscription Tiles area, supply the images that will be used to present the Apple subscription options. When customers tap anywhere on the tile, they will be taken to the iOS subscription options. Tile images should be sized accordingly.

- iPad 1 and 2 (aka iPad SD)
    - 468×135 pixels for landscape
    - 331×180 pixels for portrait
- iPad 3 (aka iPad HD)
    - 936×270 pixels for landscape
    - 662×360 pixels for portrait

Optional Library Subscription Tile URL   Enter in the Optional Library Subscription Tile URL field the URL to the web page that is displayed within an in-app browser when a subscription tile is tapped.

Optional Remote Custom Dialog URL   After successfully completing the subscription process, you can optionally have another URL appear to thank the customer, collect additional information, or promote additional products. Enter the URL to such a page in the Optional Remote Custom Dialog URL field.

Subscription Type   In the Subscription Type area, you must specify the type of subscription(s) offered by your app. If you will be providing your publication free via the Newsstand using Apple's Free Subscription option, choose that as the type and provide the Free Subscription Product ID from your iTunes Connect.

TIP   iTunes Connect is a suite of web-based tools to manage your apps in the App Store. An iTunes Connect account is required if you intend to publish from Adobe DPS to the App Store or iBooks. Visit `http://abbrv.it/DigiPubIDTools` for links to iTunes Connect and the iTunes Connect Online Application.

When using a paid subscription model, choose that option, and then click the plus sign to provide at least one product ID from your iTunes Connect and to set the duration for the subscription period. You may specify more than one subscription option.

ICONS AND SPLASH SCREENS

In the Icons And Splash Screens panel, you must provide imagery to be used in various places for your app. At the top, as you can see in Figure 9.74, are buttons for each of the devices selected in the first step for the app. Clicking each of these will reveal the unique sizes and fields for the icons and other imagery required by that device.

FIGURE 9.74
The Icons And
Splash Screens
screen for iOS
(when both iPad
and iPhone have
been selected on the
New Viewer screen)
and for Android

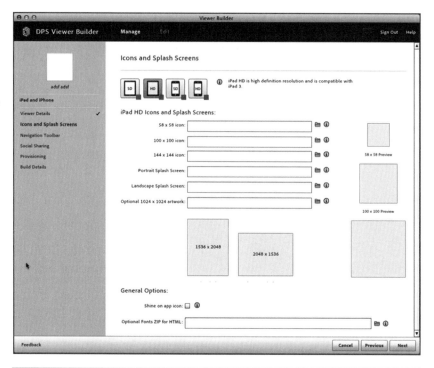

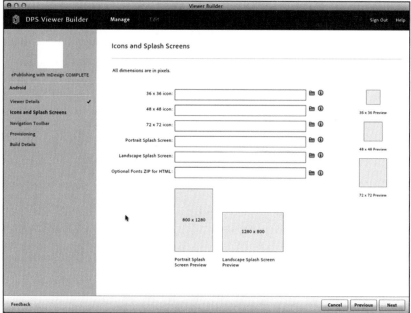

Icons   Create 72 PPI RGB PNG images (with or without transparency) to become the icons for your app in a variety of sizes. Assuming you are producing a viewer for both iPad and iPhone, you will need the following sizes of icons:

- iPad 1 and 2 (aka iPad SD)
    - 29×29 pixels
    - 50×50 pixels
    - 72×72 pixels
- iPad 3 (aka iPad HD)
    - 58×58 pixels
    - 100×100 pixels
    - 144×144 pixels
- iPhone non-Retina (aka iPhone SD)
    - 29×29 pixels
    - 57×57 pixels
- iPhone Retina (aka iPhone HD)
    - 58×58 pixels
    - 114×114 pixels

The Icons section is the same for Android but with different icon sizes available—36×36, 48×48, and 72×72 pixels.

Splash Screens   When your viewer app is first launched, it displays a splash screen for three seconds. Create 72 PPI RGB PNG images without transparency to serve as the splash screens in the following sizes and orientations:

- iPad 1 and 2 (aka iPad SD)
    - 768×1024 pixels for landscape
    - 1024×768 pixels for portrait
- iPad 3 (aka iPad HD)
    - 2048×1536 pixels for landscape
    - 1536×2048 pixels for portrait
- iPhone non-Retina (aka iPhone SD): 320×480 pixels (single orientation only)
- iPhone Retina (aka iPhone HD): 640×960 pixels (single orientation only)

For Android, the Splash Screens section is the same but with different pixel dimensions— 800×1280 pixels and 1280×800 pixels.

Optional Artwork   The Optional Artwork field available for each of the devices is actually to allow the inclusion of an optional large icon that will be displayed in the App Store, particularly if your app is featured by the App Store. Use a nontransparent 72 PPI RGB PNG image for this large icon, in the following sizes:

◆   iPad 1 and 2 (aka iPad SD): 512 × 512 pixels

◆   iPad 3 (aka iPad HD): 1024 × 1024 pixels

◆   iPhone non-Retina (aka iPhone SD): 512 × 512 pixels

◆   iPhone Retina (aka iPhone HD): 1024 × 1024 pixels

Shine On App Icon   Activate the Shine On App Icon check box if you want to apply the effect of a light shining on your icons.

Optional Fonts ZIP For HTML   If you've created article layouts from HTML and used fonts in that HTML that are not included by default on the selected mobile devices, you'll need to add those fonts into either the folio or the viewer. In the "Including Custom Fonts" topic in this chapter, I explain how to add them to your folio (and review how to add them here to the viewer). To include them in the viewer, which saves per-issue file size and download times when the same fonts are used across multiple issues, point the Optional Fonts ZIP For HTML field to the ZIP archive containing those fonts.

Newsstand

When employing the Apple App Store/Newsstand model to manage subscriptions of multi-issue viewers, the Newsstand screen will follow the Icons And Splash Screens screen. Here supply the necessary information Apple needs to connect your app to the Newsstand.

Enable Newsstand   Activate the Enable Newsstand option to allow your app to appear in the Apple Newsstand.

Magazine/Newspaper   Select Magazine or Newspaper to tell the Newsstand whether your app should be categorized as a magazine or newspaper.

Binding Edge   Choose from Binding Edge Left or Right to communicate in the app's icon whether it's a right-to-left publication, as would be common with English, French, Spanish, and other right-to-left written languages, or a left-to-right publication for languages such as Japanese, Hebrew, Farsi, and other written languages that read left to right.

Newsstand Icon   Yet another icon you'll need to provide is one to appear in Newsstand. This RGB, 72 PPI, nontransparent PNG will be used as your app's cover image but will be replaced by the cover image of each subsequently published issue. For iPad 1 and 2, make the image 96 × 128 pixels and, for the iPad 3, 192 × 256 pixels in size.

Navigation Toolbar (Enterprise Only)

For Enterprise Adobe DPS accounts, the next screen displayed is the navigation toolbar (Single and Professional accounts are unable to customize the default navigation toolbar). On this screen you can toggle and customize the display and functions of the navigation toolbar (see Figure 9.75).

FIGURE 9.75

The Navigation
Toolbar screen for
Enterprise accounts

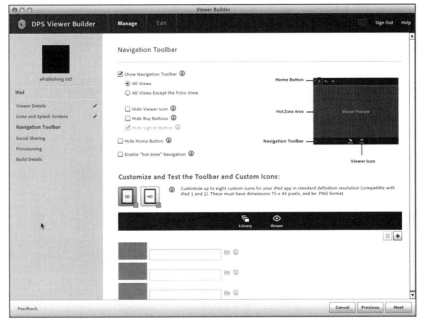

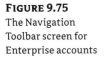

Show Navigation Toolbar   Activate the Show Navigation Toolbar check box to enable the navigation toolbar to appear at the bottom of the app window when a user taps once on the screen. Using the radio buttons beneath this option, you can specify whether the navigation toolbar appears in all views or hides in the folio view.

Hide Viewer Icon   By default a Viewer icon is included in the navigation toolbar. Tapping the Viewer icon shows the previously viewed folio. Check the Hide Viewer Icon option to remove that function.

Hide Buy Buttons   By default issues are made available to purchase individually as well as via subscription. The former method is accomplished by the inclusion of a Buy button beside the issue thumbnail. If you want to disallow purchasing of back issues individually, thus putting the emphasis on subscriptions, check the Hide Buy Buttons option.

Hide Sign In Button   A Sign In button appears on the navigation toolbar before a subscriber has signed into the app. Enabling Hide Sign In Button will remove that button from the toolbar, letting you include the sign-in functionality within the HTML that appears when a subscriber taps one of the issue icons.

Hide Home Button   Tapping the Home button in the header takes readers to the library, but so does the Library button in the navigation toolbar. If you'll be showing the navigation toolbar option you can opt to hide the Home button to remove this behavior added by decree of the Department of Redundancy Department.

Enable "Hot Zone" Navigation   Hot zones, as indicated by the diagram on the Navigation Toolbar screen, are navigation areas that, when tapped, navigate to the next (on the right) or previous (on the left) article. They are most useful when a full-screen overlay is currently displayed, allowing readers to move on to the next article without the need to first close the overlay.

In the lower section of the screen, under Customize And Test The Toolbar And Custom Icons, you can add up to eight buttons to the toolbar (see Figure 9.76). To add a button, click the plus sign just below the black navigation bar preview and then define the button's function and appearance using the following options.

FIGURE 9.76

Adding a custom button to the navigation toolbar

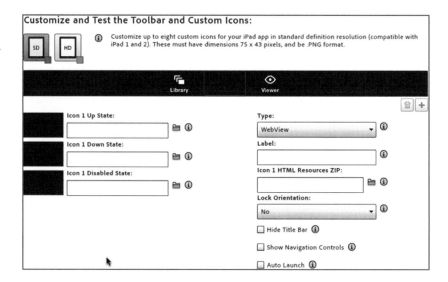

Icon States   On the left are three fields asking for transparent PNG images to use as the states of the button you're adding. Within each field provide an image to present, respectively, the up or normal state of the button, the down state, which means while the button function is active, and the disabled state, which is the state of the button if its function is not compatible with the current activity.

Type   From the Type menu, choose the function of your button, either WebView or Navigation. A WebView button lets you display the content of an HTML file, while Navigation should be used only when employing publishing systems from third-party company Woodwing to use that system's metadata for navigation purposes.

Label   Primarily for use with Woodwing publications, the Label field lets you specify an article Intent metadata field for navigation.

Icon 1 HTML Resources ZIP   Assuming you've set the Type field to WebView, the Icon 1 HTML Resources ZIP asks you to point it to the ZIP archive containing the HTML file (and its assets) for display when the subscriber taps the button. Note that subfolders are not allowed in the ZIP; the HTML file and all assets must be within the same folder and then compressed into the ZIP archive.

Lock Orientation   If the WebView content you've created will not adapt well to device rotation, set the Lock Orientation field to the orientation in which it does work. When the content appears, it will then always be in that orientation regardless of device rotation.

Hide Title Bar   When showing WebView content, a browser-like title bar is displayed by default. Toggle that display on or off with the Hide Title Bar control.

Show Navigation Controls   Similar to the title bar, WebView content includes basic browser navigation controls to enable subscribers to navigate between your WebView pages. Disabling Show Navigation Controls hides those controls.

Auto Launch   When the app library appears, you can specify one WebView object to automatically appear by activating the Auto Launch check box.

SOCIAL SHARING

One of the best ways to promote a publication is to provide the tools that let your subscribers promote it for you. On the Social Sharing screen is where you provide those tools (see Figure 9.77). Activate the check boxes beside the sharing features you'd like to include. Turning on any of them enables the Publication URL field where you should supply the URL of your publication's website. Further, activating the Enable Facebook Sharing option turns on the Facebook App ID field where you can fill in the Facebook App ID you were given when you registered your app on the Facebook developer site. Disabling all sharing check boxes will hide the Social Sharing button from the toolbar in the app.

FIGURE 9.77
The Social Sharing screen lets you help subscribers spread the word about your publications.

PROVISIONING

Apple policy requires that all apps run on the iPad must be signed by a valid certificate and provisioned. On the Provisioning screen (shown in Figure 9.78) you provide proof of the latter, the mobileprovision files; certificates are specified after generating your viewer app.

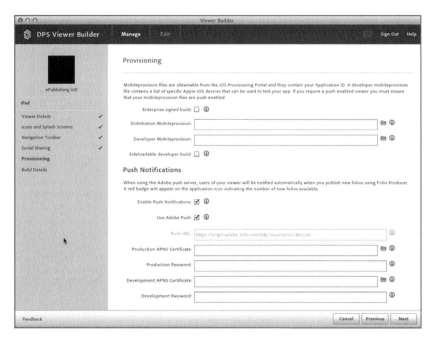

Enterprise Signed Build   Enable the Enterprise Signed Build option only if your app will be distributed solely within your own organization. Doing so will show the Intended Application ID and Enterprise Mobileprovision fields in place of Distribution Mobileprovision and Developer Mobileprovision. If your app is for general distribution, leave the option disabled, which makes the two following fields Distribution Mobileprovision and Developer Mobileprovision and enables Sideloadable Developer Build.

> **Intended Application ID**   The Intended Application ID field should be completed with the URL scheme ID of your organization, for example com.mypub.issue9.

> **Enterprise Mobileprovision**   In the Enterprise Mobileprovision field, provide the provision file obtained via the iOS Provisioning Portal.

Distribution Mobileprovision   Supply in the Distribution Mobileprovision field the provision file obtained via the iOS Provisioning Portal.

Developer Mobileprovision   In Developer Mobileprovision, point to the mobileprovision file for the development app, which will include a UDID list of iOS device IDs.

Sideloadable Developer Build   Activating the Sideloadable Developer Build option enables you to drag .folio files into your development viewer through iTunes and test them live on a device without the need to rebuild your viewer.

Enable Push Notifications   Required when using Newsstand publishing, the check box option for Enable Push Notifications changes the icon of your app on subscribers' devices to show a number indicating the count of available issues.

Use Adobe Push   Activating Use Adobe Push employs Adobe's push system for new issue and update notifications in your app. With this option selected, you'll need to also complete the following fields: Production APNS Certificate, Production Password, Development APNS Certificate, and Development Password to certify your app's access to Adobe's push service. Disabling Use Adobe Push replaces those fields with two others, Push URL and Custom Push Parameters, so that you can employ an alternate push notification system.

> **Production APNS Certificate**   In the Production APNS Certificate field, provide the production APNS certificate file to make use of Adobe's push notification server.

> **Production Password**   Enter the corresponding Production APNS Certificate password in the Production Password field.

> **Development APNS Certificate**   Load the development APNS certificate into the Development APNS Certificate field.

> **Development Password**   Supply the password corresponding to the development APNS certificate in the Development Password field.

Push URL   If push notifications are enabled but not using the Adobe push service, you must direct the app to the URL of the push notification server you are using in the Push URL field.

Custom Push Parameters   When employing a non-Adobe push notification server, the Custom Push Parameters field lets you enter the parameters required by your push notification server. Enter each parameter on a line by itself in the form of `PARAMETER_NAME=VALUE`.

Build Details

The final screen you see when building a viewer is Build Details, which lets you choose to enable Omniture Analytics on the app by activating the Report Suite Tracking Enabled check box. Once activated, the Build Details screen will provide you with the URL of the Omniture tracking server and, if different, the URL of a secure Omniture tracking server. You'll also be given at this point your Omniture report suite ID to identify your app in the Omniture analytics.

Including Custom Fonts

To embed the fonts for HTML content into Adobe DPS publications, there are two methods.

- First, you can add them, collected in a ZIP archive, to the Viewer Builder discussed a few pages back.

- You can also include them in the `HTMLResources.zip`, in a subfolder called `fonts`.

Chapter 10

Creating Interactive Magazines with Aquafadas DPS

Competing head to head with Adobe Digital Publishing Suite is a comprehensive but relatively unknown challenger from France, Aquafadas Digital Publishing Solution. Although not as popular as Adobe DPS, Aquafadas offers a much richer set of interactive elements for incorporation into digital magazines. Also working as an InDesign add-in, the Aquafadas system is more polished and professional-looking than Adobe's DPS tools, and, in nearly all other aspects, Aquafadas DPS is arguably a better, more intuitive, more feature-rich system for producing digital magazines.

- ◆ Installing Aquafadas DPS
- ◆ Starting a Publication
- ◆ Adding a New Layout
- ◆ Live-Testing Your Publication
- ◆ Panning and Zooming
- ◆ Understanding Picture-Enrichment Options
- ◆ Creating Slideshows and Galleries
- ◆ Incorporating Audio and Video
- ◆ Adding Animations and 3D Rotating Objects
- ◆ Producing Before-and-After Comparisons
- ◆ Building Read-Along Text
- ◆ Employing Scrolling Page Regions
- ◆ Using Content Replacement
- ◆ Adding Live Web Content
- ◆ Including Offline HTML, Games, and Activities
- ◆ Adding Actions and Advanced Buttons
- ◆ Applying the Finishing Touches

Installing Aquafadas DPS

If you want to use Aquafadas Digital Publishing System (Aquafadas DPS), install one or more of the following from `http://abbrv.it/DigiPubIDTools`:

◆ The Aquafadas plug-in for Adobe InDesign (Windows or Mac)

◆ Optional test tools myKiosk for iPad or iPhone and iOS Simulator (Mac only)

TIP Throughout, I've used *iPhone* to refer to both the iPhone and the iPod Touch; after all, the latter is simply a dialer-less version of the iPhone.

◆ Optional AVE AppFactory (Mac only) to convert interactive magazines into stand-alone apps for distribution

Starting a Publication

Beginning an interactive magazine for Aquafadas DPS begins very differently than creating a publication for Adobe DPS. Instead of starting with InDesign's New Document dialog and then adding the layout to a folio, you begin right within the AVE Project Manager panel, which you'll find after installing the Aquafadas plug-in for Adobe InDesign under Window ➤ Extensions ➤ AVE Project Manager (in the AVE Publishing menu, depending on the version of the installer). If this is your first publication with Aquafadas DPS, you'll likely see a blank AVE Project Manager panel, but after a few projects, it will look more like the one in Figure 10.1. The panel lists your active projects, including each project's ID number, name, and the type of project, as well as the structure of that project, all of which will make a great deal more sense shortly.

FIGURE 10.1
An AVE Project Manager panel showing several active but unselected projects

Creating a Project

At the bottom of the panel are initially six buttons when no project (aka folio) is selected; from the left, they are as follows: Create (+) begins a new project, Import and Export (upward- and downward-facing arrows) let you load and save the project list, Duplicate (two boxes) copies a highlighted project making it easy to create a new rendition of a publication while starting from the last rendition, Refresh (circular shape with arrowheads) ensures that you're seeing the latest projects and statuses in the list, and Delete (×) removes a project (forever).

There's also a seventh button, Settings (the gear icon), in the top-right corner of the panel. It opens the Preferences dialog (Figure 10.2), which offers a selection of controls.

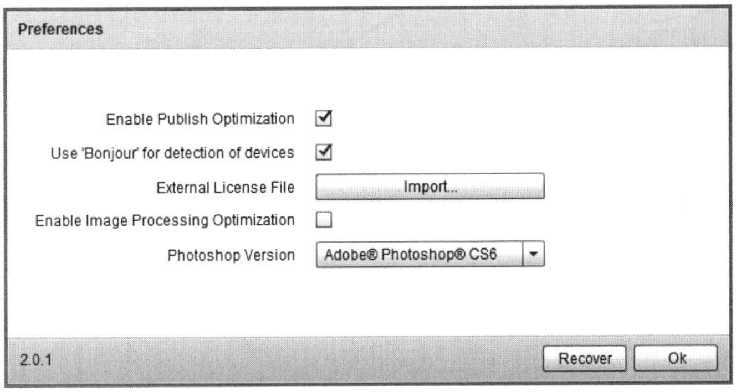

FIGURE 10.2
The Preferences dialog

Preferences

Enable Publish Optimization	☑
Use 'Bonjour' for detection of devices	☑
External License File	Import...
Enable Image Processing Optimization	☐
Photoshop Version	Adobe® Photoshop® CS6 ▾

2.0.1   Recover   Ok

Enable Publish Optimization   If activated, the Enable Publish Optimization check box tells Aquafadas to compress and optimize the content of the folio during generation for fastest previews.

Use Bonjour for the Detection of Devices   Bonjour is a third-party notification system for both Windows and Mac OS X that services and applications like Aquafadas DPS can employ to provide pop-up desktop notifications for various purposes such as when applications have updates or, in this case, when Aquafadas DPS detects the connection of a tablet or other device running the Aquafadas DPS myKiosk previewer app. Enable this option to receive such notifications if Bonjour is installed on your system.

External License File   To publish your interactive magazines, you must purchase licenses from Aquafadas. Those licenses are sometimes delivered in the form of external, XML-based license files. Clicking the Import button lets you browse for and load your license files into Aquafadas DPS.

Enable Image Processing Optimization   While designing layouts, you might use imagery that has a higher resolution than is necessary for the target display device(s) or imagery like PSDs that include layers. To save both your and your readers' disk space and file transfer times, Aquafadas DPS can automatically optimize the images used in the layout—on the page and in enrichments—by loading those images into Photoshop and downsampling them and/or merging layers.

When Enable Image Processing Optimization is enabled and an installed version of Photoshop identified in the Photoshop Version field, Aquafadas DPS will automatically process all images that require processing through Photoshop any time you publish the magazine—whether for actual publication or publishing for previewing purposes. Be warned that this process can take quite a bit of time and may even hang the publication process, so I recommend you preoptimize your images before publication and turn off Enable Image Processing Optimization.

Recover   Clicking the Recover button will attempt to identify and restore any projects from earlier versions of Aquafadas DPS or online projects that were not previously automatically detected by AVE Project Manager.

PROJECTS DISAPPEAR AFTER UPGRADING AQUAFADAS DPS INDESIGN PLUG-IN

Ideally this won't be an issue for much longer, but as of the time of this writing (and for quite a while before it), installing a new version of the Aquafadas DPS InDesign plug-in seems to make any existing projects disappear. Those projects are emphatically not gone; they are alive and well but need to be "recovered" to the new version of the AVE Project Manager panel. At the top of the AVE Project Manager panel, on the far right, click the Settings button to open the Preferences dialog. At the bottom of that dialog is the Recover button. Clicking it will cause AVE Project Manager to query the database of projects, articles, and files created by the prior version and produce a list of your existing projects. Check the box beside each project you'd like to recover—probably all of them—and then click the Recover button. After a brief wait, you'll have all your projects restored intact to the Project List in the AVE Project Manager panel.

Begin by clicking the Create button to create a new project. You'll see the New dialog appear just like in Figure 10.3. If it seems the dialog is cut off, then it probably is. All child windows of the AVE Project Manager must appear *within* the AVE Project Manager panel, even if that means they appear cut off. To resolve this situation, drag the bottom right corner of AVE Project Manager panel outward until it's large enough to fit the New window (or other subsequent child windows). You can also resize and reposition the child windows themselves—within the area of the containing AVE Project Manager panel—if you need to do so.

Let's go through the New dialog one field at a time.

Project Name   Name your project in this field. It should be named as you would like people to see it. For instance, My Digital Magazine, Vol. II, No. 6 or The H.R. Giger Exotic Pet Catalog, Spring 2014.

Project Type   Aquafadas offers tools to create several different types of digital publications, including comic books, enhanced ebooks, PDFs, and, of course, interactive magazines. Depending on the Aquafadas tools you installed, you may have several options here, though the Aquafadas plug-in for Adobe InDesign offers only two by default: AVEMag and AVEPDF. You want to choose AVEMag.

Orientation   Here's where planning the publication turns into building the publication. Within the Orientation are two check box options, Horizontal and Vertical. If you want your publication to have a landscape layout check the Horizontal option; if you want it to have a portrait layout, check Vertical. You may check one or both, but this choice applies to all articles and layouts; you cannot mix and match vertical, horizontal, and vertical and horizontal between articles in one project.

FIGURE 10.3
The New dialog

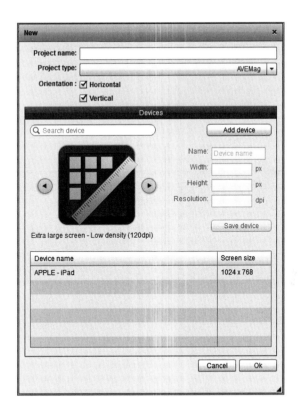

Devices   Within the Devices section you must identify at least one device so that Aquafadas DPS can build you a layout configured for that device. In the Search Device field, begin typing the name of a device to show a filtered list of matching device names. For example, to add a layout for an iPhone, iPad, Droid, MileStone, or numerous other devices, type *i* into the Search Device field; you'll see a pop-up list of all Aquafadas DPS–configured devices with an *i* in their names. Select one and click the Add Device button. Fill in a name for the device as well as the width, height, and resolution of the page, and then click Save Device to add it to the list of device layouts at the bottom.

After clicking OK, you'll have your project defined.

There's no choice of background page format at either the project or article level in Aquafadas DPS because Aquafadas DPS automatically uses a PDF-based page format. That means text and other vector elements will always look as sharp as the display device is able to handle. The same publications built for iPad 1 and 2 prior to the release of iPad 3 will have very sharp, zoomable text on the iPad 3's higher resolution without the extra overhead of double-sized images. Of course, the images in older issues of digital magazines, blown up 200 percent for the iPad 3 Retina display, may suffer quality degradation, but text and vector objects won't.

Adding Articles

Like Adobe DPS, Aquafadas DPS works on the metaphor of articles. Each article is a separate InDesign document. In the AVE Project Manager panel, highlight the project you just created. In the Project Structure pane to its right, you'll see the New and Import ID File button (see Figure 10.4).

In this case, not having any prior content, you want to choose New. Aquafadas DPS will create a new INDD document in the dimensions of the device you chose during project setup; if you added multiple devices, you'll be asked to choose one for layout creation. You'll then be prompted to save the article's INDD document somewhere on your computer or the network. Unlike DPS, Aquafadas DPS allows collaboration via local networks rather than web-based file sharing.

By default, the article is untitled. You don't want that because it will appear as "Untitled" in the table of contents and elsewhere in the final publication. Within the project thumbnail you'll find valuable information such as the number of pages in the article and the date and time of creation and modification. To the right of the number of pages you'll also see a pop-up menu icon (see Figure 10.5). This menu offers several commands that I'll get to in time. For now, select Settings to open the Article Properties dialog (see Figure 10.6). Here is where you supply a title for the article and a few other bits of information I'll cover in more depth in the "Finalizing the Publication" section later in this chapter.

FIGURE 10.5

The article's pop-up menu

FIGURE 10.6

Setting the title and description in the Article Properties dialog

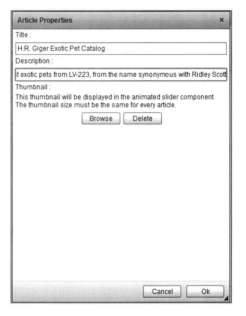

Once you've titled the article, you can hide the AVE Project Manager panel and begin designing the content of your article using all of InDesign's normal tools.

ADDING PAGES WITH THE PAGES PANEL TAKES A LONG TIME TO UPDATE AVE PROJECT MANAGER

As an experienced InDesign user—heck, even as a novice InDesign user—you'll want to add pages via the Pages panel, which is the right way to do it. There's a caveat, however: sometimes there's a delay, one that could be several minutes long, between the time you add and begin working with new pages and when they appear in the AVE Project Manager panel. The delay can be so long, in fact, that many people think that pages added via a normal method like the Pages panel or via Smart Text Reflow operations will never appear in their Aquafadas DPS projects, that pages can be added only via the AVE Project Manager panel's Add button. This isn't the case. It's merely a delay caused by the InDesign document being updated in the AVE database. However you add pages, AVE Project Manager will recognize and use them.

Importing external files into a project for Aquafadas DPS is easy:

1. Open the AVE Project Manager panel, and click the Import button between two article columns or beside the first column.

2. A typical file open dialog will ask you to locate the first file to import. Aquafadas DPS can import only one file at a time. When you click Open, the Project Manager panel will create a new article from the INDD including any pages and preview thumbnails.

3. Using the menu under the article's title and beside its page count, choose Settings, and then complete the Article Properties dialog to title and further define the article. Click OK, and you're done.

4. Repeat the last two steps as needed to import any additional articles.

Rearranging Articles

In the horizontally based AVE Project Manager panel, you can change the order of articles by dragging them left or right by their titles. If you have trouble seeing an article you want to move and the location to which you want to move it without scrolling horizontally, use the zoom slider or buttons at the bottom of the AVE Project Manager panel to reduce the display size of the article columns, fitting more columns in view.

Adding a New Layout

You are by no means required to design for both landscape and portrait reading experiences. That said, including both orientations, thus allowing the reader to read the publication with the tablet held horizontally or vertically, offers the reader a choice, whichever orientation is more comfortable, and it offers you the opportunity to include alternate content from one orientation to the next, making your publication more engaging.

Creating Layouts for Both Orientations

When you created your project in the AVE Project Manager panel, you were given the option of including a horizontal/landscape orientation, a vertical/portrait orientation, or both. (Refer to Figure 10.3 to help refresh your memory of the New project dialog box.) If you enabled both the Horizontal and Vertical check boxes or used the Project Settings button at the bottom of the main AVE Project Manager panel to later include both orientations, then every page of every article you create in that project will have two thumbnail icons in the Project Structure pane (see Figure 10.7). Thus, both orientations are already built into every page of every article in your project. You don't need to use the Pages panel to set up alternate layouts or build separate INDD documents. At this moment, however, you can't access the portrait layout; by default you begin working with the landscape version in a dual-orientation publication within Aquafadas DPS. Searching around the AVE Project Manager panel for a means of changing between the orientation layouts is pointless; the control isn't where you might expect it, especially if you're switching from Adobe DPS to Aquafadas DPS or learning both concurrently for maximum marketability of your skills. Instead, the control is on the AVE Interactivity panel, which is also available from the Window ➤ Extensions and AVE Publishing menus.

FIGURE 10.7
Each page of an article in the Project Structure pane shows thumbnails for the orientations included in the project at creation time.

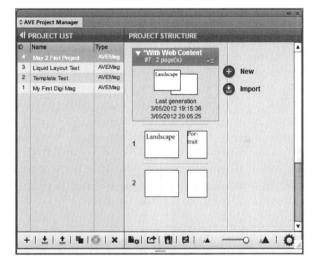

At the bottom of the AVE Interactivity panel are two page icons (see Figure 10.8). These are the orientation buttons. Clicking one or the other will instantly change the orientation of the current document—all pages. That action might *appear* to have the same effect as using Document Setup, the Pages panel, the Page tool, or the Control panel in pages mode to *genuinely* switch the entire document's page orientation from landscape to portrait, or vice versa, but that is *not* what's happening here. What's really going on is that Aquafadas DPS has made every page have two completely separate states—one portrait, one landscape, very much like multistate objects. When you use the orientation buttons at the bottom of the AVE Interactivity panel, you're actually switching between page *states* and, if you look at the AVE Project Manager panel, between the landscape and portrait thumbnails. In other words, every page is *already* landscape *and* portrait; those orientation buttons merely let you switch between those two states of the page.

FIGURE 10.8
Switching between orientations is accomplished by clicking the Change Orientation buttons at the bottom of the AVE Interactivity panel.

Wait, it gets better.

Synchronizing Content Across Layouts

With Adobe DPS you have to turn on an option for synchronizing text, and then only the source layout's text should be edited if you want to update the text across all layouts. Once the text is changed, you also then have to update links to see that change appear on the alternate layouts. In contrast, all text frames in Aquafadas DPS are automatically synchronized to one another, and changing text in *either* orientation automatically updates the other to match.

Wait, it gets better still. Note that I didn't title this section "Synchronizing *Text* Across Layouts."

It isn't just text frames that are synchronized. *All* content is synchronized across both layouts—graphic frames, media frames, enrichments (interactive elements), and everything else. Change the content in one, and the other updates to match, automatically, instantly. If you *don't* want content to synchronize—for instance, if you want to use one image in portrait and another in landscape—you can turn off this synchronization per object via the AVE Interactivity panel.

Selecting a text frame with the black arrow Selection tool reveals three options at the top of the AVE Interactivity panel—Visible In This Orientation, Same Story, and Same Text Style.

Visible In This Orientation   This option is available for all objects, not just text frames. If checked, Visible In This Orientation includes the selected object in the current orientation; if the check box is cleared, the object will not be included in the current orientation. With this option you can easily create an object of any kind—text, graphic, vector element, multimedia, enrichment, and so on—that appears only in one orientation's layout while a completely different version of the object appears in the other orientation's layout.

When you disable the Visible In This Orientation option for an object in the background its item entry on the Layers panel is hidden for that orientation. To make the object visible again, open the Layers panel (Window ➢ Layers) and make the object visible again by clicking the far left column of the Layers panel entry until the eyeball once again appears. Then you'll have to select the object and check the Visible In This Orientation button on the AVE Interactivity panel.

Same Story   With a text frame selected, this option tells Aquafadas DPS that the frame contains the same content in one orientation as in the other, thus synchronizing the text. It's via this option that changes made to the text in one layout are instantly reflected in the other layout. If you want to have separate copy between the layouts, clear this option from one or both versions of the text frame.

Same Text Style   When Same Story is enabled on a text frame, you can synchronize the text between layouts. When Same Text Style is enabled, not only the content of the text will be synchronized but also the formatting, including paragraph, character, table, cell styles, and local formatting and overrides. Disabling this option lets you assign different styles to, or separately override the formatting of, text between layouts, much like DPS.

Note that only the *content* of frames and enrichments is synchronized between layouts. Attributes of the containers—frames—are not synchronized. You couldn't do much adaption from one orientation to the next if container attributes were synced. Instead, you can move, resize, scale, rotate, skew, and fit objects however you need to adapt to the next layout without fear of messing up the other orientation. You can even change the object style, fill and stroke, effects, and number of columns (for text frames) of the landscape-orientation and portrait-orientation objects independently from one another.

In this way, Aquafadas DPS works a lot like Layer Comps in Photoshop, recording the visibility state of a layer and the position of the objects comprising that layer, while keeping their actual content in sync.

However, changing the orientation in the Pages panel or any other standard InDesign location will not rework the page content even if you're employing a liquid layout rule to automatically rework the page content. You can either adapt all the objects to the new orientation manually or take just a couple of extra steps to use InDesign's liquid layout behaviors to automatically adapt the content to the new orientation (see the "Using Liquid Layout Behaviors" section in Chapter 9).

Importing Existing Article Layouts

Adding existing layouts to an Aquafadas DPS publication is remarkably easy. Within any project selected on the AVE Project Manager panel, click the Import button in the Project Structure pane. An Open File dialog will appear. In that dialog, navigate to and select the INDD file you want to import—the process does not currently work with IDML files. Click the Open button, and wait a moment while Project Manager imports the document to its own database, and then the document is imported. Be sure to check the Links panel before moving on; sometimes Project Manager can't find all the linked assets, in which case you'll need to relink or update links as needed.

Copying Articles Between Projects

Like most other things with Aquafadas DPS, copying an article from one project to another is quite simple. Choose Duplicate from the article's pop-up menu in the Project Structure pane of the AVE Project Manager panel—the menu, remember, is to the right of the number of pages in the article. In the resulting Duplicate the Article dialog, choose the active project into which you'd like to copy the article. Click OK, and you're done.

Live-Testing Your Publication

Always test your publications early (and often) to make sure they're doing exactly what you want, and that the enrichments behave the way you want them to behave. For that reason, let's talk about how to live-test your publication before getting to the *really* cool stuff, so that you can *see* the really cool stuff.

Aquafadas DPS publications can be previewed live on tablets, but if you have a standard account, only you can preview the project. To offer team reviewing, you'll need a collaborative Aquafadas Digital Publishing account.

As of this writing, although Aquafadas DPS can publish Android publications, the Aquafadas DPS previewer app is not available in any of the Android app stores. Thus, you're left with only the ability to preview the project on iPad. Follow these steps to do that:

1. Ensure that your creation computer is on a network that has Wi-Fi. If not, skip this tutorial and move onto the next, which lets you load projects via iTunes.

2. Make sure that your iPad is on the same Wi-Fi network as your computer.

3. Install on your iPad the free myKiosk app from the iOS App Store.

4. Inside myKiosk tap the Transfer Settings button in the top-left corner. It will display an option to enable transfers and the iPad's unique URL address on the local network. Make note of the URL.

5. In InDesign, in the AVE Project Manager panel, select the project you'd like to test and then click the Send To myKiosk button at the bottom of the panel.

6. In the dialog that appears, enter the URL provided by the myKiosk app on your iPad and the name of the author and editor of the publication. Click Send to have Aquafadas DPS transfer the project to the myKiosk iPad app.

7. When the project appears on your iPad, tap to open it and test it.

If you don't have a Wi-Fi network, you can use the myKiosk app to access applications you've made with the AVE AppFactory (Mac only) application and uploaded to your Avepublishing.

com account. By tapping the Test button at the bottom of the myKiosk iPad app, you can log into your Avepublishing.com account and access all publications uploaded to your account. Using this method instead of the Wi-Fi transfer from the AVE Project Manager panel, you can also perform more advanced tests such as simulated in-app purchases and subscriptions within your publications.

Panning and Zooming

Enabling panning or zooming on images using Aquafadas DPS is just as easy as the Adobe DPS method, but it offers several additional options you won't find in the Adobe DPS Folio Overlays panel.

1. Perform any essential cropping of your desired image in Photoshop or other software. Because panning enables the entire image to be displayed and all but negates cropping affected by leaving parts of the image outside the image frame, you'll need to physically crop the image file *before* placing it into InDesign, removing any parts you don't want readers to see.

2. Place the screen-ready image into InDesign using File ➢ Place (Ctrl+D/Cmd+D).

3. Position and scale that image as necessary. If you want to enable image panning, ensure that the image frame is smaller than the image it contains, thus cropping out parts of the image. If you want to enable zooming in on the image, scale the image down in InDesign, making its Effective PPI measurement on the Links panel larger than its Actual PPI value (see Figure 10.9).

FIGURE 10.9
The Links panel's Link Info section shows the Effective PPI and Actual PPI values for the selected image.

4. Select the image object with the black arrow Selection tool.

5. In the AVE Interactivity panel, click the Picture enrichment icon. You'll be presented with the options in Figure 10.10, which I'll explain in depth in the next section. For now, enable

the Visible In This Orientation check box at the top, and check the Use Pan&Zoom control in the middle of the panel.

FIGURE 10.10
Among the Picture enrichment options is the Use Pan&Zoom control to enable panning and zooming.

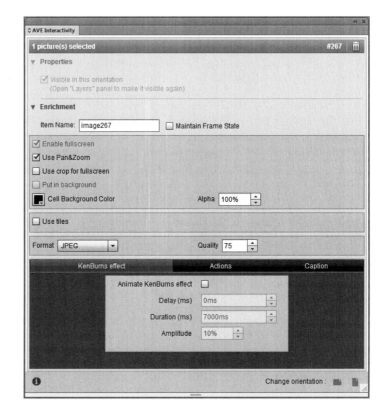

That's it. You've made an image pan and/or zoom. Test it. Now let's go back and examine the other options the Picture enrichment makes available to your images—with or without panning and zooming.

Including InDesign Vector Objects

Within InDesign you can, of course, create vector objects such as rectangles, other polygons, and ellipses; you can also draw just about any shape you can imagine with the Pen tool. You can even paste in more complicated vector objects drawn in Illustrator. To enjoy all the options Aquafadas makes available to raster those vector objects—drawn in or pasted into InDesign—you'll need to convert them to enrichments. That process is so simple it doesn't even warrant a step-by-step. Just select one or more vector objects, grouped or ungrouped, on the AVE Interactivity panel, and click the To Picture enrichment. That will tell Aquafadas DPS to treat the object or group as an enrichment, complete with optional on-touch actions. If you convert multiple, ungrouped objects at one time, each will have a separate entry in the middle of the panel. Note that, upon export, they will be grouped and rasterized as a single object.

Understanding Picture-Enrichment Options

Adding an image into an InDesign document and then creating an AVE interactive magazine from that InDesign document automatically includes the image—you don't have to use the AVE Interactivity panel at all. *Choosing* to use the panel, selecting a graphic frame with the Selection tool, and then clicking the Picture enrichment icon in the AVE Interactivity panel will convert a standard image into an enrichment. Doing so offers several options to enhance the display and behavior of the image (refer to Figure 10.10). It also enables that image to be controlled by other enrichments, but that's something I'll cover throughout the rest of the chapter. Note that Aquafadas DPS calls enrichment options "metadata," which is revealed if you hover your cursor over the trashcan icon in the top-right corner. Clicking that trashcan removes the enrichment and all options of the selected object, returning you to the enrichment selection screen despite that the button is actually labeled Remove Item's Metadata.

In the previous section, I discussed the Use Pan&Zoom control, and I discussed the Visible In This Orientation shortly before that. Let's walk through the remaining options here, many of which are common for all types of enrichments.

Item Name   Just as when working with multistate objects or any type of object-oriented programming, each object must have a unique name by which actions, interactivities, enrichments, scripts, or any other function will reference that object. The instant you convert an object from a standard InDesign frame or other object to an enrichment, the AVE Interactivity panel assigns a unique name to that object—typically something generic like "image328." This name is displayed in the Item Name field. You can leave it at the default, but if you intend to manually set actions or functions to reference that object—say, with a video object, to create buttons that play, pause, and stop that video—do yourself a favor and give it a more recognizable name such as "VideoDemo1." The software will work with it no matter if it has a default name or one you supply; renaming will simply make it easier for you to pick the object from a list that may start at "video001" and continue through "video999."

Maintain Frame State   Enrichments may contain multiple states. For example, one image might be replaced by another in a gallery or slideshow. The Maintain Frame State check box option asks how you'd like that slideshow or other multistate object to *remain* when readers leave the article/page and in case they come back. If Maintain Frame State is enabled, the object will look the same as when the reader left it. Leaving Maintain Frame State off, which is its default, resets the enrichment when the reader leaves the page or article.

Enable Fullscreen   The Enable Fullscreen option is a toggle that determines whether you will allow an image or other enrichment to be launched out of the page into full-screen mode when the reader double-taps the enrichment. With some enrichments, turning this on also enables a full-screen button in the interactive magazine; disabling the option removes that button.

Use Crop For Fullscreen   If you've cropped the image on the page in InDesign by making its graphic frame smaller than the image the frame contains and you enable the Crop For Fullscreen option, when the image is displayed full-screen (assuming full-screen display is enabled), then the full-screen version will be cropped to match the on-page version. By default this option is disabled, which shows the entire image in full-screen view regardless of any on-page cropping.

REVEAL MORE IMAGE

Leaving Use Crop For Fullscreen disabled but then cropping an image on-page creates a neat effect and interactivity for some publications. Readers can be presented with a cropped version of an image on-page, perhaps an isolation or thumbnail, and then, when they double-tap the on-page version, presented not only with a larger, zoomed version but also a version that contains more area than they had known was there. The following graphic, which is from the promotional one-off publication *X-Men Extra*, shows this effect in use, showing a cropped in-page image (left) and a fuller version (with caption) displayed in a lightbox full-screen view.

Cell Background Color and Alpha   When images and other enrichments are displayed in full-screen mode, any area not covered by the content will be given a background color. The Cell Background Color field lets you choose that full-screen background color, while the Alpha field to the right lets you control the transparency of the background.

USE A LIGHTBOX EFFECT

Lightbox is a popular effect wherein images and video are displayed with a semitransparent background color overlay revealing the pages that launched the images and video behind them. You can see the lightbox effect in use on Facebook, Pinterest, and numerous other sites and services that display images or video. Creating the lightbox effect is simple: set a cell background color (black or white are the most common, but don't limit yourself), and then set the Alpha field to somewhere between 75 and 95 percent. Setting the Alpha field to 0 percent shows the full, unfiltered page behind the pop-up image.

Use Tiles   When using Pan&Zoom you should consider enabling the option Use Tiles, which, once activated, causes two other options to appear beside it—Max Width and Tile Size.

The Max Width value is the maximum width of the *full image*, not the cropped view of it. For instance, say you have a 1,000 × 1,000-pixel image cropped and scaled down to 250 × 250 pixels on the page. Setting the Max Width field to 1,000 tells the publication to show the image at its full width; setting that field to 500 enables the picture to be zoomed only up to a maximum width of 500 pixels, or half its actual size but twice the size displayed initially within the page.

Working in conjunction with the Max Width field is the Tile Size field, which offers two options: 512 or 1024, both pixel measurements. This field is effectively a zoom step measurement; each time the reader pinches to zoom in or out, the image can be zoomed either 512 or 1024 pixels at a time.

Format and Quality   Images in enrichments can be converted to PNG or JPEG during export to Aquafadas DPS interactive magazines. The Format field lets you choose per image what that format should be. If you select JPEG, you'll also need to set a Quality value to control the quality vs. compression ratio.

KenBurns Effect   The KenBurns Effect is an option available for many enrichments. The effect itself is a type of panning and zooming made popular by American filmmaker Ken Burns, who didn't create the effect but used it so well and so extensively in his documentaries that the effect was named after him. We've all seen the Ken Burns Effect (the space is incorrectly removed in the Aquafadas DPS user interface) within many examples, including historical documentaries, in the opening sequence to the TV series *Cheers*, and within the OS X screensavers. The effect is simple; it shows a static image and then zooms in on that image to create the impression of motion. Sometimes the zooming also pans, moving around the image as it zooms, to further enhance the impression of motion. (See `http://en.wikipedia .org/wiki/Ken_burns_effect` for a video of the effect in action.) Activating this effect on images with Pan&Zoom enabled or images within a slideshow or gallery can add a little extra polish that Adobe DPS simply can't add at this time.

The options for the KenBurns Effect, which has its own tab at the bottom of the AVE Interactivity panel, are as follows (see Figure 10.11):

FIGURE 10.11
The KenBurns
Effect tab

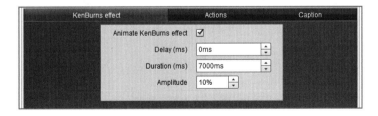

Animate KenBurns Effect   This check box option activates the Ken Burns Effect on the selected object and activates the other three fields.

Delay   Using the Delay field, set a delay in milliseconds (ms) before the animation of the effect begins.

Duration   Also measured in milliseconds, the Duration field controls the overall duration of the animation effect.

Amplitude The Amplitude field controls the amount of zoom and/or pan in the Ken Burns Effect animation. A higher value—in percent—causes greater zooming and panning.

Actions The Actions section lets you define interactive actions that occur when the object is tapped. For instance, by tapping an image, a reader might cause a separate video object to begin playing, to open an external URL, or to begin recording the reader's voice. I'll discuss Actions in depth in the "Adding Actions and Advanced Buttons" section.

Caption Finally, there's the Caption tab available for many image-based enrichments (see Figure 10.12). In place of, or in addition to, inserting the caption for an image directly on the page, Aquafadas DPS provides the option of dynamically adding it to an image, video, and certain other enrichments. Caption text will be overlaid atop the image in the first mode or displayed below the image in full-screen mode. Check the appropriate option and supply the caption in the unlabeled space below the two check boxes.

FIGURE 10.12
The Caption tab

INCLUDING INDESIGN VECTOR OBJECTS

Within InDesign you can, of course, create vector objects such as rectangles, other polygons, and ellipses; you can also draw just about any shape you can imagine with the Pen tool. You can even paste in more complicated vector objects drawn in Illustrator. To enjoy all the options Aquafadas makes available to raster those vector objects—drawn in or pasted into InDesign—you'll need to convert them to enrichments. That process is so simple it doesn't even warrant a step-by-step. Just select one or more vector objects, grouped or ungrouped, on the AVE Interactivity panel, click the To Picture enrichment. That will tell Aquafadas to treat the object or group as an enrichment, complete with optional on-touch actions (see the following image). If you convert multiple, ungrouped objects at one time, each will have a separate entry in the middle of the panel. Note that, upon export, they will be grouped and rasterized as a single object.

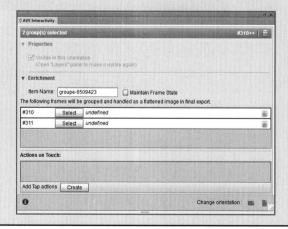

Creating Slideshows and Galleries

With print publications, many great photos are often left out of a final product because of space constraints. Just as common—particularly with catalogs—is the inverse problem, a requirement to include a large number of images—maybe color, style, or size variations of the same product or detail and isolation imagery. The necessity for a large number of images in the world of print publication, where every page costs money, often results not in increased page count but in shrinking images down below their ideal size just to fit them. Interactive magazine solves both of these problems. Any number of images can be presented in a single space, at their ideal sizes.

A slideshow is a series of images displayed sequentially. They can transition from one image to the next automatically after an interval of time, when a reader taps or swipes on them, or both. By contrast a gallery in this realm means a series of images that can also be navigated nonsequentially, usually by the reader tapping thumbnails of the images or buttons. In this section, you'll create both types.

Creating a Slideshow

Aquafadas DPS's slideshow enrichment could be a little easier to execute, but you can't argue with the depth of its options.

1. Create a graphic frame sized and placed where you need it. If you already have a graphic frame with an image in it, that will work, too. If you're creating a new frame, don't worry about placing an image into the frame unless you want one there for positioning.

2. Select the graphic frame with the black arrow Selection tool, and choose the Slideshow enrichment on the AVE Interactivity panel.

3. On the following screen, activate Visible In This Orientation, and choose Simple Slideshow as the type (see Figure 10.13); you'll work with the Slideshow with Thumbnails type a little later, in the "Creating a Gallery" section. Click the Create The Slideshow button.

FIGURE 10.13
When creating a slideshow or gallery, you must first choose the type.

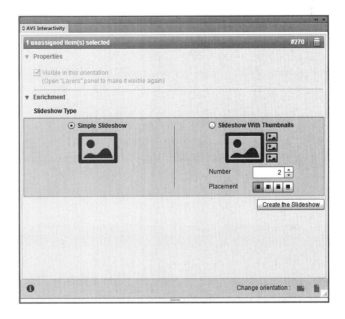

4. On the next (and final) screen, you'll see all of the options related to your slideshow (see Figure 10.14). Except for Enable Scrolling and Show Page Control, all the other options in the Enrichment section are identical to those detailed earlier in this chapter in the "Understanding Picture-Enrichment Options" section. Refer to that section for the main options, but take a moment to decide which of the three slideshow-specific options you might want to use. Here's what they are:

FIGURE 10.14
The Slideshow options (cropped to the top of the panel)

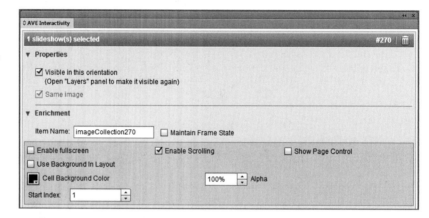

Enable Scrolling　Images used in slideshows may be of different sizes. I'll discuss fitting and resizing options shortly, but assuming you've left your images as different sizes and that one or more are too large to fit the screen, activating the Enable Scrolling option lets readers scroll around in images that are larger than the screen. If the option is disabled, images will be cropped to the screen.

Show Page Control　If enabled, the Show Page Control option displays dots beneath the slideshow to communicate to the reader how many slides are in the slideshow and which slide is currently displayed.

Start Index　Slideshow enrichments contain multiple images, and each image is assigned an index number. This index number can be used by buttons and actions to display specific images in the slideshow out of sequence. Index numbering occurs automatically, starting from the number you specify in the Start Index field. For example, if Start Index equals 1, then the first slide listed on the left in the Contents tab will be image number 1, the one below it image 2, and so on.

5. The lower half of the AVE Interactivity panel is where you manage all the images in the slideshow as well as timings and any effects applied to those images. Begin with the Contents tab (see Figure 10.15) and click the Files button at the bottom of the image list. If that button reads Feed, click the down arrow beside it and select Files. I'll explain the Feed option later, in the "Creating a Web-Fed Slideshow" section.

When the Open dialog appears, select any and all images in the same folder that you'd like in your slideshow. If you want to include images from multiple folders, select the ones you need from a single folder now, and then use the File button to add the images from subsequent folders. It's helpful if your images are all the same size and orientation, though not required.

6. Once you've added all your images, they'll appear in the image list on the left side of the Contents tab (see Figure 10.15). Selecting one displays it on the right, on the Crop tab. Now you need to decide if and how the image will be fit or cropped.

FIGURE 10.15
Each slideshow image appears in the list on the left, while the Crop tab lets you crop them to fit within the slideshow's frame.

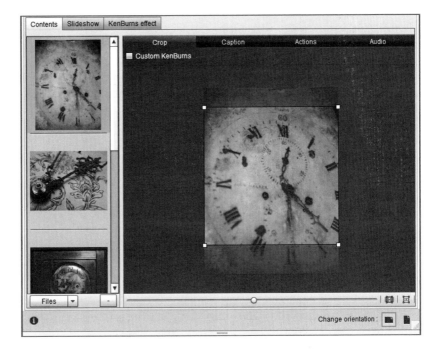

Over your image will likely appear a crop box. The area within the box is the part of the image that will be shown in the slideshow. The aspect ratio of the crop box is determined by the dimensions of the graphic frame you created to house the slideshow. Changing the frame dimensions after creating the slideshow will not alter the crop box dimensions, which is why it's important to size and place the graphic frame before turning it into a slideshow enrichment. Drag the control corners to resize the crop area or drag from within the box to move the crop area.

An alternative to manually cropping are the two fitting buttons—Fill Frame and Fit Content—in the lower right corner of the Crop tab (highlighted in Figure 10.16).

You can also choose to employ the Ken Burns Effect (again, discussed in the "Understanding Picture Enrichment Options" section) on this image so that it automatically zooms and pans to display what can't fit within the space defined by the slideshow's graphic frame. To do that, enable the Custom KenBurns check box in the upper-left corner of the Crop tab, set the Duration option as needed, and then adjust the two crop frames— one green for the start of the effect and the other red for the end (see Figure 10.16).

You can also synchronize the Ken Burns Effect for each image to an audio track, which we'll get into after the next step.

To get a better view as you work, move the slider beneath the image preview to zoom in or out.

FIGURE 10.16
With the Custom KenBurns option checked, you can set options for the Ken Burns Effect, including the start and end views of the image.

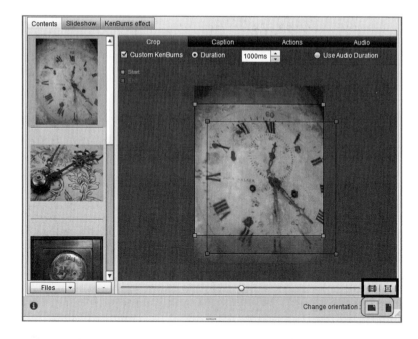

7. Switch to the Caption tab (Figure 10.17). If you want to show a caption for the slide, enter that caption in the large white area and enable the appropriate option above that—whether to show the caption when the slide is shown on the page and whether to show the caption when the slide is shown in full-screen mode.

FIGURE 10.17
The Caption tab lets you add captions to the in-page and/or full-screen views of the image.

8. The Actions tab we'll discuss in depth in the "Adding Actions and Advanced Buttons" section toward the end of this chapter, so let's skip it for now. On the Audio tab you're given the option of including audio in the slideshow (see Figure 10.18). Moreover, this audio can play throughout the entire slideshow, or a separate soundtrack can be played for each image in the slideshow.

FIGURE 10.18
Adding an audio track to the slide

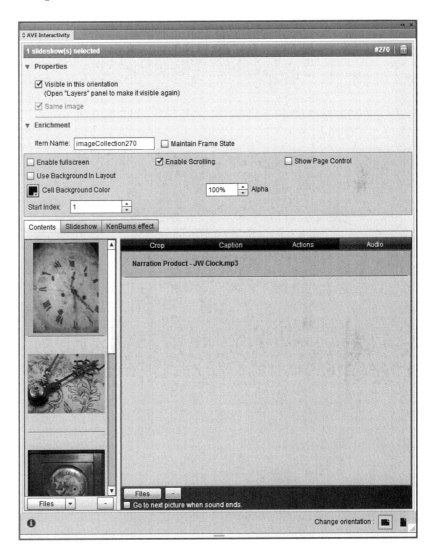

Click the Files button at the bottom of the tab to add one or more MP3 audio files the same way you previously added images to the slideshow. Adding multiple audio files will cause each to play in order. If the order is incorrect, simply drag the entries in the list to reorder them.

Beneath the Files button is the Go To Next Picture When Sound Ends option. Highlighting one or more audio files in the list and then enabling this option creates a slideshow cued to the soundtrack—each sound plays out entirely and then switches to the next slide and plays the next sound file while that slide displays. Activating Use Audio Duration within the KenBurns Effect options on the Crop tab synchronizes the animation of the Ken Burns pan and zoom to the length of the corresponding audio track.

AQUAFADAS SLIDESHOWS ARE AMAZING!

Slideshows with audio tracks are impressive—and even better, slide shows synchronized to audio tracks and slides animated via pan and zoom effects contemporized to the length of that audio!

Think about the possibilities. How about creating a virtual art museum where images and narrative tour readers through a selection of pieces? For that matter, as a designer you could present your portfolio not just as silent images but as images with you explaining verbally the challenges unique to each piece. What about a nature slideshow wherein each photograph of an animal is accompanied by a recording of the sound that animal makes? Along the same lines, a kids' book—or even a language lesson for adults—where a picture or word is shown and an announcer properly pronounces the corresponding word. Maybe you want to take this personal. You could use this feature to create a personal scrapbook or photo album complete with audio tracks—baby's first word along with a picture, saying "I do" as your best wedding photo displays, and so on.

---

9. Now select the second image in the image list on the left and crop or fit it, give it a caption and caption options, and choose its actions and audio. Repeat for each image in the slideshow.

10. After you've set the options for all your images, above the image list switch from the Contents tab to the Slideshow tab (Figure 10.19). There you choose whether to enable auto play—I know, it's not obvious that that's what you're being asked. If Enable Animation is deselected, then slides will advance only when the reader taps or swipes (or, when using a gallery, by tapping the trigger thumbnail). If you check the box beside Enable Animation, it will start the slideshow automatically when the reader reaches that page, and it will use the swipe or fade animation specified below that check box. Check the box beside Enable Animation, and then set the remaining three options.

FIGURE 10.19
The Slideshow tab

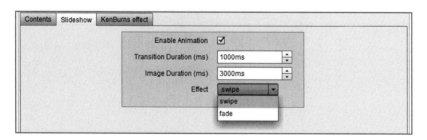

Transition Duration   Measured in milliseconds, the Transition Duration field controls the length of the transition effect, and whether the swipe or fade happens quickly or slowly.

Image Duration   Image duration is the length of time each image remains on screen before transitioning to the next slide, also measured in milliseconds. Set the field appropriately but note that audio synchronization trumps this setting if both are used.

Effect   The Effect drop-down field offers two choices—Swipe, a peeling transition effect, and Fade, which smoothly melts or fades each slide into its replacement.

11. Finally, on the KenBurns Effect tab, you can activate and set the options for a Ken Burns Effect across the entire slideshow rather than, or in addition to, Ken Burns Effects applied individually to specific images.

Creating a Web-Fed Slideshow

One other nifty feature of Aquafadas DPS's slideshow enrichment is the ability to pull images from an *RSS* or *ATOM* feed. This enables you to control the content of a slideshow remotely, without having to update the published app, and even to pull imagery from multiple sources. For instance, you could populate a slideshow from your Flickr photo stream, and the moment you upload new photos to Flickr, those images are viewable in your digital magazine (that is, assuming the reader is actively online, which is the only real drawback to keep in mind).

Creating a web-fed slideshow is simple:

1. Follow the first four steps in the "Creating a Slideshow" tutorial.

2. When you get to step 5, instead of choosing Files beneath the file list, select Feed.

3. Choosing Feed adds a cute RSS illustration to the files list (see Figure 10.20). In the bottom-right corner of that illustration is an easily missed, gear-like configuration button (highlighted in the figure). Click it.

FIGURE 10.20
Setting the source to Feed displays an RSS feed icon on the Contents tab.

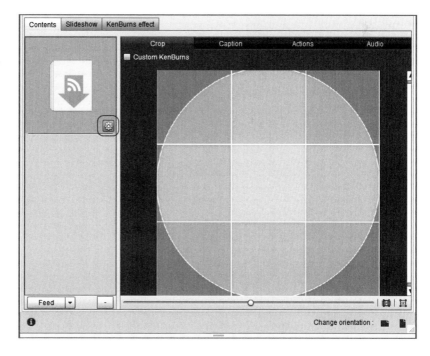

4. In the resulting dialog, fill in the URL field with the complete URL of the RSS or Atom feed supplying the images for the gallery (see Figure 10.21). Then fill in the remaining options, explained next.

FIGURE 10.21
Adding the RSS or ATOM feed data

Limit   An RSS or Atom feed may contain many items, perhaps more than you need. If you have access to the script generating the feed, you can limit the number of items (images) included in the feed at that end. If not or if you don't want to limit the whole feed for this one use, you can set the Limit field to a whole number equal to the number of images you want to fetch from the feed. For example, your feed may present the latest 50 images or posts, but in the interactive magazine you want to show only the most recent 10; you'd then set the Limit field to 10. To include all entries in the feed, set the Limit field to 0.

Offset   When the slideshow fetches the most recent so many entries from the feed, it will start at the top, *the* most recent item, and continue to each next most recent item until it's reached the number set in the Limit field. Sometimes you might not want the slideshow to fetch the most recent items. Maybe you want to have a delay between something appearing in the feed and in the slideshow, such that you have time to review new imagery before it appears in your magazine. Or maybe you have multiple slideshows fed by the same RSS or Atom feed, the first slideshow showing the most recent ten images and the second slideshow displaying the next most recent, images numbered 11 through 20. In those cases, you'd need to set an offset value, a number of items up from the most recent to skip before the slideshow grabs the content. Set the Offset field to the number of items you want skipped; setting it to 0 doesn't skip any.

Cache Time-to-Live   To save on memory and disk storage space, both of which are big considerations in terms of both mobile devices and the data plans that give them Internet access, Aquafadas included the option to cache, or store locally, the previously fetched results of the RSS or Atom feed for a time. For example, if you set the Cache Time-to-Live field to 1 (meaning one hour), the slideshow will wait an hour before it redownloads content from the feed. I highly recommend setting this value to something other than 0, or no caching. Think critically about how often you update the content for the slideshow feed; do you really update it every hour? Do you update it once a day? Then why not save the reader some bandwidth and set the cache time to 24 hours.

5. Once you've configured your feed, you can click the plus-sign button at the bottom of the AVE Interactivity panel to add another RSS or Atom feed, if desired. Otherwise, click the back arrow above the fields you just completed to return to the standard slideshow options.

6. Finish up by setting all the other standard options for your slideshow.

TIP   You can mix web-fed and local images in a slideshow. Just add one or more Feed items and one or more File objects to the Contents tab.

Creating a Gallery

Creating a gallery with Aquafadas DPS is nearly identical to creating a slideshow without trigger images. It is, however, a whole lot easier and faster than creating a gallery in Adobe DPS—no multistate objects, and no buttons panel, just the AVE Interactivity panel:

1. Begin the same way as with a slideshow, by creating a graphic frame sized and placed where you need it—with or without an image in it.

2. Select the graphic frame and choose the Slideshow enrichment in the AVE Interactivity panel.

3. On the following screen, activate Visible In This Orientation, choose Slideshow With Thumbnails, and indicate in the Number field how many images will be in the gallery.

4. Beneath the Number field, choose a placement for the trigger thumbnails. (You can change it later if you want.)

5. From here you're back to the same interface and options as with a standard slideshow. Add your pictures, set their options, set the slideshow and object options, and place images into the trigger or thumbnail frames.

PRODUCING BEFORE-AND-AFTER COMPARISONS

In Aquafadas DPS, before-and-after comparisons can be incorporated into your digital publications with a higher degree of interactivity (and style) than simply placing two pictures side-by-side on the page.

1. In InDesign create a graphic frame to hold the before-and-after enrichment; all images will be shown in this one graphic frame and may also be displayed as a full-screen pop-up.

2. Select the frame with the black arrow Selection tool; then on the AVE Interactivity panel, select the Comparator enrichment.

3. In the resulting options, activate the Visible In This Orientation check box and name the enrichment. If you want the comparison to appear as a full-screen pop-up, activate Enable Fullscreen and set the background color and transparency for the areas of the pop-up beyond the comparator itself.

4. Check Show Text Captions, and then supply the caption text for the left and right images—something like "before" and "after"—if you want to have captions appear.

5. Beneath the Before and After tabs, click the Files button to add one or more images to be displayed as the before images.

Incorporating Audio and Video

As covered in Chapter 8, audio and video can be deployed in your interactive publications to foster greater reader engagement and to present content that simply isn't possible in print publishing.

Inserting Audio

Adding on-the-page audio in Aquafadas DPS is limited to adding just the audio file, which automatically generates an OS-standard player bar during playback. There is no poster function as is built into Adobe DPS; instead, the system lets you visually represent the audio with the unfettered freedom of designing directly on the page. In other words, if you want the audio to have a poster (an image, such as a speaker icon or album cover, to visually represent the audio file), place an image on the page behind or near the audio enrichment frame.

1. Create a new graphic frame and select it with the black arrow Selection tool.

2. In the AVE Interactivity panel, click the Audio enrichment icon.

3. Set the Visible In This Orientation option to active, and then fill in the basic enrichment options such as Item Name and Maintain Frame State, if desired.

4. In the middle section of the panel, you'll see a File button, which is actually a drop-down field (see Figure 10.22). From this field choose either the URL or the File option. The former lets you point to the full URL of an MP3 hosted online, including it during play time in the interactive magazine if the reader has an active Internet connection. The latter option, File, is the more commonly used one because it lets you click the File button to the right of the File field and select a local sound file for inclusion.

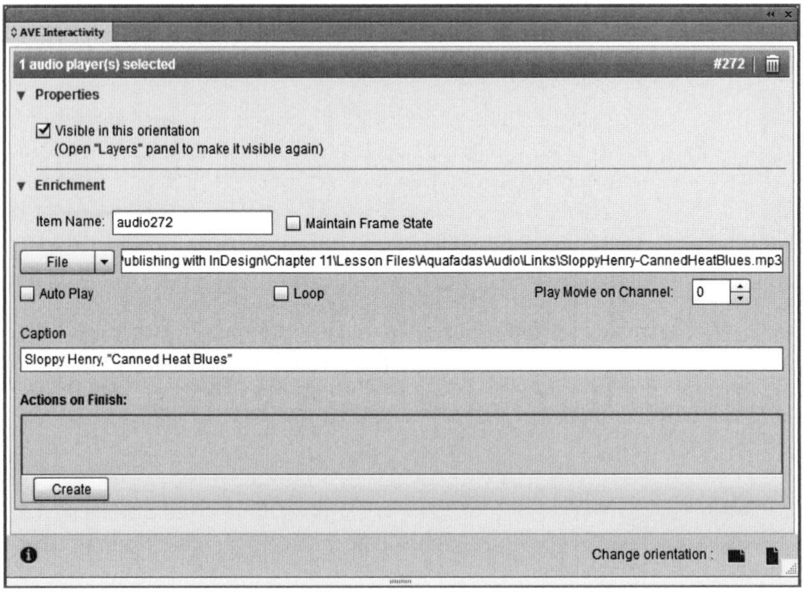

FIGURE 10.22
Setting the options in the Audio enrichment

5. Set the remaining options. Choose Auto Play if you want the sound to play automatically when the page loads. Activating Loop will continuously play the sound in a loop, such as with ambient music or a soundtrack. And Play Movie on Channel lets you play the sound effect on a specific, arbitrary channel number, thus enabling multiple audio tracks to play simultaneously, each on a different channel.

6. Fill in the Caption field to give your audio a caption. The caption will display as the audio plays, so use this not for background or ambient sounds, but when a textual explanation of what the reader is hearing is desired. Adding a descriptive caption (or a complete transcript as the caption) is especially important for accessibility reasons, to communicate the content to the hearing-impaired.

7. Finally, assign any actions to occur when the audio finishes playing. See the "Adding Actions and Advanced Buttons" section for more about that.

TIP   Because Aquafadas DPS does not place the audio into the frame on the page, but adds the MP3 only during publication, you cannot use InDesign's Media panel to preview audio objects.

Within Aquafadas DPS workflows you can include audio in your interactive magazine in these other ways, discussed in depth in Chapter 8, "Covering the Basics of Interactive Publications," or elsewhere in this chapter:

◆   Link to an external audio file via a hyperlink (see the "Utilizing Hyperlinks of All Types" section in Chapter 8).

◆   Include audio that is embedded within or controlled by a page on the Web (see the "Integrating Live Web Content" section in Chapter 8).

◆   Seed, or even control, slideshows and galleries with one or more soundtracks and clips (see the "Creating a Gallery" topic).

◆   Add an action to just about any enrichment that plays one or more MP3 files (see the "Adding Actions and Advanced Buttons" section).

◆   Add an action to just about any enrichment that records speech or other audio from the reader (assuming the reader's device includes a microphone) and then optionally play back that recording (see the "Adding Actions and Advanced Buttons" section).

Including Video

Video enrichments are most commonly used to embed video clips that readers will activate and watch embedded in-page or full-screen—and you can either leave that choice to the reader or force your video to always play full-screen. But that's not all you can do with video. Aquafadas's video enrichment shares many attributes with its image and audio enrichments, including an optional Ken Burns Effect as well as the ability to execute actions after the video plays, actions such as loading up the next video, opening a URL, or showing or hiding other objects. But that's not all you can with video. By toggling just a couple of options, you can use a video as page's animated background or make it a perpetually playing design element. In either case, your video enrichment can be uncluttered by player controls and buttons.

TIP You can also include videos in Aquafadas slideshows and galleries! See the "Creating a Slideshow" topic earlier in this chapter, and, instead of importing images—or only images— throw some video files into the mix. They'll play just like images.

1. Either place a video into the layout using File ➤ Place or merely create an empty graphics frame.

2. Select the frame with the black arrow Selection tool; then, in the AVE Interactivity panel, click the Movie enrichment button.

3. Set the Visible In This Orientation option to active, and then fill in the basic enrichment options such as Item Name and Maintain Frame State, if desired.

4. In the middle section of the panel, you'll see a File button, which is actually a drop-down field (see Figure 10.23). From this field choose either the URL or the File option. The former lets you point to the full URL of a video hosted online, including it during play time in the interactive magazine if the reader has an active Internet connection. The latter option, File, is the more commonly used one because it lets you click the File button to the right of the File field and select a local video file for inclusion. Alas, even if you already placed a video file into the frame, you'll need to complete the File field.

FIGURE 10.23
Setting the AVE Interactivity options for a Movie enrichment

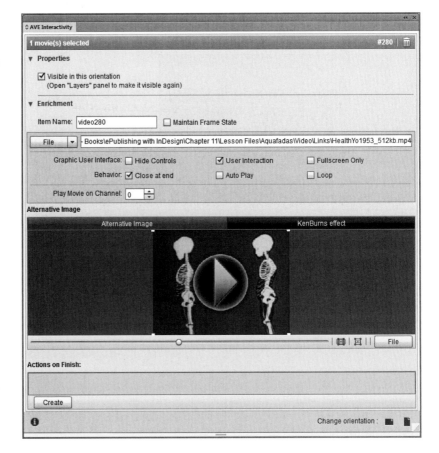

5. Set the remaining options.

Hide Controls   By default the video controls are always shown as an overlay on the video. Activating Hide Controls moves them out of the reader's way until the reader taps the video.

User Interaction   User Interaction is an important option to enable if you want your readers to be able to work with the controls or toggle the video between full-screen and in-page mode. However, if you're using video to present in-page perpetual animation or background video, you'll want to disable the User Interaction option, thus letting the video play without the risk of a reader pausing or otherwise messing it up.

Fullscreen Only   The Fullscreen Only option will make the video always play in full-screen mode rather than giving the user the choice.

Close At End   Selecting Close At End is especially important if you enable the Fullscreen Only option because it will stop the video and return to the page. Whether Fullscreen Only is active or not, this option will return to the video's poster or alternative image when the video has finished playing. Forgetting to set Close At End won't leave the reader stuck, unable to return to the document; instead, he or she will have to manually click the Close button in the video.

Auto Play   Choose Auto Play if you want the video to play automatically when the page loads.

Loop   Activating Loop will continuously play the video in a loop, which opens up the possibility of using video for animations or animated backgrounds like smartphone live wallpapers.

Play Movie On Channel   Play Movie On Channel lets you play a movie on a specific, arbitrary channel number, thus enabling multiple videos to play simultaneously, each on a different channel.

6. In the Alternative Image section in the middle of the AVE Interactivity panel, click the File button and select a static image to use to represent the video when it isn't playing. Once you've loaded the image, you'll be able to crop and fit it just like working with images in slideshows and galleries. In this same area, you can also add a Ken Burns Effect to the video itself (not the alternative image) by clicking the KenBurns Effect tab and setting options like those for slideshows, galleries, and standard images.

7. Finally, assign any actions to occur when the video finishes playing. See the "Adding Actions and Advanced Buttons" section for more about that.

INCORPORATING EXTERNAL PUBLICATIONS

Let's say you publish a periodical and in the current issue you want to tease the next issue or back issues. Or maybe you want to feature a digital comic book within another publication. Aquafadas offers two simple enrichments to help you incorporate other live digital publications into your layouts: Show AVE and AVE Comics. They work just about the same: create a graphic frame to hold the other magazine or comic, select the correct enrichment, and then navigate to the AVE or AVE Comic to incorporate. As long as the content you want to incorporate is also published, it will download to the reader's device and display in the space you've created for it.

Adding Animations and 3D Rotating Objects

At first blush, the title of this section might sound like to two totally unrelated types of interactivity. Bear with me, though; you'll soon see that, while the intent is different, they're actually both built the same way. I'll start off with the 3D rotating object; even if you want to use animation only, please go through the 3D rotating objects tutorial because the steps are the same for other types of animations.

Preparing 3D Rotating Objects

The first thing you need To add a 3D rotating object overlay is, of course, your 3D rotating object. Typically these objects are created in 3D drawing programs like the selection of applications available from Autodesk (`http://autodesk.com`), which include industry standards such as the AutoCAD line of products, 3Ds Max, Maya, and pretty much every other go-to name in 3D design and rendering. Although Autodesk is the big name and has bought up many of its competitors over the years, alternatives like SketchUp (`http://sketchup.google.com/`) from Google and Rhino 3D (`www.rhino3d.com/`) are also available. You can even create basic 3D in Photoshop Extended. And then there's 3D objects captured via photo or video cameras moving around the object in sequence.

However you get your 3D object, you or your 3D designer will need to make a video of that object rotating in all the ways you want the reader to see. For instance, if you want the reader to merely move laterally, rotating the object only horizontally (as with the book example I provided in `Lesson Files\Aquafadas\Animation and 360 Rotate`), film it rotating only horizontally; if you want readers to be able to rotate it vertically, film it that way. Filming is the easy part: 3D drawing and rendering programs let you rotate not the object but the *camera*, the view on the object, within a full 360-degree sphere. Those programs also let you record the camera movements to digital video. Naturally, photographs and live-action video captured with moving cameras will already be in digital video format.

That's what you need at this point, a video of the object rotating in three-dimensional space. Moreover, that video must be in a format that Photoshop can open. The list of compatible formats is much too long to include here—especially after Photoshop CS6—so I'll point you to Photoshop's documentation for that list. However, I will say that it'll open pretty much any common format 3D programs and video-editing applications will render, including standards like QuickTime MOV, Windows AVI, H.264 MPEG4 MP4 and M4V, 3GP, AAC, and plenty more. Once you have the video of your object rotating, it's time to make the frames.

Preparing Other Animations

If you're aren't working with 3D rotating objects but instead are using any other type of animation—everything from a cartoon character changing expressions and moving in a fixed space to text or another object traveling across the page—the preparation is a little different. First, ask yourself whether you need to use this, the Image Sequence overlay, for your animation or would it be better as an embedded video, which has its own characteristics. If video is not the way to go, then let's look at the current state of your animation.

If it's in video format, you must work through the following "Making the Frames" section. If your animation is already in a series of separate images, make sure they are either JPEG or PNG image files, with or without transparency in the latter format, and that all the individual images comprising that animation are numbered sequentially and in the same folder.

Making the Frames

When you create the 3D rotating object, you need to do so as a movie clip. But in order for readers to experience the draggable 3D rotation as if it *were* video, you actually have to convert the video to a selection of static images. The ADP rendering engine then shows those images like a slideshow, *simulating* video. As a reader drags a finger across the overlay, the document replaces one static image with another, each image being a frame from the video of the object rotating, thus giving the appearance that the reader is actually moving the object in three-dimensional space. When you interacted with my 3D rotating book, you were actually switching between the 75 different JPEG images in the Lesson Files\Adobe DPS\Animation and 360 Rotate\Links folder (see Figure 10.24).

FIGURE 10.24
Some of the 75 individual images comprising the frame of the 3D rotating book animation

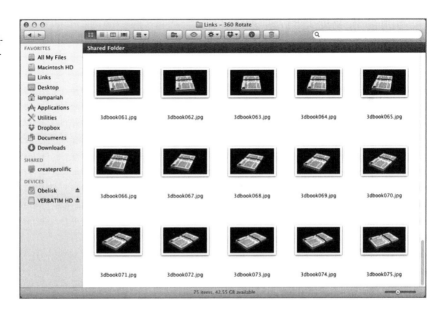

Converting the video file into those individual frame images may look daunting, but it's actually just a few clicks, relying on automation features built into Photoshop to do all the repetitive and complicated steps. Let's open Photoshop (just about any version, at least as far back as CS4) and create those images.

1. In Photoshop choose File ➤ Import ➤ Video Frames to Layers. In the Open dialog, navigate to, and open, your video file.

2. The Import Video To Layers dialog will appear next (see Figure 10.25). It will show you a preview of your video, including a Play/Stop button, buttons to move to the beginning and end of the film, and a timeline to show the progress of the film as it plays. Beneath the timeline are two black arrow start and stop markers. If you want to import frames from across the entire video, leave these markers where they are—at the beginning and end. If, however, you want to import only a range of frames, say, to limit the reader's ability to rotate the object to seeing only three sides instead of four, move the markers such that they include only the portion of the video you want to include in the interactive magazine; any frames before the left marker and after the right marker will be excluded.

Moving the markers automatically switches the Range To Import setting in the top left corner of the dialog from the default From Beginning to End option to the Selected Range Only option.

FIGURE 10.25

The Import Video
To Layers dialog

3. Now set the limit of frames.

All video, whether digital or on film, is merely a series of static images played so quickly that our brains fill in the transitions between those images, creating the illusion for us of full-motion—thus the older but more accurate description of film as "motion pictures." When we're talking about movies and television shows shown on any device—movie theater screens, television screens, mobile device screens, and so on—we need to include a high number of frames displayed rapidly, measured in frames per second (FPS). That's not what I'm talking about here.

In this case, you're not working with full-motion video. What you're creating is video that will be driven by the reader's finger, not by a projector or media player. Consequently, the transitions between frames or states of the object during rotation don't need to be as smooth as they would for movies or television. You can use fewer frames and still rely on the reader's brain to fill in the transitions between them. Fewer frames means fewer separate JPEG images, which means less disk space and bandwidth required for the reader to obtain the publication.

Instead of importing every frame and then subsequently making every frame its own JPEG image, tell Photoshop to import fewer frames. You do that by activating the Limit To Every [Blank] Frames option and filling in the blank beside it. If you enter 2 in the blank, Photoshop will import only every second frame of the movie, giving you half the number of images as frames that make up the original movie.

Determining how many frames you must include is largely a matter of trial and error. Start by setting the Limit To Every [Blank] Frames field to a high number like 6 or 8, work through the rest of the tutorial, and test the overlay live on a mobile device. If you see the rotation stutter between frames, then you've chosen too high a number and need to go back through just this "Making the Frames" section with a lower number in the Limit To Every [Blank] Frames field.

4. Disable the Make Frame Animation option, which is useful only if you're turning a video into an animated GIF or PNG (like how I snuck that cool tip in there?), and then click OK.

After a few moments of processing, Photoshop will create a separate layer on the Layers panel from each imported video frame (see Figure 10.26).

FIGURE 10.26
When the video
import to layers has
finished process-
ing, you'll find each
frame as a separate
layer on the Layers
panel.

5. Now is the time if you need to do anything to the frames, things such as color correction, special effects, and what-not. Obviously, with so many layers, you'll want to automate such processing with an action file.

6. Now choose File ➤ Scripts ➤ Export Layers To Files to have Photoshop automatically generate a separate image from each of the layers in the document. Up will pop the Export Layers To Files dialog (see Figure 10.27).

FIGURE 10.27
Exporting all the
frame layers to
individual images
via the Export Lay-
ers To Files script
dialog

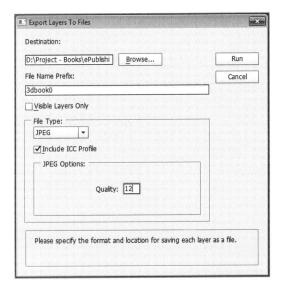

7. Set the options for output and then click Run to begin creating those individual frame images that InDesign's Folio Overlays panel requires.

Here's what those options mean in terms of the project you're currently working on.

Destination   The Destination field tells Photoshop where to save the images. To save a little time, you want to set this to be an otherwise empty folder near or under the folder containing the INDD that will house the overlay.

File Name Prefix   DPS doesn't much care what you name the images as long as they're sequentially numbered, which they will be automatically by Photoshop (sort of; see the "Filename Reversal" sidebar). Whatever you enter here as the prefix for your images, the name before the numbering, is for your reference only; DPS has no interest in it, and readers will never see the filenames.

Visible Layers Only   The Visible Layers Only check box gives you another way to limit the range of motion in the 3D rotating object. If you had noticed in the Layers panel frames that you didn't want included in the overlay, well, you probably deleted them. Alternatively, you could have simply hidden the layers and activating this option would only export the layers that aren't hidden.

File Type   Choose JPEG or PNG-24 from the File Type list, and then set the appropriate options below the field. If you select JPEG as the export file type, your option will be a numeric field for JPEG quality—0 to 12. If you opt for PNG-24, you'll be given three check boxes: Transparency, Interlaced, and Trim Layers. Disable all three. The first two are incompatible with the overlay, while the third will crop empty space from each layer/image individually, resulting in the frames of your object not lining up and the whole illusion failing faster than *The Smurfs* movie did.

When Photoshop finishes the process, you'll have a folder full of images ready for use in InDesign (just like I had in Figure 10.24).

FILENAME REVERSAL

As a consequence of this process, first generating layers from the frames in a video and then exporting those layers to individual files, the resulting files are in reverse order; if the object rotated clockwise in the original video, it will now rotate counterclockwise in the overlay. For example, 3dbook_0001_Layer 75.jpg., one of the rotating book's output files, begins numbering at 1 (0001, technically) even though that same image is the last layer, which is the last frame converted to a layer, as identified by the layer name, Layer 75, in the filename. In most cases, this reversal isn't a big problem, but if it is for your publication, you can fix it in InDesign with one option, or use a file renaming utility to rename all the images into their inverse (correct) order.

Adding the Objects

Turning the frames of an animation or an object rotating in 3D space into an enrichment is the easiest part of the whole process.

1. Back in InDesign, create a graphic frame sized and positioned as you want the 3D rotating object to appear in the interactive magazine.

2. Decide how you want that frame to look when the reader first reaches the page. If you want it to automatically show the first frame of the 3D rotating object animation, then leave the frame blank. If, however, you want to include a different image, maybe one that includes an icon or text instructing the reader to drag a finger across the image to explore the depicted object in three-dimensional space, then place that static image into the frame using File ➢ Place.

3. Select the frame with the black arrow Selection tool, and click the Animated Images enrichment icon in the AVE Interactivity panel.

4. Activate the Visible In This Orientation option, and set Item Name and Maintain Frame State as desired.

5. In the next section of the dialog, which you can see in Figure 10.28, click the plus sign button to browse for the images comprising the frames of the animation. (The dialog says to select the folder, but it really should say select the images.) Select all the images you want to include; don't try to load them one at a time. If the images are in multiple locations, click the plus sign again to browse for more images. Any that get included by mistake can be removed by highlighting them in the list and clicking the minus sign.

FIGURE 10.28
Options for the Animated Images enrichment (after adding files)

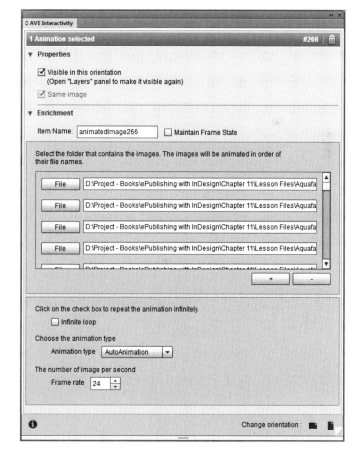

6. Finally, set the other options in the panel to complete inclusion of the enrichment.

Here's what the other options on the panel mean:

Infinite Loop Activating Infinite Loop plays the animation in perpetuity, starting over immediately upon ending, which is a great way to just let your object rotate or to use an animation design element with which readers won't directly interact.

Animation Type The Animation Type drop-down menu offers two selections: AutoAnimation and Scroll. AutoAnimation is the type you want if you're using multiple images for the animation frames. That tells ADP that merely switching between the various images will accomplish the frame-by-frame animation. Opt for the Scroll option when you're animating just a single image too large for the space in which its contained—like panning (see the "Panning and Zooming" section earlier in this chapter)—and you want to animate the movement of the image within its frame.

The remaining controls in the panel differ depending on which type of animation is chosen. Selecting AutoAnimation shows only the Frame Rate field, as you can see in Figure 10.29, while choosing Scroll hides Frame Rate and reveals fields for Scroll Direction, Scroll Velocity, and Indicator Style, as shown in Figure 10.30.

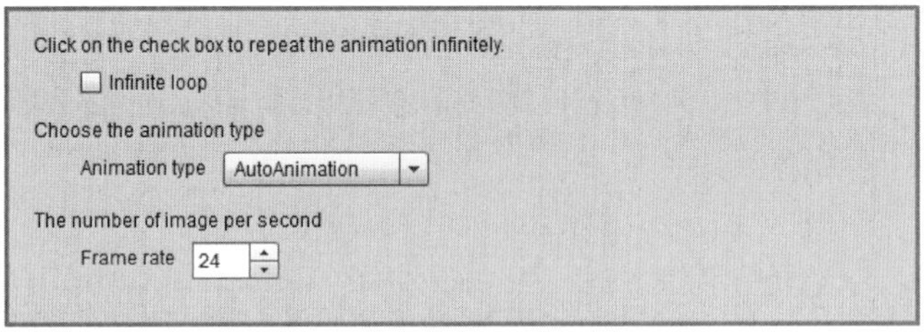

FIGURE 10.29
After choosing AutoAnimation from the Animation Type field, the only other option to set is Frame Rate.

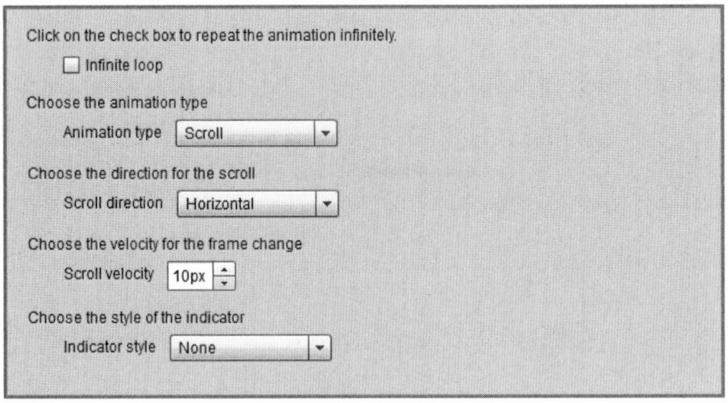

FIGURE 10.30
Setting the Animation Type to Scroll offers these options.

Frame Rate Available only when Animation Type is set to AutoAnimation, the Frame Rate is the only control needed because the animation is contained within the frame images. The Frame Rate field sets the number of frames shown per second (FPS), which is how fast the animation plays. The higher the FPS, the faster the frame images go by, which means the shorter the overall animation or the faster the object rotates, but also the less noticeable any missing frames.

Scroll Direction   From the Scroll Direction field, select the plane on which you'd like to enable scrolling of images whose Animation Type is set to Scroll; you can choose Horizontal or Vertical.

Scroll Velocity   The Scroll Velocity field asks for a measurement in pixels of how far each step of scrolling should go (in other words, how far should the image advance every time the reader taps the scroll bar).

Indicator Style   When the Animation Type is set to Scroll, you have the option of showing a scrollbar on the animated image. The Indicator Style field lets you choose that scrollbar color for contrast. You can choose Black, White, or Default, which means whatever color(s) the device's operating system says scrollbars should be. You can also choose None, which hides the scrollbars for cleaner autorunning animations.

To create other types of animations is an identical process, except, perhaps, not allowing readers to control the animation, to have the animation play automatically. For instance, open and test the ex_animation.indd file from the Lesson Files\Aquafadas\Animation and 360 Rotate folder. Sure the little guy running across the bottom is rather spastic, but he demonstrates animation in a way you can't miss. Also, notice that you can't interact with him. He's an autoplaying animation, one used for decoration.

Adding animations such as that guy is easier than including 3D rotating objects. If your animation will "travel," however, as the man runs across the page, then create *all* frames of the animation at the same size, including empty spaces. To better understand this, take a look at Figure 10.31, which is three frames/images from my animation. Notice that, although the man starts out on the right, the image encompasses the full area he'll travel, all the way across to the left edge of the page. Those areas are simply left empty, and the frame images created as PNG-24 with transparency enabled cause the background elements to shine through.

FIGURE 10.31
Three frames of the 17-frame animation, all of equal width

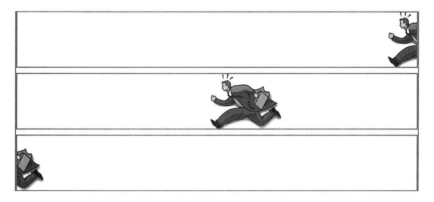

A WORKAROUND FOR CREATING 3D PANORAMAS AND SPACES

Alas, Aquafadas doesn't have a built-in enrichment for creating 3D panoramas and spaces. You can fake it, though; there are two methods to use if you want to enable readers to explore the interior of a space station, the inner workings of the human respiratory system, museum galleries, and so on.

First, if you need the reader to move along only one plane, horizontally or vertically, you can employ the Animated Picture enrichment with the Scroll animation type or, if you've taken enough photos for a smooth transition, using the AutoAnimation type and leaving it to the images to move the reader around.

The second method is to create the panoramic effect outside of InDesign using web technologies, encapsulate the effect within HTML, and use Aquafadas DPS's HTML Page enrichment to include the page and its panorama inside the interactive magazine. See the section titled "Integrating Offline HTML, Games, and Activities" later in this chapter for how to do that.

Producing Before-and-After Comparisons

Ah, the venerable before-and-after image comparison. Without this brilliant visual construct, how would the world ever know how much weight Alec Baldwin lost?

The before-and-after photo technique is employed in many, many ways, most of them more constructive and beneficial than for purposes of showing off weight loss, fashion, gossip, and poor design. Such comparisons can be incorporated into your digital publications with a higher degree of interactivity (and style) than simply placing two pictures side-by-side on the page.

Aquafadas DPS offers a purpose-built before-and-after enrichment called the Comparator.

1. In InDesign, create a graphic frame to hold the before and after enrichment; all images will be shown in this one graphic frame and may also be displayed as a full-screen pop-up.

2. Select the frame with the black arrow Selection tool; then, in the AVE Interactivity panel, select the Comparator enrichment.

3. In the resulting options, activate the Visible In This Orientation check box, and name the enrichment. At this point, you should also determine whether you'd like the comparison to remain in-page or have it appear as a full-screen pop-up. If the latter, activate the Enable Fullscreen control and set the background color and transparency for the areas of the pop-up beyond the comparator itself.

4. Check the Show Text Captions box, and then supply the caption text for the left and right images—something like "before" and "after"—if you want to have captions appear.

5. Beneath the Before tab, click the Files button to add one or more images to be displayed as the before images.

6. Do the same on the After tab for the comparison images. Note that you need the same number of before and after images, which readers will be able to cycle through in pairs.

That's it. The effect is now complete. When readers activate the enrichment, they'll be presented with a vertical bar, a window shade sort of device that can be dragged left or right, revealing in the same space either the after or before image, respectively.

Building Read-Along Text

When Aquafadas DPS hit version 2.0 in mid-2012, read-along functionality (Figure 10.32) was added, bringing this favorite feature of children's and elearning ebooks into the realm of interactive magazines but with all the power and creativity inherent in an Aquafadas enrichment.

FIGURE 10.32

Employing the Read Aloud enrichment in this edition of The Wonderful Wizard of Oz highlights each word as the narrator reads it.

Scarecrow declared he could see as well as by day. So she took hold of his arm and managed to get along fairly well.

"If you see any house, or any place where we can pass the night," she said, "you must tell me; for it is very uncomfortable walking in the dark."

Soon after the Scarecrow stopped.

"I see a little cottage at the right of us," he said, "built of logs and branches. Shall we go there?"

"Yes, indeed," answered the child. "I am all tired out."

So the Scarecrow led her through the trees until they reached the cottage, and Dorothy entered and found a bed of dried leaves in one corner. She lay down at once, and with Toto beside her soon fell into a sound sleep. The Scarecrow, who was never tired, stood up in another corner and waited patiently until morning came.

Creation of this type of enrichment is a little more involved than most others, though it's an easier process than incorporating read-along functionality into fixed-layout ebooks, which requires a nonstandard audio and text preparation phase as well as copious hand-tagging in the ebook HTML files.

1. Prepare your audio, the track of your voiceover artist reading the content. The track should be an MP3 file on either your computer or your network to be incorporated directly into the interactive magazine or hosted online and included in the publication via streaming over a live Internet connection.

   For ideal results, trim the audio such that there is no music, sound, or open air before the announcer begins speaking. If you want to play music or some other audio before the read-along track begins, add the extra sounds as a standard audio enrichment and then set an action on that audio enrichment to activate the read-along enrichment when the first finishes (see the sections "Inserting Audio" and "Actions and Advanced Buttons" in this chapter).

   Note the duration of the audio track in seconds.

2. You will need to process the audio through a text and audio syncing application, such as iKaraoke Tuneprompter, that produces KTP-format transcription files. Doing so lets you connect the spoken words of the person reading with the words in the transcript, creating

appropriate markers to cue the visual display of each word with its spoken equivalent. (You can find links to download iKaraoke Tuneprompter and tutorials to help you use it at `http://abbrv.it/DigiPubIDTools`.)

3. In InDesign, create a graphic frame to house the read-along content, which will be the text being read as well as the accompanying audio track.

4. Select the frame with the black arrow Selection tool, and choose the Read Aloud enrichment from the AVE Interactivity panel.

5. Set the standard options—Visible In This Orientation, Item Name, and Maintain Frame State—as desired (see Figure 10.33).

FIGURE 10.33
Setting the options for the Read Aloud enrichment

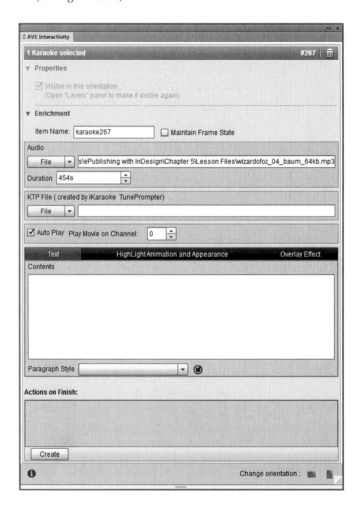

6. In the Audio section, use the File button to select either File or URL. For File, locate the local copy of the MP3 audio track; for URL, you must supply the full URL to the online-hosted soundtrack.

7. In the KPT File section, make a similar selection—File or URL—and provide the location of the KTP transcription file.

8. Decide whether you want the read-along to automatically play or wait for activation and on what channel the audio should play, and set the Auto Play and Play Movie on Channel options appropriately. Note that if you'll be activating the read-along enrichment through an action of another enrichment (or a button), you want to leave Auto Play disabled.

9. The large field in the Text tab in the middle of the panel is for the read-along text (see Figure 10.34). Paste in here the text as it will be read; the full text will be visible to the reader, with the currently spoken word highlighted, so double-check it for spelling and grammatical errors. Once you're satisfied, choose a paragraph style to apply to this text on the page from the Paragraph Style field. If you haven't yet created the style, go create it, return to this panel, and click the Refresh button to the right of the Paragraph Style field to update the list of available paragraph styles.

FIGURE 10.34
The Text area holds the text to be read.

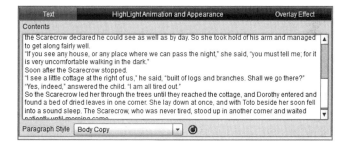

10. Switching to the Highlight Animation And Appearance tab, create the appearance of the word being actively spoken (see Figure 10.35). In other words, as a word is spoken, it can be highlighted in the text, and here is where you set all the options to govern the appearance of that highlight. Alas, you cannot use existing character styles, but as compensation, Aquafadas DPS gives you highlight effects that would be difficult to do in character styles.

FIGURE 10.35
Setting the appearance options for the highlight applied to the currently spoken word

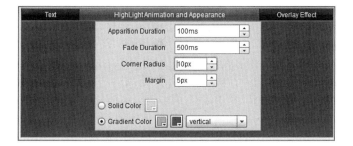

Apparition Duration The Apparition Duration determines, in measurements of milliseconds (ms), how long a highlight effect lasts. Change this value as you see fit, keeping in mind that one second equals 1,000 milliseconds.

Fade Duration As highlight effects come and go from word to word, they can be set to fade in and out, which is often more interesting than a colored background simply appearing and disappearing behind text. The Fade Duration field, which is also measured in milliseconds, determines the length of the fading effect. Lower values create faster transitions between not there and there, while longer values make the highlights fade in and out more slowly.

Corner Radius Measured in pixels, the Corner Radius field lets you round the corners of the highlight blocks that appear behind the word currently being read.

Margin When a highlight block appears behind a word, it tends to be slightly larger than the word it highlights. The amount of space on all sides is controlled by the Margin field.

Solid Color If you want the highlight to be a solid color, activate the Solid Color option and click the color swatch to access a color picker for choosing the color of the highlight.

Gradient Color Alternatively to a solid highlight block, you can use a linear gradient comprised of two colors that fade either horizontally or vertically. To use the gradient, select the Gradient Color option, pick the start and end colors from the color swatch color picker pop-ups, and then choose whether to transition the colors along the horizontal or vertical planes.

11. On the final tab, Overlay Effect, you can activate and set options for a semitransparent overlay on the entire block of text being read, the text you entered on the Text tab. Once the effect is enabled, you can choose the overlay fill color, stroke color, and stroke thickness (see Figure 10.36).

FIGURE 10.36
Specifying the
Overlay Effect
options

Employing Scrolling Page Regions

If you create a text frame in InDesign, fill that frame with placeholder text, and then reduce the size of that frame, the overset text portion of the story remains, but it generally won't be visible to the reader. The interactive magazine format, though, can allow the reader to scroll the content within that text frame—effectively, interactive magazines can include more content in a given space than will actually fit in that space. Welcome to the *TARDIS*; watch your step as you board.

Aquafadas DPS includes the ability to scroll text frames *but only text frames*. If that's all you need, just create a text frame and overset some of the text. Upon export to interactive-magazine format, Aquafadas DPS will automatically enable scrolling on that text frame, complete with up and down arrows and fading effects.

Although Aquafadas DPS does not include a native enrichment for scrolling mixed content within container frames, it does enable you to add scrollable local HTML pages to frames as well as include content located directly on the Web (just as Adobe DPS does). Check out the sections "Integrating Live Web Content" in Chapter 8 and "Including Offline HTML, Games, and Activities" in this chapter as to how to include these types of content.

Using Content Replacement

Content replacement techniques with Aquafadas DPS are quite flexible because the ability to show or hide objects and enrichments is built into the actions most enrichments can execute automatically. Thus, not only can you attach content replacement to buttons that readers must tap on to trigger, you can also replace content automatically based on non-reader-initiated events and timings. Furthermore, you can use any enrichment as variable content. Unlike Adobe DPS, Aquafadas DPS allows you to show or hide any enrichment, with or without static elements.

In Chapter 8 I listed several types of content replacements possible in both Adobe DPS and Aquafadas DPS, but you can accomplish many other types thanks to the features in Aquafadas DPS. Here are a few examples of these other types:

◆ When video and audio objects finish playing, they can show previously hidden objects, whether those objects are text, graphics, HTML widgets, animations, or other video or audio objects that autoplay and execute on-finish reveals of still more objects.

◆ Most enrichments can upon finish and, in some cases, at other times, automatically launch web addresses.

◆ As readers scroll through a section of text images, video, URLs, and other types of content can be set to appear automatically. For instance, instead of fitting all the photographs for an article as small images on the page, all visible simultaneously, a large photo area can automatically show each image as the reader reaches the relevant portion of the article.

Same-Space Content Replacement

The first example in Chapter 8, "product pages can replace one color or style of a product image with another," you've already done by creating a gallery, or a slideshow with thumbnails, in the "Creating Slideshows and Galleries" section. During that process, the thumbnails Aquafadas DPS creates for you are really buttons that call specific images in the slideshow by the images' index numbers.

Multiple Object Visibility Toggle

Because of Aquafadas DPS's superb content replacement abilities, this section includes a number of tutorials for achieving slightly different results for vastly differing projects.

Unlike Adobe DPS, Aquafadas DPS can't use multistate objects. That means the Aquafadas DPS method for tasks such as revealing the correct answers in self-tests with a single button tap is actually easier.

1. Begin with a self-test type document, or if you haven't one on hand, you can start with just a new blank document and learn the technique just as well. Of course, you'll also find

an example document—ex_self_test.indd—in the Lesson Files\Aquafadas\Content Replacement folder.

2. Create your correct answers if your self-test will provide actual answers like ex_self_test.indd (see Figure 10.37); or, if you'll be creating a multiple-choice exam like Figure 10.38, create an icon or symbol to display beside or on top of each correct answer. If you make it out of multiple objects, remember to group them together. Duplicate the correct-answer indicator as many times as needed, and position those indicators where they belong.

FIGURE 10.37
A self-test exam with answers

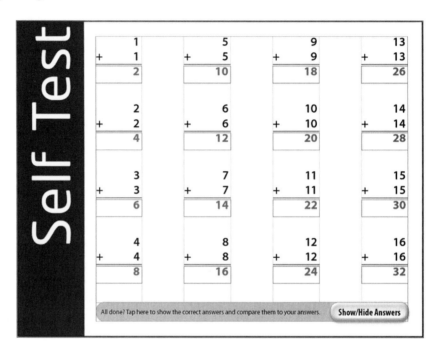

3. Select all the answers and/or indicators and group them. Although you could do this without grouping, it's usually easier to work with them as a group.

4. Select all the indicators and group them. Although you could do this without grouping, it's much easier to work with them as a group.

TIP   If you need to modify any of the components of the indicators later, including moving an indicator, leave the objects grouped and use the white arrow Direct Selection tool to select and modify the indicators or their components. This will maintain the group and the connection between the show/hide button(s) and the indicators group.

5. Create your trigger to show the correct-answer indicators. This can be a single object or a group of objects, a placed image, a vector object, a text frame, or a combination thereof. This is what readers will tap to show the correct-answer indicators.

FIGURE 10.38
A multiple-choice exam with correct-answer indicators

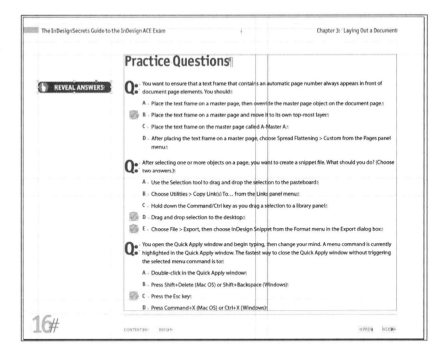

6. Create another button or trigger object to hide the correct answers. When the indicators are shown, this button will appear—usually in place of the "show answers" button—and tapping it will hide the correct-answer indicators and this "hide answers" button. Figure 10.39 shows the two buttons I created for the multiple-choice self-test.

FIGURE 10.39
My buttons for showing and hiding the correct answers

At this point, you should have three objects or sets of objects: the correct-answer indicators, the trigger to show those indicators, and the trigger to hide them.

7. Using the black arrow Selection tool, select the "show answers" button, and then choose the Button or Advanced Button enrichment on the AVE Interactivity panel. For now, I'll stick with the Button enrichment and discuss the Advanced Button enrichment later in the chapter under "Adding Actions and Advanced Buttons."

8. Set the basic options for the button—Visible In This Orientation, Item Name, and Maintain Frame State—as desired.

9. Below the Actions on Touch area, click the Create button to load the first action into the Actions On Touch list.

10. Change the Tell drop-down to Frame (Using Frame Picker); a new button will appear beside the field (see Figure 10.40).

FIGURE 10.40
After adding an action and setting the Tell field to Frame (Using Frame Picker)

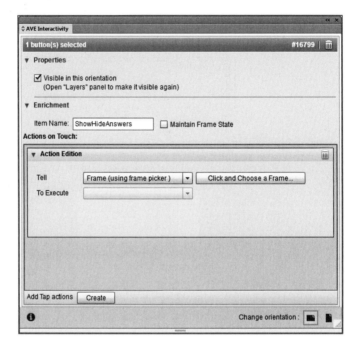

11. Click that new Click And Choose A Frame button; then, in the document, click the group containing the correct-answer indicators. When you've successfully clicked them, you'll see them surrounded by the familiar dashed line group bounding box, and in the AVE Interactivity panel, two other things will happen: the Click And Choose A Frame button will be replaced by the name of the object you just selected, which might be simply a number preceded by a hash sign, and the To Execute field will become selectable.

12. In the To Execute field, select Change Visibility. When the Visibility field appears below it, set the field to Visible.

13. Still working with the "show answers" button, add another action with the Create button. Repeat the last three steps, but this time, instead of selecting the answer indicators, select the "hide answers" button. In other words, after showing the answer indicators, the "show answers" button will also make visible the "hide answers" button. You should see something akin to Figure 10.41.

FIGURE 10.41
These two actions will show the correct answers and the "hide answers" button.

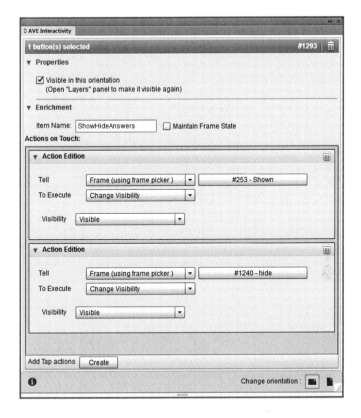

14. Add a third action.

15. In this third and final action for the "show answers" button, make the button hide itself. Use the Frame (Using Frame Picker) Tell option, select the "show answers" button, choose Change Visibility from the To Execute field, and then set the Visibility menu to Hidden. The net result will be that this one option fires three actions with a single tap: it shows the correct-answer indicators, it reveals the button that will let readers hide those answers again, and it hides itself from the view to get out of the way of the "hide answers" button. Figure 10.42 shows what these actions look like on the AVE Interactivity panel.

16. Convert the "hide answers" button into a button enrichment, and give it all the same actions as the previous button, but with the reverse visibility settings. It should hide the correct-answer indicators, reveal the "show answers" button, and hide itself, just like Figure 10.43.

FIGURE 10.42
With all three actions in place, this button is finished.

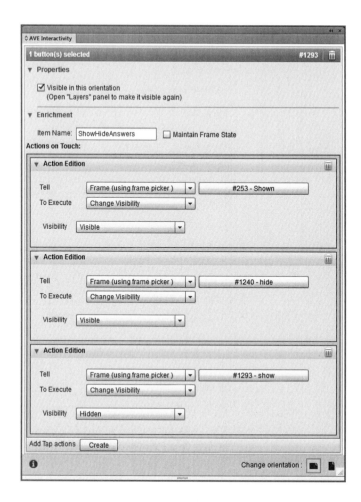

17. Select the correct-answers indicators group, and then clear the check box beside Visible In This Orientation in the AVE Interactivity panel. This will initially hide the correct answers.

18. Line up the "show answers" and "hide answers" buttons such that one is above the other and they are in the position where you'd like to publish them.

19. Select the "hide answers" button, and disable its option for Visible In This Orientation in the AVE Interactivity panel.

FIGURE 10.43
The properly configured "hide answers" button

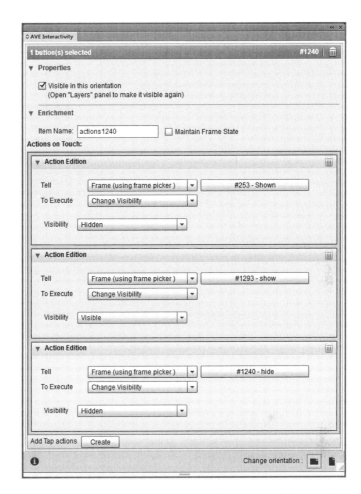

If you wanted to reveal and hide the correct answers with just a single button that did both—a "show/hide answers" toggle—you can do that even more easily.

1. Create your answer indicators as before.

2. Create a single button to trigger the revealing and hiding of the answer indicators. You might want to name it something like Show/Hide Correct Answers.

3. Turn the button into an enrichment with an action whose Tell Field is set to Frame (Using Frame Picker), and select the indicators group.

4. Set the To Execute field to Change Visibility.

5. This time, from the Visibility drop-down menu, select Toggle. Toggle will show what is hidden and hide what is shown in a single action. That's it. You're done. Just one action (see Figure 10.44). No need to add additional actions to the button because you want the button itself to always be visible.

FIGURE 10.44
Setting the Visibility field to Toggle means you can use one button for both showing and hiding answers.

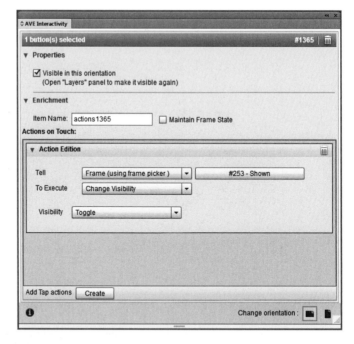

You now have a self-test whereby readers can show and hide correct-answer indicators. More importantly, the same technique can be used for many other types of content hiding and showing. Any number of objects, grouped or not—even other enrichments—can be hidden and shown; as long as you can select their frames from the Actions On Touch area or can enter their frame names using the Frame (Using Frame Name) option, you can hide them, show them, or toggle them between hidden and visible.

However, if you're getting into simultaneously showing and hiding more than a couple of objects at a time, don't use the previous method of adding a visibility action for each. Instead, there's a much easier way that involves only a single action to toggle the visibility of any number of objects in one action. For instance, maybe you produce a multilingual publication. To save production time and publication expenses, you could build all language versions in a single document, using the same articles and layouts, by attaching the display of each language's version of the content—all text; imagery with included captions, video, and audio objects; everything—to language-specific buttons. In other words, clicking the English button shows the English version of all objects, while tapping buttons labeled Español, Français, and Deutsch load Spanish, French, and German-language objects without changing pages and without replacing nonlanguage objects such as images and enrichments without written or spoken language components.

This multilingual document is the same as a media-rich children's alphabet book (see Figure 10.45).

Whether you're working with a children's alphabet book, multilingual documents, or other such sophisticated, multiobject content replacements wherein you want to be able to show and hide more than one or two objects, the following technique makes the process a breeze:

1. Using layers, segregate the content that will always appear from the set that will initially appear but later be hidden, and segregate both from the set of content that will be initially hidden but later revealed. Taking a look at `ex_animal_alphabet.indd` from the `Lesson Files\Aquafadas\Content Replacement` folder will clarify the segregation of

content. In the meantime, you can see the Layers panel for that document, for which I've built the "A" and "B" variable content, in Figure 10.46.

FIGURE 10.45
Using letters for trigger buttons, this children's book replaces text, imagery, and even other enrichments.

Tapping A shows imagery, copy, and audio for the antelope.

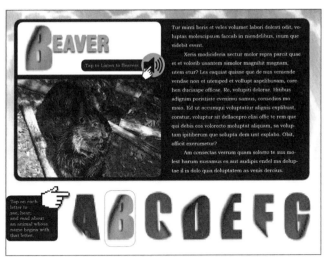

Tapping B shows similar content for beavers.

FIGURE 10.46
The Layers panel in ex_animal_alphabet.indd segregates the static content (Background) as well as the unique replaceable content for each letter (Letter A and Letter B).

2. Hide the Letter B layer by clicking off its visibility indicator in the Layers panel.

3. Create the trigger object that will show the Letter A layer and hide the Letter B layer. If you'd rather this trigger not be a button or user-activated device but prefer an automatic time- or event-based action, see the "Automated Content Replacement" step-by-step, which will walk you through doing just that. For now, make a trigger object. If you're using ex_animal_alphabet.indd or something similar, the trigger objects would be the letters at the bottom of the page.

4. With that first trigger object selected, click the Button enrichment in the AVE Interactivity panel. Set its basic options as desired.

5. At the bottom of the panel, click the Create button to load an action into the Actions On Touch list.

6. Set the Tell field to Layer, and enter in the field that appears to the right the name of the layer you will make visible, the layer you designated Letter A.

7. From the To Execute field, choose Change Visibility, and then set the Visibility field to Visible. Figure 10.47 shows the correct settings using the ex_animal_alphabet.indd lesson document.

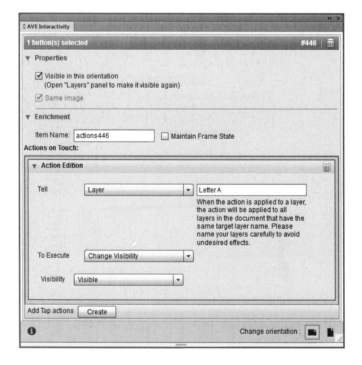

8. Create another action with the Create button below the list, following the same configuration you just did, with two exceptions. In this second action, supply the name for the layer designated as the Letter B, and then change the Visibility field to Hidden, as in Figure 10.48. This will hide the Letter B layer while simultaneously making the Letter A object visible.

FIGURE 10.48
These two actions
show the Letter A
layer while hiding
the Letter B layer.

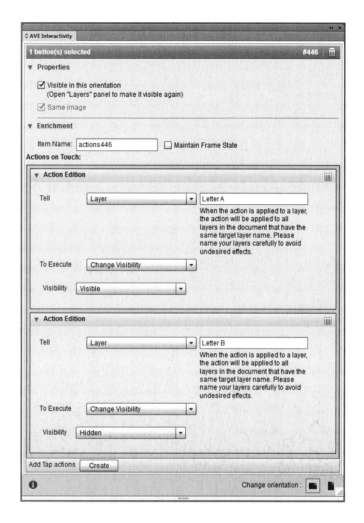

9. If your document has more than two sets of variable data, as a completed `ex_animal_`
   `alphabet.indd` would, then you'll need to add additional hiding actions for all those other
   layers. You don't, for example, want a reader to tap G and be unable to see the information
   about a giraffe because the antelope layer is still showing and blocking out other layers.

10. Repeat steps 2 to 9 for each pairing of a trigger object and variable content layer, ensur-
    ing that every trigger shows its corresponding layer but hides every one of the others.
    When you're done, you'll have a sophisticated content-replacement layout wherein
    each set of content is comprised of individual objects, not groups, and may contain
    anything Aquafadas DPS can export—text, images, vector objects (converted via the To
    Image enrichment), slideshows, videos, mazes, games, and everything else in the AVE
    Interactivity panel.

   By segregating static and enrichment content into layers—something most creatives do as a
matter of productivity anyway—and using Aquafadas DPS's built-in ability to include InDesign

layers in its publications and then selectively show and hide those layers in the publication, you can create highly adaptive user experience publications.

Relative-Location Content Replacement

Moving on to the next logical step, look at Figure 10.49, which is demonstrative of any kind of map, diagram, floor plan, chart, or detailed illustration or photograph on which a lot of information needs to be presented. In this case, it's a section of a bicycling route map (the same one used in the discussion of relative-location content replacement with Adobe DPS in the previous chapter) with various geographic features called out with icons, features such as sights to see, shopping areas, information kiosks and agencies, boat excursion launches, and so on. Tapping each marker icon reveals a pop-up with more information and multimedia related to the location identified by the marker.

FIGURE 10.49
You can control layer visibility to present contextual information in a space-efficient and reader-engaging way.

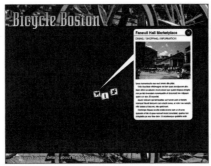 

This entire map uses the same layer visibility technique I just finished going through, but with a couple of differences.

First and foremost is the fact that the variable content, the pop-ups describing locations around Boston, aren't all in the same place as was the content in the children's alphabet book. Here, the pop-up balloons occupy different places on the page to keep them out of the way of the icon buttons that spawn them and out of the way of the bike trails and area of the map being described, something many readers will appreciate the ability to see even as they learn about the location itself. Thus, for instance, the "Faneuil Hall Marketplace" pop-up is well away from, but connected to, the location of Faneuil Hall Marketplace on the map. It does, however, cover up the New England Aquarium, which spawns a pop-up of its own. The "New England

Aquarium" pop-up, out of necessity, moves away from the area of the aquarium's icon and thus away from the space occupied by the "Faneuil Hall Marketplace" pop-up. The replaceable content therefore doesn't all stack neatly in the same place; each pop-up has its own unique position, making this type of content-replacement-relative location.

The next difference is pretty obvious: instead of static images for the antelope and beaver, the lesson file, ex_bicycle_map.indd, shows that I've replaced the static, single image required by DPS in each pop-up with an image gallery enrichment. Thus, instead of a single view of Faneuil Hall Marketplace, which includes several buildings, statues, and other areas worth showing in such a pop-up describing the area as a "To Do & See," a slideshow (with automatic Ken Burns Effect in this case) lets readers see much more of the site. I could have even added a soundtrack to the slideshow to let readers *listen* to the area, perhaps a narrator discussing the features or history of the site. The New England Aquarium pop-up has the same kind of slideshow, though I could have incorporated video of the aquarium instead or even within the slideshow.

Another difference is the presence of close buttons in the pop-ups. If you're reading both the Adobe DPS and Aquafadas DPS techniques—maybe to evaluate which is better for your needs—you know that in the Adobe DPS version of this publication I created a full-page invisible button that, when clicked, hid all the pop-ups. You could do the same thing with Aquafadas DPS, but that isn't why there's a difference between the methods of closing the pop-ups between the two systems. Rather, I *want* those close buttons on the pop-ups, like they are in Aquafadas DPS. But because Adobe DPS can't include buttons in multistate objects, I *couldn't* have them with DPS; I had to build a workaround for Adobe DPS, which was the ability for readers to tap anywhere outside the pop-up itself to close all pop-ups. The ability for Aquafadas DPS to toggle the visibility of whole layers lets me create those X-like close buttons and add the darkened background (a lightbox effect) so that the pop-ups really stand out against the map.

The ability to include enrichments in the variable content also means I'm able to include more text in the pop-ups. If you open ex_bicycle_map.indd, you'll see that both functional pop-ups contain overset text. Remember from the "Employing Scrolling Page Regions" section that Aquafadas DPS *can't* overset text; upon export, text frames containing overset text automatically become scrolling. Thus, I can include more text than will fit in the pop-up.

TIP Want to include an actual Google Maps map with all the features that entails? Consult the "Adding Live Web Content" section later in this chapter.

Automated Content Replacement

Now let's talk about some more automated content-replacement techniques, replacements that don't require the reader to actually tap anything. Let's start with a simple audio or video object that launches another audio or video object.

1. Create and position frames for two or more audio or video enrichments you'd like to play in sequence. They can be positioned in the same place, but you'll need to be able to select them individually.

2. One at a time, turn those objects into the correct type of enrichment and set the appropriate options. In my case, I'm using the ex_auto_playlist.indd lesson file with a pair of public-domain songs I've included for your listening pleasure.

3. As you can see in Figure 10.50, which shows me working with the first audio enrichment in the ex_auto_playlist.indd lesson file, the bottom of the AVE Interactivity panel

includes an Actions On Finish section. It works the same way as the Actions On Touch controls from previous step-by-steps. So, click the Create button to add an action.

FIGURE 10.50
Setting an action to play the MP3 audio enrichment attached to the frame Track2 to play automatically when the audio in that frame finishes

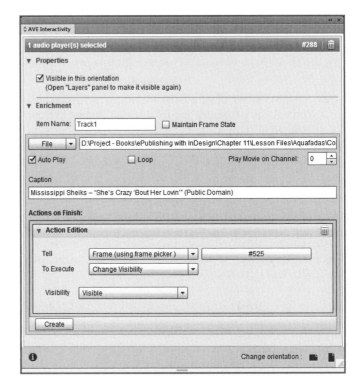

4. In the Action Edition section, set the Tell field to Frame (Using Frame Picker), click the Click And Choose A Frame button, and then select the second audio or video frame, the one you want to play automatically when this one finishes.

5. Set the To Execute field to Change Visibility and then the Visibility field to Visible.

6. Before I wrap up with this media object, add another action such that, after launching the second enrichment, this one hides itself. You're now finished with this enrichment.

7. Select the other audio or video enrichment, the one that will play second, and deselect its Visible In This Orientation option. That will hide the media until it's called by the other. Note that in ex_auto_playlist.indd I left both audio enrichment frames visible so that you don't have to go hunting through the Layers panel to access the second frame.

8. Finally, on this second audio or video object, set it to autoplay. If you need to play a third media object, repeat steps 3 through 7.

If you wanted to launch something other than another audio or video object when one such enrichment finishes playing, you could choose other actions, such as opening a URL, starting an animation, or hiding or showing an entire layer of objects—you know, anything you can do with buttons. The same Actions On Finish are available for video and animation enrichments, too.

Anchor-Based Content Replacement

The final type of content replacement I want to discuss is another automated method but one that doesn't rely on obvious events like audio, video, or animations ending. Rather, this technique works with the Anchor enrichment type; anchors are merely automatic, usually invisible (to the reader) triggers for actions.

1. Prepare but don't place into InDesign a video, an HTML page, or set of images for a slideshow.

2. Lay out the rest of your page, including text and other objects. *Don't* leave a space for the content you prepared. You'll show that content in a pop-up box above the page. Although you can also use anchors for more standard actions such as showing and hiding content within the page, selecting specific images in a slideshow, and so on, this gives me the opportunity to tell you about Aquafadas DPS's built-in pop-up functionality, too.

3. Somewhere on the page create a small graphic frame or vector shape with no fill and no stroke.

4. With the black arrow Selection tool, select this new object, and in the AVE Interactivity panel, click the Anchor enrichment.

5. In the anchor's options, activate Visible In This Orientation, and set the basic options (Figure 10.51), which are as follows:

FIGURE 10.51
The Anchor enrichment options

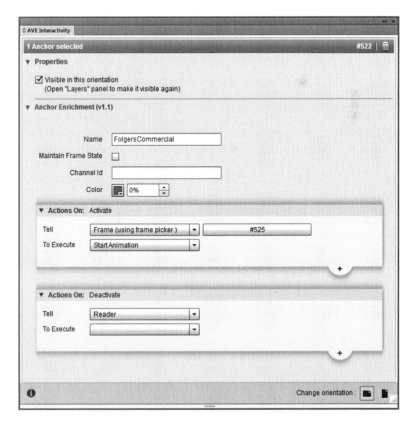

Name   Like any other object, anchors can be controlled through actions attached to other enrichments; thus, the Name field lets you assign a name to the anchor for easy targeting. Moreover, because one of the actions you can assign to most objects is one that jumps the view to an anchor, naming the anchor makes selecting it much easier than remembering what the anchor's object ID number was.

Maintain Frame State   This is the same as for the Picture enrichment type. If Maintain Frame State is enabled, if a reader leaves the article or page, upon their return, the object will look the same, at whatever state it appeared when the reader left it. Leaving Maintain Frame State off, which is its default, resets the enrichment when the reader leaves the page or article; thus, if the reader comes back, an enrichment like a slideshow has rewound to the first image again.

Channel ID   Just as video and audio enrichments can be targeted to play on specific channels anchors can be set to define those channels. Filling in a number in the Channel ID field sets all channel-based media controlled by the anchor to play in that channel.

Color and Opacity   If you'd like the anchor object to be visible to readers, set the object's fill and/or stroke as desired. However, if you'd like to change appearance, or be visible only when activated, you can click the Color field swatch and select a highlight color as well as set an opacity level to the right of the Color field.

6. In the Actions On: Activate section, set the Tell field to Reader, the To Execute drop-down to Show Popup, and the Popup Type to, well, whatever you prefer. There are three appearances of pop-ups Aquafadas DPS is capable of producing: Classic, a simple pop-up behind which the main page can be seen; Modal, a lightbox effect showing the main page dimmed or overlayed; and Fullscreen, only the pop-up itself showing and completely hiding the main page behind it.

7. Click the Edit Pop-up button, and you'll be prompted to choose the pop-up enrichment type—Movie, Slideshow, or HTML Page. This is where you get back to that content you prepared. Click the appropriate one.

8. On the following screen, you'll need to set the width and height of the pop-up in the appropriately labeled fields; they even appear if you've chosen Fullscreen as the pop-up type though they're irrelevant in that case. The rest of the screen is the standard options for the Movie, Slideshow, or HTML Page enrichments; set them as you would their on-the-page counterparts.

9. After configuring the content of the pop-up, click the left-facing arrow at the top of the panel to return to the anchor's own options. When this anchor appears on-screen, your content will automatically appear in a pop-up.

And you don't have to stop there. While configuring the anchor, you can click the plus sign beneath the Actions On: Activate group to add more actions to fire when the anchor comes on-screen, and you can configure one or more actions to fire when the anchor goes offscreen in the Actions On: Deactivate area. Anchors can fire when the anchor appears on the page, when it moves out of the view, or both. For example, if the anchor is on the second page of an article, it can be configured to fire its action when the reader scrolls to that second page; the same anchor can also be configured to fire a different action when the reader scrolls to the point of driving the anchor offscreen again.

Adding Live Web Content

Adding live web content in Aquafadas DPS is about as daunting as adding an image. Take Figure 10.52, for example. That's a digital magazine page containing imagery and text and, on the right, the live feed of my Twitter timeline. You can try it for yourself by opening `ex_ twitter.indd` from the `Lesson Files\Aquafadas\Web Content` folder and publishing the layout to myKiosk. Once there, you can interact with my Twitter feed and your own Twitter account, including signing up for an account if you don't already have one. Just make sure you're online when you try it.

FIGURE 10.52
Integrating live web content like my live Twitter feed shown on the right here makes updating readers instantaneous and does not require you to resubmit to app stores.

1. Create the graphic frame that will define the area for the live web content. This can be part of the page or an edge-to-edge frame so that the entire page is the live web content.

2. Select the graphic frame with the Selection tool, and choose the HTML Page enrichment from the AVE Interactivity panel.

3. Set the basic options for the object such as the Visible In This Orientation toggle, the Item Name, and, if desired, the Maintain Frame State toggle.

4. In the middle section of the dialog, a button may read either Folder, URL, or Feed (see Figure 10.53). That button is actually a drop-down menu that lets you choose whether to include local HTML files contained in a folder (see the section "Including Offline HTML, Games, and Activities" immediately following this section), an RSS or ATOM feed of content (I'll talk about that soon), or, with the URL option, a full and standard URL to a website or a specific page on that site. Choose URL, and supply the URL in the field to the right.

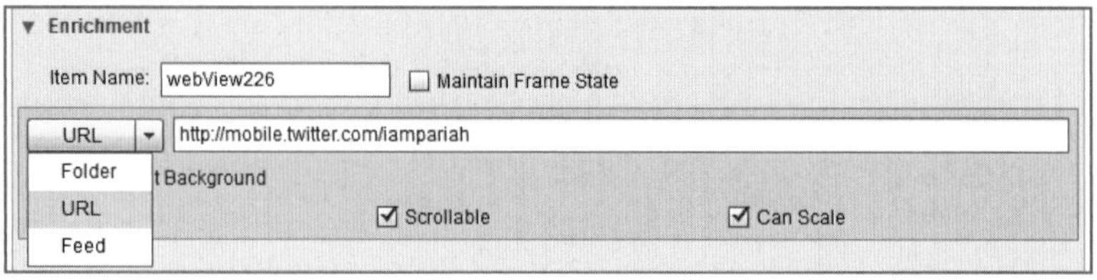

FIGURE 10.53
Web content can be
included as a local
file, as an online
URL, or as a feed for
RSS and ATOM feed
content.

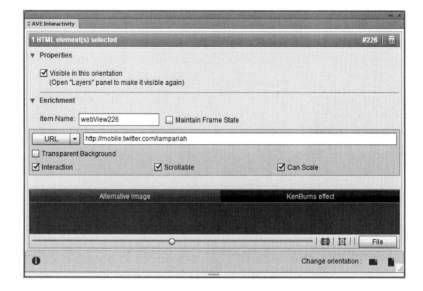

5. Set the remaining four check box options (Figure 10.54), which are as follows:

FIGURE 10.54
The complete
options for the
enrichment

Transparent Background   By default web content has an opaque background. Enabling the Transparent Background option will allow the background of the page to shine through any web content, assuming the web-based content itself is set to have a transparent background via CSS or another method.

Interaction   In most cases, you'll want to enable the Interaction option that allows users to touch, zoom, and otherwise interact with the web-based content. If, however, you're using the web-based content merely as decoration—say, serving up the latest imagery or prices—turning off that option makes the web-based content behave like any static element on the page.

Scrollable   If the incorporated web content, either the initial page or wherever readers might navigate to using hyperlinks embedded within the web content, is wider or taller than the graphic frame containing it, then enabling the Scrollable option will allow readers to scroll to see any content cropped out by the frame's viewport. You would want to disable Scrollable if your web content is fixed-size, such as would be the case with banners and other ad creative, tiny bits of content included as decoration or variable content.

Can Scale   Web pages may or may not match the size of the magazine page or the frame through which the web content is shown. Activating the Can Scale option will automatically scale that web content uniformly to fit within the width of the frame. Disabling this option on content that is wider than the frame will make it scrollable if Scrollable is also enabled; if Scrollable is disabled, the content will be cropped by the frame.

6. Click the File button at the bottom of the Alternative Image tab to select a static image to show before the web content loads and in case the reader's device isn't connected to the Internet, and if you want to add a Ken Burns Effect, use the correct tab for that.

TIP To help readers understand that they can't access your content when they're not connected to the Web, place an informative image or text behind the frame holding the web content overlay or enrichment. Your readers will thank you for it.

In addition to incorporating any web page in your publication, you can also stream the latest announcements, blog posts, or social media updates via RSS or ATOM publishing technology. Let's set up an HTML enrichment for that.

1. Create the frame to hold the content and assign the HTML Page enrichment to it.

2. Fill the standard options of Visible In This Orientation, Item Name, and Maintain Frame State, as desired.

3. This time, select Feed from the Folder/Feed/URL button. A subpanel will immediately appear (see Figure 10.55).

FIGURE 10.55
Configuring the inclusion of RSS feed content

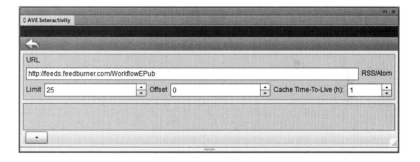

4. In the URL field, enter the full URL of a feed generated in RSS (all versions) or ATOM formats. The following are a few examples of such URLs:

◆ `http://feeds.feedburner.com/WorkflowEPub`

◆ `http://gurusunleashed.com/a/articles/indesign/feed/atom/`

◆ `http://iamPariah.com/?feed=rss2`

5. Decide how many items or blog posts you want to appear in the enrichment, and set the Limit field to that number. See the "Limit" setting under the "Creating a Web-Fed Slideshow" section earlier in this chapter for details.

6. The Offset field, if set to anything other than 0, will count down from the top of the feed, omitting that number of most recent items. For example, if you enter a value of 10, the most recent ten items in the feed will be skipped, and inclusion will begin with the 11th item.

USING OFFSETS

Offsets are most often used in two scenarios. First, when you want to impose a delay between the publication of content and it appearing inside the digital publication, an offset can keep one or more items out of the magazine until later posts push them down into the included set. Second, when you'll be including multiple blocks of content from the same feed. One frame, for instance, could be set to show the first 10 posts via the Limit field, while another frame uses an Offset value of 10 and a Limit value of 10 to show items numbered 11–20.

7. In the Cache Time-To-Live field, enter a time value, in hours, between when the enrichment first fetches the content of the feed and when it should query the feed again for new items. See the Cache Time-to-Live setting in the "Creating a Web-Fed Slideshow" section earlier in this chapter for details.

8. After setting these options, click the arrow in the top-left corner of the panel to return to the main HTML Page enrichment options where you can set other options such as Transparent Background, Interaction, and so forth.

ADDING INTERACTIVE GOOGLE MAPS USING AQUAFADAS DPS

The Map enrichment lets you include maps generated by Google Maps, including any number of markers with basic text information and different colored pins to highlight locations or areas of interest, and it can work with the reader's mobile device to highlight the reader's current position on the map. The ability to add buttons to the map that let the reader change the view and enable or disable geolocation adds on even more power.

◆ Use the plus-sign button hiding below the Marker Options section to add a marker, and set the options as you see fit: show callouts, choose colors, allow panning and zooming, and so on.

◆ On the Buttons Menu tab, you can create a buttons toolbar. In the Image field, choose an image to be the background of the toolbar.

◆ In the Items area, select each of the commands on the left, in the Disabled Item(s) list, that you'd like to include in the toolbar as buttons. Click the right-facing arrow for each desired command, thus adding commands to the Enabled Item(s) list. Any commands remaining on the left will not be available for use by readers.

◆ In Screen Manager Images, you can choose to include graphics—typically icons—to become the visual representation of buttons that let the reader take the map enrichment into full-screen mode and then return to in-page mode from full-screen.

Including Offline HTML, Games, and Activities

Not all content based on web technologies needs to be hosted live on the Web to be included in your interactive publication. True, you *want* it online to be able to update or customize the content in real time, but if you're including HTML-based content merely to provide a type of interactivity or content that Aquafadas DPS doesn't do natively, you can do that without requiring readers to be online.

Both Adobe DPS and Aquafadas DPS enable you to incorporate local HTML pages within interactive magazines, either as part of pages or as complete replacements for normal publication pages. These HTML pages can be HTML 3, 4, or 5; may include scripting such as JavaScript; and can do just about anything inside the publication that doesn't require a database or other server-side technology.

Adding Offline Web Content

The ability to include HTML in pages in your interactive magazine lets you add any HTML content that doesn't need server-side technologies, such as ASP or a database, and to let readers use that content without the requirement of a live Internet connection. And, of course, removing the necessity for a live Internet connection further enhances the experience of the HTML content just being part of the page like any other enrichment.

Including offline content using HTML and other web technologies is the same process as including content live from the Web (see the section "Adding Live Web Content"). The only change to that workflow is that, within the HTML Page enrichment options, you select Folder from the Folder/Feed/URL button. In the dialog that appears, point Aquafadas to a folder containing the HTML file you want to use. Aquafadas will also include any assets or external files referenced by the HTML, such as image files, one or more CSS style sheets, external JavaScript files, and so on, as long as they're located in the same folder as the HTML file or in a subfolder thereof, and as long as references to those files are relative (for example, `images/picture.png`) rather than absolute (for example, `MacDrive:Documents:Folder:Subfolder:images:picture.png`). The included HTML (and whatever other web technologies are incorporated thereby) can be part of the page or the whole page, depending on the size of the graphic frame you create to house it.

Dropping In Games and Activities

People spend a great deal of time using electronic games with simple premises—games such as puzzles, matching, mazes, and Sudoku. As a result, I have long advocated inclusion of games in several genres of digital publications—if you serve live web content to your readers, incorporated into the same page, while they're playing games, you stand an excellent chance of getting more content seen or read than when readers go through a publication linearly. Additionally, if your publication is advertising-supported, rotating ads in place around a game will gain you more impressions and thus more revenue.

Aquafadas DPS includes 10 HTML5-based games and activities as enrichments you can insert into your publications. Some are included free of charge; others cost a one-time licensing fee. The ones that are free may display ads that Aquafadas inserts and for which Aquafadas itself earns revenue. In case you don't like that, each of the free games has a purchasable upgrade option that removes those ads and gives you more control and customization of the game or activity. (See the "Launch Activity" section later in this chapter for more details.)

The free games and activities are as follows:

Simple Maze   The Simple Maze game lets readers take control of a marker or character and move interactively through a labyrinth from start to finish with sophisticated collision awareness. As the publisher, you may design all visual aspects of the maze—the background image, the appearance of the maze walls, and the marker or avatar—and design the maze map readers must navigate.

Matching Game　The Matching Game enrichment lets you provide pairs of images to be displayed as cards or tiles. These images will be shuffled by the Aquafadas DPS software upon display making every game unique. The images you match can be of anything, and you can customize the game's background and success and failure screens.

Simple Draw　Simple Draw asks readers to trace with their fingers atop an image. A nice feature of this particular enrichment is that it doesn't have to be same image every time. You can include a static image, but you can also specify a URL from which to grab images when readers' devices have live Internet connections. Because the model or to-be-traced image resides on the Web and is fed to the magazine via URL, you can change the image daily, hourly, or every five minutes.

These games and activities are available as add-ons:

Maze　Maze is the upgrade to Simple Maze that offers even greater customization and more detailed maps. One of the coolest features of the upgrade is the ability to let the reader use the device accelerometer instead of just a finger; this means the reader can navigate the maze tactilely by moving the tablet or smartphone. Other features include time- and event-trig-gered sounds and other actions as well as the ability to create passable edges or road blocks.

Memory　Mahjong is a matching game, and that is how sophisticated the Memory upgrade game can be. It can be a simple child's picture-matching game or something far more com-plex and worthy of adults. The upgrade enables such very useful features as greater diffi-culty, difficulty that increases as the number of face-down cards decrease, and the option of saving the score between sessions.

Jigsaw　With the Jigsaw activity you provide a JPEG or PNG image and specify the number of pieces to carve it into, and the software will randomly break up the image. Readers then have to drag the pieces into their correct places to complete the puzzle.

Slice　The Slice game shows the reader a series of images and then asks the reader to recon-struct one of the series from blocks while being timed.

Sudoku　Sudoku requires little introduction or explanation because millions are addicted to this math-based puzzler. The Sudoku activity takes the work out of building Sudoku grids by asking for just a few pieces of information, such as grid size, difficulty level, and color and typography on the grid, and then it generates an interactive game.

Draw　The Draw activity is a fully interactive coloring book. Depending on the options you set, readers can color one or many different images using a full color palette, paintbrushes, colored pencils, and erasers. Best of all, an integrated screen capture function lets readers capture and share their handiwork, spreading the word about your publication.

Each of these games and activities is added like an enrichment. Simply create a frame to hold the activity, and in the AVE Interactivity panel, select the appropriate icon from the panel. The free ones are within the main set of enrichments, while the optional upgrade modules are at the bottom of the panel (see Figure 10.56).

FIGURE 10.56
The locations of the games and activities (highlighted)

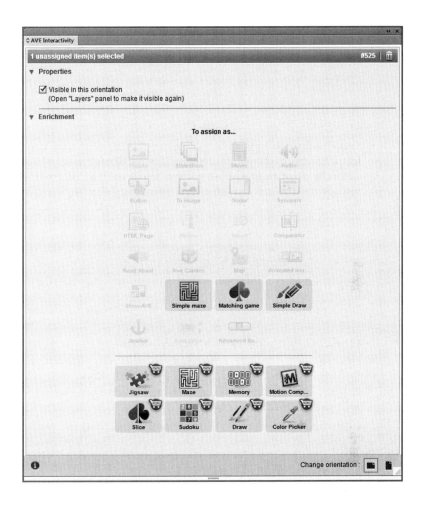

Adding Actions and Advanced Buttons

In addition to all the interactivity in the Aquafadas DPS enrichments, there are actions that can be executed by buttons and when certain events occur via other enrichments. Buttons and actions create whole new levels of interactivity, control, and creativity for you and your publications. Many of the available button and action functions you've already worked with in the process of creating different types of interactivities; others I haven't covered yet. In this section, let's look at all that stuff I haven't yet covered.

Employing Actions

In Aquafadas DPS, actions are not limited to buttons. They can be executed by other enrichments as well. For example, when a reader taps an image, an action can jump the reader to a different article, or a video. Once it has finished playing, can automatically spawn the next video, creating a playlist.

It's also important to note that although a few enrichments allow only one action at a time, most enrichments that offer actions, and especially buttons and advanced buttons, enable you to assign multiple actions to fire in rapid succession. For instance, you could play a sound (a button "click" sound, say), start three animations playing in different places on the page, and show several previously hidden frames—all from a single button tap.

Within Aquafadas DPS, actions are logically grouped according to what they control—the entire app ("reader"), for such things as navigation between articles and opening URLs, layers for altering visibility based on InDesign layers, and frames, which provide granular control of individual enrichments and other objects such as showing and hiding them, activating playback on animation, and toggling the display of the object between in-page and full-screen. Following Aquafadas DPS's action structure, let's look at the available actions grouped into their control levels.

READER-LEVEL ACTIONS

The reader is the branded myKiosk app, with your publication integrated. Actions that can run on the reader/app are the most powerful because they can call resources outside the publication and even exit the app itself. The following To Execute menu actions are available once you set the Tell menu on a button or enrichment to Reader:

Go To Article   Selecting Go To Article (AVE MAG Only) enables you to jump the reader to another article in the same publication. Simply supply the article ID, which is the number that appears below the filename in the Project Structure section of the AVE Project Manager panel, and then a Page Index value, which is the page you want to target within the article.

Go To Web   The Go To Web action lets you send readers to online resources. Just supply a URL and choose whether you want to show the online content in a pop-up window within the application or open the URL in the device's actual web browser. The Out Of Application check box is what communicates to Aquafadas your choice—leave it off to show URLs in a pop-up and activate it to open URLs in a browser.

Launch Activity   Choosing the Launch Activity action enables you to open Simple Draw, Matching Game, or Simple Maze activities in pop-up windows (see "Including Offline HTML, Games, and Activities" for more on these and other activities). Select the Launch Activity action, click the Edit Activity button, choose the activity, and then configure the activity's options just as you would if they were in-page enrichments.

Show Popup   You worked with the Show Popup action in the "Using Content Replacement" section. This action lets you create a pop-up or content overlay in three styles—Classic, Modal, or Fullscreen—to contain just about any type of content or enrichment. Just select Show Popup from the To Execute menu, choose the Popup Type option, click Edit Popup, and define the pop-up content.

Quit   Quit is a simple option—it exits the reader app on the device. There are no options, of course.

Go to Anchor   Anchors are special enrichments with a dual purpose. First, they can execute actions automatically as they come on-screen—something else you worked with in the "Using Content Replacement" section of this chapter. Their second purpose is just what you might infer from the name: anchors are nameable targets that can be used in navigation. After placing and naming an anchor, using the Go To Anchor action and then supplying the anchor name enables a button tap or automatic action to jump the reader's view to that anchor.

Layer-Level Actions

There's really only one action that can be executed on layers, and that's to change the visibility of the layer and all objects on it. Once again, we worked with this action in the "Using Content Replacement" section. Using the action is easy: put all the objects you want to show or hide onto one or more layers using InDesign's Layers panel. Then, after setting the Tell field to Layer, supply the name of the layer whose visibility you want to control, select the To Execute menu's only option (Change Visibility), and then choose the desired state from the Visibility menu (Visible, Hidden, and Toggle). That last option switches between the first two—if the layer is hidden, Toggle makes it visible; if the layer is shown, Toggle hides it. Using this action, you can manage the visibility of anything you can place on layers in InDesign, which is to say *anything*—text frames, placed images, native vector objects (converted to enrichments with the Picture enrichment), enrichments of all types, and even other buttons and advanced buttons.

Frame-Level Actions

The final two options on the Tell menu are Frame (Using Frame Picker) and Frame (Using Frame Name). Both execute actions on individual frames; the only difference between them is how you specify which frame to control, by clicking the frame or by supplying the frame's name, respectively. The actions offered for both options are identical and as follows:

Change Visibility   Choosing the Change Visibility option from the To Execute menu proffers the Visibility menu with three options: Visible, Hidden, and Toggle. By selecting one of them, you can make previously hidden frames—text, placed images, native vector objects (converted to enrichments with the Picture enrichment), enrichments of all types, and even other buttons and advanced buttons—visible or hide them if they already were visible. The Toggle option switches between the two states (visible objects disappear, and invisible objects appear) and continues to swap those two states every time the action is executed by tap or automation.

Start/Stop Animation   The Start Animation and Stop Animation actions enable you to control animated or video content frames via buttons or automation. There are no options for these actions; they simply start the animation in the targeted frame or stop that frame's animation. Careful use of this type of action can string together an array of animations that play in sequence—one plays and, as part of that enrichment's actions, automatically starts playing the next animation elsewhere on the page when the first stops.

Fullscreen   Another action without options is the Fullscreen action. Selecting it from the To Execute menu merely launches the specified frame in a full-screen view, taking over the device's display. In this way, any frame can be made to fill the screen, not only those frames or enrichments that have their own full-screen options. For example, you could include in-page a relatively small vector-based map, diagram, or chart and then, through a reader-activated tap or an automatic action from some other enrichment, launch that frame into full-screen mode to enable readers to see it in greater detail. Once in full-screen mode, a button will appear to enable readers to return to the normal page view.

Creating Advanced Buttons

Throughout the rest of the chapter, you've worked pretty heavily with the Buttons enrichment, that is, converting an object to a button to execute one or more actions. There isn't much to standard button enrichments. You have the universal Visible In This Orientation, Item Name, and Maintain Frame State options, and then you just add one or more actions. Buttons are very simple objects. Advanced Buttons, however, are a whole lot more interesting.

After converting a frame or a group of frames to the Advanced Button enrichment, you'll be greeted with the options in Figure 10.57. Set the basic options—Visible In This Orientation, Name, and Maintain Frame State—and then move down to the rest of the controls.

FIGURE 10.57
The Advanced Button enrichment offers much more than a standard Button enrichment.

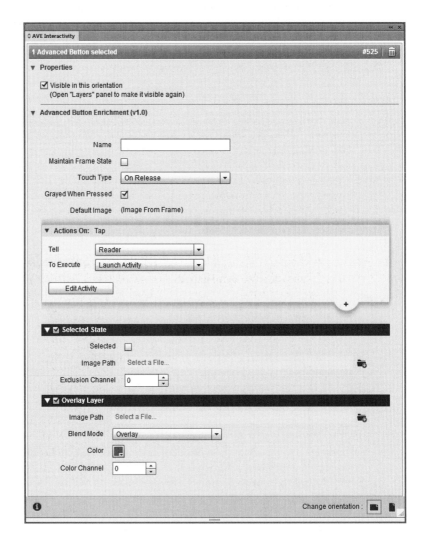

Two types or sets of actions can be executed: layer-level and frame-level. There is really only one action that can be executed on layers, and that's to change the visibility of the layer and all objects on it. Frame-level actions, which control the state of individual frames, can toggle visible or hidden, start or stop an animation or video in the frame, and toggle the frame content from whatever size it happens to be to full-screen.

Applying the Finishing Touches

Before sending your epublication out into the world to make its own way, give it the best chance at success by attending to some of the oft-overlooked details. I'll focus largely on presenting articles well in the navigation systems, identifying the contents of those articles when all that can be seen is a short blurb and a thumbnail image, and ensuring that noneditorial content stays out of the navigation systems. This will make your publications all the better as readers move away from flipping pages manually to reach the content they want.

Supplying Article Details

After carefully designing each article, you should just as carefully confirm that you've supplied the additional information to make the article look its best in the table of contents, thumbnail scrubber, slider enrichments, and elsewhere. Putting its best foot forward in all these locations means supplying an accurate title and description of the article and making sure that the thumbnail of the article provides the best visual representation possible. You can supply or edit the article details at any time by choosing Settings from the drop-down menu within the article thumbnail in the Project Structure pane of the AVE Project Manager (see Figure 10.58). That will open the Article Properties dialog in Figure 10.59.

FIGURE 10.58
Access the Article
Settings via this
menu command

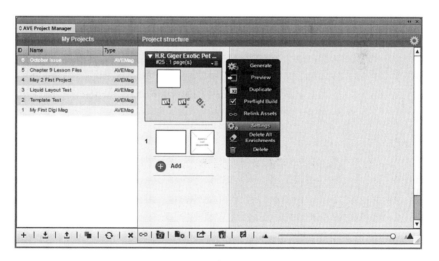

Title   The Title field is fairly self-explanatory—it's the title of the article as you want it to appear in all contents and navigational systems.

FIGURE 10.59
The properties of
the selected article

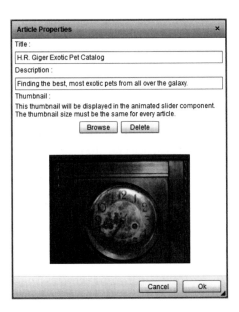

Description Often overlooked by publishers is the Description field. Leaving it blank means, in some areas, relying entirely on the title of the article to catch readers' attentions. That's usually a foolish mistake. Take advantage of this field! You can populate it with the article's dek, a hook paragraph, or just a basic description that tells readers more about the content than the title might.

Thumbnail You can stick with the default thumbnail Aquafadas DPS automatically generates as an image of the full article or supply a custom thumbnail you've created (see the sidebar "Creating Article Thumbnails" a few pages back for the whys and hows). Assuming you've already created your thumbnail graphic, click the Browse button to navigate to and select the thumbnail graphic to represent the article.

To remove a custom thumbnail and use the Aquafadas DPS automatically generated thumbnail of the article, click the Delete button and republish or repreview the article or project.

CREATING ARTICLE THUMBNAILS

By default, Aquafadas DPS creates a thumbnail from the entire article or from the first screen of a multiscreen article. Often, however, you can represent an article better with a cropped or custom thumbnail than with a version of the page shrunk down. Save your thumbnail images in PNG format (144 × 144 pixels for the iPad 3's Retina display and 70 × 70 pixels for renditions targeted to the iPad 1 and 2, Kindle Fire, and all other tablets), and use the Article Properties dialog to associate them to individual articles.

Defining Project Options

Whereas DPS splits all the options, metadata, and advanced interface customization between the Folio Properties dialog, the Folder Producer online interface, and the Viewer Builder, Aquafadas DPS keeps it altogether right in InDesign in the AVE Project Manager panel. To access these settings, highlight the desired project in the AVE Project Manager panel, and then click the Project Settings button at the bottom of the panel. Up will pop the Project Settings dialog.

The General pane of the dialog—in Figure 10.60—looks very much like the New Project dialog and allows you to change only the project name, which is the title readers will see, and to add or remove orientations from the publication.

FIGURE 10.60
The General tab of
Project Settings

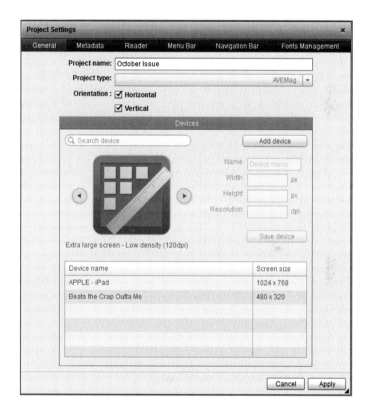

ADDING METADATA

The Metadata pane of the Project Settings dialog allows you to fill in the relevant details about the project (see Figure 10.61). Some of these details will appear to readers before they purchase the publication; some will also be used to help readers searching for apps or publications to find yours. With the exception of Title, Author, Date, Identifier, and Language, all fields are optional. All fields are also—in use, function, and accepted content and format—identical to those used in ebooks. Thus, refer to the "Editing Ebook Metadata" section in Chapter 6, "Fine-Tuning EPUBs."

FIGURE 10.61

The Metadata tab

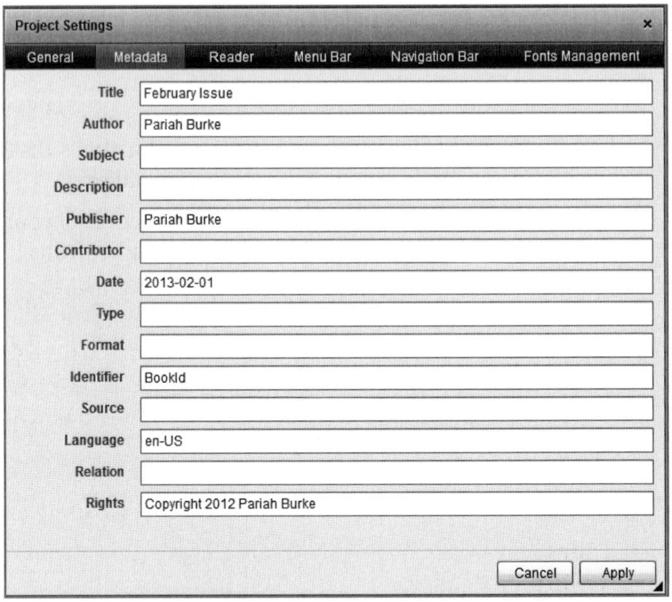

Title Enter here the title of the publication as readers will see it.

Author In the Author field, enter the publisher's name or, if the entire publication is by a single author, that person's name or nom de plume.

Subject Use the subject field to provide a brief description of the content or genre of the publication, such as Mathematics or Sports.

Description When your publication appears in your app's issue library, the Apple Newsstand, the Kindle Fire Newsstand, the Google Play store, and anywhere else, the content of the Description field will be displayed as an abstract or marketing blurb for your publication.

Publisher Enter the publisher's legal name, even if you already supplied it in the Author field.

Contributor If it's necessary to identify those who helped create the epublication supply their names here.

Date Enter the date of publication in your operating system's standard date format. Note that in the figure my date reads YYYY-MM-DD because that's how my operating system is set up. If you're in the United States and don't like efficiency as much as I do, then your date format is likely set to MM/DD/YYYY.

Type The Type field is optional and somewhat nebulous in definition. As with EPUBs (see Chapter 6), the Type field doesn't get much use yet. Its job is to differentiate specialized publications such as a dictionary, reference book, or a compilation of annotations. At the time of this writing, there is no standardized list of accepted types. Rather, it's still wide open as to what publishers might use as the type of a publication.

Format   Similarly, the Format field doesn't have a whole lot of current use. You could enter anything in there you wanted to make identification of your content easier, say, Magazine, Catalog, or Picture Book.

Identifier   Each digital magazine must have a unique identifying number. This is not an ISBN or ISSN. Rather, it's the unique number assigned to your magazine issue upon publication. If you don't yet know what that is, leave this field at its default, BookId, which will be replaced during publishing with the actual identifier.

Source   The Source field lets you identify the source of your publication if it isn't to be credited to the entities listed in the Publisher and Author fields.

Language   Each digital publication is required to list the language in which the majority of the project is written, according to ISO 639 and/or ISO 3166-1 language codes. The former, ISO 639, identifies all printed languages as two-digit codes (for example, EN for English), while ISO 3166-1, which identifies countries as two-digit codes, enables the identification of country-specific language, such as EN-US for English as used in the United States as opposed to EN-GB for *u*-heavy British English.

Consult `http://abbrv.it/DigiPubIDISO639` and `http://abbrv.it/DigiPubIDISO3166` for more information on language and country codes you can use in the Language field.

Relation   The optional Relation metadata property identifies another document to which yours might be related.

 Rights   Enter in the Rights field any notices related to copyright ownership, grant of rights, or rights licensing such as use Creative Commons Licenses (see `http://creativecommons.org`).

CHOOSING READER BEHAVIORS

On the Reader pane of Project Settings, you can set options that determine how readers (people) interact with the publication reader (software) and how it presents your publication (see Figure 10.62).

FIGURE 10.62
The Reader tab

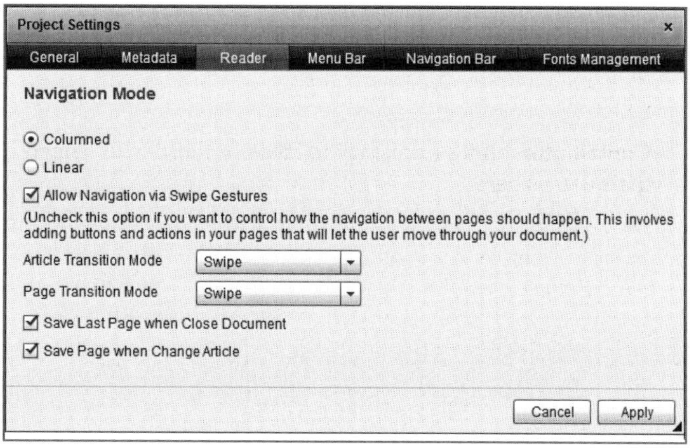

Navigation Mode   You have two options for the way page thumbnails appear to readers in the scrubber. Columned will show every article, top to bottom, whether it has one screen or several, in side-by-side columns. A relatively short single screen article thumbnail, for instance, might be side-by-side with a very tall three-screen article thumbnail. Linear mode maintains an equal height for all thumbnails, cropping deeper pages' thumbnails to be the same height as single-screen articles.

Allow Navigation Via Swipe Gestures   In most cases, you'll want to leave the Allow Navigation Via Swipe Gestures check box selected. With the option enabled, it lets readers swipe to move between articles and between screens within articles; disabling it removes that ability, requiring you to create your own navigation system via Button or Advanced Button enrichments.

Article Transition Mode   The Article Transition Mode drop down offers three behaviors readers experience when switching between articles: Swipe is the default, which lets readers swipe to change articles; Arrow displays a solid color arrow that, when tapped, changes the screen; and Arrow Overlay presents a semitransparent arrow floating atop the screen content to change screens with a tap.

Page Transition Mode   The Page Transition Mode offers the same choices and behaviors as Article Transition Mode, but its options are for moving between screens in the same article rather than switching articles.

Save Last Page When Close Document   The Save Last Page When Close Document option determines whether the reader remembers the last article and screen of that article between sessions, after a reader closes the publication, and subsequently returns the reader to that article and screen. Disabling the option starts the reader at the cover of the project every time.

Save Last Page When Change Article   When articles have multiple screens and then a reader switches to another article and returns to the first, what should the reader see? Should she be returned to the exact screen he or she left off in that multiscreen article, or should he or she be returned to the first screen of the article? That option is controlled by the Save Last Page When Change Article check box. Enabled, it remembers where the reader was for each article; disabled, it starts each article anew.

DESIGNING THE MENU BAR

One of the coolest ways to brand your interactive magazines and differentiate them from others is by customizing the user interface. Aquafadas DPS is one of the few systems capable of doing so; at the time of this writing, even DPS relies on a fixed-appearance user interface whose elements are supplied in part by the device operating system and in part by DPS itself. On the Menu Bar tab of the Project Settings dialog, you can customize your publication's menu bar with colors, imagery, and even custom button labels (see Figure 10.63).

Display Menu Bar   If you don't want any menu bar displayed at all, uncheck the Display Menu Bar box. Typically, though, you'll want to leave the option—and the menu bar—enabled so that readers can navigate your publication app.

Always Visible   By default the menu bar appears only after tapping an otherwise noninteractive portion of the screen. The check box Always Visible can alter that behavior by keeping the menu bar visible at all times.

FIGURE 10.63
Customize the
appearance of your
app's user inter-
face on the Menu
Bar tab.

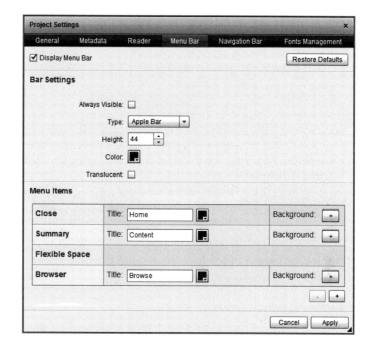

Type There are currently two styles or types of menu bars available; Apple's iOS-style and Aquafadas DPS's own style. The Type field lets you choose between them as Apple Bar and Standard, respectively.

Height By entering a value in pixels in the Height field, you can control the height of the menu bar readers see. Be careful not to make it too small for readers to interact with.

Color The Color field, which is a swatch backed by a swatch panel and HTML hex color input field, lets you choose the color of your menu bar. The default and most common color of menu bars is black, but you can choose any RGB color. Because you can also change the color of button text labels (I'll get to that momentarily), you don't necessarily have to stick to a dark menu bar background color.

Translucent Activating the Translucent check box allows the content of your publication to come through the menu bar. By default the menu bar is opaque, not allowing the publication design to be seen through it.

Menu Items The Menu Items section lets you add, remove, and customize the buttons that appear on the menu bar. Each item's title, text color, and background image (the plus sign on the right end of each line) can be set individually.

Reorder items in the Menu Items list by dragging them up or down.

To remove an item from the menu, highlight it, and then click the button adorned with a minus sign (-) beneath the list of menu items.

To add menu items, click the plus sign button (+) beneath the list of menu items. The following are the menu items available for inclusion in your menu bar:

Browser The Browser command does not open a web browser. Instead, it opens the thumbnail scrubber enabling readers to browse and navigate to articles.

Summary Similar to the browser command, the Summary command opens the TOC for reader navigation through the magazine.

Close When tapped, the Close command will close the current issue and return readers to the list of issues. In the case of one-off publications, it will return readers to the cover. If you were hoping that the Close command would actually exit the app, check out the "Adding Buttons and Actions" section of Chapter 9, "Building Interactivity into Interactive Magazines," for a way to create a button or action that exits the app.

+/- Bookmark Aquafadas DPS publications may contain bookmarks to help readers return to specific locations at later times. By adding the +/- bookmark function, you'll create a toggle button on the menu bar that lets readers create a bookmark at the current location and, if the location already has a bookmark, delete it.

+/- Note If you elect to include the +/- note command, it will enable readers to make notes about specific locations in the publication (without a button for +/- note, readers can't access that functionality). The command creates a toggle button; by tapping it once in a location, the reader may create a note at that location. Tapping the toggle a second time deletes the note.

Bookmarks/Note The Bookmarks/Note command lists the bookmarks and/or notes created by the reader throughout the publication. Tapping one of the entries in the list jumps the reader to that location.

Flexible Space The flexible space construct isn't a command or button and therefore doesn't offer customization options. Its purpose is to provide a separation between buttons. For example, if you want your menu bar to display buttons for Browser and Summary on the left and then Close on the right, you'll need to have a flexible space construct inserted in the Menu Items list before the Close command. Close will then align to the right while the flexible space fills whatever space is necessary between Summary and Close. Without the flexible space, buttons appear immediately after one another starting on the left. Multiple flexible spaces may be used to create buttons on the left, on the right, and in the center.

CONTROLLING NAVIGATION BAR DISPLAY

What Aquafadas DPS calls the *navigation bar* is what we more commonly refer to as the thumbnail scrubber, the linear view of the entire publication as thumbnails of articles that appears, along with the menu bar, by tapping once on the screen. Using the Navigation Bar tab of the Project Settings dialog, you can fine-tune the display of the navigation bar (see Figure 10.64).

Type In the Type drop-down menu, you're presented with two choices: None and Stack View. Choosing None will disable the navigation bar entirely. Choosing Stack View turns on the navigation bar and offers the remaining options for controlling it.

FIGURE 10.64
Choosing the
options for the navi-
gation bar

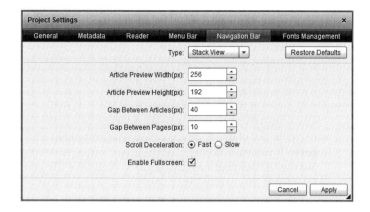

Article Preview Width and Article Preview Height   The Article Preview Width and Article Preview Height fields let you set the size (in pixels) of the thumbnail images that will display in the navigation bar. The two fields actually work together to set maximum sizes for the images—the thumbnails will always be no taller than the Height field value and no wider than the Width field value, scaled proportionately. Thumbnails are automatically generated from page content, scaled to fit the specified dimensions. Thus, for best results, pick sizes that enable a good view of the contents of the page without being so large as to dominate the screen.

Gap Between Articles   Again set in pixels, Gap Between Articles lets you set the horizontal distance between one article's thumbnail and the next article's thumbnail.

Gap Between Pages   *Pages* as Aquafadas uses the term is what we now call *screens*, the different screens of a single article. Using the Gap Between Pages field, you can set the spacing between the thumbnails comprising the Navigation Bar view on a multiscreen article.

Scroll Deceleration   When readers navigate longer documents via the navigation bar, they may swipe hard and fast to move quickly through the thumbnails. As the inertia of such a swipe comes to an end, the lateral movement along the navigation bar slows and stops. Scroll Deceleration offers you a choice of how long it takes the inertia falloff to result in stopping progression through the thumbnails: Fast means the movement comes to a stop quickly after the initial swipe progression, and Slow makes the movement gradually slow and stop.

Enable Fullscreen   Checking the box beside the Enable Fullscreen option allows the navigation bar to fill the screen. Unchecking this option keeps the navigation bar at the bottom of the screen.

Including Custom Fonts

Because mobile devices include so few onboard fonts, one the first questions often asked about digital publishing is whether fonts used in the design will be displayed on the mobile device. The answer is, yes, they will. Moreover, that's automatic except for HTML-based content you might include.

It's automatic with any page you design in InDesign because of the page output formats. If you elect to format pages as PNG or JPG when creating a new folio or article, then your type gets rasterized as part of the page anyway, negating the need for fonts. If you choose to format your pages as PDF, the PDF automatically embeds a *subset* of the fonts in use by including just the *glyphs* used in the design.

With Aquafadas DPS, the same holds true—typographic components that are not rasterized have their used fonts (or a subset of those fonts) embedded automatically. You can check on that fact by accessing the Project Settings for the publication and going to the Fonts Management tab (see Figure 10.65). If the list is empty, click the Update From Project button to refresh the list, something done automatically during publication generation. You can also embed additional fonts not currently in use in the project articles by clicking the Import Fonts button and browsing for OTF, TTF, or TTC fonts.

FIGURE 10.65
The fonts in use, and to be embedded, in this Aquafadas DPS project

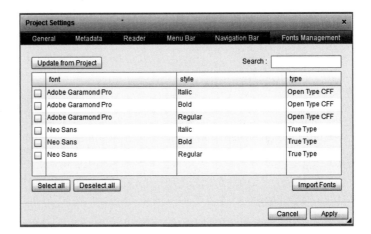

Embedding fonts is crucial to the correct display of HTML-based content you might include. Note that this doesn't mean live web content you direct readers to; rather, it's for HTML widgets and pages embedded directly within the interactive magazine. With Aquafadas DPS, just add any fonts required by the HTML layouts or components to the Fonts Management tab in the Project Settings dialog.

Glossary

alpha

In terms of software, an alpha release is one that is an early version of the software produced primarily for the testing by developers. Among the characteristics that mark software as alpha version are known bugs, incompatibilities with other software and possibly with hardware as well, and the absence of certain features planned for the retail release of the software. After alpha version comes beta version, a more stable version of the software produced for wider distribution and testing, often in real-world workflows by a select group of experts and clients. Adobe broke with the alpha and beta tradition with Digital Publishing Suite by providing the alpha version of DPS, including the InDesign plug-in Folio Producer Tools and the online DPS dashboard interface, to several large publishers. Those publishers produced the earliest DPS-powered interactive magazine–format publications despite the alpha status of the software. See also: *beta*.

anti-aliasing

Because square pixels comprise computer screens and rectangular pixels comprise television screens, an effect called aliasing (or *stair-stepping* or *jaggies*) occurs when the edges of objects don't perfectly align with the pixel grid. For example, with a capital *A*, the crossbar aligns perfectly horizontally with the pixel grid, but the lines that form the majority of the shape are diagonal, which means they cut across several columns of pixels. A single pixel may be only one color and cannot be bifurcated; thus, if a diagonal stroke in the *A* falls partially within the pixel, then the entire pixel must be colored. As the strokes progress diagonally, a series of pixels fills in, converting a smooth diagonal stroke into a stair-stepped series of square (or rectangular) pixels. Anti-aliasing is the method (with several submethods) of trying to reduce the appearance of this stair-stepping effect in pixels. The method of reduction works within

the requirements of each pixel being a solid color by altering the color of pixels to match the percentage of the pixel that would have been used, were pixel division possible. For example, if part of the *A*'s black diagonal stroke fills only half of the pixel, then the color of the pixel is changed to 50 percent gray, tricking the mind into interpreting the pixel as only half-filled. Anti-aliasing also colors pixels outside where the strokes of a letter or object land with small percentages of color to help convey the illusion of smoothness.

apps

With the rise of smartphones and tablets with limited capacity for RAM and storage space has come the age of apps. An application in the computer world is a fully functional, often complex program with many functions and features. An app, by contrast, is a specialized program that is small in terms of storage space and system requirements compared to applications and limits its features to a niche function. Although the mobile industry didn't invent the concept of apps, it did popularize it, because the software we install on our smartphones and tablets consists of, by necessity, apps and not applications. The slogan most responsible for the rise of the term *app* in popular culture was Apple's, accompanying its first-generation iPhone: "There's an app for that." The term *app* became an even bigger part of the social consciousness when Apple's slogan was satirized and adapted to many other, often humorous, situations and products, including besmirchments of Apple itself.

ATOM

ATOM refers to both an XML-based method of feeding web content and a publishing protocol used for creating and updating web resources. It's the former I most often reference in this book. ATOM was created as a replacement for Really Simple Syndication (RSS), which was the standard at the time for pushing content from a web server to readers and their software clients rather than waiting for readers to visit the website and consume the content there. The function of ATOM is the same as that of RSS, differentiated only by the geeky bits of how the two systems work. Suffice it to say that ATOM and RSS are nearly interchangeable, and any website or web-based server content can be delivered in either format (or both). See also: *RSS*.

backlighting

In terms of mobile devices, backlighting means that the device screen is illuminated from behind (the screen appears self-illuminating). Mobile phones and tablets contain backlighting, while ereaders typically don't, which is why the average person finds them comfortable for long reading sessions. Ereaders like the nontablet NOOK and early-generation Kindle devices omit backlighting to simulate the appearance of a printed book.

beta

Beta-version software is a not-ready-for-sale release of the software, often with known bugs and incompatibilities and often lacking certain features and functions planned for the retail release. Software companies such as Adobe produce beta software for release to a select but often large and well-rounded group of experts and clients so that they may test the software under real-world conditions, in real-world workflows, and provide feedback to the software maker to aid in the fixing of bugs and incompatibilities and the finalizing of the product's feature list in an expected full retail version.

bit rate

This is the rate at which bits of data are transferred from one place to another. For example, take an MP3 file with a bit rate of 128 bits per second (BPS). The quantification means that 128 bits of data will be transferred per second from the MP3 reader to the MP3 player module; thus, 128 bits of audio data may be played every second. A 256 BPS MP3 song will result in twice as much audio data as a 128 BPS version, creating a more rich and vibrant sound.

carry-over

This is a notation to readers that the current point in a threaded story is not the beginning of the story; instead, it continues here from an earlier place, as in "continued from page 10." This is also known as *carry-over line*, *continued line*, or *continue head*. See also: *jumpline*.

cloud

The word *cloud*, as used in phrases such as "the cloud" and "cloud storage," refers to the manner in which digital storage space is delivered as a service. This storage space is typically redundant and non-centralized, meaning that the data exists simultaneously on several hard drives, on several servers, and often in several global locations simultaneously to mitigate the risk of data loss or data inaccessibility due to a hard drive or connective failure at the server level. For example, with the purchase of an iPad, owners are given access to cloud-based, or online, file storage in Apple's iCloud service. All files stored in the iCloud service are available from any Internet connection in the world to all iOS devices running iOS 5 and newer, as well as computers that have the iCloud client software installed. Google, Microsoft, ASUS, Dropbox, Box.net, Rackspace, and numerous other companies offer cloud-based file storage and often other cloud-based services, some free and some paid.

Creative Commons

Creative Commons is a digital-era attempt at defining and enforcing intellectual-property law in a manner that is relevant to a world in which content is now available via electronic means to everyone, everywhere. Unlike precedent-based U.S. and international intellectual-property law, which is complex, incomplete, and inconsistently applied, not only between different countries but often between similar situations in the same country, Creative Commons offers an internationally consistent set of licenses that group rights and privileges content creators and content users can easily understand and use. The system is backed by an informative website at http://creativecommons.org that succinctly and in plain English (or Spanish or French or Japanese or…) describes what allowances content creators are granting to users and what those users may and may not legally do with the content under the chosen Creative Commons license. Tools on the website, such as a short, question-based license selector, help creators quickly and without risk grant certain licenses to their work—such as the license to distribute the work or the license to allow commercial use of the work—while retaining all other rights under U.S. and international copyright law. Some of the images used in this book and in its lesson files were used under Creative Commons licenses.

CSS

CSS stands for Cascading Style Sheets, the means by which styling is accomplished in HTML-based content. CSS style definitions and attributes such as font size, color, and much more are applied to HTML content tagged or named a particular way. CSS figures heavily into EPUB design because EPUBs are, like HTML, XML-tagged.

digital replica

Digital replica is a format of electronic publication that is effectively the print version of the publication viewed on screen. It is a replica of the print version in digital format. I often call digital replicas "app via PDF" because most digital-replica systems directly convert a PDF of a publication into an app capable of running on mobile devices. Depending on the system employed, digital replicas can often include basic interactivity such as hyperlinks and, sometimes, embedded audio and video objects.

Because of the rapidity with which digital-replica systems are changing at the time of this writing, coverage of this particular format is limited in this book. I do go in depth into the various digital-replica systems, as well as how to incorporate digital-replica publishing into your workflow in webinars, on-site consulting and training, and articles. See my website at `http://iamPariah.com` for further digital-replica and digital-publishing education and workflow needs.

Dublin Core Metadata

Refers to Dublin Core Metadata Element Set, which is an international standard set of properties or information forms that describe types of resources. Dublin Core Metadata is the set of metadata included in various documents, images, and epublications (including EPUBs), that communicate where the content came from, who created it, when it was created, who owns the rights to it, and various other relevant information describing, but not necessarily included within, the content. You can learn more about Dublin Core Metadata at `http://dublincore.org`.

Although you may think the initiative is named for the city in Ireland, its origins are less exotic—it began at a 1995 workshop in Dublin, Ohio.

end sign

This is a symbol, mark, or icon used to indicate the end of an article, particularly when the article jumps between pages.

enhanced ebook

This is a nebulous term that refers to any ebook that contains more interactivity or multimedia than a typical novel in ebook form that is merely text and basic pictures. The term is most often used in marketing to communicate to the would-be buyer of an ebook that it includes such extra features. Some consumers have consequently come to adopt the term, but, as the definition of "ebook" evolves to include more media and interactivity as standard elements, so must the definition of "enhanced ebook" evolve. Ergo, there isn't really such a thing as an enhanced ebook.

fixed-layout ebook

Often referred to as *children's ebooks*, *picture ebooks*, *photo books*, and similar monikers, fixed-layout ebooks are visually rich layouts that offer much more than standard EPUBs. Unlike standard EPUB-based ebooks, fixed-layout ebooks don't automatically reflow to fit the device on which they're viewed. Instead, they behave very much like PDFs or even digital magazines, displaying the design, typography, and page geometry exactly as designed on all devices that support fixed layout. Screen fitting is limited to zooming and whether to show a single page or a two-page spread.

This specialty type of ebook tends to be very reliant on imagery, either as inline graphics or page background images or both, and sometimes even as spread-spanning images. They support advanced typographic control and pixel-precise layout, and they can contain read-along, on-demand, or ambient audio. Limited interactivity may also be achieved through JavaScript integration. Objects can be placed anywhere on the page, aligned relative to one another, with absolute precision, and type control goes far beyond standard, flowable EPUB in the forms of support for any font (with embedding), accurate line wrapping, hyphenation, leading control, tracking (letter spacing), and even multiple columns. Fixed-layout EPUBs may have real sidebars, note or tip boxes, and live-text image captions. And, as in flowable EPUBs, all the text—even in such special features—is searchable, live text.

At the time of this writing, fixed-layout ebooks are entirely proprietary with limited device support. They can be viewed on iOS devices, Kindle Fire, NOOK tablet, and Kobo Vox, though each device manufacturer has its own unique system and format for creating fixed-layout ebooks. For instance, to make a fixed-layout ebook available in the iOS iBookstore, it must be built completely differently than the KF8-format version created to sell through the Amazon Kindle store for viewing on a Kindle Fire.

Because of the frequent changes inherent in the formats, device support, and workflows for creating the highly profitable and popular fixed-layout ebooks, fixed-layout ebooks are not discussed in detail in this book. Please consult `http://iamPariah.com` for information on the latest industry changes you need to know in order to make fixed-layout ebooks a profitable part of your business.

flush

This is the clean edge of type. For example, this page is printed with type flush left, meaning that the type aligns along the left to create a clean edge.

folio

In the Adobe Digital Publishing Suite, a folio is one or more articles or layouts built for DPS deployment.

glyph

This is a single character, pictogram, mark, or entity within a font or language.

HTML5

This is the latest generation of the Hypertext Markup Language (HTML). HTML5 supports animation, multimedia, and advanced adaptive content. When incorporated into epublications such as interactive magazines, HTML5 can fill in interactive or content-presentation features and effects that the native interactive magazine–format tools like Adobe DPS, Aquafadas DPS, and others cannot natively create. HTML5 is also an iOS-supported alternative to Adobe Flash–format animations, multimedia, and games, and it can do nearly everything Flash can do.

interactive magazine

Interactive magazine is a format of digital publication optimized for touch-based navigation and tablet viewing, and may contain a great deal of interactivity, including hyperlinks, audio and video, image and video slideshows, panoramic images, 3D rotatable objects, scrollable areas, content replacements, and embedded web content. All of this is wrapped into an app with swipe-to-page and pinch-to-zoom capabilities and visual tables of contents with or without page thumbnails. As of this writing, interactive magazines are viewable only on tablets and certain smartphones; they are not accessible on standard computers.

interactive replica

This is an alternate term for *digital replica*.

JavaScript

Developed initially by Netscape (remember that?), JavaScript is an open scripting language designed to add and control dynamic content in websites and HTML-based content and user interfaces. In terms of epublishing, JavaScript is a very popular scripting language that can be used, to varying degrees, within ebooks, *fixed-layout ebooks,* and interactive magazines.

jumpline

This is a directive to readers that a threaded story resumes at a later point, as in "continues on page 83." This is also known as a *continue line* or *jump head.* See also: *carry-over.*

KF8

This stands for Kindle Format 8, the file format launched in the first quarter of 2012 as the new standard for ebooks, *fixed-layout* ebooks, and other digital publications produced for the newest generation of Kindle devices.

lossless

In the context of this book, the term *lossless* refers to a type of image compression that reduces the file size of images without reducing the quality. PNG-24 is a lossless format, while JPEG is the opposite, employing a lossy compression method that discards pixel data in order to achieve compression.

magalog

This is an industry term describing a publication formatted as, or including, editorial content but whose primary purpose is to sell or advertise products. The term is a mash-up of *magazine* and *catalog.*

MathML

Mathematical Markup Language is a recommendation (not a standard) of the W3C for describing mathematical and scientific programs and formulae on the Web and in electronic publications. It has been under development since 1998.

open source

This refers to software whose code has been made available for use or modification, without use or licensing restriction or fee, to the general public. The popular blog and content-management software WordPress is an example of open source software.

OpenType

This is an intelligent font software based on Unicode. OpenType fonts (or simply OpenTypes) have predefined spaces for more than 65,000 glyphs from more than a dozen languages. These fonts often contain variant designs such as true small caps, swashes, contextual alternates, ordinals, and several versions of numerals in a single file, replacing several separate fonts required to achieve the same functionality in Type1 or TrueType fonts. OpenType fonts are identified on a computer by the extension `.otf`, although in many cases they bear the old TrueType `.ttf` file extension, revealing the fact that, at their cores, OpenType fonts are structured as either Type1 or TrueType. OpenType fonts are 100 percent cross-platform; the same font functions and renders identically on Windows, Mac OS 9, Mac OS X, and several flavors of Unix.

OTF

This is a file extension for OpenType fonts. See: *OpenType.*

overrides

In terms of styles, an override is a formatting option not specifically defined in the style assigned to the text, object, table, or cell. For instance, using the Cmd+Shift+I/Ctrl+Shift+I keyboard shortcut to apply italic to text is an override of a paragraph style in which the text is defined to be roman, or not italic. Overrides are indicated by a plus sign (+) beside the style name in Paragraph Style, Character Style, Object Style, Table Style, and Cell Style panels.

picture-book ebook

This is an alternate term for *fixed-layout ebook.*

pilcrow

This is a paragraph mark (¶).

poster

When working with multimedia, a poster is the static image used to represent video, animation, or audio before or during playback. In other contexts, it may be a really large picture of Justin Bieber, Blood on the Dance Floor, or that shirtless *Twilight* kid tacked up on your daughter's bedroom wall.

posterization

The term *posterization* has many definitions in various contexts ranging from photography to basketball (check `www.urbandictionary.com`). In this book I've used it in the graphic-design sense, which means the process of reducing tonal values to create sharp-contrast, poster-like areas of color. Often the process of posterization is a negative consequence of tonal and color correction actions, such as using Levels or Curves in Photoshop.

print replica

This is an alternate term for *digital replica*.

public domain

Referring to intellectual property rights, *public domain* is the total absence of intellectual property rights. A work of any type that is no longer eligible for copyright or trademark protection is "placed into the public domain," meaning that any member of the public may do anything she desires with the content, including, but not limited to, reusing the work with or without modification for commercial purposes. For example, many of the resources provided throughout this book's lesson files—particularly those from *The Wonderful Wizard of Oz*—are in the public domain, which enables me to distribute those files to you, and you to use them, without restriction or cost.

RAR

RAR is an acronym for Roshal Archive, a compression and archival scheme developed by Eugene Roshal. Like ZIP, RAR is a method for collecting multiple files into a single archive file and compressing the original files so that the archive takes up less disk space than the files it contains. See also: *ZIP*.

raster

This means pixel-based, typically in terms of imagery, as opposed to vector- or mathematic-based.

resolution-independent

Typically used in reference to imagery, this means that the artwork has no inherent resolution or reliance on pixels and will output to the highest resolution of the output device.

RSS

This is an abbreviation for RDF Site Summary, though it is just as often interpreted as Really Simple Syndication. RSS is an XML-based web content distribution format and method that "pushes" content to readers and their software rather than waiting for readers to voluntarily visit the website or other source of the content. It is the standard for such content distribution, despite the emergence of would-be replacement ATOM. In epublishing, RSS is used in numerous places, including as a means of pushing content into interactive magazines created with Aquafadas DPS and pushing newspaper and other periodical content into EPUB-based newspapers. See also: *ATOM*.

SMIL

An abbreviation for Synchronized Multimedia Integration Language, SMIL is a W3C-recommended markup language for describing and controlling multimedia content in a variety of digital publication formats. Although not yet widely used, SMIL has the potential to become a powerful component of digital publishing because of its ability to homogenize audio, video, animation, and transcripts and closed-captioning from such multimedia so that they can be accessible to a large variety of devices, applications, apps, and technologies.

subset

As used herein, this refers to font embedding. When fonts are embedded in any document—PDFs, interactive magazines, EPUBs, and so on—the entire font file is included, adding the font file's size to the overall publication size. With only a few fonts, this can dramatically increase the file sizes and transfer rates of digital publications. Subsetting was created to mitigate file size by including only the *glyphs* actually used from the font. For example, if a publication includes the letters *A–Y*, there's no need to include *Z*. Thus, the subset of the font, the letters *A*, *B*, *C*, and so on down through *Y*, will be extracted from the font and included in the publication so that those letters may render correctly, but *Z* and any other glyphs not used in the publication but present in the font will be excluded from embedding.

SVG

This is an abbreviation for Scalable Vector Graphics and is a resolution-independent, vector-based, XML-based file format initially designed to supplant Macromedia Flash as the dominant online vector graphics format. Although Adobe dropped out as one of the chief architects and proponents of SVG following Adobe's acquisition of Macromedia, mainly for the Flash technology, the SVG format has continued to flourish, owing in large part to its open source status. SVG is an important part of epublishing because it's the only vector-based format supported across all tablets and smartphones (iOS devices don't do Flash). Vector-based artwork in EPUBs must be in SVG format.

tall-screen video

As a consequence of the proliferation of mobile devices and consumers' predilection to shoot and watch video on these devices in a portrait orientation, as well as the fact that most digital publications are created in portrait orientation, video that has been rotated 90 degrees from the normal landscape, wide-screen view is becoming very popular. Tall-screen video is video recorded with a taller-than-wide orientation, which fits very nicely into portrait-oriented ebook, PDF, and interactive-magazine pages.

URI

An abbreviation for Uniform Resource Indicator, URI is an address or string of characters leading or identifying a resource in a computer network, usually the Internet. URI and URL are often used interchangeably, though there is a subtle difference between them. A Uniform Resource Locator (URL)

specifically supplies an address to a resource without naming it. A URI, by contrast, can be either a location or a name (or both). Also related is a Uniform Resource Name (URN), which identifies or names a resource without providing a location for that resource. Thus, URI encompasses both URL and URN and is therefore the more generic term to use when it refers to identifying and locating a resource in a computer network, or both.

UUID

UUID is an abbreviation for Universally Unique Identifier, which is a string of characters used to provide a relatively unique identity to objects or, as used in this book, epublications. InDesign will automatically generate a UUID upon export to EPUB when a more specific identifying number, such as an International Standard Book Number (ISBN), has not been provided. I say that the UUID is "relatively unique" because, as designed, there is no central system assigning and guaranteeing the uniqueness of the string of alphanumeric characters. InDesign will generate a unique UUID, but you can rely on its uniqueness only among other UUIDs generated by *your* single installation of InDesign on your computer. My copy of InDesign might generate the same UUID for one of *my* publications. Therefore, the name Universally Unique Identifier is a misnomer; it should be Locally Unique Identifier or Relatively Unique Identifier Within a Given Closed Environment. Don't rely on any UUID as being *actually* unique outside the immediate environment of the software and computer that generate it.

vertical video

This is another name for *tall-screen video*.

walled garden

A walled garden in the physical world is one in which the garden has been completely enclosed by a wall of stone, wood, shrubbery, or some other material. Plants cannot escape the garden, nor can the garden be invaded by plants that originate outside the wall. That concept has been applied to software, hardware, and epublications as well, with the most famous example being Apple. Apple manufactures the iPhone and iPad hardware, develops the operating system for both devices (iOS), and directly controls which apps and publications are allowed to be made available to owners of those devices. By controlling all aspects of the devices, including the content allowable on those devices, Apple maintains a walled garden. The iOS operating system and its features are designed to run only on Apple devices, preventing the plants from escaping the garden; by reviewing every app and epublication made available to iOS device users, Apple prevents plants that originate outside the wall from coming in without approval. Amazon, too, maintains a walled garden, though it's to a lesser degree—think slatted fence surround. Devices like the Kindle Fire have access only to Amazon's curated App Store, but apps from outside the App Store can be sideloaded onto the Kindle Fire even though Amazon could prevent that but apparently decided against it. Moreover, the same content available to the Kindle Fire is usually available outside of that device as well; Amazon's ebooks, emagazines, enewspapers, video, music, and other content are available to users of non-Amazon devices and operating systems, often, depending on the content type, without the need to even use Amazon-owned assets beyond the point of purchase.

widget

A widget is an app (*applet* before popularization of the term *app*) comprised of a preconfigured chunk of code and designed to perform a specific task. For example, the Facebook Like button on a website is a chunk of HTML and JavaScript code provided by Facebook and pasted into the code of millions of other websites. It's a widget that doesn't need to be configured by the user, merely copied and pasted. Widgets are also often employed in epublishing to add functions, behaviors, and dynamic content in a manner already figured out by someone else—in other words, widgets are the wheel you don't have to reinvent. Millions of widgets are available online to perform numerous functions on websites, mobile apps, and

epublications, and many organizations create their own widgets for internal use, creating copy-and-paste functionality to ease workflow.

WOFF

This is an acronym for Web Open Font Format, a font format bearing additional metadata and designed to be embedded in a web page or other XML-based content and downloaded from a server to a web browser or other client as a means of enabling web and ebook designers to use a greater variety of typefaces in designs without fear of client-side font substitution. WOFF fonts are OpenType, TrueType, or Open Font Format compressed and encoded using special algorithms. Although WOFF is not yet an international standard, it has been published by the World Wide Web Consortium Web Fonts Working Group as a Candidate Recommendation. It is already supported by all the major desktop browsers, and support is rapidly spreading through mobile browsers and ereaders. See also: *OpenType*.

XHTML

This is an abbreviation for Extensible Hypertext Markup Language. XHTML is an extension to standard HTML that makes web pages more semantically standardized and organized based on an XML framework. HTML, prior to HTML5, which was built with standardization in mind, required a specialized markup parser for devices like web browsers in order to display as intended. Many offshoots and proprietary bastardizations of HTML evolved, which created a situation in which HTML pages would not reliably render the same across all devices. XHTML was devised to address such inconsistencies by wrangling web-page markup into a single, universal entity that was based on the accepted standard of XML. The result was that XHTML could be parsed by devices that understood XML, which was almost universal by that point anyway, and it would display exactly the same across all such devices. Because of this cosmopolitan and consistent support for XHTML, EPUB and other digital publication formats require that XHTML, not HTML, be used.

XML

An abbreviation for Extensible Markup Language, XML is a markup language designed to be both human- and machine-readable. It is designed to tag, identify, and create a hierarchy from textual content. Those tags, identifications, and hierarchical indicators can then be used to organize, modify, and style the content in any number of ways by applications, apps, and devices that recognize XML. The "extensible" part of the name refers to the fact that XML is built to be a foundation markup methodology from which both specialized and more generalized systems may later be developed, and many have. XML is the basis for XHTML, RSS, ATOM, EPUB, and even less obvious file formats such as those created by Microsoft Word, Excel, and other Office products.

ZIP

A ZIP file (extension `.zip`) is a compressed archive containing other files. The format was developed in the 1980s by Phil Katz and later placed in the public domain, and is the world's most widely used format for compressing and distributing a collection of files. So efficient and popular is the ZIP archival and compression methodology that it is incorporated into many other file formats, including Microsoft Word DOCX files, JAR archives, and even, as an optional compression algorithm, TIFF images. See also: *public domain*.

Index